COLIN DRURY

Management and cost accounting

Van Nostrand Reinhold (UK)

First published in 1985 by
Van Nostrand Reinhold (UK) Co. Ltd
Molly Millars Lane, Wokingham, Berkshire,
England

Reprinted 1985, 1986 (twice), 1987

Typeset by Columns of Reading, Berkshire

Printed and bound in Great Britain by
R. J. Acford Ltd., Chichester

Library of Congress Cataloging in Publication Data

Drury, Colin.
 Management and cost accounting.

 (The VNR series in accounting and finance)
 Includes bibliographies and index.
 1. Managerial accounting. 2. Cost accounting.
I. Title. II. Series.
HF5635.D798 1985 658.1′511 85-3266
ISBN 0-442-30637-7

British Library Cataloguing in Publication Data

Drury, Colin
 Management and cost accounting.—(The VNR
 series in accounting and finance)
 1. Managerial accounting
 I. Title
 658.1′511 HF5635

ISBN 0-442-30637-7

Management and cost accounting

Contents

Preface

The aim of this book is to explain the principles involved in designing and evaluating management and cost accounting information systems. Management accounting systems accumulate, classify, summarize and report information that will assist managers in their *decision-making, planning and control activities*. A cost accounting system accumulates financial information for *stock valuation and profit measurement*. As the title suggests, this book is concerned with both management and cost accounting but emphasis is placed on the former. A major theme of this book is that different financial information is required for different purposes.

After many years of teaching management and cost accounting to various professional, undergraduate, postgraduate and post-experience courses I became convinced there was a need for a book with a more 'accessible' text. A large number of cost and management accounting text books have been published and these are generally aimed at students who are preparing for the examinations of professional accountancy bodies. Many of these books contain a detailed description of accounting techniques without any discussion of the *principles* involved in evaluating management and cost accounting systems. Such books often lack a conceptual framework, and ignore the considerable amount of research conducted in management accounting in the past two decades. At the other extreme some books focus entirely on a conceptual framework of management accounting with an emphasis on developing normative models of what ought to be. These books pay little attention to accounting techniques. My objective has been to produce a book which falls within these two extremes.

This book is intended primarily for students who are preparing for the cost and management accounting examinations of the professional accountancy bodies at the foundation and professional level. It should also be of use to degree, higher national diploma and postgraduate students who are pursuing a one or two year management accounting course and who are approaching cost and management accounting for the first time. An introductory course in financial accounting is not a prerequisite, although many students will have undertaken such a course.

A major theme of this book is that different financial information is required for different purposes, but my experience indicates that this approach can confuse students. In one chapter of a typical book students are told that costs should be allocated to products including a fair share of overhead costs; in another chapter they are told that allocated costs are irrelevant and should be disregarded. In yet another chapter they are told that costs should be related to people (responsibility centres) and not products, whereas elsewhere no mention is made of responsibility centres.

In writing this book I have devised a framework which is intended to overcome these difficulties. The framework is based on the principle that there are three ways of constructing accounting information. One is conventional cost accounting with its emphasis on producing product costs for stock valuation and profit measurement. The second is the notion of relevant cost with the emphasis on providing information to help managers to make good decisions. The third is responsibility accounting which focuses on the costs and revenues of responsibility centres.

This book consists of 24 chapters divided into six parts. The role of each chapter within the overall framework is explained briefly in Chapter 1 and in more detail in the introduction to each section of the book. The first part (Part I) consists of two chapters and provides an introduction to management and cost accounting. The following three parts reflect the three different ways of constructing accounting information. Part II consists of six chapters and is entitled Cost Accumulation for Stock Valuation and Profit Measurement. We focus here on *cost accounting* with the emphasis on allocating manufacturing costs to products to separate costs between cost of goods sold and the closing stock valuation. We also briefly consider the extent to which product costs accumulated for stock valuation and profit measurement are suitable or unsuitable for decision-making and responsibility accounting. Part III consists of six chapters and is entitled Information for Decision-Making. Here we consider the notion of relevant cost and the information which should be presented to help managers to make good decisions. Part IV consists of five chapters and is entitled Information for Planning and Control. In this we emphasize the process for integrating the decisions into a meaningful, coordinated package via the budgeting process. We also focus on responsibility accounting and the assignment of cost and revenues to managers. The emphasis here is on the accounting process as a means of providing information to help managers control the activities for which they are responsible. The behavioural aspects of management accounting are included as a separate chapter in this section. Part V consists of three chapters and is entitled The Application of Quantitative Methods to Management Accounting. The final part Divisional Performance Evaluation, consists of two chapters which deal with the problems of measuring the performance of divisional managers.

In devising a framework around the three methods of constructing financial information there is a risk that the student will not appreciate that the three categories use many common elements, that they overlap, and that they constitute a single management accounting system, rather than three separate systems. I have taken steps to minimize this risk in each section by emphasizing why financial information for one purpose should or should not be adjusted for another purpose. In short, each section of the book is not presented in isolation and an integrative approach has been taken.

When I wrote this book an important consideration was the extent to which the application of quantitative techniques should be integrated with the appropriate topics or considered separately. I have chosen to integrate quantitative techniques whenever they are an essential part of a chapter (for example, the use of probability statistics are essential to Chapter 12, Decision-Making Under Uncertainty) but my objective has been to confine them, where possible, to Part V.

This approach allows for maximum flexibility. Teachers wishing to integrate quantitative techniques with earlier chapters may do so but those who wish to concentrate on other matters will not be hampered by having to exclude the relevant quantitative portions of chapters.

Although conceived and developed as a unified whole, the book can be tailored to the individual requirements of a course and to the preferences of the individual reader. For a discussion of the alternative sequencing of the chapters see Guidelines to Using the Book in Chapter 1. The following are suggested programmes for various courses:

Foundation professional accountancy examination with a major emphasis on cost accounting: All of Part I and II, Chapters 9 and 10 of Part III plus Chapters 15–17 of Part IV.

Professional accountancy examinations at the professional or advanced level: Revision of prescribed reading for the foundation level plus the remaining chapters of the book.

A two-year management accounting course for undergraduates: Part I and Parts III to VI. If instructors wish to provide a short course on cost accounting then Chapters 3, 4 and 8 from Part II can be assigned.

A one-year degree or post-experience course in management accounting: Part I, Part III (Chapters 9-13), Part IV (Chapters 15, 16, 17 and 19) and Chapter 23 from Part VI.

Throughout this book I have kept the illustrations simple. More complex problems are set at the end of each chapter to enable students to pursue certain topics in more depth. A *Student's Manual* and an *Instructors' Guide* accompany this book. The former provides suggested answers to the problems which are asterisked after the question number and the latter answers to the remaining problems. Students are strongly recommended to purchase the accompanying manual which complements this book and contains suggested answers to over 160 questions. Both manuals provide suggestions for assignments to meet specific objectives. Where possible, the problems have been arranged in ascending order of difficulty.

Each chapter also contains a suggested list of further reading to enable students to pursue particular topics in more depth. Many of the references are the original work of writers who have played a major role in the development of management accounting. The contributions of such writers are often reflected in this book but there is frequently no substitute for original writing.

Many people have helped in the preparation of this book and I am particularly indebted to Professor John Perrin and Dick Wilson who both commented helpfully on earlier drafts; to Audrey Marsh, Dominic Recaldin and Stephen Wellings for their valuable assistance; and to Bronwen, my wife, who has somehow managed to convert my original manuscripts into one final typewritten form. My appreciation goes also to the Institute of Cost and Management Accountants, the Association of Certified Accountants and the Institute of Chartered Accountants in England and Wales for permission to reproduce examination questions. Questions from the Institute of Cost and Management Accountants examinations are designated ICMA; questions from the Association of Certified Accountants are designated ACCA; and questions from the Institute of Chartered Accountants in England and Wales and designated ICAEW. The answers in the accompanying teachers' and students' guides to this book are my own and are in no way the approved solutions of the above professional bodies.

Finally, and most importantly, I acknowledge the patience and understanding of my wife Bronwen and children Martin, Robert and Caroline.

Introduction to management and cost accounting

The objective of this section is to provide an introduction to management and cost accounting. In Chapter 1 we define accounting and distinguish between financial, management and cost accounting. We then examine the role of management accounting in providing information to managers for decision-making, planning and control. The role of each chapter within the overall framework is also explained in.this chapter. In Chapter 2 we consider the various ways in which costs and sales revenues can be classified to meet the various requirements of the different users of accounting information.

The two chapters in this section provide a framework which is used to develop the remaining sections of this book. A thorough understanding of Chapters 1 and 2 is therefore essential.

1 The scope of management accounting

There are many definitions of accounting, but the one which captures the theme of this book is the definition formulated by the American Accounting Association. It describes accounting as

the process of identifying, measuring and communicating economic information to permit informed judgements and decisions by users of the information.

In other words, accounting is concerned with providing information which will help decision-makers to make good decisions.

An inspection of the terms used in this definition will indicate that an understanding of accounting requires an understanding of the attributes of *economic information* and the process of identifying, *measuring* and *communicating information*.

In addition, we must understand the *decision-making* process and be able to identify the *users* of accounting information. The objective in this first chapter is to consider each of the components of the definition of accounting to provide a framework which will enable you to achieve a more meaningful insight into the issues and problems of accounting which are discussed in this book. We will begin by looking at the *users* of accounting information and *identifying* their requirements.

The users of accounting information

Accounting is a language which communicates financial information to people who have an interest in an organization—managers, shareholders and potential investors, employees, creditors and the government. Managers require information which will assist them in their decision-making and control activities; for example, information is needed on the estimated selling prices, costs, demand, competitive position and profitability of various products which are made by the organization. Shareholders require information on the value of their investment and the income which is derived from their shareholding. Employees require information on the ability of the firm to meet wage demands and avoid redundancies. Creditors and the providers of loan capital require information on a firm's ability to meet its financial obligations. Government agencies like the Central Statistical Office collect accounting information and require such information as the details of sales activity, profits, investments, stocks, dividends paid, the proportion of profits absorbed by taxation, and so on. In addition, the Inland Revenue needs information on the amount of profits which are subject to taxation. All this information is important for determining policies to manage the economy.

Accounting information is not confined to business organizations. Accounting information about individuals is also important and is used by other individuals; for example, credit will only be extended to an individual after the prospective borrower has furnished a reasonable accounting of his private financial affairs. Non-profit-making organizations such as churches, charitable organizations, clubs, and government units such as local

authorities, also require accounting information for decision-making, and for reporting the results of their activities. For example, a cricket club will require information on the cost of undertaking its various activities so that a decision can be made as to the amount of the annual subscription which it will charge to its members. Similarly, local authorities need information on the costs of undertaking specific activities so that decisions can be made as to which activities will be undertaken and the resources which must be raised to finance them.

The foregoing discussion has indicated that there are many users of accounting information who require information for decision-making. The objective of accounting is to provide sufficient information to meet the needs of the various users at the lowest possible cost. Obviously, the benefit derived from using an information system for decision-making must be greater than the cost of operating the system.

An examination of the various users of accounting information indicates that they can be divided into two categories:

(1) internal parties within the organization;
(2) external parties outside the organization.

It is possible to distinguish between two branches of accounting which reflect the internal and external users of accounting information. *Management accounting* is concerned with the provision of information to managers to aid them in decision-making for planning and control, whereas *financial accounting* is concerned with the provision of information to external parties outside the organization. In this book we shall focus on management accounting and for simplicity we shall concentrate mainly on the applications of management accounting to manufacturing business organizations which are operated for the purpose of making a profit. Note, however, that many of the applications are equally appropriate to non-manufacturing and non-profit organizations, and the questions at the end of each chapter include many problems which are relevant to these entities. Solutions to selected problems are contained in the Students' Manual to this book.

The meaning of information

We noted at the beginning of this chapter that our definition of accounting requires an understanding of the attributes of *economic information* and the process of *identifying*, *measuring* and *communicating* information. Anyone studying accounting must be aware of the basic aspects of information theory and information economics but before we embark on a discussion of information theory we must understood what is meant by the term 'information'.

It is possible to distinguish between information and data. Data represents facts of any kind; information can be more narrowly defined–it is a subset of data. An item of data is classed as information only if it adds to knowledge; for example, the number 100,000 taken by itself is not information because it does not add any knowledge, but the statement that 100,000 additional sales orders were received last month does add knowledge and is therefore classed as information.

Information may be obtained by direct observation or by communication. Managers normally obtain information by communication because it is not possible for them to observe all activities taking place which are under their responsibility. Instead, managers rely on information from conversations with their subordinates or the contents of formal reports, some of which will be prepared by the accountant.

Not all information is valuable. The information content of a message varies inversely with the probability of the occurrence of an event that is being reported. Suppose, for example, that you are informed that the temperature on the south coast of England on Christmas Day is expected to be less than 10 °C. Because the probability of this event is very high it is unlikely that this statement will have very much information content and it is thus of little value. If, however, you are informed that the temperature on the south coast during the Christmas period is expected to be in excess of 20 °C you may consider this information to be important and valuable because the probability of such an event is very low. This statement is valuable because it may cause you to change your planned course of action. Instead of staying at home, you may decide to visit the south coast during the Christmas period.

Accounting should concentrate on the provision of relevant information which is valuable to the recipient. In our everyday life we receive vast quantities of information in excess of our requirements but our brains act as filters, so that we act on only a small fraction of the quantity of information we receive. For example, the ears of a

pedestrian walking along a main street in a city centre pick up many sounds which are disregarded, but if the pedestrian hears the sound of a car horn the brain brings this message to the attention of the conscious mind for appropriate action. The accountant acts in a similar way when designing an accounting reporting system by filtering out unneeded information and conveying only relevant information to the decision-maker. Clearly, this filtering process should be in accordance with the users' requirements. The Report of the Committee on Managerial Decision Models (1978) defined relevant accounting information as that which bears upon or is useful to the action it is designed to facilitate or the result it is desired to produce. For example, if a manager is considering alternative courses of action both of which require the use of existing machinery, then the cash outflows (payments) for the hire of the machinery will remain the same for both alternatives. This information is not relevant to the decision because the cash flows remain unchanged for both alternatives. Only those cash flows that will be different for the individual alternatives represent relevant accounting information for the decision.

Relevance is at the heart of management accounting; if information is not relevant to some need it has no value. Thus it is important that there is a close relationship between the management accountant and all levels of management so that the management accountant can be familiar with the firm's operations and determine relevance in a manner which more precisely reflects the needs, understanding and receptivity of particular users.

Measurement theory

Measurement theory is important to accountants as it is concerned with the problem of assessing or evaluating data so that its significance is correctly stated. Measurement is concerned with assigning numbers to objects or events. Accountants play a major role in this measurement process by quantifying data. The quantification of data adds usefulness and conveys more information than strictly qualitative statements. For example, performance in ice skating, diving and gymnastic competitions when expressed in quantitative terms conveys more meaningful information of the judgements of the performance of the various competitors.

The use of numbers raises the question as to what standard of measurement should be used? Accounting uses the monetary unit as the standard of measurement to measure costs, values and benefits of alternative courses of action. The advantage of using money as a standard of measurement is that it provides a useful means of attaching a common significance to very diverse objects and events about which business decisions are made. Not all decisions, however, can be expressed in monetary terms. For example, management might consider alternative policies aimed at improving employee morale and loyalty, but these items cannot be measured in monetary terms, and other quantitative or qualitative measures will be necessary to evaluate the alternative policies.

An essential requirement of any measurement is that it should remain stable. Unfortunately, the monetary unit of measurement is not a stable measure in times of inflationary or deflationary price changes. Because of this instability it is difficult to compare objects and events which are measured in one period of time with similar objects and events measured in subsequent periods. Consequently, some adjustments to the unit of measurement are necessary to overcome the problem. We shall consider these adjustments in subsequent chapters.

In addition to the need for stability, other attributes are also important. The cost of the measurement system should not be unreasonable. In other words, the benefits from adopting the measurement system should be greater than the costs of the system. Also, the measurement unit should be understandable to the users. Finally, the basis of measurement should be relevant to the decision. In the remaining chapters of this book we shall consider alternative courses of action and discuss the extent to which they possess the measurement attributes outlined in this section.

The communication of information

A communication system consists of the transfer of messages between an originator and a recipient. The objective is for the desires of the originator of the message to influence the actions of the recipient. The transfer of the message is effected by the use of a transmitting device at the information source and the signals are picked up by a recieving device which decodes the signals

Fig. 1.1 A communication system

into a message at the destination. The transmitter and receiver are linked by a communication channel. This process is illustrated in Fig. 1.1, above.

An information source produces a message which is communicaed by a transmitting device through a *channel*. The channel is the medium used to transmit the signal which is then picked up by a receiving device and converted into a message for the recipient. In Fig. 1.1 we can see that the communication channel is subject to interference or 'noise' which can cause the signal received to differ from the signal transmitted, thus frustrating the intention of the originator of the message. Noise may be caused by processing errors such as the transposition of symbols in transit, the accidental loss of digits or the destruction of part of a report. Noise is present in all systems; it cannot be eliminated but it can be reduced, thus improving the clarity of the messages.

Let us now apply the procedure outlined in Fig. 1.1 to the accountant's role in the communication system. The information source in an accounting system consists of economic events which are normally reflected in signals received in the form of invoices, bank statements, wage slips and other documents. The accountant acts as a transmitting device by observing the economic events and encoding them by means of the preparation of accounting reports or statements. Such accounting reports or statements represent the communication channel by providing information for decision-making, explaining plans and evaluating performance. The message or accounting report may be received by a manager who will decode and interpret the report. For example, a manager may receive a report on the performance of a subordinate and may interpret the difference between planned and actual performance in terms of the remedial action required. Hence the accounting report is decoded by the manager for

use by the subordinate who is the recipient of the message. Successful communication of accounting information should mean that the messages which are conveyed in the accounting report have a significant influence on the actions of the manager.

Noise in an accounting system occurs when there are transfer errors and calculation errors and this reduces the accuracy and reliability of the output from the system. The minimization of noise in the accounting system can be achieved by ensuring that self-checking devices are built in when the data is being analysed and collected for inclusion in the accounting reports.

A further aspect of noise relates to the physical capacity of the receiver to process all the information being transmitted. The transfer of too much information can cause 'information overload', which may result in the most important aspects of the message being lost, because it is buried in a mass of other information. The action of the receiver would then be different from that which was intended by the originator of the message. According to Ackoff (1975), managers receive too much information which is of little relevance to them.

Noise can also be affected by behavioural considerations. The effectiveness of accounting information is determined by the manner in which it affects behaviour. In this sense, we may say that unless accounting information serves to produce the desired action, it has served no purpose at all. Consequently the accountant should be aware of the human process which leads managers to recognize or fail to recognize the meaning of the information which is communicated. We shall consider in Chapter 19 how accounting information affects human behaviour.

The value of information

Accountants should aim to provide the right

information to the right people in the right quantity at the right time, and at minimum cost. This raises the question as to what is the optimal quantity, content, accuracy and speed of transmitting information. These alternatives have different costs and values and it is clear that accountants should bear this in mind when collecting and presenting accounting information. For example, better quality decisions might be made by postponing a decision until more information or information of greater accuracy is available. Decisions, however, must often be made promptly if they are to have maximum influence on future events. Consequently, there is a trade-off between speed on the one hand and accuracy and quantity on the other. We should therefore compare the costs of improving information systems with the potential benefits. The relationship between the costs and value of information is illustrated in Fig. 1.2.

The diagram indicates that the cost of providing information increases at an accelerating rate as the quantity, content, accuracy and speed of transmitting information is increased. The value of information eventually decreases due to information overload at increasing levels. The optimal quantity, content, accuracy and speed of transmitting information is reflected by the dashed vertical line where the difference between the value of the information and the cost of transmitting the information is greatest.

How do we ascertain the value of the benefits of providing information? In theory we should evaluate the consequences of taking each decision with a given amount of information; we then evaluate the consequences of taking each decision when extra information is available, and we use the difference between these two figures as a measure of the value of the extra information. If this value is in excess of its cost then the information should be produced.

The various outcomes which are possible, from alternative decisions in a world of uncertainty, will be unaffected by the amount of information which is available to decision-makers at the time of making their choice. However, the information which is available will affect the perceptions of the decision-maker and so information only has value when the decision-maker's action, in the presence of information, differs from what his action would be in the absence of information. The additional value gained from the decision with extra information is known as the *gross value* of extra information, and the difference between the gross value and the cost of providing the information is called the *net value* of the extra information. Consider the situation presented in Example 1.1.

EXAMPLE 1.1

We must decide whether to accept a special order from a customer. We have two alternatives–either to accept or reject the order, and we will assume that rejection will cause no ill-feelings. The selling price of the order is £525,000. The cost of making the special items is not known with certainty but we estimate that it will be either £550,000 or £400,000 depending on how much time is needed to manufacture the item. For simplicity, we will assume that only these two outcomes are possible and there is a 50 : 50 chance of either outcome occurring.

The following outcomes are possible.

| | Outcome | |
Choices:	Low production cost	High production cost
Accept	£125,000 profit	£25,000 loss
Reject	£0	£0

The expected value of the production cost (that is, the weighted average of the possible production costs) is 50% of £550,000 plus 50% of £400,000 which equals £475,000. We shall discuss the nature of expected values and their role in the decision-making process in Chapter 12. Assuming that our decision is based on the expected value of the production cost, we will accept the order because

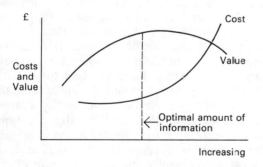

Fig. 1.2 Costs and value of information

the selling price of £525,000 is greater than the expected cost of £475,000. The expected surplus is £50,000 which consists of a 50% chance of a gain of £125,000 (if the low production cost occurs) and a 50% chance of a loss of £25,000 (if the high production cost occurs).

Would you prefer to obtain additional information prior to making the decision? Clearly the answer is yes, because if the high production outcome occurs then a loss will occur. Suppose it is posisble to buy additional information which can. in advance, indicate the actual production cost. If the information indicates that the low production cost will occur then we will accept the order and obtain a surplus of £125,000. If the information indicates that the high production cost will occur then we will not accept the order. As each message is equally likely in this case, the expected values of the possible outcomes is £62,500 which consists of 50% of £125,000 plus 50% of zero.

We can now ascertain the gross value of the information. The *gross value* is the expected value of the possible outcomes with the information (£62,500) less the expected value of the possible outcomes without the information (£50,000), which equals £12,500. We would therefore be prepared to pay up to £12,500 for the information. If we assume that the cost of the information is £10,000 then the *net value* of the information will be £2,500.

This analysis has assumed that once we have received the information we would know the exact production cost with certainty. In other words, we have assumed that we could buy perfect information. In the real world it is unlikely that the decision-maker will be able to obtain perfect information, and information which is less than perfect is called imperfect information. The principles which are applied for calculating the value of imperfect information are the same as those we applied for calculating the value of perfect information, but the calculations are more complex. For an illustration see Mace (1980).

The decision-making process

Now that we have considered the various components of our definition of accounting—that is, information, communication, and measurement—

we shall now examine the final component in the definition: decision-making. Because information produced by management accountants must be judged in the light of its ultimate effect on the outcome of decisions, a necessary precedent to an understanding of management accounting is an understanding of the decision-making process. Figure 1.3 presents a diagram of a decision-making model.

The first five stages represent the decision-making or the planning process. Planning involves making choices between alternatives and is primarily a decision-making activity. The final two stages represent the control process which is the process of measuring and correcting actual performance to ensure that the alternatives which are chosen and the plans for implementing them are carried out. Let us now consider each of the elements of the decision-making and control process.

Identifying objectives

Before good decisions can be made there must be some guiding aim or direction which will enable the decision-makers to assess the desirability of favouring one course of action over another. Hence the first stage in the decision-making process should be to specify the objectives or goals of the organization.

Considerable controversy exists as to what the objectives of firms are or should be. Economic theory normally assumes that firms seek to maximize profits for the owners of the firm (the ordinary shareholders in a limited company) or, more precisely, the maximization of shareholders' wealth. Various arguments have been used to support the profit maximization objective. There is the legal argument that the ordinary shareholders are the owners of the firm which, therefore, should be run for their benefit by trustee managers. Another argument supporting the profit objective is that profit maximization leads to the maximization of overall economic welfare. That is, by doing the best for yourself, you are unconsciously doing the best for society. Moreover, it seems a reasonable belief that the interests of firms will be better served by a larger profit than by a smaller profit so that maximization is at least a useful approximation.

Many writers have taken the view that firms do not seek to maximize profits. Baumol (1959) argues that large firms operating in markets where

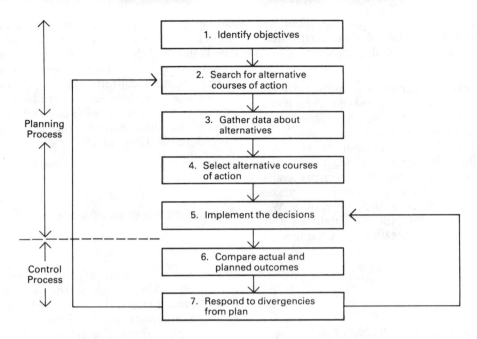

Fig. 1.3 The decision-making, planning and control process

the forces of competition are weak do not have to maximize profits to survive. As long as sufficient profits are being made to keep shareholders happy and to provide adequate internal finance, managers can pursue other objectives which reflect their own interests. Unless management has substantial holdings of shares, Baumol argues that sales revenue is likely to be a key managerial goal in the short run, and growth of sales in the long run. These views are also supported by Galbraith (1969) and Marris (1967).

Some writers (see for example Simon, 1959) believe that businessmen are content to find a plan which provides satisfactory profits rather than to maximize profits. For example, possible solutions to a problem are examined in sequence until one is found which offers a satisfactory level of performance free from unacceptable uncertainty. No further attempt is made to find an even better solution. This is known as a 'satisficing' solution.

Cyert and March (1963) have argued that the firm is a coalition of various different groups — shareholders, employees, customers, suppliers and the Government — each of whom must be paid a minimum to participate in the coalition. Any excess benefits after meeting these minimum constraints are seen as being the subject of bargaining between the various groups. In addition, a firm is subject to constraints of a

societal nature. Maintaining a clean environment, employing disabled workers and providing social and recreation facilities are all examples of social goals which a firm may pursue.

Clearly it is too simplistic to say that the only objective of a business firm is to maximize profits. Some managers seek to establish a power base and build an empire; another goal is security; and the removal of uncertainty regarding the future may override the pure profit motive. Nevertheless, the view adopted in this book is that, broadly, firms seek to maximize the value of future net cash inflows (that is, future cash receipts less cash payments) or to be more precise the *present value* of future net cash inflows.[1] The concept of 'present value' is explained in Chapter 13. The reasons for choosing this objective are as follows:

(1) It is unlikely that any other objective is as widely applicable in measuring the ability of the organization to survive in the future.
(2) It is unlikely that maximizing the present value of future cash flows can be realized in practice, but by establishing the principles necessary to achieve this objective you will learn how to increase cash flows.
(3) It enables shareholders as a group in the bargaining coalition to know how much the

pursuit of other goals is costing them by indicating the amount of cash distributed among the members of the coalition.

Our chosen objective cannot be applied to all organizatinos. Non-profit organizations such as national and local government activities, hospitals, charitable organizations and colleges do not have an objective of maximizing net cash inflows. The objectives of these organizations are to provide the maximum services within the resources available. Nevertheless, they do need to make decisions which are related to their objectives. We shall discuss the special features of planning and control in non-profit organizations in Chapters 15 and 16.

The search for alternative courses of action

The second stage in the decision-making model is a search for a range of possible courses of action (or strategies) which might enable the objectives to be acheived. If the management of a company concentrates entirely on its present product range and markets, and market shares and cash flows are allowed to decline, there is a danger that the company will be unable to generate sufficient cash flows to survive in the future. To maximize future cash flows it is essential that management identifies potential opportunities and threats in its current environment and takes specific steps immediately so that the organization will not be taken by surprise by any developments which may occur in the future. In particular, the company should consider one or more of the following courses of action:

(1) developing *new* products for sale in *existing* markets;
(2) developing *new* products for *new* markets;
(3) developing *new* markets for *existing* products.

The search for alternative courses of action involves the acquisition of information concerning future opportunities and environments; it is the most difficult and important stage of the decision-

making process. Ideally, firms should consider all alternative courses of action but, according to Cyert and March (1969), firms will, in practice, consider only a few alternatives, with the search process being localized initially. If this type of routine search activity fails to produce satisfactory solutions, the search will become more widespread. We shall examine the search process in more detail in Chapter 15.

Gather data about alternatives

When potential areas of activity are identified management should assess the potential growth rate of the activities, the ability of the company to establish adequate market shares, and the cash flows for each alternative activity for various *states of nature*. Because decision problems exist in an uncertain environment it is necessary to consider certain factors which are outside the decision-maker's control, which may occur for each alternative course of action. These uncontrollable factors are called states of nature. Some examples of possible states of nature are economic boom, high inflation, recession, the strength of competition, and so on. For a detailed discussion of the search for possible courses of action and gathering data about them see Ansoff (1984).

The course of action selected by a firm using the information presented above will commit its resources for a lengthy period of time and the overall place of the firm will be affected within its environment — that is, the products it makes, the markets it operates in and its ability to meet future changes. Such decisions dictate the firm's long-run possibilities and hence the type of decisions it can make in the future. These decisions are normally referred to as long-run or strategic decisions. Strategic decisions have a profound effect on the firm's future position and it is therefore essential that adequate data is gathered about the firm's capabilities and the environment in which it operates. We shall discuss this topic in Chapter 15. Because of their importance strategic decisions should be the concern of top management.

Besides strategic or long-term decisions management must also make decisions which do not commit the firm's resources for a lengthy

period of time. Such decisions are known as short-term or operating decisions and are normally the concern of lower-level managers. Short-term decisions are based on the environment of today, and the physical, human and financial resources presently available to the firm. These are, to a considerable extent, determined by the quality of the firm's long-term decisions. Examples of short-term decisions include the following:

(1) What selling prices should be set for the firm's products?
(2) How many units should be produced of each product?
(3) What media shall we use for advertising the firm's products?
(4) What level of service shall we offer customers in terms of the number of days required to deliver an order and the after-sales service?

Data must also be gathered for short-term decisions; for example, data on the selling prices of competitors' products, estimated demand at alternative selling prices, and predicted costs for different activity levels must be assembled for pricing and output decisions. When the data has been gathered, management must decide which courses of action to take.

Select appropriate alternative courses of action

In practice, decision-making involves choosing between competing alternative courses of action and selecting the alternative which best satisfies the objectives of an organization. Assuming that our objective is to maximize future net cash flows, the alternative selected should be based on a comparison of the differences between the cash flows. Consequently, an incremental analysis of the *net* cash benefits for each alternative should be applied. The alternatives are ranked in terms of *net* cash benefits and those showing the greatest benefits are chosen subject to taking into account any qualitative factors. We shall discuss how incremental cash flows are measured for short-term and long-term decisions and the impact of qualitative factors in Chapters 10–14.

Implementation of the decisions

Once alternative courses of action have been selected they should be implemented as part of the budgeting process. The budget is a financial plan for implementing the various decisions which management has made. The budgets for all of the various decisions are expressed in terms of cash inflows and outflows, and sales revenues and expenses. These budgets are merged together into a single unifying statement of the organization's expectations for future periods. This statement is known as a *master budget*. The master budget consists of a budgeted profit and loss account, cash flow statement and balance sheet. The budgeting process communicates to everyone in the organization the part which they are expected to play in implementing management's decisions. We shall discuss the budgeting process further in Chapter 15.

Comparing actual and planned outcomes and responding to divergencies from plan

The final stages in the process outlined in Fig. 1.2 of comparing actual and planned outcomes and responding to divergencies from plan represent the firm's control process. The managerial function of control consists of the measurement, reporting and subsequent correction of performance in an attempt to ensure that the firm's objectives and plans are achieved. In other words, the objective of the control process is to ensure that the work is done so as to fulfil the original intentions.

To monitor performance the accountant produces performance reports and presents them to the appropriate managers who are responsible for implementing the various decisions. Performance reports consisting of a comparison of actual outcomes (actual costs and revenues) and planned outcomes (budgeted costs and revenues) should be issued at regular intervals. Performance reports provide *feedback* information by comparing planned and actual outcomes. Such reports should highlight those activities which do not conform to plans so that managers can devote their scarce

time to focusing on these items. This process represents the application of *management by exception*. Effective control requires that corrective *action* is taken so that actual outcomes conform to planned outcomes.

Alternatively, the plans may require modification if the comparisons indicate that the plans are no longer attainable. The importance of monitoring plans and modifying them where necessary has been emphasized by several writers (for example see Dermer, 1977, and Bromwich, 1980) but the justification for this monitoring and modification process is best shown by the following statement of the American Accounting Association:

> Plans and objectives are, to a significant degree, a matter of expectation and expectations vary continuously with time and with changing circumstances. Thus, what was set down as to what should occur may no longer be a rational basis for guiding or evaluating actions which are intended to achieve the organization's goals when the time comes for implementation. Consequently, management needs information not only on the changing actions of members of the organization but on the changing condition of the environment in which these actions take place.
>
> As actions must be modified to accord to plans, so must the plans be modified to achieve the organization's goals. It is of particular importance that when evaluations of actions are made, the scope of judgment includes the appropriateness of the standards or plans. The environmental conditions that now pertain are relevant to this judgment, not the conditions that were expected to be encountered.

The process of taking corrective action so that actual outcomes conform to planned outcomes, or the modification of the plans if the comparisons indicate that actual outcomes do not conform to planned outcomes, is indicated by the arrowed lines in Fig. 1.3 linking stages 7 and 5 and 7 and 2. These arrowed lines represent 'feedback loops'. They signify that the process is dynamic and stress the interdependencies between the various stages in the process. The feedback loop between stages 7 and 2 indicates that the plans should be regularly reviewed and if they are no longer attainable alternative courses of action must be considered for achieving the organization's objectives. The second loop stresses the corrective action taken so that actual outcomes conform to planned outcomes. We shall discuss the planning and control process in Chapters 15 and 16.

The management process

We have noted that the objective of management accounting is to serve management by providing information for decision-making. In addition, feedback information is required for controlling the implementation of the decisions. To be aware of the information needs of management we must first understand the management function which accounting serves. Drucker (1974) suggests that management consists of the following functions: planning, controlling, organizing, communicating and motivating.

Planning

In the previous section we noted that planning has both short-term and long-term dimensions. The long-range plan summarizes management's expectation of the future during the next three to five years, or perhaps even longer. The purpose of the long-range plan is to anticipate future needs or opportunities which require specific steps to be taken now or in the near future — for example, investment in new facilities to increase capacity, and the development of new products or markets. A company should not be taken by surprise by any developments which occur gradually over an extended period of time. It is essential that a firm systematically thinks ahead since it is unlikely that its major product will be generating satisfactory profits in ten years' time. The planning process should provide answers to such questions as 'What does the firm desire?' and 'When and how are the objectives to be accomplished?' When management are agreed on the answers to these questions a programme of action can be formulated consisting of long-term and short-term plans. The latter convert the firm's long-range plans to the needs of the immediate future and consist of detailed plans in the form of the annual budget.

Control

In our discussion of the decision-making process we noted that control involves a comparison of actual performance with plans so that deviations from plan can be identified and corrective action taken. This may result in action to ensure that actual performance will conform with the original plans or, alternatively, a revision of the plans

because they are no longer feasible. The control process enables management to assess whether or not the objectives included in the long-range plan are likely to be achieved. If the objectives are unlikely to be achieved, the control process provides the appropriate response for the review of the company's objectives and long-range plans. This process gives warning of potential problems and enables the objectives and commitments to be changed before any serious damage to the company's future occurs.

Organizing

Organizing is the establishment of the framework within which required activities are to be performed and the designation of who should perform these activities. In addition, organizing requires a clear definition of a manager's responsibility and lines of authority. The process of organizing involves departmentalization by establishing divisions, departments, sections, branches, and so on. These units are created to break organizational tasks into manageable parts and it is essential that these tasks are satisfactorily coordinated if a company is to achieve its objectives efficiently. The various departments or units are linked in a hierarchy, with a formal communication structure which enables instructions to be passed downwards and information to be passed upwards to senior management. An *organization chart* clarifies an organizational structure and assists in defining authority, responsibility and accountability. A partial organization chart for a manufacturing firm is presented in Fig. 1.4.

The lines of this chart represent the formal channels of communication between the various managers. For example, the managers of the five major functions–marketing, production, finance, personnel and research and development–are directly responsible to the managing director for their operations and performance; that is, they serve in a *line relationship* to the managing director. Similarly, the managers of the machine, assembly, maintenance, and distribution departments are directly responsible to the production manager and thus a line relationship also exists here. *Staff relationships*, on the other hand, exist when one department provides a service to other departments. On most organizational charts staff relationships are presented horizontally to the line functions which they serve, whereas line relationships between subordinates and their immediate supervisors are shown by vertical lines. The

Fig. 1.4 A partial organization chart of a manufacturing company

management accounting department performs a staff function by providing line managers and other staff managers with a specialised information service, which assists them in their decision-making, planning, and control activities.

Motivating

Motivation means influencing human behaviour so that the participants identify with the objectives of the organization and make decisions which harmonize with these objectives. The emphasis is on producing a drive or incentive that influences action towards meeting the objective. An important attribute of a good manager is to be able to motivate his subordinates to act in such a way that they strive to achieve the targets set by top management. Drucker (1974) suggests that a manager motivates by making a team out of people who are responsible for various jobs and that he achieves this through the practices with which he manages:

> He does it in his own relation to the men he manages. He does it through incentives and rewards for successful work. He does it through constant communication, both from the manager to the subordinate, and from the subordinate to the manager.

The role of the management accountant in the management process

Having considered the functions of the management process we shall now briefly consider the role which the management accountant plays in helping managers to perform each of these functions.

Planning

In the planning process the management accountant helps to formulate future plans by providing information to assist in deciding what products to sell, in what markets, and at what prices, and evaluating proposals for capital expenditure. In the budgeting process the management accountant plays a major role in the short-term planning process. He is responsible for providing data on past performance which may be particularly useful as guidance for future performance. In addition, he establishes budget procedures, and timetables and coordinates the short-term plans from all sections of the business and ensures that these plans are in harmony with each other. He then assembles the various plans into one overall plan (that is, the master budget) for the business as a whole and presents this plan for top management approval.

Control

Management accounting aids the control process by producing performance reports which compare the actual outcome with the planned outcomes for each *responsibility centre*. A responsibility centre may be defined as a segment (such as a department) of an organization where an individual manager holds delegated authority and is responsible for the segment's performance.

The management accountant provides an important contribution to the control process by drawing a manager's attention to those specific activities which do not conform to plan. In other words, the management accountant assists the control function by providing prompt measurements of actions and identifying trouble spots. This management-by-exception approach frees managers from an unnecessary concern with those operations that are adhering to the plans. In addition, top management is made aware of those specific locations where the plans are not being achieved.

Organizing

The interaction of the management accounting and the organizing process is suitably described by Belkaoui (1980, p. 30). He states:

> The identification of the elements of an organizational structure most prevalent and essential

to a proper functioning of a management accounting system allows the tailoring of the internal reporting system to that structure or the suggestion of a more appropriate organization structure.

Belkaoui concludes that, while organizational structure is concerned with authority, responsibility and specialization so as to assure effective performance, management accounting–through responsibility accounting–represents the design and implementation of the accounting system for better defining and consolidating these relations.

Communication

Management accounting aids the communication function by installing and maintaining an effective communication and reporting system. For example, the budget communicates plans to those managers who are responsible for carrying them out so that they are clearly aware of what is expected of them during the forthcoming budget period. In addition, the information contained in the budget can be helpful in ensuring coordination between managers of different organizational sub-units, so that each is aware of the requirements and constraints faced by the others with whom he interacts. The performance reports produced by the accountant communicate important information to a manager by indicating how well he is doing in managing his activities and highlighting those items which need detailed investigation through the process of management-by-exception.

Motivation

Budgets and performance reports which are produced by the accountant also have an important influence on the motivation of the personnel of the organization. Budgets represent targets which are intended to motivate managers to strive to achieve the organization's objectives. Such targets are more likely to motive than a situation of vagueness and uncertainty. The performance reports are intended to motivate desirable individual performances by communicating performance information in relation to targets set. In addition, the accountant assists in motivating personnel by providing valuable assistance in identifying potential managerial problem areas and highlighting those items for detailed investiga-

tion. He provides a supportive system to enable managers to control their activities more effectively. It is important to note, however, that budgets and performance reports can cause serious behavioural problems and can be harmful to motivation if they are used and interpreted without sufficient knowledge of potential organizational behavioural problems. We shall discuss the behavioural aspects of management accounting in Chapter 19.

Cost accounting and management accounting

At the beginning of this chapter we noted that management accounting is concerned with the provision of information to managers to help them make good decisions whereas financial accounting is concerned with the provision of information to parties outside the organization. Financial accounting requires that we match costs with revenues to calculate profit. Consequently any unsold finished goods stock or partly completed stock (work in progress) will *not* be included in the cost of goods sold which is matched against sales revenue during a given period. In an organization which produces a wide range of different products or jobs it will be necessary, for stock valuation purposes, to charge the costs to each individual job. The total value of the stocks of completed jobs and work in progress plus any unused raw materials forms the basis for determining the stock valuation to be deducted from the current period's costs when calculating profit. This total is also the basis for determining the stock valuation for inclusion in the balance sheet. Costs are therefore allocated to each individual job or product to provide the necessary information for financial accounting reports. *Cost accounting* was developed to provide this information.

Kaplan (1982, p. 1) suggests that product costs which were constructed for financial accounting were being used by operating executives for decision-making. During the 1950s emphasis shifted from external users to internal users of cost accounting data, which resulted in cost data for use by management being accumulated in a different manner from that which was used for financial accounting. This shift in emphasis led to the emergence of management accounting and it is now possible to distinguish between cost account-

ing and management accounting. *Cost accounting is concerned with cost accumulation for stock valuation to meet the requirements of external reporting, whereas management accounting relates to the provision of appropriate financial information for managers to help them make better decisions*. An examination of the major texts in cost and management accounting indicates that the distinction between management accounting and cost accounting is extremely vague, with some writers referring to the decision-making aspects in terms of cost accounting and other writers using the term management accounting; the two terms are often used synonymously. In this book cost accounting will refer to the accumulation of costs for stock valuation, and this topic will be developed in Part II. The term management accounting will be applied to the provision of information for management activities such as decision-making, planning and control, and we shall focus on these aspects in Parts III–VI.

Summary of the contents of the book

Part I consists of two chapters and provides an introduction to management accounting.

Chapter 1, The Scope of Management Accounting, examines the components in the definition of accounting, and provides a framework to enable you to obtain an insight into the issues and problems of cost and management accounting.

Chapter 2, Cost and Revenue Classification, is concerned with the classification of costs and revenue for cost accounting and management accounting. In particular, we shall consider the different ways in which costs should be classified to meet the requirements of the users of accounting information.

Part II consists of six chapters and is entitled Cost Accumulation for Stock Valuation and Profit Measurement. We focus here on cost accounting with the emphasis on allocating manufacturing costs to products, to separate costs between the costs of goods sold and the closing stock valuations. We also briefly consider the extent to which product costs accumulated for stock valuation should be adjusted for decision-making and control.

Chapter 3, Accounting for Materials and Labour, is concerned with the accounting problems associated with materials and labour when calculating product costs. To help you to gain an insight into the problems a description of the clerical procedures which should be followed for the ordering, receipt and issue of materials is presented.

Chapter 4 Accounting for Overhead Expenditure, focuses on the procedure for allocating overheads to products.

Chapter 5, Accounting Entries for a Job Costing System, explains the accounting entries which should be made to record the transactions within a job costing system. There is also emphasis on the data collection system.

Chapter 6, Process Costing, and *Chapter 7*, Joint Products and By-product Costing, consider the special problems which are associated with calculating product costs in those industries which produce similar products and by-products from common resource inputs.

Chapter 8 Absorption Costing and Variable Costing, discusses the differences between absorption costing and variable costing, their strengths and weaknesses, and the circumstances where one system may be preferable to the other.

Part III also consists of six chapters and is entitled Information for Decision-making. Here we consider the information which should be presented to help managers make good decisions. To help you to understand the basic principles of the differing information requirements for various decisions we assume a world of certainty in the first three chapters. The fourth chapter introduces methods for incorporating uncertainty into the analysis. In the final two chapters we consider the measurement of benefits and costs for long-range decisions.

Chapter 9, Cost–Volume–Profit Analysis, focuses on what will happen to the financial results if a specified level of activity or volume fluctuates. In particular we concentrate on price–output decisions and compare the accountant's and the economist's approach to cost–volume–profit analysis.

Chapter 10, Measuring Costs and Benefits for Decision-making, develops the relevant cost approach to decision-making. We consider a range of decisions such as dropping a segment, special selling price decisions, the effect of scarce factors and make or buy decisions.

Chapter 11, Accounting Information for Pricing Decisions, contains a discussion of both economic and accounting approaches to pricing decisions.

Chapter 12, Decision-making Under Conditions of Risk and Uncertainty, focuses on how uncertainty can be incorporated into the analysis.

In particular, we consider the topics which have been covered in the three previous chapters, that is, cost–volume–profit analysis, pricing decisions and the measurement of costs and benefits under conditions of uncertainty.

Chapter 13 and 14, Capital Investment Decisions (1) and (2), are concerned with the measurement of benefits and costs for capital investment decisions. In Chapter 13 we introduce the basic principles for incorporating the time value of money into the analysis and in Chapter 14 we discuss the more complex problems of capital investment decisions.

Part IV consists of five chapters and is entitled Information for Planning and Control. Here we emphasize the process for integrating the decisions into a meaningful coordinated package via the budgeting process. We also focus on the control process by considering the information which is required to help management to ensure that the firm's objectives and plans are achieved.

Chapter 15, The Budgeting Process, considers the role of budgeting within the planning process and the relationship between the long-range plan and the budgeting process. We also contrast the budgeting process in non-profit organizations with the budgeting process in profit-oriented organizations.

Chapter 16, Control in the Organization, focuses on the accounting process as a means of providing accounting information to help managers control the activities for which they are responsible, and we stress the process of responsibility accounting. We also consider the special problems of control in non-profit organizations.

Chapter 17 and 18, Standard Costing Variance Analysis (1) and (2), concentrate on how the difference between planned outcomes and actual outcomes (that is, the variances) can be analysed in detail, thus enabling more effective control to be exercised. In Chapter 17 we explain how a standard costing system operates and the procedure for calculating the variances. In Chapter 18 we consider some of the criticisms of standard costing variance analysis and look at alternative approaches for providing a more meaningful analysis of variances.

Chapter 19, Behavioural Aspects of Accounting Control Systems, emphasizes that the contribution fo management accounting to the planning and control process is of a behavioural nature and highlights the important behavioural aspects of management accounting. In particular, the major research findings of the behavioural literature are discussed.

Part V consists of threee chapters and is entitled The Application of Quantitative Methods to Management Accounting.

Chapter 20, Mathematical Approaches to Cost Estimation, emphasizes the contribution of mathematical and statistical techniques in determining cost behaviour patterns, including the separation of costs into their fixed and variable elements.

Chapter 21, Quantitative Models for the Planning and Control of Stocks, examines the application of quantitative models for determining the optimum investment in stocks.

Chapter 22, The Application of Linear Programming to Management Accounting, explains linear programming techniques and considers their application to a variety of management accounting problems.

Part VI consists of two chapters and is entitled Divisional Performance Evaluation. We focus here on the problems of measuring the performance of divisional managers.

Chapter 23, Performance Measures and Control in Divisionalized Companies, considers how a financial control system might be devised which will motivate divisional managers to pursue goals which are in the best interests of the company as a whole.

Chapter 24, Transfer Pricing, focuses on various approaches to arriving at transfer prices among divisions so that the transfer price motivates divisional managers to make sound decisions and at the same time gives a divisional profit calculation which is a fair reflection of the manager's performance.

Guidelines for using this book

If you are pursuing a course of management accounting, without cost accounting, Part II (Chapters 3–8) can be omitted, as the remaining chapters do not rely heavily on this part of the book. Alternatively, you could delay reading the cost accounting chapters in Part II until you have studied Parts III and IV. If you wish to gain an insight into cost accounting but do not wish to study it in depth you may prefer to read only Chapters 3, 4 and 8 of Part II.

The chapters on the application of quantitative techniques to management accounting have been delayed until Part V. An alternative approach

would be to read Chapter 20 immediately after reading Chapter 9 on Cost–Volume–Profit Analysis, or after Chapter 16 which includes Flexible Budgeting. Chapter 21 is self-contained and may be assigned to follow any of the chapters in Part III. Chapter 22 should be read only after you have studied Chapter 18.

Summary

Accounting is defined as the process of identifying, measuring and communicating economic information to permit informed judgements and decisions by users of the information. We have distinguished between internal users (management accounting) and external users (financial accounting) and considered the meaning and communication of information and the theoretical approach to ascertaining the value of information. We have also considered a decision-making planning and control model.

To provide an awareness of the information needs of management, its various functions (that is, planning, controlling, organizing, communicating and motivating) have been discussed. We also focused on the role of management accounting within this process. Finally, we have explained the differences between cost accounting and management accounting and emphasized that cost accounting is concerned with the calculation of product costs for use in the financial accounts, whereas management accounting serves managers by providing information to help them in decision-making, planning and control.

References and further reading

Ackoff, R.L. Management Misinformation Systems, in Rappaport, A. (Ed.), *Information for Decision-making*. Prentice-Hall, 1975.

American Accounting Association. *A Statement of Basic Accounting Theory*. American Accounting Association, 1966.

Ansoff, H.I. *Implanting Strategic Management*. Prentice-Hall, 1984.

Baumol, W.J. On the theory of oligopoly. *Economica* **XXV**, 1959, pp. 187-98.

Benston, G. Cost Accounting and Managerial Decisions (An Introduction), in Benston, G. (Ed.), *Contemporary Cost Accounting and Control* 2nd edn. Dickenson Publishing Company, 1979.

Belkaoui, A. *Conceptual Foundations of Management Accounting*. Addison-Wesley, 1980.

Bromwich, M. Standard Costing for Planning and Control, in Arnold, J. Carsberg, B. and Scapens, R. (Eds), *Topics in Management Accounting*. Philip Allan, 1980.

Cyert, R.M. and March, J.G. *A Behavioural Theory of the Firm*. Prentice-Hall, 1969.

Dermer, J. *Management Planning and Control Systems*. Irwin, 1977.

Drucker, P. *Management: Tasks, Responsibilities, Practices*. Heinemann, 1974.

Galbraith, J.K. *The New Industrial State*. Pelican, 1969.

Hart, H. A Review of Some Major Recent Developments in the Management Accounting Field. *Accounting and Business Research* **11** (42), spring 1981, pp. 99-116.

Horngren, C.T. Choosing Accounting Practices for Reporting to Management, in Anton, H.R., Firmin P.A. and Grove, H.D. (Eds), *Contemporary Issues in Cost and Managerial Accounting* 3rd edn. Houghton Mifflin, 1978.

Kaplan, R.S. *Advanced Management Accounting*. Prentice-Hall, 1982.

Mace, J.R. Value of Information, in Arnold, J., Carsberg, B. and Scapens, R. (Eds), *Topics in Management Accounting*. Philip Allan, 1980, pp. 62-83.

Marris, R. *The Economic Theory of Managerial Capitalism*. Macmillan, 1967.

Parker, R.H. History of Accounting for Decisions, in Arnold J., Carsberg B. and Scapens, R. (Eds), *Topics in Management Accounting*. Philip Allan, 1980.

Report of the Committee on Managerial Decision Models, in Anton, H.R., Firmin, P.A. and Grove, H.D. (Eds), *Contemporary Issues in Cost and Managerial Accounting* 3rd edn. Houghton Mifflin, 1978, pp. 21-46.

Simon, H.A. Theories of Decision-making in Economics and Behavioural Science. *American Economic Review* **49** (3), 1959.

Solomons, D. The Historical Development of Costing, in Solomons D. (Ed.), *Studies in Cost Analysis* 2nd edn. Sweet & Maxwell, 1968.

2 Cost and revenue classification

In the previous chapter we noted that accounting is concerned with communicating information for a variety of uses. *Management accounting* serves managers by providing information to help them in decision-making, planning and control, while *cost accounting* is concerned with the calculation of product costs for use in the financial accounts. Accounting information is required for a variety of reasons and it is essential that a sound system of recording and classifying this information is established.

The objective of this chapter is to consider the various ways in which costs and sales revenues can be classified. It is important to note that there is a variety of ways in which accounting information can be classified and there is no single best classification scheme. Classification depends on the purpose for which the information is to be used. In this chapter we shall concentrate on classifying *costs* as there are many different ways of doing this, whereas the classification of *sales revenue* presents fewer problems.

Cost objectives

A cost objective is any activity for which a separate measurement of costs is desired. In other words, if the users of accounting information want to know the cost of something, this something is called a cost objective. Examples of cost objectives include the cost of a product, the cost of a service, the cost of operating a department or sales territory, or indeed anything for which one wants to measure the resources used. Staubus (1971, p. 1) states:

> Costing is the process of determining the cost of doing something, e.g. the cost of manufacturing an article, rendering a service or performing a function. The article manufactured, service rendered, or function performed is known as the object of costing. . . . Objects of costing are always activities.

We shall see that the cost collection system accumulates costs and classifies them into certain categories such as labour, material or overhead costs and then allocates these costs to cost objectives. Let us now consider this process in more detail.

Classification of costs

To simplify things here, cost objectives are divided into three broad categories: costs for *stock valuation*, costs for *decision-making*, and costs for *control*. For example, the cost of operating an existing machine is a cost objective which may be required for a comparison with the costs of operating a replacement machine. This information will fall under the broad category of costs for decision-making. In practice, cost objectives can be analysed in far more detail but a detailed identification of the many cost objectives for which cost information is required would be endless; by using the three broad categories of stock valuation, decision-making and control we can establish a useful framework for identifying how costs might be classified. (For a description of various cost terms see Management Accounting: Official Terminology, 1982.) Let us now consider alternative ways in which costs may be classified for each of these three broad categories. A summary of possible cost classifications is presented in Exhibit 2.1.

We shall now consider each of the cost objectives and possible approaches to classifying costs

Exhibit 2.1 Cost objectives and possible cost classifications

Cost objective	Possible methods of cost classifications
(1) Costs for stock valuations	Period and product costs Elements of manufacturing costs Job and process costs
(2) Costs for decision-making	Cost behaviour Relevant costs Sunk costs Opportunity costs Marginal and incremental costs
(3) Costs for control	Controllable and uncontrollable costs Cost behaviour

and also look at various approaches to classifying sales revenues.

Cost accounting: classification of costs for stock valuation and profit measurement

For stock valuation and profit measurement we must distinguish between *unexpired costs* (assets) and *expired costs* (expenses). Unexpired costs are the resources which have been acquired and which are expected to contribute to future revenue; they are recorded as assets in the balance sheet. When they have been consumed in the generation of revenue and have no future revenue-producing potential they are considered to be *expired costs* (expenses) in the profit and loss account. For example, the costs incurred in producing goods for

Fig. 2.1 Expired and unexpired costs

resale where such goods remain unsold and held in stocks, are recorded as unexpired costs in the balance sheet. When the goods are sold, these unexpired costs become expired costs (expenses) as represented in the cost of goods sold calculation, and they are matched against sales revenue to calculate profit. Hence an *expense* is a cost which has been consumed in earning revenue. The difference between expired and unexpired costs is illustrated in Fig. 2.1.

Period and product costs

The measurement of expired and unexpired costs is important in financial accounting for determining profits and valuing assets. In the United Kingdom a statement of standard accounting practice on stocks and work in progress was published by the Accounting Standards Committee in 1975 (SSAP 9). This statement requires that, for stock valuation, only *manufacturing* costs should be included in the calculation of product costs. Accountants therefore classify costs as product costs and period costs. Product costs are those costs which are identified with goods purchased or produced for resale. In a manufacturing organization they are the costs which the accountant attaches to the product and which are included in the stock valuation for finished goods, or for partly-completed goods (work in progress), until they are sold; they are then recorded as expenses and matched against sales for calculating profit. Period costs are those costs which are not included in the stock valuation and as a result are treated as expenses in the period in which they are incurred. Hence no attempt is made to attach

Fig. 2.2 Treatment of period and product costs

period costs to products for stock valuation.

In a manufacturing organization all manufacturing costs are regarded as product costs and non-manufacturing costs are regarded as period costs.[1] In retailing or wholesaling organizations goods are purchased for resale without changing their basic form. The cost of the goods purchased is regarded as a product cost and all other costs such as administration and selling and distribution expenses are considered to be period costs. The treatment of period and product costs for a manufacturing organization is illustrated in Fig. 2.2.

You will see that both product and period costs are eventually classified as expenses. The major difference is the point in time at which they are so classified. This is illustrated in the following example:

EXAMPLE 2.1

A company produces 100,000 identical units of a product during Period 1. The costs for the period are as follows:

Manufacturing costs:	£	
Direct labour	400,000	
Direct materials	200,000	
Manufacturing overheads	200,000	800,000
Non-manufacturing costs		300,000

During Period 1 the company sold 50,000 units for £750,000 and the remaining 50,000 units were unsold at the end of the period. There was no opening stock at the start of the period. The profit and loss account for Period 1 will be as follows:

		£
Sales (50,000 units)		750,000
Manufacturing costs: Direct labour	400,000	
(products costs) Direct materials	200,000	
Manufacturing overhead	200,000	
	800,000	
Less Closing stock (50% or 50,000 units)	400,000	
Cost of goods sold (50% or 50,000 units)		400,000
Gross profit		350,000
Less Non-manufacturing costs (period costs)		300,000
Net profit		50,000

Fifty per cent of the production was sold during the period and the remaining 50% was produced for stocks. Half of the product costs are therefore identified as an expense for the period and the remainder is included in the closing stock valuation.[2] If we assume that the closing stock is sold in the next accounting period, the remaining 50% of the product costs will become expenses in the next accounting period. However, all the period costs became an expense in this accounting period, because this is the period to which they relate. Note that only product costs form the basis for the calculation of cost of goods sold, and that period costs do not form part of this calculation.

Because non-manufacturing costs represent a significant proportion of total costs it appears appropriate to ask why accountants have not included these costs as part of the product cost. The reasons are as follows:

(1) Assets represent future benefits and manufacturing costs incurred in making a product can be expected to generate future revenues to cover the cost of production. However, there is no guarantee that non-

manufacturing costs will generate future revenue because they do not represent value added to any specific product. Non-manufacturing costs should not therefore be included in the stock valuation.

(2) The incurrence of some non-manufacturing costs, particularly in relation to distribution (for example, delivery costs), do not occur when the product is being stored and it is incorrect to include such costs as part of the stock valuation.

Elements of manufacturing costs

In manufacturing organizations the calculation of product costs consists of three elements: direct materials, direct labour and manufacturing overhead. For stock valuation the costs of a product are collected as follows:

	£
Direct materials	xxx
Direct labour	xxx
Prime cost	xxx
Manufacturing overhead	xxx
Total manufacturing cost	xxx

Direct materials consist of all those materials which can be physically identified with a specific product. For example, wood which is used to manufacture a desk can easily be identified as part of the product and can thus be classified as direct materials. Alternatively, materials used for the repair of a machine which is used for the manufacture of *many* different desks are classified as *indirect materials*. These items of materials cannot be identified with any one product because they are used for the benefit of all products rather than for any one specific product. However, not all items of materials that can be identified with a specific product are classified as direct materials. For example, the nails used in the manufacture of a particular desk can be identified specifically with the desk, but because the cost is likely to be insignificant the expenses of tracing such items do not justify the possible benefits from calculating more accurate product costs. Note that indirect materials form part of the manufacturing overhead cost.

Direct labour consists of those labour costs which can be specifically traced to or identified with a particular product. Examples of direct labour costs include the wages of operatives who assemble parts into the finished product, or machine operatives engaged in the production process. By contrast the salaries of factory supervisors or the wages paid to the staff in the stores department cannot be specifically identified with the product and thus form part of the *indirect labour costs*. The wages of all employees who do not work on the product itself but who assist in the manufacturing operation are thus classified as part of the indirect labour costs. As with indirect materials, indirect labour is classified as part of the manufacturing overhead cost.

Prime cost refers to the direct costs of the product and consists of direct labour costs plus direct material costs plus any direct expenses. The cost of hiring a machine for producing a specific product is an example of a direct expense.

Manufacturing overhead consists of all manufacturing costs other than direct labour, direct materials and direct expenses. It therefore includes all indirect manufacturing labour and material costs plus indirect manufacturing expenses. Examples of indirect manufacturing expenses in a multi-product company include rent of the factory and depreciation of machinery.

To ascertain the total manufacturing cost for stock valuation, all that is required for the direct cost items is to record the amount of resources used on the appropriate documents. For example, the units of materials used in making a particular product are recorded on a stores requisition and the hours of direct labour used are recorded on job cards. Having obtained the quantity of resources used for the direct items it is necessary to ascertain the price paid for these resources. The total of the resources used multiplied by the price paid per unit of resources used provides us with the total of the direct costs or the prime cost for a product.

In contrast, it is not possible to attach overhead costs accurately to products as overhead costs are incurred for the benefit of *all* products and the amount of the overheads which should be allocated to a specific product can only be an estimate. The accountant resolves this problem by ascertaining the total overheads for a period and then sharing these costs among the products which have been manufactured during the period, on some sensible basis. Such apportionments are questionable but we shall defer a discussion of

apportioning overheads until Chapter 4.

The distinction between direct and indirect costs depends on the cost objective. We have assumed in this section that the cost objective is the product for stock valuation. Costs are classified as direct or indirect depending on their traceability to the cost objective (that is, the product). If the cost objective is to establish the cost of using various distribution channels for *decision-making* then the rental of warehouses and the salaries of storekeepers will be regarded as direct costs for each distribution channel. Similarly, for *control* the cost objective may be to compare the costs incurred in obtaining customers' orders with budgeted costs. In this situation salesmen's salaries and travelling expenses will be regarded as direct costs whereas the costs of the personnel department in appointing production, administration and sales staff will not be traceable to the cost objective. Consequently, these costs are indirect. We shall discuss cost objectives for decision-making and control later in this chapter.

Job and process costs

For stock valuation we have noted that the manufacturing cost must be calculated for each unit of output. In an organization which produces a wide range of products or jobs, and where each order is unique, and requires different amounts of labour, material and overhead, the cost of each order must be separately calculated. Such a cost accumulation system is known as a *job costing system*. An alternative cost accumulation system known as *process costing* can be applied to an organization which produces many units of the same product during a period. With a system of process costing the allocation of manufacturing cost to a specific order is unnecessary. Instead the cost of a single unit can be obtained by merely dividing the costs of production for a period by the number of units produced in that period. In other words, the cost of an order is assumed to be the *average* cost per unit of all the units which have been produced during the period multiplied by the number of units ordered.

Job costing classification is suited to industries which produce specialized or made-to-order outputs. Examples of such industries include construction, printing, machinery and shipbuilding. Because each customer's order is normally unique, average costs per unit of output are not suitable. A job costing system will give a more

accurate calculation of product costs because costs are accumulated for each specific order, but the system is expensive in terms of the clerical work involved in attaching direct costs to each specific job. We shall look at a cost accumulation for a system of job costing in Chapters 3-5.

A system of process costing is likely to be appropriate for those firms which operate in the chemical, cement, oil, paint and textile industries as there is a mass production of like items passing through a series of successive operations. Total costs are accumulated for a period for each of these operations or processes and an average cost is calculated periodically for each process. The cost of a single unit of output is calculated by adding together the average cost of each of the processes through which the products has passed. In Chapter 6 we shall consider how costs should be accumulated where a system of process costing is used.

Classification for decision-making and planning

Cost accounting is concerned with the calculation of *actual* product costs for stock valuation and profit measurement, whereas management accounting is concerned with the provision of information to help managers make good decisions. Because decisions are concerned with *future* events management requires details of expected *future* costs and revenues. *Future* costs and revenues are not included in the data collection system as the objective of this system is to accumulate *past* costs and revenues for stock valuation and profit measurement. If past costs and revenues provide a close approximation to future costs and revenues, then (with index-linking for inflation) it will be possible to extract the appropriate information for decision-making.

Additional costs and revenue classifications can be developed to facilitate an evaluation of various alternative actions for decision-making and planning, and we shall now discuss the following classifications:

(1) costs and revenue behaviour in relation to volume of activity.
(2) relevant and irrelevant costs;
(3) sunk costs;
(4) opportunity costs;
(5) incremental and marginal costs/revenues.

Cost and revenue behaviour

A knowledge of how costs and revenues will vary with different levels of activity (or volume) is essential for decision-making. Activity or volume may be measured in terms of units of production or sales, hours worked, miles travelled, patients seen, students enrolled or any other appropriate measure of the activity of an organization. Examples of decisions which require information on how costs and revenues vary with different levels of activity include:

(1) What should the planned level of activity be for the next year?
(2) Should we reduce the selling price to sell more units?
(3) Would it be wiser to pay our sales staff by a straight commission, a straight salary, or by some combination of the two?
(4) Should we purchase additional machinery to expand output?

For each of the above decisions management requires estimates of costs and revenues at different levels of activity for the alternative courses of action. The estimate of total sales revenue at different levels of activity requires a knowledge of the relationship between selling price and demand, but we shall defer our discussion of price–demand relationships until Chapters 9 and 11.

The terms 'variable', 'fixed', 'semi-variable' and 'semi-fixed' are generally used to describe how a cost reacts to changes in activity. *Variable costs* vary in direct proportion to the volume of activity, that is, doubling the level of activity will double the total variable cost. Consequently, total variable costs are linear and *unit* variable cost is constant. Figure 2.3 illustrates a variable cost where the variable cost per unit of activity is £10.[3]

Examples of variable manufacturing costs include direct labour, direct materials and power. These costs fluctuate directly in proportion to operating activity.[4] Examples of non-manufacturing variable costs include sales commissions, which fluctuate with sales value, and petrol, which fluctuates with the number of miles travelled. Suppose, for example, a firm pays its salespersons a sales commission. As sales value increases, the commissions paid will increase proportionally. If a firm pays a commission of 10% of sales value, the total commission paid will be as follows:

Month	Sales value (£)	Commission paid (£)
1	100,000	10,000
2	120,000	12,000
3	150,000	15,000

Note that variable cost (commission paid) varies proportionally with the level of activity (as expressed in sales value), whereas the unit variable cost remains unchanged at 10 p per £1 of sales.

Fig. 2.3 Variable costs

Fig. 2.4 Fixed costs

Fixed costs remain constant over wide ranges of activity for a specified time period. Examples of fixed costs include depreciation of the factory building, supervisors' salaries, and leasing charges for cars used by the salesforce. Figure 2.4 illustrates fixed costs.

You will see that the *total* fixed costs are constant for all levels of activity whereas *unit* fixed costs decrease proportionally with the level of activity. For example, if the total of the fixed costs is £5,000 for a month, the fixed costs per unit will be as follows:

Units produced	Fixed cost per unit £
1	5000
10	500
100	50
1000	5

In Fig. 2.4 the total of the fixed costs is assumed to remain unchanged for all levels of activity but in practice one might expect the total fixed costs to increase in steps in the manner depicted in Fig. 2.5.

Total fixed costs are, however, usually graphed as fixed, as shown in Fig. 2.4A, because it is assumed that firms have previously made decisions about the amount of fixed costs which are to be incurred, and at what activity levels they intend to operate. It is the fixed costs associated with these decisions that are graphed in Fig. 2.4A.

Note that the total fixed costs are assumed to remain unchanged in response to changes in the level of activity, but *they may change in response to other factors*. For example, a constant time period is assumed but if the time period is extended, the total fixed costs may change.

Consider a monthly rental charge; if the time period is extended the total rental charge will increase. Another assumption is that price levels will remain unchanged, but if prices increase then total fixed costs will also increase.

Semi-variable costs include both a fixed and a variable component. The cost of maintenance is a semi-variable cost consisting of planned maintenance which is undertaken whatever the level of activity, and a variable element which is directly related to the level of activity. The separtion of semi-variable costs into the fixed and variable components is extremely difficult in practice and we shall defer an examination of the methods used for doing this until Chapter 20.

Semi-fixed or *step* costs are fixed for a given level of activity but they eventually increase by a constant amount at some critical point. See Fig. 2.6 for an illustration of this.

We can distinguish fixed costs from semi-fixed

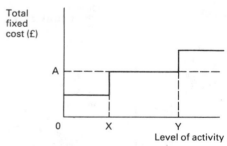

It is assumed that the firm plans to operate at a level of activity between points X and Y resulting in fixed costs of OA. The horizontal line above points X and Y is extended to the right and left signifying the planned fixed costs for the period.

Fig. 2.5 Step fixed costs regarded as a fixed cost

costs by the range between the activity levels before the steps in total fixed costs occur. In Fig. 2.5 the ranges between the steps are wider than those which occur in Fig. 2.6. In Fig. 2.5 we assume that the firm is committed to the fixed costs between activity levels X and Y and cannot increase its activity beyond Y within the current accounting period. Hence the fixed cost line is extended in both directions (as indicated by the dashed horizontal lines) and regarded as a fixed cost.

An example of a semi-fixed cost is the salaries of supervisors; assume that the supervisory staff can supervise direct labour up to 500 hours of activity per week. For each increase in 500 hours of activity per week the supervision cost will increase by the weekly wages cost of an additional supervisor.

The treatment of semi-fixed costs depends on the frequency of the steps and the amount of the increase at each point. If the steps are close together as in Fig. 2.6B, the semi-fixed costs may be approximated by a variable cost as represented by the straight line in Fig. 2.6B. If the steps are infrequent and the increase in the semi-fixed costs are small, the semi-fixed costs can be approximated by the fixed cost horizontal dashed line in the manner depicted in Fig. 2.6C. On the other hand, if the increases in semi-fixed costs are large and the steps are not too frequent (see Fig. 2.6A), the increase in the costs should be incorporated in the analysis as a step cost. The analysis will therefore include $£SF_1$ for activity levels between O and OQ_1, $£SF_2$ for activity levels between OQ_1

and OQ_2, $£SF_3$ for activity levels between OQ_2 and OQ_3, and so on.

We shall discuss the application of costs and revenues classified by behaviour throughout the remainder of the book. In particular, we shall focus on cost and revenue behaviour in Chapter 9, and in Chapter 16 when we consider flexible budgeting. The techniques for separating fixed and variable costs are introduced in Chapter 20.

Relevant and irrelevant costs and revenues

For decision-making, costs and revenues can be classified according to whether they are *relevant* to a particular decision. Relevant costs and revenues are those future costs and revenues which will be changed by a decision, whereas irrelevant costs and revenues are those which will not be affected by the decision. For example, if one is faced with a choice of making a journey by car or by public transport, the car tax and insurance costs are irrelevant as they will remain the same whatever alternative is chosen. However, petrol costs for the car will differ depending on which alternative is chosen and this cost will be relevant for decision-making.

Let us now consider a further illustration of the classification of relevant and irrelevant costs. Assume a company purchased raw materials a few years ago for £100 and that there appears to be no possibility of selling these materials or using them

Fig. 2.6 Semi-fixed costs

in future production apart from in connection with an enquiry from a former customer. This customer is preapred to purchase a product which will require the use of all these materials but he is not prepared to pay more than £250 per unit. The additional costs of converting these materials into the required product are £200. Should the company accept the order for £250? It appears that the cost of the order is £300 consisting of £100 material cost and £200 conversion cost, but this is incorrect because the £100 material cost will remain the same whether the order is accepted or rejected. The material cost is therefore *irrelevant* for the decision, but if the order is accepted the conversion costs will change by £200, and this conversion cost *is a relevant cost*. If we compare the revenue of £250 with the relevant cost for the order of £200 it means that the order should be accepted, assuming of course that no higher-priced orders can be obtained elsewhere. The following calculation shows that this is the correct decision.

	Do not accept order	Accept order
	£	£
Materials	100	100
Conversion costs	–	200
Revenue	–	(250)
Net costs	100	50

The net costs of the company are £50 less, or alternatively the company is £50 better off as a result of accepting the order. This agrees with the £50 advantage which was suggested by the relevant cost method. In this illustration the sales revenue was relevant to the decision because future revenue changed depending on which alternative was selected, but sales revenue may also be irrelevant for decision-making. Consider a situation where a company can meet its sales demand by purchasing either machine A or machine B. The output of both machines is identical but the operating costs and purchase costs of the machines are different. In this situation the sales revenue will remain unchanged irrespective of which machine is purchased (assuming of course that the quality of output is identical for both machines). Consequently, sales revenue is irrelevant for this decision; the relevant items are the operating costs and the cost of the machines.

We have now established an important principle regarding the classification of costs and revenues for decision-making, namely, that in the short term not all costs and revenues are relevant for decision-making and it is essential that we design a cost collection system which will enable us to classify costs into relevant and irrelevant categories when extracting cost information for decision-making.

Sunk costs

These costs are the cost of resources already acquired where the total will be unaffected by the choice between various alternatives. They are costs that have been created by a decision made in the past and which cannot be changed by any decision that will be made in the future. The expenditure of £100 on materials which were no longer required, referred to in the preceding section, is an example of a sunk cost. Similarly, the written down values of assets previously purchased are sunk costs. For example, if a machine was purchased four years ago for £100,000 with an expected life of five years and nil scrap value then the written down value will be £20,000 if straight line depreciation is used. This written down value will have to be written off, no matter what possible alternative future action might be chosen. If the machine was scrapped the £20,000 would be written off; if the machine was used for productive purposes, the £20,000 would still have to be written off. This cost cannot be changed by any future decision and is therefore classified as a sunk cost.

Sunk costs are irrelevant for decision-making, but they are distinguished from irrelevant costs because not all irrelevant costs are sunk coss. For example, a comparison of two alternative production methods may result in identical direct material expenditure for both alternatives, so the direct material cost is irrelevant because it will remain the same whichever alternative is chosen, but the material cost is not a sunk cost as it will be incurred in the future.

Opportunity costs

Some costs for decision-making cannot normally

be collected within the accounting system. Costs that are collected within the accounting system are based on past payments or commitments to pay at some time in the future. Sometimes it is necessary for decision-making to inpute costs which will not require cash outlays, and these imputed costs are called opportunity costs. An opportunity cost is a cost which measures the opportunity which is lost or sacrificed when the choice of one course of action requires that an alternative course of action be given up.

EXAMPLE 2.2

A company has an opportunity to obtain a contract for the production of a special component. This component will require 100 hours of processing on machine X. Machine X is working at full capacity on the production of product A, and the only way in which the contract can be fulfilled is by reducing the output of product A. This will mean a loss of revenue of £200. The contract will also result in *additional* variable costs of £1,000.

If the company takes on the contract it will sacrifice revenue of £200 from the lost output of product A. This represents an opportunity cost and should be included as part of the costs when negotiating for the contract. The contract price should at least cover the additional costs of £1,000 plus the £200 opportunity cost to ensure that the company will be better off in the short term by accepting the contract.

It is important to note that opportunity costs only apply to the use of scarce resources. Where resources are not scarce no sacrifice exists from using these resources. In Example 2.2 if machine X was operating at 80% of its potential capaicty then the decision to accept the contract would not have resulted in reduced production of product A. Consequently, there would have been no loss of revenue and the opportunity cost would be zero.

You should now be aware that opportunity costs are of vital importance for decision-making. If no alternative use of resources exists, the opportunity cost is zero, but if resources have an alternative use, and are scarce, then an opportunity cost does exist. Unfortunately the calculation of the opportunity cost of a resource is very difficult in practice but some attempt must be made to obtain a reasonable approximation. One possible approach is to use linear programming techniques to measure the opportunity costs of scarce resources, and a discussion of this topic is presented in Chapter 22. For a detailed discussion of opportunity costs see Arnold and Scapens (1981).

Incremental and marginal costs/revenues

Incremental and differential costs and revenues are the additional costs or revenues which arise from the production or sale of a group of additional units. Consider the information presented in Example 2.3.

EXAMPLE 2.3

The following are extracts from the sales budget of a company for the current year:

	£
Selling Revenues	
50,000 units at a selling price of £20 per unit	1,000,000
Selling Costs:	
Advertising	100,000
Salaries of sales staff	80,000
Travelling expenses of salespeople	50,000
Rent of sales office	10,000

During the next year management is considering establishing a new sales territory in the north of England. It is proposed to increase advertising expenditure by 30 per cent and appoint an additional salesperson at a salary of £15,000 per annum to establish a market. In addition travelling expenses are expected to increase by ten per cent per annum. The target annual sales volume at the existing selling price for the new sales territory is 10,000 units per annum. The estimated variable cost of production is £5 per unit of output. Should the company establish the new sales territory?

The decision requires details of the incremental revenues and costs which will arise from estabishing the new sales territory and the following information should be presented:

	Current costs and revenues £		Projected costs and revenues £		Incremental costs and revenues £	
Sales revenue (1)		1,000,000		1,200,000		200,000
Advertising	100,000		130,000		30,000	
Sales staff salaries	80,000		95,000		15,000	
Travelling expenses	50,000		55,000		5,000	
Rent	10,000		10,000		–	
Variable production Costs (2)	250,000	490,000	300,000	590,000	50,000	100,000

(1) Current sales revenue is 50,000 units at £20 per unit and projected sales revenue is 60,000 units at £20 per unit.
(2) Current variable production cost is 50,000 units at £5 per unit and projected variable production cost is 60,000 units at £5 per unit.

The incremental costs and revenues of establishing the new sales territory is shown in the final column of the above statement. The incremental analysis can be presented as follows:

			£
Incremental revenues			200,000
Incremental costs:	Advertising	30,000	
	Salaries	15,000	
	Travelling expenses	5,000	
	Production costs	50,000	100,000
Incremental profit			100,000

You will see from this example that incremental costs may or may not include fixed costs. If fixed costs change as a result of a decision, the increase in costs represents an incremental cost; the increase in the salaries of the sales staff is therefore an incremental cost. If fixed costs do not change as a result of a decision the incremental costs will be zero, and so the incremental cost of the rent of the sales office is zero.

Incremental costs and revenues are similar in principle to the economist's concept of marginal cost and marginal revenue. The main difference is that marginal cost/revenue represents the additional cost/revenue of one extra unit of output whereas incremental cost/revenue represents the additional cost/revenue resulting from a group of additional units of output. The economist normally represents the theoretical relationship between cost/revenue and output in terms of the marginal cost/revenue of single additional units of output. We shall see that the accountant is normally more interested in the incremental cost/revenue of increasing production and sales to

whatever extent is contemplated, and this is most unlikely to be a single unit of output.

Decision-making summary

In this section we have concentrated on possible methods of cost classification for decision-making. The application, benefits and limitations which result from classifying costs and revenues in the manner described in the preceding discussion will be considered in more detail in Chapters 9–14, when we shall concentrate on the requirements of financial information for a variety of decision-making problems. However, we shall also be considering in Chapters 3–8 whether or not costs which have been accumulated for stock valuation can also provide a reasonable approximation for decision-making. For this reason it is important that you should now understand the various methods of classifying costs for decision-making and the conflicting requirements of cost classification for stock valuation and decision-making.

Classification for control

The allocation of costs to products is inappropriate for cost control as the manufacture of the product may consist of several different operations

all of which are the responsibility of different individuals. The product cost will not therefore pinpoint costs to areas of responsibility. To overcome this problem costs and revenues must be allocated to the individuals who are responsible for their incurrence. This system is known as responsibility accounting.

Responsibility accounting is based on the recognition of individual areas of responsibility as specified in a firm's organization structure. These areas of responsibility are known as responsibility centres; a responsibility centre may be defined as a segment of an organization where an individual manager is held responsible for the segment's performance. There are three types of responsibility centre:

(1) A *cost centre* where managers are accountable for the expenses which are under their control.
(2) A *profit centre* where managers are accountable for sales revenue and expenses, for example a division of a company which is responsible for the selling and production of a product.
(3) An *investment centre* where managers are normally accountable for sales revenue and expenses but in addition are responsible for some capital investment decisions and are thus able to influence the size of the investment.

Controllable and non-controllable costs and revenues

Costs and revenues allocated to responsibility centres should be classified according to whehter or not they are controllable or non-controllable by the manager of the responsibility centre. All costs are controllable at some management level. For example, top management has authority to dispose of facilities and increase or decrease the number of managers employed. However, not all costs can be controlled at lower management levels, so there is a need for costs to be classified into their controllable and non-controllable categories in the performance reports which the accountant prepares for each responsibility centre. If costs were not classified in this way it would be difficult to evaluate a manager's performance. In

addition, managers would soon lose interest in cost control if they found that their performance was being judged on items which were outside their control.

A controllable cost may be defined as a cost which is reasonably subject to regulation by the manager with whose responsibility that cost is being identified. If this condition does not hold then clearly the cost should be classified as non-controllable by the manager of the resonsibility centre. However, such non-controllable costs may be controllable at a higher level of responsibility. For example, a responsibility centre manager may have no control over the number of supervisors employed in his department, but this decision may be made by his superior. Hence the supervision costs will be a non-controllable cost on the responsibility manager's performance report but it will be a controllable cost on his superior's performance report.

In additioon to classifying costs into their controllable and non-controllable elements a detailed analysis of controllable costs is necessary so that the responsibility centre manager and his superior can pinpoint those costs which do not conform to plan. Exhibit 2.2 illustrates a typical performance report which may be presented to a manager of a responsibility centre.

Exhibit 2.2 Responsibility centre performance report

	Department X		
Controllable costs	Budget	Actual	Variance
	£	£	£
Direct materials	16,500	15,300	1,200
Direct labour	21,000	22,000	(1,000)
Indirect labour	3,000	3,200	(200)
Idle time	500	400	100
Fuel	800	1,000	(200)
Supplies	400	500	(100)
Stationery	300	280	20
	42,500	42,680	(180)
Non-controllable costs			
Salaries	14,000	14,000	–
Depreciation	5,000	5,000	–
Insurance	2,000	2,200	(200)
	21,000	21,200	(200)

You will see that the responsibility centre manager requires that the controllable costs be classified into various important categories of expenses, and that the difference between the budgeted and actual results be emphasized. This

difference is termed the *variance* and should not be confused with the statistical variance which we shall be discussing in Chapter 12. In practice, a more detailed analysis of controllable costs may be required. For example, both direct labour and direct materials should be analysed according to labour grades and different types of materials used.

Cost behaviour

A discussion of fixed, variable, semi-variable and semi-fixed costs was presented earlier in this chapter. Classification by the behaviour of costs to changes in the level of activity is also important for control. Let us assume that the controllable costs for a responsibility centre consist entirely of variable costs. The budgeted variable cost per unit produced is £1 and the budgeted production for the next period is 400 units. The actual production for the period was 500 units and the actual costs were £480. Exhibit 2.3 presents a summary of two possible performance reports.

The *incorrect method* compares the actual costs for 500 units with the budgeted costs for 400 units. Clearly we are not comparing like with like and this comparison is inappropriate for assessing the manager's performance in the control of costs. In fact, the performance report indicates that the manager has performed rather badly regarding the control of costs. This is clearly incorrect. On the other hand, the *correct method* compares the actual costs for 500 units with costs that should have been incurred for 500 units, and correctly indicates that the manager has been successful in the control of costs.

Exhibit 2.3 clearly indicates that it is essential for cost control to compare actual and budgeted costs *for the same level of activity*. This requires that costs be initially classified into their fixed, variable, semi-fixed and semi-variable elements so that the budgeted costs can be adjusted to the level of activity under which the manager operated for the period. The system which we have outlined here is called *flexibile budgeting*.

A detailed discussion of the problems involved in classifying costs into controllable and non-controllable, and cost behaviour categories can be found in Chapters 16–19.

Exhibit 2.3 Summary of performance reports

(A) Incorrect method			(B) Correct method		
	Budget	Actual		Budget	Actual
	£	£		£	£
Variable costs	400	480	Variable costs	500	480

Summary

To meet the requirements of the various users of accounting information costs and revenues must be classified in various ways. For cost classification, costs should be identified with a cost objective, which can be defined as any activity for which a separate measurement of costs is desired. To simplify the presentation we have identified three cost objectives: costs for stock valuation, costs for decision-making and costs for control. With regard to stock valuation, we have classified costs into manufacturing and non-manufacturing categories, various elements of manufacturing costs, period and product costs, and job and process costs. For decision-making we have classified costs according to cost behaviour patterns and into relevant, sunk, opportunity, marginal and incremental costs. Finally, for cost control we have classified the costs into controllable and non-controllable costs, and fixed and variable costs.

The problems, applications and limitations of the various methods of cost classification will be pursued in detail in various chapters in the remainder of the book. For example, in Part II (Chapters 3–8) we shall concentrate on cost accumulation for product costs for stock valuation and profit measurement. In Part III (Chapters 9–14) cost information for decision-making is considered and in Part IV (Chapters 15–19) we turn our attention to cost information for planning and control. Within each of these sections we shall develop many of the aspects which we have discussed in this chapter, but it would be unwise to consider each of the various objectives of cost information in isolation, so every opportunity will be used to illustrate how cost information which is necessary to meet one cost objective may be inappropriate for another. For this reason it is important that you have a sound understanding of the alternative methods of cost classification so that you can evaluate different methods of assembling cost information.

References and further reading

Accounting Standards Committee. *Accounting for Stocks and Work in Progress* (SSAP 9), 1975.

Arnold, J. and Scapens, R. The British Contribution to Opportunity Cost Theory, in Bromwich, M. and Hopwood, A.G. (Eds), *Essays in British Accounting Research*. Pitman, 1981, pp. 155-70.

Coase, R.H. The Nature of Costs, in Solomons, D. (Ed.), *Studies in Cost Analysis*, 2nd edn. Sweet & Maxwell, 1968.

Haseman, W.C. An Interpretive Framework of Cost. *The Accounting Review* **43**(4), October 1968, pp. 738-52.

Management Accounting: Official Terminology. Institute of Cost and Mangement Accountants, 1982.

National Association of Accountants. The Use and Classification of Costs, in Solomons, D. (Ed.), *Studies in Cost Analysis*, 2nd edn. Sweet & Maxwell, 1968.

Staubus, G.J. *Activity Costing and Input–Output Accounting*. Irwin, 1971.

Problems

* Indicates that a suggested solution is to be found in the *Students' Manual*.

2.1* Classify each of the following as being usually fixed (F), variable (V), semi-fixed (SF) or semi-variable (SV):
(a) Direct labour
(b) Depreciation on machinery
(c) Factory rental
(d) Supplies and other indirect materials
(e) Advertising
(f) Maintenance of machinery
(g) Factory manager's salary
(h) Supervisory personnel
(i) Royalty payments

2.2* Which of the following costs are likely to be controllable by the head of the production department?
(a) Price paid for materials
(b) Charge for floor space
(c) Raw materials used
(d) Electricity used for machinery
(e) Machinery depreciation
(f) Direct labour
(g) Insurance on machinery
(h) Share of cost of industrial relations department

2.3 For the relevant cost data in items (1)–(7), indicate which of the following is the best classification:

(a) sunk cost (f) semi-fixed cost
(b) incremental cost (g) controllable cost
(c) variable cost (h) non-controllable cost
(d) fixed cost (i) opportunity cost
(e) semi-variable cost

(1) A company is considering selling an old machine. The machine has a book value of £20,000. In evaluating the decision to sell the machine, the £20,000 is a
(2) As an alternative to the old machine the company can rent a new one. It will cost £3,000 a year. In analysing the cost–volume behaviour the rental is a
(3) To run the firm's machines, there are two alternative courses of action. One is to pay the operator a base salary plus a small amount per unit produced. This makes the total cost of the operators a.
(4) As an alternative, the firm can pay the operators a flat salary. It would then use one machine when volume is low, two when it expands, and three during peak periods. This means that the total operator cost would now be a
(5) The machine mentioned in (1) could be sold for £8,000. If the firm considers retaining and using it, the £8,000 is a
(6) If the firm wishes to use the machine any longer, it must be repaired. For the decision to retain the machine, the repair cost is a
(7) The machine is charged to the foreman of each department at a rate of £3,000 a year. In evaluating the foreman, the charge is a

2.4* Data:

	£
Cost of motor car	5,500
Trade-in price after 2 years or 60,000 miles is expected to be	1,500
Maintenance–6 monthly service costing	60
Spares/replacement parts, per 1,000 miles	20
Vehicle licence, per annum	80
Insurance, per annum	150
Tyre replacements after 25,000 miles, four at	37.50 each
Petrol, per gallon	1.90
Average mileage from one gallon is 25 miles.	

(a) From the above data you are required:
(i) to prepare a schedule to be presented to management showing for the mileages of 5,000, 10,000, 15,000 and 30,000 miles per annum:
(1) total variable cost
(2) total fixed cost
(3) total cost

(4) variable cost per mile (in pence to nearest penny)

(5) fixed cost per mile (in pence to nearest penny)

(6) total cost per mile (in pence to nearest penny)

If, in classifying the costs, you consider that some can be treated as either variable or fixed, state the assumption(s) on which your answer is based together with brief supporting reason(s).

(ii) on the graph paper provided, to plot the information given in your answer to (i) above for the costs listed against (1), (2), (3) and (6).

(iii) to read off from your graph(s) in (ii) and state the approximate total costs applicable to 18,000 miles and 25,000 miles and the total cost per mile (in pence) at these two mileages.

(b) 'the more miles you travel, the cheaper it becomes.' Comment briefly on this statement.

(25 marks)

ICMA Cost Accounting 1
November 1982

2.5* (a) In economics, variable costs are often described as curvilinear whereas within cost accounting it is usual to assume variable costs have a linear function.

You are required to sketch two separate diagrams depicting:
(i) a curvilinear variable cost;
(ii) a linear variable cost.

(b) Explain and show by drawing two separate diagrams what is meant by:
(i) a semi-variable cost;
(ii) a stepped fixed cost;
and give ONE example of each.

(c) (i) Explain a method of depreciating an asset where the depreciation is not regarded as a fixed cost. Give the names of two common kinds of assets which may suitably be depreciated by the method you have stated.

(ii) You are required, ignoring inflation, to:
comment on the following statement, and
state whether, or not, you agree with it.

A business owning an asset with an estimated life of five years makes an annual provision for depreciation which is one fifth of the purchase price of the asset. Provided the asset lasts for exactly five years the business will, by making the depreciation entries, ensure that sufficient cash is available to replace the asset.

(20 marks)

ICMA Cost Accounting 1
November 1981

2.6* (a) 'Fixed costs are really variable: the more you produce the less they become'.

Explain the above statement and state whether or not you agree with it.

(b) You are required to *sketch* a separate graph for each of the items listed below in order to indicate the behaviour of the expense. Graph paper need not be used but your axes must be labelled.
(i) Supervisory labour
(ii) Depreciation of plant on a machine hour basis
(iii) Planned preventive maintenance plus unexpected maintenance
(iv) Monthly pay of a salesman who receives a salary of £3,000 per annum plus a commission of 1% paid on his previous month's sales when they exceed £20,000; assume that his previous month's sales totalled £30,000.

ICMA Cost Accounting 1
November 1977

2.7 From the information given below you are required to:
(a) prepare a standard cost sheet for one unit and enter on the standard cost sheet the costs to show sub-totals for:
(i) prime cost;
(ii) variable production cost;
(iii) total production cost;
(iv) total cost;
(b) calculate the selling price per unit allowing for a profit of 15% of the selling price.

The following data are given:
Budgeted output for the year 9,800 units
Standard details for one unit:
 Direct materials 40 square metres at £5.30 per square metre
 Direct wages:
 Bonding department 48 hours at £2.50 per hour
 Finishing department 30 hours at £1.90 per hour
 Budgeted costs and hours per annum:

	£	hours
Variable overhead:		
Bonding department	375,000	500,000
Finishing department	150,000	300,000
Fixed overhead:		
Production	392,000	
Selling and distribution	196,000	
Administration	98,000	

(15 marks)

ICMA Cost Accounting 1
May 1980

2.8 A theatre with seating for 1,200 persons is maintained and operated by a local authority. The theatre is used for plays by the authority's

own repertory company and is let for concerts, other productions and meetings.

In an average week details of the expenditure and income of the theatre are as follows:

	£
Expenditure:	
Artists	1,600
Salaries and wages of full time employees	600
Wage related costs	500
Part-time programme sellers and attendants	100
Maintenance, lighting and heating	550
Proportion of Recreation Department's administration costs (apportioned)	800
Scenery and equipment	400
Costumes	200
Income, other than ticket sales:	
Refreshments, net	300
Lettings	160
Sponsorship donations	100
Advertising	100

When the repertory company stages a play half of all available tickets at each price are usually sold for five evening performances. There are 300 seats at £2.00 each, 400 seats at £1.50 each and 500 seats at £1.00 each.

The local operatic society has offered to hire the theatre for one week in October 1981 for its production of 'The Desert Song' at a rental of either:

 (i) one half of the income from all tickets sold;

or (ii) £3,000.

The society would, irrespective of the hire basis chosen, provide its own programme sellers and attendants in place of those usually employed by the authority. Guaranteed local support would enable the operatic society to reduce the prices given above by £0.25 for each seat, and expect to have 75% capacity audiences for each of the seven performances planned for six evenings and one Saturday afternoon.

If the letting were approved, the authority would remain responsible for providing and paying full time employees and artistes and for maintenance, lighting and heating. It would not be obliged to pay its part-time employees nor would it incur expenditure for that week on scenery and equipment and on costumes.

You are required to prepare a report for the forthcoming meeting of the authority's Recreation and Arts Committee setting out:

 (a) in a columnar statement the expected income and expenditure and the resultant surplus or deficit for one week if the theatre is:

 (i) used by the repertory company for a play,

 (ii) let to the operatic society for 'The Desert Song', on each of the two bases stated above;

 (b) your recommendation;

 (c) three aspects or uncertainties which you would like the committee to consider.

(25 marks)
ICMA Cost Accounting 1
November 1980

2.9 The managing director of X Limited has recently returned from attending a conference on cost behaviour and is anxious to ensure that the cost reports are in accord with the various theories he has heard there. In a discussion with you he has made two major observations:

 (i) 'in general, fixed costs are actually variable because an increase in production leads to lower costs';

 (ii) 'a marginal costing approach must be right for the company because all we must be concerned with are the variable costs as the fixed costs look after themselves.'

Draft a report to the managing director outlining the major concepts involved in his observations and assessing their validity.

(25 marks)
ICMA Cost Accounting 2
May 1982

2.10* On the answer sheet provided are fifteen pairs of axes for graphs. On each one a cost curve depicting a particular set of circumstances can be drawn.

Example: Fixed costs

You are required to draw cost curves depicting each of the following independent sets of circumstances on the printed answer sheet provided:

 (i) y = x,

 (ii) y = a + bx,

 (iii) $y = a + bx + cx^2$,

 (iv) step-costs,

 (v) total cost of buying goods subject to a reduction in unit price, which applies only to further goods purchased, after a certain cumulative sum of purchases has been made,

 (vi) total cost of buying goods in short supply, so that after the purchase of a certain cumulative sum the unit price of any further goods purchased increases,

 (vii) total cost of buying electricity on a two-part tariff, being a fixed rental charge plus a

constant cost per unit used,

(viii) marginal cost of a firm with a slowly-declining long-run average cost curve,

(ix) total cost of a firm experiencing a learning-curve phenomenon,

(x) total cost of buying a transport service at a constant unit price, but for which a deferred rebate is given after a certain quantity has been purchased,

(xi) average fixed cost per unit of activity,

(xii) total cost of an incentive bonus given at a constant rate per unit of output after a certain level of output,

(xiii) total cost of telephone charges, given three elements which are–
(1) a fixed rental
(2) a certain amount of free calling time before any call charge is levied
(3) a certain amount of calling time is charged at a constant rate per unit of time up to a given maximum amount of calling time after which calling time is again free of charge,

(xiv) cost of a year's depreciation charged on the sum-of-the-years'-digits basis,

(xv) total cost of rent on a factory which is leased from the local authority under an employment generation scheme, such that the rent is a fixed certain sum which is waived if more than a certain number of direct labour-hours is worked in a year (10 marks).

*ICAEW Management Accounting
December 1981*

2.11* It is commonly suggested that a management accounting system should be capable of supplying different measures of cost for different purposes. You are required to set out the main types of purpose for which cost information may be required in a business organisation, and to discuss the alternative measures of cost which might be appropriate for each purpose.

*ICAEW Management Accounting
July 1980*

2.12* *Opportunity cost* and *sunk cost* are among the concepts of cost commonly discussed.
You are required:
(i) to define these terms precisely (4 marks),
(ii) to suggest for each of them situations in which the concept might be applied (4 marks), and
(iii) to assess briefly the significance of each of the concepts (4 marks).

*ICAEW P2 Management Accounting
December 1980*

2.13* 'The diverse uses of routinely recorded cost data give rise to a fundamental danger: information prepared for one purpose can be grossly misleading in another context' (from *Management Accounting: A Conceptual Approach* by L.R. Amey and D.A. Egginton).
Required:
Discuss to what extent the above statement is valid and explain your conclusions.

(c. 12 marks)
*ACCA P2 Management Accounting
June 1979*

Cost accumulation for stock valuation and profit measurement

In Chapter 1 we saw that *cost accounting* is concerned with the allocation of costs to each individual job or product for stock valuation and profit measurement, whereas *management accounting* is concerned with providing managers with appropriate financial information to help them make better decisions. In this section we shall concentrate on cost accounting but we will also briefly consider the extent to which product costs accumulated for stock valuation should be adjusted for decision-making and control. Readers who are pursuing a course on management accounting rather than cost accounting should proceed directly to Part III.

The objective of cost accounting is to determine unit *manufacturing* costs. These costs are necessary for financial accounting and in the next six chapters we shall be looking at how unit *manufacturing* costs are ascertained. In Chapters 3 and 4 we shall consider the procedures necessary to allocate direct materials, direct labour and overhead costs to products. In Chapter 5 the emphasis will be on the data processing system for cost accounting. The first three chapters in this section assume a job costing system where costs are charged to each individual customer's order as each order is *unique*, requiring different amounts of labour, materials and overheads. In Chapter 6 we shall consider the cost accumulation procedure for a process costing system. This is a system applicable to industries which produce many units of the same product during a particular period. In Chapter 7 we shall discuss the problems associated with calculating product costs in those industries which produce joint and by-products. The final chapter in this section is concerned with an alternative accounting treatment of fixed manufacturing overheads.

3 Accounting for materials and labour

In this chapter and the five following chapters we shall be looking at product costing, the objective of which is to determine *unit manufacturing costs*. Unit costs are necessary for financial accounting and may, under certain circumstances, be used by managers for planning and decision-making. We begin by concentrating on accounting for material and labour costs. Throughout this chapter we will examine a job costing system designed for a manufacturing organization but note that the same basic techniques are also used by service organizations; for example, accountants, consulting engineers, lawyers, garages, and so on, use job costing to provide information about the cost of work they have carried out for their clients.

In designing a system to account for material and labour costs it is important that suitable clerical procedures are introduced to ensure that costs are collected quickly and accurately. Detailed consideration of such clerical procedures and documentation is therefore necessary at this point and we begin by looking at the clerical procedure for the control and recording of materials.

Materials control procedure

Consider Fig. 3.1, which illustrates a typical procedure for the ordering, receipt and issue of materials in a manufacturing organization.

Determining optimal stock levels

The major objective of stock control is to establish and maintain the optimum level of investment in all types of stocks, from raw materials to finished goods. When establishing optimum stock levels it is necessary to ensure that sufficient stocks are maintained so that production requirements and customer demand can be met. On the other hand excessive stocks are to be avoided since this will result in unnecessary money being tied up in stocks which could be used for other profitable purposes. The optimum stock level lies somewhere between these two points.

Establishing optimum stock levels is of vital importance in controlling stock levels but our major concern in this chapter is to consider the accounting procedure for materials and supplies; we shall not consider at this stage how optimal stock levels may be established (for a full discussion of this topic turn to Chapter 21). You will see from Chapter 21 that determining optimum stock levels also enables us to establish the stock level at which materials should be replenished (the re-order point) and the quantity to be ordered (the re-order quantity).

The storekeeper is responsible for ensuring that optimal stock levels are maintained for each item of material in stock, and it is necessary that he should maintain an accurate clerical record of the *quantity* of material in stock for each stores item. The clerical record for collecting this information is called a *bin card* (see Exhibit 3.1).

Fig. 3.1 Materials control procedure

In most large organizations stock records will now be kept on a computer rather than on bin cards, and the storekeeper merely presses a few keys on a visual display unit to obtain details of a particular stock item. The storekeeper will normally be responsible for informing the purchasing department when to purchase various materials. If records are maintained manually the storekeeper must examine each bin card to find the items which need to be re-ordered. A computerized system will provide this information at the touch of a key. When items of materials have reached their re-order point the storekeeper makes out a *purchase requisition* requesting the purchasing department to obtain the re-order quantity from the appropriate supplier.

Purchase of materials

When the purchasing department receives a copy of the purchase requisition the purchasing officer will select the appropriate supplier based on the department's expert knowledge, and then complete a *purchase order* requesting the supplier to supply the materials listed on the order. A copy of the purchase order is sent to the receiving department for checking with the goods when they arrive.

Receipt of materials

When the goods are received by the stores department they are inspected and checked with the supplier's delivery note and a copy of the purchase order. The stores department then lists the materials received on a *goods received note* (GRN) and enters details in the receipts column of the appropriate bin card. Copies of the GRN are passed to the purchasing department and to the accounts department. The purchasing department will record that the order has been completed and the accounts department will check the GRN with the supplier's invoice to ensure that payment is only made in respect of goods actually received. The supplier's invoice will normally

arrive several days after the goods have been received, and the accounts department uses this invoice to price each of the items listed on the GRN. The items on the GRN are then entered in the respective column of the appropriate *stores ledger account*. An example of a stores ledger

Exhibit 3.1 A bin card

BIN CARD							
Description: Normal Quantity to Order:			Bin No.: ... Code No.: ... Maximum: ... Minimum: .. Re-order Level:				
Receipts			Issues			Balance	Remarks
Date	G.R.N. No.	Quan- tity	Date	Req. No.	Quan- tity	Quantity	

Exhibit 3.2 A stores ledger account

	STORES LEDGER ACCOUNT										
	Material: Code: Maximum Quantity: Minimum Quantity:										
Date	Receipts				Issues				Stock		
	G.R.N. No.	Quantity	Unit Price £	Amount £	Stores Req. No.	Quantity	Unit Price £	Amount £	Quantity	Unit Price £	Amount £

account can be seen in Exhibit 3.2. You will notice from this example that it is merely a record of the quantity and value of each individual item of materials in store. In most organizations these records are now stored on a computer.

Issue of materials

The production control department is responsible for maintaining scheduled production in accordance with the production budget and the planned stock levels. (For a detailed discussion of production scheduling see Lockyer, 1982.)

The formal procedure for authorizing production is for the production control department to issue a production order to the appropriate production department. Production control also determines the quantity of materials necessary to fulfil a production order and lists the required materials on *stores requisitions* which are attached to the production order. When the departmental foreman receives the production order he gives the requisitions to the storekeeper in exchange for the appropriate materials. The storekeeper then enters the details from the stores requisitions in the issue column of the appropriate bin cards (remember that a separate bin card is maintained for each of the items of material held in stock). He then forwards the stores requisition to the accounts department. For an example of a typical stores requisition see Exhibit 3.3.

When the accounts department receives the stores requisition it will price each of the items listed on the requisition. This information is obtained from the receipts column in the stores ledger account for each item of material issued. (Remember that there is a separate stores ledger account for each individual item of material in stock.) The information on the stores requisition is transferred to the quantity and value columns in the various stores ledger accounts, and a balance of the quantity and value for each of the specific items of materials is calculated. In many organizations this clerical routine is carried out by a computer.

Charging materials to jobs

The cost of each material issue should now be charged to the appropriate job number or over-

Exhibit 3.3 A stores requisition

STORES REQUISITION						
Material Required for: (Job or Overhead Account) Department:				Date:		No.
Quantity	Description	Code No.	Weight	Rate	£	Notes
Foreman:						

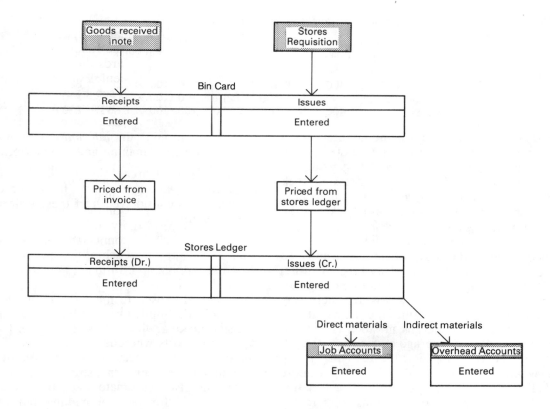

Fig. 3.2 Summary of materials accounting procedure

head account, the relevant information being obtained from the stores requisitions. You will see from Exhibit 3.3 that the job number or overhead account number should previously have been entered on to the stores requisition by the departmental foreman. The final stage is for the accounting department to record the following transactions:

(1) Reduce raw material stocks by recording the values issued in the stores ledger accounts.
(2) Record the amount of materials issued in the appropriate job or overhead account.

A summary of the accounting procedure is given in Fig. 3.2.

Pricing the issues of raw materials

You will recall from our previous discussion relating to the materials control procedure that the purchase cost which was charged to job or overhead accounts was obtained from the receipts column of the appropriate stores ledger account. We must now consider how this purchase cost is to be determined, as there are several possible methods. Consider the situation illustrated in Example 3.1.

EXAMPLE 3.1

During the quarter ending 31 March a company purchased 200 gallons of liquid on the following dates:
1 February : 100 gallons at £1 per gallon
1 March : 100 gallons at £2 per gallon
On 30 March 100 gallons were issued to job X. The liquid had been placed in a tank and it would be impossible to determine which consignment had been issued. The liquid is suitable for resale in its purchased state at £4 per gallon. For simplicity let us assume that the company incurred no labour or overhead costs and that there was no opening stock.

There are several possible methods which may be used to calculate the cost of the issue and the value of the closing stock. First, we can assume

Exhibit 3.4 Summary of transactions in Example 3.1

	Sales £	Cost of sales £	Raw materials Closing stock £	Gross profit £
First in first out (FIFO)	400	100 (100 × £1)	200 (100 × £2)	300
Last in first out (LIFO)	400	200 (100 × £2)	100 (100 × £1)	200
Average cost	400	150 (100 × £1.50)	150 (100 × £1.50)	250

that the first item received was the first item to be issued; that is *first in, first out* (FIFO). In the present example the £100 material cost would be recorded as the cost of job X and the closing stock would be valued at £200. Secondly, we can assume that the last item to be received into stock was the first item to be issued, that is *last in, first out* (LIFO). Here, a material cost of £200 would be recorded against the cost of the job and the closing stock would be valued at £100. Thirdly, since it would be impossible to determine whether the first or last consignment was issued there may be a strong case for issuing the items at the *average cost* of the materials in stock (i.e. £1.50 per gallon). Under an average cost system, the job cost would be recorded as £150 and the closing stock would be valued at £150. For a more detailed example of the problems of calculating the various issue prices of materials refer to the Appendix at the end of this chapter. A summary of the transactions set out in Example 3.1 is given in Exhibit 3.4.

In example 3.1 we assumed that it was impossible to separate physically the materials received, but there are many situations where it is possible to identify physically materials issued with a particular consignment. It is, however, too cumbersome to label each batch of materials received, and it is necessary to make some assumption about the flow of materials in and out of stores based on one of the three stores pricing methods already described. Note that FIFO, LIFO and average cost all charge the job at cost and value the stock at cost, but how do we determine which method of pricing should be used? Before we answer this question you should note that the pricing of stores issues is intended to meet the following two objectives:

(1) To allocate the material costs to the various jobs, which then form part of the stock valuation (for unsold production) and the cost of sales (for production which has been sold). Here we are concerned with profit calculations and stock valuations for external reporting.

(2) To determine the *relevant* cost of materials for decision-making and product pricing.

For management accounting *the second objective is of overriding importance*. Before proceeding further let us consider each of these objectives in more detail.

External reporting

The method chosen to meet the requirements of external reporting is likely to be unacceptable for decision-making; job costs are recorded with *actual* past costs whereas *future* costs and opportunity costs are necessary for decision-making. The method chosen for external reporting may sometimes give a satisfactory approximation of the relevant cost for decision-making but this will depend on the particular circumstances.

Let us consider the suitability of the three methods of stores pricing (FIFO, LIFO and average cost) for external reporting. Later in this chapter we shall also discuss a future orientated system of stores pricing called standard costing. FIFO appears to be the most logical method in the sense that it makes the same assumption as the physical flow of materials through an organization; that is, it is assumed that items received first will be issued first. During periods of inflation, the earliest materials which have the lowest prices will be issued first. You will remember from Exhibit 3.4 that this assumption leads to a lower cost of sales calculation and therefore a higher profit than would be obtained by using either of the other methods. Note also that the value of the raw material closing stock will be at the latest and therefore the higher prices.

We can also see by referring back to Example 3.1 and Exhibit 3.4 that, with the LIFO method, the latest and higher prices are charged to production. This results in a higher cost of sales charge and lower profits compared with using FIFO or average cost. The value of the raw material closing stock will be at the earliest and therefore lower price. Under the average cost

method, the cost of sales and the closing stock will fall somewhere between the values recorded for the FIFO and LIFO methods.

LIFO is not an acceptable method of pricing for taxation purposes, although this does not preclude its use provided that the accounts are adjusted for Inland Revenue purposes. The Statement of Standard Accounting Practice on stocks and work in progress (SSAP 9), however, states that LIFO does not bear a reasonable relationship to actual costs obtained during the period and implies that this method is inappropriate for external reporting. In view of these comments the FIFO or the average cost method should be used for external reporting. Note at this point that the value of raw material stock may not necessarily consist of the total of one of the stores pricing methods outlined. The Statement of Standard Accounting Practice on stocks and work in progress states that it is necessary to compare the cost and net realizable values for each similar group of stocks and then to value the stocks at the lower of these figures.

The accounting profession is currently in the process of introducing a system of current cost accounting for external reporting and this may eventually replace historical accounting. The LIFO method provides the closest approximation to current cost, and we may therefore see a move towards the use of LIFO for external reporting in the future.

Decision-making

We will now consider the most appropriate method of stores pricing for decision-making. We are interested here in the *future* costs of the raw materials. Note that the use of materials on a particular job will *normally* result in those items having to be replaced. In this situation the relevant material cost will be the *replacement cost*.[1] In addition, management may also require the preparation of monthly or quarterly profit and loss statements, and it can be argued that the profit calculation may be more meaningful if the stocks are valued at replacement cost. Consider the situation outlined in Example 3.2.

EXAMPLE 3.2

1 January — Allan starts business with £1,000 cash and on the same date uses this money to purchase 1,000 units of stock at £1 each.

31 December — He sells the 1,000 units at cost plus 20%.

The replacement cost at this date is £1.50 per unit. For simplicity we shall assume that there are no labour or overhead costs.

The balance sheet after each transaction will be as follows:

Balance sheet	(1)	as at 1 January	
Capital 1,000		Cash	1,000

Balance sheet	(2)	as at 1 January	
Capital 1,000		Stock	1,000
		(consisting of 1,000 units at £1)	

Balance sheet	(3)	as at 31 December	
Capital 1,000		Cash	1,200
Profit	200	(equivalent to 800 units stock at £1.50)	

These accounting statements indicate that Allan has made a profit of £200; in real terms, however, capital has not increased. In fact it has declined as Allan has not maintained his original capital intact. At the beginning of the year his capital consisted of a stock of 1,000 units, but by the end of the year the capital was equivalent to only 800 units of stock. You can see from this simplified illustration that it would be unwise for a company to use such historic cost calculations as a basis for decision-making, as a loss has been made in *real* terms. It may therefore be useful to management if internal profit statements are prepared, with the cost of sales figure calculated on the basis of stores issued being priced at their replacement cost. You can also see from Example 3.2 that the purchase cost of £1 per unit would not be satisfactory for determining the relevant cost of the materials issued on 31 December. For example, if we added a profit margin of 40% to the cost of £1 this would be insufficient to cover the replacement cost of the materials.

The most acceptable method of pricing stores issues for decision-making is replacement cost. There are, however, serious practical difficulties which arise from operating a replacement cost stores pricing system. Consider, for example, a company whose stores department issues thousands of different items of materials each day. In this situation it would be impossible to examine

the trade press or contact a supplier to ascertain the replacement cost of each item of material issued. This problem can be overcome by operating a future orientated standard costing system, and we will consider such a system later in this chapter; note for the moment that a standard costing system is not applicable to all organizations. There are, therefore, strong arguments for operating a simple method of stores pricing which will provide a reasonable approximation of replacement cost. Consider the situation outlined in Example 3.3.

EXAMPLE 3.3

On 1 January Allan commenced business with £1,500 cash. On the same day he purchased 500 units of stock at £1 each, and another 500 units on July 1 at £2 each. On December 31 he sells 500 units of stock at £2.40 each. The replacement cost of the stock at this date was also £2.40.

We can see from this example that the relevant cost of the materials issued on 31 December is the replacement cost at this date of £2.40 per unit. The cost accounting system should record the issue on this date at £2.40 per unit, and any internal profit statement should result in a zero profit calculation since the revenue from the sale of 500 units is just sufficient to replace the 500 units. Let us see how closely FIFO, LIFO and average cost methods meet these requirements.

	FIFO	LIFO	Average cost
	£	£	£
Issue cost	1	2	1.50
profit	700 (£1,200 sales less £500 cost of sales)	200 (£1,200 sales less £1,000 cost of sales)	450 (£1,200 sales less £750 cost of sales)

You will see that LIFO provides the closest approximation to replacement cost. The difference between the replacement cost and the cost derived from each of the stores pricing methods depends very much on the rate of stock turnover. The faster the stock turnover, the shorter the time period from acquisition of the raw material to the sale and therefore the closer historic cost will be to replacement cost. When there is a fast stock turnover, FIFO should provide a satisfactory approximation, and in such circumstances the choice of the stores pricing method may not be too critical for decision-making. There would be a strong case for using the same stores pricing method as that used for external reporting.

Where a firm does not have a fast stock turnover, there may be strong arguments for using LIFO if this gives a reasonable approximation to replacement cost; the latest purchase price is normally used and this will be the nearest to replacement cost (for a discussion of the arguments in favour of using LIFO in an inflationary environment see Copeland et al., 1971). There may be situations, however, where the LIFO method does not result in the latest purchase price being used. This situation may occur when stocks are built up and then run down before further purchases are made; some materials will be issued at the earlier purchase prices. Refer again to Example 3.3; if no further purchases were made, then the next 500 units will be issued at the earliest purchase price of £1. In normal circumstances, however, this kind of situation is unlikely to arise frequently and there may still be strong arguments for using LIFO for decision-making in a slow stock-turnover firm.

The use of LIFO for decision-making may cause administration problems as it is unacceptable for external reporting. There is a possibility that two systems of stores pricing may be operating at the same time—one for internal reporting and another for external reporting. (For a discussion of the disparity in methods of handling stock valuation between management and financial accounts see Dangerfield and Stephenson, 1973.)

Many firms operate a *standard costing system* and use *standard costs* for material issues. A standard cost is a target cost of what *future* purchases of material should cost when buying efficiently. The emphasis on future costs should lead to a closer approximation of replacement cost than FIFO or average cost, and a standard cost is therefore an acceptable pricing method for decision-making. The Statement of Standard Accounting Practice on stocks and work in progress states that standard costs can be used for external reporting, provided they are reviewed frequently to ensure that they bear a reasonable approximation of actual costs obtained during the period. This means that a standard cost system

may be an acceptable method of stores pricing for meeting both the internal and external requirements. The problem with using standard costs is that they are established within a standard costing system and, to justify the setting up of such a system, *repetitive* operations are necessary. When operations are not repetitive it is necessary to establish standard costs for each separate operation; this is often very time consuming and expensive, and the costs of operating such a system may exceed the benefits. At this stage, however, we shall not consider further the merits of standard costing as the topic is dealt with in depth in Chapters 17 and 18.

Let us now examine the conclusions which we can draw from our discussion so far on stores pricing. We need to allocate material costs to jobs for external reporting. We also want to determine the *relevant* materials costs for decision-making. External reporting requirements are based on *historical* costs whereas relevant costs for management accounting *are future costs or replacement costs*. A sound stores pricing system cannot normally meet these conflicting requirements, but firms will generally require a pricing system that *approximately* meets such requirements. You will recall that, in certain situations, to achieve this may necessitate the operation of two separate pricing systems. To overcome this problem a stores pricing system can be adopted based on the use of standard costs. Note at this stage that with regard to cost control it is also necessary to ensure that each responsibility centre is identified with the appropriate cost of any materials that have been issued to that centre. (For a detailed discussion of cost control turn to Chapter 16.)

Treatment of stores losses

To achieve accurate profit measurement the clerical record in respect of each item of materials in stock must be in agreement with the actual stock held. This means that the actual stock must be physically counted and compared with the clerical record. To do this effectively there must be either a complete periodic stockcount or some form of continuous stocktaking. The former refers to a situation where all the stores items are counted at one point in time, whereas the latter involves a sample of stores items being counted regularly, on, say, a daily basis. If there is continuous stocktaking production is unlikely to be disrupted.

Sometimes it may be found that the actual stock level is different from the clerical or computer records. The reasons for this may be as follows:

(1) an entry having been made in the wrong stores ledger account or bin card;
(2) the items having been placed in the wrong physical location;
(3) arithmetical errors made when calculating the stores balance on the bin card, or stores ledger when a manual system is operated;
(4) theft of stock.

When a discrepancy arises the individual stores ledger account and the bin card must be adjusted so that they are both in agreement with the actual stock. Assume, for example, that the actual stock is less than the clerical or computer record. The quantity and value of the appropriate stores ledger account and bin card (quantity only) must be reduced and the difference charged to a factory overhead account for stores losses.

Treatment of transportation costs

Ideally, delivery charges made by suppliers should be included as part of the purchase price of the materials so that these costs can be charged as direct costs. Wherever possible materials should be charged directly to cost objectives rather than being grouped as indirect costs and apportioned to cost objectives. The delivery charge will normally be shown separately on the invoice for the consignment of materials delivered. When the invoice is for one kind of material only, there is no problem in accounting for the materials, as the delivery charge merely needs to be added to the cost of the materials and the resulting total entered in the receipts of column of the appropriate stores ledger account. When the delivery charge refers to several different types of material the charge must be apportioned to each of the materials delivered. Such an apportionment could be made according to either the value or the weight of the materials. Alternatively, the clerical work could be simplified by charging transportation costs to a factory overhead account and apportioning these costs as part of the factory overhead procedure.

What is our objective in accounting for materials? The answer is that it is to charge the costs to the appropriate cost objective. Our cost objective

in this chapter is the product. When the delivery charge is apportioned to each of the materials received the charge is treated as a direct cost. This method is more accurate than the alternative method of charging the materials to the factory overhead account. The method which should be adopted in practice depends on the actual amount of the transport costs. If these costs are negligible then it is preferable to simplify the clerical work and charge them to a factory overhead account.

Treatment of materials handling costs

The term materials handling costs refers to the expenses involved in receiving, storing, issuing and handling materials. One approach is to include these items as part of the cost of materials by establishing a separate materials handling rate. Consider, for example, a situation where the materials handling costs for a period were £250,000 and the materials issued during the period were valued at £1 million. In this situation the materials handling costs could be charged out at a rate of 25% of the cost of material issued, which would mean £250,000 being charged to production for materials handling. Alternatively, the materials handling rate could be established on the basis of the weight of material issued, if this would provide a better indication of how much of the materials handling charge each item of materials had incurred.

Note, however, that establishing a separate materials handling rate is time consuming and for this reason many companies include these costs with those of manufacturing overheads and charge them to production as part of the normal factory overheads. This procedure will be outlined in the next chapter.

Accounting for labour

Accounting for labour costs can be classified into the following categories:

(1) *Labour cost accounting* which is concerned with identifying the amount of labour cost to be charged to individual jobs and overhead accounts.
(2) *Payroll accounting* which is concerned with recording the amounts due to employees,

the Inland Revenue or pension funds etc., for labour services.

Labour cost accounting

Where a manufacturing organization operates a job costing system, information on the time spent by *productive* workers on various activities is obtained from documents such as job cards, time sheets, idle time cards, and so on. When an operative commences a job the foreman or time keeper will enter the time at which he starts the job on a job card or time sheet. Both these documents will contain the job number or overhead account number. When the job is completed the finishing time is entered on the job card or time sheet, the hourly rate of pay is applied, and the labour cost can then be calculated.

Alternatively, if a productive worker is unoccupied for short periods because of a machine breakdown or because he is waiting to start the next job, an idle time card will be used to record the amount of idle or waiting time incurred. The objective of labour cost accounting is to record the time spent by all operatives on each activity on a separate job card or time sheet and then to apply the appropriate hourly rate. The labour costs are then charged to each of these activities; hence job cards, time sheets, idle time cards and so on are the source documents for analysing production labour costs to various jobs or overhead accounts.

In respect of certain categories of unproductive labour, such as supervisors and general labourers, it may not be possible to analyse the amount of time spent on various activities. The labour cost for these workers should be obtained from their personal record cards and charged to general factory or departmental overhead accounts for supervision or general labour. These costs are then allocated to products following the overhead allocation procedure which is outlined in the next chapter. A summary of the labour cost accounting procedure is given in Fig. 3.3.

In addition to accumulating labour costs for product costing *it is also necessary to analyse labour costs to responsibility centres for cost control.* To control labour costs effectively such costs must be charged to those persons responsible for their incurrence so that comparisons can be made against planned costs for each category of labour. However, we shall not discuss the problem of cost control at this stage as our objective in this

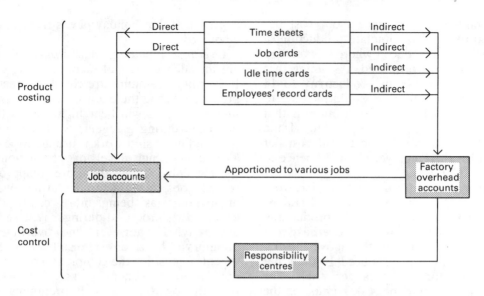

Fig. 3.3 Labour cost accounting procedure

chapter is to concentrate on product costing and not the control of costs. A further discussion of cost control will be deferred to Chapter 16.

Payroll accounting

Payroll accounting requires the provision of certain information relating to employees' attendance time, details of absenteeism, hourly rates of pay, and details of various deductions such as tax and national insurance. Clock cards or absenteeism reports provide the basic information for the calculation of attendance time, and the employee's personal record card provides details of the various deductions. Where incentive payment systems are in operation piecework tickets contain details of the number of items produced by each employee and this is multiplied by the rate per item to give the total weekly wage. Where bonus schemes are in operation the total payment will be based on an attendance time (the time rate wage) plus a bonus. The time rate wage is obtained from the clock card and the bonus details from the job card. Under a bonus scheme a set time is allowed for each job and a bonus is paid based on the proportion of time which is saved. An illustration of a bonus system is given in Example 3.4.

EXAMPLE 3.4

The time allowed for a specific operation is 20 hours and the actual time taken by an employee was 16 hours. A bonus system is in operation where employees receive a bonus of 50% of the time saved. The hourly wage rate is £5 per hour.

The employee, having worked for 16 hours, will receive a time rate wage of £80 (16 hours at £5) plus a bonus of £10 (50% of 4 hours saved at £5 per hour). In the situation described in this example, the time allowed will previously have been recorded on the job card, and the actual time taken will be entered on the card when the job is completed. The bonus can then be calculated on the face of the job card. The next stage is for the information on the job card to be transferred to the employee's record card which becomes the basis for determining the total weekly bonus to be included on the payroll. In many organizations the payroll accounting function is now likely to be carried out by a computer.

Incentive schemes

The objective of an incentive scheme is to reduce the cost per unit produced. For example, assume that a worker is paid £3 per hour and in 1 hour

produces 10 units. The average labour cost per unti will be 30 pence. To stimulate production, a piecework system is introduced where workers are paid 25 pence per unit produced. Assuming that this results in an increase in productivity to 14 units per hour; the hourly rate would increase to £3.50 (14 × 25 pence). The overall effect is that there is an increase in the hourly rate of the employee and a reduction in the labour cost per unit produced for the employer (from 30 pence to 25 pence).

The employer could afford to pay a piecework rate in excess of 25 pence per unit and still be better off if there is an increase in production, because of the reduction in fixed overhead per unit. For example, assume in the above illustration that 10 workers each produced 10 units per hour and worked for 40 hours per week. The weekly production would be 4,000 units. If the fixed overheads per week were £4,000 then the fixed overhead per unit would be £1. However, if all 10 workers increased production to 14 units per hour under a piecework system, then weekly production would increase to 5,600 units, and the fixed overhead per unit produced would be reduced to 71.4 pence (£4,000/5,600 units). The introduction of the incentive scheme will be worthwhile provided that the increased output can be sold at a price which is in excess of the cost of production.

Accounting treatment of various labour cost items

Holiday pay, overtime and shift premiums

Holiday pay received by employees whose labour cost is normally regarded as direct should be charged to jobs by means of an inflated hourly rate. For example, if the employee is normally paid £5 per hour for a 40 hour week and is entitled to six weeks annual holiday then he will receive a total of £1,200 holiday pay (six weeks at £200 per week). Assuming that the employee works the remaining 46 weeks, his attendance time will amount to 1,840 hours (46 weeks at 40 hours per week). Dividing £1,200 by 1,840 hours gives an addition of approximately 65 pence per hour to the employee's hourly wage rate to ensure that the holiday pay is recovered. The advantage of this approach is that holiday pay is treated as a direct labour cost.

Overtime premiums and shift-work premiums are included as part of manufacturing overheads. If overtime premiums are charged directly to jobs produced during the overtime or night shift period then these jobs will bear higher costs than those produced during a regular working week. Overtime and night shift work is usually necessitated by a generally high level of production, not by specific jobs. It is therefore inappropriate to record jobs manufactured during overtime or night hours as being more costly than their counterparts produced during, say, a regular eight hour day. If, however, the overtime or shift premiums are a direct result of a customer's urgent request for the completion of the order and not due to the general pressure of factory work, then the overtime or shift premiums should be charged directly to the job. It is important that overtime and shift premiums are also analysed by responsibility centres for cost control purposes.

Let us now examine the comments made in the preceding paragraph with the aid of a simple illustration. Consider a situation where an employee is paid time and a half for weekly hours worked in excess of 40 hours. Assume that the employee works for 50 hours and that the 10 hours of overtime were spent on job X. The hourly wage rate is £5. The employee's weekly wage will be calculated as follows:

Normal time rate wage: 50 hours at £5 = £250
Overtime premium ($\frac{1}{2}$ × 10 hours at £5) = £ 25
 ————
 £275

The normal time rate wage will be allocated to the various jobs on which the employee was engaged during the period, but if the overtime was a result of general factory pressure than it would be unreasonable to charge the overtime premium to job X merely because it was scheduled to be produced during the overtime period. In such circumstances it would be preferable to charge the overtime premium to the appropriate factory overhead account, the total of which would be apportioned to *all* jobs worked on during the period.

Piecework and bonus payments

Let us now consider the accounting problems

associated with incentive payment schemes. The earnings of an employee on piecework are computed for each payroll period by multiplying the agreed rate per piece times the number of good units produced. There will usually also be a specified minimum weekly wage, so that if an employee's production falls below the weekly minimum, he will be paid at the time rate rather than the piecework rate for that period. For example, if an individual is paid on the basis of 20 pence per piece with a £4 per hour guaranteed wage rate and works 38 hours during the week, his minimum wage for the week is £152 (38 × £4) even though his week's output might only be 600 pieces, which would entitle him to only £120 on a piecework basis. The difference between the guaranteed minimum wage of £152 and the actual wage of £120 will normally be charged to the appropriate factory overhead account.

A further problem with piecework schemes is that time may be spent on work for which no piecework rate has been established. This is known as *non-rated work*. Non-rated work will be paid at the normal hourly wage rate. Time spent on non-rated work should therefore be charged to jobs or overhead accounts at the relevant hourly rates, as would be the case if the company had no piece rate system. If any additional payment is made to employees to compensate them for the lack of rated work then these additional payments should be charged to a factory overhead account.

Where bonus systems are in existence the job time will be recorded on the job card and the bonus can also be calculated on this card. The time rate element and the bonus element can then be charged to the specific job or overhead account on which the bonus was earned.

Employment costs

In addition to the wage and salary payments to employees, the employer will incur a number of other costs which are incidental to the employment. These costs include such items as the employer's share of national insurance contributions and pension fund contributions. Employment costs are frequently recorded as manufacturing overheads, to the extent that they relate to manufacturing workers, but it is preferable to calculate an average hourly rate for employment costs and add this to the hourly wage

rate paid to the employees. For example, the employer may be responsible for employment costs of £30 for an operative who is paid £4 per hour for a 40 hour week. Here we can establish that the employment costs are 75 pence per hour and this cost can be added to the hourly wage rate of £4 per hour giving a total rate of £4.75 per hour. This approach is conceptually preferable to the alternative of charging the £30 to an overhead account as employment costs are a fundamental part of acquiring labour services.

Idle time

During the production process, lost time may occur for several reasons such as temporary lack of work, bottlenecks, or machine breakdowns. The cost of idle time could be included as part of the employee's labour cost in a similar manner to that described for employment costs, but this approach is inappropriate as idle time costs do not occur in respect of all the employees. Therefore not all jobs will be charged with a share of the idle time costs. Idle time normally results from poor production scheduling and a lack of sales orders. As this affects all jobs rather than just a few the idle time should be apportioned to *all* jobs. Also it is preferable in relation to cost control for the idle time to be charged to a separate account for each department rather than for it to be absorbed as part of the direct labour cost. If this procedure is followed the cost of idle time will be regarded as a factory overhead and can be reported to management at frequent intervals.

Labour costs for decision-making

Earlier in this chapter in our discussion on ascertaining the relevant cost of materials for decision-making, it was suggested that the replacement cost method should be used. This is because there may be a lengthy time lag from the date of acquisition of the material to the date of reimbursement in the form of sales revenue. In the case of labour there is normally a much shorter time lag from the time of payment for this resource until reimbursement of the sales revenue,

and the replacement cost and acquisition cost of labour are likely to be the same. Therefore, in those situations where labour is likely to be a relevant cost, the actual cost of labour will be included as part of the relevant cost. Determining the relevant labour costs for decision-making is not an easy task, and consideration of this problem will be deferred to Chapter 10.

Summary

In this chapter we have examined in some detail the accounting problems associated with materials and labour. To gain an insight into the problems involved, a description of the clerical procedures necessary for the ordering, receipt and issue of materials was presented. Three alternative methods of interpreting the cost of materials issued — first in first out (FIFO), last in first out (LIFO) and the average cost method — have been considered and analysed.

We have established that the issue price of materials is required for product costs to calculate the cost of goods sold for external reporting, or for the work in progress or finished goods stock valuation if the product remained unsold at the end of the period. The material cost is also required for decision-making, and we have noted that replacement cost is preferable for this purpose, but that FIFO or the average cost method is required for external reporting. Of the three stores pricing methods considered we have concluded that LIFO provides the most suitable approximation of relevant costs for decision-making, but as this method is likely to be unacceptable for external reporting its adoption may mean having to use two different and separate methods of stores pricing. This possibility was rejected because of the additional work involved in operating two systems. To overcome the conflict which exists between the cost information requirements for both external reporting and decision-making we concluded that *materials should be recorded and issued at a standard cost*.

In our discussion of accounting for materials it was emphasized that in addition to charging material costs to products, it is also necessary to charge responsibility centres with materials costs for cost control. We concluded our discussion of material costs by considering the accounting treatment of stores losses, transportation costs and material handling costs.

After considering the accounting problems associated with material costs we turned our attention to accounting for labour. We classified the problems of accounting for labour into two categories — labour cost accounting and payroll accounting, and concentrated on the clerical procedures necessary for each of these aspects. We also examined the accounting treatment of various labour costs — holiday pay, overtime and shift premiums, piecework and bonus payments, employments costs and idle time. Finally, labour costs for decision-making were briefly discussed and it was suggested that if labour is a relevant cost then the actual labour cost incurred is likely to be an appropriate cost for decision-making.

References and further reading

Accounting Standards Committee. *Accounting for Stocks and Work in Progress* (SSAP 9).

Bastable, C.W. and Merriwether, J.D. FIFO in an Inflationary Environment. *Journal of Accountancy (USA)* March 1975, pp. 49-56.

Biddle, G.C. Accounting Methods and Management Decisions: The Case of Inventory Costing and Inventory Policy. *Journal for Accounting Research* 1981. Studies on Economic Consequences of Financial and Managerial Accounting; Effects on Corporate Incentive and Decisions.

Copeland, R.M., Wojdak, J.F. and Shank, J.K. Use LIFO to Offset Inflation. *Harvard Business Review* May-June 1971.

Copeland, R.M. and Shank, J.L. LIFO and the Diffusion of Innovation. *Journal of Accounting Research Selected Studies* 1971, pp. 196-230.

Dangerfield, B.C. and Stephenson, E. Stock Valuation in the Consumer Durables Manufacturing Industry. *Accounting and Business Research* Winter 1973, pp. 2-13.

Davis, H.Z. The Effects of LIFO Inventory Costing on Resource Allocation: A Comment. *Accounting Review* LVI, October 81, pp. 975-76.

Derstine, R.P. and Huefner, R.J. LIFO–FIFO, Accounting Ratios and Market Risk. *Journal of*

Accounting Research **12**(2), Autumn 1974, pp. 216-34.

Dopuch, N. and Ronen, J. The Effects of Alternative Inventory Valuation Methods — An Experimental Study. *Journal of Accounting Research* **11**(2), Autumn 1973, pp. 191-211.

Halperin, R. The Effects of LIFO Inventory Costing on Resource Allocation: A Public Policy Perspective. *Accounting Review* **LIV** January 1977, pp. 58-71.

Lockyer, K.G. *Production Management.* Pitman, 1982.

Sunder, S. Optimal Choice Between FIFO and LIFO. *Journal of Accounting Research* **14**(2), Autumn 1976, pp. 277-300.

Problems

*Indicates that a suggested solution is to be found in the *Students' Manual*.

3.1* With reference to a material control system you are required to:
 (a) explain the meaning of:
 (i) perpetual inventory;
 (ii) continuous stocktaking;
 (b) explain the source and purpose of the undermentioned documents:
 (i) goods received note;
 (ii) materials transfer note;
 (iii) purchase requisition;
 (iv) materials returned note;
 (c) draw a specimen of a materials returned note.

(20 marks)
ICMA Cost Accounting 1
November 1980

3.2* (a) Three students, K. L. and M, are equal partners in a joint venture which involves them, on a part-time basis, in buying and selling sacks of product F. The transactions for the six months ended 30 September were as stated below. You are to assume that purchases at the unit costs given were made at the beginning of each month and that the sales were made at the end of each month at the fixed price of £1.50 per sack.

Month	Purchases		Sales
	Sacks	Unit cost	Sacks
		£	
April	1,000	1.00	500
May	500	1.20	750
June	1,000	1.00	Nil
July	Nil	—	600
August	500	1.20	650
September	500	1.30	600

In October the student partners held a meeting to review their financial position and to share out the profits but there was disagreement because each partner had priced the issues on a different basis. K had used FIFO, L had used LIFO and M had used a weighted average, basing his weighted average on the whole of the six months' purchases. It was however, agreed that the stock remaining at the end of September should be stored until next April.

You are required to:
 (i) show the records which each student kept of the transactions;
 (ii) show the amount each student ought to receive if the whole of the profit arising from each method of pricing the issues were distributed;
 (iii) comment briefly on the acceptablity of the three different results arising from the transactions.

(b) In the context of a manufacturing business, explain briefly what is meant by *the last sentence* of the following statement.

The Statement of Standard Accounting Practice No. 9 on Stocks and Work-in-Progress (SSAP 9) states in an explanatory note, paragraph 3 that 'In order to match costs and revenue, "costs" of stocks and work in progress should comprise that expenditure which has been incurred in the normal course of business in bringing the product or service to its present location and condition. Such costs will include all related production overheads, even though these may accrue on a time basis.'

(25 marks)
ICMA Cost Accounting 1
November 1979

3.3 A shop stocks winter coats which sell at £55 each. To avoid overstocking and because of limited space, the deliveries from four manufacturers, at differing prices, are made to the shop on a weekly basis at opening time on Monday mornings. During October the deliveries and sales of the coats were as shown below and there was an opening stock of 10 coats which had been purchased in September at £29 each.

	Coats bought		
Week No.			Number of
	Number	Cost each	coats sold
		£	
1	20	30	15
2	30	33	33
3	40	29	35
4	30	35	39

Trading accounts are prepared monthly and from the information given above you are required to:
 (a) prepare stock records for the transactions based on the three methods of pricing issues listed below:

(i) FIFO;
(ii) LIFO;
(iii) weighted average calculated at the end of the month (work to two decimal places of £1);
(b) recommend which method you would advise the shop management to use and why;
(c) show the gross margins to the nearest £1 and as a percentage of the sales turnover for each of the three methods of pricing issues;
(d) comment on the type of information you would require to determine whether the gross margin figures are good, poor or indifferent.

(25 marks)
ICMA Cost Accounting 1
November 1981

3.4* At the beginning of November the opening stock of a particular component was 440 units, total value £2,200.
During the month the following supplies were received:

 8.11.1979 400 units, total value £1,800
 15.11.1979 400 units, total value £2,200
 22.11.1979 400 units, total value £2,400

There is a standard carriage charge included in the above amounts, of £100 per delivery, for transporting the components to the factory. The invoice for the goods received on 22 November had not been received by the end of the month.
Shown below are the issues from store during November:

 2.11.1979 300 units. 16.11.1979 500 units
 9.11.1979 50 units, 20.11.1979 20 units
 13.11.1979 300 units, 28.11.1979 30 units

The components issued on 9 November were used in the general plant maintenance programme and those issued on 20 November were incorporated into plant and equipment being constructed by the company's engineers to mechanize part of the manufacturing process. All other issues were made direct to production for inclusion in the output of the company's products, the issue on 28 November being to replace components damaged by incorrect handling.
On 21 November 40 units were returned to store from production and, at the end of the month, the closing stock was 440 units.
Required:
(a) Record the month's transactions in a stores account for this component indicating very clearly the account into which (or from which) the corresponding entry should be posted. You should assume the company operates an historic batch costing system, fully integrated with the financial accounts, and

uses a first in, first out method of pricing material issues. (17 marks)
(b) Briefly contrast the effects of using first in, first out with the last in, first out method of pricing material issues from store. (5 marks)
(Total 22 marks)
ACCA Foundation Costing
December 1979

3.5* (a) Outline a suitable system for collecting the material cost of each job in a manufacturing company employing historic job costing.
(8 marks)
(b) Zeppo Ltd manufactures a range of products from one basic material. In September the opening stock of the material was 650 kilos and, at the end of the month a physical count revealed a stock of 900 kilos, which was 250 kilos less than that shown by the inventory records. Except for the returns to the supplier shown below, all material recorded as being issued from store was consumed by production.
The material costs £2 per kilo. At the beginning of September the amount owing to creditors for supplies of this material was £3,800 and during the month Zeppo Ltd paid these creditors £7,200 and returned £600 of faulty material. At the end of the month the amount owing to the creditors concerned was £4,000.
The company operates an historic batch costing system fully integrated with the financial accounts.
Required:
(i) Calculate the value of material issued to production during September and record the month's transactions for the material in a stores account showing both quantities and value. You should clearly indicate the account into which (or from which) the corresponding entry should be posted. (9 marks)
(ii) Briefly consider the possible reasons for the stock loss revealed by the physical count.
(5 marks)
(22 marks)
ACCA Foundation Costing
December 1980

3.6* The Managing Director of a company manufacturing one product, a standard sized office desk, asks you as the recently appointed works accountant to investigate the material control procedures operating in the factory. You have arranged for a physical stock count of raw materials, work-in-progress and finished goods to take place at the beginning and end of April. The results of this stock-taking and other data relevant to the consumption of material during April are shown below.

Physical stocktaking	Opening stock at beginning of April	Closing stock at end of April
Finished goods	650 desks	925 desks
Work-in-progress degree of completion:	300 desks	160 desks
Timber	66.67% complete[a]	75.0% complete
Varnish	25.0% complete	37.5% complete

(^a i.e. the 300 desks had been issued with 66.67% of the timber necessary to complete the desk.)

(*a* i.e. the 300 desks had been issued with 66.67% of the timber necessary to complete the desk.)

Raw materials:		
Timber	40,000 square feet	55,000 square feet
Varnish	1,600 litres	700 litres

Other data	
Sales	4,600 desks

	Timber	Varnish
Works Manager's estimate of material consumption per desk, including an allowance for normal waste	30 square feet.	0.47 litres
Purchase price of opening stock	£1.40 per square foot.	£1.20 per litre

Purchases of materials:		
5 April	125,000 square feet at £1.50 per square foot.	400 litres at £1.10 per litre

19 April	70,000 square feet at £1.70 per square foot.	1,800 litres at £1.30 per litre

Value of material issued to production:

12 April	£120,000	£1,200
26 April	£164,000	£1,550

The value of material issued to production has been obtained by using the following methods of pricing material issues:

> Timber—last in, first out
> Varnish—first in, first out

Required:
(a) Calculate the quantity of timber and varnish issued on *each* of the dates shown in the question and the consequent book-stocks of each material at the end of April. Compare the closing book-stocks of each material with the results of the physical stock count.

(9 marks)

(b) Calculate the total quantity of each material which, according to the works manager's estimates, should have been consumed and compare with the quantities of materials actually consumed. (6 marks)

(c) Discuss the possible reasons for any differences revealed by your comparisons in (a) and (b) above. (7 marks)

(22 marks)

ACCA Level 1 Costing
June 1983

3.7 S. Poynter Public Limited Company, an engineering company constructing special purpose equipment to customer specification, employs a system of job costing to determine the actual cost of products manufactured. Shown below is the incomplete stores account, for month 11, of one component used in the construction of the equipment.

Question 3.7

Stores Account–Component XYZ

Date	Quantity Units	Price £	Value £	Date	Quantity Units	Price £	Value £
1.11.81				2.11.81			
Opening stock	35	2.00	70	Job 123	25		
5.11.81				10.11.81			
Creditors	40	2.25	90	Job 147	38		
13.11.81				24.11.81			
Creditors	30	2.50	75	Job 151	48		
23.11.81				30.11.81			
Creditors	50	2.80	140	Closing stock	44		
	155		375		155		

Ten of the components issued on 24 November to Job 151 were to replace units which had been previously issued to that job but had been damaged and scrapped as a result of incorrect installation.

Required:

(a) Calculate the value of the closing stock of Component XYZ using the following methods of pricing material issues:
 (i) first in, first out;
 (ii) last in, first out. (6 marks)

(b) Using the weighted average method of pricing, calculate the value of the components issued on 24 November. Explain how the ten components issued to replace those previously damaged should be treated in the cost accounts and briefly outline the reasons for your recommended treatment.
(Calculations should be to two decimal places only.) (8 marks)

(c) During month 11 the total wages earned by the direct operatives in one department were made up as follows:

	£
Basic pay (£3 per hour)	4,800
Overtime earnings (basic time rate plus overtime premium)	1,440
Shift premium	360
Total wages	£6,600

Overtime, which is paid at basic time rate plus one-half, is worked as a means of generally increasing the output of the factory. Analysis of the direct workers' returned work tickets reveals that 280 hours was non-productive time, 60 hours were spent producing capital equipment for the company and the remainder of the time was spent on jobs.

Required:

Using appropriate journal entries show how the above wages should be recorded in the cost accounting system, which is not integrated with the financial accounts.

(8 marks)
(22 Marks)
*ACCA Foundation Costing
December 1981*

3.8 XYZ Ltd are considering introducing an incentive scheme. Current production for the period is 100 units and total wages paid are £600 for this production. Material costs are £5 per unit. Fixed overheads are £1,000 for the period and the current selling price is £25.

Management decide to introduce a piecework system paying £9 for each unit produced based on an estimate that production for the period will double to 200 units.

Your managing director asks you to provide a financial evaluation of the scheme and to indicate any other factors which cannot be quantified but which may be affected by the introduction of the scheme.

3.9* Betayet Ltd is a small company manufacturing one type of component in a single operation. The company employs 10 direct workers on a basic 40 hour week at £3 per hour with a guaranteed minimum weekly wage of £120 per operative. The maximum amount of overtime which may be worked, paid at time rate plus one third, is in total 200 hours per week. Additional direct workers cannot be recruited.

The average time for one operative to manufacture one component is 40 minutes.

Demand for the product varies considerably; the minimum weekly output is 450 units, but for a significant part of the year the company cannot satisfy total demand despite working the maximum overtime hours available. The nature of the component is such that stocks of work in progress or finished goods cannot be stored.

After appropriate studies have been made an incentive scheme has been proposed, based upon a standard operator time of 30 minutes per component, in which operatives will be paid £2 for each component produced. The guaranteed minimum wage would still apply and, if required, overtime would continue to be worked, up to the maximum shown above, and be paid at the previous time rate premium.

The selling price of the component is £9 per unit, material costs £2 per unit, variable overheads varying with hours worked £3 per labour hour, and fixed overheads £1,200 per week.

Required:

(a) Produce columnar revenue accounts, comparing weekly profits at the following activity levels:
 I Under the current wages scheme at,
 (i) minimum weekly output
 (ii) current maximum output
 II Under the proposed incentive scheme, with labour achieving standard efficiency, at,
 (i) minimum weekly output
 (ii) current maximum output
 (iii) proposed maximum output
(11 marks)
Briefly explain the reasons for the change in profit caused by the incentive scheme.
(4 marks)

(b) Assuming the incentive scheme is adopted and labour achieved standard efficiency, calculate the effect on company profits of a labour dispute in which 100 hours of direct operatives' time were lost, and not paid for, during a week in which demand was:
 (i) 450 units
 (ii) greater than the proposed maximum level

of output

Carefully explain your calculations.

(7 marks)
(22 marks)
ACCA Foundation Costing
June 1980

3.10* (a) Shown below is a summary of the previous week's payroll data for the Moulding Department in Peal Public Limited Company, a company manufacturing two different types of telephone receiver.

	Direct workers	Indirect workers
Hours worked:		
Ordinary time	3,600 hours	800 hours
Overtime	630 hours	80 hours
Basic hourly rate of pay	£3,60	£2.10
Net wages paid[a]	£12,864	£1,420

Analysis of direct workers' time:
Productive time:

Type 1 Receiver–4,800 units	2,400 hours
Type 2 Receiver–1,500 units	1,125 hours
Non-productive down time	705 hours

The Moulding Department employs 90 direct and 20 indirect operatives. All operatives are paid at hourly time rates; overtime, which is regularly worked to meet budgeted production targets, is paid at time rate plus one third.

The company operates a batch costing system, using actual costs, which is fully integrated with the financial accounts.

(*a* Note for Hong Kong students–wages are paid after deduction of tax at source.)

Required:
Construct the Moulding Department's Wages Control Account for the previous week *clearly* indicating the accounts into which the corresponding entries would be posted. (9 marks)
(b) The works manager of Peal PLC is considering introducing a piece-work incentive scheme for the direct workers in the Moulding Department. Work Study Services have examined the manufacturing process in the Moulding Department and consider that the operation to produce Type 1 Receivers should be performed, under normal conditions, by one operative in 24 minutes, for a Type 2 Receiver the corresponding time is 36 minutes. Unavoidable non-productive down-time is expected to remain at approximately 20% of productive time.

Having considered the above times the works manager suggests that direct operatives should be paid a piece-rate of £1,90 for each Type 1 Receiver produced; £2.85 for each Type 2 Receiver produced; and non-productive down-time should be paid at £2.50 per hour.

As the accountant of Peal PLC you have been asked to appraise the above scheme. It should be assumed that the previous week's payroll data shown in (a) above represents an average week in the Moulding Department, although the weekly volume of production and consequent wages do fluctuate around this mean figure. No further information has been provided.

Required:
(i) Examine the effect of the proposed scheme on the labour costs in the Moulding Department.
Any assumptions you consider necessary should be clearly stated.

(7 marks)

(ii) Briefly discuss any additional considerations which would need to be thoroughly examined before the feasibility of the proposed incentive scheme could be finally assessed.

(6 marks)
(22 marks)
ACCA Level 1 Costing
June 1982

3.11 (a) Distinguish between a straight piece work scheme and a premium bonus scheme.
(b) In addition to the schemes mentioned in (a) above, there are other payment by results schemes; from the data given below you are required to identify and state what type of scheme is in operation. Also list *two* advantages which might accrue to an employer operating such a scheme.

Each employee is paid a minimum of £16 for an 8 hour day for which a quota of 16 units of production has been agreed. An incentive is paid to each employee who produces more than 16 units in 8 hours but it is physically impossible for more than 20 units to be produced in that time. If 17–20 units are produced in one day the rate of remuneration for *every* unit produced by one person is on the following basis.

Good units produced per day	Remuneration per unit £
17	1.03
18	1.07
19	1.12
20	1.20

(c) From the data given below you are required to draw, on the graph paper provided, a graph which shows the *hourly group remuneration cost* at the four different output levels, viz:

Output in units

240 to 300
301 to 360
361 to 420
421 to 500

The calculated group labour costs per hour and the units relating to each amount must be shown on the appropriate axes of the graph.

Data:

A team of eight men is required to operate an expensive piece of plant. A group bonus scheme is in operation and three shifts of 8 hours each are worked each day. The agreed quota is 300 units of output per shift and if this quantity or less is produced the basic rates of pay apply. However, if more than 300 units are produced per shift, higher remuneration is payable to all members of the team. Such higher remuneration is based on percentage additions to the basic pay. The percentage increases are:

For output per shift of (units)	Increase %
301 to 360	20
361 to 420	40
421 to 500	50

For each grade of employee the basic rate of pay is as follows:

Grade	Number of men	Hourly rate £
Senior technicians	2	4.50
Operatives	4	3.00
Apprentices	2	1.50

(20 marks)

ICMA Cost Accounting 1
May 1981

3.12 The Board of Directors of an expanding engineering company manufacturing a range of domestic saucepans and kitchen utensils appointed a Management Accountant in November 19X0. His initial task was to build up an information system for use in internal control. When the appointment was confirmed, the importance of knowing the profit position of the company at short intervals, in contrast with the present profit reporting (half-yearly with a considerable delay after the period end), had been stressed.

After spending some six months finding out about the business, getting to know the staff and preparing standard product costs, the new accountant had produced various control statements, the results of which were summarized in a monthly profit statement. By using the audited accounts for the half-year ended 30 June 19X1 as a starting point, he produced the final profit statement showing a profit of £221,440 for the year ending 31 December, and it was presented to the Managing Director about ten working days after the year end.

Whilst preparing the information during the six months, the Management Accountant had become concerned about the possibility of error in the records of material consumption. This information was supplied to him by the Stores Controllers' staff, who had the responsibiity for recording all aspects of materials from ordering to issuing to production. The recording system had been devised and operated for a number of years by the present Buyer/Stores Controller who had been with the company since its very early days. Although the Accountant had examined, and accepted as adequate, the methods of recording, the six months operating period had brought to light several discrepancies and inconsistencies in records as well as examples of bad stock-keeping which had not been fully explained or investigated deeply.

Two months later the audited financial accounts of the company were produced showing a net profit (before tax) of £146,120.

After a detailed comparison of the two results, the Management Accountant was able to report that about £1,400 of the difference was due to omissions on his part, and the need to make some expense estimates. The remaining £74,000 was due to the difference between the raw material consumption as recorded day by day, and the calculated consumption in the financial accounts on the basis of:

Opening stock plus purchases less closing stock

The opening and closing stocks were based on physical stock counts at the year end.

You are required to comment on the discrepancy in materials usage, and suggest an outline programme of investigation into possible reasons for it. Include any suggestions which may help to avoid a similar situation in the future.

Appendix 3.1: Stores pricing methods

In Chapter 3 we used a simple example to illustrate three different methods of stores pricing. We will look here at a more complex problem illustrated in Example 3A.1.

EXAMPLE 3A.1

The purchases and issues of a raw material for a five month period were as follows:

1 July	Received	2,000 units at £10 per unit
9 July	Received	520 units at £10.50 per unit
18 July	Issued	1,400 units
5 August	Received	800 units at £11.50 per unit
22 August	Received	600 units at £12.50 per unit
15 September	Issued	1,240 units
14 October	Issued	480 units
8 November	Received	1,000 units at £11 per unit
24 November	Issued	760 units

There was no opening stock of the raw material.

The stores ledger cards when issues are priced respectively according to the FIFO, LIFO and average cost methods are given in Exhibit 3A.1.

FIFO

Note that the issue of 1,240 units on 15 September is at three different purchase prices. This is because 1,400 units out of the earliest purchase of 2,000 units have already been issued. The remaining 600 units are therefore the first items to be issued out of the 1,240 units on 15 September. The next earliest purchase of 520 units are now issued leaving a balance of 120 units to be issued from the purchase of 5 August. The closing stock consists of the final purchase for the period of 1,000 units plus 40 units from the 22 August purchase which have not yet been issued.

LIFO

The issue of 480 units on 14 October consists of 160 units at the 5 August purchase price at £11.50. This is because all the units for the latest purchase on 22 August have previously been issued together with 640 units at the next latest purchase on 5 August. Only 160 units from the 5 August purchase are available for issue. The balance of 320 units issued is at £10 as all the previous later purchases have already been issued. Hence LIFO does not always ensure that the issues are at the latest purchase price. The closing stock consists of 240 units at the latest purchase price of £11 plus 800 units at the earliest purchase price of £10.

Average cost method

With the average cost method the items are issued at the average cost per unit. This is calculated by dividing the total amount in stock by the total quantity in stock, after each new purchase. For example, the average cost per unit for the July 9 and August 22 purchases is calculated as follows:

$$9 \text{ July} \quad = \frac{£25,460}{2,520 \text{ units}} = £10.1032$$

$$22 \text{ August} = \frac{£28,016}{2,520 \text{ units}} = £11.1175$$

Note from Exhibit 3A.1 that each item is issued at the latest average price and that this average price only changes when a new purchase is received.

The use of computers

From the discussion in this chapter you will have noted that the operation of a stores pricing system is very tedious. Consider how tedious the calculations would be for a company with thousands of different items of raw materials! Fortunately, a computer can be programmed to operate a stores pricing system, and programs are available from softwear manufacturers at a very low cost for use with microcomputers. It is most unlikely, therefore, that stores pricing will be carried out manually even in a small business.

Exhibit 3A.1

Stores ledger account — FIFO method

Material: Code: Maximum Quantity:
Minimum Quantity:

Date	Receipts				Stores Req.	Issues			Stock		
	G.R.N No.	Quantity	Unit Price £	Amount £		Quantity	Unit Price £	Amount £	Quantity	Unit Price £	Amount £
July 1		2,000	10.0	20,000					2,000		20,000
9		520	10.50	5,460					2,520		25,460
18						1400	10.0	14,000	1,120		11,460
Aug. 5		800	11.50	9,200					1,920		20,600
Aug. 22		600	12.50	7,500					2,520		28,160
Sept 15						600	10.0				
						520	10.50				
						120 1240	11.50	12,840	1,280		15,320
Oct 14						480	11.50	5,520	800		9,800
Nov 8		1,000	11.0	11,000		200	11.50		1,800		20,800
Nov 24						560 760	12.50	9,300	·1,040		11,500

The closing stock represents: 40 units at £12.50 per unit = £ 500
 1,000 units at £11.00 per unit = £11,000
 —————
 £11,500
 —————

Stores ledger account — LIFO method

Material: Code: Maximum Quantity:
Minimum Quantity:

Date	Receipts				Stores Req.	Issues			Stock		
	G.R.N No.	Quantity	Unit Price £	Amount £		Quantity	Unit Price £	Amount £	Quantity	Unit Price £	Amount £
July 1		2,000	10.0	20,000					2,000		20,000
9		520	10.50	5,460					2,520		25,460
18						520	10.50				
						880 1400	10.00	14,260	1.120		11,200
Aug 5		800	11.50	9,200					1,920		20,400
22		600	12.50	7,500					2,520		27,900
Sept 15						600	12.50				
						640 1240	11.50	14,860	1,280		13,040
Oct 14						160	11.50				
						320 480	10.00	5,040	800		8,000
Nov 8		1,000	11.00	11,000					1,800		19,000
Nov 24						760	11.00	8,360	1.040		10,640

The closing stock represents: 800 units at £10.00 per unit = £ 8,000
 240 units at £11.00 per unit = £ 2,640
 —————
 £10,640
 —————

Stores ledger account — average cost

Material: Code: Maximum Quantity:
Minimum Quantity:

Date	Receipts				Issues				Stock		
	G.R.N. No.	Quantity	Unit Price £	Amount £	Stores Req.	Quantity	Unit Price £	Amount £	Quantity	Unit Price £	Amount £
July 1		2,000	10.0	20,000					2,000	10.0	20,000
9		520	10.50	5,460					2,520	10.1032	25,460
18						1400	10.1032	14,144	1,120		11,316
Aug 5		800	11.50	9,200					1,920	10.6854	20,516
Aug 22		600	12.50	7,500					2,520	11.1175	28,016
Sept 15						1240	11.1175	13,785	1,280		14,231
Oct 14						480	11.1175	5,336	800		8,895
Nov 8		1,000	11.00	11,000					1,800	11.0528	19,895
Nov 24						760	11.0528	8,400	1,040		11,495

4 Accounting for overhead expenditure

In Chapter 3 we discussed the procedure for accounting for labour and materials for calculating product costs. This chapter is concerned with the procedure for allocating overheads to products. Overhead expenditure consists of indirect labour, indirect materials and indirect expenses. In other words overheads are those costs which are not directly attributable to cost objectives such as a product, process, sales territory, customer group etc. Some examples of specific items of overhead expenditure include supervision, rent and rates, and lighting and heating for product costing. These items may, however, be directly attributable to another cost objective — for example, if the cost objective is a sales territory then they may be direct costs.

For product costing manufacturing overheads must be allocated to jobs. The justification for this is that all manufacturing overheads are incurred in the production of the firm's output, and so each unit of the product produced receives some benefit from these costs. It follows that each unit of output should be charged with some of the overhead costs. It is also a requirement of the Statement of Standard Accounting Practice (SSAP 9) on stocks and work in progress that all manufacturing overheads must be applied to jobs when calculating profit and determining the stock valuation entry in the balance sheet.

Because external reporting requires that we should charge manufacturing overheads to products, most of this chapter will be devoted to apportioning manufacturing overheads to products for stock valuation. In addition to external reporting demands, managers require details of product costs to assist them in making decisions on product pricing and product mix. They also require information to assist them in controlling their costs. Chapter 10 deals with costs for decision-making, and Chapter 16 deals with cost control, but the different accounting treatment of overheads for decision-making and cost control will be briefly discussed in this chapter. We begin by outlining the procedure by which overheads are apportioned to products.

An overview of the procedure of apportioning overheads to products

An overview of the procedure is illustrated in Fig. 4.1.

In relation to *cost control*, overhead costs are initially collected by responsibility centre and object of expenditure, for example Department X Idle Time, Department Y Indirect Materials, and so on. These costs are periodically totalled and listed on a performance report, which also includes budgeted costs. This report highlights those costs which are in excess of budget.

In relation to *product costing* it is necessary to apportion these overhead costs to particular products. The normal procedure is to re-allocate the costs of the responsibility centres to the various *production* departments and then to apportion the overheads to the various jobs passing through each of the production departments.

What basis should we use to apportion manufacturing overheads to each unit of production?

Fig. 4.1 An overview of the overhead apportionment procedure

Most frequently used are input factors such as direct labour hours, machine hours or direct labour costs. For a discussion of other input factors see Appendix 4.2. Total departmental overheads generally depend on the level of an input factor such as direct labour hours. For example, the greater the direct labour hours the greater will be the expenditure on indirect labour, indirect materials and other overhead costs. The selection of the input factor should be the one which corresponds most closely with the total overhead expenditure of each department. Scatter diagrams and regression analysis are the tools for selecting the appropriate input factor; these techniques are discussed in detail in Chapter 20.

When the appropriate input factor has been selected an overhead rate per unit of input factor is calculated for each department and this is applied to all jobs passing through the depart-

Although the objective of this chapter is to illustrate the allocation of overheads for stock valuation, note that the approach outlined in the preceding paragraphs might be used by any organization which receives reimbursement for the *services* it performs. For example, the general and administrative expenses of a firm of accountants, or a garage, is apportioned to the individual client or customer. Similarly, in a non-profit organization, such as a local authority, the general and administrative expenses will be allocated to *programmes* such as education, leisure, or social services.[1]

Blanket overhead rates and departmental overhead rates

A blanket overhead rate refers to a situation where a single overhead rate is established for the factory as a whole and this rate is charged to all jobs irrespective of the departments in which they were produced. If we assume that the total factory overheads for a particular period are £120,000, and that 60,000 direct labour hours are worked during the period, then the blanket overhead rate will be £2 per direct labour hour and all jobs passing through the factory will be charged at this rate.

A blanket overhead rate may not be a satisfactory method of apportioning overheads in a situation where a factory consists of a number of departments and all jobs do not spend an equal amount of time in each of these departments. Let us assume that the £120,000 overheads and the 60,000 direct labour hours are the totals of three production departments and that these totals can be analysed to departments A, B and C as follows:

	Department A	Department B	Department C	Total
Overheads	£12,000	£100,000	£8,000	£120,000
Direct labour hours	20,000	20,000	20,000	60,000
Overhead rate per direct labour hour	60 pence	£5	40 pence	£2

ment. Each job is charged with overhead based on the amount of the input factor used to produce it. For example, if direct labour hours is selected as an input factor for a particular department and the overhead rate is £5 per direct labour hour, then a job which spends 10 hours in the department will be charged with overhead of £50.

In this illustration it may be more meaningful to establish separate departmental overhead rates rather than to use an overall blanket rate of £2 per hour. Consider a situation where job Z requires 20 direct labour hours in Department C but does not pass through Departments A and B. If a blanket overhead rate is used then job Z will be

charged £40, consisting of 20 direct labour hours at £2 per hour. If a departmental overhead rate is used then job Z will be charged £8 consisting of 20 direct labour hours at 40 pence per hour. Which method should be used? The logical answer must be to establish separate departmental overhead rates so that job Z is charged only with a fair share of the overheads of Department C. If the blanket overhead rate was applied, all the factory overhead rates would be averaged out and job Z would be indirectly charged with some of the overheads of Department B. This would not be satisfactory as job Z does not pass through Department B and this department incurs a large amount of the overhead expenditure. We can conclude from this example that a blanket overhead rate is only satisfactory when all jobs spend approximately the same time in each department. If all jobs do *not* spend approximately the same time in each department then, to ensure that all jobs are charged with their fair share of overheads, it is necessary to establish separate overhead rates for each department. Let us now examine the procedure for calculating these rates.

Procedure for calculating departmental overhead rates

From Fig. 4.1 you will see that the procedure involves the following:

(1) the allocation of overheads to production and service departments;
(2) the apportionment of service department overheads to production departments;
(3) the calculation of appropriate departmental overhead rates;
(4) charging overhead to jobs.

Let us now consider this procedure in detail.

Allocation of overheads to production and service departments

We established in the previous section the advantage of using separate overhead rates for each department. In respect of such items as the salaries of supervisors or indirect materials, there is little difficulty as these items can be physically located to specific departments, and the overhead expenditure can be charged directly to those departments which actually incurred the expenditure.

There are certain items of overhead expenditure, however, which cannot be allocated to specific departments because they are incurred for the benefit of many departments. In respect of these items it is necessary to establish a logical basis for apportioning the overheads.

The following tabulation summarises some commonly used apportionment bases:

Cost	Basis of apportionment
Rent, rates, lighting and heating	Area
Employee-related expenditure: works management, works canteen, time and wages office	Number of employees
Depreciation and insurance of plant and machinery	Value of items of plant and machinery

The problem with cost apportionment is that it is not possible to allocate costs in a universally acceptable manner. Several alternative methods of apportioning costs may be adopted, which cannot be said to be either right or wrong. More than one method may be acceptable in particular circumstances, and consequently the allocation of overhead costs is often arbitrary. The objective must be to choose a method which has the closest cause-and-effect relationship with the cost objective. The end result of this stage is that all manufacturing overheads will be allocated to factory production and service departments.

Apportionment of services department overheads to production departments

Service departments are those which exist to provide services of various kinds to other units of the organization, for example stores and maintenance departments. They render essential services which support the production process, but they do not deal directly with the products. Consequently, their costs must be apportioned to production departments which actually work on the manufactured product. The method which is

chosen to apportion service department costs to production departments should be related to the benefits which the production departments derive from the service rendered. For example, the total expenditure of the stores department can be apportioned to the production departments on the basis of the number of stores requisitions issued. Similarly, maintenance department costs can be apportioned on the basis of the time recorded in the various production departments by the maintenance staff. Once the service department costs have been apportioned to production departments all factory overhead expenditure will be allocated to *production* departments only. This enables an overhead rate for each production department to be established, and this rate is then charged to all jobs which pass through the various production departments.

Calculation of appropriate departmental overhead rates

The final stage is to allocate the overheads of each production department to jobs which pass through that department. The most frequently used methods are those based on time — for example, direct labour hours, machine hours and direct wages. For a description of other methods which are sometimes used, turn to Appendix 4.2. In respect of a non-machine department, direct labour hours is the most appropriate method whereas in the case of a machine department a machine hour rate is preferable. This is illustrated in Exhibit 4.1.

Charging overhead to jobs

If we assume that job X spends 10 hours in Department A, 6 hours in Department B and 5 machine hours in Department C, then the overhead charged to job X will be £49. This charge is calculated as follows:

Assembly Department A: 10 direct labour
hours at £1 per
hour = £10

Assembly Department B: 6 direct labour
hours at £4 per
hour = £24

Machine Department C: 5 machine hours
at £3 per hour = £15

£49

Note that if *all* jobs spend the stated proportion of time in each department (10 : 6 : 5) it will be unnecessary to analyse overheads to departments, as a blanket overhead rate would yield the same overhead allocation. It would be rare, however, for such a situation to occur in practice in an organization which uses job costing. Let us now apply each of the stages which we have outlined to calculate the departmental overhead rates from the information contained in Example 4.1.

EXAMPLE 4.1

The annual overhead costs for a factory which has three production departments (two machine shops and one assembly shop) and two service departments (stores and maintenance departments) are as follows:

	£	£
Indirect wages and supervision:		
Machine shop: X	100,000	
Y	99,500	
Assembly	92,500	
Stores	10,000	
Maintenance	60,000	362,000
Indirect materials:		
Machine shop: X	100,000	
Y	100,000	
Assembly	40,000	
Stores	4,000	
Maintenance	9,000	253,000
Lighting and heating	50,000	
Rent and rates	100,000	
Insurance of machinery	15,000	
Depreciation of machinery	150,000	
Insurance of buildings	25,000	
Salaries of works management	80,000	420,000
		1,035,000

Exhibit 4.1 Calculation of overhead absorption rates

	Assembly Department A	Assembly Department B	Machine Department C
Overheads allocated	£80,000	£160,000	£240,000
Direct labour hours	80,000	40,000	10,000
Machine hours	–	–	80,000
Overhead rate	£1 per direct labour hour	£4 per direct labour hour	£3 per machine hour

The following information is also available:

	Book value of machinery £	Area occupied (sq. metres)	Number of employees	Direct labour hours	Machine hours
Machine shop: X	800,000	10,000	30	200,000	100,000
Y	500,000	5,000	20	150,000	50,000
Assembly	100,000	15,000	30	200,000	
Stores	50,000	15,000	10		
Maintenance	50,000	5,000	10		
	1,500,000	50,000	100		

Maintenance department records indicate that the amount of time spent on maintenance work in other departments was as follows:

Machine shop X	12,000 hours
Machine shop Y	8,000 hours
Assembly	5,000 hours
	25,000 hours

Details of total materials issues (i.e. direct and indirect materials) to the production departments are

as follows:

Machine shop X	£400,000
Machine shop Y	£300,000
Assembly	£100,000
	£800,000

To allocate the items listed in Example 4.1 to the production and service departments we must prepare an overhead analysis sheet, as shown in Exhibit 4.2.

Exhibit 4.2 Overhead analysis sheet

Item of expenditure	Basis of apportionment	Total £	Production departments Machine shop X £	Machine shop Y £	Assembly £	Service departments Stores £	Maintenance £
Indirect wages & supervision	Actual	362,000	100,000	99,500	92,500	10,000	60,000
Indirect materials	Actual	253,000	100,000	100,000	40,000	4,000	9,000
Lighting and heating	Area	50,000	10,000	5,000	15,000	15,000	5,000
Rent and rates	Area	100,000	20,000	10,000	30,000	30,000	10,000
Insurance of machinery	Book value of machinery	15,000	8,000	5,000	1,000	500	500
Depreciation of machinery	Book value of machinery	150,000	80,000	50,000	10,000	5,000	5,000
Insurance of buildings	Area	25,000	5,000	2,500	7,500	7,500	2,500
Salaries of works management	Number of employees	80,000	24,000	16,000	24,000	8,000	8,000
(1)		1,035,000	347,000	288,000	220,000	80,000	100,000
Reapportionment of service Departmental costs:							
Stores	Value of materials issued		40,000	30,000	10,000	(80,000)	
Maintenance	Technical estimate	–	48,000	32,000	20,000		(100,000)
(2)		1,035,000	435,000	350,000	250,000	–	–
Machine hours and direct labour hours			100,000	50,000	200,000		
Machine hour overhead rate			£4.35	£7.00			
Direct labour hour overhead rate					£1.25		

The overhead expenditure is initially allocated to production and service departments as indicated in line (1). The service department costs in line (1) of £80,000 and £100,000 are then reapportioned to production departments. Line (2) represents the analysis of manufacturing overheads to production departments only. Let us now consider in turn each of the items in the overhead analysis sheet.

Allocation of overheads to production and service departments

Indirect wages and materials cannot be allocated to specific jobs, but they can normally be allocated specifically to the appropriate departments. These items are therefore directly charged to departments on an actual basis. The remaining items listed on the overhead analysis sheet cannot be directly charged to departments on an actual basis. Thus an appropriate method for apportioning the overheads to departments has to be established. We can assume that rent and rates, lighting and heating, and insurance of buildings are related to the total floor area of the buildings, and the benefit obtained by each department can therefore be ascertained according to the proportion of floor area which it occupies. The total floor area of the factory in this example is 50,000 square metres and machine shop X occupies 20% of this and machine shop Y occupies a further 10%. Consequently 20% of rent and rates, lighting and heating and insurance of buildings will be apportioned to machine shop X, and 10% will be apportioned to machine shop Y. The insurance premium paid and depreciation of machinery are generally regarded as being a function of the book value of the machinery. Because the book value of machinery for machine shop X is 8/15 of the total book value and machine shop Y is 5/15 of the total book value then 8/15 and 5/15 of the insurance and depreciation of machinery is apportioned to machine shops X and Y. We can assume that the amount of time which works management devotes to each department is related to the number of employees in each department; as 30% of the total employees are employed in machine shop X, then 30% of the salaries of works management will be apportioned to this department.

Apportionment of service department overheads to production departments

We have now completed stage 1: the allocation of all overhead expenditure to production and service departments. The second stage is to reapportion the service department costs to production departments according to the benefits they have received. We will assume that the value of materials issued provides a suitable approximation of the benefit which each of the production departments receive from the stores department. Therefore 50% of the value of materials is issued to machine shop X resulting in 50% of the total costs of the stores department being apportioned to machine shop X. The maintenance department records the amount of time during which its staff are employed on maintenance work in other departments, and this provides the basis for estimating the benefits which each production department obtains from the maintenance department. As 12,000 hours out of the 25,000 hours worked in the maintenance departments are devoted to machine shop X then 48% of the costs are apportioned to machine shop X.

Calculation of overhead rates

The factory overheads have now been analysed to production departments. The next stage is to establish an overhead rate for each department for charging to the jobs which pass through the various departments. We shall assume that the company uses a machine hour rate for the machine departments and a direct labour hour rate for the assembly department. The overhead rates are calculated by applying the following formula:

$$\frac{\text{Departmental overheads}}{\text{Departmental direct labour hours or machine hours}}$$

The calculations are as follows:

$$\text{Machine shop X} = \frac{£435,000}{100,000 \text{ machine hours}}$$
$$= £4.35 \text{ per machine hour}$$

$$\text{Machine shop Y} = \frac{£350,000}{50,000 \text{ machine hours}}$$
$$= £7 \text{ per machine hour}$$

$$\text{Assembly department} = \frac{£250,000}{200,000 \text{ direct labour hours}}$$
$$= £1.25 \text{ per direct labour hour}$$

The overhead rates are related to time but as the overheads of the machine departments are pre-

dominantly machine oriented a machine hour rate is used. In the assembly department, however, no machine work is performed and a direct labour hour rate is therefore calculated for this department.

Charging overhead to jobs

The final stage is to charge overhead to jobs passing through the production departments. If we assume that job number 80 spends 3 hours in machine shop X, 2 hours in machine shop Y and 1 hour in the assembly department, then the overhead charged to this job will be £28.30. The calculation is as follows:

Machine shop X : 3 hours at £4.35 per hour
Machine shop Y : 2 hours at £7 per hour
Assembly department : 1 hour at £1.25 per hour

The overhead allocation procedure is more complicated where service departments serve each other. In Example 4.1 it was assumed that the stores department does not provide any services for the maintenance department and that the maintenance department does not provide any services for the stores department. An understanding of situations where service departments do serve each other is not, however, necessary for a general understanding of the overhead procedure, and the problem of service department reciprocal cost allocations is therefore dealt with in Appendix 4.1.

Pre-determined overhead rates

Our discussion in this chapter has assumed that the *actual* overheads for an accounting period have been charged to the products. However, the calculation of overhead rates based on the actual overheads incurred during an accounting period causes a number of problems. First, the job cost calculations have to be delayed until the end of the accounting period as the overhead rate calculations cannot be obtained before this date, but information on job costs is required quickly if it is to be used for periodic stock and profit calculations or for decision-making. Secondly, one may argue that the timing problem can be resolved by calculating actual overhead rates at more frequent intervals, say on a monthly basis, but the objection to this proposal is that a large

amount of overhead expenditure is fixed whereas activity will vary from month to month, giving large fluctuations in the overhead rates. Consider Example 4.2.

EXAMPLE 4.2

The fixed overheads for XYZ Ltd are £240,000 per annum, and monthly production varies from 4,000 hours to 10,000 hours. The monthly overhead rate for fixed overhead will therefore fluctuate as follows:

Monthly overhead	£20,000	£20,000
Monthly production	4,000 hours	10,000 hours
Monthly overhead rate	£5 per hour	£2 per hour

Fixed overhead expenditure remains constant each month but monthly production fluctuates because of holiday periods and seasonal variations in demand. Consequently, the overhead rate varies from £2 per hour to £5 per hour. It would be unreasonable for a job worked on in one month to be charged at £5 per hour for overhead and an identical job worked on in another month to be charged at only £2 per hour.

Such fluctuating overhead rates are not representative of typical, normal production conditions. Management has committed itself to a specific level of fixed costs in the light of foreseeable needs for beyond one month. Thus, where production fluctuates, monthly overhead rates may be volatile. An average, annualized rate based on the relationship of total annual overhead to total annual activity is more representative of typical relationships between total costs and volume than a monthly rate. What is required is a *normal* product cost based on average long-term production rather than an actual product cost which is affected by month-to-month fluctuations in production volume. Taking these factors into consideration it is preferable to establish an estimated overhead rate based on annual *estimated overhead expenditure and activity*. Consequently the procedure outlined in the previous sections for calculating departmental overhead rates should be *based on standard activity levels and not actual activity levels*. We shall consider how we might determine standard activity levels later in this chapter.

Under and over recovery of overheads

The effect of calculating overhead rates based on estimated annual overhead expenditure is that it

Fig. 4.2 Illustration of under recovery of factory overheads

will be most unlikely that the overhead charged to production will be the same as the actual overhead incurred. Consider a situation where the estimated annual fixed overheads are £200,000 and the estimated annual activity is 100,000 direct labour hours. The estimated fixed overhead rate will be £2 per hour. Assume that actual overheads are £200,000 and are therefore identical to the estimate, but that actual activity is 90,000 direct labour hours instead of the estimated 100,000 hours. In this situation only £180,000 will be charged to production. This calculation is based on 90,000 direct labour hours at £2 per hour, giving an under recovery of overheads of £20,000.

Consider an alternative situation where the actual overheads are £195,000 instead of the estimated £200,000 and actual activity is 100,000 direct labour hours which is identical to the original estimate. In this situation 100,000 direct labour hours at £2 per hour will be charged to production giving an over recovery of £5000. This example illustrates that *there will be an under or over recovery of overheads whenever actual activity or overhead expenditure is different from the calculations used to estimate the overhead rate.*

The question now arises as to how the under or over recovery of overheads should be accounted for. In theory one should go back and share the under/over recovery among all the jobs worked on during the year. In practice this would not be worthwhile, and furthermore such historical information is probably of no further use to management. Another possibility would be to carry these costs forward to future accounting periods, but it can be argued that one should not adjust for a failure to recover past costs in future accounting periods as such a practice results in a distortion of performance figures.

The normal procedure is to treat any under or over recovery of overhead as a period cost. In other words the under or over recovery of overhead should be written off against the profit and loss statement in the current accounting period. This procedure is illustrated in Fig. 4.2.

Note that any under or over recovery of overhead is not allocated on jobs. Also note that the under recovery is recorded as an expense of the current accounting period, and that none of this adjustment is included in the stock valuation. Not all accountants would agree with treating the under/over recovery of overheads as a period cost adjustment. For example, Horngren (1982) advocates that such amounts could be apportioned between cost of goods sold for the current period and closing stocks. This argument is based on the assumption that the under/over recovery is due to incorrect estimates of activity and overhead expenditure which leads to incorrect allocations being made to the cost of sales and closing stock accounts. The proposed adjustment is an effort to rectify this incorrect allocation.

Note that the UK Statement of Standard Accounting Practice on Stocks and Work in Progress (SSAP 9) recommends that the under/over recovery of overheads should be regarded as a period cost adjustment. It states that the allocation of overheads in the valuation of stocks and WIP needs to be based on the company's *normal level of activity* and that any under/over recovery should be written off in the current year. Remember that we are discussing here how to treat any under or over recovery for the purpose of external reporting and its impact on the stock valuation and profit calculation.

Measuring capacity

When the estimated overhead rates are calculated it is apparant that these rates will be significantly influenced by the estimated volume level. Total fixed overheads will remain unchanged for various activity levels and the fixed overhead rate will fluctuate with changes in estimates of volume. This problem applies only to fixed overhead and the greater the proportion of fixed overheads in an organization's total cost the more acute is the problem. Consider the following example.

EXAMPLE 4.3

The estimated annual fixed manufacturing overheads for a department of a company are £1 million. Calculate the departmental fixed overhead rate assuming that estimated activity is (A) 100,000 hours and (B) 80,000 hours.

The estimated fixed overhead rate is calculated as follows:

$$\frac{\text{Total fixed overheads}}{\text{Total hours}}$$

This formula gives fixed overhead rates of £10 and £12.50 per hour. Clearly the choice of the volume level may significantly affect product cost calculations, stock valuations and the profit and loss account. For this reason some writers have argued that capacity levels should be included in published financial statements (see Bierman, 1975). It is therefore important to establish which volume base should be used for calculating the fixed overhead rate, and we shall now consider three different volume measures.

(1) *Normal volume* is the anticipated average level of activity which will satisfy average customer demand over a period of years, say 3–5 years, and thus includes seasonal, cyclical and trend factors.
(2) *Annual budgeted volume* is the expected level of activity over the coming year.
(3) *Practical capacity* is the estimated *maximum* level of activity at which departments can operate.

Let us now illustrate these volume measures with the following data:

Annual fixed factory overhead		£720,000
Average annual normal volume		85,000 direct labour hours
Annual practical capacity		100,000 direct labour hours
Annual budgeted volume — year	1	65,000 direct labour hours
	2	95,000 direct labour hours
	3	80,000 direct labour hours
	4	100,000 direct labour hours

We will assume normal volume and practical capacity will remain unchanged from years 1 to 4, that fixed overhead expenditure will not change, and that actual expenditure will be the same as budgeted expenditure. The effect of using the different volume measures is illustrated in Exhibit 4.3.

Exhibit 4.3 Comparison of annual budgeted volume, normal volume and practical capacity for overhead absorption

		Annual budgeted volume			Normal volume			Practical capacity		
Year	Annual budgeted volume	Overhead rate[a] £	Overhead charged[b] £	Under/ (over) recovery £	Overhead rate[c] £	Overhead charged £	Under/ (over) recovery £	Overhead rate[d] £	Overhead charged £	Under/ (over) recovery £
1	65,000	11.08	720,000	–	8.4706	550,588	169,412	7.20	468,000	252,000
2	95,000	7.58	720,000	–	8.4706	804,705	(84,705)	7.20	684,000	36,000
3	80,000	9.00	720,000	–	8.4706	677,647	42,353	7.20	576,000	144,000
4	100,000	7.20	720,000	–	8.4706	847,060	(127,060)	7.20	720,000	–
							£ 0			

[a] Fixed factory overhead ÷ annual budgeted volume.
[b] It is assumed that actual volume is identical to budgeted volume.
[c] £720,000 budgeted overheads/85,000 direct labour hours.
[d] £720,000 budgeted overheads/100,000 direct labour hours.

If *normal volume* is used as the volume measure the overhead rate will be £8.4706 per direct labour hour. In year 1 the overhead charged to production will be £8.4706 times 65,000 direct labour hours giving a charge of £550,588. Actual overheads are assumed to be the same as the budgeted overheads of £720,000 giving an under recovery of £169,412. The overheads charged to production and the under/over recovery of overheads for the remaining years have been calculated in a similar manner.

The overhead rate using *practical capacity* as a measure of volume is calculated in a similar manner with fixed overheads of £720,000 being divided by the maximum practical capacity of 100,000 hours. Hence the overhead rate of £7.20 per hour. Since actual activity in year 1 is assumed to be 65,000 hours, then 65,000 hours at £7.20 (£468,000) will be charged to production. The under recovery will be £252,000.

When the overhead rate is calculated using the *annual budgeted volume*, the changes in budgeted annual volume will lead to a change in the overhead rate from year to year. Because actual volume is assumed to be identical to budgeted volume there will be no under or over recovery when annual budgeted volume is used as a volume measure. Note that Exhibit 4.3 is designed to stress only the computation of overhead rates using different volume measures. Total fixed overheads are assumed to be constant each year, so that we can ignore the effects of changes in fixed overhead costs. Changes in fixed overhead expenditure can, however, affect the overhead rate regardless of the volume measure used to set the rate.

How do we interpret the result which we have obtained from Exhibit 4.3? Any under recoveries of overhead are assumed to measure the cost of not producing a target volume, that is, the loss from idle capacity. When we use normal volume as a volume measure we are trying to measure the cost of failing to achieve the normal volume. Alternatively, if the practical capacity measure is used we are trying to measure the cost of failing to achieve maximum practical capacity. In Exhibit 4.3 we assumed that the *actual* volume was equal to the annual *budgeted* volume, which gave zero under or over recovery when the annual budgeted volume was used. However, if the *actual* volume is less than the *budgeted* volume then an under recovery of fixed overheads will occur which represents the cost of failing to meet the budgeted volume. Having described the three alternative volume measures let us now consider the arguments for and against the use of each of these measures.

Normal volume

The advantage of using normal volume is that this measure provides a better approximation of the long-run average costs of providing a firm's operating capacity as seasonal and cyclical variations and trend factors are averaged out. For example, in Exhibit 4.3 volume ranges from 65,000 to 100,000 hours over the four years but the average annual volume over the four year period is 85,000 hours. The proponents of this method argue that long-run average costs are more meaningful than costs which fluctuate from year to year because of seasonal and cyclical variations.

The main argument against using a normal volume measure is that it is extremely difficult to produce realistic estimates of normal volume because of the difficulty in estimating normal sales volume when cyclical fluctuations occur.

Annual budgeted volume

The proponents of the budgeted volume measure argue that it is advantageous because each year's fixed overhead cost must stand by itself, in other words the objective is that each year's overhead should be charged to the production of that year regardless of the relationship of that year's activity to average long-run activity. This measure is also attractive from the practical point of view as it is easier to obtain more realistic forecasts for a single year. The disadvantage is that it does not highlight the cost of failing to achieve long-run production capacity.

Practical capacity

The objective of management may be to operate the plant at maximum practical capacity. If so, there may be advantages in using this measure because the under recovery of overhead will give an approximation of the failure to achieve maximum capacity. The disadvantage is that this measure will yield a low fixed overhead rate and therefore low product costs for stock valuation purposes. In addition there is likely to be a

continuous under recovery of fixed overheads as maximum practical capacity is unlikely to be achieved.

Significance of volume measures for control

Our previous discussion has suggested that an under recovery of overheads provides an approximation of the cost of failing to meet the appropriate volume measure. This information may be useful for control purposes and in the short term the annual budgeted volume may provide the most suitable feedback information; managers may see the annual budgeted volume as the most realistic target against which to measure unused capacity. Measuring the cost of failing to meet the budgeted volume will be discussed in Chapters 17 and 18 but at this stage we should note that the whole concept of measuring the cost of failing to meet target volume in terms of under recovered fixed overheads is questionable. For a detailed discussion of this topic see Horngren (1978).

Significance of volume measures for product pricing

In job costing organizations it is not uncommon for selling price to be determined by adding a percentage profit margin to actual cost. Clearly the volume level that is selected for calculating the fixed overhead rate may significantly affect the product cost and hence the selling price. Normal volume indicates the long-run average cost of providing a firm's operating capacity, and the resulting selling prices represent a long-run selling price. If, however, the company operates in a competitive market and demand for its products is elastic then it is preferable to take into account short-term changes in demand when determining selling prices. In this situation budgeted volume should be used to set the selling prices.

Using maximum practical capacity as a volume measure will mean lower product costs and lower selling prices than the alternative volume measures. There is a danger that the company will not be able to achieve consistently practical capacity and this could result in unrealistically low selling prices being set which fail to cover total company costs. Practical capacity is therefore only an appropriate volume measure to be used as a basis for selling prices when it is likely that maximum practical capacity will be attained.

There are many other factors, besides cost, which must be considered when determining a company's selling prices. Demand and competition are of particular importance. Also, any pricing decision should be based on cost–volume–profit relationships and relevant costs. These factors are discussed in Chapters 9 and 10. A complete discussion of cost information for pricing decisions will be deferred until Chapter 11.

Non-manufacturing overheads

In respect of external reporting, only manufacturing overheads form part of the product costs. Non-manufacturing overheads are regarded as period costs and are disposed of in exactly the same way as the under/over recovery of manufacturing overheads outlined in Figure 4.1.[2] For *external reporting* it is therefore unnecessary to allocate non-manufacturing overheads to products. However, in job costing organizations it is not uncommon for selling price to be based on estimates of *total* cost or even actual cost. For example, housing contractors and garages often charge for their services by adding a percentage profit margin to actual cost. Thus in relation to *product pricing* it may be appropriate to allocate non-manufacturing overheads to products. For an illustration of cost-based pricing methods see the General Motor Corporation case study.[3]

Some non-manufacturing costs may be a direct cost of the product. Delivery costs, salesmen's salaries and travelling expenses may be directly identifiable with the product, but it is likely that the majority of non-manufacturing overheads cannot be allocated directly to specific products. On what basis should we apportion non-manufacturing overheads? The answer is that we should select an input factor which corresponds most closely with non-manufacturing overheads. The problem is that input factors such as direct labour hours, machine hours and direct labour cost are not necessarily those which are closely related to non-manufacturing overheads, as most non-manufacturing overheads are fixed costs and do not vary with changes in the input factor. An alternative approach is to allocate non-manufacturing overheads on the ability of the products to bear such costs. This approach can be implemented by allocating non-manufacturing costs to products on the basis of their manufacturing costs. This procedure is illustrated in Example 4.4.

EXAMPLE 4.4

The estimated non-manufacturing and manufacturing costs of a company for the year ending 31 December are £500,000 and £1 million respectively. The non-manufacturing overhead absorption rate is calculated as follows:

$$\frac{\text{Estimated non-manufacturing overheads}}{\text{Estimated manufacturing costs}}$$

In precentage terms each product will bear a charge for non-manufacturing overheads of 50% of manufacturing cost.

Accountants are clearly on weak ground when allocating non-manufacturing overheads as these cost allocations are very arbitrary. Consequently, it may be preferable not to allocate non-manufacturing overheads to products, but to add a percentage profit margin to each product so that it provides a profit contribution and a contribution to non-manufacturing overheads. For a discussion of how cost information can be used in determining selling prices see Chapter 11.

Overheads for decision-making

In respect of short-term decision-making, the overhead rates calculated in this chapter may be inappropriate. It may be preferable to analyse the overhead rate into fixed and variable elements. This would assist in approximating the relevant cost and would give additional information to management for decision-making. In the short-term, only the variable cost may be relevant for certain decisions but in the long term all costs must be considered. It is therefore necessary to develop separate fixed and variable overhead rates so that management can consider the short-term and long-term implications of various decisions. In addition separate overhead rates are required for estimating costs over various ranges of activity. A detailed discussion of which overhead costs should be used for decision-making is deferred to Chapter 10. At this stage it is important to remember that the overhead calculations suggested in this chapter are necessary for stock valuation, but that such calculations may be inappropriate when used in a decision-making context.

Overheads for control

In order that overheads can be effectively controlled it is essential that these costs are allocated to the individuals who can influence them; they should be allocated to responsibility centres. In addition it is important that overheads should be correctly separated into their controllable and non-controllable elements for each responsibility centre. Responsibility heads cannot be held responsible for items beyond their control, and incorrect identification is likely to cause conflict. As a general rule indirect labour and materials or items charged to departments on an actual basis are controllable. On the other hand, apportionments, such as rent and rates, and those service department allocations where the responsibility head cannot directly influence the quantity of the service consumed should be regarded as non-controllable.

Accounting reports may still include overheads which the head of a responsibility centre cannot control but these overheads should be clearly distinguished from controllable overheads. They will be included because even though a manager may not be able to control them directly he may be able to influence them indirectly — for example, large personnel costs. By paying more attention to training and giving due consideration to human problems, staff turnover may be reduced and this may eventually lead to a reduction in personnel costs. Drawing the attention of managers to the amount of costs not directly controlled by them, but which have been apportioned to them, may encourage managers to make a greater effort to influence such costs. Generally, overhead apportionments play a secondary role in the control of overheads.

We shall not pursue our discussion on the control of overheads further at this stage as this topic is discussed in detail in Chapter 16. It will merely be repeated here that *the allocation of overheads to products is appropriate for stock valuation and profit measurement but such calculations are inappropriate for cost control.*

Summary

In this chapter we have argued that it is preferable to charge overheads to products using *departmental* overhead rates rather than using a *blanket* overhead rate whenever products spend an unequal proportion of time in each department. As a result there is a need to establish a procedure for calculating departmental overhead rates. The procedure must include the following stages:

(1) the allocation of overheads to production and service departments;
(2) the apportionment of service department overheads to production departments;
(3) the calculation of appropriate departmental overhead rates which are then used to charge to jobs passing through each department.

These points were illustrated in Example 4.1. It was suggested that departmental overhead rates should be established on the basis of the input factor which corresponds most closely with the total overhead of each department. The most frequently used overhead rates are the direct labour hour method for non-machine departments and the machine hour rate for machine departments. The direct wages percentage, units of output, direct materials and prime cost percentage methods are discussed in Appendix 4.2, but they can only be recommended in certain circumstances.

As the use of actual overhead rates causes a delay in the calculation of product costs, and the use of monthly overhead rates causes fluctuations in monthly overhead rates, it was suggested that predetermined annual overhead rates should be used. However, the use of annual predetermined overhead rates gives an under or over recovery of overhead whenever actual overhead expenditure or activity is different from budget. Any under or over recovery of overhead is generally regarded as a period cost adjustment and written off to the profit and loss account, although some writers argue that the under/over recovery should be apportioned between the cost of sales and closing stocks.

We have examined three different levels of measuring activity — that is, normal volume, annual budgeted volume and practical capacity. The use of each measure gave us a different overhead rate which caused product costs and stock valuations to differ. The under or over recovery of overhead also varied depending on which volume measure was used.

After discussing manufacturing overheads we noted that non-manufacturing overheads were recorded as period costs and were not charged to the products. The major objective of the present chapter has been to concentrate on accounting for overheads for stock valuation and profit measurement calculations. We have also briefly contrasted the differing requirements of analysing overheads for decision-making and control and noted that for short-term decision-making only variable overheads should be allocated to the product.

To conclude this chapter, note that many people argue in favour of using an alternative system of allocating overheads to products, namely variable costing. This is a system which charges only variable manufacturing overheads to products; fixed manufacturing overheads are regarded as period costs and are not allocated to products. For a discussion of the arguments for and against the different methods of allocating overheads to products see Fremgen (1977). Many of the problems identified in this chapter would no longer apply if a system of variable costing was adopted. A detailed discussion of variable costing can be found in Chapter 8.

Finally, the whole discussion of overhead allocation reflects the assumption that external reporting will use historic cost accounting. There are strong arguments in favour of stock valuations and cost of sales calculations being based on current costs rather than historic costs. For a discussion of current cost accounting see Lee (1980, Chapter 8). If external reporting abandons historic cost accounting then it will be necessary to revise the procedure of accounting for overheads.

References and further reading

Accounting Standards Committee. *Accounting for Stocks and Work in Progress* (SSAP 9), 1977.

Anthony, R.N. and Dearden, J. *Management Control Systems*. R.D. Irwin, 1980.

Bierman, H. Capacity Measures in Financial Accounting. *Accounting and Business Research* Autumn 1975, pp. 305-308.

Dhaliwal, D.S. Cost Allocation and Resource Requirement Planning. *Accounting and Business Research* 9(34) Spring 1979, pp. 163-8.

Eckel, L.G. Arbitrary and Incorrigible Allocations. *The*

Accounting Review **51**(3), October 1976, pp. 764-77.

Fremgen, J.M. The Direct Costing Controversey — An Identification of Issues. *The Accounting Review* January 1964, pp. 43-51; also in Benston, G. (Ed.), *Contemporary Issues in Cost Accounting and Control.* Dickenson, 1977.

French, D.P. and Russell, A.H. An Approximate Method for the Allocation of Reciprocal Service Costs. *Accounting and Business Research* **12**(48), Autumn 1982, pp. 265-72.

Gordon, L.A. Allocating Service Departments Costs. *Accounting and Business Research* Winter 1974, pp. 3-8.

Hong, H.K. Reciprocal Service Costs Allocation and Sensitivity. *Accounting and Business Research* **11**(42), Spring 1981, pp. 117-20.

Horngren, C.T. *Cost Accounting: A Managerial Emphasis.* Prentice Hall, 1982, Chapter 4.

Horngren, C.T. A Contribution Margin Approach to the Analysis of Capacity Utilisation, in Anton, H.R., Firmin, P.A. and Grove, H.D. (Eds), *Contemporary Issues in Cost and Managerial Accounting*, Houghton Mifflin, 1978.

Kaplan, R.S. *Advanced Management Accounting.* Prentice Hall, 1982, Chapter 11.

Lee. T.A. *Income Value and Measurement* 3rd edn. Van Nostrand Reinhold (UK), 1980.

Liao, S.S. The Matching Concept and Cost Allocation. *Accounting and Business Research* **9**(35), Summer 1979, pp. 228-36.

Livingstone, J.L. Matrix Algebra and Cost Allocation. *The Accounting Review* **XLIII**, July 1968, pp. 503-508.

Rowse, R. and Leo, K.J. Defining Operating Capacity. *The Australian Accountant* April 1976, pp. 148-52.

Thomas, A.L. Goals for Joint-cost Allocation. *Abacus* December 1982, pp. 166-75.

Vatter, W.J. Limitations of Overhead Allocation, in Thomas, W.E. (Ed.), *Readings in Cost Accounting Budgeting and Control* 5th edn, South Western Publishing Co., 1978.

Verrecchia, E.E. An Analysis of Two Cost Allocation Cases. *Accounting Review* **LVII**, July 1982, pp. 579-93.

Wall, M.C. Is the Allocation of Overhead Costs Necessary. *The Australian Accountant* November 1970, pp. 479-87.

Zimmerman, J.L. The Costs and Benefits of Cost Allocations. *Accounting Review* **LIV**, July 1979, pp. 504-21.

Problems

*Indicates that a suggested solution is to be found in the *Students' Manual.*

4.1* (a) Explain why pre-determined overhead absorption rates are preferred to overhead absorption rates calculated from factual inform-ation after the end of a financial period.
(b) The production overhead absorption rates of factories X and Y are calculated using similar methods. However, the rate used by factory X is lower than that used by factory Y. Both factories produce the same type of product. You are required to discuss whether or not this can be taken to be a sign that factory X is more efficient than factory Y.

(20 marks)
ICMA Cost Accounting 1
November 1979

4.2* (a) Specify and explain the factors to be con-sidered in determining whether to utilize a single, factory-wide recovery rate for all production overheads or a separate rate for each cost centre, production or service department. (12 marks)
(b) Describe three methods of determining fixed overhead recovery rates and specify the circum-stances under which each method is superior to the other methods mentioned. (8 marks)
(20 marks)
ACCA P2 Management Accounting
June 1981

4.3* From the data given you are required to:
(a) prepare an 'overhead analysis sheet' showing the basis for apportionments made (calcu-lated to the nearest £1);
(b) calculate (to two decimal places of £1) an overhead absorption rate based on direct labour hours for:
 (i) the assembly department;
 (ii) the finishing department;
(c) state briefly, for each overhead item or group of items, why the basis of apportionment was chosen;
(d) for purposes of apportioning costs, state what other information you would have preferred to have used for any of the items instead of the information given.
Data:
 The information given relates to a four-week accounting period. In addition to the cost centres listed there is an 'occupancy' cost centre which is charged with all the costs concerned with occupa-tion of the building. The total of this cost centre should be apportioned before the stores costs are apportioned.

Department:	Machining	Assembly	Finishing	Stores
Area occupied, in sq. feet	24,000	36,000	16,000	4,000
Plant and equipment, at cost, in £000	1,400	200	60	10
Number of employees	400	800	200	20
Direct labour hours	16,000	32,000	4,000	–
Direct wages	£32,600	£67,200	£7,200	–
Number of requisitions on stores	400	1,212	200	–

Allocated costs:

	Total £	Machining £	Assembly £	Finishing £	Stores £
Indirect wages	34,000	9,000	15,000	4,000	6,000
Indirect materials	2,400	400	1,400	600	–
Maintenance	2,100	1,400	600	100	–
Power	2,200	1,600	400	200	–
Total:	£40,700	£12,400	£17,400	£4,900	£6,000

Other costs:

	£
Rent	2,000
Rates	600
Insurance on building	200
Lighting and heating	400
Depreciation on plant and equipment	16,700
Wage related costs (holiday pay, graduated national insurance and company pension scheme)	28,200
Factory administration and personnel	7,100
Insurance on plant and equipment	1,670
Cleaning of factory premises by outside contract cleaners	800
	£57,670

(30 marks)
ICMA Cost Accounting 1
May 1979

4.4 From the information given below you are required to:
(a) prepare a statement of the estimated costs for each cost centre, stating any assumptions you have made;
(b) comment on why you have included or excluded the interest;
(c) comment on whether the Recreation Committee should make decisions concerning the future operations of the snack bar and/or the licensed bar on the basis of the results depicted for these two activities.

A local authority has borrowed £1 million at an interest rate of 15% per annum and built a sports centre. The activities and their cost centre numbers are listed below.

(4.4 *continued*)

Cost centre no.	Activity
1	Swimming pool, adults
2	Swimming pool, children
3	Gymnasium/badminton courts
4	Squash courts
5	Table tennis
6	Snack bar
7	Licensed bar
8	Administration

Estimated annual operating costs (other than staff salaries):

	£000
Rates and insurance	50
Fuel and electricity	20
Repairs and maintenance	15
Chemicals for both swimming pools	6
Security	10
Cleaning materials	5
Salary related costs (employer's National Insurance and pension contributions)	17
Provisions for snack bar	20
Provisions for licensed bar	16

Additional information:

Cost centre no.	Activity	Staff salaries £000	Capital cost £000	Estimated revenue £000	Area occupied sq. metres
1	Swimming pool, adults	16	350	50	1,750
2	Swimming pool, children	5	100	10	350
3	Gymnasium/badminton	8	200	14	750
4	Squash	4	100	12	250
5	Table tennis	6	75	4	260
6	Snack bar	10	75	60	160
7	Licensed bar	6	50	34	80
8	Administration	30	50	–	400
		85	1,000	184	4,000

It has been agreed that:
(i) costs associated with administration are to be apportioned to cost centres 1 to 7 on the basis of estimated revenue;
(ii) any surplus or deficit arising on the snack bar and the licensed bar are to be apportioned over cost centres 1 to 5 in accordance with the following percentages:

Cost centre no.	1	2	3	4	5
%	40	10	20	20	10

(30 marks)
*ICMA Cost Accounting 1
November 1981*

4.5 AEF Ltd is a retail organization which operates three sales departments and an administration department in a large supermarket complex. Each sales department has a manager responsible for its operation to the general manager and its own prescribed gross margin related to selling price.

Exceptionally, the general manager permits the departmental managers to reduce the selling price of a product by giving a quantity discount, a special price for a large order or for an item of out-dated stock.

The following data are given:

	Audio and video equipment £	Electrical appliances £	Furniture £
Stock at 1 April:			
Cost	120,000	80,000	200,000
At full sales value	200,000	110,000	280,000
Transactions during April:			
Purchases	150,000	40,000	160,000
Net sales	215,000	63,000	224,000
Price reductions approved	5,000	3,000	7,000

Expenditure incurred during April was:

Item	Amount £	Basis of apportionment to sales and administration departments
Rates	4,000	} Area occupied
Light and heat	2,000	
Advertising	35,250	
Transport	25,850	Sales value for month
Insurance	3,525	before any reductions
Miscellaneous	1,175	
Canteen	4,125	Number of employees
Salaries and wages	24,910	See detailed
Depreciation	3,750	information given below
Administration	2,500	Direct

Other detailed information for April was:

Department	Salaries and wages £	Depreciation £	Number of employees	Area occupied sq. feet
Audio and video equipment	11,900	500	27	6,000
Electrical appliances	2,000	750	4	2,000
Furniture	6,000	1,000	15	5,000
Administration	5,010	1,500	9	3,000
Total	£24,910	£3,750	55	16,000

Each month the total costs of the administration department are apportioned to the three sales departments on the basis of the sales values for the month before any reductions.

You are required, using the data given to:
(a) calculate the value of stock at 30 April for balance sheet purposes;
(b) prepare a tabulated profit and loss statement for each sales department for April;
(c) discuss an alternative system of accounting which you consider would produce more realistic results to aid management.

(30 marks)
ICMA Cost Accounting 2
May 1980

4.6* A factory with three departments uses a single production overhead absorption rate expressed as a percentage of direct wages cost. It has been suggested that departmental overhead absorption rates would result in more accurate job costs. Set out below are the budgeted and actual data for the previous period, together with information relating to job No. 657.

Hours in thousands

		Direct wages £000's	Direct labour	Machine	Production overhead £000's
Budget:					
Department:	A	25	10	40	120
	B	100	50	10	30
	C	25	25	–	75
Total:		150	85	50	225
Actual:					
Department:	A	30	12	45	130
	B	80	45	14	28
	C	30	30	–	80
Total:		140	87	59	238

During this period job No. 657 incurred the actual costs and actual times in the departments as shown below:

	Direct material £	Direct wages £	Direct labour hours	Machine hours
Department: A	120	100	20	40
B	60	60	40	10
C	10	10	10	–

After adding production overhead to prime cost, one-third is added to production cost for gross profit. This assumes that a reasonable profit is earned after deducting administration, selling and distribution costs.

You are required to:
(a) calculate the current overhead absorption rate;
(b) using the rate obtained in (a) above, calculate the production overhead charged to job No. 657 and state the production cost and expected gross profit on this job;
(c) (i) comment on the suggestion that departmental overhead absorption rates would result in more accurate job costs; and
 (ii) compute such rates, briefly explaining your reason for each rate;
(d) using the rates calculated in (c) (ii) above, show the overhead, by department and in total, that would apply to job No. 657;
(e) show the over/under absorption, by department and in total, for the period using:
 (i) the current rate in your answer to (a) above, and
 (ii) your suggested rates in your answer to (c) (ii) above.

(20 marks)
ICMA Cost Accounting 1
November 1977

4.7 (a) Distinguish between 'budget cost allowance' and 'overhead absorption'.

(b) A department uses an overhead absorption rate of £2 per hour to absorb the departmental variable and fixed overhead.

Activity level in hours	Budget cost allowance £
3,200	7,040
3,600	7,520
4,800	8,960

From the information given above you are required to calculate:
(i) the total budgeted fixed overhead; and
(ii) the normal activity level on which the £2 rate was based.

(c) A manufacturing company with machining and assembly departments seeks your advice about methods of absorbing production overhead.

From the information given below you are required to:
(i) list four methods of absorbing production overhead and show the rates for each department in respect of the four methods;
(ii) compile a comparative statement showing, for each of the four methods chosen in (i) above, the total production cost attributable to Job 987;
(iii) state for *each* department which rate you recommend should be used and why;
(iv) re-calculate (or re-state) the total production cost attributable to Job 987 on the basis of your answer to (c) (iii) above.

Data for the year:	Machining department	Assembly department
Direct material	£100,000	£40,000
Direct labour	£250,000	£480,000
Production overhead	£300,000	£120,000
Direct labour hours	120,000	180,000
Machine hours	100,000	50,000

Data relating to Job 987	Machining department	Assembly department
Direct material	£8,000	£2,000
Direct labour	£2,500	£4,500
Direct labour hours	1,000	1,500
Machine hours	800	300

(30 marks)
ICMA Cost Accounting 1
May 1981

4.8* Shown below is next year's budget for a small engineering factory manufacturing two different products in two production departments, namely a machine shop and an assembly department. A canteen is also operated as a separate department.

Product	A	B
Selling price, per unit	£60	£70
Sales volume	1,500 units	3,000 units
Increase (decrease) in finished stocks	500 units	(500) units
Material cost, per unit	£8	£5
Direct labour:	hours per unit	hours per unit
Machine shop (£3 per hour)	5	6
Assembly department (£2 per hour)	4	4
Machining:		
Machine shop	3	8
Assembly department	1	–

	Machine shop	Assembly dept.	Canteen	Total
Production overhead:	£	£	£	£
Variable	26,000	9,000	–	35,000
Fixed	42,000	30,000	16,000	88,000
	£68,000	£39,000	£16,000	£123,000
Number of employees	15	9	1	
Floor area	4,000 sq. ft.	1,000 sq. ft.	1,000 sq. ft.	

Required:
(a) Establish an appropriate overhead absorption rate for each production department and calculate the total budgeted cost per unit of each product. You must clearly state and briefly justify the methods of overhead absorption used. (17 marks)
(b) Assuming the company operates a full absorption costing system calculate the impact on budgeted profit if, next year, the actual results are as predicted except that sales and production of product A are 300 units higher than budget. (5 marks)
(Total 22 marks)
ACCA Foundation Costing
December 1979

4.9 Bookdon Public Limited Company manufactures three products in two production departments, a machine shop and a fitting section; it also has two service departments, a canteen and a machine maintenance section. Shown below are next year's budgeted production data and manufacturing costs for the company.

Product	X	Y	Z
production	4,200 units	6,900 units	1,700 units
Prime cost:			
Direct materials	£11 per unit	£14 per unit	£17 per unit
Direct labour–			
Machine shop	£6 per unit	£4 per unit	£2 per unit
Fitting section	£12 per unit	£3 per unit	£21 per unit
Machine hours, per unit	6 hours per unit	3 hours per unit	4 hours per unit

Budgeted overheads:	Machine shop	Fitting section	Canteen	Machine maintenance section	Total
	£	£	£	£	£
Allocated overheads	27,660	19,470	16,600	26,650	90,380
Rent, rates, heat and light					17,000
Depreciation and insurance of equipment					25,000
Additional data:					
Gross book value of equipment	£150,000	£75,000	£30,000	£45,000	
Number of employees	18	14	4	4	
Floor space occupied–					
square metres	3.600	1,400	1,000	800	

It has been estimated that approximately 70% of the Machine Maintenance Section's costs are incurred servicing the Machine Shop and the remainder incurred servicing the Fitting Section.

Required:

(a) (i) Calculate the following budgeted overhead absorption rates:

A machine hour rate for the Machine Shop.

A rate expressed as a percentage of direct wages for the Fitting Section.

All workings and assumptions should be clearly shown. (12 marks)

(ii) Calculate the budgeted manufacturing overhead cost per unit of Product X.
(2 marks)

(b) The production director of Bookdon PLC has suggested that, 'as the actual overheads incurred and units produced are usually different from that budgeted and as a consequence profits at each month end are distorted by over/under absorbed overheads, it would be more accurate to calculate the actual overhead cost per unit each month end by dividing the total number of all units actually produced during the month into the actual overheads incurred'.

Critically examine the production director's suggestion. (8 marks)
(22 marks)

ACCA Level 1 Costing
June 1982

4.10 Superdoop PLC is a manufacturing company operating three production departments. Shown opposite are next year's budgeted manufacturing costs, per unit, for each of the three products manufactured by the company.

(continued on p. 81)

	Product X		Product Y		Product Z	
	£	£	£	£	£	£
	per unit	per unit	per unit	per unit	per unit	per unit
Direct materials		24.0		36.0		48.0
Direct wages:						
Department A	10.0		8.0		14.0	
Department B	12.0		15.0		21.0	
Department C	6.0		3.0		2.0	
	——	28.0	——	26.0	——	37.0
Production overheads:						
Department A	11.2		8.0		4.8	
Department B	6.0		7.5		10.5	
Department C	2.5		2.5		2.5	
	——	19.7	——	18.0	——	17.8
Total budgeted manufacturing cost per unit		71.7		80.0		102.8

Prime costs are variable, production overhead contains both fixed and variable elements.

The company operates a full absorption costing system and next year's budgeted overhead absorption rates, based upon next year's budgeted overheads and activity, are:

Department A	Department B	Department C
£1.60 per machine hour	50% of direct wages	£2.50 per unit

Next year's budgeted total direct wages for Department B, analysed by product are:

Product X	Product Y	Product Z
£158,400	£412,500	£147,000

Stocks of work-in-progress are not carried.
Required:
(a) Describe the circumstances in which it would be appropriate to use each of the absorption methods indicated in the question.

(8 marks)

(b) Calculate next year's total budgeted overheads for each of the three departments in Superdoop PLC.

(c) Assume that, next year, the actual results are exactly as those predicted in the budget except that production of Product Z is 200 units higher than that budgeted and, as a consequence, the overheads over-absorbed in the three departments are as follows:

Department A	Department B	Department C
£840	£1,680	£200

Analyse the overheads incurred in Departments A and B between fixed and variable.

(8 marks)
(22 marks)

ACCA Level 1 Costing
December 1982

4.11* Shown below is next year's budget for the Forming and Finishing departments of Tooton Ltd. The departments manufacture three different types of component which are incorporated into the output of the firm's finished products.

Component	A	B	C
Production	14,000 units	10,000 units	6,000 units
Prime costs:	£ per unit	£ per unit	£ per unit
Direct materials			
—Forming dept.	8	7	9
Direct labour			
—Forming dept.	6	9	12
—Finishing dept.	10	15	8
	24	31	29

Manufacturing times:
Machining
–Forming dept.	4 hrs per unit	3 hrs per unit	2 hrs per unit

Direct labour
–Forming dept.	2 hrs per unit	3 hrs per unit	4 hrs per unit
–Finishing dept.	3 hrs per unit	10 hrs per unit	2 hrs per unit

	Forming Department £	Finishing Department £
Variable overheads	200,900	115,500
Fixed overheads	401,800	231,000
	£602,700	£346,500

Machine time required and available	98,000 hours	–
Labour hours required and available	82,000 hours	154,000 hours

The Forming department is mechanized and employs only one grade of labour, the Finishing department employs several grades of labour with differing hourly rates of pay.

Required:

(a) Calculate suitable overhead absorption rates for the Forming and Finishing departments for next year and include a brief explanation for your choice of rates.

(6 marks)

(b) another firm has offered to supply next year's budgeted quantities of the above components at the following prices:

Component A £30,　　Component B £65,
Component C £60

Advise management whether it would be more economical to purchase any of the above components from the outside supplier. You must show your workings and, considering cost criteria only, clearly state any assumptions made or any aspects which may require further investigation.

(8 marks)

(c) Critically consider the purpose of calculating production overhead absorption rates.

(8 marks)

(22 marks)

ACCA Foundation Costing
June 1980

4.12* (a) In a factory with four production departments and two service departments, the operating costs for the month of October were as shown below. The cost of running the canteen is apportioned to each department on the basis of the estimated use of the canteen by the employees in each department. Similarly, the cost of the boiler house is apportioned on the basis of the estimated consumption of power used by each department.

Cost for October were:		£
Production department:	1	200,000
	2	500,000
	3	300,000
	4	400,000
Service department:		
Canteen		50,000
Boiler house		100,000
Total		£1,550,000

The service departments are apportioned as follows:

		Canteen %	Boiler house %
Production department:	1	10	20
	2	30	10
	3	20	30
	4	30	20
Service department:			
Canteen		–	20
Boiler house		10	–
		100	100

You are required to prepare a cost statement showing the costs of operating the four production departments after the costs of the service departments have been re-apportioned to each production department.

(b) Comment briefly on the problems associated with apportioning service department costs to production departments.

(15 marks)

ICMA Cost Accounting 1
November 1982

4.13 The Isis Engineering Company operates a job order costing system which includes the use of predetermined overhead absorption rates. The company has two service cost centres and two production cost centres. The production cost centre overheads are charged to jobs via direct labour hour rates which are currently £3.10 per hour in production cost centre A and £11.00 per hour in production cost centre B. The calculations involved in determining these rates have excluded any consideration of the services that are provided by each service cost centre to the other.

The bases used to charge general factory overhead and service cost centre expenses to the production cost centres are as follows:

(i) general factory overhead is apportioned on the basis of the floor area used by each of the production and service cost centres,

(ii) the expense of service cost centre 1 are charged out on the basis of the number of personnel in each production cost centre,

(iii) the expenses of service cost centre 2 are charged out on the basis of the usage of its services by each production cost centre.

The company's overhead absorption rates are revised annually prior to the beginning of each year, using an analysis of the outcome of the current year and the draft plans and forecasts for the forthcoming year. The revised rates for next year are to be based on the following data:

	General factory overhead	Service cost centres 1	2	Production cost centres A	B
Budgeted overhead for next year (before any reallocation)	£210,000	£93,800	£38,600	£182,800	£124,800
% of factory floor area	–	5	10	15	70
% of factory personnel	–	10	18	63	9
Estimated usage of services of service cost centre 2 in forthcoming year	–	1,000 hrs	–	4,000 hrs	25,000 hrs
Budgeted direct labour hours for next year (to be used to calculate next year's absorption rates)	–	–	–	120,000 hrs	20,000 hrs
Budgeted direct labour hours for current year (these figures were used in the calculation of this year's absorption rates)	–	–	–	100,000 hrs	30,000 hrs

(a) Ignoring the question of reciprocal charges between the service cost centres, you are required to calculate the revised overhead absorption rates for the two production cost centres. Use the company's established procedures. (6 marks)

(b) Comment on the extent of the differences between the current overhead absorption rates and those you have calculated in your answer to (a). Set out the likely reasons for these differences. (4 marks)

(c) Each service cost centre provides services to the other. Recalculate next year's overhead absorption rates recognizing the existence of such reciprocal services and assuming that they can be measured on the same bases as those used to allocate costs to the production cost centres. (6 marks)

(d) Assume that:
(i) General factory overhead is a fixed cost.
(ii) Service cost centre 1 is concerned with inspection and quality control with its budgeted expenses (before any reallocations) being 10% fixed and 90% variable.
(iii) Service cost centre 2 is the company's plant maintenance section with its budgeted expenses (before any reallocations) being 90% fixed and 10% variable.
(iv) Production cost centre A is labour intensive with its budgeted overhead (before any reallocation) being 90% fixed and 10% variable.
(v) Production cost centre B is highly mechanized with its budgeted overhead (before any reallocations) being 20% fixed and 80% variable.

In the light of these assumptions, comment on the cost apportionment and absorption calculations made in parts (a) and (c) and suggest any improvements that you would consider appropriate. (6 marks)
(22 marks)

ACCA Level 2 Management Accounting
June 1983

4.14 Kaminsky Ltd manufactures belts and braces. The firm is organized into five departments. These are belt-making, braces-making, and three service departments (maintenance, warehousing, and administration).

Direct costs are accumulated for each department. Factory-wide indirect costs (which are fixed for all production levels within the present capacity limits) are apportioned to departments on the basis of the percentage of floor-space occupied. Service department costs are apportioned on the basis of estimated usage, measured as the percentage of the labour hours operated in the service department utilized by the user department.

Each service department also services at least one other service department.

Budgeted data for 1981 are as follows:

	Belts	Braces	Admin-istration	Main-tenance	Ware-housing	Company Total
1. Output and sales (units)						
Output capacity	150,000	60,000				
Output budgeted	100,000	50,000				
Sales budgeted	100,000	50,000				
2. Direct variable costs (£000s)						
Materials	120	130	–	20	30	300
Labour	80	70	50	80	20	300
Total	200	200	50	100	50	600
3. Factory-wide fixed indirect costs (£000s)						1,000
4. Floor-space (%)	40	40	5	10	5	100
5. Usage of service department labour-hours (%)						
Administration	40	40	–	10	10	100
Warehousing	50	25	–	25	–	100
Maintenance	30	30	–	–	40	100

(a) You are required to calculate the total cost per unit of belts and braces respectively, in accordance with the system operated by Kaminsky Ltd. (12 marks)

(b) In addition to the above data, it has been decided that the selling prices of the products are to be determined on a cost-plus basis, as the unit total cost plus 20%.

Two special orders have been received, outside the normal run of business, and not provided for in the budget.

They are as follows:
 (i) an order for 1,000 belts from Camfam, an international relief organization, offering to pay £5,000 for them;
(ii) a contract to supply 2,000 belts a week for 50 weeks to Mixon Spenders, a chainstore, at a price per belt of 'unit total cost plus 10%'.

You are required to set out the considerations which the management of Kaminsky Ltd should take into account in deciding whether to accept each of these orders, and to advise them as far as you are able on the basis of the information given.

(8 marks)

(c) 'Normalized overhead rates largely eliminate from inventories, from cost of goods sold, and from gross margin any unfavourable impact of having production out of balance with the long-run demand for a company's products.'

You are required to explain and comment upon the above statement. (5 marks)

ICAEW Management Accounting
December 1980

Appendix 4.1: Inter-service department transfers

Service departments provide services for other service departments as well as for production departments. For example, a personnel department provides services for other service departments such as the power generating plant, maintenance department and stores. The power generating department also provides heat and light for other service departments and so on. When such interactions occur the allocation process can become complicated. Difficulties arise because each service department begins to accumulate charges from other service departments from which it receives services, and these must be reallocated back to the user department. Once it has begun, this allocation and reallocation process can continue for a long time before a solution is found. The problem is illustrated in Example 4A.1.

EXAMPLE 4A.1

A company has three production departments and two service departments. The overhead analysis sheet provides the following totals of the overheads analysed to production and service departments.

		£
Production department	X	48,000
	Y	42,000
	Z	30,000
Service department	1	14,040
	2	18,000
		152,040

The expenses of the service departments are apportioned as follows:

	Production departments			Service departments	
	X	Y	Z	1	2
Service department 1	20%	40%	30%	–	10%
Service department 2	40%	20%	20%	20%	–

Let us now use this example to illustrate three different methods of allocating the service department costs.

(1) Repeated distribution method.
(2) Simultaneous equations method.
(3) Specified order of closing method.

Repeated distribution method

Where this method is adopted the service department costs are repeatedly allocated in the specified percentages until the figures become too small to be significant. See Exhibit 4A.1. You can see from line 2 of Exhibit 4A.1 that the overheads of service department 1 are allocated according to the prescribed percentages. As a result some of the overheads of service department 1 are transferred to service department 2. In line 3 the overheads of service department 2 are allocated, which means that service department 1 receives some further costs. The costs of service department 1 are again allocated and service department 2 receives some

Exhibit 4A.1 Repeated distribution method

Line	Production departments			Service departments		Total
	X	Y	Z	1	2	
1 Allocation as per overhead analysis	48,000	42,000	30,000	14,040	18,000	152,040
2 Allocation of service department 1	2,808 (20%)	5,616 (40%)	4,212 (30%)	(14,040)	1,404 (10%)	
					19,404	
3 Allocation of service department 2	7,762 (40%)	3,881 (20%)	3,880 (20%)	3,881 (20%)	(19,404)	
4 Allocation of service department 1	776 (20%)	1,552 (40%)	1,165 (30%)	(3,881)	388 (10%)	
5 Allocation of service department 2	154 (40%)	78 (20%)	78 (20%)	78 (20%)	(388)	
6 Allocation of service department 1	16 (20%)	31 (40%)	23 (30%)	(78)	8(10%)	
7 Allocation of service department 2	4 (40%)	2 (20%)	2 (20%)	–	(8)	
8 Total overheads	59,520	53,160	39,360	–	–	152,040

further costs. This process continues until line 7 by which time the costs have become so small that any further detailed apportionments are unnecessary. As a result the total overheads in line 8 of £152,040 are allocated to production departments only.

Simultaneous equation method

When this method is used simultaneous equations are initially established as follows:

Let X = Total overhead of service department 1
Let Y = Total overhead of service department 2

The total overhead which is transferred in to service departments 1 and 2 can be expressed as:

$$X = 14,040 + 0.2Y$$
$$Y = 18,000 + 0.1X$$

Rearranging the above equations:

$$X - 0.2Y = 14,040 \qquad (1)$$
$$- 0.1X + Y = 18,000 \qquad (2)$$

We can now multiply equation (1) by 5 and equation (2) by 1, giving

$$5X - Y = 70,200$$
$$-0.1X + Y = 18,000$$

Adding the above equations together we have

$$4.9X = 88,200$$
$$\text{Therefore } X = 18,000 \ (88,200/4.9)$$

Substituting this value for X in equation (1), we have

$$18,000 - 0.2Y = 14,040$$
$$\text{Therefore } - 0.2Y = -3,960$$
$$\text{Therefore } Y = 19,800$$

We now apportion the values of X and Y to the production departments in the agreed percentages.

You will see from line 2 that the value for X (service department 1) of £18,000 is allocated in the specified percentages. Similarly, in line 3 the value for Y (service department 2) of £19,800 is apportioned in the specified percentages. As a result the totals in line 4 are in agreement with the totals in line 8 of the repeated distribution method.

Specified order of closing

If this method is used the service departments' overheads are allocated to the production departments in a certain order. The service department which does the largest proportion of work for other service departments is closed first; the service department which does the second largest proportion of work for other service departments is closed second; and so on. Return charges are not made to service departments whose costs have previously been allocated. Let us now apply this method to the information contained in Example 4A.1. The results are given in Exhibit 4A.2.

The costs of service department 2 are allocated first (line 2) because 20% of its work is related to service department 1, whereas only 10% of the work of service department 1 is related to service department 2. In line 3 we allocate the costs of service department 1 but the return charges are not made to department 2. This means that the proportions allocated have changed as 10% of the costs of service department 1 have not been allocated to service department 2. Therefore 20% out of a 90% total or 2/9 of the costs of service department 1 are allocated to department X.

You will see that the totals allocated in line 4 do not agree with the totals allocated under the repeated distribution or simultaneous equation methods. This is because the specified order of closing method sacrifices accuracy for clerical convenience. However, if this

Line	X	Y	Z	Total
1 Allocation as per overhead analysis	48,000	42,000	30,000	120,000
2 Allocation of service department 1	3,600 (20%)	7,200 (40%)	5,400 (30%)	16,200
3 Allocation of service department 2	7,920 (40%)	3,960 (20%)	3,960 (20%)	15,840
4	59,520	53,160	39,360	152,040

Exhibit 4A.2 Specified order of closing method

Line	Production departments			Service departments		Total
	X	Y	Z	1	2	
1 Allocation as per overhead analysis	48,000	42,000	30,000	14,040	18,000	152,040
2 Allocate service department 2	7,200 (40%)	3,600 (20%)	3,600 (20%)	3,600 (20%)	(18,000)	
3 Allocate service department 1	3,920 (2/9)	7,840 (4/9)	5,880 (3/9)	(17,640)	–	
4	59,120	53,440	39,480	–	–	152,040

method provides a close approximation to an alternative accurate calculation then there are strong arguments for its use.

In practice the problems of service department allocations are likely to be far more complex than is apparent from the simple example illustrated in this appendix. For example, it is likely that more than two service departments will exist. However, it is possible to solve the allocation problem by using computer facilities based on mathematical models. For example, with the aid of computer facilities, matrix algebra can be easily applied to situations where many service departments exist. For a discussion of the application of the matrix method to the reciprocal allocation of service department costs see Kaplan (1982).

Appendix 4.2: Overhead absorption rates

In the main body of this chapter we argued that overheads should be apportioned to products on the basis of an input factor which corresponds most closely with the overhead expenditure of each department. It was suggested that for a non-machine department the direct labour hour method is the most suitable and for a machine department the machine hour method is preferable. In other words, overheads should be apportioned to jobs on the basis of the amount of time each job spends in a production department. However, several other methods are used for apportioning overheads and questions on these methods are sometimes set in examinations. In view of this we shall consider here the following methods:

Direct wages percentage,
Units of output,
Direct materials percentage,
Prime cost percentage

Each of these methods is illustrated using the information given in Example 4A.2.

EXAMPLE 4A.2

The budgeted overheads for a department for the next accounting period are £200,000. In addition the following information is available for the period:

Estimated direct wages	£250,000
Estimated direct materials	£100,000
Estimated output	10,000 units

Direct wages percentage method

The direct wages percentage overhead rate is calculated as follows:

$$\frac{\text{Estimated departmental overheads} \times 100}{\text{Estimated direct wages}}$$

Using the information given in Example 4A.2:

$$\frac{£200,000}{£250,000} \times 100 = 80\% \text{ of direct wages}$$

If we assume that direct wages cost for a product is £20 then overheads of £16 (80% × £20) will be charged to the product.

The direct wages percentage method is suitable where uniform wage rates apply within a department. In such a situation this method will yield exactly the same results as the direct labour hour method. However, consider a situation where wage rates are not uniform. Job X and job Y spend 20 hours in the same production department but job X requires skilled labour and job Y requires unskilled labour with direct wages costs respectively of £100 and £50. If we apply the direct wages percentage overhead rate of 80% we would charge overhead of £80 to job X and £40 to job Y. If both jobs spend the same amount of time in the department are such apportioned amounts fair? The answer would appear to be negative and the direct wages percentage method should only therefore be recommended when similar wage rates are paid to direct employees in a production department.

Units of output method

If this method is used the overhead rate is calculated as follows:

$$\frac{\text{Estimated departmental overhead}}{\text{Estimated output}}$$

Using the information given in Example 4A.2 this would give an overhead rate of £20 per unit produced. The units of output method is only suitable where all units produced within a department are identical. In other words, it is best suited to a process costing system, and it is not recommended for a job costing system where all jobs spend a different amount of time in each production department. If, for example, two of the units produced in Example 4A.2 required 100 hours and 2 hours respectively, then they would both be charged £20. Such an apportionment would not be logical.

Direct materials percentage method

The direct materials percentage overhead rate is calculated as follows:

Estimated departmental overheads

Estimated direct materials

Using the information given in Example 4A.2:

$$\frac{£200,000}{£100,000} = 200\% \text{ of direct materials}$$

If we assume that the direct material cost incurred by a product in the department is £50 then the product will be charged with £100 for a share of the overheads of the department.

If the direct materials percentage overhead rate is used the overheads charged to jobs will bear little relationship to the amount of time which jobs spend in each department. Consequently, this method of recovery cannot normally be recommended, unless the majority of overheads incurred in a department are related to materials rather than time. In particular, the method is appropriate for charging materials handling expenses to products as was suggested in Chapter 3. For the remainder of factory overheads, however, it is preferrable to establish overhead rates based on either direct labour hours or machine hours.

Prime cost percentage method

The prime cost percentage overhead rate is calculated as follows:

$$\frac{\text{Estimated departmental overheads}}{\text{Estimated prime cost}} \times 100$$

Using the information given in Example 4A.2 you will see that the estimated prime cost is £350,000 which consists of direct wages of £250,000 plus direct materials of £100,000. The calculation of the overhead rate is:

$$\frac{£200,000}{£350,000} \times 100 = 57.14\%$$

A job which incurs £100 prime cost in the department will be charged £57.14 for the departmental overheads.

As prime cost consists of direct wages and direct materials the disavantages which apply to the direct materials and direct wages percentage methods also apply to the prime cost percentage method of overhead recovery. Consequently, the prime cost method is not recommended.

5 Accounting entries for a job costing system

This chapter is concerned with the accounting entries necessary to record transactions within a job costing system. The system on which we shall concentrate our attention is one in which the cost and financial accounts are combined in one set of accounts; this is known as an *integrated cost accounting system*. An alternative system, where the cost and financial accounts are maintained independently, is known as an *interlocking accounting system*. The integrated cost accounting system is generally considered to be preferable to the interlocking system as the latter involves a duplication of accounting entries.

Control accounts

The recording system is based on a system of control accounts. A control account is a summary account, where entries are made from *totals* of transactions for a period. For example, the balance in the stores ledger control account will be supported by a voluminous file of stores ledger accounts which will add up to agree with the total in the stores ledger control account. Assuming 1000 items of materials were received for a period which totalled £200,000, then an entry of the total of £200,000 would be recorded on the debit (receipts side) of the stores ledger *control* account. This will be supported by 1000 separate entries in each of the individual stores ledger accounts. The total of all these *individual* entries will add up to £200,000. A system of control accounts enables one to check the accuracy of the various accounting entries, as the total of all the *individual* entries in the various stores ledger accounts should agree with the control account, which will have received the *totals* of the various transactions. The file of all the individual accounts (for example, the individual stores ledger accounts) supporting the total control account is called the subsidiary ledger.

We will now examine the accounting entries necessary to record the transaction outlined in Example 5.1. A manual system is described so that the accounting entries can be followed but the normal practice is now for these accounts to be maintained on a computer. You will find a summary of the accounting entries set out in Exhibit 5.1, where each transactions is prefixed by the appropriate number in parentheses to give a clearer understanding of the necessary entries relating to each transaction. In addition, the appropriate journal entry is shown for each transaction together with a supporting explanation.

EXAMPLE 5.1

The following are the transactions of AB Ltd. for the month of April.
Transaction Number
1 Raw materials of £182,000 were purchased on credit
2 Raw materials of £2,000 were returned to the supplier because of defects
3 The total of stores requisitions for direct materials issued for the period was £165,000

4 The total issues for indirect materials during the period was £10,000

5 Gross wages of £185,000 were incurred during the period consisting of:

Wages paid to employees	£105,000
PAYE due to Inland Revenue	£ 60,000
National Insurance contributions due	£ 20,000

6 All the amounts due in transaction 5 were settled by cash during the period

7 The allocation of the gross wages for the period was as follows:

Direct wages	£145,000
Indirect wages	£ 40,000

8 The employer's contribution for national insurance deductions was £25,000

9 Indirect factory expenses of £41,000 were incurred during the period

10 Depreciation of factory machinery was £30,000

11 Overhead expenses charged to jobs by means of factory overhead absorption rates was £140,000 for the period

12 Non-manufacturing overhead incurred during the period was £40,000

13 The cost of jobs completed and transferred to finished goods stock was £300,000

14 The sales value of goods withdrawn from stock and delivered to customers was £400,000 for the period

15 The cost of goods withdrawn from stock and delivered to customers was £240,000 for the period

Recording the purchase of raw materials

The entry to record the purchase of materials in transaction 1 is:

Dr Stores ledger control account 182,000
 Cr Creditors control account 182,000

This accounting entry reflects the fact that the company has incurred a short-term liability to acquire a current asset consisting of raw material stock. Each purchase is also entered in the receipts column of an individual stores ledger account (a separate record is used for each item of materials purchased) for the quantity received, unit price and amount. In addition a separate credit entry is made in each individual creditor's account. Note that the entries in the control accounts form part of the system of double entry, whereas the separate entries in the individual accounts are detailed subsidiary records which do not form part of the double entry system.

The entry for transaction 2 for materials

returned to suppliers is:

Dr Creditors control account 2,000
 Cr Stores ledger control account 2,000

An entry for the returned materials is also made in the appropriate stores ledger records and in the individual creditor's accounts.

Recording the issue of materials

The storekeeper issues materials from store in exchange for a duly authorized stores requisition. For direct materials the job number will be recorded on the stores requisition and for indirect materials the overhead account number will be entered on the requisition. The issue of *direct* materials involves a transfer of the materials from stores to production. For transaction 3 material requisitions will have been summarized and the resulting totals will be recorded as follows:

Dr Work in Progress Account 165,000
 Cr Stores Ledger Control Account 165,000

This accounting entry reflects the fact that raw material stock is being converted into work in progress stock. In addition to the above entries in the control accounts, the individual jobs will be charged with the cost of the material issued so that job costs can be calculated. Each issue is also entered in the issues column on the appropriate stores ledger record.

The entry for transaction 4 for the issue of *indirect* materials is:

Dr Factory overhead control account 10,000
 Cr Stores ledger control account 10,000

In addition to the entry in the factory overhead control account the cost of material issued will be entered in the individual overhead accounts. These separate overhead accounts will normally consist of individual indirect material accounts for each responsibility centre. Periodically, the totals of each responsibility centre account for indirect materials will be entered in performance reports for comparison with the budgeted indirect materal cost.

After transactions 1–4 have been recorded the stores ledger control account would look like this:

Stores ledger control account

(1) Creditors	182,000	(2) Creditors	2,000	
		(3) Work in progress	165,000	
		(4) Factory overhead A/C	10,000	
		Balance c/d	5,000	
	182,000		182,000	
Balance B/d	5,000			

Accounting procedure for labour costs

Accounting for labour costs can be divided into the following two distinct phases:

(1) Computations of the gross pay for each employee and calculation of payments to be made to employees, government, pension funds etc. (payroll accounting)
(2) Allocation of labour costs to jobs, overhead account and capital accounts (labour cost accounting).

An employee's gross pay is computed from information on the employee's personal record, and attendance or production records. For each employee, a separate record is kept showing the employee's employment history with the company, current rate of pay and authorized deductions such as national insurance, pension plans, savings plans, union dues, and so on. The clock card contains details of attendance time; job cards provide details of bonuses due to employees; and if a piecework system is in operation the piecework tickets will be analysed by employees and totalled to determine the gross wage. The gross wages are calculated from these documents and an entry is then made in the payroll for each employee showing the gross pay, tax deductions and other authorized deductions. The gross pay less the deductions gives the net pay, and this is the amount of cash paid to each employee.

The payroll gives details of the total amount of cash due to employees and the amounts due to the Inland Revenue, Pension Funds and Savings Funds etc. To keep the illustration simple at this stage transaction 5 includes only deductions in respect of tax (PAYE) and national insurance. The accounting entries for transaction 5 are

Dr Wages control account	185,000	
Cr PAYE account		60,000
Cr National Insurance contributions account		20,000
Cr Wages accrued		105,000

The credit entries in transaction 5 will be cleared by a payment of cash. The payment of wages will involve an immediate cash payment but some slight delay may occur with the payment of tax and national insurance as the final date for payment of these items is normally a few weeks after the payment of wages. The entries for the cash payments for these items (transaction 6) are

Dr PAYE account	60,000	
Dr National Insurance contributions account	20,000	
Dr Wages accrued account	105,000	
Cr Cash/bank		185,000

Note that the credit entries for transaction 5 merely represent the recording of amounts due for future payments. The wages control account, however, represents the gross wages for the period and it is the amount in this account which must be allocated to the job, overhead and capital accounts. Transaction 7 gives details of the allocation of the gross wages. The accounting entries are

Dr Work in progress control account	145,000	
Dr Factory overhead control account	40,000	
Cr Wages control account		185,000

In addition to the total entry in the work in progress control account, the labour cost will be charged to the individual job accounts. Similarly, the total entry in the factory overhead control account will be supported by an entry in each individual overhead account for the indirect labour cost incurred. These individual overhead accounts will normally consist of separate responsibility centre accounts for indirect labour. The information from these accounts will be available for recording in the appropriate responsibility performance reports.

Transaction 8 represents the employer's contribution for national insurance payments. The

national insurance deductions in transaction 5 represented the employees' contributions where the company acts merely as an agent, paying these contributions on behalf of the employee. The employer is also responsible for making a contribution in respect of each employee. In Chapter 3 it was pointed out that in some companies the employer's contributions are regarded as part of factory overhead but that it is preferable to add these contributions to the gross wage and charge an inflated hourly rate to each job. To keep the accounting entries simple here, the employer's contributions will be charged to the factory overhead account. The accounting entry for transaction 8 is therefore

Dr Factory overhead
 control account 25,000
 Cr National Insurance
 contributions account 25,000

The National Insurance contributions account will be closed with the following entry when the cash payment is made:

Dr National Insurance
 contributions account 25,000
 Cr Cash/bank 25,000

After recording these transactions the wages control account would look like this:

Wages control account

(5)	Wages accrued A/c	105,000	(7) Work in progress	145,000
(5)	PAYE Tax A/c	60,000	(7) Factory overhead A/c	40,000
(5)	National Insurance			
	account	20,000		
		185,000		185,000

Accounting procedure for manufacturing overheads

Accounting for manufacturing overheads involves entering details of the actual amount of manufacturing overhead incurred on the debit side of the factory overhead control account. The total amount of overheads charged to production is recorded on the credit side of the factory overhead account. In the previous chapter we established that manufacturing overheads are charged to production using estimated overhead rates. It is most unlikely, however, that the actual amount of overhead incurred which is recorded on the debit

side of the account will be in agreement with the amount of overhead charged to jobs which is recorded on the credit side of the account. The difference represents the under or over recovery of factory overheads which is transferred to the profit and loss account, in accordance with the requirements of the Statement of Standard Accounting Practice on Stocks and Work in Progress (SSAP 9).

Transaction 9 represents various indirect expenses which have been incurred and which will eventually have to be paid in cash, for example rent, rates and lighting and heating. Transaction 10 includes other indirect expenses which do not involve a cash commitment. For simplicity it is assumed that depreciation of factory machinery is the only item which falls into this category. The accounting entries for transactions 9 and 10 are

Dr Factory overhead
 control account 71,000
 Cr Expense creditors
 control account 41,000
 Cr Provision of
 depreciation account 30,000

In addition, subsidiary entries, not forming part of the double entry system, will be made in individual overhead accounts. These accounts will be headed by the title of the responsibility centre followed by the object of expenditure. For example, it may be possible to charge indirect materials directly to specific responsibility centres and separate records can then be kept of the indirect materials charge for each centre. It will not, however, be possible to allocate rent, rates and lighting and heating directly to responsibility accounts, and entries should be made in individual overhead accounts for these items. Such expenses could, if so requested by management, be apportioned to responsibility centres according to, say, floor area but note that they should be regarded as non-controllable by the responsibility centres.

Transaction 11 refers to the total overheads which have been charged to jobs using the

estimated overhead absorption rates. The accounting entry in the control accounts for charging overheads to jobs is

> Dr Work in progress control
> account 140,000
> Cr Factory overhead
> control account 140,000

In addition to this entry the individual jobs are charged so that job costs can be calculated. When these entries have been made the factory overhead control account would look like this:

Factory overhead control account

(4) Stores ledger control account	10,000	(11) Work in progress		
(7) Wages control account	40,000	control account	140,000	
(8) Employer's National		Balance — Under		
Insurance contributions		recovery of overhead		
account	25,000	transferred to costing		
(9) Expense creditors account	41,000	profit and loss account	6,000	
(10) Provision for depreciation				
account	30,000			
	146,000		146,000	

The debit side of this account indicates that £146,000 overhead has been incurred, but examination of the credit side indicates that only £140,000 has been charged to jobs via overhead absorption rates. The balance of £6,000 represents an under recovery of factory overhead, which is regarded as a period cost to be charged to the costing profit and loss account in the current accounting period. The reasons for this were explained in the previous chapter.

Non-manufacturing overheads

You will have noted in the previous chapter that non-manufacturing overhead costs are regarded as period costs and not product costs, and non-manufacturing overheads are not therefore charged to the work in progress control account. The accounting entry for transaction 12 is

> Dr Non-manufacturing
> overheads 40,000
> Cr Expense creditors 40,000

At the end of the period the non-manufacturing overheads will be transferred to the profit and loss account as a period cost by means of the following accounting entry:

> Dr Profit and loss account 40,000
> Credit non-
> manufacturing over-
> heads account 40,000

In practice, separate control accounts are maintained for administrative, marketing and financial overheads, but to simplify this example all the non-manufacturing overheads are included in one control account. In addition, subsidiary records will be kept which analyse the total non-manufacturing overheads by individual accounts, for example office stationery account, salesmen's travelling expenses account, etc. Note that these accounts do not form part of the double entry system, but represent a detailed breakdown of the total entries included in the non-manufacturing overhead control account.

Accounting procedures for jobs completed and products sold

When jobs have been completed they are transferred from the factory floor to the finished goods store. The total of the job accounts for the completed jobs for the period is recorded as a transfer from the work in progress control account to the finished goods stock account. The accounting entry for transaction 13 is

> Dr Finished goods stock
> account 300,000
> Cr Work in progress
> control account 300,000

When the goods are removed from the finished goods stock and delivered to the customers, the revenue is recognized. It is a fundamental principle of financial accounting that only costs associated with earning the revenue are included

Exhibit 5.1 Summary of accounting transaction for AB Ltd

Stores ledger control account

(1) Creditors	182,000	(2) Creditors		2,000
		(3) Work in progress		165,000
		(4) Factory overhead A/c		10,000
		Balance c/d		5,000
	182,000			182,000
Balance B/d	5,000			

Work in progress control account

(3) Stores ledger A/c	165,000	(13) Finished goods Stock A/c		300,000
(7) Wages control A/c	145,000			
(11) Factory overhead A/c	140,000	Balance c/d		150,000
	450,000			450,000
Balance B/d	150,000			

Factory overhead control account

(4) Stores ledger A/c	10,000	(11) Work in progress A/c		140,000
(7) Wages control A/c	40,000	Balance — under recovery transferred to costing P & L A/c		6,000
(8) National Insurance contributions A/c	25,000			
(9) Expense creditors A/c	41,000			
(10) Provision for depreciation	30,000			
	146,000			146,000

Finished goods stock account

(13) Work in progress A/c	300,000	(15) Cost of sales A/c		240,000
		Balance c/d		60,000
	300,000			300,000
Balance B/d	60,000			

Cost of sales account

(15) Finished goods stock A/c	240,000	Transferred to costing P & L A/c	240,000	

Non-manufacturing overhead control account

(12) Expense creditors	40,000	Transf to costing P & L A/c	40,000

Provision for depreciation account

		(10) Factory overhead A/c	30,000

Creditors account

(2) Stores ledger A/c	2,000	(1) Stores ledger A/c	182,000

Wages control account

(5) Wages accrued A/c	105,000	(7) Work in progress A/c		145,000
(5) PAYE tax A/c	60,000	(7) Factory overhead A/c		40,000
(5) National Insurance account	20,000			
	185,000			185,000

Wages accrued account

(6) Cash/bank	105,000	(5) Wages control A/c	105,000

Sales A/c

Transferred to costing P & L A/c	400,000	(14) Debtors A/c	400,000

PAYE taxation account

(6) Cash/bank	60,000	(5) Wages control A/c	60,000

Debtors A/c

(14) Sales A/c	400,000

National Insurance contributions account

(6) Cash/bank	20,000	(5) Wages control A/c	20,000
(8) Cash/bank	25,000	(8) Factory overhead A/c	25,000
	45,000		45,000

Expense creditors account

		(9) Factory overhead A/c	41,000
		(12) Non-manufacturing overhead	40,000

Costing profit and loss account

Sales		400,000
Less cost of sales		240,000
Gross profit		160,000
Less Under recovery of factory overhead	6,000	
Non-manufacturing overhead	40,000	46,000
Net profit		114,000

Exhibit 5.2 Flow of accounting entries in an integrated accounting system

as expenses. The cost of those goods which have been delivered to customers must therefore be matched against the revenue due from delivery of the goods so that the gross profit can be calculated. Any goods which have not been delivered to customers will be included as part of the finished stock valuation. The accounting entries to reflect these transactions are

Transaction 14	Dr Debtors control account	400,000	
	Cr Sales account		400,000
Transaction 15	Dr Cost of sales account	240,000	
	Cr Finished goods stock account		240,000

Costing profit and loss account

At frequent intervals management may wish to ascertain the profit to date for the particular period. The accounting procedure outlined in this chapter provides a data base from which a costing profit and loss account may easily be prepared. The costing profit and loss account for AB Ltd based on the information given in Example 5.1 is set out in Exhibit 5.1. As cost control procedures should exist at responsibility centre levels management may find the final profit calculation sufficient when it is combined with a summary of the various performance reports. Alternatively, management may prefer the profit statement to be presented in a format similar to that which is necessary for external reporting. Such information can easily be extracted from the subsidiary records. For example, the factory and non-

manufacturing overhead control accounts are supported by detailed individual accounts such as factory depreciation, factory lighting and heating, office salaries and so on. The items in the costing profit and loss account can therefore be easily replaced with those items normally presented in the financial accounts by extracting from the subsidiary records the appropriate information. The accounting procedure outlined in Exhibit 5.1, however, provides the data base for ascertaining the job costs and stock valuations which are essential to external reporting. In addition, information in the subsidiary records provides the data base from which the accountant can extract relevant decision-making and control information to suit the needs of the various users of accounting information.

tained in the cost accounts to record the corresponding entry which, in an integrated accounting system, would normally be made in one of the financial accounts (creditors, debtors accounts etc.). This account is called a cost control or general ledger adjustment account.

Using an interlocking accounting system to record the transactions listed in Example 5.1 the entries in the creditors, wages accrued, PAYE taxation, National Insurance contribution, expense creditors, provision for depreciation and debtors accounts would be replaced by the following entries in the cost control account:

Cost control account

(2)	Stores ledger control	2,000	(1)	Stores ledger control account	182,000
(14)	Sales account	400,000	(5)	Wages control account	185,000
	Balance c/d	215,000	(8)	Factory overhead control account	25,000
			(9)	Expense creditors account	41,000
			(12)	Non-manufacturing overhead account	40,000
			(10)	Factory overhead account	30,000
				Profit and loss account (profit for period)	114,000
		617,000			617,000
				Balance B/d	215,000

The entries in the remaining accounts will be unchanged.

Interlocking accounting

Interlocking account is a system where the cost and financial accounts are maintained independently of each other, and in the cost accounts no attempt is made to keep a separate record of the financial transactions. Examples of financial transactions include entries in the various creditors, debtors and capital accounts. To maintain the double entry records an account must be main-

Contract costing

Contract costing is a system of job costing that is applied to relatively large cost units which normally take a considerable length of time to complete. Building and construction work, civil engineering and shipbuilding are some examples of industries where large contract work is undertaken, and where contract costing would be appropriate.

A contract account is maintained for each contract. All the direct costs of the contract are debited to the specific contract and overheads are apportioned in the manner prescribed in Chapter 4. The contract price is credited to the contract account and each contract account therefore becomes a small profit and loss account.

Because of the considerable length of time which is taken to complete a contract it is necessary to determine the profit to be attributed to each accounting period. Financial accounting normally recognizes revenue when the goods are delivered but such an approach is inappropriate for long-term contracts, as profits on large contracts would not be reported until they were completed. The profit and loss account would not reflect a fair view of the profitability of the company during the year but show only the results of contracts which had been completed before the year end. To overcome this problem it is preferable to take credit for ascertainable profit while contracts are in progress.

The statement of standard accounting practice on stocks and work in progress (SSAP 9) provides the following guidance on the ascertainable profit to be taken up for a particular period:

The profit, if any, taken up needs to reflect the proportion of the work carried out at the accounting date and to take into account any known inequalities of profitability in the various stages of a contract. Many businesses, however, carry out contracts where the outcome cannot reasonably be assessed before the conclusion of the contract and in such cases it is prudent not to take up any profit. Where the business carries out contracts and it is considered that their outcome can be assessed with reasonable certainty before their conclusion, then the attributable profit should be taken up, but the judgement involved should be exercised. with prudence.

If, however, it is expected that there will be a loss on a contract as a whole, provision needs to be made (in accordance with the prudence concept), for the whole of the loss as soon as it is recognised.

Let us now prepare some contract accounts and determine the ascertainable profit to be taken up for an accounting period.

EXAMPLE 5.2

A construction company is currently undertaking three separate contracts and information relating to these contracts for the previous year, together with other relevant data are shown below:

	Contract A £000s	Contract B £000s	Contract C £000s
Contract price	1760	1485	2420
Balances B/fwd at beginning of year:			
Completed work	–	418	814
Material on site	–	20	30
Written down value of plant and machinery	–	77	374
Wages accrued	–	5	10
Profit previously transferred to profit and loss A/c	–	–	35
Transactions during year:			
Materials delivered to sites	88	220	396
Wages paid	45	100	220
Salaries and other costs	15	40	50
Written down value of plant issued to sites	190	35	–
Head office expenses apportioned during the year	10	20	50
Balances C/fwd at end of year:			
Material on site	20	–	–
Written down value of plant and machinery	150	20	230
Wages accrued	5	10	15
Value of work certified at end of year	200	860	2,100
Cost of work not certified at end of year	–	–	55

The agreed retention rate is 10% of the value of work certified by the contractees' architects. Contract C is scheduled for handling over to the contractee in the near future and the site engineer estimates that the extra costs required to complete the contract, in addition to those tabulated above, will total £305,000. This amount includes an allowance for plant depreciation, construction services, and for contingencies.

You are required to prepare a cost account for each of the three contracts and recommend how much profit or loss should be taken up for the year.

Before we compile the accounts, some of the terms used in Example 5.2 require an explanation.

A customer is likely to be required under the terms of the contract to make *progress payments* to the contractor throughout the course of the work. The amount of the payments will be based on the sales value of the work carried out, as assessed by the architect or surveyor in the *architect's certificate*. A certificate provides confirmation that work to a certain sales value has been completed, and that some payment to the contractor is now due. The amount of the progress payment will consist of:

(1) the sales value of work carried out and certified by the architect; less
(2) a retention; less
(3) the payments made to date.

So if the architect's certificate assesses the value of work carried out to be £300,000 and if the retention is 10%, and if £230,000 has already been paid in progress payments, the current payment will be

£300,000 − £30,000 retention −
£230,000 previous payment = £40,000

There is frequently a contract clause which entitles the customer to withold payment of *retention money* for a proportion of the value of work certified for a specified period after the end of the contract. During this period the contractor must make good all contractual defects. When the defects have been satisfactorily completed the customer will release the retention money.

Let us now prepare the cost accounts for contracts A, B and C:

Contract accounts

	A £000s	B £000s	C £000s		A £000s	B £000s	C £000s
Cost of contract to date B/fwd		418	814	Wages accrued B/fwd		5	10
Materials on site B/fwd		20	30	Materials on site C/fwd	20		
Plant on site B/fwd		77	374	Plant on site C/fwd	150	30	230
Materials control A/c	88	220	396	Cost of work not certified C/fwd			55
Wages control A/c	45	100	220	Cost of work certified (balance) C/fwd	183	915	1,654
Salaries	15	40	50				
Plant control A/c	190	35					
Apportionment of head office expenses	10	20	50				
Wages accrued C/fwd	5	10	15				
	353	940	1,949		353	940	1,949
Cost of work certified B/fwd	183	915	1,654	Value of work certified	200	860	2,100
Profit taken this period			282	Loss taken		55	
Profit taken previous periods			35				
Profit not taken	17		129				
	200	915	2,100		200	915	2,100
Cost of work not certified B/fwd			55	Wages accrued B/fwd	5	10	15
Materials on site B/fwd	20						
Plant on site B/fwd	150	20	230				

You will see that the contract accounts are divided into three sections. The objectives of the first section is to determine the costs which should be matched against the value of work certified so as to calculate the profit to date. The costs to be matched against the value of work certified are shown on the line marked 'Cost of work certified' which is entered on the credit side of the account. You should note that unexpired costs such as the *cost* of work not certified and the written down value of the plant at the end of the period are carried forward to the third section of the contract accounts. This section represents the unexpired costs of the current period which will become an expired cost in future periods. The third section of the account should therefore be regarded as a future cost section.

In the second section of the contract accounts the cost of the completed work is matched against the value of the completed work so that the profit to date can be calculated. The profits/(losses) on the three contracts to date are as follows:

	£000s
Contract A	17
Contract B	(55)
Contract C	446

The problem is to determine how much profit should be taken up for the year on incomplete work. According to SSAP 9 the concept of prudence should be applied, and you are recommeded to adopt the following guidelines:

(A) If the contract is in its early stages, no profit should be taken. Profit should only be taken when the outcome of the contract can be assessed with reasonable certainty. You will see from Example 5.2 that the contract price for Contract A is £1,760,000 but the value of work certified is only £200,000. The contract is therefore only approximately one-eighth complete and it is recommended that no profit is taken.

(B) If a loss is incurred, the prudence concept should be applied, and the total loss should be recognized in the period in which it is incurred. Consequently, the loss of £55,000 on Contract B is recognized in the current accounting period.

(C) If the contract is nearing completion, the size of the eventual profit should be foreseen with reasonable certainty and there is less need to be excessively prudent in determining the amount of profit to be recorded in the profit and loss account.

With regard to Contract C the value of work certified is approximately 87% of the contract price and the anticipated profit is calculated as follows:

	£000s
Cost of work certified	1654
Cost of work not certified	55
Estimated costs to complete	305
Estimated cost of contract	2014
Contract price	2420
Anticipated profit	406

The profit taken is calculated using the following formula:

$$\frac{\text{Cash received to date } (0.90 \times £2100)}{\text{Contract price } (£2420)}$$
\times Estimated profit from the contract $(£406) \simeq £317,000$

You should note that other more prudent approaches are sometimes used to determine the profit earned to date. The profit for the current period consists of the profit to date (£317,000) less the profit of £35,000 previously transferred to the profit and loss account. The profit taken to the profit and loss account for the current period is therefore £282,000.

(D) Where substantial costs have been incurred on a contract, and it is not nearing completion (say it is in the region of 35–85% complete) the following formula is often used to determine the attributable profit to date:

$$\text{Profit taken} = \tfrac{2}{3} \times \text{Notional profit} \times \frac{\text{Cash received}}{\text{Value of work certified}}$$

The notional profit is the value of work certified to date minus the cost of work certified. This formula is one approach to applying the prudence concept.

Work in progress valuation

The Statement of Standard Accounting Practice on Stocks and Work in Progress (SSAP 9) states

that the gross amount of long-term contract work in progress should be stated in the accounts at cost plus attributable profits (if any) less foreseeable losses (if any). The work in progress valuation for Example 5.2 is calculated as follows:

Other entries in the balance sheet will include:

	£000s
Materials on site	20
Plant on site	400
Accruals	30

WIP	Contract A £000s	Contract B £000s	Contract C £000s
Cost of work completed to date	183	915	1,709
Add profit (loss) taken to date	____	(55)	317
	183	860	2,026
Less progress payments received	180	774	1,890
	3	86	136

Alternatively, the work in progress can be expressed as follows:

	Contract A £000s	Contract B £000s	Contract C £000s
Cost of work completed but not certified			55
Add retentions	20	86	210
	20	86	265
Less profit not taken	17	____	129
	3	86	136

Summary

In this chapter we have examined the accounting entries necessary to record transactions within a job costing system. Discussion has been concentrated on an integrated accounting system and the accounting transactions have been illustrated with a comprehensive example. A major feature of the system is the use of control accounts. A summary of the accounting entries, where all purchases and expenses are settled in cash, is shown diagrammatically in Exhibit 5.2. We have also examined a system of contract costing which is the name given to a system of job costing that is applied to relatively large cost units which normally take a considerable length of time to complete.

References and further reading

Accounting Standards Committee. *Accounting for Stocks and Work in Progress* (SSAP 9).

Holgate, P. And Now . . . it's not the SSAP 9 News. *Accountancy Age* 12 July, 1984, p. 9.

Kennedy, A. and Sugden, K. Contract W.I.P. What's in Progress?. *Management Accounting* July/August, 1984, pp. 32-4.

Problems

*Indicates that a suggestion solution is to be found in the *Students' Manual*.

5.1* You are required, using the information given below for the month of April 1980, in respect of D Manufacturing Company Limited to:
 (a) write up the integrated accounts;
 (b) prepare a trading and profit and loss account

for April, 1980;

(c) compile a trial balance as at 30th April, 1980.

(1) List of balances as at 1 April 1980:

	£000
Land and buildings	500
Plant, machinery and office equipment	800
Provision for depreciation, plant machinery and office equipment	200
Material stores	80
Work in progress	40
Finished goods stock	20
Debtors	260
Creditors	100
Bank overdrawn	50
Share capital	1,100
Share premium	200
Profit and loss, appropriation: credit balance	35
Creditor for PAYE and national insurance	15

2. Transactions for the month of April 1980:

	£000
Cash received from debtors	190
Cash paid to creditors	70

	Gross wages £000	PAYE & National Insurance £000	
Direct wages paid	40	10	30
Indirect wages paid	20	5	15
Administrative staff salaries paid	30	10	20
Selling staff salaries paid	20	5	15
Cash paid to creditor for PAYE and National Insurance			30
Cash paid, expenses: production			20
administration			10
Depreciation: production plant and machinery			20
administrative office equipment			5
Employer's contribution, national insurance:			
production			5
administration			3
selling			2
Materials received and invoiced			50
Materials price variance, adverse: extracted as materials are received			5
Materials issued to production from stores			40
Materials issued to production maintenance			8
Transfers from work in progress to finished goods stock			110
Sales on credit			160
Production cost of goods sold			112

Production overhead is absorbed on the basis of 200% on direct wages.

Administration and selling costs are treated as period costs.

(25 marks)

ICMA Cost Accounting 1
May 1980

5.2 IA Limited operates an integral accounting system and, based on the data given below, you are required to prepare the relevant ledger accounts for the month ended 31 October 1982 and a trial balance at that date.

Trial balance at 1 October 1982

	£	£	£
Capital and reserves			1,210,000
Debtors		60,000	
Creditors			75,000
Plant and machinery		240,000	
Provision for deprecia- tion, plant and machinery			60,000
Freehold buildings		400,000	
Stocks:			
Raw materials		350,000	
Work in process 1:			
direct materials	35,300		
direct wages	24,200		
production overhead	60,500		
	———	120,000	

(*continued* on p. 102)

Work in process 2:

direct materials	63,500	
direct wages	34,600	
production overhead	51,900	
		150,000
Finished goods		30,000
Bank		31,000
Sales		500,000
Cost of sales		370,000
Abnormal loss		4,500
Administration overhead		60,000
Selling and distribution overhead		40,000
Production overhead, over/under absorbed		10,500
	£1,855,500	£1,855,500

Transactions for the month ended 31 October 1982 included:

	£
Direct wages incurred:	
process 1	42,400
process 2	64,600
Direct wages paid	100,000
Production salaries paid	85,000
Production expenses paid	125,000
Paid to creditors	165,000
Received from debtors	570,000
Administration overhead paid	54,000
Selling and distribution overhead paid	42,000
Materials purchased on credit	105,000
Materials returned to suppliers	5,000
Materials issued to:	
process 1	68,000
process 2	22,000
Goods sold on credit:	
at sales prices	550,000
at cost	422,400

	Direct materials £	Direct wages £
Abnormal loss in:		
process 1	800	600
process 2	1,400	800
Transfer from process 1 to process 2	76,300	47,400
Transfer from process 2	273,900	69,800

Provision for depreciation of plant and machinery is on a straight line method at 20% per annum on cost.

(30 marks)
*ICMA Cost Accounting 2
November 1982*

5.3 CD Ltd, a company engaged in the manufacture of specialist marine engines, operates an historic job cost accounting system which is not integrated with the financial accounts.

At the beginning of May 1980 the opening balances in the Cost Ledger were:

	£
Stores ledger control account	85,400
Work in progress control account	167,350
Finished goods control account	49,250
Cost ledger control account	302,000

During the month the following transactions took place:

		£
Materials:	Purchases	42,700
	Issues to production	63,400
	to general maintenance	1,450
	to construction of manufacturing equipment	7,650
Factory wages:	Total gross wages paid	124,000

£12,500 of the above gross wages were incurred on the construction of manufacturing equipment, £35,750 were indirect wages and the balance was direct.

Production overheads:
Actual amount incurred, excluding items shown above, was £152,350; £30,000 was absorbed by the manufacturing equipment under construction and under absorbed overhead written off at the end of the month amounted to £7,550.

Royalty payments:
One of the engines produced is manufactured under licence. £2,150 is the amount which will be paid to the inventor for the month's production of that particular engine.

Selling overheads: £22,000
Sales: £410,000.
The company's gross profit margin is 25% on factory cost.

At the end of May stocks of work in progress had increased by £12,000. The manufacturing equipment under construction was completed within the month, and transferred out of the cost ledger at the end of the month.

Required:
prepare the relevant control accounts, costing profit and loss account, and any other accounts you consider necessary to record the above transactions in the cost ledger for May 1980.

(22 marks)
*ACCA Foundation Costing
June 1980*

5.4* (a) The cost accountant and the financial accountant of C Limited have each completed their final accounts for the year. Shown overleaf are the

manufacturing, trading and profit and loss accounts, together with a statement reconciling the cost and financial profits. You are required to show the following accounts in the cost ledger:

 (i) raw materials;
 (ii) work in progress;
(iii) finished goods;
(iv) profit and loss.

Manufacturing, trading and profit and loss account for the year ended 31 December 1981

	£000	£000		£000	£000
Raw material:			Trading account,		
Opening stock	110		cost of goods		
Purchases	640		manufactured		1,000
	750				
Less: Returns	20				
	730				
Closing stock	130				
		600			
Direct wages					
Paid	220				
Accrued	20				
		240			
Prime cost		840			
Production expenses		162			
Work-in-progress:					
Opening stock	25				
Closing stock	27				
		(2)			
		1,000			1,000

	£000	£000		£000	£000
Finished goods:			Sales	1,530	
Opening stock	82		Less: Returns	30	
Manufactured	1,000				1,500
	1,082				
Closing stock	72				
		1,010			
Gross profit		490			
		1,500			1,500
Administration expenses		200	Gross profit		490
Sales expenses		70	Discount received		10
Discount allowed		20			
Debenture interest		10			
Net profit		200			
		500			500

	£000	£000	£000
Profit shown in the financial account			200
Items not shown in the cost accounts:			
Discount allowed		20	
Debenture interest		10	
Sales expenses		70	
Discount received		(10)	
		—	90
			290
Difference in stock valuation:			
Opening stock, raw materials	7		
Opening stock, finished goods	9		
Closing stock, raw materials	15		
	—	31	
Closing stock, work-in-progress	(5)		
Opening stock, work-in-progress	(3)		
Closing stock, finished goods	(4)		
	—	(12)	
		—	19
Profit shown in the cost account			309

Notes:
Production overhead is absorbed at a rate of $66\frac{2}{3}\%$ of wages.
Administration overhead is written off in the period in which incurred.

(b) Discuss briefly the reasons for including in a cost accounting system notional interest on capital locked up in stock and its treatment in preparing a reconciliation of cost and financial profits.

(25 marks)
ICMA Cost Accounting 2
May 1982

5.5 NIA Limited operates a non-integrated accounting system. At the end of April, the financial accountant has produced the final accounts, shown below. Based on these accounts and data supplied by the cost accountant, a reconciliation statement has been prepared, also as shown below.

You are required to prepare the following accounts as they would appear in the cost ledger:
 (i) raw material stores;
 (ii) work in progress;
 (iii) finished goods.

Manufacturing, trading and profit and loss account, for April 1979

	£	£		£
Raw materials:			Cost of goods	
Opening stock	60,500		manufactured,	
Purchases	320,000		carried down	602,000
	380,500			
Closing stock	65,000			
		315,500		
Direct wages		125,000		
Production over-head		160,000		
Work in progress:				
Opening stock	36,700			
Closing stock	35,200			
		1,500		
		£602,000		£602,000

	£	£		£
Finished goods:			Sales	1,000,000
Opening stock	45,600			
Goods manu-factured	602,000			
	647,600			
Closing stock	47,600			
		600,000		
Gross profit, carried down		400,000		
		£1,000,000		£1,000,000

	£		£
Administration expenses	110,000	Gross profit, brought down	400,000
Selling and distribution expenses	150,000	Discount received	30,000
Discount allowed	50,000		
Debenture interest	20,000		
Net profit	100,000		
	£430,000		£430,000

Statement reconciling the profit of financial accounts and cost accounts

		£	£	£
Profit as per financial accounts				100,000
Differences in stock valuation:				
Add: Raw materials:	closing stock	750		
Work-in-progress:	opening stock	900		
Finished goods:	opening stock	1,300		
	closing stock	500		
			3,450	
Less: Raw materials:	opening stock	1,100		
Work-in-progress:	closing stock	500		
			1,600	
				1,850

Other items

Add: Discount allowed	50,000		
Debenture interest	20,000		
		70,000	
Less: Discount received		30,000	
			40,000
			141,850
Production overhead, over absorbed			2,000
Profit, as per cost accounts			£139,850

ICMA Cost Accounting 2
May 1979

5.6* Dearncroft PLC, a company manufacturing special purpose plastic fittings for the building industry, operates a batch costing system, using actual costs, which is not integrated with the financial accounts.

At the end of period 8 there was a fire in the company's main store, the result of which was that all the material stock records were destroyed, together with all the materials held in store. The work in progress and finished goods physical stock fortunately were not damaged. Immediately the fire damage had been cleared away a physical stock count and valuation of the work in progress and finished goods stocks was undertaken. These closing stock values, together with other relevant data summarizing the activities of the company during period 8, are shown below.

Stocks:	At beginning of Period 8	At end of Period 8
Materials	£16,740	All destroyed
Work in progress	£17,500	£22,160
Finished goods	£ 5,490	£ 8,770

Transactions during Period 8:

Purchases of materials	£44,390
Gross wages paid	£24,420
(Analysis of work tickets shows that £16,200 of the above wages represents direct work spent on jobs)	
Production overheads, excluding any relevant items above	£26,580
Sales	£96,000

It should be assumed that all material issues during Period 8 were charged direct to production.

The company operates a marginal (variable) costing system in the cost ledger, stocks are valued at variable cost and wages are regarded as variable. The variable production overhead absorption rate is 80% of direct wages and fixed production overheads in Period 8 amounted to £21,000.

The selling price of the company's products is calculated by adding a contribution margin of $66\frac{2}{3}\%$ on to variable factory cost.

Required:

(a) Calculate the estimated cost of the closing stock of materials destroyed by the fire.

(10 marks)

(b) It has been suggested that the claim on the insurance company for the loss of stocks should be based, not on historic costs, but on replacement costs, and that in future material issues to production also should be charged using replacement costs.

(i) Briefly outline how you would support a claim to the insurance company based on replacement costs. (3 marks)

(ii) Comment upon the implications of charging material issues to production using replacement costs. (4 marks)

(c) Briefly comment upon the implications of valuing stocks of work in progress and finished goods using the marginal (variable) cost approach. (5 marks)

(22 marks)

ACCA Level 1 Costing
December 1982

5.7* Shown below is one week's basic payroll data for the assembly department of Wooden Ltd, a manufacturer of a range of domestic furniture.

	Direct workers	Indirect workers
Total attendance time	800 hours	350 hours
Basic hourly rate of pay	£1.50	£1.00
Overtime hours worked	100 hours	40 hours
Shift premium	£150	£50
Group bonus	£160	£70
Employees' deductions:		
Income Tax	£250	£100
National Insurance	£75	£35
Employer's contributions:		
National Insurance	£125	£55

Overtime, which is paid at basic time rate plus one-half, is used as a means of generally increasing the factory output. However, 20% of the overtime shown above, for both direct and indirect workers, was incurred at the specific request of a special customer who requires, and is paying for, a particular batch of coffee tables to be completed quickly.

Analysis of the direct workers' time from returned work tickets shows:

Productive time	590 hours
Non-productive time:	
Machine breakdown	50 hours
Waiting for materials	40 hours
Waiting for instructions	45 hours
Idle time	75 hours

Required:
(a) Assuming the company operates an historical batch costing system, fully integrated with the financial accounts, write up the assembly department's wages, work in progress and production overhead control accounts, and other relevant accounts. (14 marks)
(b) Explain the reasons for, and effect on product costs of, your treatment of the following items:
 (i) Employer's National Insurance contributions
 (ii) Group bonus
 (iii) Overtime earnings.

(8 marks)
(22 marks)
ACCA Foundation Costing
June 1979

5.8 Shown below are extracts from the previous month's production and overhead budgets for the Finishing Department of a manufacturing company.

Budgeted production:

Product A	560 units
Product B	340 units
Product C	205 units

The standard hour content of each product is:

Product A	3 standard hours per unit
Product B	5 standard hours per unit
Product C	4 standard hours per unit

The budgeted overheads at two specified levels of activity are:

Activity level	4,500 standard hours	3,700 standard hours
	£	£
Depreciation	9,540	9,540
Inspection services	4,250	4,250
Indirect materials	1,125	925
Maintenance of plant	3,300	3,140
Indirect labour	10,900	9,780
Electricity	2,700	2,220
	£31,815	£29,855

It should be assumed that the fixed cost content of the above overheads remains constant at all levels of activity and that the variable content varies with standard hours produced.

Actual production activity and overhead expenditure in the finishing department for the previous month were:
Production:

Product A	610 units
Product B	330 units
Product C	230 units

Actual overhead expenditure:

	£
Depreciation	9,600
Inspection services	4,220
Indirect materials	1,264
Maintenance of plant	3,230
Indirect labour	11,110
Electricity	2,520
Total	£31,944

The company operates a full absorption costing system and the budgeted overhead absorption rate for a particular month is based upon the standard hours of budgeted production for that month.
Required:
(a) Produce the finishing department's production overhead control account for the previous month. All workings should be clearly shown. (11 marks)
(b) Analyse the under/over absorbed overhead calculated in (a) above. Make whatever calculations you consider necessary. (7 marks)

(c) Outline possible reasons for the under/over absorbed overhead. (4 marks)

(22 marks)

ACCA Level 1 Costing
June 1983

5.9 XY Constructions Ltd is building an extension to a college operated by the Education Authority. Work on the college extension commenced on 1 April 1981 and after one year, on 31 March 1982, the data shown below were available.

You are required to:
 (i) prepare the account for the contract for the year ended 31 March 1982;
 (ii) show in relation to the contract an extract from the balance sheet as at 31 March 1982.

During the year:	£000
Plant sent to site	100
Direct materials received at site	460
Direct wages incurred	350
Direct expenses incurred	45
Hire of tower crane	40
Indirect labour costs	70
Supervision salaries	42
Surveyors fees	8
Service costs	18
Hire of scaffolding	20
Overhead incurred on site	60
Head office expenses apportioned to contract	70
Cash received rom the Education Authority	1,000

At 31 March 1982	£000
Value of plant on site	75
Work certified, valued at	1,250
Cost fo work not certified	250
Wages accrued	30
Service costs accrued	2
Materials unused on site	40

(b) Discuss the valuation of work in progress, with particular reference to contract building work.

(25 marks)

ICMA Cost Accounting 1
May 1982

5.10* A construction company is currently undertaking three separate contracts and information relating to these contracts for the previous year, together with other relevant data, is shown on p. 109.

The cost of operating the construction services department, which provides technical advice to each of the contracts, is apportioned over the contracts in proportion to wages incurred.

Contract STU is scheduled for handing over to the contractee in the near future and the site estimates that the extra costs required to complete the contract in addition to those tabulated above will total £138,000. This amount includes an allowance for plant depreciation, construction services and for contingencies.

Required:
(a) Construct a cost account for each of the three contracts for the previous year and show the cost of the work completed at the year end. (9 marks)
(b) (i) Recommend how much profit or loss should be taken, for each contract, for the previous year. (7 marks)
 (ii) Explain the reasons for each of your recommendations in (b)(i) above. (6 marks)

(22 marks)

ACCA Level 1 Costing
December 1983

5.11 Jigantic Ltd is a building company engaged in the construction of hospitals and other major public buildings; most of the contracts undertaken extend over a three or four year period.

Shown below are the expenses incurred for the year ended 31 May 1981, together with other operating details, for three of the contracts in which the company is currently engaged.

	Contract A £000s	Contract B £000s	Contract C £000s
Contract price	4,000	10,200	12,000
Value of work certified by contractees' architects	2,350	7,500	11,000
Cash received from contractees	2,000	6,750	9,900
Work in progress at 1.6.1980	–	2,400	6,700
Cost incurred during the year:			
Materials	1,100	1,600	1,050
Labour	700	1,150	975
Other expenses, excluding depreciation	350	475	775
Plant and equipment:			
Written down value at 1.6.1980	300	800	700
Written down value at 30.5.1981	600	525	175
Purchases during the year	725	400	125
Cost of work not yet certified	75	–	800

Problem 5.10

	Contract MNO £000s	Contract PQR £000s	Contract STU £000s	Construction services dept. overhead £000s
Contract price	800	675	1,100	
Balances brought forward at beginning of year:				
Cost of work completed	–	190	370	–
Material on site	–	–	25	
Written down value of plant and machinery	–	35	170	12
Wages accrued	–	2	–	
Profit previously transferred to profit/loss A/c	–	–	15	–
Transactions during year:				
Material delivered to sites	40	99	180	–
Wages paid	20	47	110	8
Payments to sub-contractos	–	–	35	–
Salaries and other costs	6	20	25	21
Written down value of Plant:				
issued to sites	90	15	–	–
transferred from sites	–	8	–	–
Balances carried forward at the end of year:				
Material on site	8	–	–	–
Written down value of plant and machinery	70	–	110	5
Wages accrued	–	5	–	–
Pre-payments to sub-contractors	–	–	15	–
Value of work certified at end of year	90	390	950	–
Cost of work not certified at end of year	–	–	26	–

(5.11 *continued*)

The agreed retention rate is 10% of the value of work certified by the contractees' architects.

Contract C is nearing completion and the site manager estimates that costs, additional to those tabulated above, of £425,000 will be incurred in order to complete the contract. He also considers that the plant and equipment on site will be worthless by the time the contract is complete.

The nature of the work undertaken by Jigantic Ltd is such that it may be regarded as reasonable for the company to include in its annual accounts a prudent estimate for profit attributable to that part of the work on each contract certified as complete at the end of each accounting year.

The opening stock of work in progress shown above includes an estimated profit of £1,150,000 for Contract C, but none for Contract B as, at the beginning of the year, work on this project had

only recently commenced.

The directors of Jigantic Ltd propose to incorporate into the company's profit and loss account for the year ended 31 May 1981 the following amounts of profit/(loss) for each contract:

Contract A	Nil
Contract B	£720,000
Contract C	£2,400,000

Required:

(a) Making whatever calculations you consider necessary, carefully explain whether you agree with the proposed profit/(loss) figures for the above contracts. If you consider any of the proposed amounts are inappropriate suggest, with supporting explanations and calculations, a more suitable figure.

(15 marks)

(b) Show the relevant entries for each contract, incorporating any revised profit/(loss) figures, on the balance sheet of Jigantic Ltd as at 31 May 1981.

(7 marks)

(22 marks)

ACA Foundation Costing
June 1981

6 Process costing

In the previous three chapters we have examined the cost accumulation procedure for a job costing system where costs are charged to each individual customer's order, as each order is unique and requires different amounts of labour, material and overhead. In this chapter we shall consider the cost accumulation procedure for an alternative system called process costing.

A process costing system is used in those industries where the end products are more or less identical. With this system no attempt is made to allocate the manufacturing cost to a specific order. Instead, the cost of an individual order for a single unit can be obtained by dividing the costs of production for a particular period by the number of units produced during that period. In other words, the cost of the order is assumed to be the *average*
cost of all units produced during the period.

A system of process costing is employed in mass production industries where like units usually pass through a series of production stages which are called processes, for example the chemical, cement, oil, paint and textile industries. Process costing may also be used in firms which produce a variety of products provided that the overall production process can be broken down into sub-operations of a continuous repetitive nature.

Our objective here is to examine the cost accumulation procedure which is necessary for stock valuation and profit measurement for a process costing system. We shall also discuss briefly at the end of the chapter how cost information should be accumulated for decision-making and cost control. We begin with a description of the flow of costs.

Flow of costs in a process costing system

In a process costing industry production moves from one process (or department) to the next until final completion occurs. Each production department performs some part of the total operation and transfers its completed production to the next department where it becomes the input for further processing. The completed production of the last department is transferred to the finished goods stock.

The cost accumulation procedure follows this production flow. Control accounts are established for each process (or department) and direct costs and manufacturing overhead are allocated to each process. The procedure for direct costs is the same as that which is applied to a job costing system with materials and labour being charged to the appropriate process, but a process costing system is easier to operate than a job costing system because the detailed work of allocating costs to many individual cost units is unnecessary. Also many of the costs which are indirect in a job costing system may be regarded as direct in a process costing system. For example, supervision or depreciation which is confined to one department would be treated as part of the direct costs of that department in a process costing system as these costs are directly attributable to the cost objective (that is, the department or process). However, supervision and depreciation are normally regarded as indirect costs in a job costing system because such costs are not directly attributable to an individual job.

As production moves from process to process, costs are transferred with it. The costs of Process

Exhibit 6.1 The flow of costs in process costing system

A are transferred to Process B; Process B costs are then added to this cost and the resulting total cost is transferred to Process C; Process C costs are then added to this cost. Therefore, the cost becomes *cumulative* as production proceeds and the addition of the costs from the last department's costs determines the total cost. The flow of costs from department to department is illustrated in Exhibit 6.1 and a comparison of job costing and process costing is made in Exhibit 6.2.

Normal and abnormal losses

Certain losses are inherent in the production process and cannot be eliminated. For example, liquids may evaporate, part of cloth cut to make a suit may be lost, and losses occur in cutting wood to make furniture. These losses occur under efficient operating conditions and are referred to as normal or uncontrollable losses.

In addition to losses which cannot be avoided, there are some losses which are not expected to occur under efficient operating conditions, for example the improper mixing of ingredients, the use of inferior materials and the incorrect cutting of cloth. These losses are not an inherent part of the production process and are referred to as abnormal or controllable losses.

Normal and abnormal losses require a different accounting treatment. Normal losses are absorbed

by the good production whereas abnormal losses are not included in the process costs but are removed from the appropriate process account and reported separately as an abnormal loss. The abnormal loss is treated as a period cost and written off to the profit and loss account at the end of the period. The accounting treatment for normal and abnormal losses is illustrated in Exhibit 6.3.

Let us now look at some unit cost calculations.

EXAMPLE 6.1

1,200 gallons of liquid were introduced into a process at a cost of £1,200, and a normal loss of 200 gallons occurred.

The cost per unit is based on the *normal output* from an input of 1,200 gallons. An output of 1,000 gallons is expected giving a cost per gallon of £1.20. If a normal loss was not inherent in the production process the cost per unit would have been £1. The higher unit cost is calculated on the basis that 1,000 gallons is the output which is expected under normal efficient operating conditions and it is this unit cost of *normal* production which is appropriate for decision-making, control and stock valuation. However, a distinction must be made between losses which are within tolerable limits (normal) and included in the product costs, and losses which are excessive (abnormal) and which should be treated as period costs.

Exhibit 6.2 A comparison of job and process costing

Process Costing

No attempt is made to allocate costs to individual units of production. Direct costs and factory overhead costs are allocated to Process A, Process B and so on. When units are completed they are transferred to finished goods stock at *average* unit cost.

Consists of stock of *like units* valued at average unit cost of production.

Job Costing

Direct costs and factory overheads are allocated to individual units of production.

Consists of stock of *unlike units.*

Exhibit 6.3 Accounting treatment for normal and abnormal losses

EXAMPLE 6.2

1,200 gallons of liquid were introduced into a process at a cost of £1,200. From past experience and technical estimates a normal loss of one-sixth of the input is expected, but the actual output for the period was only 900 gallons.

You can see that an actual loss of 300 gallons occurred where a loss of 200 gallons was expected. This additional loss of 100 gallons is an abnormal loss. The correct procedure is to establish the cost per gallon of the *expected* output, which is

$$\frac{\text{Cost of production}}{\text{Expected output}} = \frac{£1,200}{1,000} = £1.20$$

Note that the unit cost is the same whether 1,000 gallons or 900 gallons are produced. The distribution of the input costs is as follows:

Completed production transferred to next process or finished goods store	900 gallons at £1.20 per gallon	£1,080
Abnormal loss	100 gallons at £1.20 per gallon	120
		£1,200

Abnormal loss can only be controlled in the future by establishing the cause of the abnormal loss and taking appropriate remedial action. The entries in the process account will look like this:

the profit and loss account as a period cost. The stock valuation will not therefore include any abnormal expenses. The overall effect is that abnormal losses are correctly allocated to the period in which they arise and are not carried forward as a future expense in the closing stock valuation.

Accounting for the sale of scrap[1]

There are situations where the process losses can be sold for some small value. When this is the case the resulting sales revenue should be offset against the costs of the appropriate process for which the loss occurred.

EXAMPLE 6.3

1,200 units were introduced into a process at a cost of £1,200. The output from the process was 1,000 units. The normal loss is one-sixth of the input and any lost units have a scrap value of 50 p per unit.

Process account

	Units	Unit cost	£		Units	Unit cost	£
Input costs	1,200	1.00	1,200	Normal loss	200	–	–
				Abnormal loss	100	1.20	120
				Output transferred to next process	900	1,20	1,080
			1,200				1,200

You will see that no entry is made in the account for the normal loss (except for an entry in the unit column). The transfer to the next process or to finished goods stock is based on the costs of normal production. The abnormal loss is removed from the process costs and reported separately as a loss in an abnormal losses account. This draws the attention of management to those losses which may be controllable. At the end of the accounting period the abnormal loss account is written off to

The calculation of the cost per unit of output is as follows:

$$\frac{\text{Cost of production less scrap value of normal loss}}{\text{Expected output}}$$

$$= \frac{£1100}{1000} = £1.10$$

The entries in the process account will be

Process account

	Units	Unit cost	£		Units	Unit cost	£
Input cost	1,200	1.00	1,200	Normal loss	200	–	100
				Output transferred to next process	1,000	1.10	1,100
			1,200				1,200

The sales value of the normal loss is credited to the process account and a corresponding debit will be made to the cash account. When an abnormal loss occurs the resulting sales revenue from the sale of the additional lost units should be offset against the abnormal loss.

EXAMPLE 6.4

1,200 units were introduced into a process at a cost of £1,200. The output from the process was 900 units. The normal loss is one-sixth of the input and any lost units have a scrap value of 50 p per unit.

Note that the cost per unit of output remains unchanged from the previous example. The calculation is as follows:

$$= \frac{\text{Cost of production less scrap value of normal loss}}{\text{Expected output}}$$

$$= \frac{£1,100}{1,000} = £1.10$$

As we wish to ascertain the cost of *normal* production only, the scrap value of the normal loss can be deducted in ascertaining the cost per unit. The sales value for the additional 100 units lost represents revenue of an abnormal nature and should not be used to reduce the process unit cost. This revenue is offset against the abnormal loss which is of interest to management. The net cost incurred in the process is £1,050 (£1,200 costs less £150 scrap) and the distribution of this cost is:

			£
Transferred to next process:	900 units at £1.10 per unit		990
Abnormal loss:	100 units at £1.10 per unit	110	
	Less Scrap value (100 × 50 p)	50	60
			1050

The entries in the process account will be:

Process account

	Units	Unit cost	£		Units	Unit cost	£
Input costs	1,200	1.00	1,200	Normal loss	200	–	100
				Abnormal loss	100	1.10	110
				Transferred to next process	900	1.10	990
			1,200				1,200

Abnormal loss account

		£		£
Process account		110	Cash sale for units scrapped	50
			Balance transferred to profit and loss account	60
		110		110

It may be argued that when the sales revenue is very small the sale proceeds of the scrap should be offset against the overheads for the period. The sales value would then be credited to the overhead account and not allocated to the specific process and abnormal losses accounts, but this procedure is not theoretically correct as sales revenue should be regarded as *direct* revenue rather than as *indirect* revenue. On the other hand, where the value is small, the additional clerical work of allocating the sale to the process and abnormal losses accounts may not be justified.

Abnormal gains

On occasions the actual loss in a process may be less than expected, in which case an abnormal gain results. The value of the gain is calculated in the same way as the abnormal loss and removed from the process account. The resulting gain is credited to the profit and loss account.

EXAMPLE 6.5

1,200 units were introduced into a process at a cost of £1,200. A normal loss of one-sixth of the input was expected but the actual output for the period was 1,100 units

As the output was 100 units greater than expected there was an abnormal gain. The cost per unit is as follows:

$$\frac{\text{Cost of production}}{\text{Expected output}} = \frac{£1,200}{1,000} = 1.20$$

and the distribution of the input cost is:

Completed production transferred to next process: 1100 units at £1.20	1320
Less Abnormal gain: 100 units at £1.20	(120)
	1200

The entries in the process account will be:

<div align="center">Process account</div>

	Units	Unit cost	£		Units	Unit cost	£
Input cost	1,200	1.00	1,200	Normal loss	200	–	–
Abnormal gain	100	1.20	120	Transferred to next process	1,100	1.20	1,320
			1,320				1,320

You will see that 1,100 units are passed to the next process at the cost per unit of *normal output*. The gain is credited to an abnormal gain account and transferred to the credit of the profit and loss account at the end of the period. This procedure ensures that the stock valuation is not understated by the inclusion of gains of an abnormal nature.

When units lost have a scrap value and an abnormal gain occurs then the abnormal gain must be reduced to reflect the fact that some scrap is lost.

EXAMPLE 6.6

1,200 units were introduced into a process at a cost of £1,200. The output from the process was 1,100 units. The normal loss was one-sixth of the input and any lost units have a scrap value of 50 p per unit.

The cost per unit is as follows:

$$\frac{\text{Cost of production less scrap value of normal loss}}{\text{Expected output}}$$
$$= \frac{£1,100}{1,000} = £1.10$$

The net cost incurred in the process is £1,150 (£1,200 less 100 units scrap at 50 p) and the distribution of this cost is:

		£
Transferred to the next process: 1,100 units at £1.10 per unit		1,210
Less Abnormal gain: 100 units at £1.10	£110	
Lost sales of scrap: 100 units at 50 p	(50)	60
		1,150

The accounting entries are shown on the opposite page:

Process account

	Units	Unit cost	£		Units	Unit cost	£
Input cost	1,200	1.00	1,200	Normal loss	200	–	100
Abnormal gain	100	1.10	110	Transferred to next process	1,100	1.10	1,210
			1,310				1,310

Abnormal gain account

	£		£
Normal loss account	50	Process account	110
Profit and loss account	60		
	110		110

Normal loss account (income due)

	£		£
Process account	100	Abnormal gain account	50
		Cash from scrap sold (100 × 50 p)	50
	100		100

Note that the *cost per unit is based on a normal production cost per unit* and is not affected by the fact that an abnormal gain occurred or that scrap sales of £50 did not materialize. The objective is to produce a cost per unit based on normal operating efficiency.

The abnormal gain is removed from the process account and is valued at the cost per unit of normal production. However, as 100 units were gained there was a loss of scrap sales from 100 units, and this lost income is offset against the abnormal gain. The net gain is therefore £60, and this is the amount which should be transferred to the credit of the profit and loss account.

The process account is credited with the expected sales value of the normal loss of £100 (200 units at 50 p) as the objective is to record in the process account normal production costs. Because the normal loss of 200 units does not occur the company will not obtain a scrap sales value of £100. This problem is resolved by making a corresponding debit entry in a normal loss account of £100 which represents the *amount due* from the sale of scrap from the expected normal loss. The amount due (£100) is then reduced by £50 to reflect the fact that only 100 units were lost. This is achieved by crediting the normal loss account and debiting the abnormal gain account with £50 so that the balance of the normal loss account shows the actual amount of cash received

for scrap income due (that is, £50 which consists of 100 units at 50 p per unit).

Opening and closing work in progress

To simplify the introduction of a process costing system, we have initially ignored the problem of opening and closing work in progress. However, if opening or closing stocks of work in progress exist, the calculation of the cost per unit requires some additional computations. It is obvious that partly completed production (WIP) will have a lower unit cost than fully completed production. Consequently, when opening and closing stocks of work in progress exist unit costs cannot be computed by simply dividing the total cost by the number of units still in the process. For example, if 8,000 units were started and completed during a period and another 2,000 units were partly completed, then these two items cannot be added together to ascertain the unit cost. We must convert the work in progress into finished equivalents (also referred to as *equivalent production*) so that the unit cost can be obtained.

To do this we must estimate the percentage degree of completion of the work in progress and multiply this percentage by the number of units in progress at the end of the period. If the 2,000

partly completed units were 50% complete we could express this as an equivalent production of 1,000 fully completed units. This would then be added to the completed production of 8,000 units to give a total equivalent production of 9,000 units. The cost per unit can then be calculated in the normal way. For example, if the costs for the period were £18,000 then the cost per unit completed would be £2 and the distribution of this cost would be as follows:

Completed units transferred to next
 process: 8,000 units at £2 £16,000
Work in progress: 1,000 equivalent
 units at £2 £ 2,000
 —————
 £18,000

Elements of costs with different degrees of completion

A complication which may arise concerning equivalent units is that in any given stock of work in progress not all of the elements which make up the total cost may have reached the same degree of completion. For example, materials may be added at the start of the process and are thus fully complete, whereas labour and manufacturing overheads may be added throughout the process. Materials may be 100% complete, while labour and overheads may only be partially complete. Where this situation arises separate equivalent production calculations must be made for each element of cost. In the remainder of this chapter, the term 'conversion cost' will be used to describe the sum of direct labour and overheads.

EXAMPLE 6.7

The following information refers to process A.

Opening work in progress	Nil
Units introduced into the process	14,000
Units completed and transferred to process B	10,000
Closing work in progress	4,000
Material cost added during the period	£70,000
Conversion cost added during the period	£48,000

Materials are introduced at the start of the process and conversion costs are applied uniformly throughout the process. The closing work in progress is estimated to be 50% complete.

You are required to compute the cost of the completed production transferred to process B, and the cost of the closing work in progress.

The following statement provides an ideal basis for computing the cost per unit.

Cost element	Total cost £	Completed units	WIP Equivalent units	Total equivalent units	Cost per unit £
Materials	70,000	10,000	4,000	14,000	5.00
Conversion cost	48,000	10,000	2,000	12,000	4.00
	118,000				9.00

Value of work in progress
Materials	4,000 units at £5 =	£20,000	
Conversion cost	2,000 units at £4 =	£ 8,000	£28,000
Completed units	10,000 units at £9	———	£90,000
			£118,000

Process A account

Materials	70,000	Completed units transferred to process B	90,000
Conversion cost	48,000	Closing WIP C/fwd	28,000
	———		———
	£118,000		£118,000
	═══		═══
Opening WIP B/fwd	28,000		

You will see from the above statement that the work in progress of 4,000 units is considered to be fully complete regarding materials. As materials are *issued at the start of the process*, any partly completed units must be fully complete as far as materials are concerned. Regarding conversion cost the 4,000 units in progress are only 50% complete and therefore the equivalent production for this element of cost is 2,000 units. To compute the value of work in progress the unit costs are multiplied separately by the materials and conversion cost work in progress equivalent production figures. Only one calculation is required to ascertain the value of completed production. This is obtained by multiplying the total cost per unit of £9 by the completed production. Note that the cost of the output of £118,000 is in agreement with the cost of the input of £118,000.

Previous process cost

As production moves through processing, the output of one process becomes the input of the next process. The next process will carry out additional conversion work and may add further materials. It is important to distinguish between these different cost items and this is achieved by labelling the transferred cost from the previous process 'previous process cost' and treating this item as a separate element of cost. Note that this element of cost will always be fully complete as far as closing work in progress is concerned.

Let us now extend the previous example and consider how the completed production of process A will be dealt with in *process B*.

EXAMPLE 6.8

	Process B
Opening work in progress	Nil
Units transferred from process A	10,000 units
Closing work in progress	1,000 units
Units completed and transferred to finished goods stock	9,000 units
Costs for the period: Cost of production transferred from process A	£90,000
Conversion costs	£57,000
Materials	£36,000

Materials are *introduced at the end of the process* and conversion costs are applied uniformly throughout the process. The closing work in progress is estimated to be 50% complete.

You are required to compute the cost of completed production transferred to finished stock, and the cost of the closing work in progress.

To do this we must produce a statement, similar to the one in the previous example, to calculate the values of work in progress and completed production.

Cost element	Total cost £	Completed units	WIP Equivalent units	Total equivalent units	Cost per unit £
Previous process cost	90,000	9,000	1,000	10,000	9.00
Materials	36,000	9,000	–	9,000	4.00
Conversion cost	57,000	9,000	500	9,500	6.00
	183,000				19.00

Value of work in progress		£	
Previous process cost	1,000 units at £9	9,000	£
Materials		Nil	
Conversion cost	500 units at £6	3,000	12,000
Completed units 9,000 units at £19			171,000
			183,000 ←

Process B account

Previous process cost	90,000	Completed production		
Materials	36,000	transferred to finished		
Conversion cost	57,000	stock		171,000
		Closing work in		
		progress C/fwd		12,000
	183,000			183,000
Opening WIP B/fwd	12,000			

You will see that the previous process cost is treated as a separate process cost and, as this element of cost will not be added to in process B, the *closing work in progress must be fully complete as far as previous process cost is concerned*. Note that after the first process, materials may be issued at different stages of production. In process B materials are not issued until the end of the process and the closing work in progress will not have reached this point; the equivalent production for the closing work in progress will therefore be zero for materials.

Normally, material costs are introduced at one stage in the process and not uniformly throughout the process. If the work in progress has passed the point at which the materials are added then the materials will be 100% complete. If this point has not been reached then the equivalent production for materials will be zero.

Opening work in progress

When opening stocks of work in progress exist an assumption must be made regarding the allocation of this opening stock to the current accounting period to determine the unit cost for the period. Two alternative assumptions are possible. First, one may assume that opening work in progress is inextricably merged with the units introduced in the current period and can no longer be identified separately — the *weighted average method*. Second, one may assume that the opening work in progress is the first group of units to be processed and completed during the current month — the *first-in, first-out method*. Let us now compare these methods using the information contained in Example 6.9.

EXAMPLE 6.9

A company has two processes, Process X and Process Y. Material is introduced at the *start* of Process X, and additional material is added to Process Y when the process is *seventy per cent* complete. Conversion costs are applied uniformly throughout both processes. The completed units of Process X are immediately transferred to Process Y, and the completed production of Process Y is transferred to finished goods stock. Data for the period includes the following:

	Process X	Process Y
Opening work in progress	6,000 units 3/5 converted consisting of Materials £24,000 and Conversion costs £15,300.	2,000 units 4/5 converted consisting of previous process cost of £30,600, Materials £4,000 and Conversion costs £12,800.
Units started during the period	16,000 units	18,000 units
Closing work in progress	4,000 units 3/4 complete	8,000 units 1/2 complete
Material costs added during the period	£64,000	£20,000
Conversion costs added during the period	£75,000	£86,400

The first stage is to calculate the number of units completed during the period. The calculations for each process are as follows:

	Process X	Process Y
Opening work in progress	6,000	2,000
Units introduced during period	16,000	18,000
Total input for period	22,000	20,000
Less Closing work in progress	4,000	8,000
Balance — Completed Production	18,000	12,000

Weighted average method

The calculation of the unit cost for process X is

Process X — Weighted average method

Cost element	Opening WIP £	Current cost £	Total cost £	Completed units	WIP equiv. units	Total equiv. units	Cost per unit £
Materials	24,000	64,000	88,000	18,000	4,000	22,000	4.0
Conversion cost	15,300	75,000	90,300	18,000	3,000	21,000	4.3
			178,300				8.3

Work in progress:	Materials 4,000 units at £4	£16,000	
	Conversion costs 3,000 at £4.30	£12,900	28,900
Completed Units:	18,000 units at £8.30		149,400
			178,300

Process X account

Opening work in progress B/fwd	39,300	Completed production transferred to Process Y		149,400
Materials	64,000	Closing work in progress		
Conversion cost	75,000	C/fwd		28,900
	178,300			178,300
Opening work in progress B/fwd	28,900			

You can see from the statement of unit cost calculations that the opening work in progress is assumed to be completed in the current period. The current period's costs will include the cost of finishing off the opening work in progress and the cost of the work in progress will be included in the total cost figure. The completed units will include the 6,000 units in progress which will have been completed during the period. The statement therefore includes all the costs of the opening work in progress and the resulting units, fully completed. In other words we have assumed that the opening work in progress is intermingled with the production of the current period to form one homogeneous batch of production. The equivalent number of units for this batch of production is divided into the costs of the current period, plus the value of the opening work in progress, to calculate the cost per unit.

Let us now calculate the unit cost for Process Y using the weighted average method.

Process Y — Weighted average method

Cost element	Opening WIP value £	Current period cost £	Total cost £	Completed units	WIP equiv. units	Total equiv. units	Cost per unit £
Previous process cost	30,600	149,400	180,000	12,000	8,000	20,000	9.00
Materials	4,000	20,000	24,000	12,000	–	12,000	2.00

| Conversion cost | 12,800 | 86,400 | 99,200 | 12,000 | 4,000 | 16,000 | 6.20 |
| | 47,400 | | 303,200 | | | | 17.20 |

Value of work in progress
Previous process cost — 8,000 units at £9 72,000
Material Nil
Conversion cost — 4,000 units at £6.20 24,800 96,800

Completed units
12,000 units at £17.20 206,400

303,200

Process Y account

Opening work in progress	47,400	Completed production transferred to finished stock	206,400	
Transferred from process X	149,400	Closing work in progress C/fwd	96,800	
Materials	20,000			
Conversion cost	86,400			
	303,200		303,200	
Opening work in progress B/fwd	96,800			

From the calculation of the unit costs you can see that the previous process cost is fully complete as far as the closing work in progress is concerned. Note that *materials are added when the process is 70% complete* but the closing work in progress is only 50% complete. At the stage in question no materials will have been added to the closing work in progress and the equivalent production will be zero. As with Process X it is necessary to add the opening work in progress cost to the current cost. The equivalent production of opening work in progress is ignored as this is included as being fully complete in the completed units column. Note also that the completed production cost of Process X is included in the current cost column for 'The Previous Process Cost' in the unit cost calculation for Process Y.

First-in, first-out (FIFO) method

The FIFO method of process costing assumes that the opening work in progress is the first group of units to be processed and completed during the current period. The opening work in progress is charged separately to completed production, and the cost per unit is based only on the *current period* costs and production for the current period. The closing work in progress is assumed to come from the new units started during the period. Let us now use Example 6.9 to illustrate the FIFO method for Process X and Y.

Process X — FIFO method

Cost element	Current period costs £	Completed units less opening WIP equiv. units	Closing WIP equiv. units	Current total equiv. units	Cost per unit £
Materials	64,000	12,000 (18,000−6,000)	4,000	16,000	4.0
Conversion cost	75,000	14,400 (18,000−3,600)	3,000	17,400	4.31
	139,000				8.31

Completed production:	Opening WIP	39,300			
	Materials 12,000 units at £4	48,000			
	Conversion cost 14,400 units at £4.31	62,069	149,369		
Work in progress:	Materials 4,000 units at £4	16,000			
	Conversion cost 3,000 units at £4.31	12,931	28,931		
			178,300		

From this calculation you can see that the average cost per unit is based on *current period* costs divided by the *current* total equivalent units for the period. The latter figure *excludes the equivalent production for opening work in progress* as this was performed in the previous period. Note that the closing work in progress is multiplied by the current period average cost per unit. The closing work in progress includes only the current costs and does not include any of the opening work in progress which is carried forward from the previous period. The objective is to ensure that the opening work in progress is kept separate and is identified as part of the cost of the completed production. The opening work in progress of £39,300 is not therefore included in the unit cost calculations, but is added directly to the completed production.

Let us now calculate the units costs for process Y:

Process Y — FIFO method

Cost element	Current costs £	Completed units less opening WIP equiv. units	Closing WIP equiv. units	Current total equiv. units	Cost per unit £
Previous process cost	149,369	10,000	8,000	18,000	8.2983
Materials	20,000	10,000	Nil	10,000	2.0
Conversion cost	86,400	10,400	4,000	14,400	6.0
	255,769				16.2983

Cost of completed production:
Opening WIP	47,400	
Previous process cost: 10,000 units at £8.2983	82,983	
Materials: 10,000 units at £2	20,000	
Conversion cost: 10,400 units at £6	62,400	212,783

Cost of closing work in progress:
Previous process cost: 8,000 units at £8.2983	66,386	
Materials	Nil	
Conversion cost: 4,000 units at £6	24,000	90,386
		303,169

Note that in this calculation the *opening* work in progress is 80% completed and the materials are added when the process is 70% complete. The materials will have been added to the opening work in progress, and the opening work in progress equivalent units for materials will therefore be 2,000 units. Note also that the previous process cost of £149,369 represents the cost of completed production of process X which has been transferred to Process Y.

The closing work in progress valuations and the charges to completed production are fairly similar for both methods. The difference in the calculations between FIFO and weighted average methods is likely to be insignificant where the quantity of stocks and the input prices do not fluctuate violently from month to month. Both methods are acceptable for product costing purposes but it appears that the FIFO process costing method is rarely used in practice (see Horngren, 1967). In the remainder of this chapter we shall therefore use the weighted average method.

Equivalent production and normal losses

Earlier in this chapter we established that normal losses should be considered as part of the cost of the good production. We need to know, however, at what stage in the process the loss occurs so that we can determine whether the whole loss should be charged to completed production, or whether some of the loss should also be charged to the closing work in progress. If the loss occurs near the end of the process, or is discovered at the point of inspection, only the units which have been completed during the period should be charged with the cost of the loss. Alternatively, the loss could be assumed to occur at a specific point, earlier in the process. For a discussion of losses occurring part-way through a process see the appendix at the end of this chapter.

Generally, it is assumed that normal losses take place at the stage of completion where inspection occurs. Where such an assumption is made the *normal loss will not be charged to the closing work in progress* as the loss is related only to units which have reached the inspection point.

EXAMPLE 6.10

A department with no opening work in progress introduces 1,000 units into the process; 600 are completed, 300 are half completed and 100 units are lost (all normal). Losses are detected upon completion. Material costs are £5,000 (all introduced at the start of the process) and conversion costs are £3,400.

To calculate the value of the normal loss we prepare the normal unit cost statement, but with a separate column for the number of units lost.

Element of cost	Total cost £	Completed units	Normal loss	WIP equiv. units	Total equiv. units	Cost per unit £
Materials	5,000	600	100	300	1,000	5.0
Conversion cost	3,400	600	100	150	850	4.0
	8,400					9.0

Value of work in progress

Materials: 300 units at £5	1,500		
Conversion cost: 150 units at £4	600	2,100	
Completed units: 600 units at £9	5,400		
Normal loss: 100 units at £9	900	6,300	
		8,400	

Note here that all of the cost of the normal loss is added to the completed production, as it is

detected at the completion stage. The closing work in progress will not have reached this stage and therefore does not bear any of the loss. The cost per unit completed after the allocation of the normal loss is £10.50 (£6,300/600 units).

Equivalent production and abnormal losses

Where abnormal losses are incurred the correct procedure is to produce the normal unit cost statement, but with the addition of two separate columns for the units lost; one for normal losses and one for abnormal losses.

EXAMPLE 6.11

A department with no opening work in progress introduces 1,000 units into the process; 600 are completed, 250 are 20% complete and 150 units are lost consisting of 100 units of normal loss and 50 units of abnormal loss. Losses are detected upon completion. Material costs are £8,000 (all introduced at the start of the process) and conversion costs are £4,000.

The unit cost calculations are:

Element of cost	Total cost £	Completed units	Normal loss	Abnormal loss	WIP equiv. units	Total equiv. units	Cost per unit £
Materials	8,000	600	100	50	250	1,000	8
Conversion cost	4,000	600	100	50	50	800	5
	12,000						13

Value of work in progress				
Materials	250 units at £8	2,000		
Conversion cost	50 units at £5	250	2,250	
Completed units	600 units at £13	7,800		
Add normal loss	100 units at £13	1,300	9,100	
Abnormal losss	50 units at £13		650	
			12,000	

You can see that the normal loss has been charged to completed units only. The abnormal loss is charged to a separate account and written off as a period cost to the profit and loss account. The entries in the process account will be:

Process account

Materials	8,000	Transfer to next process	9,100
Conversion cost	4,000	Abnormal loss written off to profit and loss account	650
		Closing work in progress C/fwd	2,250
	12,000		12,000

Note that there is an argument for apportioning the normal loss of £1,300 between the completed units and the abnormal loss. If the normal loss is of a significant value then there are strong arguments for doing this as the normal loss is part of the cost of production. The true cost of the abnormal loss should be charged at the cost per unit of *normal output*. In the unit cost statement for Example 6.11 you will see that the completed production is 600 units and the abnormal loss is 50 units. The normal loss of £1,300 is therefore apportioned pro rata to completed production and the abnormal loss. The calculations are as follows:

Completed units 600/650 × £1,300 = 1,200
Abnormal loss 50/650 × £1,300 = 100

The revised value for completed production would

then be £9,000 (7,800 + 1,200) and for the abnormal loss the value would be £750 (650 + 100).

Process costing for decision-making and cost control

The detailed calculations which we have made in this chapter are necessary for calculating profit and valuing stocks. For example, the process work in progress forms part of the balance sheet stock valuations, and the transfers to succeeding processes become part of the work in progress of these processes or form part of the finished stock. If the finished stock is sold then these costs become part of the cost of goods sold for profit calculations. The calculations of unit costs, process work in progress valuations and the completed units valuation transferred to the next process are therefore necessary to determine the balance sheet stock valuation and the cost of goods sold figure.

It is most unlikely that this same information will be appropriate for decision-making and cost control. In particular, process *total* unit costs will not be relevant for decision-making. What is required is an analysis of costs into their fixed and variable elements for each process. A detailed discussion of those costs which *are* relevant for decision-making will be deferred to Chapter 10, but it is important that you should note at this point that the costs should be assembled in a different way.

Cost control

In respect of cost control we must ensure that the actual costs which are included on a performance report are the costs incurred for *the current period only* and do not include any costs which have been carried forward from previous periods. This principle can be illustrated using the information given in Example 6.9 for Process X. The relevant facts are repeated in Example 6.12.

EXAMPLE 6.12

Material is introduced into Process X at the start of the process and conversion costs are added uniformly throughout the process. Details of Process X for the period are as follows:

Opening work in progress	6,000 units	3/5 converted consisting of materials £24,000 and conversion costs £15,300.
Units started during the period	16,000 units	
Closing work in progress	4,000 units 3/4 complete	
Units completed during the period	18,000 units	
Materials added during the period	£64,000	
Conversion costs added during the period	£75,000	

The budgeted costs for the period are £3.80 per unit for materials and £4 per unit for conversion costs. You are required to produce a cost control performance report for the period.

The unit cost statement given in Example 6.9 for Product X was as follows:

Cost element	Opening WIP value	Current cost	Total cost	Completed units	WIP equiv. units	Total equiv. units	Cost per unit
Materials	24,000	64,000	88,000	18,000	4,000	22,000	4.00
Conversion cost	15,300	75,000	90,300	18,000	3,000	21,000	4.30

This statement is *not* appropriate for cost control, as it includes the value of work in progress brought forward from the previous period. Also the total equivalent units includes the opening work in progress equivalent units partly-processed in the previous period. The inclusion of previous period costs and production *is* appropriate for stock valuation and profit measurement, as the objective is to match costs (irrespective of when they were incurred) with revenues, but it is *not* appropriate to include previous costs for cost control. The objective of cost control is to compare the actual costs of the *current* period with the budgeted cost for the equivalent units produced during the *current* period. We wish to measure a manager's performance for the current period and to avoid this measure being distorted by carrying forward costs which were incurred in the previous period. We must therefore calculate the equivalent units produced during the *current* period by deducting the equivalent units produced during the previous period from the total number

of equivalent units. The calculation is:

	Total equivalent units	Opening WIP equiv. units	Equiv. units produced during period
Materials	22,000	6,000	16,000
Conversion cost	21,000	3,600 (3/5 × 6,000)	17,400

Note that materials are introduced at the start of the process, and the 6,000 units opening work in progress will have been fully completed in the previous period as far as materials are concerned. We can now present a cost control performance report for this process.

Performance report

	Budgeted cost £	Current period actual cost £	Difference £
Materials	60,800 (16,000 units at £3.80)	64,000	3,200 Adverse
Conversion cost	69,600 (17,400 units at £4)	75,000	5,400 Adverse

From this report you will see that we are comparing like with like; that is, both the budgeted costs and the actual costs refer to the equivalent units produced during the *current* period.

Note that information required for cost control must be analysed in far more detail than that presented in the performance report here. For example, the different types of materials and conversion costs must be listed and presented under separate headings for controllable and non-controllable expenses. The essential point to note, however, is that *current* period actual costs must be compared with the budgeted cost for the *current periods* production.

Batch costing

It is not always possible to classify cost accumulation systems into job costing and process costing systems. Where manufactured goods have some common characteristics and also have some individual characteristics the cost accumulation system may be a combination of both the job costing and process costing systems. For example, the production of footwear, clothing and furniture often involves the production of batches, which are variations of a single design and require a sequence of standardized operations. Let us consider a company which makes kitchen units. Each unit may have the same basic frame, and require the same operation, but the remaining operations may differ; some frames may require sinks, others may require to be fitted with work tops; different types of door may be fitted to each unit, some may be low-quality doors and others may be of a higher quality. The cost of a kitchen unit will therefore consist of the basic frame plus the conversion costs of the appropriate operations. The principles of the cost accumulation system are illustrated in Exhibit 6.4.

The cost of each product consists of the cost of operation 1 plus a combination of the conversion costs for operations 2 to 5. The cost per unit produced for a particular operation *consists of the average unit cost of each batch produced for each operation*. It may well be that some products may be subject to a final operation which is unique to that product. The product cost will then consist of the average *cost* of a combination of operations 1 to 5 plus the *specific cost* of the final unique operation. The cost of the final operation will be traced specifically to the product using a job costing system. The final product cost therefore

Exhibit 6.4 A batch costing system

Product	Operations 1	2	3	4	5	Product cost
A	✓	✓	✓			A = Cost of operations 1, 2, 3
B	✓			✓	✓	B = Cost of operations 1, 4, 5
C	✓	✓		✓		C = Cost of operations 1, 2, 4
D	✓		✓		✓	D = Cost of operations 1, 3, 5
E	✓	✓			✓	E = Cost of operations 1, 2, 5

consists of a combination of process costing techniques and job costing techniques. This system of costing is referred to as *operation costing* or *batch costing*. Skinner (1978) suggests that process costing is rarely used in a continuous manufacture process, and that in practice operation costing is most commonly used.

Summary

In this chapter we have examined the cost accumulation procedure necessary for a process costing system for stock valuation and profit measurement. A process costing system is an average cost system which is appropriate for those industries where the units of final output are identical. The cost of an individual order for a single unit can be obtained by merely dividing the costs of production for a period by the units produced for that period. Examples of industries where a system of process costing is appropriate include chemical, cement, oil, paint and the textile industries.

The accounting treatment for normal and abnormal losses has been explained and illustrated. Normal losses are inherent in the production process and cannot be eliminated; their cost should be borne by the good production. Abnormal losses are avoidable, and the cost of these losses should not be charged to products but reported separately as an abnormal loss and written off as a period cost to the Profit and Loss Account. Scrap sales (if any) which result from the losses should be apportioned to the appropriate Process Account (for normal losses) and the Abnormal Loss Account (for abnormal losses).

We have established that where stocks of work in progress are in existence it is necessary in order to create homogeneous units of output to convert the work in progress into finished equivalent units of production. As materials are normally introduced at the start or end of the process and conversion costs are added uniformly throughout the process it is necessary to keep a separate record of these items of cost. When materials are added at the start of the process the materials element of the WIP is 100 per cent complete. Alternatively, if materials are added at the end of the process they are zero complete. Costs transferred from previous processes are recorded separately for unit cost calculations as they are always regarded as 100 per cent complete.

We have discussed and examined two alternative methods of apportioning the opening work in progress costs to production; the weighted average and the first in first out methods. If the weighted average method is used both the units and the value of the opening work in progress are merged with the current period costs and production to calculate the average cost per unit. Using the first in first out method the opening work in progress is assumed to be the first group of units to be processed and completed during the current month. The opening work in progress is therefore charged separately to completed production, and the cost per unit is based only on *current* costs and production for the period. The closing work in progress is assumed to come from the new units which have been started during the period.

Finally, we have briefly contrasted the differing ways in which cost information should be accumulated for decision-making and cost control. In respect of decision-making we are interested in the additional future costs and revenue resulting from a decision, and only incremental costs may be relevant for short-term decisions. In respect of cost control it is only *current* costs and production which should be included in performance reports as we are interested in a manager's performance in the current period and wish to avoid distorting the report with costs carried forward from the previous period.

References and further reading

Corcoran, A.W. A matrix approach to process cost accounting. *Management Accounting (USA)*, November 1966, 48-53.

Forrester, D.A.R. Process costing in text and content. *Management Accounting (UK)* November 1982, 34-6.

Horngren, C.T. Process costing in perspective: Forget FIFO. *Accounting Review* July 1967.

Mock and Grove. An investigation of subjective measurement: A field test of percentage of completion measurement. In *Measurement, Accounting and Organizational Information*, 1979. Wiley.

Partington, C. Process costing — a comment. *Abacus* June 1980.

Reimund, F. A process model for costing. *Management Accounting (USA)* January 1975, 45-7.

Schwan, E.S. Process costing for reaction accounting. *Management Accounting (USA)* September 1974, 45-50.

Skinner, R.C. Process costing. *Abacus* December 1978, 160-71; and a reply to Partington in *Abacus* June 1980.

Problems

*Indicates that a suggested solution is to be found in the *Students' Manual*.

6.1* (a) In a process costing system state what is meant by: (i) normal loss, and (ii) abnormal loss, and indicate how you would treat these items in the cost accounts.

(b) A company makes one product which passes through two processes. From the data given below which relates to period 4, you are required to show the transactions which would appear in the two process accounts, finished goods account, abnormal loss account and the abnormal gain account.

Process 1
Material: 5,000 kg at £0.5 per kg
Labour: £800
Production overhead 200% on labour

Process 2
Materials: 4,000 kg at £0.8 per kg
Labour: £1,753
Production overhead 100% on labour

Normal losses are 20% of input in process 1 and 10% of input in process 2 but without further processing any losses are able to be sold as scrap for £0.3 per kg from process 1 and £0.7 per kg from process 2.

The outputs for period 4 were:

3,800 kg from process 1
7,270 kg from process 2

There was no work in process at the beginning or end of period 4 and no finished goods stock at the beginning of the period.

(20 marks)
ICMA Cost Accounting 1
May 1981

6.2 'No Friction' is an industrial lubricant which is formed by subjecting certain crude chemicals to two successive processes. The output of Process 1 is passed to Process 2 where it is blended with other chemicals. The process costs for Period 3 were as follows:

Process 1
Material — 3,000 kg. @ £0.25 per kg
Labour — £120
Process plant time — 12 hours at £20 per hour

Process 2
Material — 2,000 kg. @ £0.4 per kg
Labour — £84
Process plant time — 20 hours @ £13.50 per hour

General overhead for Period 3 amounted to £357 and is absorbed into process costs on a process labour basis.

The normal output of Process 1 is 80% of input and of Process 2, 90% of input.

Waste matter from Process 1 is sold for £0.20 per kg and that from Process 2, for £0.30 per kg.

The output for Period 3 was as follows:

Process 1 2,300 kg
Process 2 4,000 kg

There was no stock or work in process at either the beginning or the end of the period and it may be assumed that all available waste matter had been sold at the prices indicated.

You are required to show how the foregoing data would be recorded in a system of cost accounts.

6.3 Product B is made by means of three processes. Material is put into process at the start of process 1 and the output transferred to process 2. The output of process 2 is transferred to process 3 and the completed product of process 3 is transferred to finished goods stock.

The data for the week ended 31 October 1980 relating to product B are given below:

Process	Description		Units	Stage of completion %	Cost £
1	Work in process, at start		20	50	270
	Input:	Material	270		3,240
		Labour and overhead			840
	Output:	Transferred to process 2	290		
2	Input:	Material added			530
		Labour and overhead			1,540
	Output:	Transferred to process 3	240		
	Work in process, at end:				
		Material added	50	50	
		Labour and overhead		80	
3	Work in process, at start:		90		

	Transferred cost		2,025
	Labour and overhead	$33\frac{1}{3}$	105
Input:	Labour and overhead		1,015
Output:	Transferred to finished goods stock	300	
	Work in process, at end	30	$66\frac{2}{3}$
Finished goods:			
	Stock at start	100	2,700
	Sold	324	

No units were lost in production and the weighted average basis of pricing is to be used.

You are required to prepare for the week ended 31 October 1980.

(a) the three manufacturing process accounts, showing in each:
 (i) the unit cost;
 (ii) the value of work in process;
 (iii) the cost of production transferred;
(b) the finished goods stock account.

<div align="right">(30 marks)

ICMA Cost Accounting 2

November 1980</div>

6.4* A company producing a single product from one process has an opening work in process of 3,200 units which were complete as to material but only 75% complete as to labour and overhead. These units at the end of September had been valued as follows:

	£
Direct materials	14,000
Direct wages	6,500
Production overhead	
(200% on direct wages)	13,000

During the month of October a further 24,800 units were put into process and the following costs charged to the process:

	£
Direct materials	96,000
Direct wages	59,125
Production overhead	118,250

Normal loss by evaporation was 500 units and 25,000 completed units were transferred to finished stock.

Work in process at the end of October was 2,500 units which were complete as to material and half complete as to labour and overhead.

The average method of pricing is used.

You are required to prepare, for the month of October, a cost of production report or other suitable statement(s) for the operating management to show:

(a) production cost per unit in total and by element of cost;
(b) the total cost of production transferred to finished stock;

(c) the valuation of closing work in process in total and by element of cost.

<div align="right">(20 marks)

ICMA Cost Accounting 1

November 1982</div>

6.5 Prepare the process account using the average cost basis from the following information in respect of Process 1:

	Units	Material cost £	Conversion cost £
Work in process at start	1,000	11,000	3,200
Input this period	9,000	109,000	52,000
Transferred to Process 2	7,200		
Work in process at end (50% completed)	1,200		

The normal process loss is 800 units for the period and is assumed to be lost at the end of the process. All materials are added at the start of the process, and conversion cost can be assumed to be incurred evenly throughout the process. During this period it is known that there have been some additional losses due to an accidental increase in temperature, when some units were at the 75% stage of completion. The cost of normal expected loss is all carried by units completed and transferred.

6.6* A concentrated liquid fertilizer is manufactured by passing chemicals through two consecutive processes. Stores record cards for the chemical ingredients used exclusively by the first process show the following data for May 1979:

Opening stock	4,000 litres	£10,800
Closing stock	8,000 litres	£24,200
Receipts into store	20,000 litres	£61,000

Other process data for May is tabulated below.

	Process 1	Process 2
Direct labour	£4,880	£6,000
Direct expenses	£4,270	–
Overhead absorption rates	250% of direct labour	100% of direct labour
Output	8,000 litres	7,500 litres

Opening stock of work in process	Nil	Nil
Closing stock of work in process	5,600 litres	Nil
Normal yield	85% of input	90% of input
Scrap value of loss	Nil	Nil

In Process 1 the closing stock of work in process has just passed through inspection, which is at the stage where materials and conversion costs are 100% and 75% complete respectively.

In Process 2 inspection is the final operation.

Required:

(a) Prepare the relevant accounts to show the results of the processes for May 1979 and present a detailed working paper showing your calculations and any assumptions in arriving at the data shown in those accounts.
(18 marks)

(b) If supplies of the required chemicals are severely restricted and all production can be sold immediately, briefly explain how you would calculate the total loss to the company if, at the beginning of June, 100 litres of the correct mix of chemicals were spilt on issue to Process 1.
(4 marks)
(22 marks)

ACCA Foundation Costing
June 1979

6.7 XY Copiers Ltd produces the Kwikflip Copier in batches of 1,000. Each copier contains a special chemical unit plus various other chemicals and activating components. The assembly operations include the merging of the special unit with some of the other chemicals under prescribed humidity conditions, an operation which is not always successful. Experience indicates a success rate of 95% which the company has accepted as standard performance.

On 1 May, production of Batch 47 was commenced and the necessary chemical units and other materials for the batch were issued from stores, the cost price thereof being £6,175.

During May, wages amounting to £1,788 were booked to batch no. 47 at the rate of 75% of labour cost was apportioned thereto.

At the end of May, 840 copiers of Batch 47 had been completed of which 60 had proved unsuccessful and, having no value, were scrapped. Production of the remainder of the batch had passed the critical chemical merging stage and were expected to pass final inspection; half of these were estimated to be 80% complete so far as labour and overhead costs were concerned, and the remainder, 50% complete. The average cost method is used.

You are required to write up the work in progress account showing full details of your workings.
(20 marks)

6.8* The Lewis Company manufacture a product on a continuous process basis which passes through one department. The product uses three different items of materials. Materials A and B are introduced at the start of the process and material C is introduced when the process is 60% complete. Labour and overhead costs are added continuously throughout the process and overhead is charged at 100% of the direct labour cost.

The work in progress at the start of the accounting period consisted of 3,000 units 20% complete valued at £17,880 consisting of £12,600 for material A, £2,400 material B and conversion costs of £2,880.

During the period 20,000 units were started and the following costs were incurred:

Material A	£84,000
Material B	£16,000
Material C	£19,200
Direct labour	£44,400

The completed production for the month was 15,000 units and the closing work in progress consisted of 4,000 units which were 50% complete. Because of an error an unexpected loss occurred and all the opening work in progress was spoilt. This loss was discovered when the opening work in progress was 40% complete. Normal loss is as expected and this is detected at the 90% stage.

You are required to produce the process account for the period and show your calculations of the cost per unit, closing work in progress and cost of completed production. Use the weighted average method.

6.9* Shown below is the previous month's operating data for Process 3, the final manufacturing operation in the production of standard sized insulation blocks.

Work in process:
 Opening stock 400 blocks, total cost £1,000
 Closing stock 500 blocks

The degree of completion of both opening and closing stocks of work in process was:

Previous process costs	100%
Process 3 materials	80%
Conversion costs	60%

During the month 4,500 blocks were transferred from Process 2 at a total cost of £9,000. Other costs charged to Process 3 during the month were:

Materials	£4,360
Labour and overhead	£2,125

Process inspection occurs when Process 3 materials are 60% complete and conversion costs 30% complete and normally no losses are expected at this stage. However, during the month 300 blocks were rejected at inspection and sold as scrap for £1 each.

The company operates the first in, first out method of charging opening stock to production.
Required:
(a) Prepare the Process 3 account and an abnormal loss account recording the data shown above. Include a detailed working paper showing all your calculations. (17 marks)
(b) Explain the reasons for valuing stocks of work in process. (5 marks)
(22 marks)

ACCA Foundation Costing
December 1980

6.10 No Strings Ltd makes a single product, and uses a process costing system. The following data relate to the month of June 1980:

Opening work in process	3,200 units, each one-half completed
Closing work in process	3,600 units, each one-third completed
Product completed during June	4,000 units

Opening work in process (in £):
Direct labour	3,200
Direct materials	12,800
Overheads	6,400

Variable costs incurred during June 1980 (in £):
Direct labour	8,820
Direct materials	15,400

Direct materials are used at the first stage of the production process, whereas the labour cost is incurred evenly throughout that process. Overhead is charged to product at a rate of £2 per £1 of direct labour cost.

You are required to calculate in respect of June 1980:
 (i) the number of equivalent units of product made in the month (2 marks),
 (ii) the number of units of product started in the month (2 marks),
 (iii) assuming a FIFO flow of costs, the average variable cost of each unit of product which is both started and finished in the month (2 marks),
 (iv) assuming a FIFO flow of costs, the total cost (including overheads) of the units of product completed during the month (2 marks),
 (v) assuming a FIFO flow of costs, the cost of the closing work in process, showing the total and the separate amounts for direct labour, direct materials and overheads (2 marks).

ICAEW Management Accounting
July 1980

6.11 Shown on page 133 is an extract from the accountant's working papers for the process cost accounts, for May 1982, of the final two operations in a factory producing one particular type of industrial chemical.

Process 5 costs (in addition to the cost of transfers from Process 4):

Materials	£10,175
Conversion costs	£18,000

Normally a loss of 10% of input is expected in Process 5; all losses may be sold as scrap at £2 per kilo.
Required:
(a) Calculate the total cost of the 8,000 kilos of chemical transferred from Process 4 to Process 5 during May 1982. (5 marks)
(b) Calculate the total cost, incurred by Process 4 during May 1982, for each of the following:
 (i) Materials transferred from Process 3.
 (ii) Process 4 materials.
 (iii) Process 4 conversion costs.
(10 marks)
(c) Prepare the Process 5 Account for May 1982. (7 marks)
(22 marks)

ACCA Level 1 Costing
June 1982

6.12 (a) You are required to explain and discuss the alternative methods of accounting for normal and abnormal spoilage. (8 marks).
(b) Weston Harvey Ltd assembles and finishes trapfoils from bought-in components which are utilized at the beginning of the assembly process. The other assembly costs are incurred evenly throughout that process. When the assembly process is complete, the finishing process is undertaken. Overhead is absorbed into assembly, but not finishing, at the rate of 100% of direct assembly cost.

It is considered normal for some trapfoils to be spoiled during assembly and finishing. Quality control inspection is applied at the conclusion of the finishing process to determine whether units are spoiled.

It is accepted that the spoilage is normal if spoiled units are no more than one-eighteenth of the completed good units produced. Normal spoilage is treated as a product cost, and incorporated into the cost of good production. Any spoilage in excess of this limit is classed as abnormal, and written off as a loss of the period in which it occurs.

Trapfoils are valuable in relation to their weight and size. Despite vigilant security precautions it is common that some units are lost, probably by pilferage. The cost of lost units is written off as a loss of the period in which it occurs. This cost is measured as the cost of the bought-in components plus the assembly process, but no finishing cost is charged.

Weston Harvey uses a FIFO system of costing.
The following data summarize the firm's activities during November 1981:

Problem 6.11

	Process 4 kg		kg
Opening stock	3,000	Transfers to Process 5	8,000
Transfers from Process 3	11,000	Loss	2,000
		Closing stock	4,000
	14,000		14,000

	Materials transferred from Process 3	Process 4 materials	Process 4 conversion costs
Cost per equivalent whole unit of production	£2.80 per kg	£.175 per kg	£2.50 per kg
Degree of completion:			
Opening stocks	100%	70%	60%
Losses	100%	60%	45%
Closing stocks	100%	80%	70%

Normally no losses are expected in Process 4.

The company operates the first in, first out method of charging opening stock to production and, at the beginning of May 1982, the value of the opening stock in Process 4 was £16,400.

	Process 5 kg		kg
Opening stock	Nil	Transfers to finished goods store	7,400
Transfers from Process 4	8,000	Loss	600
		Closing stock	Nil
	8,000		8,000

(6.12 continued)

Opening work in process:

Bought in components	£60,000
Direct assembly cost to 31 October 1981	£25,000
No. of units (on average one-half assembled)	50,000

Direct costs incurred during November 1981:

Bought in components received	£120,000
Direct assembly cost	£40,000
Direct finishing costs	£30,000

Production data for November, 1981: Trapfoils

Components received into assembly for	112,000
Good units completed	90,000
Spoiled units	10,000
Lost units	2,000

None of the opening work in process had at that stage entered the finishing process. Similarly, nor had any of the closing work in process at the end of the month. The units in the closing work in process were on average one-third complete as to assembly; none had entered the finishing process.

You are required:

(i) to calculate the number of units in the closing work in process (3 marks),

(ii) to calculate the number of equivalent units processed in November 1981, distinguishing between bought-in components, assembly, and finishing (6 marks),

(iii) to calculate the total costs to be accounted for in the month of November 1981, subdivided into the amounts for good units produced, spoilage, lost units, and closing work in process (8 marks).

(25 marks)

ICAEW Management Accounting
December 1981

6.13* PC Manufacturing Company operates a process costing system and the following information relates to process A for the month of March:

Opening work in process of 1,000 units 40% complete, consisting of £17,400 for

direct materials and £10,000 for conversion costs.

Production completed for March was 8,200 units with materials added for the month of £162,600 and conversion costs in the month of £173,920.

Closing work in process was 800 units which was 20% complete.

There are no losses in process. All materials are introduced at the start of the process and conversion costs are incurred uniformly throughout the process. Process A is the initial process and the completed production is then transferred to Process B.

You are required:
(a) To prepare a schedule of equivalent production and cost per unit and the process account for the month of March.
(b) Assuming that the company operates a standard cost system using the following standards per finished unit:

Direct materials	£20
Conversion costs	£23

Prepare a performance report for the month of March showing the *total* variances only for current performance.

Appendix 6.1: Losses which occur part way through a process

It is possible that losses may occur at a point in time before the end of the production process. For example, chemicals may be added part way through a process and spillage may occur at this point resulting in process losses. Let us assume that a normal loss of 100 units and an abnormal loss of 50 units are identified when the process is 50% complete. If materials are added prior to this stage, then any materials or previous process cost will be 100% complete. An entry of 100 units and 50 units will be made in the normal loss and abnormal losses columns of the unit cost calculation statement in respect of materials and previous process cost. If materials are added after the halfway stage then no materials will have been added to the spoilt units and a nil entry is required in both the normal and abnormal losses columns.

Regarding the conversion costs, they will have been added uniformly throughout the process and, once the spoilt units have been identified, no further conversion costs will be incurred. Equivalent production for the normal and abnormal losses will therefore be 50% for conversion cost, and an entry of 50 and 25 units, respectively, will be made in the normal and abnormal loss columns. The normal and abnormal losses will then be valued in the same way as illustrated in the examples in this chapter.

Whether or not the closing work in progress should be charged with any of the normal loss depends on whether the work in progress is more or less than 50% complete. If it is more than 50% complete then the closing work in progress will have passed the point where the loss occurs and it should be charged with some of the normal loss. If it is less than 50% complete then all of the normal loss should be charged to the completed units. Example 6.1A illustrates the procedure for recording spoilt units which are identified part way through the process.

EXAMPLE 6.1A

A department with no opening work in progress introduces 1,000 units into the process; 600 are completed, 250 are 20% complete and 150 units are lost consisting of 100 units normal loss and 50 units abnormal loss. *Losses are detected when production is 50% complete.* Material costs are £8,000 (all introduced at the start of the process), conversion costs are £2,900 and the previous process cost is £10,000.

The calculation of the unit cost is shown opposite.

From this calculation you can see that materials and the previous process cost are 100% complete when the loss is discovered. However, spoilt units will not be processed any further once the loss is detected and the lost units will be 50% complete in respect of conversion costs. Note also that the closing work in progress has not reached the point where the loss is detected, and so the full amount of the normal loss is charged to the completed units.

Let us now assume that in Example 6.1A the 250 units in the closing work in progress were 60% complete. As the closing work in progress has passed the point where the loss is detected, the normal loss should be apportioned between the completed units and the closing work in progress. The correct procedure would be to make the following entries in the completed units and work in progress equivalents column of the previous unit cost statement for Example 6.1A:.

	Completed units	WIP equiv. units
Previous process cost	600	250
Materials	600	250
Conversion cost	600	150

Element of cost	Total cost £	Completed units	Normal loss	Abnormal loss	WIP equiv. units	Total equiv. units	Cost per unit £
Previous process cost	10,000	600	100	50	250	1,000	10.00
Materials	8,000	600	100	50	250	1,000	8.00
Conversion cost	2,900	600	50	25	50	725	4.00
	20,900						22.00

Value of work in progress
Previous process cost	250 units at £10	£2,500	
Materials	250 units at £8	2,000	
Conversion cost	50 units at £4	200	4,700

Completed units
600 units at £22	13,200	
Add Normal loss: 100 units at £10 (previous process cost)	1,000	
100 units at £8 (materials)	800	
50 units at £4 (conversion cost)	200	15,200

Abnormal loss
Previous process cost:	50 units at £10	500	
Materials	50 units at £8	400	
Conversion cost	25 units at £4	100	1,000
			20,900

The revised unit costs can now be calculated, and the cost of the completed units and the value of the normal and abnormal loss can be ascertained in the same way as illustrated in the previous unit cost statement.

The value of the normal loss will be apportioned for each element of cost in the ratio of completed units and work in progress equivalent units as follows:

The apportioned values of the normal loss are then added to the completed units and closing work in progress valuations. For an illustration of the above appraoch you should refer to the answer to problem 6.6 which is shown in the *Students' Manual*.

	Completed units	WIP equiv. units
Previous process cost	600/850 of normal loss	250/850 of normal loss
Materials	600/850 of normal loss	250/850 of normal loss
Conversion cost	600/750 of normal loss	150/750 of normal loss

7 Joint product and by-product costing

Joint/common costs are an important topic in accounting literature. Joint costs are important generally, in overhead allocation including service and non-profit organizations. In this chapter we shall concentrate on one particular aspect of the joint cost problem, that is joint and by-product costs. Joint products and by-products arise in situations where the production of one product makes inevitable the production of other products. When a group of individual products is simultaneously produced, and each product has a significant relative sales value, the outputs are usually called *joint products*. Those products which are part of the simultaneous production process and have a minor sales value when compared with the joint products are called *by-products*. As their name implies, by-products are those products which result incidentally from the main joint products. By-products may have a considerable absolute value, but the crucial classification test is that the sales value is small when compared with the values of the joint products. Joint products are crucial to the commercial viability of an organization, whereas by-products are incidental. In other words, by-products do not usually influence the decision as to whether or not to produce the main product, and they normally have little effect on the prices set for the main (joint) products. Examples of industries which produce both joint and by-products include chemicals, oil refining, mining, flour milling and gas manufacturing.

A distinguishing feature of the production of joint and by-products is that the products are not identifiable as different individual products until a specific point in the production process is reached, known as the *split-off point*. All products may separate at one time, or different products may emerge at intervals. Before the split-off point, costs cannot be traced to particular products. For example, it is not possible to determine what part of the cost of processing a barrel of crude oil should be allocated to petrol, kerosine or paraffin. After the split-off point, joint products may be sold or subjected to further processing. If the latter is the case, any further processing costs can easily be traced to the specific products involved. Figure 7.1 illustrates a simplified production process for joint and by-products.

You will notice from this illustration that, at the split-off point, joint products A and B and by-product C all emerge, and that it is not possible to allocate costs of the joint process directly to the joint products or by-products. After the split-off point further processing costs are added to the joint products before sale, and these costs can be specifically attributed to the joint products. By-product C in this instance is sold at split-off point without further processing, although sometimes by-products may be further processed after the split-off point before they are sold on the outside market.

For external reporting it is necessary that the stock valuation includes an apportionment of the joint costs of production, as well as any directly attributable additional costs of further processing (if any). Note, however, that *joint cost apportionments are of little use for decision-making*. Let us first consider the various methods of apportioning joint costs to products for stock valuation, and then go on to discuss which costs are relevant for decision-making.

Methods of apportioning joint costs to joint products

If all the production for a particular period was sold the problem of allocating joint costs to products would not exist. Stock valuations would not be necessary and the calculation of profit

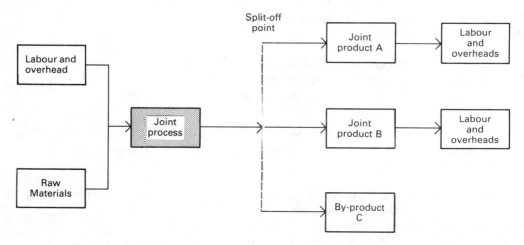

Fig. 7.1 Production process for joint and by-products

would merely require the deduction of total cost from total sales. However, if stocks are in existence at the end of the period, cost apportionments to products are necessary. As any such apportionments are bound to be subjective and arbitrary, this area will involve the accountant in making decisions which are among the most difficult to defend. All one can do is to attempt to choose an apportionment method which seems to provide a rational and reasonable method of distribution. The methods which can be used to apportion joint costs up to split-off point can be divided into the following two categories:

(1) Methods assumed to measure benefits received from the joint product costs by the individual products based on *physical measures* such as weight, volume etc.

(2) Methods assumed to measure the ability to absorb joint costs based on apportioning joint costs relative to the *market values* of the products.

In Exhibit 7.1 products X, Y and Z all become finished products at the split-off point. The question is how much of the £60,000 joint costs should be allocated to each product? The £60,000 cannot be specifically identified with any of the individual products as the products themselves were not separated before split-off point, but some method must be used to split the £60,000 among the three products so that closing stocks may be valued and profit calculated.

Physical measures methods

Using this method the cost allocation is a simple apportionment of cost in proportion to volume. Each product is assumed to receive similar benefits from the joint costs and is therefore charged with its proportionate share of the total

Exhibit 7.1 Illustration of apportionment of joint costs

cost. We can compute the cost apportionment using this method as follows:

Product	Units produced	Proportion to total	Joint costs apportioned	Cost per unit
X	4,000	$1/3$	20,000	£5
Y	2,000	$1/6$	10,000	£5
Z	6,000	$1/2$	30,000	£5
	12,000		£60,000	

Note that this method assumes that the cost per unit is the same for each of the products. This may be a reasonable assumption where each of the products are obtained from the same material and have undergone the same production process, but where the market prices of the products differ widely such an assumption would not be reasonable as some products may yield high profits while others may show losses. This would give a misleading product profit calculation. Let us look at the product profit calculation using the information given in Exhibit 7.1:

Product	Sales revenue £	Total cost £	Profit (loss) £	Profit/ sales (%)
X	30,000	20,000	10,000	$33\frac{1}{3}$
Y	50,000	10,000	40,000	80
Z	20,000	30,000	(10,000)	(50)
	100,000	60,000	40,000	40

You will see from these figures that the allocation of the joint costs bears no relationship to the revenue-producing power of the individual products. Product Z is charged with the largest share of the joint costs but has the lowest total sales revenue; product Y is charged the lowest share of the joint costs but has the highest total sales revenue. The physical measures method is not therefore very satisfactory, and its weakness can be further highlighted if we assume that 80% of the production of X, Y and Z were sold during the period. The appropriate stock valuations and corresponding sales value of each product would be:

		Stock valuations	
		Cost	Sales
Product		(1) £	value (1) £
X		4,000	6,000
Y		2,000	10,000

Z		6,000	4,000
		12,000	20,000

(1) 20% of total cost and sales revenue.

It appears inappropriate to value the stock of product Z at a price higher than its market value and at a valuation three times higher than that of product Y, when in fact product Y is more valuable in terms of potential sales revenue. A further problem is that the joint products must be measurable by the same unit of measurement. Difficult measurement problems arise in respect of products which consist of solids, liquids and gases and it is necessary to find some common base. For example, in the case of coke, apportionments can be made on the basis of theoretical yields extracted from a ton of coke.

The main advantage of using a physical measures basis is simplicity, but this is outweighed by its many disadvantages.

Sales value method

When this method is used joint costs are allocated to joint products in proportion to their sales value, on the assumption that higher selling prices indicate higher costs; it ensures that profit margins are uniform for the joint products. To a certain extent this method could better be described as a means of apportioning profits or losses, according to sales value, rather than a method for apportioning costs. Using the information in Exhibit 7.1 the apportionments under the sales value method would be:

Product	Units produced	Sales value £	Proportion of sales value to total (%)	Costs apportioned £
X	4,000	30,000	30	18,000
Y	2,000	50,000	50	30,000
Z	6,000	20,000	20	12,000
		100,000		60,000

The revised product profit calculations would be:

Product	Sales revenue £	Total cost £	Profit/ (loss)	Profit/ sales (%)
X	30,000	18,000	12,000	40
Y	50,000	30,000	20,000	40
Z	20,000	12,000	8,000	40
	100,000	60,000	40,000	

If we assume that 80% of the production is sold the stock valuations would be:

Stock valuations

Product	Cost (1)	Sales value (1)
X	3,600	6,000
Y	6,000	10,000
Z	2,400	4,000
	12,000	20,000

(1) 20% of total cost and sales revenue.

The sales value method overcomes the criticisms made in respect of the physical measures method but can itself be criticized as it is based on the assumption that sales revenue determines prior costs. For example, an unprofitable product with low sales revenue will be apportioned with a small share of joint costs thus giving the impression that it is generating profits.

In Exhibit 7.1 we have assumed that all products are sold at the split-off point and that no additional costs are incurred beyond the split-off point. In practice, however, it is likely that joint products will be processed individually beyond the split-off point, and market values may not exist for the products at this stage. To estimate the sales value at split-off point it is therefore necessary to use the sales value at the point of sale and work backwards. This method is called the *net realizable value method* and is illustrated in Exhibit 7.2.

The calculations are as follows:

Product	Sales value £	Costs beyond split-off point £	Estimated net realizable value at split-off point	Proportion to total (%)	Joint costs apportioned
X	36,000	8,000	28,000	28	16,800
Y	60,000	10,000	50,000	50	30,000
Z	24,000	2,000	22,000	22	13,200
	120,000	20,000	100,000		60,000

Exhibit 7.2 Illustration of net realizable value method

You will see that the costs incurred beyond the split-off point have been deducted from the sales value at the point of sale to estimate the *net realizable value* at split-off point.

Joint product costs £100,000

Split-off point

Sale of 5,000 units of Product X at £16 per unit: £80,000

Sale of 5,000 units of Product Y at £8 per unit: £40,000

Total sales revenue £120,000

Which method?

How do we choose the best method for allocating joint costs to products for stock valuation? The answer to this question depends on why a stock valuation is required. Is it to spread the cost in proportion to the physical units produced, or is it to arrive at a cost which is indicative of the revenue generating power of the various joint products in stock? Most accountants would argue in favour of the latter, and *the method of allocating joint costs which provides the closest approximation to the revenue generating power of the joint products is the net realizable value method*. This is therefore the method which is recommended for stock valuation.

Limitations of joint cost allocations for decision-making

Our previous discussion has concentrated on the allocation of joint costs for stock valuation and profit measurement. Joint product costs calculated for stock valuation are entirely inappropriate for decision-making. For short-term decision-making *relevant costs* should be used — these represent the additional costs which a product incurs, or those costs which will be eliminated if the product is not made. Consequently, joint cost allocations should not be used when making short-term decisions as they are expected to remain unchanged in the short run.[1] Let us consider the situation illustrated in Example 7.1.

EXAMPLE 7.1

A company incurs joint product costs of £100,000 for the production of two joint products, X and Y. Both products can be sold at split-off point. However, if additional costs of £6,000 are incurred on Product Y

then it can be converted into product Z and sold for £10 per unit. The joint costs and the sales revenue at split-off point are illustrated in the following diagram:

You are required to advise management whether or not Product Y should be converted into Product Z.

The joint costs of £100,000 will be incurred irrespective of which decision is taken, and are not relevant for this decision. The information which is required for the decision is a comparison of *the additional costs with the additional revenues from converting Product Y into Product Z*. The following information should therefore be provided:

	£
Additional revenue from converting Product Y into Product Z (5,000 × £2)	10,000
Additional conversion costs	6,000
Additional profit from conversion	4,000

The proof that profits will increase by £4,000 if conversion takes place is as follows:

	Convert to Product Z £	Do not convert £
Sales	130,000	120,000
Total costs	106,000	100,000
Profits	24,000	20,000

The general rule is that it will be profitable to extend the processing of a joint product so long as the additional revenues exceed the additional costs, but note that the *variable portion* of the *joint costs* will be relevant for some decisions. For an illustration of a situation where joint variable costs are relevant for decision-making see Example 7.2.

EXAMPLE 7.2

A company incurs joint production costs of £300,000 for the production of two joint products, A and B. Both products require further processing before they can be sold. Details of the expected costs and revenues of the joint products are given in the following diagram:

Product A Further variable processing costs of £80,000

Product A Sales value: 10,000 units at £40 per unit

Product B Further variable processing costs of £20,000

Product B Sales value: 2000 units at £30 per unit

Joint product cost £300,000

Split-off point

The joint costs of £300,000 consist of £240,000 fixed costs and a variable cost of £5 per unit of output. A new customer has approached the company with an offer to purchase 600 units of product B at a price of £25 per unit. The sale will not affect the market price to the other customers. Should the company accept this offer?

You can see from this example that the *further* processing variable costs of joint products A and B are £8 and £10 per unit respectively. The fixed portion of the joint costs of £240,000 will remain unchanged even if the customer's offer is accepted and any apportionment of these costs to products should be excluded for decision-making. However, the variable costs of the joint process of £5 per unit will lead to additional costs if the customer's order is accepted, and so should be included in our analysis. Nevertheless, such costs should not be apportioned to the products for decision-making. To decide whether or not to accept the offer we must compare the additional costs with the additional revenues.

Unless we are sure that we can sell as much of Product A as we produce, we cannot analyse the potential sale of an additional 600 units of product B by comparing the revenue and cost of Product B by itself. To increase production of Product B we need to incur additional variable costs of £5 per unit of output *in the joint production process*. As the production of 600 units of Product B will lead to an output of 3,000 units of Product A in the joint process, the variable costs of the joint process will be £18,000 (3600 × £5). The additional costs associated with the production of 600 units of Product B will therefore be:

Further processing variable costs of *Product B* (600 units at £10 per unit)	£6,000
Variable costs of *joint process* (3,600 units at £5 per unit)	£18,000
	£24,000

The additional revenue from the sale of 600 units of Product B is £15,000 (600 units at £25 per unit).

Because of the £18,000 variable cost from the joint process, the additional revenue from the sale of Product B cannot cover, by itself, the increase in the total costs of the firm. The company will need to process and sell additional units of Product A if the customer's order is to be profitable.

Producing an additional 3,000 units of Product A will increase the variable costs of Product A by £24,000 (3,000 units at £8 per unit) after the split-off point. The additional costs arising from acceptance of the customer's order will therefore be

Excess of variable costs over revenues from the sale of Product B (£24,000 − £15,000)	£9,000
Variable costs of Product A (3,000 units at £8)	£24,000
	£33,000

To cover these costs the company must obtain additional sales revenue from Product A. If a separate market can be found, the selling price of the 3,000 units of Product A must be in excess of £11 (£33,000/3,000 units) if acceptance of the customer's order is to be profitable. This analysis, of course, assumes that the agreed price will not affect the selling price to existing customers. Alternatively, if the company cannot find a market for the 3,000 units of Product A at a selling price which is in excess of £11 per unit, it could consider selling the 3,000 units at the split-off point rather than after further processing. The company would then have to find a market to cover the £9,000 excess of variable costs over revenues from the sale of Product B at split-off point.

Accounting for by-products

By-products are products which have a minor sales value and which emerge incidentally from the production of the major product. As the

major objective of the company is to produce the joint products, it can justifiably be argued that the joint costs should be charged only to the joint products and that the by-products should not be charged with any portion of the joint costs which are incurred before the split-off point. Any costs which are incurred in producing by-products after the split-off point can justifiably be charged to the by-product as such costs are incurred for the benefit of the by-product only.

By-product revenues or by-product net revenues (the sales revenue of the by-product less the additional further processing costs after the split-off point) can be accounted for by either of the following methods:

Method 1 Allocating the net sales revenue due from the *actual sales* of the by-product.
Method 2 Allocating the net sales revenue due from the *actual production* of the by-product.

There are two possible interpretations of the resulting net sales revenue figure for whichever method is used. The net revenue can either be *deducted from the costs* of the main product or it

can be *recorded as other income* and added to the sales revenue in the profit and loss account. We will now examine the two methods and the alternative interpretations of the net revenue figure using the information given in Example 7.3.

EXAMPLE 7.3

In the manufacture of Product A, a by-product called By-product B emerges at the end of processing. The following data was recorded for period one:

	£
Production costs before separation of the two products	60,000
Costs of processing By-product B after separation (4,000 units at 10 p)	400
Production for the period:	
Product A 20,000 units	
By-product B 4,000 units	
Sales for the period:	
Product A, 15,000 units at £5 per unit	
By-product B, 2,000 units at £1 per unit	

There was no opening stock at the start of the period. You are required to produce the profit statements showing:

Exhibit 7.3 Method 1: Allocation of net revenue due from the actual sales of the by-product

			(A) Deducted from costs £		(B) Other income £
Revenue:					
Sale of Product A — 15,000 units at £5			75,000		75,000
Net revenue from By-product B — 2,000 units at £0.90					1,800
					76,800
Cost of sales:					
Production Costs of A			60,000		60,000
Less Net revenue from sale of by-product:					
Sale of By-product B	2,000				
Less Costs after separation (2000 × 10 p)	200	1,800			
		58,200			
Less Closing stock of Product A(1)		14,550	43,650	15,000(2)	45,000
Gross profit			31,350		31,800

(1) $\dfrac{5,000 \text{ units closing stock}}{20,000 \text{ units production}} \times £58,200$

(2) $\dfrac{5,000 \text{ units closing stock}}{20,000 \text{ units production}} \times £60,000$

(A) net revenue deducted from the costs of the main product,
(B) net revenue being recorded as other income

for each of Methods 1 and 2.

The relevant information is set out in Exhibits 7.3 and 7.4.

You will see that Method 1 allocates the net revenue due from the actual sales of 2,000 units of the by-product. The 2,000 unsold units are allocated when the by-product is sold in the future accounting periods. To simplify the example the by-product closing stock of 2,000 units at 10 p, and the associated production costs of £200, have been excluded from the calculations as their net effect is zero. The difference of £450 between the two profit figures is reflected in the following stock valuation attached to Product A:

	£
Cost reduction method	14,550
Other income method	15,000
Stock difference	450

When net revenue is deducted from costs, 25% of the net revenue of £1,800 is not recorded as a cost deduction until the 5,000 units stock of Product A are sold.[2] When the net revenue is recorded as other income, the full benefit of £1,800 is recorded in the current accounting period.

Let us now consider the second method of accounting for by-product costs.

When this method is used you will see that net revenue based on *production* and *not sales* is included in the statement. The difference between the two profits is again reflected in the following stock valuations attached to Product A:

	£
Cost reduction method	14,100
Other income method	15,000
Stock difference	900

As explained in our consideration of Method 1, the stock difference (£900) arises because 25% of the net revenue of £3,600 is not recorded as a cost deduction until the 5,000 units stock of Product A are sold.

You will see that when the net revenue is recorded as other income, Method 2 yields £1,800 more profit than Method 1. The reason for this difference is that the net revenue is recognized on the number of units of the by-product *produced*, whereas Method 1 recognizes net revenue on the number of units of the by-product *sold*. As 4,000 units are produced but only 2,000 units are sold, an additional net revenue of £1,800, consisting of 2,000 unsold units, is recognized with Method 2. However, when net revenue is recorded as a

Exhibit 7.4 Method 2: Allocation of net revenue based on actual production

		(A) Deducted from costs £		(B) Other income £
Revenue:				
Sale of Product A — 15,000 units at £5		75,000		75,000
Net revenue from By-product B — 4,000 units at £0.90				3,600
				78,600
Cost of sales:				
Production costs of A		60,000		60,000
Less Net revenue from sale of by-product:				
Revenue due from production of By-product B	4,000			
Less costs after separation	400	3,600		
		56,400		
Less closing stock of product A ($\frac{1}{4} \times 56,400$)		14,100	42,300	15,000($\frac{1}{4}$) 45,000
Gross profit			32,700	33,600

ACCOUNTING FOR BY-PRODUCTS / 143

deduction from costs, only 75% of the additional net revenue of £1,800 is recorded as a cost deduction, and this accounts for the difference of £1,350 profits between Method 1 and 2. Only 75% of the net revenue of £1,800 is recorded as a cost reduction as 15,000 out of 20,000 units produced were sold in the current period; the remaining 25% will be recorded as a cost deduction when the 5,000 units are sold in the next accounting period.

The choice between Methods 1 and 2 should reflect trading circumstances. If the sale of the unsold production of the by-product cannot be guaranteed or if the market values are unstable, then it may be appropriate to defer recognition of the net revenue until sales have been made. However, if future sales are certain and market price is unlikely to fluctuate there is a case for recognizing by-product net revenue at the production stage. This ensures that the unit costs of the main product are reduced during the period in which production occurs. The major criticism of recognizing net revenue at the production stage is that it leads to a premature recognition of profit, but if the amounts involved are not material this problem can safely be ignored. Once a particular accounting method has been chosen, it should be followed consistently for a period of years so that valid comparisons can be made of the trend in by-product total revenues.

By-products, scrap and waste

The terms by-products, scrap and waste are used to refer to outputs with little or no value. Because different people use these different terms to refer to the same thing we shall briefly discuss the distinction between them.

Waste is a term used to describe material which has no value, or even negative value if it has to be disposed of at some cost. Examples include gases, sawdust, smoke and other unsaleable residues from the manufacturing process. Waste presents no accounting problems because it has no sales value and therefore it is not included in the valuation of stock.

By-products, as we have already seen, are those products which have a minor sales value and which emerge incidentally from the production of the major products.

Scrap also emerges as a consequence of the joint production process but it is distinct from by-products in the sense that it is the leftover part of raw materials, whereas by-products are different from the material which went into the production process. Metal shavings and sawdust would normally be classified as scrap, whereas minor chemicals emerging from a chemical process would normally be classified as a by-product. The term scrap is usually limited to material which has some use, as being sold or re-processed. When a product of minor sales value is processed beyond the split-off point it should be considered to be a by-product and not scrap, although the fact that a product will not be processed beyond the split-off point does not necessarily mean that it should be considered as scrap. The major distiguishing feature is that by-products are different from the materials that went into the production process.

The accounting procedure for scrap and by-products are fairly similar and the accounting treatment which has already been outlined for by-products can also be applied to scrap. However, if the sales revenue from scrap is insignificant then the revenue due from the *actual production* for the period should be credited to the joint process.

Defective units

Defective units are those units which do not meet quality standards but which can be rectified and sold either as firsts or seconds. Rectification should only be undertaken if incremental revenue is expected to exceed incremental costs. The costs of rectification should normally be charged to the departmental factory overhead account and thus spread over all the production for the period. Let us assume, for example, that out of an order of 100 units, 10 units are found to be defective. The original cost accumulations were £1,000, and the cost of rectification is £100. The accounting entries would be as follows:

		Dr	Cr
Original cost accumulations:	Work in progress account	1,000	
	Stores control, wages control and factory overhead accounts		1,000
Cost of rectification:	Departmental factory overhead account	100	
	Stores control, wages control and factory overhead accounts		100
Transfer to finished stock:	Finished goods stock	1,000	
	Work in progress account		1,000

It is important that defective work should be avoided. Periodic control reports are required showing the order number on which the defective units occurred, the reason why the units were rejected as defective, and the cost of rectifying the defective units.

Summary

The distinguishing feature of joint products and by-products is that they are not separately identifiable as different products before the split-off point. To meet the requirements of financial accounting it is necessary to trace all product-related costs to products so that costs can be allocated to finished goods and to the cost of goods sold. Consequently, joint costs need to be apportioned to products. The apportionment methods which we have considered are based on physical volume and sales value. We have seen that the physical units method can lead to a situation where the recorded joint product cost stock valuation is in excess of net realizable value, and this method of apportionment is not recommended.

We have established that the apportionment of joint costs for decision-making is unacceptable. Such decisions should be based on a comparison of the additional costs with the additional revenues. We examined this principle in the light of two basic decisions: (1) whether to sell products at the split-off point or whether to process further; and (2) whether to accept an order below the current selling price.

Two methods of accounting for by-products have been considered; one method allocates net sales revenue *due from the actual sales* of the product and the second method allocates the net sales revenue *due from actual production*. The resulting net sales revenue can be deducted from the joint product costs, or recorded as other income for both methods. Finally, as the terms by-products, scrap and waste are subject to different interpretations we have considered briefly the distinguishing features of these items.

References and further reading

Balachandran, B.V. and Ramakrishnan, R.T.S. Joint cost allocation: A unified approach. *Accounting Review* **LVI**, January 1981, 85-96.

Bierman, H., Jr. Inventory valuation: The use of market prices. *The Accounting Review* **XLII**, October 1967, 731-7.

Feller, R.E. Joint products in the petroleum industry. *Management Accounting (USA)* September 1977, 41-5.

Griffin, C.H. Multiple products costing in petroleum refining. In Solomons, D. (Ed.), *Studies in Cost Analysis* 2nd edn. Sweet & Maxwell, 1968.

Hardy, J.W. and Orton, B.B. An approach to joint cost allocations. *Journal of Accountancy (USA)* October 1981, 105-8.

Hartley, R.V. Decision-making when joint products are involved. *The Accounting Review* **XLIX**, October 1971, 746-55.

Jensen, D.L. The role of costs in pricing joint products: A case of production in fixed proportions. *The Accounting Review* July 1974, 465-76.

Kaplan, R.S. *Advanced Management Accounting*. Prentice Hall, 1982, Ch. 12.

Louderback, J.G. Another approach to allocating joint costs: A comment. *The Accounting Review* July 1976, 683-5.

Manes, R. and Smith, V.L. Economic joint cost theory and accounting practice. *The Accounting Review* **XL**, January 1965, 31-5.

Mepham, M.J. Joint production costs. *Management Accounting* February 1978, pp. 64-8.

Moriarty, S. Another approach to allocating joint costs. *The Accounting Review*, October 1975, 791-5.

Nurnberg, H. Joint and by-product costs. In S. Davidson and Weil, R.L. (Eds), *Handbook in Cost Accounting*. McGraw-Hill, 1978, Ch. 18.

Slater and Wootton, *Joint and by-product Costing in the UK*. Institute of Cost and Management Accounting, 1984.

Thomas, A.L. On joint cost allocations. *Cost and Management (USA)*. September–October 1974.

Problems

*Indicates that a suggested solution is to be found in the *Students' Manual*.

7.1* Three joint products are produced by passing chemicals through two consecutive processes.

Output from the first process is transferred into the second process, from which the three joint products are produced and immediately sold.

The previous month's operating data for the processes is tabulated below:

	Process 1	Process 2
Direct material (25,000 kg at £4 per kg)	£100,000	–
Direct labour	£62,500	£69,000
Overheads	£45,000	£69,000
Normal loss	10% of input	Nil
Scrap value of loss	£2 per kg	–
Output	23,000 kg	Joint Product A 9,000 kg
		Joint Product B 8,000 kg
		Joint Product C 6,000 kg

There were no opening or closing stocks in either process and the selling prices of the output from Process 2 were:

Joint Product A	£24 per kg
Joint Product B	£18 per kg
Joint Product C	£12 per kg

Required:

(a) Prepare an account for Process 1, together with any loss or gain accounts you consider necessary to record the month's activities.
(8 marks)

(b) Calculate the profit attributable to each of the joint products by apportioning the total costs from Process 2:
 (i) according to weight of output
 (ii) by the market value of production.
(6 marks)

(c) Critically examine the purpose of apportioning process costs to joint products. (8 marks)
(22 marks)
ACCA Level 1 Costing
December 1982

7.2 (a) A chemical, Exalete, passes through processes A and B before completion. In Process B, a by-product Exaletent is produced which, after further processing in Process C, is sold at a profit of $16\frac{2}{3}\%$ of selling price.

You are required, from the data given for the month of April, to prepare accounts for:

 (i) Processes, A, B and C;
 (ii) abnormal loss;
 (iii) abnormal gain.

	Process		
	A	B	C
Output in units	4,200	3,800	100
Normal loss in process:			
% of input	20	5	–
	£	£	£
Scrap value of any loss in process, per unit	1.5	5	–
Costs:			
Direct materials introduced (5,000 units)	30,000	–	–
Direct materials added	10,000	3,100	100
Direct wages incurred at £3 per hour	12,000	14,700	300
Direct expenses	7,500	1,170	–

Production overhead for the month, £72,000, is absorbed by a labour hour rate.

(b) Define and explain briefly the accounting treatment of:
 (i) by-products;
 (ii) joint products.

(25 marks)
ICMA Cost Accounting 2
May 1983

7.3* (a) Polimur Ltd operates a process which produces three joint products, all in an unrefined condition. The operating results of this process, for October 1979, are shown below.

Output from process:	Product A	100,000 kg
	Product B	80,000 kg
	Product C	80,000 kg

The month's operating costs were £1,300,000. The closing stocks were 20,000 kg of A, 15,000 kg of B and 5,000 kg of C. The value of the closing stock is calculated by apportioning costs according to weight of output. There were no opening stocks and the balance of the output was sold to a refining company at the following prices:

Product A £5 per kg Product C £9 per kg
Product B £4 per kg

Required:
Prepare an operating statement showing the relevant trading results for October 1979.
(6 marks)

(b) The management of Polimur Ltd have been considering a proposal to establish their own refining operations.
The current market prices of the refined products are:

Product A £17 per kg Product C £20.50 per kg
Product B £14 per kg

The estimated unit costs of the refining operation are:

Product	A	B	C
	£ per kg	£ per kg	£ per kg
Direct materials	0.50	0.75	2.50
Direct labour	2.00	3.00	4.00
Variable overheads	1.50	2.25	5.50

Prime costs would be variable. Fixed overheads, which would be £700,000 monthly, would be direct to the refining operation. Special equipment is required for refining Product B and this would be rented, at a cost not included in the above figures, of £360,000 per month.

It may be asumed that there would be no weight loss in the refining process and that the quantity refined each month would be similar to October's output shown in (a) above.

Required:

Prepare a statement which will assist management to evaluate the proposal to commence refining operations. Include any further comments or observations you consider relevant.　(16 marks)

(Total 22 marks)

ACCA Foundation Costing
December 1979

7.4　(a) Explain briefly the distinction between joint products and by-products.

(b) Discuss briefly the problems involved in calculating the cost of manufacture of joint products with particular reference to the apportionment of pre-separation point costs.

A common method of apportioning these pre-separation point costs is by physical measurement; outline two other methods.

(c) In a process line of the JP Manufacturing Company Ltd, three joint products are produced. For the month of October the following data were available:

Product:	X	Y	Z
Sales price per kg	£5	£10	£20
Post-separation point costs	£10,000	£5,000	£15,000
Output in kg	2,500	1,000	1,500

Pre-separation point costs amounted to £20,000.

The joint products are manufactured in one common process, after which they are separated and may undergo further individual processing. The pre-separation point costs are apportioned to joint products, according to weight.

You are required:

(i) to prepare a statement showing the estimated profit or loss for each product and in total;

(ii) as an alternative to the costing system used in (i) above, to present a statement which will determine the maximum profit from the production of these joint products.

The sales value of each product at separation point is as follows:

X = £3　　Y = £4　　Z = £6

(30 marks)

ICMA Cost Accounting 2
November 1977

7.5　FPI Ltd is in the food processing industry and, in one of its processes, three joint products are manufactured. Traditionally, the company has apportioned work incurred up to the joint products pre-separation point on the basis of weight of output of the product.

You have recently been appointed cost accountant, and have ben investigating process costs and accounting procedures.

You are required to prepare statements for management to show:

(a) the profit or loss of each product as ascertained using the weight basis of apportioning pre-separation point costs;

(b) the optimal contribution which could be obtained from the manufacture of these products.

The following process data for October are given:

		Product A £	Product B £	Product C £
Costs incurred up to separation point	£96,000			
Costs incurred after separation point		20,000	12,000	8,000
Selling price per tonne:				
Completed product		500	800	600
Estimated, if sold separation point		250	700	450
		tonnes	tonnes	tonnes
Output		100	60	80

The cost of any unused capacity after the separation point should be ignored.

(25 marks)

ICMA Cost Accounting 2
November 1979

7.6*　(a) Discuss the problems which joint products and by-products pose the management accountant, especially in his attempts to produce useful product profitability reports. Outline the usual accounting treatments of joint and by-products and indicate the extent to which these treatments are effective in overcoming the problems you have discussed. In your answer clearly describe the differences between joint and by-products and provide an example of each.

(14 marks)

(b) A common process produces several joint products. After the common process has been completed each product requires further specific,

and directly attributable, expenditure in order to 'finish off' the product and put it in a saleable condition. Specify the conditions under which it is rational to undertake:
 (i) the common process, and
 (ii) the final 'finishing off' of each of the products which are the output from the common process.
Illustrate your answer with a single numerical example.

(6 marks)
(Total 20 marks)
ACCA P2 Management Accounting
December 1981

7.7* Hawkins Ltd produces two joint products, Boddie and Soull. A further product, Threekeys, is also made as a by-product of one of the processes for making Soull. Each product is sold in bottles of one litre capacity.

It is now January 1983. You are a cost accountant for Hawkins Ltd. You have been instructed to allocate the company's joint costs for 1982 between Boddie and Soull, but *not* to the by-product Threekeys.

During 1982, 2,000,000 litres of a raw material, Necktar, costing £3,000,000, were processed in Department Alpha with no wastage. The processing costs were £1,657,000.

50% of the output of Department Alpha was unfinished Boddie, for which there was no external market. It was transferred to Department Beta, where it was further processed at an additional cost of £8,1000,000. Normal wastage by evaporation was 16% of the input of unfinished Boddie. The remaining good output of finished Boddie was sold for £10 per litre in the outside market.

The other 50% of the output from the joint process in Department Alpha was in the form of processed Necktar. It was all transferred to Department Gamma, as there was no outside market for processed Necktar. In Department Gamma it was further processed, with no wastage, at a cost of £30,900,000.

72% of the output of Department Gamma was in the form of unfinished Soull, for which there was no external market. It was transferred to Department Delta, where it was subjected to a finishing process at a further cost of £719,000. Normal spoilage of $16\frac{2}{3}$% of the input to the finishing process was experienced. The spoiled material was disposed of without charge, as effluent. The remaining finished Soull was sold in the outside market for £60 per litre.

The remaining 28% of the output of Department Gamma was in the form of finished Threekeys, the by-product. It was sold in the outside market for £8 per litre, but due to its

dangerous nature special delivery costs of £70,000 were incurred in respect of it.
You are required:
 (i) to allocate the appropriate joint costs between Boddie and Soull on the basis of relative sales value, treating the net realizable value of Threekeys as an addition to the sales value of Soull (6 marks),
 (ii) to prepare a statement showing the profit or loss attributed to each of the three products and the total profit or loss, for 1982, on the basis of the information above and allocating joint costs as in (i) above (4 marks), and
 (iii) to show with reasons whether Hawkins Ltd should continue to produce all three products in 1983, assuming that input/output relationships, prices and sales volumes do not change (3 marks).
ICAEW Management Accounting
December 1982

7.8 The following information relates to the affairs of ODJB Ltd in 1980. ODJB manufactures three products from a joint process:

(£000s except units produced)	Product			
	Shields	Ragas	Spargos	Total
Units produced	20,000	20,000	20,000	60,000
Sales value at split-off	A	B	200	600
Joint costs	180	C	D	360
Sales value if processed further	470	E	290	F
Additional costs of further processing	G	100	100	300
Gain (or loss) from further processing	H	10	J	K

Joint costs are allocated in proportion to sales value at split-off.

You are required to calculate the ten missing amounts designated by the letters A–K in the above table (5 marks).
ICAEW Management Accounting
July 1981

7.9* Stover Chemicals operates four manufacturing processes. Process 1 yields three joint products (X, Y and Z) in fixed proportions. Although each of these products could be sold at the split-off point (and there exists a ready market for each in this state) they are normally processed further; X in process 2, Y in process 3, and Z in process 4. This additional processing enhances their saleable values as follows:

Selling prices per litre

	X	Y	Z
Product sold at split-off point	£0.80	£0.30	£1.30
Product sold after further processing	£1.20	£0.70	£1.75

The process accounts for the last operating period, when the plant was operating at full capacity, can be summarized as follows:

Process 1

	Litres	£		Litres	£
Opening work in pogress	4,000	1,200	Production transferred		
Direct material	99,000	9,900	X to process 2	50,000	25,000
Processing expense		39,500	Y to process 3	30,000	15,000
			Z to process 4	20,000	10,000
			Closing work in progress	3,000	600
	103,000	£50,600		103,000	£50,600

Process 2

	Litres	£		Litres	£
Opening work in progress	2,000	1,267	Sales revenue	50,000	60,000
Input from Process 1	50,000	25,000	Closing work in progress	2,000	1,267
Processing expense		13,333			
Profit to profit and loss account		21,667			
	52,000	£61,267		52,000	61,267

Process 3

	Litres	£		Litres	£
Opening work in progress	1,000	650	Sales revenue	30,000	21,000
Input from process 1	30,000	15,000	Loss to profit and loss account		3,000
Processing expense		9,000	Closing work in progress	1,000	650
	31,000	£24,650		31,000	£24,650

Process 4

	Litres	£		Litres	£
Opening work in progress	2,000	1,700	Sales revenue	20,000	35,000
Input from process 1	20,000	10,000	Closing work in progress	2,000	1,700
Processing expense		14,000			
Profit to profit and loss account		11,000			
	22,000	£36,700		22,000	£36,700

The costs incurred and the processing efficiency for the period to which the above accounts relate can be assumed to be representative of current conditions. The joint costs in process 1 have been apportioned on the basis of the output (in litres) of X, Y and Z. All work in progress is complete as far as material content is concerned and (except for the closing work in progress in process 1) it is half processed. The closing work in progress in process 1 is one-quarter processed.

You are required:

(a) to comment on the relative profitability of the products, in particular consider the loss arising on product Y in process 3 (3 marks);

(b) to comment on the company's policy of processing all three products beyond the split-off point (3 marks);

(c) to restate the process accounts for processes 3 and 4 using sales values (at the split-off point) as the basis for the joint cost allocation (5 marks);

(d) to restate the process accounts for processes 1 and 4 using the sales values at the split-off point as transfer prices in transferring production from process 1 to the other processes (5 marks);

(e) to discuss the utility of each version of the process accounts (one version in the question and two in your solution) and to comment on the joint cost allocation problem (6 marks).

(22 marks)

ACCA Level 2 Management Accounting
June 1982

7.10 A chemical company has a contract to supply annually 3,600 tonnes of product A at £24 a tonne and 4,000 tonnes of product B at £14.50 a tonne. The basic components for these products are obtained from a joint initial distillation process. From this joint distillation a residue is produced which is processed to yield 380 tonnes of by-product Z. By-product Z is sold locally at £5 a tonne and the net income is credited to the joint distillation process.

The budget for the year ending 30 June 1981 includes the following data:

repair costs and reduce all production in the year by 10%. Supplies of the products can be imported to meet the contract commitment at a cost of £25 a tonne for A and £15 a tonne for B.

Experiments have also shown that the joint distillation plant operations could be changed during the year such that either:

(i) The output of distillate for product A would increase by 200 tonnes with a corresponding reduction in product B distillate. This change would increase the joint distillation variable costs for the whole of that operation by 2%.

or

(ii) The residue for by-product Z could be mixed with distillate for products A and B proportionate to the present output of these products. By intensifying the subsequent processing for products A and B acceptable quality could be obtained. The intensified operation would increase product A and B separable fixed costs by 5% and increase the evaporation loss for the whole operation to 11% and 21% respectively.

You are required to:

(a) calculate on the basis of the original budget:
 (i) the unit costs of products A and B; and
 (ii) the total profit for the year;

(b) calculate the change in the unit costs of products A and B based on the reduced production;

(c) calculate the profit for the year if the shortfall of production is made up by imported products;

(d) advise management whether either of the alternative distillation operations would improve the profitability calculated under (c) and whether you recommend the use of either.

(30 marks)

ICMA P3 Management Accounting
May 1980

| | Joint process | Separable costs | | |
		Product A	Product B	By-product Z
Variable cost per tonne of input, in £	5	11	2	1
Fixed costs for year, in £	5,000	4,000	8,000	500
Evaporation loss in process as percentage of input	6	10	20	5

Since the budget was compiled it has been decided that an extensive five-week overhaul of the joint distillation plant will be necessary during the year. This will cost an additional £17,000 in

7.11 A chemical company produces amongst its product range two industrial cleaning fluids, A and B. These products are manufactured jointly. In 1979 total sales are expected to be restricted because home trade outlets for fluid B are limited to 54,000 gallons for the year. At this level plant capacity will be under-utilized by 25%.

From the information given below you are required to:
(a) draw a flow diagram of the operations;
(b) calculate separately for fluids A and B for the year 1979:
 (i) total manufacturing cost;
 (ii) manufacturing cost per gallon;
 (iii) list price per gallon;
 (iv) profit for the year;
(c) calculate the breakeven price per gallon to manufacture an extra 3,000 gallons of fluid B for export and which would incur selling, distribution and administration costs of £1,260;
(d) state the price you would recommend the company should quote per gallon for this export business, with a brief explanation for your decision.

The following data are given:

1. Description of processes.

Process 1: Raw materials L and M are mixed together and filtered. There is an evaporation loss of 10%.

Process 2: The mixture from process 1 is boiled and this reduces the volume by 20%. The remaining liquid distils into 50% extract A, 25% extract B, and 25% by-product C.

Process 3: Two parts of extract A are blended with one part of raw material N, and one part of extract B with one part of raw material N, to form respectively fluids A and B.

Process 4: Fluid A is filled into one-gallon labelled bottles and fluid B into six-gallon preprinted drums and they are then both ready for sale. 1% wastage in labels occurs in this process.

2. Costs

	Cost per gallon £
Raw material: L	0.20
M	0.50
N	2.00

	Cost £
Containers: 1-gallon bottles	0.27 each
6-gallon drums	5.80 each
Bottle labels, per thousand	2.20

	Per gallon of input processed £
Direct wages: Process 1	0.11
2	0.15
3	0.20
4	0.30

Manufacturing overhead:

Process	Fixed per annum £	Variable, per gallon of input processed £
1	6,000	0.04
2	20,250	0.20
3	19,500	0.10
4	14,250	0.10

By-product C is collected in bulk by a local company which pays £0.50 per gallon for it and the income is credited to process 2.

Process costs are apportioned entirely to the two main products on the basis of their output from each process.

No inventories of part-finished materials are held at any time.

Fluid A is sold through agents on the basis of list price less 20% and fluid B at list price less 33⅓%.

Of the net selling price, profit amounts to 8%, selling and distribution costs to 12% and administration costs to 5%.

Taxation should be ignored.

(30 marks)
ICMA P3 Management Accounting
November 1978

8 Absorption costing and variable costing

In the previous chapters we looked at the proced-
ures necessary to ascertain product or job costs for
stock valuation to meet the requirements of external
reporting. The approach which we adopted was to
allocate *all* manufacturing costs to products and to
value unsold stocks at their total cost of manufac-
ture. Non-manufacturing costs were allocated not to
the products but were charged direct to the profit
statement and excluded from the stock valuation. A
costing system based on these principles is known
as an *absorption* or *full costing* system.

In this chapter we are going to look at an
alternative costing system known as *variable cost-
ing*, *marginal costing* or *direct costing*. Under this
alternative system only variable manufacturing costs

are allocated to products and included in the stock
valuation. Fixed manufacturing costs are not allo-
cated to the product but are considered as period
costs and are charged directly to the profit state-
ment. Both absorption costing and variable costing
systems are in complete agreement regarding the
treatment of non-manufacturing costs as period
costs. The disagreement between the proponents of
absorption costing and the proponents of variable
costing is concerned with whether or not manu-
facturing fixed overhead should be regarded as a
period cost or a product cost. An illustration of the
different treatment of fixed manufacturing overhead
for both absorption and variable costing systems is
shown in Exhibit 8.1.

Problem of terminology

Absorption costing is sometimes referred to as full
costing. You can avoid becoming confused by this
if you simply remember that absorption costing
and full costing are used to refer to a system in
which all the fixed manufacturing overheads are
allocated to products. The alternative system,
which allocates only variable manufacturing costs
to products, should correctly be referred to as
variable costing, although the terms direct costing
and marginal costing are also frequently used.
This is unfortunate as neither direct costs nor
marginal costs are quite the same as variable
costs. Direct costs are those which can be
specifically identified with a product; they include
direct labour and materials but exclude variable
overheads. So to use the term direct costing when

it specifically excludes variable overheads is not at
all appropriate. The term marginal costing is also
inappropriate as economists use this term to
describe the cost of producing one additional unit.
Applying this definition may lead to fixed costs
being included in a situation when the production
of an additional unit will result in an increase in
fixed costs, for example the appointment of an
additional supervisor, or an increase in capacity
due to the purchase of an additional machine.
Many accountants use the term marginal cost to
mean *average* variable cost. Because marginal cost
may be interpreted in different ways by account-
ants and economists it is better not to use the term
when referring to stock valuation. For all these
reasons we shall be using the term variable costing

Exhibit 8.1 Absorption and variable costing systems

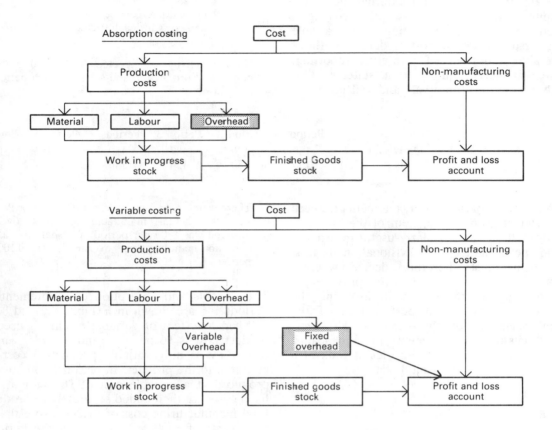

throughout this book to describe a system of costing where only the variable manufacturing costs are allocated to the product.

External and internal reporting

Many writers have argued the cases for and against variable costing for stock valuation for external reporting (see Fremgen, 1977 for a summary of the arguments). One important requirement for external reporting is consistency. It would be unacceptable if companies changed their methods of stock valuation from year to year. In addition, inter-company comparison would be difficult if some companies valued their stocks on an absorption cost basis while other

companies did so on a variable cost basis. Furthermore, the users of external accounting reports need reassurance that the published financial statements have been prepared in accordance with generally accepted standards of good accounting practice. Therefore there is a strong case for the acceptance of one method of stock valuation for external reporting. In the United Kingdom a statement of standard accounting practice on stocks and work in progress was published by the Accounting Standards Committee (SSAP 9). This states

In order to match costs and revenue, cost of stocks and work in progress should comprise that expenditure which has been incurred in the normal course of business in bringing the product or service to its present location and condition. Such costs will include all related production overheads, even though these may accrue on a time basis.

The effect of this statement in SSAP 9 was to require absorption costing for external reporting.

In spite of the fact that absorption costing is required for external reporting, the variable costing versus absorption costing debate is still of considerable importance for internal reporting. Management may require profit statements at monthly or quarterly intervals and will no doubt

	£
Unit selling price	10
Unit variable cost	6
Fixed costs for each period	300

Normal activity is expected to be 150 units per period and production and sales for each period are as follows:

	Period 1	Period 2	Period 3	Period 4	Period 5	Period 6
Units sold	150	120	180	150	140	160
Units produced	150	150	150	150	170	140

wish to receive separate profit statements for each major product group or segment of the business. This information is particularly useful in evaluating the performance of divisional managers. Management must therefore decide whether absorption costing or variable costing provides the more meaningful information in assessing the economic and managerial performance of the different segments of the business. However, before discussing the arguments for and against absorption and variable costing, let us look at a simple illustration of both methods.

EXAMPLE 8.1

The following information is available for periods 1–6 for a company which produced a single product:

There were no opening stocks at the start of Period 1 and the actual manufacturing fixed overhead incurred was £300 per period. We shall also assume that non-manufacturing overheads are £100 per period.

The variable and absorption cost statements for Periods 1–6 are shown in Exhibits 8.2 and 8.3.

When a system of variable costing is used the product cost is £6 per unit and *includes variable costs only* as only variable production costs are allocated to the product. In period 1 150 units are produced at a variable cost of £6 per unit. The fixed costs are then added separately to produce a total manufacturing cost of £1,200. Note that the fixed costs of £300 are charged in the period in which they are incurred.

In period 2, 150 units are produced but only 120

Exhibit 8.2 Variable costing statements

	Period 1 £	Period 2 £	Period 3 £	Period 4 £	Period 5 £	Period 6 £
Opening stock	–	–	180	–	–	180
Production cost	900	900	900	900	1020	840
Closing stock	–	(180)	–	–	(180)	(60)
Cost of sales	900	720	1080	900	840	960
Fixed costs	300	300	300	300	300	300
Total costs	1200	1020	1380	1200	1140	1260
Sales	1500	1200	1800	1500	1400	1600
Gross profit	300	180	420	300	260	340
Less non-manufacturing costs	100	100	100	100	100	100
Net profit	200	80	320	200	160	240

Exhibit 8.3 Absorption costing statements

	Period 1 £	Period 2 £	Period 3 £	Period 4 £	Period 5 £	Period 6 £
Opening stock	–	–	240	–	–	240
Production cost	1200	1200	1200	1200	1360	1120
Closing stock	–	(240)	–	–	(240)	(80)
Cost of sales	1200	960	1440	1200	1120	1280
Adjustment for under/ (over) recovery of overhead	–	–	–	–	(40)	20
Total cost	1200	960	1440	1200	1080	1300
Sales	1500	1200	1800	1500	1400	1600
Gross profit	300	240	360	300	320	300
Less non-manufacturing costs	100	100	100	100	100	100
Net profit	200	140	260	200	220	200

units are sold. Therefore 30 units remain in stock at the end of the period. In order to match costs with revenues the sales of 120 units should be matched with costs for 120 units. As 150 units were produced we need to value the 30 units in stock and deduct this sum from the production cost. Using the variable costing system the 30 units in stock are valued at £6 per unit. Closing stock of £180 will then be deducted from the production costs, giving a cost of sales figure of £720. Note that the closing stock valuation does not include any fixed overheads.

The 30 units of closing stock in period 2 become the opening stock for period 3 and therefore an expense for this period. The production cost for the 150 units made in period 3 is added to this opening stock valuation. The overall effect is that costs for 180 units are matched against sales for 180 units. The profits for periods 4–6 are calculated in the same way. Let us now consider in Exhibit 8.3 the profit calculations when closing stocks are valued on an absorption costing basis.

When using the *absorption costing method*, fixed overheads are allocated to individual products and are included in the production costs. In Example 8.1 the fixed overheads for each period are £300 and the normal activity is 150 units, so fixed overheads are charged to the product at £2 per unit. The product cost now consists of variable cost plus a fixed manufacturing cost, making a

total of £8 per unit. The production cost for period 1 (150 units at £8) is £1,200.

Now compare the absorption costing statement with the variable costing statement for period 1. With absorption costing the fixed cost is included in the production cost figure, whereas with variable costing only the variable cost is included. With variable costing the fixed cost is charged separately and is not included in the cost of sales figure. Note also that the closing stock of 30 units for period 2 is valued at £8 per unit in the absorption costing statement whereas the closing stock is valued at only £6 in the variable costing statement.

In calculating profits, the matching principle which has been applied in the absorption costing statement is the same as that described for variable costing. However, complications arise in periods 5 and 6; in period 5, 170 units were produced, so the production cost of £1,360 includes fixed overheads of £340 (170 units at £2). The total fixed overheads incurred for the period are only £300 so £40 too much has been charged. This over recovery of fixed overhead is recorded as a *period cost adjustment*. (A full explanation of under and over recoveries of overheads and the reasons for period cost adjustments was presented in Chapter 4, and if you are unsure of this concept please refer back now to the section headed Under and Over Recovery of Overheads).

In period 6, 140 units were produced at a cost of £1,120, which included only £280 for fixed overheads. As a result there is an under recovery of £20 which is written off as a period cost. You can see that an under or over recovery of fixed overhead occurs whenever actual production differs from the normal level of activity of 150 units, as the calculation of the fixed overhead rate of £2 per unit was based on the assumption that actual production would be 150 units per period.

Variable costing and absorption costing: a comparison of their impact on profit

A comparison of the variable costing and absorption costing statements produced from the information contained in Example 8.1 reveals the following differences in profit calculations:

(A) The profits calculated under the absorption costing and variable costing systems are identical for periods 1 and 4.
(B) The absorption costing profits are higher than the variable costing profits in periods 2 and 5.
(C) The variable costing profits are higher than the absorption costing profits in periods 3 and 6.

Let us now consider each of these in a little more detail.

Production equals sales

In Periods 1 and 4 the profits are the same for both methods of costing; in both periods production is equal to sales and stocks will neither increase nor decrease. Therefore, if opening stocks exist, the same amount of fixed overhead will be carried forward as an expense to be included in the current period in the opening stock valuation, as will be deducted in the closing stock valuation from the production cost figure. The overall effect is that with an absorption costing system the only fixed overhead which will be included as an expense for the period will be the amount of fixed overhead which is incurred for the period. *Thus, whenever sales are equal to production the profits will be the same for both the absorption costing and variable costing systems.*

Production exceeds sales

In periods 2 and 5 the absorption costing system produces higher profits; in both periods production exceeds sales. Profits are higher for absorption costing when production is in excess of sales because stocks are increasing. The effect of this is that a greater amount of fixed overheads in the closing stock is being deducted from the expenses of the period than is being brought forward in the opening stock for the period. For example, in period 2 the opening stock is zero and no fixed overheads are brought forward from the previous period. However, a closing stock of 30 units means that a £60 fixed overhead has to be deducted from the production cost for the period. In other words only £240 is being charged for fixed overhead with the absorption costing system whereas the variable costing system charges the £300 fixed overhead incurred for the period. The effect of this is that profits are £60 greater with the absorption costing system. As a general rule, *if production is in excess of sales, the absorption costing system will show a higher profit than the variable costing system.* For a discussion of a situation where this might not occur see Ijiri *et al.* (1965).

Sales exceed production

In periods 3 and 6, the variable costing system produces higher profits; in both periods sales exceeds production. When this situation occurs stocks decline and a greater amount of fixed overheads will need to be brought forward as an expense in the opening stock than is being deducted in the closing stock adjustment. For example, with the absorption costing system, in period 6, 30 units of opening stock are brought forward so that a fixed cost of £60 is included in the stock valuation. However, a closing stock of 10 units requires a deduction of £20 fixed overheads from the production costs. The overall effect is that an additional £40 fixed overheads is included as an expense within the stock movements, and a total of £340 fixed overheads is charged for the period. The variable costing system on the other hand would charge fixed overheads for the period of only £300. As a result profits are £40 greater with the variable costing system. As a general rule, *if sales are in excess of production, the variable costing system will show a*

higher profit than the absorption costing system. (For an exception see Ijiri *et al.*, 1965).

Impact of sales fluctuations

The profit calculations *for an absorption costing system* can produce some strange results. For example, in period 6 the sales volume has increased but profits have declined, in spite of the fact that both the selling price and the cost structure have remained unchanged. A manager whose performance is being judged in period 6 is likely to have little confidence in an accounting system which shows a decline in profits when sales volume has increased and the cost structure and selling price has not changed. The opposite occurs in period 5. In this period the sales volume declines but profit increases. The situations in periods 5 and 6 arise because the under or over recovery of fixed overhead is treated as a period cost, and such adjustments can at times give a misleading picture of profits.

In contrast, the variable costing profit calculations show that when sales volume increases profit also increases. Alternatively when sales volume decreases profit also decreases. These relationships continue as long as the selling price and cost structure remain unchanged. Looking again at the variable costing profit calculations you will note that profit declines in period 5 when the sales volume declines, and increases in period 6 when the sales volume also increases. The reasons for these changes are that, with a system of variable costing, profit is a function of sales volume only, when the selling price and cost structure remain unchanged. However, with absorption costing profit is a function of both sales volume *and* production volume.

Some arguments in support of variable costing

Variable costing provides more useful information for decision-making

The separation of fixed and variable costs helps to provide relevant information about costs for making decisions. Relevant costs are required for a variety of decisions, for example whether to make a component internally or whether to purchase externally, also problems relating to product-mix. These decisions will be discussed in Chapter 10. In addition the estimation of costs for different levels of activities requires that costs are split into their fixed and variable elements. The assumption is that only with a variable costing system will such an analysis of costs be available. It is therefore assumed that projection of future costs and revenues for different activity levels, and the use of relevant cost decision-making techniques, are possible only if a variable costing system is adopted. Nevertheless, there is no reason why an absorption costing system cannot be used for external reporting and costs can also be analysed into their fixed and variable elements for decision-making. The advantage of variable costing is that the analysis of variable and fixed costs is highlighted. (Such an analysis is not a feature of an absorption costing system.)

Variable costing removes from profit the effect of stock changes

We have seen that with variable costing profit is a function of sales volume, whereas with absorption costing profit is a function of both sales and production. We have also learned, using absorption costing principles, that it is possible for profit to decline when sales volumes increase. Where stock levels are likely to fluctuate significantly, profits may be distorted when they are calculated on an absorption costing basis as the stock changes will significantly affect the amount of fixed overheads charged to an accounting period.

Fluctuating stock levels are less likely to occur when one measures profits on an annual basis, but on a monthly or quarterly basis seasonal variations in sales may cause significant fluctuations. As profits are likely to be distorted by an absorption costing system there are strong arguments for using variable costing methods when profits are measured at *frequent* intervals. Because *frequent* profit statements are presented only for management the argument for variable costing is stronger for management accounting. Financial accounts are presented for public release annually or at half-yearly intervals; because significant changes in stock levels are less likely on an annual basis the argument for the use of variable costing in financial accounting is not as strong.

A further argument for using variable costing for internal reporting is that the internal profit

statements may be used as a basis for measuring managerial performance. Managers may deliberately alter their stock levels to influence profit when an absorption costing system is used; for example, it is possible for a manager to defer deliberately some of the fixed overhead charge by unnecessarily increasing stocks over successive periods.[1]

Variable costing avoids fixed overheads being capitalized in unsaleable stocks

In a period when sales demand decreases a company can end up with surplus stocks on hand. With an absorption costing system only a portion of the fixed overheads incurred during the period will be charged as an expense because the remainder of the fixed overhead will be included in the valuation of the surplus stocks. If these surplus stocks cannot be disposed of the profit calculation for the current period will be misleading as fixed overheads will have been deferred to later accounting periods. However, there may be some delay before management concludes that the stocks cannot be sold without a very large reduction in the selling price. The stocks will therefore be over-valued and a stock write-off will be necessary in a later accounting period. The overall effect may be that the current period's profits will be overstated. (For an example of this situation see Exhibit 8.4.)

Some arguments in support of absorption costing

Absorption costing does not understate the importance of fixed costs

Some people argue that decisions based on a variable costing system may concentrate only on sales revenues and variable costs and ignore the fact that fixed costs must be met in the long run. For example, if a pricing decision is based on variable costs only, then sales revenue may be insufficient to cover all the costs. It is also argued that the use of an absorption costing system, by allocating fixed costs to a product, ensures that fixed costs will be covered. These arguments are incorrect. Absorption costing will not ensure that

fixed costs will be recovered if actual sales volume is less than the estimate used to calculate the fixed overhead rate. (A discussion of the limitations of using absorption cost as a basis for setting selling prices is presented in Chapter 11.) The argument that a variable costing system will cause managers to ignore fixed costs is based on the assumption that such managers are not very bright! A failure to consider fixed costs is due to faulty management and not to a faulty accounting system.

Absorption costing avoids fictitious losses being reported

In a business which relies on seasonal sales and in which production is built up outside the sales season to meet demand, the full amount of fixed overheads incurred will be charged, in a variable costing system, against sales. However, in those periods where production is being built up for sales in a later season, sales revenue will be zero but fixed costs will be recorded as an expense. The result is that losses will be reported during out-of-season periods and large profits will be reported in the periods when the goods are sold.

By contrast in an absorption costing system fixed overheads will be deferred and included in the closing stock valuation and will be recorded as an expense only in the period in which the goods are sold. Losses are therefore unlikely to be reported in the periods when stocks are being built up. In these circumstances absorption costing appears to provide the more logical profit calculation. Examples of the profit calculations for absorption and variable costing systems for a company whose sales are subject to a seasonal demand are shown in Exhibits 8.6 and 8.7.

Absorption costing is theoretically superior to variable costing

The proponents of absorption costing argue that asset services represented by fixed manufacturing costs are just as much expended in the production of goods and services as are the services represented by variable costs. They argue that because all these assets are needed to produce a finished product all the related costs should be charged to the units produced. Let us now consider this argument.

The variable costing v. absorption costing debate

The debate is about whether fixed manufacturing costs are costs of the product made or costs for the period in which they are incurred. The proponents of absorption costing argue that fixed manufacturing costs are a product cost whereas the proponents of variable costing argue that such costs are a period cost. The period cost argument assumes that fixed manufacturing costs expire with the passage of time regardless of production activity and that these costs are incurred for the benefit of operations during a given period of time. This benefit is unchanged by the actual level of operations during the period and the benefit expires at the end of the period.

The product cost argument is based on the principle that the fixed costs are assigned to the product rather than the period, because it is the product which generates the revenue. The time period is viewed as being purely incidental to the operations of the firm. It is argued that revenue derives from the sale of the product and therefore all the production costs must be matched with revenue in the period of sale.

Cost obviation concept

The definition of an *asset* is critical to the debate. The American Accounting Association defined assets as *aggregates of service potentials available for or beneficial to expected operations*. One could say that assets have service potentials to the extent that they save costs in the *future*. This interpretation is called the *cost obviation concept*, and the proponents of variable costing have used it to argue that variable costing is superior to absorption costing. For example, Wetnight (1958) argued that variable costing meets the future benefit test better than absorption costing in the following way:

> If this test of future benefit is applied to the two methods of costing it can be seen that variable costing most closely meets the requirements. In the first place, there is a future benefit from the incurrence of variable costs. These costs will not need to be incurred in a future period. However, in the case of fixed costs, no future benefit exists, since these costs will be incurred during the future period, no matter what the level of operations.

Sorter and Horngren (1962), writing on the cost obviation concept, state:

> If the total future cost of an enterprise will be decreased because of the presence of a given cost, the cost is relevant to the future and is an asset; if not, that cost is irrelevant and is expired.

Thus, one could argue that the production of goods for stock in one period enables a firm to realize revenue in a future period without reincurring the variable costs of producing the stock. Alternatively, the availability of stocks in one period does not stop fixed costs being incurred in a future period. Variable costs are therefore relevant to future periods but fixed costs are not. In other words, variable costs are product costs but fixed costs are period costs.

Revenue production concept

Another interpretation of the service potential of an asset is to view an asset in terms of its capacity to contribute to the production of revenue in the future. This is the revenue production concept. This interpretation distinguishes between assets and expenses according to whether or not the costs incurred will contribute to the realization of revenue in the future. The revenue production concept assumes that any cost essential in making a product which may reasonably be expected to be sold represents a cost of obtaining sales revenue. Hence these costs should be deferred and included in the stock valuation so that they may be matched with revenue in the calculation of profit for the period of sale. In other words, the revenue production interpretation of service potential implies adherence to the absorption costing method of valuing stocks.

Relevant costing

Horngren and Sorter (1962) pursued the cost obviation concept further and presented a theory of stock valuation based on relevant costing. This important contribution moves away from a strict adherence to either variable costing or absorption costing methods for stock valuation. In some circumstances only variable costs are included in the stock valuation while in other circumstances both fixed and variable costs are included. The

decision on whether fixed manufacturing costs should be included in the stock valuation is not therefore clear cut, and Horngren and Sorter would argue that it depends on the circumstances.

Horngren and Sorter state that in using relevant costing only one basic assumption is required, and that is that a cost should only be carried forward as an asset if, and only if, it has a favourable economic effect on expected future costs or future revenues. Therefore, a cost cannot represent a future benefit if its absence will not influence the obtaining of future revenues or the incurrence of future costs. For example, if an item can be replaced and used in normal operations at zero incremental or opportunity cost, its presence or its physical amount does not represent service potential; in other words, its absence would have no impact on total future costs or revenues. Therefore, *if a given cost will not influence either total future revenue or total future costs, it is not an asset*.

Sorter and Horngren use an example of a paper manufacturing company with a Batch A1 in stock consisting of £40,000 variable costs and £60,000 fixed production overheads. They also assume that if Batch A1 was not in hand, a similar batch, Batch A2, could be produced in the next period by utilizing otherwise idle capacity. Therefore, no additional fixed costs would have to be *incurred* and the total expected incremental costs of Batch A2 would be the £40,000 variable production costs. It is also assumed that Batches A1 and A2 cannot both be sold. The relevant costing approach would recognize only the £40,000 as representing economic benefit, and the £60,000 fixed cost cannot qualify as an economic good. If Batch A1 can be replaced in normal operations at variable cost, its presence or its physical amount represents economic benefit only in the amount of variable costs that will not have to be incurred in the future. In other words, if Batch A1 were not on hand, £40,000 would be the only future outlay necessary to restore the enterprise to an equivalent economic position.

Note that the relevant costing approach would support absorption costing *if future sales demand exceeded productive capacity* (for example, if Batch A1 were not in hand there would be no spare capacity to produce it in the next period) as future sales would be lost for ever because of a shortage of stocks. Production of Batch A1 in the current period will therefore change future revenues. Hence the costs of using the capacity (that is, the fixed costs) have a favourable economic effect on future revenues and should be included in the stock valuation.

Horngren and Sorter provide a further illustration relating to the depreciation of machinery. They argue that if depreciation is most closely related to *time expiration* (due to obsolescence, technical change, and so on) this depreciation cannot form part of the product cost unless the utilization of a machine in a particular period will make possible future sales which would otherwise be lost for ever. If, on the other hand, depreciation is most closely related to *production* rather than time, it is properly treated as a product cost because the decision to produce a unit in period 1 rather than in period 2 affects the service potential of the fixed asset. Each decision of this kind affects the asset's useful life, whereas with time-based depreciation such a decision has no effect on useful life.

Internal profit measurement

The relevant costing approach emphasizes that the choice between absorption costing and variable costing depends on the particular circumstances, and one cannot argue that one method is superior for all situations. There are times when variable costing will produce the more meaningful profit calculations and other times when absorption costing will produce a more meaningful calculation. Consider the following example.

EXAMPLE 8.2

A company *with a normal production capacity of 100 units* produces 100 units per period for four periods. The variable cost per unit is £5 and the period's fixed overheads are £1,000. The company produces a speciality product and there is no comparable market price. However, the company is able to sell only 10 units per period at the previous market price of £20 per unit for the first three periods. At the end of period 4 the total production to date of 370 units, which consists of 90 units of unsold production for each of the first three periods plus 100 units produced in period 4, is sold for a temporary distress price of £6 per unit.

The absorption costing and variable costing statements relating to this information are set out in Exhibits 8.4 and 8.5.

Exhibit 8.4 Absorption costing statements

	Period 1 £	Period 2 £	Period 3 £	Period 4 £	Total £
Sales	200 (10 × £20)	200	200	2,220 (370 × £6)	
Less Cost of sales	150 (10 × £15)	150	150	5,550 (370 × £15)	
Profit/(loss)	50	50	50	(3,330)	(3,180)
Closing stock valuation	1,350 (90 × £15)	2,700 (180 × £15)	4,050 (270 × £15)	–	

Exhibit 8.5 Variable costing statements

	Period 1 £		Period 2 £		Period 3 £		Period 4 £		Total £
Sales		200 (10 × £200)		200		200		2,220 (370 × 6)	
Less Variable cost of sales	50 (10 × £5)		50		50		1,850 (370 × £5)		
Fixed overheads	1,000	1,050	1,000	1,050	1,000	1,050	1,000	2,850	
Profit/(loss)		(850)		(850)		(850)		(630)	(3,180)
Closing stock valuation		450 (90 × 5)		900 (180 × 5)	1,350	(270 × 5)			

Note from Exhibit 8.4 that profits of £50 per periods are reported for the first three periods and that in period 4 a loss of £3,330 is reported. The cost per unit consists of a variable cost of £5 plus a fixed cost of £10 per unit (£1,000/100 units). Therefore, when 10 units are sold for each of the first three periods costs of £150 per period are matched against sales. The remaining 90 units of unsold stock are valued at £15 per unit, including £10 per unit for fixed overheads. The result is that £900 fixed overheads (90 units at £10) are deferred as expenses in each of the first three periods. In period 4, when all the production is sold, the closing stock at the end of period 3, valued at £4,050, plus the cost of production of £1,500 for period 4 is matched against sales. This gives a loss of £3,330. Let us now look at the variable costing profit statements. This information is presented in Exhibit 8.5.

You can see that the cost of sales for each of the first three periods includes only the variable cost of £50 (10 units at £5 per unit). The full amount of fixed overheads is charged against sales in the period in which the overhead is incurred. The unsold production of 90 units in each of the first three periods is valued at a variable cost of £450. In period 4 the cost of sales consists of the closing stock at the end of period 3, valued at £1,350, plus the variable cost of production of £500 for the 100 units produced and sold in period 4.

If we compare the profit and losses in the statements presented in Exhibits 8.4 and 8.5 we can see that the variable costing statement appears to give management more meaningful information. With variable costing management is made aware that it is failing to sell enough goods to cover the fixed costs and this failure is reflected in the losses incurred in each of the first three periods. The absorption costing statement, however, indicates that the company is making a profit in the first three periods in spite of the fact that sales revenue is insufficient to cover fixed costs. In period 4 a large loss occurs. Although the total loss for the first four periods is the same with both

Exhibit 8.6 Absorption costing statements

	Period 1 £	Period 2 £	Period 3 £	Period 4 £	Total £
Sales	200 (10 × £20)	200	200	7,400 (370 × £20)	
Less Cost of sales	150	150	150	5,550	
Profit	50	50	50	1,850	2,000

Exhibit 8.7 Variable costing statements

	Period 1 £		Period 2 £		Period 3 £		Period 4 £		Total £
Sales		200		200		200		7,400	
Less Variable cost of sales	50		50		50		1,850		
Fixed overheads	1,000	1,050	1,000	1,050	1,000	1,050	1,000	2,850	
Profit/(loss)		(850)		(850)		(850)		4,550	2,000

methods, some may argue that absorption costing produces misleading profit calculations. In this case variable costing appears to present a clearer picture of the performance each period.

Let us now consider a situation in which absorption costing provides management with a more meaningful profit calculation. We shall use Example 8.2 but assume that the company is a fireworks manufacturer and is deliberately building up stocks to meet the seasonal demand in period 4. We shall also *assume that all sales, including those in period 4, are at £20 per unit and not £6 per unit*. The profit calculations are set out in Exhibits 8.6 and 8.7.

Both methods produce the same total profits of £2,000 but the variable costing method produces a loss of £850 for each of the first three periods and a very large profit in period 4. With the absorption costing method the majority of the fixed overhead is deferred until the production is sold and a small profit is recorded in each of the first three periods. As stocks are deliberately being built up to meet seasonal demand, the losses shown under a variable costing system appear to be misleading. Absorption costing profit statements present a clearer picture of the performance each period for this particular company.

We have seen that variable costing produces more meaningful profit calculations in the first situation and that absorption costing provides more meaningful profit calculations in the second situation. We must conclude, therefore, that the choice of whether or not we include fixed overheads in a stock valuation will depend on the circumstances. The selection of absorption costing or variable costing systems should take into account the trading circumstances in which a company operates, and the profit calculation should provide the closest approximation to the true economic facts.

We already know that for internal profit calculations the choice of absorption costing or variable costing systems can have a critical influence on the monthly or quarterly profit calculations. However, with external reporting, stocks are unlikely to fluctuate very much from one accounting year end to the next, and the choice of absorption costing or variable costing is unlikely to produce serious distortions in profit calculations. In addition, the users of external accounting information require assurances that the annual profits are calculated according to a set of consistent accounting principles. For this reason, Statement of Standard Accounting Practice No. 9 recommends that all companies use one common method (absorption costing) for external reporting.

Current cost accounting

The absorption costing versus variable costing debate applies only when stocks are valued at historic cost. If external reporting abandons historical cost accounting in favour of current cost accounting (when stocks are valued at net realizable value or replacement cost rather than original acquisition cost) the debate is no longer relevant as the cost of sales will be calculated at current cost and not historical cost. For a discussion of current cost accounting see Lee (1980). Even if stocks are still valued on a historical cost basis in the external accounts there are strong arguments for adopting current cost valuations for internal reporting. However, as long as historical costs are presented externally, there is a strong possibility that management may continue to produce internal profit calculations on the same basis, and the variable costing and absorption costing debate will not doubt continue.

Summary

In this chapter we have examined and compared absorption costing systems and variable costing systems. With an absorption costing system, fixed manufacturing overheads are apportioned to the products, and these are included in the stock valuation. With a variable costing system, only variable manufacturing costs are identified to the product; fixed manufacturing costs are regarded as period costs and written off to the profit and loss account. Both variable and absorption costing systems treat non-manufacturing overheads as period costs.

An illustration of the stock valuations and profit calculations for both systems was presented, and we noted that when production was equal to sales both systems yielded identical profits. However, when production exceeded sales, absorption costing showed the higher profits. Variable costing yielded the higher profits when sales exceeded production. Nevertheless, total profits over the life of the business will be the same for both systems. Differences arise merely in the profits attributed to each accounting period.

The proponents of variable costing claim that it provides more useful information for decision-making but it was argued that similar relevant cost information can easily be provided with an absorption costing system. The major advantage of variable costing is that profit is reflected as a function of sales, whereas in an absorption costing system profit is a function of both sales and production. For example, we established that with absorption costing, when all other factors remain unchanged, sales can increase but profit may decline. By contrast, with a variable costing system, when sales increase profits also increase. A further advantage of variable costing is that fixed overheads are not capitalized in unsaleable stocks.

The arguments which we have considered in support of absorption costing include:

(1) Absorption costing does not underestimate the importance of fixed costs.
(2) Absorption costing is theoretically superior to variable costing.
(3) Absorption costing avoids fictitious losses being reported.

Only one third of these appears to be justified.

Critical to the debate about whether fixed manufacturing costs are product costs or period costs is the definition of an asset. An asset is defined as an aggregate of service potentials, available for, or beneficial to, expected operations. Two interpretations of service potential have been considered: the cost obviation concept and the revenue production concept. The former supported variable costing whereas the latter supported absorption costing.

We have also examined the relevant cost theory of stock valuation. The relevant costing approach emphasized that the choice of absorption costing or variable costing depends on the particular circumstances, and that one method is not superior for all situations. We looked at situations when variable costing was superior to absorption costing and vice versa, and we concluded that the decision as to whether or not fixed overheads should be included in the stock valuation would also depend on the particular circumstances (see Example 8.2). Finally, we stressed that if external reporting abandons historical cost accounting in favour of current cost accounting the variable absorption costing debate will no longer be relevant.

References and further reading

Accounting Standards Committee (1977). *Accounting for Stocks and Work in Progress* (SSAP 9).

Accounting Standards Committee (1980). *Current Cost Accounting* (SSAP 16).

American Accounting Association. *Accounting and Reporting Standards for Corporate Financial Statements and Preceding Statements and Supplements* (1957), page 4.

Amerman, G. Facts about direct costing for profit determination. *Journal of Accounting Research* April 1954, 161.

Fremgen, J.M. The direct costing — An identification of issues. *The Accounting Review* January 1964, 43-51; also in Benston, G.J. (Ed.), *Contemporary Cost Accounting and Control*. Dickenson Publishing Company, 1977.

Gordon, A.L. and Cook, H.J. Absorption costing and fixed factors of production. *Accounting Review* January 1973, 128-30.

Green, D. A moral to the direct costing. *Journal of Accounting Research* 4(1), Spring 1966, 119-20.

Horngren, C.T. and Sorter, G.H. Asset recognition and economic attributes — The relevant costing approach. *The Accounting Review* 37, July 1962, 394; also in Benston, G.J. (Ed.), *Contemporary Cost Accounting and Control*. Dickenson Publishing Company, 1977.

Ijiri, Y., Jaedicke, R.K. and Livingstone, J.L. The effect of inventory costing methods on full and direct costing. *Journal of Accounting Research* 3(1), Spring 1965, 63-74.

Largay, J. Microeconomic foundations of variable costing. *Accounting Review* January 1973, 115-119.

Lee T.A. *Income and Value Measurement.* Van Nostrand Reinhold (UK), 1980, Ch. 7.

Lentilhon. Direct costing — Either . . . or. *The Accounting Review* October 1964, 880-83.

Nielsen, O. A predecessor of direct costing. *Journal of Accounting Research* 4(1), Spring 1966, 119-20.

Staubus, G.J. Direct relevant or absorption costing. *Accounting Review* January 1963, 64-73.

Wetnight, R.B. Direct costing passes the future benefit test. *NAA Bulletin* 39, August 1958, 84..

Problems

*Indicates that a suggested solution is to be found in the *Students' Manual*.

8.1* In product costing the costs attributed to each unit of production may be calculated by using either
 (i) absorption costing, or
 (ii) marginal (or direct or variable) costing.

Similarly, in departmental cost or profit reports the fixed costs of overhead or service departments may be allocated to production departments as an integral part of the production departments' costs or else segregated in some form.
Required:
Describe absorption and marginal (or direct or variable) costing and outline the strengths and weaknesses of each method.

(c. 11 marks)
ACCA P2 Management Accounting
June 1979

8.2* (a) Comment briefly on the two most important features which you consider distinguish marginal costing from absorption costing.

(b) For decision making purposes, a company uses the following figures relating to product B for a one-year period.

Activity:	50%	100%
Sales and production, in thousands of units	200	400
	£000	£000
Sales	1,000	2,000
Production costs:		
Variable	400	800
Fixed	200	200
Selling, distribution and administration expenses:		
Variable	200	400
Fixed	300	300

The normal level of activity for the current year is 400,000 units. The fixed costs are incurred evenly throughout the year and actual fixed costs are the same as budgeted.

There were no stocks of product B at the start of the quarter in which 110,000 units were produced and 80,000 units were sold.

From each of the questions (i) to (iv) below, you are required to select the appropriate answer. You must support each answer with an explanatory calculation.

(i) The amount of fixed production costs absorbed by product B in the first quarter, using absorption costing, is:

	£
1	80,000
2	40,000
3	110,000
4	55,000
5	None of these.

(ii) The over/(under) absorption of fixed production costs in the first quarter is:

	£
1	(5,000)
2	5,000
3	10,000
4	15,000
5	None of these.

(iii) The net profit (or loss) for the first quarter using absorption costing, is:

	£
1	(115,000)
2	50,000
3	(175,000)
4	125,000
5	None of these.

(iv) The net profit (or loss) for the first quarter, using marginal costing, is:

	£
1	35,000
2	(340,000)
3	65,000
4	(115,000)
5	None of these.

(20 marks)
ICMA Cost Accounting 1
May 1979

8.3* The unit cost of production for a firm which produces a single product is as follows:

	£
Direct materials	2.60
Direct labour	3.00
Variable overhead	0.40
Fixed overhead	1.00
	7.00

The fixed overhead calculation is based on budgeted level of activity of 150,000 units and budgeted manufacturing fixed overheads of £150,000 for each quarter. The budgeted selling and administration overheads are £100,000 per quarter (all fixed). The selling price for the product is £10 per unit. The production and sales for each quarter were as follows:

	Quarter 1	Quarter 2	Quarter 3	Quarter 4
Production (units)	150,000	170,000	140,000	150,000
Sales (units)	150,000	140,000	160,000	160,000

There was no opening stock in Quarter 1 and assume that actual costs were identical to estimated costs.
You are required:
(A) To produce in columnar form absorption and variable costing profit statements.
(B) To comment on the results for each quarter and the year as a whole.

8.4 (a) From the information given below you are required to prepare profit statements for the year based on:
(i) marginal costing,
(ii) absorption costing, and
(iii) to comment on the difference in the profit figures you report for (i) and (ii) above.
JB Ltd produces a single product which is bottled and sold in cases. The normal annual level of operations, on which the production fixed overhead absorption is based, is 36,000 cases.
Data for the last financial year were as follows:

Production	40,000 cases
Sales	32,000 cases

	Per case
	£
Selling price	60
Costs:	
Production:	
Direct labour	12
Direct material	14
Variable overhead	8

	£
Fixed overhead (budgeted and incurred)	216,000
Selling and administration costs:	
Fixed	50,000
Variable	15% of sales revenue

There was no opening stock of finished goods and the work in progress stock may be assumed to be the same at the end of the year as it was at the beginning of the year.
(b) For making decisions based on cost data, the distinction between fixed and variable costs is important.
You are required to:
(i) explain why the above statement is true;
(ii) give brief details of *two problems* associated with the determination of fixed and variable costs;
(iii) list *three* types of decisions where the division between fixed and variable costs is important.

(30 marks)
ICMA Cost Accounting 1
May 1982

8.5* MS Ltd manufactures one product only, sold for £100 each. There is given below a budgeted profit and loss statement for one year based on sales and production at a normal level of activity.

Profit and loss statement

	£000	£000
Sales		1,000
Costs:		
Direct material	300	
Direct wages	200	
Production overhead: variable	50	
fixed	200	
Administration overhead: fixed	100	
Selling overhead: fixed	50	
		900
Net profit		£100

Budgets have been prepared for year ending 30 June 1981 and year ending 30 June 1982. In the budget to 30 June 1981 sales have been shown as only 80% of the normal level of activity while production has been included at the normal level of activity. In the budget for year ending 30 June 1982 sales have been shown as achieving the normal level of activity while production has been reduced to 80% of the normal level of activity to utilize stock made previously.

(a) You are required to prepare a budgeted profit and loss statement for each of the years ending 30 June 1981 and 1982, based on a system of:
 (i) absorption costing;
 (ii) marginal costing.
(b) Discuss briefly the effect on profit of these two different systems.

(25 marks)
ICMA Cost Accounting 2
May 1980

8.6 Rumbles Ltd manufactures a single product, with a variable manufacturing cost of £12 per unit and a selling price of £20 per unit. Fixed production overheads are £90,000 per period. The company operates a full absorption costing system and the fixed overheads are absorbed into the cost of production, on the basis of a normal activity of 15,000 units per period, at a rate of £6 per unit. Any under or over absorbed overheads are written off to the profit and loss account at the end of each period. It may be assumed that no other expenses are incurred.

Summarized below are the company's manufacturing and trading results, showing quantities only, for periods 2 and 3.

	Period 2	Period 3
Opening stock	5,000 units	11,000 units
Production	17,000 units	13,000 units
	22,000 units	24,000 units
Less Closing stock	11,000 units	6,000 units
Sales	11,000 units	18,000 units

The managing director of Rumbles Ltd, who has recently returned from a course on marginal costing, has calculated that as sales have increased by 7,000 units in period 3, the company's profits should increase by £56,000. However, the results produced by the accountant show that profits in period 2 were £34,000 and in period 3 were £24,000. The managing director is somewhat surprised!

Required:
(a) Produce columnar revenue accounts, for both periods, showing how the profits of £24,000 and £34,000 were obtained. (5 marks)
(b) Carefully explain, with supporting calculations:
 (i) the reasons for the reduction in reported profits between the two periods.
 (5 marks)
 (ii) how the Managing Director has calculated that profits should increase by £56,000 in Period 3. (2 marks)
 (iii) why profits have not increased by £56,000 in Period 3. (5 marks)
 (17 marks)
ACCA Foundation Costing
December 1980

8.7 Using the information given below, prepare profit statements for the months of March and April 1978 using:
(a) marginal costing;
(b) absorption costing.

	£
Per unit:	
Sales price	50
Direct material cost	18
Direct wages	4
Variable production overhead	3
Per month:	
Fixed production overhead	99,000
Fixed selling expenses	14,000
Fixed administration expenses	26,000
Variable selling expenses, 10% of sales value	

Normal capacity was 11,000 units per month.

	March units	April units
Sales	10,000	12,000
Production	12,000	10,000

(20 marks)

ICMA Cost Accounting 1
May 1978

8.8 Bittern Ltd manufactures and sells a single product at a unit selling price of £25. In constant price-level terms its cost structure is as follows:

Variable costs:	Production materials	£10 per unit produced
	Distribution	£1 per unit sold
Semi-variable costs:	Labour	£5,000 per annum, plus £2 per unit produced
Fixed costs:	Overheads	£5,000 per annum

For several years Bittern has operated a system of variable costing for management accounting purposes. It has been decided to review the system and to compare it for management accounting purposes with an absorption costing system.

As part of the review you have been asked to prepare estimates of Bittern's profits in constant price-level terms over a three-year period in three different hypothetical situations, and to compare the two types of system generally for management accounting purposes.

You are required:
(a) in each of the following three sets of hypothetical circumstances, to calculate Bittern's profit in each of years t_1, t_2 and t_3, and also in total over the three-year period t_1 to t_3, using, first, a variable costing system, and then a full-cost absorption costing system with fixed cost recovery based on a normal production level of 1,000 units per annum:
 (i) Stable unit levels of production, sales and inventory

	t_1	t_2	t_3
Opening stock	100	100	100
Production	1,000	1,000	1,000
Sales	1,000	1,000	1,000
Closing stock	100	100	100

(5 marks)

 (ii) Stable unit level of sales, but fluctuating unit levels of production and inventory

	t_1	t_2	t_3
Opening stock	100	600	400
Production	1,500	800	700
Sales	1,000	1,000	1,000
Closing stock	600	400	100

(5 marks)

 (iii) Stable unit level of production, but fluctuating unit levels of sales and inventory

	t_1	t_2	t_3
Opening stock	100	600	400
Production	1,000	1,000	1,000
Sales	500	1,200	1,300
Closing stock	600	400	100

(5 marks)

(Note: All the data in (i)–(iii) above are volumes, not values)

(b) to write a short comparative evaluation of variable and absorption costing systems for management accounting purposes, paying particular attention to profit measurement, and using your answer to part (a) to illlustrate your arguments if you wish. (10 marks)

ICAEW Management Accounting
July 1979

8.9* The Miozip Company operates an absorption costing system which incorporates a factory-wide overhead absorption rate per direct labour hour. For 1980 and 1981 this rate was £2.10 per hour. The fixed factory overhead for 1981 was £600,000 and this would have been fully absorbed if the company had operated at full capacity, which is estimated at 400,000 direct labour hours. Unfortunately, only 200,000 hours were worked in that year so that the overhead was seriously underabsorbed. Fixed factory overheads are expected to be unchanged in 1982 and 1983.

The outcome for 1981 was a loss of £70,000 and the management believed that a major cause of this loss was the low overhead absorption rate which had led the company to quote selling prices which were uneconomic.

For 1982 the overhead absorption rate was increased to £3.60 per direct labour hour and selling prices were raised in line with the established pricing procedures which involve adding a profit mark-up of 50% to the full factory cost of the company's products. The new selling prices were also charged on the stock of finished goods held at the beginning of 1982.

In December 1982 the company's accountant prepares an estimated profit and loss account for 1982 and a budgeted profit and loss account for 1983. Although sales were considered to be depressed in 1981, they were even lower in 1982 but, nevertheless, it seems that the company will make a profit for that year. A worrying feature of

the estimated accounts is the high level of finished goods stock held and the 1983 budget provides for a reduction in the stock level at 31 December 1983 to the (physical) level which obtained at 1 January 1981. Budgeted sales for 1983 are set at the 1982 sales level.

The summarized profit statements for the three years to 31 December 1983 are as follows:

Summarized profit and loss accounts

	Actual 1981		Estimated 1982		Budgeted 1983	
	£	£	£	£	£	£
Sales revenue		1,350,000		1,316,250		1,316,250
Opening stock of finished goods	100,000		200,000		357,500	
Factory cost of production	1,000,000		975,000		650,000	
	1,100,000		1,175,000		1,007,500	
Less: Closing stock of finished goods	200,000		357,500		130,000	
Factory cost of goods sold		900,000		817,500		877,500
		450,000		498,750		438,750
Less: Factory overhead under-absorbed		300,000		150,000		300,000
		150,000		348,750		138,750
Administrative and financial costs		220,000		220,000		220,000
	Loss	(£70,000)		£128,750	Loss	(£81,250)

(a) You are required to write a short report to the board of Miozip explaining why the budgeted outcome for 1983 is so different from that of 1982 when the sales revenue is the same for both years. (6 marks)

(b) Restate the profit and loss account for 1981, the estimated profit and loss account for 1982 and the budgeted profit and loss account for 1983 using marginal factory cost for stock valuation purposes. (8 marks)

(c) Comment on the problems which *may* follow from a decision to increase the overhead absorption rate in conditions when cost plus pricing is used and overhead is currently under-absorbed. (3 marks)

(d) Explain why the majority of businesses use full costing systems whilst most management accounting theorists favour marginal costing. (5 marks)

N.B. Assume in your answers to this question that the value of the £ and the efficiency of the company have been constant over the period under review. (22 marks)

ACCA Level 2 Management Accounting
December 1982

8.10 The Waverley Co. Ltd has just been set up in order to manufacture and sell three products; A, B and C. Details of planned production and sales quantities for each of these for the next two years are shown below:

Planned activity—units (000s)

	Year 1			Year 2		
	A	B	C	A	B	C
Production	30	20	10	30	20	10
Sales	24	16	4	24	10	12

The proposed pattern of production is considered to be the normal long-term pattern but the sales expected in the first two years are not representative of the anticipated long-term position.

It is expected that the sales price and the variable cost per unit will be stable for at least two years; details of these are:

	Sales price (per unit) £	Variable cost (per unit) £
A	8	2
B	12	4
C	12	3

The manufacturing process requires that all production be subjected to both manual operations and mechanical processing. Details of labour and machine production hours required for each unit produced are:

	Labour hours (per unit)	Machine hours (per unit)
A	2	1
B	3	1
C	2	2

Total fixed production overhead costs will be £280,000 in each year.

The managing director wishes to ascertain both the total profit (before administration costs etc.) expected for each of the first two years and the profitability of each product. Accordingly he has asked each of the three applicants for the job of management accountant to produce the information he requires but is surprised that the figures they produce display little similarity. It appears that one candidate has utilized direct costing whereas the other two have utilized absorption costing but with each using a different basis for overhead recovery. Before making a decision as to whom to employ the managing director wishes to ascertain which one of the sets of figures provided is 'correct' and which two sets are, therefore, 'wrong' and so seeks your advice.

Required:

(a) Prepare the three statements the managing director is likely to have received and which show:
 (i) the total profit (before considering administration costs etc.) for each of the first two years; and
 (ii) the profitability of each product.
 (c. 10 marks)

(b) Comment on the reasons for any similarities and/or differences in the three sets of figures provided in (a) above. In your comments suggest any improvements which could be made to the application of the absorption costing methods. Advise the managing director which candidate's set of figures provides the 'correct' answer and which are 'wrong'.
 (c. 7 marks)

(c) It is decided to increase the production of the

first year only by 20% in order to provide additional buffer stocks. Calculate the cost to Waverley Ltd of holding such additional stocks for a full year if the appropriate cost of financing the additional stocks is 12% per annum. (Ignore any obsolescence and costs of storage.)
 (c. 3 marks)
 (Total 20 marks)
ACCA Professional 2 Management Accounting December 1979

8.11 Synchrodot Ltd manufactures two standard products, product 1 selling at £15 and product 2 selling at £18. A standard absorption costing system is in operation and summarized details of the unit cost standards are as follows:

Standard costs data: Summary

	Product 1 £	Product 2 £
Direct material cost	2	3
Direct labour cost	1	2
Overhead (fixed and variable)	7	9
	£10	£14

The budgeted fixed factory overhead for Synchrodot Ltd is £180,000 (per quarter) for product 1 and £480,000 (per quarter) for product 2. This apportionment to product lines is achieved by using a variety of 'appropriate' bases for individual expense categories, e.g. floor space for rates, number of work-staff for supervisory salaries etc. The fixed overhead is absorbed into production using practical capacity as the basis and any volume variance is written off (or credited) to the profit and loss account in the quarter in which it occurs. Any planned volume variance in the quarterly budgets is dealt with similarly. The practical capacity per quarter is 30,000 units for product 1 and 60,000 units for product 2.

At the March board meeting the draft budgeted income statement for the April/May/June quarter is presented for consideration. This shows the following:

	Product 1		Product 2	
Budgeted sales quantity	30,000 units		57,000 units	
Budgeted production quantity	24,000 units		60,000 units	
Budgeted sales revenue	£450,000		£1,026,000	
Budgeted production costs				
Direct material	£48,000		£180,000	
Direct labour	24,000		120,000	
Factory overhead	204,000		540,000	
	£276,000		£840,000	
Add:				
Budgeted finished goods				
Stock at 1 April 1981	(8,000 units)	80,000	(3,000 units)	42,000
	£356,000		£882,000	
Less:				
Budgeted finished goods				
Stock at 30 June 1981	(2,000 units)	20,000	(6,000 units)	84,000
Budgeted manufacturing cost of budgeted sales	£336,000		£798,000	
Budgeted manufacturing profit	£114,000		£228,000	
Budgeted administrative and selling costs (fixed)	30,000		48,000	
Budgeted profit	£84,000		£180,000	

The statement causes consternation at the board meeting because it seems to show that product 2 contributes much more profit than product 1 and yet this has not previously been apparent.

The sales director is perplexed and he points out that the budgeted sales programme for the forthcoming quarter is identical with that accepted for the current quarter (January/February/March) and yet the budget for the current quarter shows a budgeted profit of £120,000 for each product line and the actual results seem to be in line with the budget.

The production director emphasizes that identical assumptions, as to unit variable costs, selling prices and manufacturing efficiency, underly both budgets but there has been a change in the budgeted production pattern. He produces the following table:

Budgeted production	Product 1	Product 2
January/February/March	30,000 units	52,500 units
April/May/June	24,000 units	60,000 units

He urges that the company's budgeting procedures be overhauled as he can see no reason why the quarter's profit should be £24,000 up on the previous quarter and why the net profit for product 1 should fall from £4.00 to £2.80 per unit sold, whereas for product 2 it should rise from £2.11 to £3.16.

You are required:

(a) To reconstruct the company's budget for the January/February/March quarter. (6 marks)

(b) To restate the budgets (for both quarters) using standard marginal cost as the stock valuation basis. (8 marks)

(c) To comment on the queries raised by the sales director and the production director and on the varying profit figures disclosed by the alternative budgets. (8 marks)

(22 marks)

ACCA Level 2 Management Accounting
June 1982

Part III

Information for decision-making

The objective of this Part, which contains six chapters, is to consider the provision of financial information which will help managers to make better decisions. Chapters 9–12 are concerned with short-term decisions based on the environment of today, and the physical, human and financial resources which are presently available to a firm; these decisions are, to a considerable extent, determined by the quality of the firm's long-term decisions. An important distinction between long-term and short-term decisions is that the former cannot easily be reversed whereas the latter can often be changed. The actions which follow short-term decisions are frequently repeated and it is possible for different actions to be taken in the future. For example, the setting of a particular selling price or product mix can often be changed fairly quickly. With regard to long-term decisions, such as capital investment, which involves, for example, the purchase of new plant and machinery, it is not easy to change a decision in the short-term. Resources may only be available for major investments in plant and machinery at lengthy intervals, and it is unlikely that plant replacement decisions will be repeated in the short term.

In Chapters 9–12 we will examine how accounting information can be applied to three different forms of short-term decisions. Chapter 9 — Cost–Volume–Profit Analysis — focuses on what will happen to the financial results if a specific level of activity or volume fluctuates. This information is required for making optimal short-term output decisions. Chapter 10 — Measuring Costs and Benefits for Decision-Making — examines how costs and benefits should be measured for a range of short-term decisions. Chapter 11 — Accounting Information for Pricing Decisions — is concerned with the provision of financial information for pricing decisions. Chapters 9–11 assume a world of certainty, whereas Chapter 12 introduces methods for incorporating uncertainty into the analysis, and the topics covered in Chapters 9–11 are re-examined under conditions of uncertainty.

The final two chapters in this section are concerned with long-term decisions. Chapter 13 looks at the techniques which are used for evaluating capital investment decisions and introduces the concept of the time value of money. A number of assumptions are made to simplify the discussion but in Chapter 14 these assumptions are relaxed and we consider how capital investment techniques can be applied to more complex situations.

In Chapters 9–14 we assume that the objective of an organization is to maximize its net cash inflows although terms such as profit, costs and revenues are also used. It is assumed that profit is equivalent to the difference between the cash inflows and outflows, and also that revenues are equivalent to cash inflows and costs are equivalent to cash outflows. Financial accounting distinguishes between these terms because costs/ revenues and cash flows must be allocated to different accounting periods when periodic profit and loss accounts and balance sheets are produced. With regard to decision-making, the objective is not to allocate the profits or cash flows to particular accounting periods, but to consider their incremental future effect. Consequently, *total* incremental profits will equal *total* incremental cash flows and it is not therefore necessary to distinguish between them.

9 Cost–volume–profit analysis

In the previous chapters we have considered how costs should be accumulated for stock valuation and profit measurement, and we have stressed that costs should be accumulated in a different way for decision-making and cost control. In the next six chapters we shall look at the presentation of financial information for decision-making. We begin by considering how the management accountant can be of assistance in providing answers to questions about the consequences of following particular courses of action. Such questions might include 'What would be the effect on profits if we reduce our selling price and sell more units?' 'What sales volume is required to meet the additional fixed charges from a proposed plant expansion?' 'Should we pay our sales people on the basis of a salary only, or on the basis of a commission only, or by a combination of the two?' These and other questions can be answered using cost–volume–profit analysis.

Cost–volume–profit (CVP) analysis is a systematic method of examining the relationship between changes in volume (that is, output) and changes in total sales revenue, expenses and net profit. As a model of these relationships, CVP analysis simplifies the real-world conditions which a firm will face. Like most models which are abstractions from reality, CVP analysis is subject to a number of underlying assumptions and limitations, which will be discussed later in this chapter; nevertheless, it is a powerful tool for decision-making.

The objective of CVP analysis is to establish what will happen to the financial results if a specified level of activity or volume fluctuates. This information is vital to management as one of the most important variables influencing total sales revenue, total costs and profits is output or volume. For this reason output is given special attention, as knowledge of this relationship will enable management to identify the critical output levels, such as the level at which profit will be maximized, or the level at which neither a profit nor a loss will occur (that is, the break-even point).

CVP analysis is based on the relationship between sales revenue, costs and profit *in the short run*, the short run being a period in which the output of a firm is restricted to that available from the current operating capacity. In the short run some inputs can be increased but others cannot. For example, additional supplies of materials and unskilled labour may be obtained at short notice but it takes time to expand the capacity of plant and machinery. Thus output is limited in the short run because plant facilities cannot be expanded. It also takes time to reduce capacity, and therefore in the short run a firm must operate on a relatively constant stock of production resources.

The theoretical relationship between total sales revenue, costs and profits with volume has been developed by economists. As the economists' model provides the theoretical foundations for the accountants' model, an understanding of the former is essential in order to understand the underlying principles on which the accountants' CVP analysis is based.

The economists' model

An economists' model of CVP behaviour is presented in Fig. 9.1. You will see that the total revenue line is assumed to be curvilinear, which indicates that the firm is only able to sell increasing quantities of output by reducing the selling price per unit; thus the total revenue line

Fig. 9.1 Economists' cost–volume graph

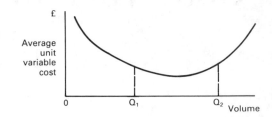

Fig. 9.2 Economists' variable cost function

does not increase proportionately with output. To increase the quantity of sales it is necessary to reduce the unit selling price, which results in the total revenue line rising less steeply, and eventually beginning to decline. This is because the adverse effect of price reductions outweighs the benefits of increased sales volume.

The total cost line AD shows that between points A and B total costs rise steeply at first as the firm operates at the lower levels of the volume range. This reflects the difficulties of operating efficiently a plant which was designed for much larger volume levels. Between points B and C the total cost line begins to level out and rise less steeply. This is because the firm is now able to operate the plant within the efficient operating range and can take advantage of specialization of labour, normal production runs, and smooth production schedules. In the upper portion of the volume range the total cost line between points C and D rises more and more steeply as the cost per unit increases. This is because the output per direct labour hour declines when the plant is operated beyond the activity level for which it was designed: bottlenecks develop, production schedules become more complex, and plant breakdowns begin to occur. The overall effect is that the cost per unit of output increases and causes the total cost line to rise steeply.

The dashed horizontal line from point A in Fig. 9.1 represents the cost of providing the basic operating capcity and is the economists' interpretation of the total fixed costs of the firm. Note also from Fig. 9.1 that the shape of the total revenue line is such that it crosses the total cost line at two points. In other words, there are two output levels at which the total costs are equal to the total revenues; or more simply, there are two break-even points.

It is the shape of the *variable* cost function in the economists' model which has the most significant influence on the total cost function; this is illustrated in Fig. 9.2. The economist assumes that the average *unit* variable cost declines initially, reflecting the fact that as output expands a firm is able to obtain bulk discounts on the purchase of raw materials and can benefit from the division of labour; this results in the labour cost per unit being reduced. The economist refers to this situation as *increasing returns to scale*. The fact that *unit* variable cost is higher at lower levels of activity causes the total cost line between points A and B in Fig. 9.1 to rise steeply. From Fig. 9.2 you can see that the *unit* variable cost levels out between output levels Q_1 and Q_2 and then gradually begins to rise. This is because the firm is operating at its most efficient output level and further economies of scale are not possible in the short term. However, beyond output level Q_2 the plant is being operated at a higher level than that for which it was intended and bottlenecks and plant breakdowns occur. The effect of this is that output per direct labour hour declines and causes the variable cost per unit to increase. The economist describes this situation as *decreasing returns to scale*.

It is the shape of the variable cost function which causes the total cost line to behave in the manner indicated in Fig. 9.1. Between points B and C the total cost line rises less steeply, indicating that the firm is operating in the range where unit variable cost is at its lowest. Between points C and D the total cost line rises more steeply as the variable cost per unit is increasing due to decreasing returns to scale.

Marginal revenue and marginal cost presentation

The normal presentation of the economists' model

Fig. 9.3 Economists' marginal revenue and marginal costs diagrams and total revenue and total costs diagrams

wards to concave upwards. Let us now compare the accountants' CVP diagram, or break-even model as it is sometimes called, with the economists' model.

The accountants' cost–volume–profit model

The diagram for the accountants' model is presented in Fig. 9.4. Note that the dashed line represents the economists' total cost function which enables a comparison to be made with the accountants' total cost function. The accountants' diagram assumes a variable cost and a selling price which are constant per unit; this results in a linear relationship for total revenue and total cost as volume changes. The effect is that there is only one break-even point in the diagram, and the profit area widens as volume increases. The most profitable output is therefore at maximum practical capacity. Clearly, the economists' model appears to be more realistic as it assumes that the total cost curve is non-linear.

Relevant range

The accountants' diagram is not intended to provide an accurate representation of total cost and total revenue throughout all ranges of output. The objective is to represent the behaviour of total cost and revenue over the range of output at which a firm expects to be operating in the future. This range of output is represented by the output range between points X and Y in Fig. 9.4. The term *relevant range* is used to refer to the output range at which the firm expects to be operating in the future and is equivalent to normal capacity which was discussed in Chapter 4. This relevant range also broadly represents the output levels which the firm has had experience of operating in the past and for which cost information is available.

You can see from Fig. 9.4 that between points X and Y the shape of the accountants' total cost

is in terms of the marginal revenue and marginal cost curves. Marginal revenue represents the increase in total revenue from the sale of one additional unit. Figure 9.3 is in two parts with the lower diagram presenting the traditional marginal revenue and marginal cost diagram; the top diagram repeats Fig. 9.1. A comparison of the two diagrams in Fig. 9.3 enables us to reconcile the traditional marginal revenue and marginal cost diagram with the total cost and total revenue presentation. Economic theory states that the profit maximizing output level is the point at which marginal cost equals marginal revenue. This occurs at point A on the lower diagram at output level Q_p. Note that in the top diagram this is the point at which the difference between the total revenue and total cost line is the greatest. The point where total revenue reaches a maximum, point B, is where marginal revenue is equal to zero.[1] Also note that the marginal cost curve reaches a minimum at point D where the total cost curve (at point C) changes from concave down-

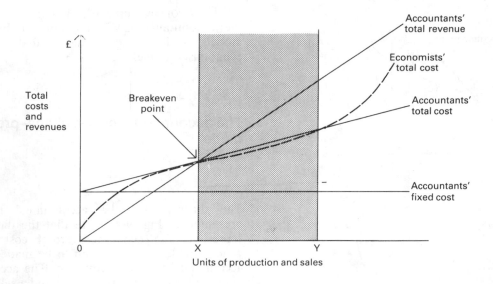

Fig. 9.4 Accountants' cost–volume–profit diagram

line is very similar to that of the economist. This is because the total cost line is only intended to provide a good approximation within the relevant production range. Within this range the accountant assumes that the variable cost per unit is the same throughout the entire range of output, and the total cost line is therefore linear. There is some empirical evidence which suggests that variable cost per unit is constant. For example, separate studies by Dean (1949) and Johnson (1972) indicate that organizations do have cost functions which are approximately linear. However, output observations were not made for very low and very high output levels; that is output outside the relevant production range. These findings suggest that cost functions are approximately linear within the relevant production range but that it is unwise to make this assumption for production levels outside the relevant range. It would be more appropriate if the accountant's total cost line was presented for the relevant range of output only, and not extended to the vertical axis or to the output levels beyond Y in Fig. 9.4.

Fixed cost function

Note also that the accountants' fixed cost function

in Fig. 9.4 meets the vertical axis at a different point to that at which the economists' total cost line meets the vertical axis. The reason for this can be explained from Fig. 9.5. The fixed cost level of OA may be applicable to, say, activity level Q_2 to Q_3, but if there was a prolonged strike or economic recession output might fall below Q_1, and this could result in redundancies and shutdowns. Therefore, fixed costs may be reduced to OB if activity falls drastically. Alternatively, additional fixed costs may be incurred if output is greater than Q_3. The fixed cost line might then consist of a series of step functions rather than the straight horizontal line depicted in Fig. 9.4. However, since the chances are very remote that activity will be less than Q_2 or greater than Q_3, the fixed costs line for output levels between Q_2 and Q_3 is extended to the left and the right; but you should remember that the point where it meets the vertical axis (that is, point A) is higher than the costs which would be incurred if the company went on a standby or caretaker basis. The fixed cost line for output levels below Q_1 (that is, OB) represents the cost of providing the basic operating capacity, and this line is the equivalent of the point where the economists' total cost line meets the vertical axis in Fig. 9.4. Because the accountant assumes that the firm will operate in the relevant range between Q_2 and Q_3, the accountants' fixed cost line OA in Fig. 9.5 represents the

Cost (£)

Relevant range

0 Q₁ Q₂ Q₃

Units of production and sales

Fig. 9.5 Accountants' fixed costs

fixed costs for the relevant output range only and does not represent the costs of providing the basic operating capacity.

Total revenue function

Let us now compare the total revenue line for the accountant and the economist. We have seen that the accountant assumes that selling price is constant over the relevant range of output, and therefore the total revenue line is a straight line. The accountants' assumption about the revenue line is a realistic one in respect of most firms which operate in industries where the short-run prices are inflexible over the relevant range of output. A further factor reinforcing the assumption of a fixed selling price is that competition may take the form of non-price rather than price competition. For example, firms may attempt to increase volume by such means as advertising, rather than by changing the selling price. Moreover, beyond the relevant range, increases in output may only be possible by offering substantial reductions in price. As it is not the intention of firms to operate outside the relevant range, the accountant makes no attempt to produce accurate revenue functions outside this range. It may be more meaningful in Fig. 9.4 if the total revenue line was presented for output levels X and Y within the relevant range, instead of being extended to the left and right of these points. For a detailed discussion reconciling the differences between the accountants' and economists' CVP analysis see Bell (1978).

Changes in fixed costs and selling prices

The accountants diagram becomes more complex when we consider the effects of changes in fixed costs or selling prices. The expansion of output beyond a certain point may require increments of fixed costs such as additional supervision and machinery, the appointment of additional sales-men and the expansion of the firm's distribution facilities. Such increases are incorporated in Fig. 9.6. Note from Fig. 9.6 that if the current output level is OQ_1, additional fixed facilities will be required if output is to be increased beyond this level. The profits for the various output levels are represented by the difference between the total cost line CDBE and the total revenue line. If the maximum sales demand is OY, profits will be less than if the maximum sales demand is OQ_1. If management is confident that sales will be in the region of OQ_2 then additional fixed facilities should be acquired to extend the output potential to a maximum of OQ_2. At this point profits are greater than at output level OQ_1. But should any further additional fixed facilities be acquired to increase output beyond OQ_2? If management considers that any output beyond OQ_3 is unlikely to be sold, a decision should be made to acquire only the additional facilities represented by the first step in the diagram as profits are greater at OQ_2 than OQ_3.

Once a decision has been made to provide a productive capacity equal to a maximum of OQ_2, a separate graph may be presented with the total cost line extended in both directions giving a total cost function of ABF. In this revised graph the step increases in fixed costs will not be included as management has already made the decision to operate in the output range between Q_1 and Q_2. The revised graph will be presented to manage-ment and can be used to demonstrate the effect of different output levels on profit. Confusion can be avoided if the total cost line is not extended in either direction outside the output range Q_1–Q_2, although Vickers (1978) argues that there may be some justification in extending the total cost line to the vertical axis (that is, to the left of OQ_1), if a step increase in fixed costs is not easy to reverse. This may occur if additional machinery is installed which can not be sold easily or which management wishes to keep to ensure that sufficient productive

Fig. 9.6 Increase in fixed costs

capacity will be available in the future.

Thus, a more complex graph may be constructed initially to assist in making output decisions, but once a decision has been made, a firm will be committed in the short term to trading conditions which are reflected in the total cost line similar to the line AB in Fig. 9.6. This total cost line, together with the appropriate fixed cost line and revenue line, may be presented in a revised graph which summarizes the decision which has previously been taken. It is this form of summary presentation which was used as a basis for comparing the accountants' and the economists' CVP presentation earlier in this chapter.

Changes in selling price

Management may also have to decide whether or not to reduce the unit selling price in order to increase output. Figure 9.7 shows the appropriate information graphically to enable such a decision to be made for a single product firm. You can see from Fig. 9.7 that in order to increase output

beyond OQ_1 the unit selling price must be reduced. This fact is illustrated by the step decline in the total revenue line from point A to point B. However, a decision to reduce the selling price must depend on an estimate of the amount by which demand will be increased as a result of the price reduction. If the firm is confident that it can sell OQ_1 at the existing selling price and a reduced selling price will only result in an increase in demand to OQ_3, profits will be higher if the selling price is not reduced. Alternatively, if the firm is confident that the sales demand will increase to OQ_2 if the selling price is reduced, profits will be higher if the price reduction is implemented.

If management decides that demand will be sufficient to warrant a reduction in the selling price a revised graph summarizing the position can be produced. This revised graph would be similar to Fig. 9.7, but with the total revenue line OA deleted, and showing the total revenue line as OBC. If we assume that price lists, advertising and price labelling of the product will be based on the decision to sell at the lower selling price, a selling price alteration may be difficult to implement in the short-term. Therefore, once the pricing decision has been made the total revenue

Fig. 9.7 The effect on output of a reduction in selling price

line OBC will be the appropriate revenue function for CVP decisions during the forthcoming period. In other words, the revised graph will represent a summary of a decision which has already been taken, and it will show top management how total costs, revenues and profits will change as output changes. Given that the cost and revenue functions have already been determined at the decision-making stage, the area of uncertainty is the actual level of output. The summary graph provides a useful representation of how costs, revenues and profits will behave according to the many possible output levels which may actually materialize.

A mathematical approach to cost–volume–profit analysis

Instead of using a diagram to present CVP information we can use mathematical relationships. The mathematical approach is a quicker and more flexible method of producing the appropriate information than the graphical approach, and is a particularly appropriate form of input to a computer financial model.

When developing a mathematical formula for producing CVP information you should note that one is assuming that selling price and costs remain constant per unit of output. Such an assumption may be valid for unit selling price and variable cost, but remember that in Chapter 2 we noted that fixed costs are a constant *total* amount whereas *unit cost* changes with output levels. As a result, profit per unit also changes with volume. For example, if fixed costs are £10,000 for a period and output is 10,000 units, the fixed cost will be £1 per unit. Alternatively, if output is 5,000 units, fixed cost will be £2 per unit. Profit per unit will not therefore be constant over varying output levels and it is incorrect to unitize fixed costs for CVP decisions.

We can develop a mathematical formula from the following relationship:

Net profit = (Units sold × unit selling price) −

$$\left[\begin{array}{c} (\text{Units sold} \times \text{Unit variable cost}) + \\ \text{Total fixed costs} \end{array} \right]$$

The following symbols can be used to represent the various items in the above equation:

NP = net profit
x = units sold
P = selling price

b = unit variable cost
a = total fixed costs

The equation can now be expressed in mathematical terms:

$$NP = Px - (a + bx)$$

CVP analysis assumes that the firm's total costs can be separated into their fixed and variable components. (We shall see in Chapter 20 that it is not often obvious which costs are fixed and which are variable, and that statistical techniques are necessary to segregate costs into their appropriate categories.)

Using the data contained in Exhibit 9.1 we can now answer the following questions:

(1) What is the output level at which Tatcher Ltd breaks even (that is, makes neither a profit or a loss)?

(2) How many units must be sold to obtain £30,000 profit?

(3) What is the profit which will result from a 10% reduction in variable costs and a £10,000 decrease in fixed costs assuming that current sales can be maintained?

(4) What is the selling price which would have to be charged to show a profit of £30,000 on sales of 8,000 units?

(5) What additional sales volume is required to meet £8,000 extra fixed charges from a proposed plant expansion?

For a more detailed discussion of further practical applications of CVP analysis, see Wilson (1972).

(1) Break-even point in units
Since $NP = Px - (a + bx)$, the break-even point is at a level of output (x) where

$$a + bx = Px - NP$$

Substituting the information in Exhibit 9.1 we have

Exhibit 9.1 Tatcher Ltd: data for cost–volume–profit example

Fixed costs per annum	£60,000
Unit selling price	£20
Unit variable cost	£10
Existing sales	8,000 units
Relevant range of output	4,000 – 12,000 units

$$60,000 + 10x = 20x - 0$$
$$\therefore 60,000 = 10x$$
$$\therefore x = 6,000 \text{ units (or £120,000 total sales at £20 per unit)}$$

An alternative method, called the *contribution margin approach*, can also be used. *Contribution margin is equal to sales minus variable expenses.* Because the variable cost per unit and the selling price per unit are assumed to be constant, the contribution margin per unit is also assumed to be constant. In Exhibit 9.1 note that each unit sold generates a contribution of £10 per unit which is available to cover fixed costs and, after they are covered, to contribute to profit. When we have obtained sufficient total contribution to cover fixed costs the break-even point is achieved, and the alternative formula is

$$\text{Break-even point in units} = \frac{\text{Fixed costs}}{\text{Contribution per unit}}$$

The contribution margin approach can be related to the mathematical formula approach; consider the penultimate line of the formula approach; it reads

$$60,000 = 10x$$
$$\therefore x = \frac{60,000}{10}$$

giving the contribution margin formula:

$$\frac{\text{Fixed costs}}{\text{Contribution per unit}}$$

The contribution margin approach is therefore a restatement of the mathematical formula, and either technique can be used; it is a matter of personal preference.

(2) Units to be sold to obtain a £30,000 profit

Using the equation NP = Px−(a + bx) and substituting the information in Exhibit 9.1, we have

$$30,000 = 20x-(60,000 + 10x)$$
$$90,000 = 10x$$
$$\therefore x = \underline{9,000 \text{ units}}$$

If we apply the contribution margin approach and wish to achieve the desired profit, we must obtain sufficient contribution to cover the fixed costs (that is, the break-even point) plus a further contribution to cover the desired profit. Hence the equation using the contribution margin approach is:

$$\text{Units sold for desired profit} = \frac{\text{Fixed costs} + \text{Desired profit}}{\text{Contribution per unit}}$$

This is merely a restatement of the penultimate line of the mathematical formula, which reads

$$90,000 = 10x$$
$$\therefore x = \frac{90,000}{10}$$

(3) Fixed costs reduced by £10,000 and a 10% reduction in variable cost

Substituting in the formula NP = Px − (a + bx), we have

$$NP = 20(8,000) − [50,000 + 9(8,000)]$$
$$\therefore NP = 160,000 − (50,000 + 72,000)$$
$$\therefore NP = \underline{£38,000}$$

(4) Selling price to be charged to show a profit of £30,000 on sales of 8,000 units

Substituting in the formula we have:

$$30,000 = 8,000P − [60,000 + 10(8,000)]$$
$$\therefore 30,000 = 8,000P − 140,000$$
$$\therefore 8,000P = 170,000$$
$$\therefore P = £21.25 \text{ (that is, an increase of £1.25 per unit)}$$

(5) Additional sales volume to meet £8,000 additional fixed charges

The contribution per unit is £10 and fixed costs will increase by £8,000. Therefore an extra 800 units must be sold to cover the additional fixed costs of £8,000.

The profit–volume ratio

This ratio is the contribution expressed as a percentage of sales:

$$\text{Profit–volume ratio} = \frac{\text{Contribution}}{\text{Sales revenue}} \times 100$$

In Exhibit 9.1 the contribution is £10 per unit and the selling price is £20 per unit; the profit–volume ratio is 50%. This means that for each £1 sale a contribution of 50 p is earned. Because we assume that selling price and contribution per unit are constant, the profit–volume ratio is also assumed to be constant. Given an estimate of total sales revenue it is possible to use the profit–volume ratio to estimate total contribution. For example, if total sales revenue is estimated to be £200,000, the total contribution will be £100,000 (50% of £200,000). To calculate the profit we deduct fixed costs of £60,000; thus a profit of £40,000 will be obtained from total sales revenue of £200,000.

Relevant range

It is vital to remember that the formulae presented in this section can only be used for decisions which apply within the relevant range. Outside this range the unit selling price and the variable cost are no longer deemed to be constant per unit and any results obtained from the formulae, which fall outside the relevant production range, will be incorrect.

Margin of safety

The margin of safety indicates by how much sales

may decrease before a company will suffer a loss. Using Exhibit 9.1 where unit selling price and variable cost were £20 and £10 respectively and fixed costs were £60,000, we noted that the break-even point was 6,000 units or £120,000 sales value. If sales are expected to be 8,000 units or £160,000, the margin of safety will be 2,000 units or £40,000. Alternatively, we can express the margin of safety in a percentage form based on the following ratio:

Percentage margin of safety

$$= \frac{\text{Expected sales} - \text{Break-even sales}}{\text{Expected sales}}$$

$$= \frac{£160,000 - £120,000}{£120,000} = 33\tfrac{1}{3}\%$$

Constructing the break-even chart

Using the data in Exhibit 9.1 we can construct the break-even chart for Tatcher Ltd (see Fig. 9.8). In constructing the graph the fixed costs are plotted as a single horizontal line at the £60,000 level. Variable costs at the rate of £10 per unit of volume are added to the fixed costs to enable the total cost line to be plotted. The total revenue line is plotted at the rate of £20 per unit of volume. The constraints of the relevant range consisting of two vertical lines are then added to the graph; beyond these lines we have little assurance that the CVP relationships are valid.

The point at which the total sales revenue line cuts the total cost line is the point where Tatcher Ltd makes neither a profit nor a loss. This is the break-even point and is 6,000 units or £120,000 total sales revenue. The distance between the total sales revenue line and the total cost line at a volume below the break-even point represents losses which will occur for various output levels below 6,000 units. Similarly, if the company operates at a volume above the break-even point, the difference between the total revenue and the total cost lines represents the profit which results from output levels above 6,000 units.

Alternative presentation of cost–volume–profit analysis

Contribution graph

In Fig. 9.8 the fixed cost line is drawn parallel to the horizontal axis and the variable cost is the difference between the total cost line and the fixed cost line. An alternative to Fig. 9.8 for the data contained in Exhibit 9.1 is illustrated in Fig. 9.9. This alternative presentation is called a contribution graph. In Fig. 9.9 the variable cost line is drawn first at £10 per unit of volume. The fixed costs are represented by the difference between the total cost line and the variable cost line. Because fixed costs are assumed to be a constant sum throughout the entire output range, a constant sum of £60,000 for fixed costs is added to the variable cost line which results in the total cost line being drawn parallel to the variable cost line. The advantage of this form of presentation is that the total contribution is emphasized in the graph, and is represented by the difference between the total sales revenue line and the total variable cost line.

Profit–volume graph

The break-even and contribution charts do not highlight the profit or loss at different volume levels. To ascertain the profit or loss figures from a break-even chart it is necessary to determine the difference between the total cost and the total revenue lines. The profit–volume graph is a more convenient method of showing the impact of changes in volume on profit. A profit–volume graph is illustrated in Fig. 9.10. The horizontal axis represents the various levels of sales volume, and the profits and losses for the period are recorded on the vertical scale. You will see from Fig. 9.10 that profits or losses are plotted for each of the various sales levels and these points are connected by a profit line. The break-even point occurs at the point where the profit line intersects the horizontal line at an output level of 6,000 units. If sales are zero, the maximum loss will be the amount of the fixed costs, as a company

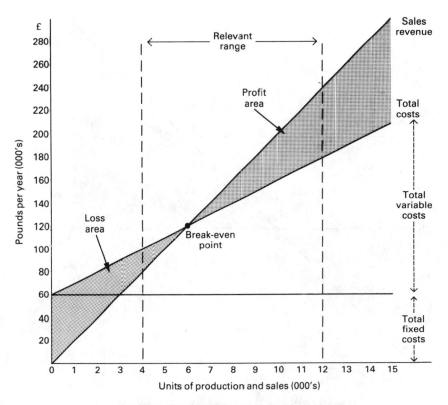

Fig. 9.8 Break-even chart for Exhibit 9.1

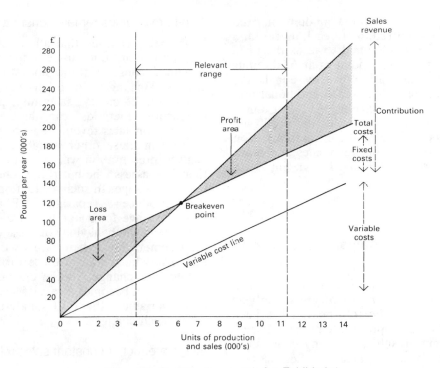

Fig. 9.9 Contribution graph for Exhibit 9.1

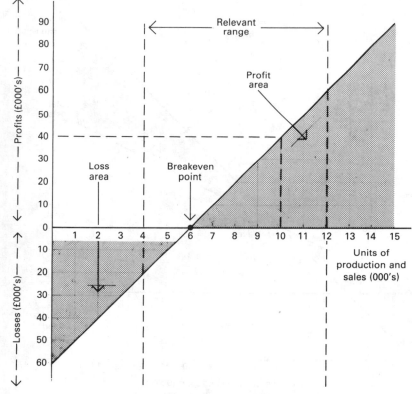

Fig. 9.10 Profit–volume graph for Exhibit 9.1

should not lose more than the amount of fixed costs which it has incurred. With each unit sold, a contribution of £10 is obtained towards the fixed costs, and the break-even point is at 6,000 units when the total contribution exactly equals the total of the fixed costs. With each additional unit sold beyond 6,000 units a surplus of £10 per unit is obtained. If 10,000 units are sold, the profit will be £40,000 (4,000 units at £10 contribution). You can see this relationship between sales and profit at 10,000 units from the dashed line in Fig. 9.10.

Cost–volume–profit analysis assumptions

It is essential that anyone preparing or interpreting CVP information is aware of the underlying assumptions on which the information has been prepared. If these assumptions are not recognized, serious errors may result and wrong conclusions may be drawn from the analysis. Let us now consider these important assumptions.

All other variables remain constant

It has been assumed that all variables other than the particular one under consideration have remained constant throughout the analysis. For example, changes in other variables such as production efficiency, sales mix, price levels and production methods can have an important influence on sales revenue and costs. If significant changes in these other variables occur the CVP analysis presentation will be incorrect.[2] One must therefore assess whether these other variables are likely to change. In such a situation all one can do is to produce a separate CVP analysis at the planning stage for a number of different assumptions about the behaviour of these other variables. Management must then base its decisions on the most likely behaviour of those variables which are subject to change. It is essential that, once management becomes aware of any changes in the other variables, the CVP analysis is altered to reflect such changes.

Single product or constant sales mix

CVP analysis assumes that either a single product

is sold, or if a range of products is sold that sales will be in accordance with a predetermined sales mix. When a predetermined sales mix is used it can be depicted in the CVP analysis by assuming average revenues and average variable costs for the given sales mix. Consider the situation described in Example 9.1.

EXAMPLE 9.1

A company sells two products — product X and product Y — and the budgeted sales are divided equally between the two products. The estimated contribution is £12 per unit for product X and £8 per unit for product Y. An analysis of the actual sales for the period indicated that 75% were for product Y and 25% were for product X. What are the break-even points for budgeted and actual sales if the annual fixed costs are £180,000? Assume tha actual costs and selling prices are identical to budget.

At the budget stage the CVP analysis will be based on an *average unit contribution* of £10 (50% × £12 + 50% × £8) but because the actual sales mix changes the actual *average unit contribution* will be £9 (25% × £12 + 75% × £8). The break-even points are as follows:

Budget = £180,000 ÷ £10 = 18,000 units
(consisting of 9,000 of X and 9,000 of Y)
Actual = £180,000 ÷ £9 = 20,000 units
(consisting of 5,000 of X and 15,000 of Y)

From these figures you will see that the break-even point is not a unique number; it varies depending on the composition of the sales mix. Because the actual sales mix is different from the budgeted sales mix the actual average unit contribution is different from that used in the budgeted break-even calculation. Thus the break-even point and the expected profits or losses at various output levels will also change. Any CVP analysis must therefore be interpreted carefully if the initial product mix assumptions do not hold. For a discussion of the application of CVP analysis in multi-product companies, where changes in product mix occur, see Anderson (1975) and Klipper (1978).

Profits are calculated on a variable costing basis

The analysis assumes that the fixed costs incurred during the period are charged as an expense for that period. Therefore variable costing profit calculations are assumed. If absorption costing profit calculations are used it is necessary to assume that production is equal to sales. If this situation does not occur the stock levels will change and the fixed overheads charged for the period will be different from the amount actually incurred during the period. Under absorption costing, only when production equals sales will the amount of fixed overhead incurred be equal to the amount of fixed overhead charged as an expense. For a discussion of how CVP analysis can be adapted to a system of absorption costing when stock levels change, see Ghosh (1980).

Total costs and total revenue are linear functions of output

The analysis assumes that the unit variable cost and the selling price are constant. For a discussion of curvilinear CVP analysis see Goggans (1965).

Analysis applies to relevant range only

Earlier in this chapter we noted that CVP analysis is appropriate only for decisions taken within the relevant production range, and that it is incorrect to project cost and revenue figures beyond the relevant range.

Application of cost–volume–profit analysis to non-manufacturing decisions

Much of the discussion in this chapter has assumed a manufacturing setting. However, CVP analysis can also be applied to non-manufacturing decisions. Consider Example 9.2.

EXAMPLE 9.2

The Recovery District General Hospital operates a separate department specifically for private health patients. In 19X0 the patients paid a fixed fee of £85 per day for the use of hospital facilities, and this fee is expected to remain unchanged for 19X1. In addition, the patients pay an extra fee to the physicians for their services. This is a private arrangement between the patient and the physician and has no effect on the finances of the hospital. For the year ending 31 December 19X0, the department

received revenue of £1,396,125 for private health care. Actual expenditure charged to the department for 19X0 was as follows:

	Basis of allocation	
	Patient-days £	Bed capacity £
Meals	220,000	
Porters' salaries		12,000
Laundry	120,000	
Laboratory	260,000	
Maintenance	37,000	
General administrative services		237,000
Other expenses	20,000	
	*657,000	249,000

(*All variable expenses)

It is estimated that all the costs will increase by 10% in 19X1. In addition rent and rates of £400,000 was charged directly to the department as it is the sole occupier of a separate building within the hospital grounds. This figure is expected to increase to £500,000 for 19X1. The salaries of the nursing staff are charged to the department at the end of the year according to the following schedule:

Annual patient-days	Nurses supplied (assumed)
Less than 7,000	3
7,000–10,000	4
10,000–13,000	5
Over 13,000	8

The average salary of the nursing staff for 19X1 is estimated at £7,000 per annum (actual for 19X0 £6,500 p.a.). The department has a maximum capacity of 60 beds but in 19X0 a number of beds were unoccupied because of insufficient demand and there have been demands from a number of parties that the department is losing money and should be closed down.

You are required to present the appropriate financial information for consideration to assist in the decision whether or not to close down the department. You are also required to indicate any additional information which should be obtianed before the final decision is taken.

The preliminary workings are as follows:

Maximum patient-days = 21,900 (365 × 60 maximum patients)
Number of patient-days for 19X0 = 16,425 (£1,396,125 ÷ £85 per day)
Unit variable cost per patient-day for 19X0 = £40 (£657,000 ÷ 16,425)

Unit variable cost per patient-day for 19X1 = £44

The financial information should include the following:

Calculation of the profit for 19X0:

		£
16,425 patient-days at a contribution of £45 per day (£85 − £40)		739,125
Less Fixed costs: Porter's salary and general admin. services	249,000	
Rent and rates	400,000	
Nursing staff	52,000	701,000
Profit:		38,125

Estimated profit for 19X1 assuming 19X0 demand:

16,425 patient-days at a contribution of £41 per day (£85 − £44)		673,425
Less Fixed costs: Meals and general admin. services	273,900	
Rent and rates	500,000	
Nursing staff	56,000	829,900
Loss:		(156,475)

Break-even point to cover all fixed costs based on a fee of £85 per day:
Minimum fixed costs: (273,900 + 500,000 + 21,000 for 3 nursing staff) £794,900
∴ Break-even point = 19,387 patient-days (794,900 ÷ £41 contribution)

This exceeds 13,000 patient days. Therefore 8 nurses must be employed to break-even.

∴ Revised fixed costs (273,900 + 500,000 + 8 nurses at £7,000 each) = £829,900
Break-even point = 20,241 patient days (829,900 ÷ 41) or 55.46 patients average throughout the year.

Break-even point to cover fixed costs specific to private department:
Relevant fixed costs = £500,000
(It is assumed that other fixed costs will still continue even if the department is closed down)
Break-even point to cover specific fixed costs is 12,195 patient-days (£500,000 ÷ £41 unit contribution) or an average of 33 patients throughout the year.

Required fee per day to break even in 19X1 (assuming 19X0 demand):
A contribution of £50.53 per patient day is required to break even:

$$\frac{£829,900}{16,425} = \frac{\text{Fixed costs}}{\text{Patient days}}$$

To obtain a contribution of £50.53 it is necessary to add the variable cost of £44 giving a fee per patient day of £94.53.

CVP analysis therefore enables the accountant to present the following information to management:

(A) There is insufficient revenue to cover a fair share of fixed costs — an average of 55 patients are required throughout the year for 19X1 and one must question whether this situation is likely to occur. (The average for 19X0 was 45 patients (16,425 ÷ 365)).

(B) To cover the short-term relevant costs the department requires an average of 33 patients if we assume that the other fixed costs will continue.

(C) The department provides an estimated contribution of £673,425 towards the fixed costs of the hospital. Assuming that the department's facilities cannot provide any alternative revenue if the department is closed down, then keeping the department open will provide a contribution of £673,425 which could not otherwise be obtained.

The following additional information should be considered before the final decision is made:

(1) What is the alternative use of the department if it is closed down? Will it lead to additional alternative revenue, or enable a better service to be offered, for example by giving more space?

(2) The non-financial benefits of closing the department should be considered even though it may not be possible to quantify them. For example, what additional service will be offered from the eight nursing staff if the department is closed?

(3) The final decision may well consider other factors, such as the political implications, but the quantitative information is one important variable to the final decision.

(4) Can the fee of £85 per day be increased? CVP analysis can be used to indicate the fee which is required to obtain a target profit level for different levels of demand.

Summary

CVP analysis is concerned with examining the relationship between changes in volume and changes in total revenue and costs. In this chapter we have compared the economists' model and the accountants' model of CVP behaviour. The major differences are that the total cost and the total revenue functions are curvilinear in the economists' model, whereas the accountants' model assumes linear relationships. However, we noted that the accountants' model was intended to predict CVP behaviour only within the relevant range, where a firm is likely to be operating on constant returns to scale. A comparison of the two models suggested that within the relevant production range the total costs and revenue functions were fairly similar. Empirical studies also indicate that, within specified output limits, organizations do have cost functions which are approximately linear.

We have seen that for decision-making a numerical presentation provides more precise information than a graphical one. Given that the cost and revenue functions will already have been determined at the decision-making stage, the major area of uncertainty relates to the actual level of output. The graphical approach provides a useful representation of how costs, revenues and profits will behave for the many possible output levels which may actually materialize.

It is essential when interpreting CVP information that you are aware of the following important assumptions on which the analysis is based:

(1) All other variables remain constant.
(2) The analysis is based on a single product or constant sales mix.
(3) Profits are calculated on a variable costing basis.
(4) Total costs and revenues are a linear function of output.
(5) The analysis applies to the relevant range only.

Finally, it must be stressed that in this chapter we have not incorporated uncertainty into the CVP analysis (CVP analysis under conditions of uncertainty will be discussed in Chapter 12).

References and further reading

Anderson, L.K. Expanded break-even analysis for a multi-product company. *Management Accounting (USA)* July 1975, 30-32.

Bell, A.L. Break-even charts versus marginal graphs. *Management Accounting (USA)* February 1969; also in *Accounting for Managerial Decision-Making*, De Coster, D.T., Ramanathan, K.V. and Sundem, G.L. Wiley, 1978, pp. 124-32.

Broster, E.J. The role of price elasticity of demand in profit planning. *Journal of Business Finance* Autumn 1971, 18-27.

Dean, J.F. Cost structures of enterprise and break-even techniques. *American Economic Review* May 1949, 150-60.

Gambling, T.E. Some observations on break-even budgeting and programming to goals. *Journal of Accounting Research* **3**(1), No. 1, Spring 1965, 159-65.

Ghosh, B.C. Fixed costs in break-even analysis. *Management Accounting* May 1980, 50-51.

Givens, H.R. An application of curvilinear break-even analysis. *The Accounting Review* **41**(1), January 1966, 141-3.

Goggans, T. Break-even analysis and curvilinear function. *The Accounting Review* October 1965.

Hartl, R.J. The linear total revenue curve in cost–volume–profit analysis. *Management Accounting* March 1975, 49-52.

Johnston, J. *Statistical Cost Accounting*. McGraw-Hill, 1972.

Klipper, H. Break-even analysis with variable product mix. *Management Accounting (USA)* April 1978, 51-4.

Manes, R. A new dimension to break-even analysis. *Journal of Accounting Research* **4**(1), Spring 1966, 87-100.

Middleton, K. A critical look at break-even analysis. *Australian Accountant* May 1980, 264-8.

Richardson, A.W. Some extensions with the application of cost–volume–profit analysis. *Cost and Management* September–October 1978, 30-35.

Singh, P.S. and Chapman, G.L. Is linear approximation good enough? *Management Accounting (USA)* January 1978, 53-5.

Solomons, D. Break-even analysis under absorption costing. In Rappaport, A. (Ed.), *Information for Decision-Making*. Prentice-Hall, 1974, pp. 100-104.

Vickers, D. On the economics of break-even. *The Accounting Review* **XXXV**(3), July 1960, 405-412; also in Anton, H.R., Firmin, P.A., Gove, H.D. (eds), *Contemporary Issues in Cost and Management Accounting*. Houghton Mifflin, 1978, pp. 272-82.

Wilson, J.D. Practical applications of cost–volume–profit analysis. In Anton, H.R. and Firmin, P.A. (Eds), *Contemporary Issues in Cost Accounting*. Houghton Mifflin, 1972, pp. 260-74.

Problems

*Indicates that a suggested solution is to be found in the *Students' Manual*.

9.1 (a) From the data given below you are required to present on graph paper a profit–volume (P/V) graph to show the expected company performance based on the budget for one year.

	£000s
Sales	600
Marginal cost	350
Fixed cost	150

Determine the break-even point and the margin of safety.

(b) Discuss briefly the limitations of a profit–volume graph.

(15 marks)
ICMA Cost Accounting 2
November 1977

9.2* ZED PLC manufactures one standard product which sells at £10.

You are required:

(a) to prepare, from the data given below, a graph showing the results for the six months ended 30 April and to determine:
 (i) the fixed costs;
 (ii) the variable cost per unit;
 (iii) the P/V ratio;
 (iv) the break-even point;
 (v) the margin of safety;

Month	Sales units	Profit/(loss) £
November	30,000	40,000
December	35,000	60,000
January	15,000	(20,000)
February	24,000	16,000
March	26,000	24,000
April	18,000	(8,000)

(b) to discuss the limitations of such a graph;
(c) to explain the use of the relevant range in such a graph.

(20 marks)
ICMA Cost Accounting 2
May 1983

9.3 (a) MC Ltd manufactures one product only, and for the last accounting period has produced the simplified profit and loss statement shown below:

Profit and loss statement

	£	£
Sales		300,000
Costs:		
Direct materials	60,000	
Direct wages	40,000	
Prime cost	100,000	
Variable production overhead	10,000	
Fixed production overhead	40,000	
Fixed administration overhead	60,000	
Variable selling overhead	40,000	
Fixed selling overhead	20,000	
		270,000
Net profit		£30,000

You are required to construct a profit–volume graph from which you should state the break-even point and the margin of safety.
(b) Based on the above, draw separate profit–volume graphs to indicate the effect on profit of each of the following:
 (i) an increase in fixed cost;
 (ii) a decrease in variable cost;
 (iii) an increase in sales price;
 (iv) a decrease in sales volume.

(25 marks)
ICMA Cost Accounting 2
November 1979

9.4 A company has decided that its profit on turnover is insufficient and, after investigation, has concluded that it must attempt to change its mix of sales.
 You are required to:
(a) to present on graph paper a profit–volume (P/V) graph to show:
 (i) the results of the budgeted sales mix for the year; and
 (ii) the expected results if the sales mix were changed to that recommended by the sales director;
(b) comment on the results shown on your graph.
 Budgeted data for the year:

	£000
Total budgeted sales value	5,000
Total fixed overhead	800

Sales of individual products

Product	Mix %	Total variable costs £000
W	40	1,500
X	10	600
Y	30	1,200
Z	20	600

Proposed budget for the year:
 The sales director is faced with severe competition in his market, so does not believe that he can increase total sales. However, he believes that if he discontinues product X, he can increase sales of the remaining products, so that the original total budgeted sales value would be unchanged. His recommendation is based on an estimate that the sales mix should be:

		%
Product:	W	40
	Y	20
	Z	40

(20 marks)
ICMA Cost Accounting 2
November 1978

9.5* XYZ Ltd produces two products and the following budget applies for 19X1:

	Product X £	Product Y £
Selling price	6	12
Variable costs	2	4
Contribution margin	4	8
Fixed costs apportioned	£100,000	£200,000
Units sold	70,000	30,000

You are required to calculate the break-even points for each product and the company as a whole and comment on your findings.

9.6* M Ltd manufactures one standard product, the standard marginal cost of which is as follows:

	£
Direct material	10.00
Direct wages	7.50
Variable production overhead	1.25
	£18.75

The budget for the year includes the following:

Output, in units		80,000
		£
Fixed overhead:	production	1,000,000
	administration	600,000
	marketing	500,000
Contribution		2,500,000

Management, in considering this budget for the coming year, is dissatisfied with the results likely to arise. A board meeting held recently discussed possible strategies to improve the situation and the following ideas were proposed:
(1) The production director suggested that the selling price of the product should be reduced by 10%. This, he feels, could increase the

output and sales by 25%. It is estimated that fixed production overhead would increase by £50,000 and fixed marketing overhead by £25,000.

(2) The finance director suggested that the selling price should be increased by 10%. It is estimated that if the current advertising expenditure of £100,000 were to be increased by £400,000, sales could be increased to

90,000 units. Fixed production overhead would increase by £25,000 and marketing overhead by £20,000.

(3) The managing director seeks a profit of £600,000. He asks what selling price is required to achieve this if it is estimated that:

an increase in advertising expenditure of £360,000 would result in a 10% increase in sales, and

fixed production overhead would increase by £25,000 and marketing overhead by £17,000.

(4) The marketing director suggested that with an appropriate increase in advertising expenditure sales could be increased by 20% and a profit on turnover of 15% obtained. It is estimated that in this circumstance fixed production overhead would increase by £40,000 and marketing overhead by £25,000. What additional expenditure on advertising would be made to achieve these results?

(5) The chairman has received an approach from a department store to supply on a long-term contract 20,000 units per annum at a special discount. Existing sales would not be affected and fixed production overhead would be increased by £50,000 per annum. How much special discount could be given if by accepting the contract the profit of the company were to be increased to £675,000 per annum?

You are required to compile a forecast profit statement for the year for each of the proposals given and comment briefly on each.

(25 marks)
ICMA Cost Accounting 2
May 1981

9.7* Fosterjohn Press Ltd is considering launching a new monthly magazine at a selling price of £1 per copy. Sales of the magazine are expected to be 500,000 copies per month, but it is possible that

the actual sales could differ quite significantly from this estimate.

Two different methods of producing the magazine are being considered and neither would involve any additional capital expenditure. The estimated production costs for each of the two methods of manufacture, together with the additional marketing and distribution costs of selling the new magazine, are summarized below:

	Method A	Method B
Variable costs	55 p per copy	50 p per copy
Specific fixed costs	£80,000 per month	£120,000 per month
Semi-variable costs		

The following estimates have been obtained:

350,000 copies	£55,000 per month	£47,500 per month
450,000 copies	£65,000 per month	£52,500 per month
650,000 copies	£85,000 per month	£62,500 per month

It may be assumed that the fixed cost content of the semi-variable costs will remain constant throughout the range of activity shown.

The company currently sells a magazine covering related topics to those that will be included in the new publication and consequently it is anticipated that sales of this existing magazine will be adversely affected. It is estimated that for every ten copies sold of the new publication, sales of the existing magazine will be reduced by one copy.

Sales and cost data of the existing magazine are shown below:

Sales	220,000 copies per month
Selling price	85 p per copy
Variable costs	35 p per copy
Specific fixed costs	£80,000 per month

Required:
(a) Calculate, for each production method, the net increase in company profits which will result from the introduction of the new magazine, at each of the following levels of activity:

500,000 copies per month
400,000 copies per month
600,000 copies per month (12 marks)

(b) Calculate, for each production method, the amount by which sales volume of the new magazine could decline from the anticipated 500,000 copies per month, before the company makes no additional profit from the introduction of the new publication.

(6 marks)
(c) Briefly identify any conclusions which may be drawn from your calculations. (4 marks)

(22 marks)
ACCA Foundation Costing
December 1980

9.8 Tweed Ltd is a company engaged solely in the manufacture of jumpers which are bought mainly for sporting activities. Present sales are direct to retailers but in recent years there has been a steady decline in output because of increased foreign competition. In the last trading year (19X1) the accounting report indicated that the company produced the lowest profit for 10 years. The forecast for 19X2 indicates that the present deterioration in profits is likely to continue. The company considers that a profit of £80,000 should be achieved to provide an adequate return on capital. The managing director has asked that a review be made of the present pricing and marketing policies. The marketing director has completed this review and passes the proposals on to you for evaluation and recommendation, together with the profit and loss account for year ending 31 December 19X1.

Tweed Ltd profit and loss account for year ending 31 December 19X1

	£	£	£
Sales revenue (100,000 jumpers at £10)			1,000,000
Factory cost of goods sold:			
Direct materials	100,000		
Direct labour	350,000		
Variable factory overheads	60,000		
Fixed factory overheads	220,000	730,000	
Administration overhead		140,000	
Selling and distribution overhead:			
Sales commission (2% of sales)	20,000		
Delivery costs (variable per unit sold)	50,000		
Fixed costs	40,000	110,000	980,000
Profit			20,000

The information to be submitted to the managing director includes the following three proposals:

(i) To proceed on the basis of analyses of market research studies which indicate that the demand for the jumpers is such that a 10% reduction in selling price would increase demand by 40%.

(ii) To proceed with an enquiry which the marketing director has had from a mail order company about the possibility of purchasing 50,000 units annually if the selling price is right. The mail order company would transport the jumpers from Tweed Ltd to its own warehouse and no sales commission would be paid on these sales by Tweed Ltd. However, if an acceptable price can be negotiated, Tweed Ltd would be expected to contribute £60,000 per annum towards the cost of producing the mail order catalogue. It

would also be necessary for Tweed Ltd to provide special additional packaging at a cost of £0.50 per jumper. The marketing director considers that in 19X2 the sales from existing business would remain unchanged at 100,000 units based on a selling price of £10 if the mail order contract is undertaken.

(iii) To proceed on the basis of a view held by the marketing director that a 10% price reduction, together with a national advertising campaign costing £30,000 may increase sales to the maximum capacity of 160,000 jumpers.

Required:
(a) The calculation of break-even sales value based on the 19X1 accounts.
(b) A financial evaluation of proposal (i) and a calculation of the number of units Tweed Ltd would require to sell at £9 each to earn the target profit of £80,000.
(c) A calculation of the minimum prices which would require to be quoted to the mail order company, first, to ensure that Tweed Ltd would, at least, break even on the mail order contract, second, to ensure that the same overall profit is earned as proposal (i) and, third, to ensure that the overall target profit is earned.
(d) A financial evaluation of proposal (iii).

9.9 (a) A break-even chart is depicted on p. 192 for Windhurst Ltd.
You are required:
 (i) to identify the components of the break-even chart labelled p, q, r, s, t, u, v, w, x, and y (5 marks),
 (ii) to suggest what events are represented at the values of x which are labelled m and n on the chart (3 marks),
 (iii) to assess the usefulness of break-even analysis to the senior management of a small company (7 marks).
(b) Hackett Ltd produces gudgeons and bludgeons. The company's budget for 1981 includes the following data:

	Gudgeons	Bludgeons
Unit selling price	£10	£5
Contribution margin ratio	40%	60%

The budget is designed to show a figure of profit or loss for each product, after apportioning joint fixed costs of £100,000 in proportion to the number of units of each product sold. For 1981 gudgeons are budgeted to show a profit of £14,000, and bludgeons a loss of £2,000. The number of units of each product sold is expected to be equal.

You are required to write a report to the managing director of Hackett Ltd advising him on

the basis of the information given whether to implement any of the following three proposals:
(i) to increase the price of bludgeons by 25%, in the expectation that the price elasticity of demand over this range of prices will be unity (4 marks),
(ii) to make changes to the production process which would reduce the joint fixed costs by 12½% and increase the variable costs of each product by 10% (3 marks),
(iii) to introduce both of the above changes (3 marks).

ICAEW Management Accounting
December 1980

9.10* Mr Belle has recently developed a new improved video cassette and shown below is a summary of a report by a firm of management consultants on the sales potential and production costs of the new cassette.

Sales potential
The sales volume is difficult to predict and will vary with the price, but it is reasonable to assume that at a selling price of £10 per cassette, sales would be between 7,500 and 10,000 units per month. Alternatively, if the selling price was reduced to £9.00 per cassette sales would be between 12,000 and 18,000 units per month.

Production costs
If production is maintained at or below 10,000 units per month, then variable manufacturing costs would be approximately £8.25 per cassette and fixed costs £12,125 per month. However, if production is planned to exceed 10,000 units per month, then variable costs would be reduced to £7.75 per cassette, but the fixed costs would increase to £16,125 per month.

Mr Belle has been charged £2,000 for the report by the management consultants and, in addition, he has incurred £3,000 development costs on the new cassette.

If Mr Belle decides to produce and sell the new cassette it will be necessary for him to use factory premises which he owns, but are leased to a colleague for a rental of £400 per month. Also he will resign from his current post in an electronics firm where he is earning a salary of £1,000 per month.

Required:
(a) Identify in the question an example of
 (i) an opportunity cost,
 (ii) a sunk cost. (3 marks)

(b) Making whatever calculations you consider appropriate, analyse the report from the consultants and advise Mr Belle of the potential profitability of the alternatives shown in the report.

Any assumptions considered necessary or matters which may require further investigation or comment should be clearly stated.

(19 marks)
(22 marks)

ACCA Level 1 Costing
December 1983

9.11 (a) The current average weekly trading results of the Swish Restaurant in Sumtown are shown below:

	£	£
Turnover		2,800
Operating costs:		
Materials	1,540	
Power	280	
Staff	340	
Building occupancy costs	460	
		2,620
Profit		£180

The average selling price of each meal is £4; materials and power may be regarded as a variable cost varying with the number of meals provided. Staff costs are semi-variable with a fixed cost element of £200 per week; the building occupancy costs are all fixed.

Required:

Calculate the number of meals required to be sold in order to earn a profit of £300 per week. (3 marks)

(b) The owners of the restaurant are considering expanding their business and using under-utilized space by diversifying into:

either (1) take away foods
or (2) high quality meals

The estimated sales and costs of each proposal are shown below:

	Take away foods	High quality meals
Sales volume, per week	720 meals	200 meals
	£	£
Average selling price, per meal	1.60	6.00
Variable costs, per meal	0.85	4.66
Incremental fixed costs, per week	610.00	282.00

The sales estimate for both of the above proposals is rather uncertain and it is recognized that actual sales volume could be up to 20% either higher or lower than that estimated.

If either of the above proposals were implemented it has been estimated that the existing restaurant's operations would be affected as follows:

(i) As a result of bulk purchasing, material costs incurred would be reduced by 10 p per meal. This saving would apply to all meals produced in the existing restaurant.

(ii) Because more people would be aware of the existence of the restaurant it is estimated that turnover would increase. If the 'take-away food' section were opened then for every ten take-away meals sold the existing restaurant's sales would increase by one meal; alternatively if the 'high quality meals' section were opened then for every five such meals sold the existing restaurant's sales would increase by one meal.

A specific effect of implementing the 'take-away food' proposal would be a change in the terms of employment of the staff in the existing restaurant, the result of which would be that the staff wage of £340 per week would have to be regarded as a fixed cost.

Required:

Calculate, for each of the proposed methods of diversification:

(i) The additional profit which would be earned by the owners of the restaurant if the estimated sales were achieved. (8 marks)

(ii) The sales volume at which the owners of the restaurant would earn no additional profit from the proposed diversification. (5 marks)

(c) Carefully consider the conclusions which may be drawn from your calculations in (b) above.

(6 marks)
(22 marks)

ACCA Level 1 Costing
June 1982

9.12 (a) Stoic Ltd manufactures wooden and plastic garden furniture of three types. It is considering possible amendments to its pricing and production policies.

Stoic prepares profit and loss statements by product line. Costs are segregated into fixed and variable categories, and a full-cost absorption system is used to allocate overheads and indirect costs to product lines. The allocations are made

consistently from period to period on a variety of bases, according to what has been accepted as equitable in the past.

For the quarter to 31 March 1980 the budgeted figures are as follows (in £):

'Total' basis	Benches	Chairs	Tables
Sales	50,400	88,000	72,000
Cost of sales	56,000	74,000	28,200
Gross profit (loss)	(5,600)	14,000	43,800
Operating and distribution costs	11,000	16,880	11,900
Operating profit (loss)	(16,600)	(2,880)	31,900
'Unit' basis			
Selling price	14.00	22.00	30.00
Direct variable costs:			
Cost of sales	13.00	12.00	6.00
Operating and distribution	2.00	2.40	2.50
Allocated costs:			
Cost of sales	2.56	6.50	5.75
Operating and distribution	1.06	1.82	2.46

Little variation is expected in the inventories of raw materials, work-in-progress, or finished goods during the quarter. You have been retained as a consultant to advise Stoic's board on its policies relating to pricing and production.

You are required to determine as accurately as possible the effect on Stoic's financial performance of each in turn of the following five independent proposals (i.e. assuming that everything not specified in the particular proposal remains the same):

 (i) the product line Benches is discontinued; (2 marks)

 (ii) the product line Benches is discontinued with a consequential decrease of 400 units in the sales of product line Tables; (3 marks)

 (iii) the selling price of product line Benches is increased to £16.00 per unit, with a consequential decrease of one-sixth in the number of Benches sold; (3 marks)

 (iv) the product line Benches is discontinued, and the plant used to make a replacement new product line, Garden Gnomes. Expected sales of Garden Gnomes would be 3,200 sets at a price of £19.00 per set. The variable cost of sales would be £12.00 per set, and the variable operating and distribution costs would be £4.10 per set. The total overhead and indirect costs previously allocated to product line Benches would be allocated to product line Garden Gnomes; (3 marks)

 (v) part of the plant in which the product line Benches is made is adapted to make product line Chairs. The output and sales of Chairs would be increased to 5,000 units (each sold at a unit price of £21.00), and the output and sales of Benches reduced to 2,400 units (each sold at a unit price of £17.00).

(4 marks)

(b) the Epicure Private Nursing Home budgets are as follows for 1980:

No. of beds available	80 per day
Inpatientdays	26,000 per annum

Fees (£) Inpatient			
fees	1,300,000		

Costs (£)	Variable	Fixed	Total
Direct supplies	100,000		100,000
Direct salaries	800,000		800,000
Patient service			
overhead	58,000	102,000	160,000
Administration	108,000	150,000	258,000
	1,066,000	252,000	1,318,000

You are required to calculate:

(i) the contribution margin ratio; (2 marks)
(ii) the break-even point in both inpatient-days and inpatient fees; (2 marks)
(iii) the margin of safety ratio (to two places of decimals) if the Home operates at full capacity; (2 marks)
(iv) the break-even point in inpatient days if direct salaries were increased to £826,000, making total variable costs £1,092,000, all matters not specified remaining the same; (2 marks) and
(v) the break-even point in inpatient days if fixed patient service overheads were increased to £120,000, making total fixed costs £270,000, all other matters remaining the same (2 marks).

ICAEW Management Accounting
(December 1979)

9.13 At the initial planning meeting of Walton Ltd it was tentatively agreed that the sales mix in the forthcoming year would result in each of the three products generating the following proportions of total sales revenues:

Product	Percentage of sales revenue produced %
A	20
B	20
C	60
	100

Utilizing the above figures the management accountant produced a budgeted product profitability report on a full cost basis as follows:

	Product					
	A £	B £	C £			
Sales price, per unit	10	20	25			
Cost, per unit						
direct material	1.5	2.0	6.0			
Direct labour	1.0	2.0	2.5			
Variable overhead	3.0	4.0	4.0			
Fixed overhead	1.0	2.0	8.0			
Depreciation:						
General	–	1.0	3.0			
Variable	1.5	1.5	4.0	5.0	–	3.0
Total costs, per unit	8.0	15.0	23.5			
Profit, per unit	£2.0	£5.0	£1.5			

The management accountant's explanation of the report included the following:
(i) The report is based on total sales of £5

million, which is the best estimate of sales for the forthcoming year.
(ii) Sales and production are intended to be equal, and hence there will be no change in the stock levels.
(iii) Planned production and sales are in total less than normal capacity and so the figures utilized in the product profitability report will lead, at the level of sales on which the report is based, to an under-recovery of fixed production overheads as follows:

	£
Fixed overheads	70,000
General depreciation	20,000

(iv) Apart from the planned under-recovery mentioned above, all production overheads are included in the product profitability report.
(v) 'General' depreciation is the time based depreciation of production machinery and is independent of activity levels. 'Variable' depreciation is the depletion of rights purchased 3 years ago which entitle Walton to produce products A and B which are patented in the USA. These rights entitle Walton to produce an agreed limited number of products A and B over a further seven years; however, at current and planned rates of production, the quantity limit will be exhausted within three or four years.
(vi) Non-production overheads are excluded from the report. These amount to:

	£
Salaries	140,000
Accommodation expenses	40,000
Depreciation of office buildings (in accordance with SSAP 12)	70,000

(vii) Apart from depreciation all other expenses involve cash flow.

(viii) Following an agreement with trade union representatives concerning guaranteed payments to production workers, it is decided to treat the labour costs inherent in this original plan as a fixed cost.

The managing director is concerned that the plans rely heavily on product C which has the lowest profit per unit and asks whether it would be possible to reduce the dependence on product C. The marketing manager feels that total sales value will be unaltered if the sales mix were changed, with less emphasis on C and more on the profitable product B, and suggests that the following production and sales mix would be feasible:

Product	Percentage of sales revenue produced %
A	20
B	50
C	30

This alternative will not alter selling price or variable costs per unit and fixed costs will also be unaltered. The marketing manager is reluctant, for competitive and strategic reasons, to reduce the sales revenue of any product below 20% of total sales.

The managing director states, 'Walton needs profit and cash flow; therefore I hope both the original and revised plans provide these'.

Required:
(a) Calculate the profit and cash flow implied by the original plan. (6 marks)
(b) (i) Calculate the sales required in order that the revised plan produces a profit and cash flow equal to that derived in (a) above. (6 marks)
 (ii) Advise Walton of the best plan to pursue if the objective is to maximize
 (1) profit
 (2) cash flow. (2 marks)
(c) List and comment on the three major practical difficulties in the analysis you have pursued above. To what extent do these deficiencies reduce the usefulness of your results?

(6 marks)
(Total 20 marks)
ACCA P2 Management Accounting December 1981

9.14 The product range of Cotten Ltd consists of three product lines. The estimates of some variable costs, sales prices and the tentative activity levels for the forthcoming year are:

	Product		
	K	L	M
Production and sales— units (000s)	50	40	40
Per unit details	£	£	£
Sales price	10	15	20
Costs: Labour	2	2	6
Materials	1	3	3
Delivery costs	2	1	3

There will be no opening stocks of any product at the beginning of the year and it is intended that sales will equal production.

In addition to the above costs there is also expected to be variable production overhead, which will be 50% of the direct labour cost, and the following production and non-production overheads:

	(£000s)
(i) Assembly area occupancy costs	60
(ii) Operating and depreciation costs of production machinery	50
(iii) Other production overheads	234
(iv) Selling expenses	85
(v) Administrative expenses	95
(vi) Advertising costs	76

Apart from cost (iii), all of costs (i)–(vi) are fixed and cannot be reduced or avoided unless all activity ceases. Costs (iv)–(vi) will not increase over the feasible range of activity levels and costs (i)–(iii) will only increase if additional factory capacity and machinery are installed. 'Other production overheads' comprise some costs specific to a particular product line and some general production overheads; none of these costs depend on the level of activity except that the specific production overheads for each product could be avoided if production of that product ceased entirely.

The managing director feels that as all Cotten's activities are caused by the three product types, all costs should be allocated between those products and this would enable a useful product profitability report to be prepared.

In the discussions between the managing director and the management accountant concerning the problems of apportioning the fixed costs to individual products, the following points emerge:
(i) The tentative plans imply the following proportional usage of the factory space used in the assembly function and of the production machinery:

	% of total usage		
	K	L	M
Assembly capacity	50	40	10
Production machinery	10	30	60

The proposed activity levels leave little assembly and machinery capacity unused. Any increase or decrease in activity levels will cause a corresponding increase or decrease in assembly and machinery usage.

(ii) Selling expenses relate to salaries and other costs of sales staff. It is generally agreed among sales staff that although each *unit* of K and L is equally difficult to sell, it requires twice the time and effort to sell each *unit* of M.

(iii) The 'other production overheads' which are specific to each product are:

(£000s)

K	30
L	15
M	5

(iv) Those 'other production overheads' which are not specific to any one product line are thought to be difficult to apportion. However, it is suggested that apportionment in accordance with variable production costs is likely to be the most suitable method.

(v) Administrative expenses and advertising costs relate to all activities and are not specific to any product line. The suggested method of apportionment is in accordance with sales revenues.

The managing director points out that although the tentative plans are likely to be adhered to it is possible that these will be changed following a further planning meeting. At this further planning meeting it may be decided to increase the activity of some products, and perhaps reduce or cease production of others, in order to increase the expected profit. However, any increase in activity may cause the constraint on assembly capacity or production machinery to become operative.

Required:

(a) Provide, preferably in a single statement in tabular form, the following:
 (i) the profit of each product line calculated in accordance with the wishes of the managing director, and
 (ii) information which will be useful at the forthcoming planning meeting in assisting any discussions concerning expansion, contraction or cessation of product lines.
 (10 marks)

(b) Use the information produced in (a) above to
 (i) show separately for each product line the effect on profit of
 (a) a 10% increase in activity, and

(b) complete cessation of that product line, and

(ii) rank the products in order of their desirability from the viewpoint of maximizing profit under conditions where the constraints on
 (a) assembly capacity, and
 (b) production machinery
are *separately* operative. Assume all three product lines are produced.
 (5 marks)

(c) Using the tentative plans show the cost per unit of each product for the purposes of stock valuation in accordance with the absorption costing approach of SSAP 9 to be used in the event of any stock remaining at the year end.

Explain, but do not attempt to calculate, the effect of any change in activity levels on the per unit stock valuation figures derived. Give an example of one major factor which could alter the per unit stock valuation figures in the context of Cotten's plans and cost structures.
 (5 marks)
 (20 marks)

ACCA P2 Management Accounting
December 1980

9.15* Shown on the next page is a typical cost-volume-profit chart.

Required:

(a) Explain to a colleague who is not an accountant the reasons for the change in result on the above cost–volume–profit chart from a loss at point (a) to a profit at point (b).
 (3 marks)

(b) Identify and critically examine the underlying assumptions of the above type of cost–volume–profit analysis and consider whether such analyses are useful to the management of an organization
 (14 marks)
 (17 marks)

ACCA Level 1 Costing
June 1983

9.16* The graphs on the next page show cost-volume-profit relationships as they are typically represented in (i) management accounting, and (ii) economic theory. In each graph TR = total revenue, TC = total cost, and P = profit.

(i) Management accounting (ii) Economic theory

You are required to compare these different representations of cost–volume–profit relationships identifying, explaining and commenting on points of similarity and also differences (15 marks).

ICAEW Management Accounting
December 1981

9.17* 'A break-even chart must be interpreted in the light of the limitations of its underlying assumptions . . .' (From *Cost Accounting: a managerial*

9.15

9.16

(i) Management Accounting

(ii) Economic Theory

emphasis by C.T. Horngren.)

Required:

(a) discuss the extent to which the above state-ment is valid and both describe and briefly appraise the reasons for *five* of the most important underlying assumptions of break-even analysis.

(c. 14 marks)

(b) For any *three* of the underlying assumptions provided in answer to (a) above, give an example of circumstances in which that assumption is violated. Indicate the nature of the violation and the extent to which the breakeven chart can be adapted to allow for this violation.

(c. 6 marks)
(Total 20 marks)
ACCA P2 Management Accounting
December 1979

9.18* The accountant's approach to cost–volume–profit analysis has been criticized in that, among other matters, it does not deal with the following:

(a) situations where sales volume differs radically from production volume;

(b) situations where the sales revenue and the total cost functions are markedly non-linear;

(c) changes in product mix;

(d) risk and uncertainty.

Explain these objections to the accountant's conventional cost–volume–profit model and suggest how they can be overcome or ameliorated.

(17 marks)
ACCA Level 2 Management Accounting
December 1982

10 Measuring costs and benefits for decision-making

In Chapter 1 we examined a general model for decision-making, and noted that a decision involves a choice between various alternative courses of action to accomplish some objective or goal. Consequently, a prerequisite for the decision-making process is to identify the objectives of the organization so that the decision-maker can assess the desirability of chosing one course of action instead of another. We noted that there is considerable controversy about what the objectives of particular firms are or should be, but the view adopted was that firms generally seek to maximize the present value of future cash flows (that is, present value of future cash inflows less present value of future cash outflows). The implication of this objective is that a firm should identify and select those opportunities which will maximize future cash flows.

To ensure that those opportunities which will result in the maximization of future cash flows are selected it is necessary to measure the cash inflows (benefits) and cash outflows (costs) for each opportunity. In this chapter we will consider how costs and benefits of potential opportunities should be measured to maximize future cash flows. In particular we shall consider the measurement of relevant *costs* for decision-making, but note that similar principles should be applied to measure *benefits*

(that is, sales revenue). In Chapter 11 we shall also take into account pricing and marketing considerations.

We assume, for this chapter, that future costs and benefits are known with certainty; decision-making under conditions of uncertainty will be considered in Chapter 12. In addition, our discussion will be restricted to measuring costs and benefits for short-term or operating decisions. The added problems which apply in respect of long-term decisions will be considered in Chapters 13 and 14.

We begin by introducing the concept of relevant cost and applying this principle to the following decision-making problems:

(1) dropping a segment,
(2) special selling price decisions,
(3) decision-making and the influence of limiting factors,
(4) make or buy decisions,
(5) replacement of equipment decisions.

We shall then consider in more detail the specific problems which arise in assessing the relevant costs of materials and labour, and conclude with a comprehensive decision-making problem which consolidates the various aspects of financial information which are required for decision making.

Measuring relevant costs and benefits

The relevant costs and benefits required for decision making are only those which will be affected by the decision. Costs and benefits which are independent of a decision are obviously not relevant and need not be considered when making

that decision. The relevant financial inputs for decision-making purposes are therefore *future cash flows which will differ between the various alternatives being considered*. In other words, only differential (or incremental) cash flows should be

taken into account and cash flows which will be the same for all alternatives are irrelevant. For example, let us consider a situation where an individual is uncertain as to whether he should purchase a monthly rail ticket to travel to work or whether he should use his car. Assuming that the individual will keep his car, whether or not he travels to work by train, the cost of his road fund licence and insurance will be irrelevant since these costs remain the same irrespective of his mode of travel. The cost of his petrol will, however, be relevant as this cost will vary depending on which method of transport he chooses. Let us now move on to consider an example in a business environment.

EXAMPLE 10.1

A company is considering the alternatives of either purchasing a component from an outside supplier or producing the component itself. The estimated costs to the company of producing the component are as follows:

	£
Direct labour	100
Direct materials	300
Variable overheads	50
Fixed overheads	100
	550

The outside supplier has quoted a figure of £500 for supplying the component. Should the company buy or make the component?

The comparative cost statements for the two alternatives are as follows:

	Company to manufacture component £	Company to purchase component £
Direct labour	100	–
Direct material	300	–
Variable overhead	50	–
Fixed overheads	100	100
Suppliers purchase price	–	500
	550	600

It is assumed in this example that the share of fixed overheads apportioned to the component will still be incurred whether or not the company purchases the component from an outside supplier. Fixed overheads are therefore irrelevant in deciding which alternative to choose. It is also assumed that the company will not incur the direct

labour, material and variable overhead costs if the component is purchased from the outside supplier; these costs will be different depending on which alternative is chosen and are therefore relevant in making the decision. The supplier's purchase price is also a relevant cost as it will be different for each of the alternatives. We should therefore present the cost statements for the two alternatives using only relevant costs as follows:

	Company to manufacture component	Company to purchase component
Direct labour	100	–
Direct materials	300	–
Variable overheads	50	–
Suppliers purchase price	–	500
	450	500

It is important that great care is taken in presenting financial information for decision making. If, in Example 10.1, the company had produced the same component in the previous period then the component would be valued at £550 for stock valuation as all manufacturing costs should be taken into account when stock is valued. For decision-making purposes only future costs that will be relevant to the decision should be included. *Costs accumulated for stock valuation purposes must not therefore be used for decision-making purposes.*

When you are trying to establish which costs are relevant to a particular decision you may find that some costs will be relevant in one situation but irrelevant in another. In Example 10.1 direct labour was considered to be a relevant cost, based on the assumption that the company will hire additional labour on a casual basis to produce the component. But now consider what the relevant labour cost will be if the company has a temporary excess supply of labour and intends to obtain the necessary labour hours from its existing labour force at no extra cost? In this situation the labour cost will be the same whichever alternative is chosen and will not be a relevant cost.

Let us now take the example a stage further: direct materials will not be a relevant cost if the company has purchased the materials in the past and now finds that they are surplus to requirements. If the materials have no alternative use and cannot be sold then the cost will be the same irrespective of which alternative is chosen. Therefore the cost of direct materials is not a relevant

cost in this situation.

The above examples show that the identification of relevant costs depends on the circumstances. In one situation a cost may be relevant but in another situation the same cost may not be relevant. It is not therefore possible to provide a list of costs which would be relevant in particular situations. In each situation you should follow the principle that *the relevant costs are future costs that differ among alternatives*. It is necessary that the accountant should be aware of all the circumstances under which a decision will be taken and ascertain full details of the changes that will result from the decision, and then proceed to select the relevant financial information to present to management.

Quantitative and qualitative factors

In many situations it is difficult to quantify in monetary terms all the important elements of a decision. Those factors which can be expressed in monetary terms only with much difficulty or imprecision are classified as *qualitative factors*. It is essential that qualitative factors are brought to the attention of management during the decision-making process, as otherwise there may be a danger that a wrong decision will be made. For example, the cost of manufacturing a component internally may be more expensivve than purchasing from an outside supplier. However, the decision to purchase from an outside supplier could result in the closing down of the company's facilities for manufacturing the component. The effect of such a decision might lead to redundancies and a decline in employees' morale which could affect future output. In addition the company will become dependent on an outside supplier, who may not always deliver on time. The company may not then be in a position to meet customers' requirements. In turn this could result in a loss of customer goodwill and a decline in future sales.

It may not be possible to quantify in monetary terms the effect of a decline in employees' morale or loss of customer goodwill but the accountant in such circumstances should present the relevant quantifiable financial information and draw attention to those qualitative items which may have an impact on future profitability.[1]

In circumstances such as those given in the above example, management must estimate the likelihood of the supplier failing to meet the company's demand for future supplies and the likely effect on customer goodwill if there is a delay in meeting orders. If the component can be obtained from many suppliers and repeat orders for the company's products are unlikely then the company may give little weighting to these qualitative factors. Alternatively, if the component can be obtained from only one supplier and the company relies heavily on repeat sales to existing customers, then the qualitative factors will be of considerable importance. In the latter situation the company may consider that the quantifiable cost savings from purchasing the component from an outside supplier are insufficient to cover the risk of the qualitative factors occurring.

Let us now move on to apply the relevant cost approach to a variety of decision-making problems.

Dropping a segment

A segment consists of a product, type of customer, geographical region or any other part of a firm that can be considered for expansion or reduction. A simple example is that of an organization which sells its products through different sales territories, where one or more of the territories is being evaluated with the possibility of being dropped. Let us consider the following example.

EXAMPLE 10.2

National Ltd is a wholesaler who sells its products to a wide range of retailers. Marketing is done through three geographical areas: the South, the Midlands and the North. The estimates of the costs and revenues for each sales territory for the next accounting period are as follows:

	South £	Midlands £	North £	Total £
Sales	800,000	900,000	900,000	2,600,000
Cost of goods sold	400,000	450,000	500,000	1,350,000
Gross profit	400,000	450,000	400,000	1,250,000

	South £		Midlands £		North £	Total £	
Selling costs:							
Salesmen's salaries	80,000		100,000		120,000		
Sales office and manage-ment expenses	40,000		60,000		80,000		
Advertising	50,000		50,000		50,000		
Salesmens' expenses	50,000	220,000	60,000	270,000	80,000	330,000	
Headquarters administration expenses		80,000		90,000		90,000	
Warehousing costs		32,000		36,000		36,000	
Total costs		332,000		396,000		456,000	1,184,000
Net profit (or loss)		68,000		54,000		(56,000)	66,000

The products are packaged and despatched from a central warehouse and it is estimated that 50% of the costs are variable and the remainder are fixed. All of the selling costs are fixed with the exception of salesmens' expenses which are variable with sales revenue. All of the administration expenses of the headquarters are common and unavoidable to all alternatives and have been apportioned to sales territories on the basis of sales value. In view of the loss should the North area be closed?

Let us examine the position if it is decided that the North area should be closed. The cost and revenue estimates for the area indicate that the cost of sales, all of the selling costs and the variable warehousing costs will be different, and therefore *relevant*. The warehousing and admin-istration fixed costs will still continue and are *irrelevant*. It is assumed that all the fixed selling costs will be eliminated if the North area is closed and that the cost of goods sold does not include any fixed costs. We can now list the relevant costs and revenues for the North area.

		£
Sales revenue		900,000
Less Relevant costs:		
Cost of goods sold	500,000	
Selling costs	330,000	
Warehousing variable costs	18,000	848,000
Excess of relevant revenues over relevant costs		52,000

You can see from this calculation that future cash flows will decline by £52,000 if the North area is closed because the company will lose a contribu-tion of £52,000 towards the administration and warehousing fixed costs. Whenever a segment of a business can provide a contribution towards meet-ing common and unavoidable (general) fixed costs it should not be closed or dropped, always assuming that the facilities have no alternative use, which would yield a higher contribution, and that the sales in the other segments are unaffected by the decision. The projected profit statements if the North area is closed are as follows:

	South £		Midland £		Total £
Sales		800,000		900,000	1,700,000
Less Variable costs:					
Cost of goods sold	400,000		450,000		
Salesmens' expenses	50,000		60,000		
Warehousing costs	16,000	466,000	18,000	528,000	994,000
Contribution		334,000		372,000	706,000
Less Specific fixed costs:					
Salesmens' salaries	80,000		100,000		
Sales office and management expenses	40,000		60,000		
Advertising	50,000	170,000	50,000	210,000	380,000
Contribution to general fixed costs		164,000		162,000	326,000
Less General fixed costs:					
Administration	260,000				
Warehouse	52,000				312,000
Net profit					14,000

Total profit is reduced by £52,000. You may have noted that the presentation of this profit statement is different to that shown in Example 10.2. This alternative presentation shows the effect of eliminating a segment by emphasizing the difference between the relevant costs and relevant revenues on the line labelled 'Contribution to general fixed costs'. If the information in Example 10.2 had been presented in this way, the attention of management would have been drawn to the fact that the North area is making a contribution towards the general fixed costs. Consequently profits will be increased or losses reduced by continuing to sell in the North area.

The discussion earlier in this chapter may have given the impression that relevant costs consist only of variable costs. However, Example 10.2 shows that some fixed costs may change when a particular alternative is being considered and can become relevant costs. It can be stated, however, as a general rule that *common and unavoidable fixed costs which are allocated to cost objectives on the basis of apportionments are not relevant for decision-making purposes*.

Special selling-price decisions

EXAMPLE 10.3

A company produces a single product and has budgeted for the production of 100,000 units during the next quarter. The cost estimates for the quarter are as follows:

	£
Direct labour	600,000
Direct materials	200,000
Variable overheads	200,000
Fixed overheads	400,000
	1,400,000

The company has received orders for 80,000 units during the coming period at the generally accepted market price of £18 per unit. It appears unlikely that orders will be received for the remaining 20,000 units at a selling price of £18 per unit but a customer is prepared to purchase the remaining 20,000 units at a selling price of £12 per unit. Should the company accept the offer?

At first sight it would appear that the company should reject the offer as the estimated costs of producing 100,000 units are £1,400,000, or £14 per unit. A study of the cost estimates, however, indicates that the fixed overheads of £400,000 will remain the same irrespective of whether or not the order is accepted. We shall assume that the company has not committed itself to paying £600,000 for direct labour and can hire sufficient labour to produce only 80,000 units if necessary. The labour cost will therefore be £6 per unit giving a total of £480,000 if 80,000 units are produced. Direct materials and variable overheads will also be proportionately reduced if only 80,000 units are produced. These variable costs are therefore relevant costs as they will be different, depending on whether the special order is accepted. We can now compare the estimated relevant costs with the relevant revenues if the order for 20,000 units is accepted:

		£	£
Additional revenue (20,000 units at £12)			240,000
Less Relevant costs: Direct labour			
(£6 per unit)	120,000		
Direct materials			
(£2 per unit)	40,000		
Variable overheads			
(£2 per unit)	40,000	200,000	
Excess of relevant revenues over relevant			
costs (i.e. contribution)			40,000

The company will obtain a contribution towards fixed overheads of £40,000 and this will increase profits by £40,000 as is shown in the following profit statement:

	Order not accepted (80,000 units)		Order accepted	
Sales	1,440,000	(80,000 × £18)		1,680,000
Less Variable cost of sales:				
Direct labour	480,000		600,000	
Direct material	160,000		200,000	
Variable overheads	160,000	800,000	200,000	1,000,000

Contribution	640,000	680,000
Less fixed overheads	400,000	400,000
Profit	240,000	280,000

Two important factors must be considered before recommending acceptance of the order. First, it is assumed that the future selling price will not be affected by selling the 20,000 units to a specific customer at a price below the going market price. If this assumption is incorrect, then competitors may engage in similar practices of reducing their selling prices in an attempt to unload spare capacity. This may lead to a fall in the market price which in turn would lead to a fall in profits from *future* sales. The loss of future profits may be greater than the short-term gain obtained from accepting special orders at prices below the existing market price. Second, the decision to accept the order prevents the company from accepting other orders which may be obtained during the period at the going market price. In other words it is assumed that no better opportunities will present themselves during the period.

A comparison of relevant costs with relevant revenues emphasizes the £40,000 short-run advantage from the acceptance of the order. Management should consider whether the £40,000 short-term advantage will be offset by the longer-term disadvantages outlined above. That is, management must decide if they are prepared to forgo £40,000 now in order to protect the long-run market advantages.

Decision-making and the influence of limiting factors

When a company is operating at full capacity future net cash flows may be restricted by its ability to increase output. For example, output may be restricted by shortage of labour, materials, equipment or factory space etc. When sales demand is in excess of the company's productive capacity it is essential that the factor responsible for limiting output is identified and that the greatest possible contribution to profit is obtained each time that this scarce or *limiting factor* is used. Consider Example 10.4.

EXAMPLE 10.4

A company produces three products and is reviewing the production and sales budgets for the next accounting period. The following information is available for the three products:

	Product X	Product Y	Product Z
Contribution per unit	£12	£10	£6
Machine hours required per unit	6 hours	2 hours	1 hour
Estimated sales demand	200 units	200 units	200 units
Required machine hours	1,200 hours	400 hours	200 hours

Machine capacity is limited to 1,200 hours and is insufficient to meet total sales demand. You have been asked to advise as to which products should be produced during the period.

In this situation the company's ability to increase its output and profits/net cash inflows is limited by the availability of machine capacity. You may think, when first looking at the available information, that the company should give top priority to producing product X since this yields the highest contribution per unit sold, but this assumption would be incorrect. To produce each unit of product X, 6 scarce machine hours are required whereas products Y and Z use only 2 hours and 1 hour respectively of scarce machine hours. By concentrating on producing products Y and Z the company can sell 200 units of each product and still have some machine capacity left to make product X. If the company concentrates on producing product X it will only be able to meet the maximum sales demand of product X and will have no machine capacity left to make products Y or Z. The way in which you should determine the optimum production plan is to calculate the contribution per limiting factor for each product and then to rank the products in order of profitability based on this calculation. Using the figures in the present example the result would be as follows:

	Product X	Product Y	Product Z
	£12	£10	£6
Contribution per machine hour	£2 (6 hours)	£5 (2 hours)	£6 (1 hour)
Ranking	3	2	1

The company can now allocate the 1,200 scarce machine hours in accordance with the above rankings. The first choice should be to produce as much as possible of product Z. The maximum sales are 200 units and production of this quantity will result in the use of 200 machine hours thus leaving 1,000 unused hours. The second choice should be to produce as much of product Y as possible. The maximum sales of 200 units will result in the use of 400 machine hours. Production of both products Z and Y require 600 machine hours, leaving a balance of 600 hours for the production of product X, which will enable 100 units of product X to be produced. We can now summarize the allocation of the scarce machine hours:

Production	Machine hours used	Balance of machine hours available
200 units of Z	200	1,000
200 units of Y	400	600
100 units of X	600	–

This production programme results in the following total contribution:

	£
200 units of Z at £6 per unit contribution	1,200
200 units of Y at £10 per unit contribution	2,000
100 units of X at £12 per unit contribution	1,200
Total contribution	4,400

Always remember that it is necessary to consider other qualitative factors before the production programme is determined. For example, customer goodwill may be lost causing a fall in future sales if the company is unable to supply all three products to, say, 150 of its regular customers.

Difficulties may arise in applying this procedure when there is more than one scarce resource. It could not be applied if, for example, labour hours were *also* scarce and the contribution per labour hour resulted in product Y being ranked first, followed by products X and Z. In this type of situation where more than one resource is scarce it is necessary to resort to linear programming methods in order to determine the optimal production programme. The application of linear programming to decision-making when there are several scarce resources will be examined in Chapter 22.

Make or buy decisions

At the beginning of this chapter we looked at a make or buy decision situation in the form of Example 10.1 to illustrate the concept of *relevant costs*. Let us now use this same example to develop an understanding of *relevant costs* in a situation where there are also other factors called *opportunity costs*.

EXAMPLE 10.1

A company is considering the alternatives of either purchasing a component from an outside supplier or producing the component itself. The estimated costs to the company of producing the component are as follows:

	£
Direct labour	100
Direct materials	300
Variable overheads	50
Fixed overheads	100
	550

The outside supplier has quoted a figure of £500 for supplying the component.

It was assumed that the company had *spare capacity* and that the relevant cost of producing the component was £450 compared with the suppliers' price of £500. Let us now assume that the company is working at *full capacity*. In such a situation it is necessary to consider the planned work that will be carried out using the relevant productive facilities if the component *is not* produced by the company. If the component *is* produced by the company then the production of some of the existing planned work will have to be reduced, resulting in a lost contribution. This lost contribution represents the *opportunity cost* of producing the component internally. For a review of the literature on opportunity costs see Arnold and Scapens (1981).

If we assume that production of the component will require 20 *scarce* machine hours and that these scarce machine hours are currently being used to produce product A which yields a contribution of £8 per machine hour, then, if the component is produced internally, there will be a lost contribution or *opportunity cost* of £160. Hence the relevant cost of producing the component internally will be as follows:

	£
Direct labour	100
Direct materials	300
Variable overheads	50
Opportunity cost of scarce resources	160
	610

This means that cash flows will be reduced by £610 if the component is produced (sales revenue on displaced work will be £610) but additional cash flows of £500 will be incurred as a result of purchasing the component from the supplier. The component should therefore be purchased because there will be a net saving in cash flows of £110. Such a decision would, of course, assume that there were no significant qualitative factors to be taken into account such as a supplier who delivers inferior quality materials or who fails to meet agreed delivery dates.

Replacement of equipment

Replacement of equipment is a capital investment or long-term decision which requires the use of discounted cash flow procedures. These procedures are discussed in detail in Chapter 13, but one aspect of replacement of equipment which we will consider at this stage is how to deal with the written down value of old equipment.[2] This is a problem which has been known to cause difficulty, but the correct approach is to apply the principle of relevant costs, and we will now examine in Example 10.5 the role of the book value of old equipment in a replacement decision. To avoid any possible confusion it will be assumed here that £1 of cash inflow or outflow in year 1 is equivalent to £1 of cash inflow or outflow in, say, year 3. Such an assumption would in reality be incorrect, and you will see why this is so in Chapter 13, but by adopting this assumption at this stage, the replacement problem can be simplified and we can focus our attention on the treatment of the book value of the old equipment in the replacement decision.

EXAMPLE 10.5

A company owns a machine which was purchased three years ago for £18,000. Depreciation based on a useful life of six years with no salvage value has been recorded each year. The present written down value of the equipment is £9,000. Management is considering replacing this machine with a new machine which will reduce the variable operating costs. The new machine will cost £7,000 and will have an expected life of three years with no scrap value. The variable operating costs are 30 p per unit of output for the old machine and 20 p per unit for the new machine. It is expected that both machines will be operated at their maximum capacity of 20,000 units per annum. The current disposal or sale value of the old machine is £4,000, and it will be zero in three years time.

The total costs over a period of three years for each of the alternatives are:

	Retain present machine £	Buy replacement machine £	
Variable operating costs:			
20,000 units at 30 p for 3 years	18,000		
20,000 units at 20 p for 3 years		12,000	
3-year depreciation charges of old machine	9,000		
Final depreciation write off of old machine		9,000 }	= 5,000 loss
Sale value of old machine		(4,000) }	on sale
Capital cost of new machine		7,000	
Total cost	27,000	24,000	

The costs of operating the replacement machine are £3,000 less than the costs of operating the existing machine. The book value of £9,000 for the old machine is not a relevant cost since it will still have to be written off whichever alternative is chosen. If the present machine is retained, three years depreciation at £3,000 per annum will be written off in the company's financial accounts, reducing the current book value of £9,000 to zero. If the new machine is purchased, a loss of £5,000 on the sale of the old machine will be incurred immediately. The loss on disposal of the old machine is calculated as follows:

Written down value of machine	9,000
Less Sale proceeds	4,000
Loss on sale	£5,000

The entries in the financial accounts for depreciation or the loss on sale of the old machine will be:

	Retain present machine £	Buy replacement machine £
Annual depreciation charge of old machine	9,000	–
Loss on sale of old machine	–	5,000

The difference between the two alternatives is £4,000; that is the amount of the sale proceeds of the old machine. The only relevant item for replacement decisions is therefore the sale proceeds of the present machine. Hence depreciation charges and the loss on the sale of the old machine should be ignored for the purpose of decision-making.[3] (For a discussion of situations where depreciation may be a relevant cost for decision-making purposes see Ross, 1968.) An alternative presentation of relevant cash flows for the purchase of the replacement machine is as follows:

	£
Savings on variable operating costs (3 years)	6,000
Sale proceeds of existing machine	4,000
	10,000
Less Purchase cost of replacement machine	(7,000)
Savings on purchasing replacement machine	3,000

Problems in determining the relevant costs of materials

So far in this chapter we have assumed, when considering various decisions, that any materials required would not be taken from existing stocks, but would be purchased at a later date and so the estimated purchase price would be the relevant material cost. A more difficult problem arises when materials are taken from existing stock. In this situation the relevant cost of materials for a particular job (say job X) depends on their alternative use. The alternative use of the materials will be either to sell them or to use them on other jobs. Hence the cost of using the materials on job X results in an *opportunity cost* consisting of either (i) the net sales revenue if the materials are sold, or (ii) the expense that will be

avoided if the materials are used on some other job; that is, the payment that will be saved for the materials minus the cost of holding the existing materials until they are required. Whichever of these two amounts is the greater may be regarded as the relevant cost of using the materials. We will now consider these two possibilities in Example 10.6.

EXAMPLE 10.6

A company has a stock of 10 units of materials which were purchased at £100 per unit. The company is considering a request from a customer for an order which will require the use of this stock of materials. If the materials are not used for the order then they will be used on job Y at a later date. It is estimated that it will cost £130 per unit to replace the materials if the customer's order is accepted. The current net realizable value of the materials is £1,100.

If the company does not use the materials on the customer's order it can sell them for £1,100 but this will mean that the company will have to replace them at a cost of £1,300. Of these two alternatives the company should keep the materials in stock and avoid having to pay out £1,300 in the future. The decision to allocate the materials to the customer's order will result in future cash flows differing by £1,300, and so the relevant cost of materials for the order will be £1,300.

Let us now consider a situation where the relevant material cost is the net realizable value. Assume that the materials in Example 10.6 have no alternative use (apart from being sold) other than to be used on another job as a substitute for materials which normally cost £120 per unit. However, it will be necessary to adapt the materials for use on this other job at a cost of £200. The net realizable value from the sale of the materials is £1,100 but the costs that will be avoided if the materials are adapted and used on another job will be £1,000 (£1,200 − £200). If the materials are not used on the customer's order, the company should sell them for £1,100 in preference to using them on another job at a net cost saving of £1,000. The decision to allocate the materials to the customer's order will therefore result in a loss of cash receipts of £1,100, and the relevant cost of materials for the order in this situation will be £1,100. For a more detailed discussion of the problems of determining the relevant costs of materials see Coase (1968).

Problems in determining the relevant cost of labour

We have assumed in earlier discussions in this chapter that direct labour costs represented the additional costs resulting from a decision, and direct labour costs have therefore been considered to be relevant costs. Let us consider now the situation where spare capacity exists and where the labour force is to be maintained in the short term; it is then likely that the direct labour cost incurred by a company will remain the same for all alternative decisions. The labour cost will be *irrelevant* for decision-making purposes. Our earlier assumption would be correct where casual labour is used and where workers can be hired on a daily basis; a company may then adjust the employment of labour to exactly the amount required to meet the production requirements. The labour cost will increase if the company accepts additional work and will decrease if production is reduced. In this situation the labour cost will be a *relevant cost* for decision-making purposes.

In a situation *where full capacity exists* and additional labour supplies are unavailable in the short term, and where no further overtime working is possible, the only way that labour resources could then be obtained for a specific order would be to reduce existing production. This would release labour for the order but the reduced production would result in a lost contribution, and this lost contribution must be taken into account when ascertaining the relevant cost for the specific order. The relevant labour cost per hour where full capacity exists is therefore the hourly labour rate plus an opportunity cost which

supply and if the company accepts the order it will be necessary to reduce production of product X. Details of the cost per unit and the selling price of product X are as follows:

		£
Selling price		40
Direct labour (4 hours at £5 per hour)	20	
Other variable costs	12	32
Contribution		8

What is the minimum selling price the company should accept for the special order?

In this example the relevant labour cost is £7 per hour consisting of the hourly wage rate of £5 plus the lost contribution of £2 per hour from product X. (The contribution of product X is £8 and requires 4 direct labour hours resulting in a contribution of £2 per hour.) Hence the relevant costs for the special order are as follows:

	£
Variable cost (excluding direct labour)	1,000
Direct labour (1,000 hours at £7 per hour)	7,000
	8,000

A selling price of £8,000 takes into account the lost contribution from product X and represents the minimum selling price that the company should accept if it wishes to ensure that future cash flows will remain unchanged. The acceptance of the order means that production of product X must be reduced by 250 units. We can now check that the relevant cost calculation is correct by comparing the contribution from the special order with the contribution that would have been obtained from product X.

	Product X (250 units)		Special order	
Sales		10,000		8,000
Less Direct labour	5,000		5,000	
Variable cost	3,000	8,000	1,000	6,000
Contribution		2,000		2,000

This statement shows that the contribution will be unchanged if the selling price of the special order is equivalent to the relevant cost of the order.

You may have noted that the hourly labour cost will continue whichever alternative is accepted and therefore may be concerned that the relevant cost consists of the hourly labour cost plus the lost contribution per hour. The reason for including the hourly labour cost is because a decision to

consists of the contribution per hour which is lost by accepting the order. Let us consider such a situation in Example 10.7.

EXAMPLE 10.7

A company has received an enquiry from a customer for a special order which will require 1,000 skilled labour hours and which will incur other variable costs of £1,000. Skilled labour is currently in short

create labour hours by reducing production of other work will result in a loss of sales and variable costs (excluding labour). That is, there will be a loss of contribution *before charging the labour costs* of £28 or £7 per hour in Example 10.7. This is just another way of saying that the relevant labour cost is the hourly wage rate of £5 plus the lost contribution per hour of £2.

There is a tendency for *indirect* labour costs to remain unchanged between certain ranges of activity and then to increase in discrete steps as activity increases. (A discussion of step cost functions can be found in Chapter 2.) When considering the acceptance of additional orders, it is necessary to question whether or not the acceptance will result in an increase in the company's indirect labour costs. If the answer is yes, then the increase in costs should be regarded as a relevant cost. These factors must also be taken into account when considering contraction decisions. You should assess which indirect labour costs will be avoided if activity is reduced or if a department is closed down, and only those costs which will be avoided by the decision should be regarded as relevant costs.

Emphasis on the short term

The concept of relevant cost is based on the principle that in the short term a company has incurred certain fixed costs to provide the basic operating capacity. As these costs have already been incurred they will remain unchanged in the short term, whatever future decisions are taken. In the long term these fixed costs must be met if a company is to survive, and it is essential that relevant cost is regarded as a short-term cost. So long as relevant revenues are in excess of relevant costs for each decision, profits will be increased or losses decreased. However, a policy of minimizing losses can only be continued for a short period, as in the long term a company must generate profits if it is to stay in business. Let us now consider Example 10.8.

EXAMPLE 10.8

A firm has undertaken to hire certain plant and machinery at a cost of £50,000 for the quarter ending 31 March, and the rent has already been paid in advance. The firm is a producer of large-scale equipment to order. A customer has offered to pay £80,000 for a special job which will incur a material

cost of £10,000 and a labour cost of £40,000. Labour can be hired casually as required. The market for large-scale equipment is badly depressed and it is most unlikely that any other orders will be forthcoming. There are no alternative uses for the plant and machinery. Let us assume at this stage that no other costs exist. Should the company accept the order?

The correct short-term decision is yes, as the relevant costs are £50,000 and the proposed selling price is £80,000. Acceptance of the order reduces the loss by £30,000 as is shown in the following profit statements:

	Profit/loss if contract is accepted		Profit/loss if contract is not accepted	
		£		£
Revenue		80,000		Nil
Rent	50,000		50,000	
Labour	40,000		–	
Materials	10,000	100,000	–	50,000
Profit/(loss)		(20,000)		(50,000)

By accepting the order the firm is making the most of its past incorrect decision of committing itself to fixed costs of £50,000. As it is now committed to these fixed costs, any business which is in excess of short-term relevant costs should be accepted. It is important, however, that the firm should also try to ensure that revenue is sufficient to cover the longer-term fixed costs (£50,000 per quarter in this example). If the company meets this requirement then it will make profits, but it cannot continue to operate in the long term if it ignores fixed costs, as it will make only losses.

In the long term *all* costs are relevant since *all* costs can eventually be changed by a management decision to liquidate the business. Let us now move on a stage further and assume that the circumstances remain exactly the same as in Example 10.8 for the future accounting periods but the customer requests a repeat order. Will the relevant costs still be £50,000 for the repeat order? The answer to this question depends on whether the firm has committed itself to the hire of the plant and machinery in future accounting periods. If it has not already committed itself then the decision on hiring should again be based on whether the plant and machinery will be put to profitable use. If the plant and machinery will only be used for this particular customer's order then the relevant cost of the order will be £100,000, consisting of the labour, materials and rental costs. A selling price of less than £100,000 will not ensure that future sales revenue is in excess of

future costs.

The rental costs are now *relevant* as acceptance of the customer's order will mean that the company will decide to hire the plant and machinery for a further period and incur costs of £50,000. In other words the rental costs will now be different if the customer's order is accepted, and the firm should only hire the plant and machinery if the customer is prepared to pay more than £100,000. We can see from this example that in the longer term all fixed costs are relevant costs.

A comprehensive example

We will conclude this chapter with a comprehensive decision-making problem, in the form of Example 10.9, which will enable us to consolidate the various items which we have considered so far. The answer is presented in Exhibit 10.1.

EXAMPLE 10.9

Brown Ltd is a company which has in stock some materials of type XY which cost £75,000 but which are now obsolete and have a scrap value of only £21,000. Other than selling the material for scrap there are only two alternative uses for them.

Alternative 1
Converting the obsolete materials into a specialized product which would require the following additional work and materials:

Material A	600 units
Material B	1,000 units
Direct labour:	
5,000 hours unskilled	
5,000 hours semi-skilled	
5,000 hours highly skilled	15,000 hours
Extra selling and delivery	
expenses	£27,000
Extra advertising	£18,000

The conversion would produce 900 units of saleable product and these could be sold for £300 per unit.

Material A is already in stock and is widely used within the firm. Although present stocks together with orders already planned will be sufficient to facilitate normal activity, any extra material used by adopting this alternative will necessitate such materials being replaced immediately. Material B is also in stock but it is unlikely that any additional supplies can be obtained for some considerable time because of an industrial dispute. At the present time material B is normally used in the production of product Z which sells at £390 per unit and incurs total variable

cost (excluding material B) of £210 per unit. Each unit of product Z uses four units of material B.

The details of materials A and B are as follows:

	Material A £	Material B £
Acquisition cost at time		
of purchase	100 per unit	10 per unit
Net realizable value	85 per unit	18 per unit
Replacement cost	90 per unit	–

Alternative 2
Adapting the obsolete materials for use as a substitute for a sub-assembly which is regularly used within the firm. Details of the extra work and materials required are:

Material C	1,000 units
Direct labour:	
4,000 hours unskilled	
1,000 hours semi-skilled	
4,000 hours highly skilled	9,000 hours

1,200 units of the sub-assembly are regularly used per quarter at a cost of £900 per unit. The adaptation of material XY would reduce the quantity of the sub-assembly purchased from outside the firm to 900 units for the next quarter only. However, as the volume purchased would be reduced some discount would be lost, and the price of those purchased from outside would increase to £1,050 per unit for that quarter.

Material C is not available externally but is manufactured by Brown Ltd. The 1,000 units required would be available from stocks but would be produced as extra production. The standard cost per unit of material C would be as follows:

	£
Direct labour, 6 hours unskilled labour	18
Raw materials	13
Variable overhead, 6 hours at £1	6
Fixed overhead, 6 hours at £3	18
	55

The wage rates and overhead recovery rates for Brown Ltd are

Variable overhead	£1 per direct labour hour
Fixed overhead	£3 per direct labour hour
Unskilled labour	£3 per direct labour hour
Semi-skilled labour	£4 per direct labour hour
Highly skilled labour	£5 per direct labour hour

The unskilled labour is employed on a casual basis and sufficient labour can be acquired to exactly meet the production requirements. Semi-skilled labour is part of the permanent labour force but the company has temporary excess supply of this type of labour at the present time. Highly skilled labour is in short supply and cannot be increased significantly in the short term; this labour is presently engaged in

Exhibit 10.1 A comparison of alternatives 1 and 2 with the sale of material XY

Alternative 1 — Conversion v. Immediate sale			£
(1) Sales revenue: 900 units at £300 per unit			270,000
Less Relevant costs:			
(2) Material XY opportunity cost		21,000	
(3) Material A (600 units at £90)		54,000	
(4) Material B (1,000 uinits at £45)		45,000	
(5) Direct labour:			
Unskilled (5,000 hrs at £3)	15,000		
Semi-skilled	Nil		
Highly skilled (5,000 hrs at £11)	55,000	70,000	
(6) Variable overheads (15,000 hrs at £1)		15,000	
(7) Selling and delivery expenses		27,000	
(7) Advertising		18,000	
(8) Fixed overheads		Nil	250,000
Excess of relevant revenues			20,000

Alternative 2 — Adaptation v. Immediate sale			
(9) Saving on purchase of sub-assembly:			
Normal spending (1,200 units at £900)		1,080,000	
Revised spending (900 units at £1,050)		945,000	135,000
Less Relevant costs:			
(2) Material XY opportunity cost		21,000	
(10) Material C (1,000 units at £37)		37,000	
(5) Direct labour:			
Unskilled (4,000 hrs at £3)	12,000		
Semi-skilled	Nil		
Skilled (4,000 hrs at £11)	44,000	56,000	
(6) Variable overheads (9,000 hrs at £1)		9,000	
(8) Fixed overheads		Nil	123,000
Net relevant savings			12,000

Notes

(1) There will be additional sales revenue of £270,000 if alternative 1 is chosen.

(2) Acceptance of either alternative 1 or 2 will mean a loss of revenue of £21,000 from the sale of the obsolete material XY. This is an opportunity cost which must be covered whichever alternative is chosen. The original purchase cost of £75,000 for material XY is a sunk cost and is irrelevant.

(3) Acceptance of alternative 1 will mean that material A must be replaced at an additional cost of £54,000.

(4) Acceptance of alternative 1 will mean that material B will be diverted from the production of product Z. The excess of relevant revenues over relevant cost for product Z is £180 and each unit of product Z uses four units of material. The lost contribution (excluding the cost of material B which is incurred for both alternatives) will therefore be £45 for each unit of material B that is used in converting the raw materials into a specialized product.

(5) Unskilled labour can be matched exactly to the company's production requirements. The acceptance of either alternative 1 or 2 will cause the company to incur additional unskilled labour costs of £3 for each hour of unskilled labour that is used. It is assumed that the semi-skilled labour would be retained and that there would be sufficient excess supply for either alternative at no extra cost to the company. In these circumstances semi-skilled labour will not be a relevant cost. Skilled labour is in short supply and can only be obtained by reducing production of product L,

resulting in a lost contribution of £24 or £6 per hour of skilled labour. We have already established that the relevant cost for labour which is in short supply is the hourly labour cost plus the lost contribution per hour, so the relevant labour cost here will be £11 per hour. If this point is not clear refer back now to Example 10.7.

(6) It is assumed that for each direct labour hour of input, variable overheads will increase by £1. As each alternative uses additional direct labour hours, variable overheads will increase giving a relevant cost of £1 per direct labour hour.

(7) As advertising, selling and distribution expenses will be different if alternative 1 is chosen, these costs are clearly relevant to the decision.

(8) The company's fixed overheads will remain the same whichever alternative is chosen, and so fixed overheads *are not* a relevant cost for either alternative.

(9) The cost of purchasing the sub-assembly will be reduced by £135,000 if the second alternative is chosen, and so these savings *are* relevant to the decision.

(10) The company will incur additional variable costs of £37 for each unit of material C that is manufactured, so the fixed overheads for material C *are not* a relevant cost.

meeting the demand for product L which requires 4 hours of highly skilled labour. The contribution from the sale of one unit of product L is £24.

An alternative presentation of this information, which you may prefer, is as follows:

	Sale of obsolete materials for scrap	Alternative 1	Alternative 2
Relevant revenues less relevant costs	£21,000	£41,000	£33,000

Difference = £20,000

Difference = £12,000

Given this information you are required to present cost information advising whether the stocks of material XY should be sold, coverted into a specialized product (alternative 1) or adapted for use as a substitute for a sub-assembly (alternative 2).

When considering a problem such as this there are many different ways in which the information may be presented. The way in which we shall deal with the problem here is to compare each of the two stated alternatives with the other possibility of selling off material XY for its scrap value of £21,000. Exhibit 10.1 sets out the relevant information and shows that of the three possibilities alternative 1 is to be preferred.

We show here the sale of the obsolete materials as a separate alternative, and so the opportunity cost of material XY, amounting to £21,000 (Exhibit 10.1, item 2) is not included in either alternative 1 or 2 as it is brought into the analysis under the heading 'Sale of obsolete materials for scrap'. Consequently, in both alternatives 1 and 2 the relevant revenues less relevant costs figure is increased by £21,000. The difference between alternatives 1 and 2 and the sale of the obsolete materials are still, however, £20,000 and £12,000 respectively, which gives an identical result to that obtained in Exhibit 10.1.

Summary

In this chapter we have described the principles involved in determining the relevant cost of alternative courses of action. We found that a particular cost can be relevant in one situation but irrelevant in another situation. The important point to note is that *relevant costs represent those future costs which will be changed by a particular decision, while irrelevant costs are those which will not be affected by that decision.* In the short term, total profits will be increased (or total losses decreased) if a course of action is chosen where relevant revenues are in excess of relevant costs. We noted that not all of the important inputs relevant to a decision can always be easily quantified, but that it is essential that any qualitative factors relevant to the decision should be taken into account in the decision-making process.

We have considered a variety of decision-making problems in the form of Examples 10.1 to 10.9, and the last of which consolidated the various aspects of relevant costs. The important point which you should remember from these examples is that *relevant costs are crucial for short-term decisions, but that in the long term revenues must be sufficient to cover all costs.*

References and further reading

Amey, L.R. On opportunity costs and decision-making. *Accountancy* July 1968.

Arnold, J. Budgets for decisions. In Arnold, J., Carsberg, B. and Scapens, R. (Eds), *Topics in Management Accounting*. Philip Allan, 1980.

Arnold, J. and Scapens, R. The British contribution to opportunity cost theory. In Bromwich, M. and Hopwood, A.G. (Eds), *Essays in British Accounting Research*. Pitman, 1981.

Coase, R.H. The nature of costs. In Solomons, D. (Ed.), *Studies in Cost Analysis* 2nd edn. Sweet & Maxwell, 1968.

Dillon, R.D. and Nash, J.F. The true relevance of relevant costs. *The Accounting Review* January 1978.

Edwards, R.S. The rationale of cost accounting. In Solomons, D. (Ed.), *Studies in Cost Analysis* 2nd edn. Sweet & Maxwell, 1968.

Manes, R.P., Soong, H.P. and Jensen, R. Relevant costs of intermediate goods and services. *The Accounting Review* **LVII**, July 1982, 594-606.

Ross, M.H. Depreciation and user cost. In Solomons, D. (Ed.), *Studies in The Accounting Review* January 1978.

Problems

*Indicates that a suggested solution is to be found in the *Students' Manual*.

10.1* Two decision-making problems are faced by a company which produces a range of products and absorbs production overhead using a rate of 200% on direct wages. This rate was calculated from the following budgeted figures:

	£
Variable production costs	64,000
Fixed production costs	96,000
Direct labour costs	80,000

Problem 1
The normal selling price of product X is £22 and production cost for one unit is:

	£
Raw materials	8
Direct labour	4
Production overhead	8
	£20

There is a possibility of supplying a special order for 2,000 units of product X at £16 each. If the order were accepted the normal budgeted sales would not be affected and the company has the necessary capacity to produce the additional units.

Problem 2
The cost of making component Q, which forms part of product Y, is stated below:

	£
Raw material	4
Direct labour	8
Production overhead	16
	£28

Component Q could be brought from an outside supplier for £20.

You are required, assuming that fixed production costs will not change, to:
(a) state whether the company should:
 (i) accept the special order in *Problem 1*;
 (ii) continue making component Q or buy it from outside in *Problem 2*;
 both your statements must be supported by details of costs;
(b) comment on the principle you have followed in your cost analysis to arrive at your answers to the two problems.

<div align="right">

ICMA Cost Accounting 1
May 1979
</div>

10.2* The management of Springer PLC is considering next year's production and purchase budgets.

One of the components produced by the company, which is incorporated into another product before being sold, has a budgeted manufacturing cost as follows:

	£
Direct material	14
Direct labour (4 hrs at £3 per hr)	12
Variable overhead (4 hrs at £2 per hr)	8
Fixed overhead (4 hrs at £5 per hr)	20
Total cost	54 per unit

Trigger PLC has offered to supply the above component at a guaranteed price of £50 per unit.

Required:
(a) Considering cost criteria only, advise management whether the above component should be purchased from Trigger PLC. Any calculations should be shown and assumptions made, or aspects which may require further investigation should be clearly stated. (6 marks)
(b) Explain how your above advice would be affected by each of the two *separate* situations shown below.
 (i) As a result of recent government legisla-

tion if Springer PLC continues to manufacture this component the company will incur additional inspection and testing expenses of £56,000 per annum, which are not included in the above budgeted manufacturing costs. (3 marks)

(ii) Additional labour cannot be recruited and if the above component is not manufactured by Springer PLC the direct labour released will be employed in increasing the production of an existing product which is sold for £90 and which has a budgeted manufacturing cost as follows:

	£
Direct material	10
Direct labour (8 hrs at £3 per hr)	24
Variable overhead (8 hrs at £2 per hr)	16
Fixed overhead (8 hrs at £5 per hr)	40
	90 per unit

All calculations should be shown.
(4 marks)

(c) The production director of Springer PLC recently said:

'We must continue to manufacture the component as only one year ago we purchased some special grinding equipment to be used exclusively by this component. The equipment cost £100,000, it cannot be resold or used elsewhere and if we cease production of this component we will have to write off the written down book value which is £80,000.'

Draft a brief reply to the production director commenting on his statement. (4 marks) (17 marks)
ICCA Level 1 Costing December 1982

10.3 (a) Identify the distinguishing characteristics of direct costs. (3 marks)

(b) A research project, which to date has cost the company £150,000, is under review. It is anticipated that, should the project be allowed to proceed, it will be completed in approximately one year when the results would be sold to a government agency for £300,000.

Shown below are the additional expenses which the managing director estimates will be necessary to complete the work.

Materials—£60,000
This material, which has just been received, is extremely toxic and if not used on the project

would have to be disposed of by special means, at a cost of £5,000.

Labour—£40,000
The men are highly skilled and very difficult to recruit. They were transferred to the project from a production department and, at a recent board meeting, the works director claimed that if the men were returned to him he could earn the company each year £150,000 extra sales. The accountant calculated that the prime cost of those sales would be £100,000 and the overhead absorbed (all fixed) would amount to £20,000.

Research staff—£60,000
A decision has already been taken that this will be the last major piece of research undertaken, and consequently when work on the project ceases the staff involved will be made redundant. Redundancy and severance pay have been estimated at £25,000.

Share of general building services—£35,000
The managing director is not very sure what is included in this expense. He knows, however, that the accounts staff charge similar amounts every year to each department.

Required:
Assuming the estimates are accurate, advise the managing director whether the project should be allowed to proceed. You must carefully and clearly explain the reasons for your treatment of each expense item. (14 marks) (17 marks)
ACCA Foundation Costing June 1979

10.4 (a) Next year's forecasted trading results for Caribee Ltd, a small company manufacturing three different types of product, are shown below.

Product	A	B	C	Total
Selling price, per unit	£10	£12	£8	
	£000s	£000s	£000s	£000s
Sales	100	96	32	228
Variable cost of sales:				
Prime cost	40	38	13	91
Variable overhead	20	18	11	49
Share of general fixed overhead	30	27	10	67
Profit/(loss)	10	13	(2)	21

Required:
(i) Explain how the company's forecasted profits would be affected if product C were discontinued. It should be assumed that sales of the remaining products would not be affected; any other assumptions made should be included with your

explanation. (4 marks)

(ii) Additional advertising for product B would cost £8,000 next year; this amount is not included in the forecasts shown above. Calculate the minimum extra sales, in units, of product B required to cover this additional cost. (4 marks)

(iii) Calculate the increase in sales volume of product A necessary to compensate for a 10% reduction in the selling price of the product. Carefully explain why the increase in volume is proportionately greater than the reduction in selling price. (5 marks)

(b) The production director of Caribee Ltd has just been informed that next year's supplies of a material used in the manufacture of each of the three products will be restricted to 92,000 kilos; no substitute materials is available and the estimated consumption of this restricted material, per product, is:

Product A 8 kilos per unit
Product B 4 kilos per unit
Product C 1 kilo per unit

The sales director estimates that the maximum demand for each product is that which is shown in the original forecast in (a) above; also he decides that advertising or adjustments to selling price are not possible.

Assume that stocks of materials, work in progress or finished goods cannot be carried.
Required:
Calculate the optimum quantities of products A, B and C which should be manufactured next year in order to maximize company profits. (9 marks)

(22 marks)
ACCA Foundation Costing
June 1981

10.5 (a) Write a brief note to show clearly the distinction between service (or operating) costing and uniform costing.
(b) As assistant to the accountant of a public passenger transport authority, you have been asked to:
 (i) prepare a statement showing the profitability of routes R1, R2 and R3 including the contribution per vehicle and contribution per mile *after deducting all direct costs*;
 (ii) comment on a proposal that route R3 be discontinued;
 (iii) comment on a proposal to reduce the service on route R3 by half on the assumption that only 4 vehicles would be used, operating for a total of 100,000 miles per annum and that the estimated

revenue from passengers would be reduced by £40,000 per annum. (You may assume that any surplus vehicles could be readily sold for their written down values).

The latest information available for the last twelve months is as follows:

Routes	R1	R2	R3	Total
Number of vehicles used	12	16	8	36
Total mileage on each route in thousands	300	400	200	900
	£000	£000	£000	£000
Revenue from passengers	210	296	116	622
Direct costs, variable	150	200	100	450
Direct costs, fixed (specific to vehicles)	36	48	24	108
Fixed costs, apportioned (garage maintenance and administration)	24	32	16	72

(20 marks)
ICMA Cost Accounting 1
May 1980

10.6* Shortbun, a perishable product which cannot be stored, is produced in one department of E.F. PLC. The department is engaged exclusively in the manufacture of shortbuns and employs only one grade of labour. At present there are 105 operatives in the department, all working a 40 hour week and overtime is not permitted. The operatives are paid £3 per hour with a quaranteed wage of £120 per week. The production capacity of the department is frequently restricted because additional operatives of the required skill cannot be recruited.

Demand for shortbuns is variable: the minimum weekly demand is 6,000 units, and the maximum is estimated to be 9,000 units per week.

The estimated production cost, selling price and consequent profit per unit of shortbun is:

	£	£
Selling price		5.00 per unit
Material	1.00	
Labour (0.6 hrs × £3)	1.80	
Variable overhead	0.60	
Fixed overhead	0.90	4.30
Profit		0.70 per unit

Variable overheads vary with units produced, the fixed overhead absorption rate is based upon an activity of 7,000 units per week.

The department manager is rather puzzled by a recent remark made by the works accountant. The accountant had been referring to the cost of

machine breakdowns which had resulted in operatives being idle for 210 hours in two successive weeks. In the first week, when demand for shortbuns had been 6,500 units, the accountant claimed that the cost of the 210 hours idle time was zero. In the second week, when demand for shortbuns had been 7,500 units, the accountant claimed that the cost of the

	Area occupied, in acres	Yield per acre, in tonnes

Fixed overhead, per annum £54,000

210 hours idle time had been £1,190.

Required:

(a) Carefully explain to the department manager how the accountant has calculated the cost of the idle time for each of the two weeks described above. (10 marks)

(b) The department manager is considering two alternative proposals for extending capacity to satisfy potential demand for shortbuns. These are:

(i) Introduce an incentive scheme for all shortbuns produced in the department. Operatives would be paid £2 for each unit produced. The manufacturing time would be reduced to 0.50 hours per unit and the guaranteed weekly wage would be withdrawn.

(ii) When demand exceeds current manufacturing capacity, purchase frozen shortbuns from another supplier at £4 per unit. Further processing would not be required and the product could be sold to the customers of E.F. PLC during the week in which they were purchased.

Required:

(i) If the incentive scheme were introduced, calculate the weekly sales, in units, required to earn a profit equal to that currently earned at maximum capacity. (5 marks)

(ii) Making whatever calculations you consider necessary compare the relative profitability of introducing the incentive scheme with buying out the additional shortbuns as and when required. (7 marks)
(22 marks)
ACCA Foundation Costing
December 1981

10.7* A market gardener is planning his production for next season and he asked you, as a cost accountant, to recommend the optimal mix of vegetable production for the coming year. He has given you the following data relating to the current year:

	Potatoes	Turnips	Parsnips	Carrots
Area occupied, in acres	25	20	30	25
Yield per acre, in tonnes	10	8	9	12
	£	£	£	£
Selling price per tonne	100	125	150	135
Variable costs per acre:				
fertilizers	30	25	45	40
seeds	15	20	30	25
pesticides	25	15	20	25
direct wages	400	450	500	570

The land which is being used for the production of carrots and parsnips can be used for either crop, but not for potatoes or turnips. The land being used for potatoes and turnips can be used for either crop, but not for carrots or parsnips. In order to provide an adequate market service, the gardener must produce each year at least 40 tonnes each of potatoes and turnips and 36 tonnes each of parsnips and carrots.

(a) You are required to present a statement to show:

(i) the profit for the current year;

(ii) the profit for the production mix which you would recommend.

(b) Assuming that the land could be cultivated in such a way that any of the above crops could be produced and there was no market commitment, you are required to:

(i) advise the market gardener on which crop he should concentrate his production;

(ii) calculate the profit if he were to do so; and

(iii) calculate in sterling the break-even point of sales.
(25 marks)
ICMA Cost Accounting 2
May 1980

10.8 As the first management accountant employed by a manufacturer of power tools you have been asked to supply financial results by product line to help in marketing decision making.

The following account was produced for the year ended 30 September 1981:

	£000	£000
Sales		1,200
Cost of goods sold:		
Materials	500	
Wages	300	
Production expenses	150	
Marketing costs	100	
		1,050
Net profit		150

A statistical analysis of the figures shows the following variable element in the costs:

	%
Materials	90
Wages	80
Production expenses	60
Marketing costs	70

Below is given, as percentages, the apportionment of the sales and the variable elements of the costs among the five products manufactured.

	Product					Total
	A	B	C	D	E	
Sales	30	15	7	28	20	100
Materials	40	20	10	20	10	100
Wages	15	25	10	25	25	100
Production expenses	30	10	10	30	20	100
Marketing costs	10	30	20	30	10	100

From the information given you are required to:
(a) (i) prepare a statement for the year showing contribution by products;
 (ii) comment on these contributions;
(b) calculate the following:
 (i) the breakeven sales level;
 (ii) the order of sales preference for additional orders to maximize contribution as a percentage of sales;
 (iii) a revised mix of the £1,200,000 sales to maximize contribution assuming that existing sales by products can only be varied 10% either up or down;
 (iv) a product mix to maximize contribution if manpower availability were reduced by 10% but the product mix could be varied by up to 20%; and
 (v) the percentage commission which could be offered to an overseas agent on an order of £30,000 worth each of products A, C and E and obtain a 20% contribution on the total sales value.

(30 marks)
ICMA P3 Management Accounting
November 1981

10.9 Following a fire at the factory of Elgar Ltd, the management team met to review the proposed operations for the next quarter. The fire had destroyed all the finished goods stock, some of the raw materials and about half of the machines in the forming shop.

At the meeting of the management team the following additional information was provided.
(i) Only 27,000 machine hours of forming capacity will be available in the forthcoming quarter. Although previously it was thought that sales demand would be the only binding limitation on production it has now become apparent that for the forthcoming quarter the forming capacity would be a limiting factor.
(ii) It will take about three months to reinstate the forming shop to its previous operational capacity. Hence the restriction on forming capacity is for the next quarter only.
(iii) Some details of the product range manufactured by Elgar are provided in the following table:

	Product				
	A	B	C	D	E
Sales price	£50	£60	£40	£50	£80
Units of special material required for production					
W or X	2	2	2	1	3
Y	–	–	–	–	6
Z	1	2	1	1	–
Other direct material costs	£6	£12	£6	£5	£13
Other variable production costs	£8	£4	£8	£4	£4
Fixed production costs (based on standard costs)	£6	£3	£6	£3	£3
Forming hours required	5	6	2	10	6

(iv) The forecasts of demand, in units, for the forthcoming quarter are:

Product	A	B	C	D	E
Units demanded	2,000	2,000	4,000	3,000	4,000

It was originally intended that the number of units produced would equal the units demanded for each product.

(v) Due to a purchasing error there is an excess of material W in stock. This has a book value of £6 per unit which is also its current replacement cost. This could be sold to realize £4 per unit after sales and transport costs. Material X could be used instead of material W; material X is not in stock and has a current replacement cost of £5 per unit.

(vi) Material Y was in stock at a book value of £2 per unit, which is its normal cost if ordered 3 months in advance, but the stocks of this material were entirely destroyed by the fire. In order to obtain the material quickly a price of £3 per unit will have to be paid for the first 3,000 units obtained in the quarter and any additional units required will cost £6 per unit. These special prices will apply only to this quarter's purchases.

(vii) Some of the stock of material Z was destroyed by the fire. The remaining stocks of 2,000 units have a book value of £7 per unit. The replacement price for Z is currently £8 per unit.

(viii) As a result of the fire it is estimated that the fixed production costs will be £42,000 for the next quarter and the administration and office overheads will amount to £11,500.

(ix) The demand figures shown in note (iv) include a regular order from a single customer for

3,000 units of C, and
3,000 units of E.

This order is usually placed quarterly and the customer always specifies that the order be fulfilled in total or not at all.

Required:

(a) *Ignoring the information contained in note (ix) for this section of the question*, determine the optimum production plan for the forthcoming quarter and prepare a statement which indicates to the management of Elgar the estimated financial results of their planned production, in terms of total contribution, net current operating profit and financial accounting profit. (12 marks)

(b) Prepare a statement which clearly shows the management of Elgar Ltd the financial consequences of both the acceptance and the rejection of the order mentioned in note (ix). Advise Elgar on the desirability of acceptance of the order in total. Indicate what further information would be useful in arriving at a decision whether to accept or reject the order. (8 marks)

(Total 20 marks)

ACCA P2 Management Accounting
December 1981

10.10* Itervero Ltd, a small engineering company, operates a job order costing system. It has been invited to tender for a comparatively large job which is outside the range of its normal activities and, since there is surplus capacity, the management are keen to quote as low a price as possible. It is decided that the opportunity should be treated in isolation without any regard to the possibility of its leading to further work of a similar nature (although such a possibility does exist). A low price will not have any repercussions on Itervero's regular work.

The estimating department has spent 100 hours on work in connection with the quotation and they have incurred travelling expense of £550 in connection with a visit to the prospective customer's factory overseas. The following cost estimate has been prepared on the basis of their study:

Inquiry 205H/81
Cost estimate

	£
Direct material and components	
2,000 units of A at £25 per unit	50,000
200 units of B at £10 per unit	2,000
Other material and components to be bought in (specified)	12,500
	64,500
Direct labour	
700 hrs of skilled labour at £3.50 per hr	2,450
1,500 hrs of unskilled labour at £2 per hr	3,000
Overhead	
Department P—200 hrs at £25 per hr	5,000
Department Q—400 hrs at £20 per hr	8,000
Estimating department	
100 hrs at £5 per hr	500
Travelling expenses	550
Planning department	
300 hrs at £5 per hr	1,500
	£85,500

The following information has been brought together:

Material A: This is a regular stock item. The stock holding is more than sufficient for this job. The material currently held has an average cost of £25 per unit but the current replacement cost is £20 per unit.

Material B: A stock of 4,000 units of B is

currently held in the stores. This material is slow-moving and the stock is the residue of a batch bought seven years ago at a cost of £10 per unit. B currently costs £24 per unit but the resale value is only £18 per unit. A foreman has pointed out that B could be used as a substitute for another type of regularly used raw material which costs £20 per unit.

Direct labour: The workforce is paid on a time basis. The company has adopted a 'no redundancy' policy and this means that skilled workers are frequently moved to jobs which do not make proper use of their skills. The wages included in the cost estimate are for the mix of labour which the job ideally requires. It seems likely, if the job is obtained, that most of the 2,200 hours of direct labour will be performed by skilled staff receiving £3.50 per hour.

Overhead—Department P: Department P is the one department of Itervero Ltd that is working at full capacity. The department is treated as a profit centre and it uses a transfer price of £25 per hour for charging out its processing time to other departments. This charge is calculated as follows:

	£
Estimated variable cost per machine hour	10
Fixed departmental overhead	8
Department profit	7
	£25

Department P's facilities are frequently hired out to other firms and a charge of £30 per hour is made. There is a steady demand from outside customers for the use of these facilities.

Overhead—Department Q: Department Q uses a transfer price of £20 for charging out machine processing time to other departments. This charge is calculated as follows:

	£
Estimated variable cost per machine hour	8
Fixed departmental overhead	9
Department profit	3
	£20

Estimating department: The estimating department charges out its time to specific jobs using a rate of £5 per hour. The average wage rate within the department is £2.50 per hour but the higher rate is justified as being necessary to cover departmental overheads and the work done on unsuccessful quotations.

Planning department: This department also uses a charging out rate which is intended to cover all departmental costs.

(a) You are required to restate the cost estimate by using an opportunity cost approach. Make any assumptions that you deem to be necessary and briefly justify each of the figures that you give. (10 marks)
(b) Discuss the relevance of the opportunity cost approach to the situation described in the question and consider the problems which are likely to be encountered if it is used in practice. (6 marks)
(c) Briefly discuss the general applicability of opportunity cost in business decision making where a choice exists among alternative courses of action. (6 marks)

(22 marks)
ACCA Level 2 Management Accounting
June 1982

10.11 The Aylett Co. Ltd has been offered a contract which, if accepted, would significantly increase next year's activity levels. The contract requires the production of 20,000 kg of product X and specifies a contract price of £100 per kg. The resources used in the production of each kg of X include:

		Resources per kg of X
Labour	—Grade 1	2 hrs
	Grade 2	6 hrs
Material	—A	2 units
	B	1 litre

Grade 1 labour is highly skilled and although it is currently under-utilized in the firm it is Aylett's policy to continue to pay grade 1 labour in full. Acceptance of the contract would reduce the idle time of grade 1 labour. Idle time payments are treated as non production overheads.

Grade 2 is unskilled labour with a high turnover and may be considered a variable cost.

The costs to Aylett of each type of labour are

Grade 1	£4 per hour
Grade 2	£2 per hour.

The materials required to fulfil the contract would be drawn from those materials already in stock. Material A is widely used within the firm and any usage for this contract will necessitate replacement. Material B was purchased to fulfil an expected order which was not received; if material B is not used for the contract it will be sold. For accounting purposes FIFO is used. The various values and costs for A and B are:

	A per unit £	B per litre £
Book value	8	30
Replacement cost	10	32
Net realizable value	9	25

A single recovery rate for fixed factory overheads is used throughout the firm even though some fixed production overheads could be attributed to single products or departments. The overhead is recovered per productive labour hour and initial estimates of next year's activity, which excludes the current contract, show fixed production overheads to be £600,000 and productive labour hours of 300,000. Acceptance of the contract would increase fixed production overheads by £228,000.

Variable production overheads are accurately estimated at £3 per productive labour hour.

Acceptance of the contract would be expected to encroach on the sales and production of another product, Y, which is also made by Aylett Ltd. It is estimated that sales of Y would then decrease by 5,000 units in the next year only. However, this forecast reduction in sales of Y would enable attributable fixed factory overheads of £58,000 to be avoided. Information on Y is as follows:

	Per unit
Sales price	£70
Labour—grade 2	4 hrs
Materials—relevant variable costs	£12

All activity undertaken by Aylett is job costed using full, or absorption, costing in order to derive a profit figure for each contract — if the contract for X is accepted it will be treated as a separate job for routine costing purposes. The decision to accept or reject the contract will be taken in sufficient time to enable its estimated effects to be incorporated in the next year's budgets and also in the calculations carried out to derive the overhead recovery rate to be used in the forthcoming year.

Required:
(a) Advise Aylett on the desirability of the contract. (8 marks)
(b) Show how the contract, if accepted, will be reported on by the routine job costing system used by Aylett. (6 marks)
(c) Briefly explain the reasons for any differences between the figures used in (a) and (b) above. (6 marks)

(20 marks)
ACCA P2 Management Accounting December 1980

10.12 Johnson trades as a chandler at the Savoy Marina. His profit in this business during the year to 30 June 1981 was £12,000. Johnson also undertakes occasional contracts to build pleasure cruisers, and is considering the price at which to bid for the contract to build the *Blue Blood* for Mr B.W. Dunn, delivery to be in one year's time. He has no other contract in hand, or under consideration, for at least the next few months.

Johnson expects that if he undertakes the contract he would devote one-quarter of his time to it. To facilitate this he would employ G. Harrison, an unqualified practitioner, to undertake his book-keeping and other paper-work, at a cost of £2,000.

He would also have to employ on the contract one supervisor at a cost of £11,000 and two craftsmen at a cost of £8,800 each; these costs include Johnson's normal apportionment of the fixed overheads of his business at the rate of 10% of labour cost.

During spells of bad weather one of the craftsmen could be employed for the equivalent of up to three months full-time during the winter in maintenance and painting work in the chandler's business. He would use materials costing £1,000. Johnson already has two inclusive quotations from jobbing builders for this maintenance and painting work, one for £2,500 and the other for £3,500, the work to start immediately.

The equipment which would be used on the *Blue Blood* contract was bought nine years ago for £21,000. Depreciation has been written off on a straight-line basis, assuming a ten-year life and a scrap value of £1,000. The current replacement cost of similar new equipment is £60,000, and is expected to be £66,000 in one year's time. Johnson has recently been offered £6,000 for the equipment, and considers that in a year's time he would have little difficulty in obtaining £3,000 for it. The plant is useful to Johnson only for contract work.

In order to build the *Blue Blood* Johnson will need six types of material, as follows:

| Material code | No. of units | | Price per unit (£) | | |
	In stock	Needed for contract	Purchase price of stock items	Current purchase price	Current resale price
A	100	1,000	1.00	3.00	2.00
B	1,100	1,000	2.00	0.90	1.00
C	–	100	–	6.00	–
D	100	200	4.00	3.00	2.00
E	50,000	5,000	0.18	0.20	0.25
F	1,000	3,000	0.90	2.00	1.00

Materials B and E are sold regularly in the chandler's business. Material A could be sold to a local sculptor, if not used for the contract. Materials A and E can be used for other purposes, such as property maintenance. Johnson has no other use for materials D and F, the stocks of which are obsolete.

The *Blue Blood* would be built in a yard held on a lease with four years remaining at a fixed annual rental of £5,000. It would occupy half of this yard, which is useful to Johnson only for contract work.

Johnson anticipates that the direct expenses of the contract, other than those noted above, would be £6,500.

Johnson has recently been offered a one-year appointment at a fee of £15,000 to manage a boat-building firm on the Isle of Wight. If he accepted the offer he would be unable to take on the contract to build *Blue Blood*, or any other contract. He would have to employ a manager to run the chandler's business at an annual cost (including fidelity insurance) of £10,000, and would incur additional personal living costs of £2,000.

You are required:

(a) to calculate the price at which Johnson should be willing to take on the contract in order to break even, based exclusively on the information given above (15 marks), and

(b) to set out any further considerations which you think that Johnson should take into account in setting the price at which he would tender for the contract (10 marks).

Ignore taxation.

ICAEW Management Accounting
July 1981

10.13* The original budget for the K department of Hilton Ltd for the forthcoming year was as follows:

Budget for forthcoming year—K department
Budgeted sales and production—30,000 units

	Per unit of output £	Total for 30,000 units £000
Sales revenue	10.0	300
Manufacturing costs		
Material A—1 litre per unit	2.0	60
Material B—1 kilo per unit	1.5	45
Production labour	2.0	60
Variable overhead	1.0	30
Fixed manufacturing overhead	2.0	60
	8.5	255
Non-manufacturing costs	1.0	30
Total costs	9.5	285
Budgeted net profit for year	0.5	15

As part of Hilton's long term strategic plan the K department was due to be closed at the end of the forthcoming year. However, rumours of the closure have resulted in the majority of K's labour force leaving the firm and this has forced the abandonment of the original budget for the department.

The managing director has suggested that the department could be closed down immediately or, by employing contract labour, could be operated to produce 10,000 or 20,000 units in the year. With the exception of the foreman (see Note (v)), the few remaining members of K's production labour force would then be re-deployed within the firm.

The following further information is available:

(i) Each hour of contract labour will cost £3.00 and will produce one unit of the product. Contract labour would have to be trained at a fixed cost of £20,000.

(ii) There are 30,000 litres of material A in stock. This material has no other use and any of it not used in department K will have to be disposed of. Costs of disposal will be £2,000 plus £0.50 per litre disposed of.

(iii) There are 15,000 kilos of material B in stock. If the material is not used in department K then up to 10,000 kilos could be used in another department to substitute for an equivalent weight of a material which currently costs £1.8 per kilo. Material B originally cost £1.5 per kilo and its current market price (buying or selling) is £2.0 per kilo. Costs to Hilton of selling any surplus material B will amount to £1.00 per kilo sold.

(iv) Variable overheads will be 30% higher, per unit produced, than originally budgeted.

(v) Included in 'Fixed manufacturing overheads' are
 (a) £6,000 salary of the departmental foreman,
 (b) £7,000 depreciation of the machine used in the department.

If the department is closed immediately the foreman, who will otherwise retire at the end of the year, will be asked to retire early and paid £2,000 compensation for agreeing to this.

The only machine used in the department originally cost £70,000 and could currently be sold for £43,000. This sales value will reduce to £40,000 at the end of the year and, if used for any production

during the year, will decrease by a further £500 per 1,000 units produced.

(vi) All other costs included in 'Fixed manufacturing overhead' and all 'Non-manufacturing costs' are apportionments of general overheads none of which will be altered by any decision concerning the K department.

(vii) The sales manager suggests that a sales volume of 10,000 units could be achieved if the unit sales price were £9.00. A sales volume of 20,000 units would be achieved if the sales price per unit were reduced to £8 and an advertising campaign costing £15,000 were undertaken.

rented out for one year at a rental of £8,000. (2 marks)

(ii) The quoted level of efficiency of the contract labour is the *average* for productiion of the first 5,000 units and any additional production would reflect the effects of the 90% learning curve which will be experienced. Show also the revised contract labour costs. (5 marks)

(20 marks)

Ignore taxation and the time value of money.

*ACCA P2 Management Accounting
June 1981*

10.14 The budgeted product profitability report of Midland Ltd for each of its products for the forthcoming year is as follows:

Product	V £000	W £000	X £000	Y £000	Z £000	Total £000
Sales	4,400	4,900	6,500	5,100	9,100	30,000
Manufacturing costs						
Materials	220	660	1,320	1,100	1,650	4,950
Labour	500	800	1,500	1,400	1,800	6,000
Production overhead— variable	250	350	400	500	720	2,220
Production overhead— fixed	350	600	1,100	1,000	950	4,000
	1,320	2,410	4,320	4,000	5,120	17,170
Transport and delivery costs						
Transport	120	360	720	600	650	2,450
Packaging	200	100	200	100	300	900
	320	460	920	700	950	3,350
Selling and advertising expenses	720	545	525	555	755	3,100
Administration	660	735	975	765	1,365	4,500
Total cost	£3,020	£4,150	£6,740	£6,020	£8,190	£28,120
Profit	£1,380	£750	£(240)	£(920)	£910	£1,880

Required:
(a) Advise Hilton Ltd of its best course of action regarding department K, presenting any data in tabular form. (13 marks)
(b) For each of the following separate circumstances show how the advice given in (a) above is altered.
 (i) Immediate closure of department K would enable its factory space to be

The management accountant provides the following additional information concerning the basis on which the above report was prepared:
 (i) Material costs are a combination of variable material cost and a 10% surcharge which is added to the basic variable material cost in order to recover the fixed costs of storage and stores administration.

(ii) Labour is to be considered a variable cost.

(iii) Fixed production overhead comprises some directly attributable fixed costs which are allocated to their appropriate product together with an apportionment of general fixed production overhead. The general fixed production overhead amounts to £3,000,000 and is apportioned in proportion to labour costs, i.e. 50% of labour costs. The attributable fixed cost is avoidable if the product to which it relates is not produced.

(iv) Transport charge comprises a fixed cost of £450,000 and a variable charge. The fixed cost is apportioned to products in proportion to their material costs.

(v) Selling and advertising expenses comprise advertising expenses directly related, and therefore directly attributed, to each product and a sales commission which equals 5% of sales revenues. Advertising costs are avoidable fixed costs.

(vi) Administration is a fixed cost and is apportioned in proportion to sales revenue.

(vii) Packaging is a variable cost.

The managing director feels that products X and Y should not be produced as they both result in a loss.

The marketing manager makes two points:

(1) Sales of any product can be increased by up to 40% of the sales figures contained in the above report merely by pursuing an additional extensive advertising campaign. If any product were selected to have its sales increased the additional advertising campaign would cost three times the currently planned cost of advertising that product. The relationship between advertising costs and increased sales applies to each product and is a proportional relationship, e.g. sales could increase by 20% if advertising were increased by 150%.

(2) By reducing sales (and production) of product X the demand for *either* V or W will rise depending upon which product is offered as a substitute for X. If V is offered as the substitute then each £1 reduction in sales of X will cause an increase in sales of V of £0.45. If W is the substitute then each £1 reduction in sales of X will cause an increase in sales of W of £0.50.

Required:

(a) Advise the managing director of the desirability of ceasing production of products X and Y and prepare a statement which shows the effect that not producing X and Y will

have on the profits of Midland Ltd. (c. 8 marks)

(b) (i) Show the effect of pursuing the advertising campaign mentioned by the marketing manager in order to increase sales of each product by 40%. Indicate which products it would be worthwhile advertising. (ii) If only £1,200,000 is available for advertising indicate which products should then be advertised? (c. 5 marks)

(c) Should sales (and production) of X be reduced in favour of either V or W? If so, which product should be offered as a substitute for X? Show the effect of reducing sales of X to zero. (c. 5 marks)

(d) Give two examples of an attributable fixed production overhead cost (c. 2 marks)

(Total 20 marks)

ACCA P2 Management Accounting
December 1979

10.15 You have just been appointed management accountant to a company that markets three products. These are sold to a wide range of industries and marketing is done through three geographical areas: South, Midland and North.

For the year ending 31 December 1981 the company presents you with the budget as shown on p. 224:

Your investigations into the budgeted figures reveal the following:

Sales and cost of goods.

Product:	D	E	F
Units sold in thousands:			
Area: South	33.0	44.0	33.0
Midland	13.2	17.6	13.2
North	19.8	26.4	19.8
Per unit:	£	£	£
Standard selling price	12	10	8
Standard variable production costs	5	4.50	4

Fixed production overhead included in cost of goods sold is £160,000 per annum.

Warehousing costs (packaging and despatch are done in each area).

Area:	South	Midland	North
	£	£	£
Freight costs, negotiated rates per unit of product sold	0.70	0.75	0.80

Budget for year ending 31 December 1981

Area:	South £000	Midland £000	North £000	Total £000
Sales	1,100	440	660	2,200
Cost of goods sold	575	230	345	1,150
Gross profit	525	210	315	1,050
Warehousing cost				
Freight	77	33	52.8	162.8
Supplies	44	17.6	26.4	88
Wages and salaries	74	29.6	44.4	148
	195	80.2	123.6	398.8
Selling costs				
Salesmen's: salaries	30	–	–	30
commissions	22	–	52.8	74.8
expenses	23	–	–	23
Agents' commissions	–	22	–	22
Sales office and management	24.5	9.8	14.7	49
Advertising	95	38	57	190
	194.5	69.8	124.5	388.8
Administration costs	120	48	72	240
Total	509.5	198	320.1	1,027.6
Net profit (or loss)	15.5	12	(5.1)	22.4

Warehouse:

Supplies per unit	0.40	0.40	0.40
Wages per unit	0.65	0.45	0.45
Supervision salaries, per annum	14,000	4,000	9,000

Selling costs.

In South area there are six salesmen each paid a basic wage of £5,000 per annum with a commission of 2% of sales. Their fixed expenses are £2,000 per annum each and variable expenses are 1% of sales.

In Midland area, manufacturers' agents are used. They receive a commission of 5% of sales from which they have to meet all their expenses. However, they can also sell products of other manufacturers provided these are not directly competitive.

In North area there are three salesmen paid solely by a commission of 8% of sales. From this they have to meet all their expenses.

The salaries of the company sales manager and his assistant together with their expenses, total £25,000 per annum. Of the total advertis-

ing £130,000 is national advertising under the direction of the company sales manager.
Other sales office and advertising costs.

Area:	South £	Midland £	North £
Local sales office costs	12,000	4,000	8,000
Local advertising	40,000	5,000	15,000

Administration costs, per annum.

Fixed costs relating to the whole company are £140,000.

The remainder varies with the number of orders which are budgeted at: South 32,000; Midland 6,000; North 12,000.

The company uses a cut-off rate of 14% per annum in deciding on capital expenditure projects.

You are to deal with each of the following four requirements independently of one another. Assume that items not affected by the suggested changes stay the same; ignore taxation and inflation.

(a) State with reasons whether, in view of the loss shown in the budget presented to you,

you agree with a proposal to close the North area.

(b) Calculate what extra sales value would need to be made in the Midland area to cover additional local advertising of £15,000 there and provide an extra profit of £10,000. Assume that the average value per order remains constant.

(c) Calculate the benefit or otherwise of a proposal to change in Midland area from manufacturers' agents to a salaried sales force of three salesmen paid on the same basis as those in South area if an increase in sales of 15% were achieved (representing an increase of 10% of the number of orders) as a result of the change.

(d) Explain, with supporting calculations, whether you would approve of a proposal to change the basis of remuneration of salesmen in North area to that operating in South area. The change would require the immediate payment of £3,500 to each salesman in North area as compensation, and, as a result of the change, sales would alter as follows:

Year	Proportion of 1981 budget	
	Sales	Number of orders received
	%	%
1981	95	98
1982	100	100
1983	105	105

(30 marks)
*ICMA P3 Management Accounting
May 1980*

10.16 Mardel Ltd is a vertically integrated company engaged in the extraction, treatment, and distribution of Mardel.
Supply sources
It draws its supplies of raw Mardel from three sources.

Source A: This is wholly owned by Mardel Ltd and is located 250 miles from the company's treatment plant. At source A maximum output is 6,000 tonnes per annum and extraction involves variable costs of £6 per tonne with fixed costs of £1,500 per annum. Another company has offered to buy at source up to the maximum output of this source for £6.75 per tonne.

Source B: This is owned equally by the company and a sole trader, X, in partnership. It is located 250 miles from the company's treatment plant and has a maximum output of 18,000 tonnes per annum. Its fixed costs of £5,000 per annum are shared equally by the partners and its variable extraction costs are £6 per tonne. The partnership agreement requires each partner to extract a minimum of 5,000 tonnes per annum. The sole trader X has indicated that he does not wish to extract more than his minimum this year, so the remaining 8,000 tonnes is available to Mardel Ltd if it so wishes. For every tonne of this 8,000 tonnes, Mardel's costs would be one-half of the variable cost plus £4.50 payment to X.

Source C: This is wholly owned by the company, is located 500 miles from the treatment plant and has a maximum output of 30,000 tonnes per annum. Variable costs are £4.25 per tonne and fixed costs £6,000 per annum.

Transport and plant
Mardel Ltd owns a fleet of carriers that can carry 17.5 million tonne-miles per annum of raw Mardel. The fixed costs of the fleet are £70,000 per annum and the variable costs £0.005 per tonne-mile. There is an active market for chartering in or chartering out of these carriers at £0.011 per tonne-mile.

Mardel Ltd's treatment plant has a capacity of 40,000 tonnes per annum of raw Mardel and there is no physical loss in the conversion of raw to treated Mardel. Variable costs are £0.25 per tonne, fixed costs are £40,000 per annum.

Customers
Mardel Ltd's customers are of two types:
 contract customers with long-term commitments at fixed prices;
 spot customers who indicate their willingness to purchase specific quantities at specific prices over the year.
There are two contract customers:

CC1 takes 4,000 tonnes per annum. The price is £12.50 per tonne delivered to a location 8 miles from the treatment plant.

CC2 takes 4,000 tonnes per annum direct from the treatment plant. The price is £11.75 per tonne but if Mardel supplies to CC2's competitor (SC4) at a lower price, then the price to CC2 must be reduced to that level.

There are nine potential spot customers for the coming year:

Customer	Quantity 1,000 tonnes	Price per tonne £	Delivery	Distance from treatment plant in miles
SC1	4	12.50 ⎤	Ex	–
SC2	6	9.25 ⎮	treatment	–
SC3	4	8.50 ⎮	plant	–
SC4	2	11.15 ⎦		–
SC5	5	11.50 ⎤		30
SC6	2	12.45 ⎮	To	2
SC7	3	15.00 ⎬	customer's	20
SC8	6	12.50 ⎮	factory	26
SC9	3	12.50 ⎦		10

Mardel Ltd will, when required, provide its own lorries for delivery from the treatment plant to its customers. Fixed costs are £3,000 per annum and variable costs £0.10 per tonne-mile.

You are required to:

(a) recommend for the coming year what extraction, treatment, selling, and transportation action Mardel Ltd should take if it is to maximize its profit;

(b) calculate what profit for the year would result from your recommendations. (30 marks) *ICMA P3 Management Accounting November 1980*

10.17* Explain why some figures which are validly incorporated into routine management accounting statements reporting on the efficiency or profitability of a department or product, may not be relevant for decision-making purposes concerning those same departments or products.

Outline the relevant costs for decision-making purposes. (20 marks)

ACCA P2 Management Accounting December 1981

11 Accounting information for pricing decisions

In the previous chapter we looked at how costs and benefits should be measured. Our objective was to provide the relevant financial information to assist management in selecting those opportunities which would lead to the maximization of future net cash inflows. We concentrated mainly on the determination of the relevant costs which are required for making various decisions. In this chapter we shall consider the determination of total cash inflows. Cash inflows are determined by the volume of sales multiplied by the selling price. In the long run an organization's total cash inflows must exceed its cash outflows if it is to survive. Consequently the pricing decision is one of the most crucial and difficult decisions which a firm has to make. The objective of this chapter is to consider what contribution accounting information can make to a firm's pricing decisions.

Accounting information is often an important input to pricing decisions. In some firms, selling prices are derived directly from cost information by estimating future product costs and adding a suitable profit margin. In other firms, an established market price is accepted. Nevertheless, cost information is still of considerable importance for determining the relative profitability of different products so that management can establish a target product mix and output to

which its marketing effort should be directed. Kaplan (1982) states:

> If the firm is selling a standard commodity, actively traded in commodity markets, then the firm will almost surely be a price taker, accepting the price given in the marketplace. In this situation the firm may need to determine its scale of operations, its production technology, or whether to be in this market at all, but it will not have to worry about how to set price. This function will be efficiently carried out in the marketplace.
>
> Usually, however, a firm has some flexibility in its pricing decisions and has the option of trading off higher prices against lower output. The firm's objective is to determine the combination of price and output that maximizes total contribution margin.

The theoretical solution to pricing decisions is presented in the economists' pricing model which explains how the optimum selling price is determined. A knowledge of this model provides a suitable framework for discussing the cost information which is appropriate for pricing decisions. The economists' model for pricing decisions is therefore the starting point of this chapter.

The economists' pricing model

Demand curves

The central feature of the economic model is the assumption that the firm will attempt to set the selling price at a level where profits are maximized. For monopolistic/imperfect competition the model assumes that the lower the price, the larger will be the volume of sales.[1] This relationship is depicted in Fig. 11.1, which is known as a demand curve.

Fig. 11.1 A demand curve

Points A and B represent two of many possible price/quantity combinations. You will·see that at a price of P_A, the quantity demanded will be Q_A, while at the lower price of P_B the quantity demanded will increase to Q_B. The economist describes the sensitivity of demand to changes in price as *the price elasticity of demand*. Demand is elastic when there are substitutes for a product, or when customers do not value the product very highly; the result is that a small increase/decrease in price causes a large decrease/increase in the quantity demanded. Alternatively, demand is inelastic when customers place a high value on the product, or when no close substitutes exist; the result is that a small increase/decrease in price causes only a small decrease/increase in the quantity demanded (see Fig. 11.2).

If you compare these two graphs you will see that in graph (A) an increase in price from P_A to

P_B results in only a small reduction in the quantity demanded, whereas in graph (B) the same increase in price results in a large reduction in the quantity demanded. For a discussion of attempts to measure elasticity of demand in practice see Wills (1971).

Establishing the optimum selling price

The precise quantification of the relationship between the selling price and the quantity demanded is very difficult in practice, but let us assume here that management has produced an estimate of the sales demand at various selling prices. This information is set out in Exhibit 11.1.

Exhibit 11.1 Estimate of sales demand at different price levels

Price £	Unit of sales Demand	Total revenue £	Marginal revenue £
40	10	400	
38	11	418	18
36	12	432	14
34	13	442	10
32	14	448	6
30	15	450	2
28	16	448	−2

Fig. 11.2 Price elasticity of demand

You will note that if the price is reduced from £40 to £38 the total revenue will increase by £18, and that each successive price reduction causes incremental or marginal revenue to increase by successively smaller amounts. This process eventually results in a decline in total revenue when the price per unit is reduced from £30 to £28.

To determine the optimum selling price (that is, the price at which total profits are maximized) it is also necessary for management to estimate the total costs for each of the sales levels given in Exhibit 11.1; this cost information is set out in Exhibit 11.2.

Exhibit 11.2 Estimate of total costs at different volume levels

Price £	Demand and output	Total costs £	Marginal cost £
40	10	360	
38	11	364	4
36	12	370	6
34	13	378	8
32	14	388	10
30	15	400	12
28	16	414	14

The final stage is to calculate the profit for each sales level and select the most profitable price–volume combination. The profit calculations are obtained by combining the information given in Exhibits 11.1 and 11.2 (see Exhibit 11.3).

Exhibit 11.3 Estimate of profits at different output levels

Price £	Units sold	Total revenue £	Total cost £	Profit £
40	10	400	360	40
38	11	418	364	54
36	12	432	370	62
34	13	442	378	64
32	14	448	388	60
30	15	450	400	50
28	16	448	414	34

You can see from this exhibit that profits are maximized at a selling price of £34 when 13 units are sold.

Graphical presentation

The economist will normally present the information contained in Exhibits 11.1 to 11.3 in graphical form: see Fig. 11.3.

The shape of the graphs for the total revenue and the total cost lines is based on the explanations outlined in Chapter 9. If we refer to the top diagram in Fig. 11.3 it indicates that the difference between total revenue and total cost increases as long as total revenue is climbing more rapidly than total cost. When total cost is climbing more rapidly than total revenue (that is, unit marginal cost exceeds unit marginal revenue) a decision to increase the number of units sold will actually reduce the total profit. The difference between total cost and total revenue is the greatest at a volume level of 13 units; the price required to generate this demand is £34 and this is the optimum selling price.

The lower part of Fig. 11.3 shows the cost and revenue information in terms of marginal revenue and marginal cost. Marginal revenue represents the increase in total revenue from the sale of one additional unit, and marginal cost represents the increase in total cost when output is increased by one additional unit. Note that the *marginal revenue line* slopes downwards to the right as demand increases reflecting the fact that the slope of the *total revenue line* decreases as demand increases. Similarly, the marginal cost line slopes upwards because of the assumption that total cost increases as output increases.

Exhibit 11.1 and the demand/price curve in the lower part of Fig. 11.3 indicates that to increase sales demand from 10 units to 11 units it is necessary to reduce the selling price from £40 to £38. This increases total revenue from £400 to £418, the difference of £18 being the marginal revenue of the eleventh unit (shown in the graph as the height of the marginal revenue line at that point). The marginal revenues for the twelfth, thirteenth and fourteenth units are £14, £10 and £6, respectively. The marginal cost is calculated by assessing the cost of one extra unit (or batch, etc.), and this information is presented in Exhibit

Fig. 11.3 The economists' model for establishing
optimum price

the top part of the graph, it will cut the total cost and the total revenue curves at the point where the difference between these two lines is the greatest. In other words, it cuts the total cost and total revenue curves at the points where the profits are maximized. The graphs in the lower and upper sections of Fig. 11.3 are therefore related, and this dual presentation clearly indicates that the point where the difference between total cost and total revenue is the greatest is where marginal revenue is equal to marginal cost. The selling price which causes marginal revenue to be equal to marginal cost represents the optimum selling price.

Oligopoly and perfect competition

The basic notion that marginal cost should equal marginal revenue to determine the optimum selling price is common under all market structures. In *perfect competition*, the selling price is given, and economic analysis is used to determine what level of output will be most profitable to the firm. Under perfect competition the mechanics of the approach may differ but the underlying theory is the same. If we apply the basic theory to *oligopolies* it closely approximates the model previously presented. In an oligopoly there are a few large sellers, each with a large share of the market. In a market where there are few competitors interdependence in decision-making becomes the dominant consideration. The revenue of a given seller depends upon the reactions of competitors to changes in its selling prices. An action taken by one firm will cause a reaction by others, and the optimal price and output decisions depend on how the competing firms react. The appropriate pricing policy becomes a problem of strategy and it is impossible to make sweeping generalizations. However, Savage and Small (1977) lay down the following general principles for oligopoly pricing:

(1) The fact that each seller knows that a price cut will be met promptly usually destroys the effect of overt price cuts as a means of extending market shares.

11.2. For example, the marginal cost is £4 for the eleventh unit and £6 for the twelfth unit. The marginal cost is plotted in Fig. 11.3 and the *optimum price is determined by the intersection of the marginal revenue and marginal cost curves*; this is at a price of £34 when sales demand will be 13 units. Note that the intersection of the graphs occurs at a demand just in excess of 13 units. Clearly, we must work in whole units demanded and therefore the optimal output is 13 units. The demand curve is also included in the lower part of Fig. 11.3 and to obtain the optimum price it is necessary to extend a vertical line upwards from the intersection of the marginal cost and marginal revenue curves. The point where this line cuts the demand curve provides us with the optimum selling price.

Note that if the vertical line at the point of intersection of the marginal cost and marginal revenue curve is extended further upwards into

(2) Many businesses in this situation believe that their demand curve is inelastic for price cuts but elastic for price increases.

(3) Most oligopolists do not use price changes as their main competitive weapon but prefer rigid prices.

(4) Rigid prices cannot be held to uncompromisingly in a dynamic world. Therefore businesses tend to resort instead to other devices such as (a) non-price competition, (b) price leadership, or (c) collusion, as an escape from the dilemma posed by the need to adjust to a changing business environment, with the need to maintain a precarious oligopoly price structure. However, price leadership and collusion may be restrained by law as 'restrictive practices'.

Thus a model which includes only price incorporates only a portion of the factors which contribute to a product's sales demand. However, the basic economic model can be adapted to incorporate other variables which influence demand using multiple regression techniques. For a discussion of the application of multiple regression models to estimate sales demand see Maurice and Smithson (1981).

Fourth, the economic model assumes that firms are profit maximizers, but many legal and social goals and constraints influence management's desire for profit. For example, stability, growth and security are other important goals to managers and they may be obtainable only at the expense of profit maximization.

For all these reasons we should not be surprised if many firms do not price their products so that marginal revenue equals marginal cost.

Problems with the economists' model

While the theoretical model developed by economists is sound, it is difficult to apply it directly in practice. The difficulties can be grouped into four categories. First, the economist assumes that a firm's demand curve is known. The precise quantification of the demand schedule for a firm's products is not easy. Consider a firm which sells a wide range of products. The prediction of sales demand for each of the products at different prices cannot be made in a very exacting manner. The most that a firm can hope for is to obtain an approximation of the demand curve.

Second, we noted in Chapter 9 that the accountants' total cost and marginal cost functions for various output levels are likely to provide only an approximation of the true cost function. The marginal cost curve can only be computed after considerable analysis, judgement and arbitrary allocations. For a detailed discussion of the probloems see Kaplan (1982).

Third, there are many other factors which influence the quantity demanded besides price. For example, the amount and quality of the sales effort, the design and packaging of the product, the channels of distribution and the credit terms offered all have an important influence on price.

Cost-based pricing formulas

Probably the most widely used method of pricing a product is to estimate the unit cost and then add a percentage mark-up to this cost to provide a reasonable level of profit. Such an approach is termed *cost-plus pricing*. In a survey of pricing procedures in the UK, Skinner (1970) found that 70% of the firms used cost-plus pricing. The cost-plus approach has been adopted because of the need to ensure that the selling price is greater than the total cost of a product so that a firm can generate profits and survive in the future.[2]

Cost-based pricing formulas encompass a variety of different methods which are used to establish the cost. For example, total cost, manufacturing cost or relevant cost may form the basis for the calculation of 'cost' in the formula. The 'plus' will also vary depending on which cost figure is used. For example, if total cost is used the mark-up will be added to provide an acceptable profit per unit. Alternatively, if total manufacturing cost is used, the 'plus' which is added must be sufficient to cover non-manufacturing overheads and to provide an acceptable profit per unit. Let us consider in more detail some cost-based pricing formulas.

Total cost plus

The price of the product is calculated by the accumulation of expected future costs per unit produced. An example of a typical price calculation is as follows:

		£
Direct materials		10
Direct labour		15
Factory overheads: Fixed	10	
Variable	5	15
Total manufacturing cost		40
Non-manufacturing overheads:		
Fixed	10	
Variable	0	10
Total cost		50
Add Profit margin (20% on total cost)		10
Selling price		60

One problem which arises if this method is adopted is the difficulty of allocating non-manufacturing costs to products. For example, it is not possible to estimate how much of the administrative overheads are attributable to a specific product as these costs are common and unavoidable to all alternatives.

Manufacturing cost plus

If this cost is used as a basis for the formula, a cost of £40 would be arrived at, using the information in the above example. To this figure a higher mark-up would need to be added to cover non-manufacturing overheads as well as to provide a profit contribution. For example, the calculation may be as follows:

Total manufacturing cost	40
Add Profit margin (50% on manufacturing cost)	20
Selling price	60

If the percentage margin which is added is increased to 50%, the selling price will be the same as for the total cost plus method, but the manufacturing cost-plus method has the advantage of avoiding the problem of estimating the amount of non-manufacturing overhead which should be allocated to the product. However, this may be illusory as management has to ensure that the profit margin percentage is sufficient to cover all the non-manufacturing overheads which must be

recovered in the selling price.

One advantage of this approach is that cost is based on the same figure as that used for stock valuation and, if the firm has produced similar products in the past, the estimate of total manufacturing cost can be obtained simply by adjusting past costs for future expected price changes.

Relevant cost plus

You will recall from our discussion in the previous chapter that certain costs will remain unchanged in the short term and are not relevant for short-term decisions. Those costs which do change as a result of selling the product are the relevant costs. The advantage of the relevant cost-plus approach is that management can see that any selling price above the relevant cost will provide a contribution towards the fixed costs of the company. Also if management is not made aware of the relevant costs there is a danger that the firm might lose profitable trade at a selling price which is below 'Total or manufacturing cost plus', thus missing the opportunity of obtaining a contribution towards fixed costs.

Using the price calculation in the 'Total cost plus' illustration and assuming that only the variable costs are relevant, the relevant cost will be £30. If we assume that spare capacity exists and that a customer is prepared to pay £40 for the product then the relevant cost approach indicates that short-term profits will increase (or losses will decrease) by £10 if the order is accepted. This approach is particularly useful in a situation where a company cannot sell any more of its products to its normal market but has covered its fixed costs in sales to this market. If the company has some spare capacity it may try to sell to another market at a lower price but above relevant cost; a contribution towards fixed costs will be obtained and profit will increase.

Relevent cost information enables a more flexible approach to pricing to be adopted by clearly indicating the cost below which the price must not fall if the company wishes to avoid decisions which will contribute to short-term losses. It is also possible to add a very large margin to the relevant cost to estimate a longer-term selling price for normal sales. For example, if a margin of 100% is added to the relevant cost of £30, the selling price will be £60, the same as using the other methods. Clearly, if this method of

pricing is adopted a company should ensure that the method of establishing selling prices is not based on small percentage margins above the relevant cost. If this does occur there is a danger that sales revenue will not be sufficient to cover total fixed costs. In the long run both variable and fixed costs must be recovered from selling prices if the firm is to generate sufficient cash flows to survive. In a survey of the use of cost data in pricing decisions of companies in the USA, Govindarajan and Anthony (1983) found that manufacturing or total cost is still the predominant base which is used in cost-plus pricing.

Now that we have considered the cost to be used in the pricing formula the next stage is to examine the 'plus' which should be added.

Establishing target mark-up percentages

Target mark-up percentages are likely to be varied from product line to product line to correspond with well established differences in custom, competitive position and likely demand. For example, luxury goods with a low sales turnover may attract high profit margins whereas non-luxury goods with a high sales turnover may attract low profit margins. Consider the sales of a jeweller compared with the sales of a super-market: a jeweller operates on a low sales turnover and a high profit margin, whereas a supermarket operates on a high sales turnover and a low profit margin.

Another approach is to estimate the amount of investment which is attributable to a product and then set a price which ensures a satisfactory return on investment for a given volume. For example, assume that cost per unit is £10 and that the annual volume is 10,000 units. If £100,000 investment is required and the target rate of return is 15%, the target mark-up will be

$$\frac{15\% \times £100,000}{10,000 \text{ units}} = £1.50 \text{ per unit}$$

The target price will be £10 plus £1.50 or £11.50 per unit.

Note that once the target selling price has been calculated it is rarely adopted without amendment. The price is adjusted upwards or downwards depending on such factors as the future capacity which is available, the extent of competition from other firms, and management's general knowledge of the market. For example, if

the price calculation is much lower than that which management considers the customer will be prepared to pay then the price may be increased. Alternatively, if similar products are selling at prices well below the calculated price then it may be necessary to adjust the calculated price downwards.

We may ask ourselves the question 'Why should cost-based pricing formulas be used when the final price is likely to be altered by management?' The answer is that cost-based pricing formulas provide an initial approximation of the selling price. It is a target price and is important information, although by no means the only information which should be used when the final pricing decisions is made. Management should use this information, together with their knowledge of the market and their intended pricing strategies, before the final price is set.

Limitations of cost-plus pricing

Ignores demand

The main objection to cost-plus pricing is that it ignores demand. The price is set by adding a margin to cost and this may bear no relationship to the price–demand relationship. It is assumed that prices should depend solely on costs. For example, a cost-plus formula may suggest a price of £20 for a product where the demand is 100,000 units, whereas at a price of £25 the demand might be 80,000 units. Assuming that the variable cost for each unit sold is £15, the total contribution will be £500,000 at a selling price of £20, compared with a total contribution of £800,000 at a selling price of £25. Thus cost-plus pricing formulas might lead to incorrect decisions. Baxter and Oxenfeldt (1968) comment on this criticism of cost-plus pricing formulas as follows:

> On the other hand, inability to estimate demand accurately scarcely excuses the substitution of cost information for demand information. Crude estimates of demand may serve instead of careful estimates of demand but cost gives remarkably little insight into demand.

Circular reasoning

There are a number of objections which apply

Unit fixed cost is calculated by dividing total fixed cost by estimated volume. The unit fixed cost is used in the selling price calculation. The selling price will influence sales demand thus affecting management's estimate of future volume. This will cause a change in unit fixed cost which in turn will lead to a revised selling price and estimate of future volume. Hence it is possible for this circular process to continue indefinitely.

Fig. 11.4 An illustration of circular reasoning

specifically to the total cost and manufacturing cost-plus methods of pricing. For example, the approaches involve circular reasoning because price changes affect the volume of sales, which in turn affect unit fixed costs which will also lead to further price changes. This process is illustrated in Fig. 11.4. Consider a situation where total fixed costs are £1,000 and fixed cost per unit is calculated on the basis of a *normal production* volume of 100 units; the fixed cost per unit will be £10. This approach requires that some assumption must be made about future volume prior to ascertaining the cost and calculating selling prices. It seems to be somewhat illogical to use a volume level in the formula to determine cost, which in turn is used to determine selling price.

Let us now assume that *actual sales demand* is 50 units. To calculate the fixed overhead per unit for the next period management may estimate that *normal volume* will be 50 units. The fixed overhead rate per unit based on this volume will now be £20 per unit instead of the original calculation of £10. The cost-based pricing formula will lead to a price increase which may be an

incorrect decision to make at a time when demand is falling.

Common fixed costs

Another problem with cost-plus formulas which include fixed costs is that fixed overheads are apportioned to products on some arbitrary basis. There are many different ways by which fixed costs can be apportioned and the effect of this is that the cost will be different depending on which apportionment method is used. The overall effect of arbitrary apportionments is that the selling price calculation will vary according to which apportionment method is used.

Pricing floor

It is often claimed that cost-based pricing formulas serve as a pricing 'floor' shielding the seller from a loss. This argument is, however, incorrect as it is quite possible for a firm to lose money even though every product is priced higher than the estimated unit cost. The reason for this is that, if sales demand falls below the activity level which was used to calculate the fixed cost per unit, the total sales revenue may be insufficient to cover the total fixed costs. Cost-plus pricing will only ensure that all the costs will be met and the target profits earned if the sales volume is equal to or more than the activity level which was used to estimate total unit costs.

Reasons for using cost-based pricing formulas

Considering the limitations of cost-plus pricing, why is it that these techniques are frequently used in practice? Baxter and Oxenfeldt (1968) suggest the following reasons:

They offer a means by which plausible prices can be found with ease and speed, no matter how many products the firm handles. Moreover, its imposing computations look factual and precise, and its prices may well seem more defensible on moral grounds than prices established by other means. Thus a monopolist threatened by a public inquiry might reasonably

feel that he is safeguarding his case by using cost-plus pricing.

Encourages price stability

Perhaps one of the major reasons for the wide-spread use of cost-plus pricing methods is that it may help a firm to predict the prices of other firms. For example, if a firm has been operating in an industry where average mark-ups have been 40% in the past, it may be possible to predict that competitors will be adding a 40% mark-up to their costs. Assuming that all the firms in the industry have similar cost structures it will be possible to predict the price range within which competitors may price their products. If all the firms in an industry price their products in this way it may encourage price stability. For example, Simmonds (1982) suggests that it may be possible to assess the cost–volume–profit relationship of competitors in order to predict their pricing responses.

Target mark-ups adjusted

In response to the main objection that cost-based pricing formulas ignore demand, note that the actual price which is calculated by the formula is rarely adopted without amendments. The price is adjusted upwards or downwards after taking account of the number of sales orders on hand, the extent of competition from other firms, the importance of the customer in terms of future sales, and the policy relating to customer relations. Therefore, it is argued that management attempts to adjust the mark-up based on the state of sales demand and other factors which are of vital importance in the pricing decision. For a discussion of target mark-up adjustments see Qualls (1977).

Minor revenue producing products

The final reason for the extensive use of cost-based pricing formulas is that many firms have so many products that it would be impossible to analyse price–volume relationships for them all. By adopting cost-based pricing formulas for the less important revenue-earning products management may be able to devote more time to establishing price–volume relationships for the more important products. For example, an

analysis of a company's estimates total sales revenue might indicate that approximately 80% of its total sales revenue is earned from about 20% of its products. This type of analysis is known as *Pareto analysis*, and is based on observations by Pareto (1848–1923) that a very small proportion of items usually accounts for the majority of value. More sophisticated pricing methods should be applied to the small proportion of products which jointly account for 80% of the total sales revenue. For the remaining 80% of the products which generate 20% of the total sales revenue there may be strong arguments for using cost-based pricing formulas. This will enable top management to delegate the pricing decision to lower levels of management, thus freeing themselves to concentrate on the pricing decisions for those products which are essential for a company's survival.

Relevant costs for pricing decisions

Taking into account the problems associated with using cost-based pricing formulas and the argument that a more sophisticated pricing approach should be adopted for a company's major revenue earning products, we must ask the question, 'What cost information should be provided for the *major pricing decisions?*' You will recall that in the previous chapter it was argued that cost information for decision-making should be based on relevant costs and should not include irrelevant costs such as common and unavoidable fixed overheads. Because the pricing decision is a major decision in any organization, the arguments which apply to decision-making in general must also apply to pricing decisions. In other words, relevant cost and revenue information should be provided for pricing decisions. Let us consider an example of how relevant cost information can be applied to a pricing decision.

EXAMPLE 11.1

XYZ Ltd is introducing a new product. The company intends to hire machinery to manufacture the product at a cost of £200,000 per annum. However, this will only enable 60,000 units per annum to be produced, although additional machines can be hired at £80,000 per annum. Each machine hired enables capacity to be increased by 20,000 units per annum but it is not possible to increase production beyond 90,000 units because of shortage of space. The minimum rental period is for one year

Exhibit 11.4 Relevant cost information for a pricing decision

Units produced	50,000 £	60,000 £	70,000 £	80,000 £	90,000 £
Relevant cost[3] (that is, Variable cost)	300,000	360,000	420,000	480,000	540,000
Specific fixed cost (hire of machinery)	200,000	200,000	280,000	280,000	360,000
Total cost specific to the product	500,000	560,000	700,000	760,000	900,000
Required contribution to general fixed costs and profit	200,000	200,000	200,000	200,000	200,000
Total specific costs plus required contribution	700,000	760,000	900,000	960,000	1,100,000
Specific cost per unit (£)	10	9.33	10.00	9.50	10.00
Specific cost plus required contribution per unit (£)	14	12.67	12.86	12.00	12.22

and the variable cost is estimated to be £6 per unit produced. There are no other fixed costs which can be specifically allocated to the product but management considers that this product should provide a target contribution of £200,000 towards fixed overheads and profit. You are required to provide relevant financial information to management for the pricing and output decision.

You should present management with the relevant cost information for a wide range of possible output levels, clearly indicating those costs which are relevant *future* costs. In addition you should present those costs which are sunk and irrelevant, but which are specific to the product and which should be recovered if the revenue from the product is to cover its long-term costs. The required information is set out in Exhibit 11.4.

Selling in different markets at different prices

A company may not sell all of its output at one price; it may sell in different markets at different prices. For example, output which cannot be sold in the main market may be disposed of at a different price in an overseas market, or the same product may be sold under different brand names at different selling prices. The appropriate cost information, similar to that presented in Exhibit 11.4, should be provided by the accountant to assist management in setting selling prices.

The relevant cost per unit in Exhibit 11.4 represents the additional future cost per unit from the manufacture of the product; it is equivalent to the variable cost per unit if the company is

committed to the hire of machinery. This unit cost represents the minimum short-run selling price per unit. In times of a recession the sales personnel should be instructed to negotiate the highest selling price above £6 unit variable cost. Similarly, if the firm is *disposing of excess production* which is unsold in the main market, the variable cost per unit represents the minimum selling price for units sold in the secondary market.

For sales in the main market, the selling price in the long term should cover *at least* those costs which can be specifically identified with the product. In the long term the selling price should also be sufficient to provide a contribution towards the general fixed costs and the profit. The specific cost per unit represents the *minimum* acceptable selling price per unit in normal trading circumstances. The sales personnel should be instructed to negotiate a selling price above the specific cost per unit so that a contribution towards general fixed costs and profit is obtained. One possibility is for management to assign an appropriate share of general fixed costs and a target profit to the product. In Example 11.1 this is £200,000 which gives a *target* long-run selling price calculation which varies from £12 to £14. The possible range of selling prices if we assume that the policy is to sell as much as possible in the main market and to dispose of the unsold production in secondary markets is as follows:

Minimum short-run price	£6.00 variable cost
Minimum long-run price	£9.33 – £10 specific cost per unit
Target long-run price	£12 – £14

Note that these selling prices represent minimum prices, and the sales personnel should be

instructed to negotiate the best price they can above the minimum level. The long-run selling prices will vary depending on the estimated sales demand, and they should be negotiated within the given ranges based on an assessment of likely demand.

Selling all the output at the same selling price

When a product is being sold at a single price, an effort should be made to estimate the demand at various selling prices. Estimates of demand may be derived from informed judgements of marketing personnel based on their knowledge of the firm's customers and prices of competing products, statistical analysis of historical data or market surveys. For a detailed discussion of the techniques for estimating the impact of price on sales volume see Harvey and Thompson (1980), who argue that there is no logical reason for retaining the cost-plus approach to pricing and that the only valid method is to use demand forecasting across a range of prices. Example 11.1 will be used to illustrate such an approach. Let us also assume that the marketing management has estimated the maximum selling prices which will be necessary to sell various levels of output in Example 11.1. Assume that the estimated selling prices for a range of output from 50,000 units to 90,000 units are as follows:

Units sold	50,000	60,000	70,000	80,000	90,000	90,000[4]
Selling price (£1)	22	20	19	18	17	15
Total sales revenue (£)	1,100,000	1,200,000	1,330,000	1,440,000	1,530,000	1,350,000

We can now combine these estimates of total revenue with the estimate of total cost specific to the product contained in Exhibit 11.4. (If the machine hire capacity decision has not been taken then the machine hire will be a relevant cost.) The

combined information is set out in Exhibit 11.5.

When this information is presented to management they will see that a selling price of £18 and the hire of 80,000 units machine capacity will maximize short-term profits, assuming that the estimate of sales demand is correct. Alternatively, a lower selling price of, say, £15 may be chosen to discourage competition and ensure that a larger share of the market is obtained in the future. At a selling price of £15 management will be able to sell its maximum production of 90,000 units. The information contained in Exhibit 11.5 indicates to management that it is estimated that short-term profits will decline by £230,000 (£680,000 − £450,000) if the £15 selling price is adopted. Management can see, therefore, that the cost of adopting a lower than optimal price is £230,000. This cost must be compared with the expected longer-term benefits of reduced competition and a larger share of the market in the future which will result from adopting the £15 selling price.

Sensitivity analysis

The accountant can also extract from Exhibit 11.5 details of the sensitivity of results to variations in policy. For example, if management is undecided whether to charge a selling price of £19 or £18, it would be of interest to know how many additional units must be sold at £18 to ensure that the same profit is obtained as would be if the selling price was £19. At a selling price of £19 the contribution to general fixed costs is £630,000 and the total specific fixed costs are £280,000. Thus, to obtain a contribution of £630,000 to general fixed costs, a

Exhibit 11.5 Revenues and costs for various selling prices

Units sold	50,000	60,000	70,000	80,000	90,000	90,000
Unit selling price (£)	22	20	19	18	17	15
Total revenue (£)	1,100,000	1,200,000	1,330,000	1,440,000	1,530,000	1,350,000
Total cost specific to the product (£)	500,000	560,000	700,000	760,000	900,000	900,000
Contribution to general fixed costs (£)	600,000	640,000	630,000	680,000	630,000	450,000

total contribution of £910,000 is required. When the selling price is reduced to £18 a contribution of £12 per unit is obtained on each sale. Dividing this unit contribution into the required total contribution of £910,000, we get a sales quantity of 75,833 units.

Hence 75,833 units must be sold at £18 to obtain the same total contribution as that which is earned when the selling price is £19. In other words, how confident is management that a reduction in selling price from £19 to £18 will lead to an increase in sales from 70,000 units to 75,833 units? If they are confident that the proposed sales level will be achieved, the selling price of £18 should be selected.

Allowing for uncertainty

The procedure suggested in the previous paragraphs is dependent on management being able to provide sound estimates of sales demand at different selling prices, but this is a very difficult task. One way of resolving the problem is to provide an upper and lower estimate of sales demand for each selling price, and management can then compare the total contribution for each of these levels at each selling price. The resulting upper and lower contribution levels enables management to choose the selling price which appears to offer the best chance of maximizing long-term profits. Alternatively, subjective probabilities of demand for each selling price can be established, and risk profiles can be developed for each alternative price indicating the likelihood of achieving various total contributions. We shall consider this approach in Chapter 12.

Pricing reviews

Once a selling price has been established it should be reviewed at regular intervals and a new price should be arrived at by applying the procedure outlined in the previous section. Sizer (1976) suggests that an essential first stage in the pricing decision is a comprehensive monitoring system which signals the need for a pricing review, and he suggests that such a system might collect some or all of the information contained in Exhibit 11.6. This type of monitoring is likely to identify some of the shifts in demand which are occurring in the market place.

Exhibit 11.6 Price monitoring system

1 Sales, in units and value:
 (a) previous year comparisons
 (b) different markets/channels comparisons
 (c) budget v. actual comparisons
 (d) forecast v. budget comparisons
 (e) forecast v. actual comparisons
2 Competitors' prices and conditions of sale
3 Enquiries from potential customers about a product
4 Sales at 'below list' prices:
 (a) measured as a percentage of total sales
 (b) revenue as a percentage of sales at full list price
5 Types of customers getting the most and largest price reductions
6 Market shares in individual markets
7 Present and forecast product costs:
 (a) production, marketing, etc.
 (b) fixed, variable
8 Product unit and total contributions in different markets
9 Price complaints:
 (a) from customers
 (b) from salesmen
10 Stocks of finished goods at different points in distribution chain
11 Customers' attitudes to company's prices, packaging, etc.
12 Number of lost customers (brand switching)
13 Enquiries and subsequent purchases

Specific products made to order

When a company produces goods which are tailored specifically to a customer's order, each order will be unique. It will not be possible to apply the procedure outlined in the previous paragraphs as each product will be different. The approach which should be taken is for the accountant to provide management with an estimate of the relevant cost of producing the goods. This cost will represent the minimum price at which an order should be accepted and should be used only for short-run decisions or for special pricing decisions.

In addition, it is necessary to estimate the normal annual activity for the production facilities and to calculate a rate per unit of normal activity for charging out the common and unavoidable fixed costs. However, management must be made aware that this rate per unit is appropriate only for a specific level of activity. Alternative fixed overhead charges per unit of activity must also be calculated for different activity levels. Manage-

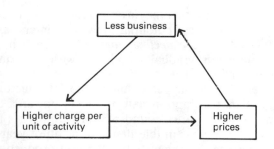

As business declines the revised charges per unit of activity will increase because total fixed costs remain unchanged, but the revised activity estimate will be lower. If this revised cost per unit is used as a basis for increasing the selling price, this will result in less business if conditions remain unchanged. So, if cost-based prices are used, and conditions remain unchanged, the pricing policy will cause future demand to decline.

Fig. 11.5 An illustration of the possible effects of using cost-plus pricing

ment should then check the actual activity against the budgeted activity throughout the year, and periodically revise the estimate of annual activity. This information can then be used to establish revised overhead charges per unit of activity, which should be fed back to the pricing executive. The pricing executive may therefore be working on a number of rates throughout the year.

It is essential that the cost information is used in a flexible manner. When the estimated budgeted activity is revised downwards there will be an increase in the overhead charge per unit of activity. It may be incorrect to use the increased overhead charge as a justification for increasing the selling price when activity is declining; a reduction in selling price may be more appropriate. Figure 11.5 illustrates how an inflexible use of cost information can lead to incorrect pricing decisions. Nevertheless, adopting the approach which has been described ensures that the pricing executive is at least made aware of a target cost, and the objective should be to negotiate a price above this cost. If this is not possible and the current state of the order book is poor, the pricing executive should be prepared to negotiate the best possible price above the relevent cost.

Where a company is operating at full capacity, management should normally set the price above the total cost and achieve at least the target profit per unit. A further point to note is that if recent price quotations have met with ready acceptance by a customer, the company may be justified in increasing the provision for total profit on quotations for new work. Alternatively, when negotiating with a new customer who appears likely to provide the company with a large volume of repeat business, a price below the total cost but above the relevant cost may be appropriate.

Choosing a pricing policy

Cost information is only one of many variables which must be considered in the pricing decision. The final price which is selected will depend upon the pricing policy of the company. A price skimming or pricing penetration policy might be selected.

Price skimming

A price skimming policy is an attempt to exploit those sections of the market which are relatively insensitive to price changes. For example, high initial prices may be charged to take advantage of the novelty appeal of a new product when demand is initially inelastic. A skimming pricing policy offers a safeguard against unexpected future increases in costs, or a large fall in demand after the novelty appeal has declined. Once the market becomes saturated the price can be reduced to attract that part of the market which has not yet been exploited.

A skimming pricing policy should not be adopted when a number of close substitutes are already being marketed. Here the demand curve is likely to be elastic and any price in excess of that being charged for a substitute product by a competitor is likely to lead to a large reduction in sales. Another problem with price skimming is that prices will be high initially and this may encourage competitors to enter the market, leading to an increased supply becoming available in the future and a reduction in the selling price. Thus a company may initially make higher short-term profits by adopting a skimming pricing policy, but this may not maximize profits in the long run. This form of pricing policy is more appropriate when it is difficult for competitors to enter the market, for example when the product

has patent protection or where a large amount of capital investment is required.

Penetration pricing

A penetration pricing policy is based on the concept of charging low prices initially with the intention of gaining rapid acceptance of the product. Such a policy is appropriate when close substitutes are available or when the market is easy to enter. The low price discourages potential competitors from entering the market and enables a company to establish a large share of the market. This can be achieved more easily when the product is new than later on when buying habits have become established.

Product life cycle

Many products have a life cycle which consists of an introductory, a growth, a maturity and a decline stage. At the *introductory stage* the product is launched and there is minimal awareness and acceptance of it. Sales begin to expand rapidly at the *growth stage* because of the introduction of promotions and greater customer awareness, but this begins to taper off at the *maturity stage* as potential new customers are exhausted. At the *decline stage* sales diminish as the product is gradually replaced with new and better versions of it.

Sizer (1980b) suggests that at the introductory stage it may be appropriate to shade upwards or downwards the price found by normal analysis to create a more favourable demand in future years. For example, he suggests that limited production capacity may rule out low prices. Therefore a higher initial price than that suggested by normal analysis may be set and progressively reduced, if and when (A) price elasticity of demand increases or (B) additional capacity becomes available. Alternatively, if there is no production capacity constraint, a lower price than that suggested by normal analysis may be preferred. Such a price may result in a higher sales volume and a slow competitive reaction, which will enable the company to establish a large market share and to earn higher profits in the long term.

At the maturity stage, the firm will be less concerned with the future effects of current selling prices and should adopt a selling price which will maximize short-term profits.

Summary

In this chapter we have considered how accounting information can be used by management in making pricing decisions. For many firms a single market price, or at least a relatively narrow range of market prices for its product, exists. For other firms, where each customer's order is unique, selling prices are derived directly from cost information by estimating future costs and adding a suitable profit margin.

The optimal selling price is that price which determines the optimal volume at which total profits are maximized. This is where marginal revenue equals marginal cost. However, optimal selling prices are not easy to determine in practice because of the difficulty in estimating a product demand curve. Consequently many firms use cost-based pricing formulas where cost is defined as total cost, manufacturing cost or relevant cost. Cost-based pricing formulas are subject to a number of limitations. First, demand is ignored and, second, the approach requires that some assumption is made about future volume prior to ascertaining the cost and calculating the selling prices. This may lead to an increase in the selling price when demand is declining and vice versa. Third, cost includes arbitrary apportionments of common and unavoidable fixed costs which will still continue if the product is not made. Fourth, there is no guarantee that the total sales revenue will be in excess of total costs even when each product is priced above 'cost'.

There are several reasons why cost-based pricing formulas are frequently used in practice. One possible justification is that cost-based pricing methods encourage price stability by enabling firms to predict the prices of their competitors. Also target mark-ups can be adjusted upwards or downwards according to expected demand thus ensuring that demand is indirectly taken into account.

For the major pricing decisions details of relevant product costs and specific product costs should be presented to management and this information should be used in a flexible manner. Where possible estimates of selling prices for various demand levels should be prepared by marketing management. By comparing the cost and revenue estimates for various demand levels it is possible to estimate the selling price which maximizes profits.

References and further reading

Anthony, R.N. A case for historical costs. *Harvard Business Review* November–December 1976, 69-79.

Arnold, J. An approach to pricing and output decisions when prices are changing. *Journal of Business Finance and Accounting* **4**(4), Winter 1977, 383-406.

Atkins, B. and Skinner, R. How British industry prices. *Industrial Market Research* 1975, 5.

Baxter, W.T. and Oxenfeldt, A.R. Costing and pricing: The cost accountant versus the economist. *Business Horizons IV* Winter 1961, 77/90. Reprinted in Solomons, D. (Ed.), *Studies in Cost Analysis* 2nd edn. Sweet & Maxwell, 1968.

Brenner, V.C. An evaluation of product pricing models. In Benston, G.J. (Ed.), *Contemporary Cost Accounting and Control*. Dickenson Publishing Company, 1977.

Flower, J.F. The case of the profitable bloodhound. *Journal of Accounting Research* **4**(1), Spring 1966, 16-36.

Gabor, A. How to price. *Management Today* January 1979, 55-7.

Govindarajan, V. and Anthony, R.N. *Management Accounting (USA)* July 1983, 30-34.

Hague, D.C. *Pricing in Business*. Allen & Unwin, 1971.

Harper, W.M. The pitfalls in fixing prices. *Accountancy* January 1972, 61-3.

Harrison, R. and Wilkes, F.M. Jaguar's pricing policy. *European Journal of Marketing (US)* Winter 1973, 242-6.

Harvey, M. and Thompson, T. The cost-plus pricing fallacy. *Accountancy* August 1980, 124-6.

Kaplan, R.S. *Advanced Management Accounting*. Prentice-Hall, 1982, Ch. 7.

Maurice, S.C. and Smithson, C.W. *Managerial Economics*. R.D. Irwin, 1981, Ch. 4.

Puxty, A. Pricing a new product. *Management Accounting* July/August 1980, 28-30.

Oxendfeldt, A.R. A decision-making structure for pricing decisions. *Journal of Marketing (USA)* January 1973, 48-53.

Qualls, P.D. Market structure and the cyclical flexibility of price cost margins. *Journal of Business* **52**(2), April 1977, 305-25.

Savage, C.I. and Small, J.R. *Introduction to Managerial Economics*. Hutchinson, 1977, Ch. 9.

Scapens, R.W., Gameil, M.Y. and Cooper, J. Accounting information for pricing decisions. In Cooper, D., Scapens, R. and Arnold, J. (Eds), *Management Accounting Research and Practice*. Institute of Cost and Management Accountants, 1983.

Shipley, D.D. Pricing objectives in British manufacturing industry. *Journal of Industrial Economics* June 1981, 429-44.

Silberston, A. Surveys of applied economics: Price behaviour of firms. *The Economic Journal LXXX* September 1970, 511-75.

Simmonds, K. Strategic management accounting for pricing: A case example. *Accounting and Business Research* **12**(47), Summer 1982, 206-14.

Sizer, J. The accountants' contribution to the selling price decision. In Arnold, J., Carsberg, B. and Scapens, R. (Eds), *Topics in Management Accounting*. Phillip Allen, 1980a.

Sizer, J. *An Insight into Management Accounting*. Penguin, 1980b, Chs. 11, 12.

Sizer, J. Export market analysis and pricing strategies. *Management Accounting* January 1983, 30-3.

Sizer, J. Pricing policy in inflation: A management accountant's perspective. *Accounting and Business Research* Spring 1976, 107-24.

Sizer, J. Pricing and the portfolio matrix. *Management Accounting* February 1982, 32-5.

Skinner, R.C. The determination of selling prices. *Journal of Industrial Economics* July 1970.

Smith, A.F. Target pricing: The job coster's dilemma. *Management Accounting* May 1979, 18-22.

Wilkes, F.M. and Harrison, R. Classified pricing rules, cost-plus pricing and the capacity constrained firm. *Journal of Business Finance and Accounting* **2**(1), Spring 1975, 19-38.

Wills, G. How significant is pricing discretion. *Management Accounting* December 1971, 355-9.

Problems

*Indicates that a suggested solution is to be found in the *Students' Manual*.

11.1* Discuss the extent to which cost data is useful in the determination of pricing policy. Explain the advantages and disadvantages of presenting cost data for possible utilization in pricing policy determination using an absorption, rather than a direct, costing basis. (14 marks)
ACCA P2 Management Accounting June 1981

11.2* At one of its regular monthly meetings the board of Giant Steps Ltd was discussing its pricing and output policies. Giant Steps Ltd is a multi-product firm, operating in several distinct but related competitive markets. It aims to maximize profits.

You are required to comment critically and concisely on *any four* of the following six statements which were included in the taped record of the meeting:

(i) Profit is maximized by charging the highest possible price.

(ii) The product manager's pricing policy should be to set a price which will maximize demand, by ensuring that contribution per unit is maximized.

(iii) Allocation of overheads and joint costs

(iv) Allocation of overheads and joint costs is a way of accountants grabbing power and influence from marketing and production people.

(v) Our management accounts must be consistent with our published accounts, so we must follow SSAP 9 on overhead allocation.

(vi) Expenditure on Research and Development would be a past or sunk cost, and no matter what decision about output or price was eventually made it would have no bearing on the recovery of that expenditure. (12 marks)

ICAEW Management Accounting
December 1982

11.3* 'In providing information to the product manager, the accountant must recognize that decision-making is essentially a process of choosing between competing alternatives, each with its own combination of income and costs; and that the relevant concepts to employ are future incremental costs and revenues and opportunity cost, not full cost which includes past or sunk costs.' (Sizer, 1975)

Descriptive studies of pricing decisions taken in practice have, on the other hand, suggested that the inclusion of overhead and joint cost allocations in unit product costs is widespread in connection with the provision of information for this class of decision. Furthermore, these costs are essentially historic costs.

You are required to:

(a) explain the reasoning underlying the above quotation (10 marks),

(b) suggest reasons why overhead and joint cost allocation is nevertheless widely used in practice in connection with information for pricing decisions (10 marks), and

(c) set out your own views as to the balance of these arguments (5 marks).

(25 marks)

ICAEW Management Accounting
July 1982

11.4* You are the newly appointed financial controller of the Guillemot Publishing Co Ltd (GPC). You advise the editorial committee, which has on its agenda a proposal to publish a lavishly-illustrated *Golfer's Annual for 1980*. The editorial committee has to decide whether, and on what terms, to publish the book.

On the basis of past experience the marketing manager estimates that the number of copies that could be sold in the UK market during the year commencing 1 October 1979 would vary with the retail price charged, as follows:

Retail price (£)	5	10	11	12	13	14	15	16	20
Expected sales (000 copies)	15	10	9	8	7.5	7	6.5	6	3
Maximum likely variation (±) around expected sales (000 copies)	5	2	2	2	1.5	1	0.5	1	2

Three-quarters of these sales would be expected during November and December 1979, and the rest by July 1980. Unsold copies would then be disposed of at nominal prices, or pulped.

The production manager estimates that the cost of setting, printing, binding and jacketing (inclusive of all materials) would be as follows:

Copies produced (000)	15	10	9	8	7.5	7	6.5	6	3
Production cost (£000)	22.5	20	18.9	17.6	17.25	16.8	16.25	15.9	15
Cost per copy (£)	1.5	2.0	2.1	2.2	2.3	2.4	2.5	2.65	5.0

The editorial costs to be incurred in preparing the book for publication are reliably estimated at a fixed sum of £5,000.

It has also been the company's practice to charge general fixed overheads (such as premises, exhibitions, book fairs, utilities, etc.) against publications on the following basis, in order to absorb costs and as an incentive to increase print-runs and gain economies of scale:

	Print run (No. of copies)	Charge per copy	Example of charge Print-run	Charge
Up to	7,000	£1.50	7,000	£10,500
More than	7,000	£1.00	8,000	£8,000

The variable costs of sales are known to be as follows:

Cost	% of full retail price
Discount or margin allowed to bookseller	$33\frac{1}{3}$
Distribution (warehousing, despatch, accounts)	10
Royalties to author on UK sales	10

The marketing budget would be fixed at £5,000 for this publication. It would also be necessary to provide 200 copies free of charge for potential reviewers and other purposes.

(a) You are required to prepare a statement for the editorial committee of the financial implications of the proposal to publish *Golfer's Annual for 1980*, and to advise them on the print-run and the retail price. (20 marks)

(b) It is now one week later. Against your advice, the editorial committee decided to place an order to have 3,000 copies printed, for sale at a retail price of £20 each in the UK market. No print order has yet been placed. An enquiry has now been received from an American publisher, offering to take for joint publication 6,000 copies at a unit price of £1.50 per copy ex works, the American publisher to bear all carriage costs and to pay royalties on these books direct to the author six-monthly in arrears.

You are required to show, in the context of the editorial committee's previous decision,

(i) the change in GPC's financial position that would arise from accepting the American publisher's terms (3 marks), and

(ii) the unit price at which GPC would have to sell 6,000 copies to the American publisher in order simply to break-even on that particular deal. (2 marks)

(Note: the answer to part (b) of this question does not depend on your answer to part (a)).

ICAEW Management Accounting July 1979

11.5 Woodwind Ltd manufactures and sells three products, Baubles, Bangles and Beads, holding respectively 10%, 6% and 8% of the national market for them. It has no plans to produce any other product. It is generally believed in the industry that demand for each of the products is little affected by demand for the other two. Like the other smaller firms in the industry, Woodwind Ltd has always followed the prices set by the market leader, Goodman Ltd. Woodwind Ltd is operating at well below full capacity and faces no foreseeable production constraints.

For the year to 30 June 1980 the following historic cost management accounts were produced for Woodwind Ltd. (All data are in £000.)

Question 11.5	Baubles	Bangles	Beads	Total	Nature of cost (V = variable; F = fixed)
Rent, rates and insurance	602	494	562	1,658	F—allocated by floor area
Direct labour	2,752	1,306	1,465	5,523	V
Indirect labour	882	424	460	1,766	F—allocated by direct labour
Energy	194	192	194	580	F—allocated by cubic space
Materials and supplies	1,568	968	960	3,496	V
Depreciation	1,130	854	730	2,714	F—allocated by plant value
Total manufacturing cost	7,128	4,238	4,371	15,737	
Selling expenses	1,820	916	940	3,676	F—allocated by sales value
Administration	690	260	356	1,306	F—allocated by time spent
Interest	104	80	106	290	F—allocated by asset value
Total cost	9,742	5,494	5,773	21,009	
Sales (less cash discount)	10,354	5,208	5,344	20,906	
Profit (loss)	612	(286)	(429)	(103)	

Unit sales (in thousand dozens):	Baubles	Bangles	Beads	Total	
Actual	2,160	1,034	970	4,164	
Budget	2,000	1,000	1,000	4,000	
Unit selling price per dozen: (before discounts)	£5.00	£5.20	£5.40	£5.15	(average)

Beads have shown a loss in the management accounts for four of the last five years (including the year to 30 June 1980). Bangles showed a small loss in the year to 30 June 1979. Sales in the industry have declined slowly for the past three years. Goodman Ltd has just announced a reduction in the price of its brand of Baubles to

11.6 French Ltd is about to commence operations utilizing a simple production process to produce two products, X and Y. It is the policy of French to operate the new factory at its maximum output in the first year of operations. Cost and production details estimated for the first year's operations are:

Product	Production resources per unit		Variable cost per unit		Fixed production overheads directly attributable to product £000	Maximum production, units 000
	Labour hours	Machine hours	Direct labour (£)	Direct materials (£)		
X	1	4	5	6	120	40
Y	8	2	28	16	280	10

£4.50 per dozen, effective immediately.

Woodwind Ltd's marketing director has estimated that, if Woodwind makes a similar price reduction immediately, then its unit sales of Baubles in the year to 30 June 1981 will be 2,000,000 dozen; that if it maintains its price at £5.00 per dozen sales will be 1,400,000 dozen units; and that if the price is dropped to £4.25 per dozen unit sales will be 2,200,000 dozen units. He estimates also that, barring price changes relative to competitors, sales of Bangles and Beads will be 1,000,000 dozen units each in the year to 30 June 1981.

You are required to set out the various issues which the directors of Woodwind Ltd should consider in relation to their production and pricing policies at their meeting to be held on 20 July 1980, and to write a short report to the Board summarizing the advice which you would offer to them.

*ICAEW Management Accounting
July 1980*

There are also general fixed production overheads concerned in the manufacture of both products but which cannot be directly attributed to either. This general fixed production overhead is estimated at £720,000 for the first year of operations. It is thought that the cost structures of the first year will also be operative in the second year.

Both products are new and French is one of the first firms to produce them. Hence in the first year of operations the sales price can be set by French. In the second and subsequent years it is felt that the market for X and Y will have become more settled and French will largely conform to the competitive market prices that will become established. The sales manager has researched the first year's market potential and has estimated sales volumes for various ranges of selling price. The details are:

Product X Range of per unit sales prices £ £	Sales volume (000s)	Product Y Range of per unit sales prices £ £	Sales volume (000s)
Up to 24.00	36	Up to 96.00	11
24.01 to 30.00	32	96.01 to 108.00	10
30.01 to 36.00	18	108.01 to 120.00	9
36.01 to 42.00*	8	120.01 to 132.00	8
		132.01 to 144.00	7
		144.01 to 156.00*	5

*Maximum price.

The managing director of French wishes to ascertain the total production cost of X and Y as, he says, 'Until we know the per unit cost of production we cannot properly determine the first year's sales price. Price must always ensure that total cost is covered and there is an element of profit — therefore I feel that the price should be total cost plus 20%. The determination of cost is fairly simple as most costs are clearly attributable to either X or Y. The general factory overhead will probably be allocated to the products in accordance with some measure of usage of factory resources such as labour or machine hours. The choice between labour and machine hours is the only problem in determining the cost of each product — but the problem is minor and so, therefore, is the problem of pricing.'

Required:

(a) Produce statements showing the effect the cost allocation and pricing methods mentioned by the managing director will have on
 (i) unit costs,
 (ii) closing stock values, and
 (iii) disclosed profit for the first year of operations.
(c. 8 marks)

(b) Briefly comment on the results in (a) above and advise the managing director on the validity of using the per unit cost figures produced for pricing decisions.
(c. 4 marks)

(c) Provide appropriate statements to the management of French Ltd which will be of direct relevance in assisting the determination of the optimum prices of X and Y for the first year of operations. The statements should be designed to provide assistance in each of the following, separate, cases:
 (i) year II demand will be below productive capacity;
 (ii) year II demand will be substantially in excess of productive capacity.
In both cases the competitive market sales prices per unit for year II are expected to be

X—£30 per unit
Y—£130 per unit

Clearly specify, and explain, your advice to French for each of the cases described.
(Ignore taxation and the time value of money.)
(c. 8 marks)
(Total 20 marks)
*ACCA P2 Management Accounting
June 1980*

11.7* (a) Nantderyn Products has two main products, Exco and Wyeco, which have unit costs of £12 and £24 respectively. The company uses a mark-up of $33\frac{1}{3}\%$ in establishing its selling prices and

the current prices are thus £16 and £32. With these prices, in the year which is just ending, the company expects to make a profit of £300,000 from having produced and sold 15,000 units of Exco and 30,000 units of Wyeco. This programme will have used all the available processing time in the finishing department. Each unit of Exco requires an hour of processing time in this department and every unit of Wyeco correspondingly requires half an hour.

Fixed overhead was £360,000 for the year and this has been charged to the products on the basis of the total processing hours used. All other costs may be assumed variable in relation to processing hours. In the current year it is estimated that £60,000 of the fixed overhead will be absorbed by Exco and £300,000 by Wyeco. With the existing selling prices it is considered that the potential annual demand for Exco is 20,000 units and that for Wyeco, 40,000 units.

You are required to comment critically on the product mix adopted by Nantderyn Products. Calculate what would have been the optimal plan given that there was no intention of changing the selling prices. (8 marks)

(b) For the forthcoming year increased capacity has been installed in the finishing department so that this will no longer be a constraint for any feasible sales programme. Annual fixed overhead will be increased to £400,000 as a consequence of this expansion of facilities, but variable costs per unit are unchanged.

A study commissioned by the sales director estimates the effect that alterations to the selling prices would have on the sales that could be achieved. The following table has been prepared:

	Exco		Wyeco	
Price	£13.50	£18.50	£29.00	£35.00
Demand in 000	30	10	60	20

It is thought reasonable to assume that the price/demand relationship is linear. Assuming that the company is now willing to abandon its cost-plus pricing practices, if these can be shown to be deficient, you are required to calculate the optimal selling price for each product and the optimal output levels for these prices. State clearly any assumptions that you find it necessary to make. (8 marks)

(c) The paradox is that, while cost-plus pricing is devoid of any theoretical justification, it is widely used in practice.'
Discuss possible justifications for this use. (6 marks)

(22 marks)
*ACCA Level 2 Management Accounting
December 1983*

11.8* Alvis Taylor has budgeted that output and sales

of his single product, flonal, will be 100,000 units in 1982. At this level of activity his unit variable costs are budgeted to be £50 and his unit fixed costs £25. His sales manager estimates that the demand for flonal would increase by 1,000 units for every decrease of £1 in unit selling price (and vice versa), and that at a unit selling price of £200 demand would be nil.

Information about two price increases has just been received from suppliers. One is for materials (which are included in Alvis Taylor's variable costs), and one is for fuel (which is included in his fixed costs). Their effect will be to increase both the variable costs and the fixed costs by 20% in total over the budgeted figures.

Alvis Taylor aims to maximize profits from his business.

You are required, in respect of Alvis Taylor's business:

(a) to calculate, *before the cost increases*:
 (i) the budgeted contribution and profit at the budgeted level of sales of 100,000 units, and
 (ii) the level of sales at which profits would be maximized, and the amount of those maximum profits (7 marks),

(b) to show whether and by how much Alvis Taylor should adjust his selling price, in respect of the increases in, respectively:
 (i) fuel costs
 (ii) materials costs (6 marks),

(c) to show whether and by how much it is worthwhile for Alvis Taylor, following the increases in costs, to spend £1,000,000 on a TV advertising campaign if this were confidently expected to have the effect during 1982 (but not beyond then) that demand would still fall by 1,000 units for every increase of £1 in unit selling price (and vice versa), but that it would not fall to nil until the unit selling price was £210 (5 marks), and

(d) to comment on the results which you have obtained in (a)–(c) above and on the assumptions underlying them (7 marks).

(25 marks)
ICAEW Management Accounting
December 1981

11.9 (a) Scott St. Cyr wishes to decide whether to lease a new machine to assist in the manufacture of his single product for the coming quarter, and also to decide what price to charge for his product in order to maximize his profit (or minimize his loss).

In the quarter just ended his results were as follows:

	£000	£000
Sales (200,000 units)		600
Less: Cost of goods sold		
Production wages: fixed	20	
piecework	90	
	110	
Materials	400	
		510
Gross profit		90
Less: Royalties (50 p per unit sold)	100	
Less: Administration (fixed cost)	30	
		130
Loss		(40)

St. Cyr expects that, during the coming quarter,
 (i) fixed basic wages (£20,000), fixed administration costs (£30,000) and the royalty rate will not change, and
 (ii) the piecework rate will increase to 50 p per unit.

Qualtiy control is very difficult and a high proportion of material is spoiled. A new machine has become available which can be delivered immediately. Tests have shown that it will eliminate the quality control problems, resulting in a halving of the usage of materials. It cannot be bought but can be leased for £115,000 per quarter.

The product has a very short shelf life and is produced only to order. St. Cyr estimates that, if he were to change the unit selling price, demand for the product would increase by 1,000 units per quarter for each one penny decrease in the selling price (so that he would receive orders for 500,000 units if he were to offer them free of charge), and would decrease by 1,000 units per quarter for each one penny increase in the unit selling price (so that at a price of £5 his sales would be zero).

You are required to advise Scott St. Cyr whether, in the coming quarter, he should lease the new machine and also the price which he should charge for his product, in order to maximize his profits (15 marks).

(b) Christian Pass Ltd operates in an entirely different industry. However, it also produces to order, and carries no inventory.

Its demand function is estimated to be $P = 100 - 2Q$ (where P = unit selling price in £ and Q = quantity demanded in thousands of units).

Its total cost function is estimated to be $C = Q^2 + 10Q + 500$ (where C = total cost in £000 and Q is as above).

You are required in respect of Christian Pass Ltd to:

(i) calculate the output in units which will maximize total profit, and to calculate the corresponding unit selling price, total profit, and total sales revenue (5 marks), and

(ii) calculate the output in units which will maximize total revenues, and to calculate the corresponding unit selling price, total loss, and total sales revenue (5 marks).

ICAEW Management Accounting
July 1981

11.10 (a) Some businesses which supply two or more markets from a single source charge a higher price for sales to the home market than for export sales. They may justify this pricing policy by saying that they need to recover their research and development costs, plus production overheads, against home demand.

You are required to explain briefly the rationale for such a differential pricing policy and to comment critically on it (5 marks).

(b) The Jackass Motor Company of Ruritania has just developed a new motor car called the Midi which it is planning to launch in the near future. The home market in Ruritania is highly competitive, and prices are low by international standards. In contrast, the neighbouring country of Lusitania tends to have much higher car prices. These are largely the consequence of Lusitanian Government efforts to assist the relatively inefficient domestic motor industry in Lusitania. Government regulations have been imposed in both countries, for reasons of safety, which make it impossible for anyone other than a motor manufacturer to import or export cars between the two markets. It would be quite possible, therefore, for Jackass to charge differ-

ent prices in the two markets if it considered it profitable to do so. Market research has indicated that demand functions for the two countries are likely to be:

Ruritania: Price (£) = $4{,}940 - 0.05Q$, and
Lusitania: Price (£) = $6{,}000 - 0.10Q$

where Q represents monthly sales quantities.

Jackass's single plant is close to the border between the two countries, so that its costs are unaffected by any decision to switch car supplies from one market to the other. Its total cost function for Midi production has been estimated as:

Total cost (£) = 50 million + 2,000Q + $0.01Q^2$

where Q again represents monthly quantities.

All Lusitanian sales prices have been converted back into Ruritanian pounds. The two countries have a fixed exchange rate, and Jackass's decisions will not be affected by taxation considerations. Jackass seeks to maximize its profits.

You are required to:

(i) calculate Jackass's monthly profit or loss if it confines its sales solely to its home market of Ruritania (5 marks),

(ii) calculate the monthly profit or loss should it decide to sell in both Ruritania and Lusitania (8 marks), and

(iii) set out and explain the changes in both price and monthly quantity sold in Ruritania, and in total monthly profits or losses of Jackass, by comparing your answers to (i) and (ii) above (7 marks).

(25 marks)
ICAEW Management Accounting
July 1982

12 Decision-making under conditions of risk and uncertainty

In Chapters 9 to 11 we considered the use of a *single* representative set of estimates for predicting future costs and revenues when alternative courses of action are followed. For example, in Chapter 11 we used a single representative estimate of demand for each selling price. However, the outcome of a particular decision may be affected by an uncertain environment which cannot be predicted, and a single representative estimate does not therefore convey all the information which might reasonably influence a decision.

Let us now look at a more complicated example; consider a situation where a company has two mutually exclusive potential alternatives, A and B, which each yield receipts of £5,000. The estimated costs of alternative A can be predicted with considerable confidence and are expected to fall in the range of £4,000 to £4,200; £4,100 might be considered a reasonable estimate of cost. The estimate for alternative B is subject to much greater uncertainty as this alternative requires high precision work involving operations which are unfamiliar to the company's labour force. The estimated costs are between £3,500 and £4,500, but £4,000 is selected as a representative estimate. If we consider single representative estimates, alternative B appears preferable as the estimated profit is £1,000 compared with an estimate profit of £900 for alternative A; but a different picture may emerge if we take into account the range of possible outcomes. Alternative A is expected to yield a profit of between £800 and £1,000, whereas the range of profits for alternative B is between £500 and £1,500. Management may consider it preferable to opt for a fairly certain profit of between £800 and £1,000 for alternative A rather than take the chance of earning only £500 from alternative B (even though there is the possibility of earning a profit of £1,500 at the other extreme).

This example demonstrates that there is a need to incorporate the uncertainty relating to each alternative into the decision-making process, and in this chapter we shall consider the various methods of doing this. We shall then look at the application of these methods to pricing decisions and CVP analysis under conditions of uncertainty.

A decision-making model

In Chapter 1 we considered a general model for decision-making and noted that decision problems have some definable structure containing certain basic elements. Figure 12.1 shows the elements of a decision model under conditions of risk and uncertainty.

You can see that a decision model has the following characteristics:

(1) An *objective* or target which a decision-maker is hoping to achieve, for example, maximization of profits, or present value of cash flows. The quantification of an objective is often called an objective function; it is used to evaluate the alternative courses of action and to provide the basis for choosing the best alternative.

Fig. 12.1 A decision-making model under conditions
of uncertainty

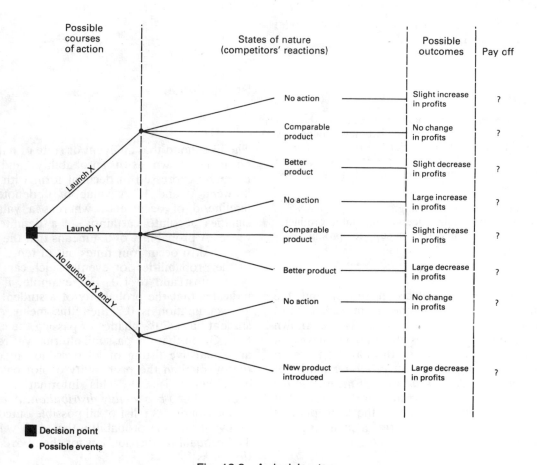

Fig. 12.2 A decision tree

(2) The search for alternative *courses of action* which will enable the objective to be achieved.

(3) Because decision problems exist in an uncertain environment it is necessary to consider those uncontrollable factors which are outside the decision-maker's control and which may occur for each alternative course of action. These uncontrollable factors are called *events* or *states of nature*. For example, in a product launch situation possible states of nature could consist of events such as a similar product being launched by a competitor at a lower price, or no similar product being launched.

(4) A set of *outcomes* for the various possible combinations of actions and events. Each outcome is conditionally dependent on a specific course of action and a specific state of nature.

(5) A measure of the value or *payoff* of each

possible outcome in terms of the decision-maker's objectives. Payoffs are normally expressed in monetary terms such as profits or cash flows but in some problems we may be interested in other payoffs such as time, market share, and so on.

(6) *Selection* of a course of action.

The essential characteristics of a decision model are illustrated in Example 12.1

EXAMPLE 12.1

DM Ltd is reviewing its marketing policy for the next budget period. It has developed two new products, X and Y, but it only has sufficient resources to launch one of them. The appropriate states of nature relate to the activities of its competitors and are as follows:

(1) competitors do nothing,
(2) competitors introduce a comparable product,
(3) competitors introduce a superior product.

The elements of the decision model and the hypothetical possible outcomes from each state of nature are illustrated in Fig. 12.2. This is known as a decision tree. In this diagram we have not measured the value (that is, the payoff) for each possible course of action, but *in the remainder of the chapter we shall look at ways of measuring the poyoff* where various outcomes are possible. Let us begin by discussing some of the concepts and techniques which are necessary for analysing risk and uncertainty.

Risk and uncertainty

A distinction is often drawn by decision theorists between risk and uncertainty. Risk is applied to a situation where there are several possible outcomes and there is relevant past experience to enable statistical evidence to be produced for predicting the possible outcomes. Uncertainty exists where there are several possible outcomes,

but there is little previous statistical evidence to enable the possible outcomes to be predicted. Most business decisions can be classified in the uncertainty category but the distinction between risk and uncertainty is of little importance in our analysis and we shall use the terms interchangeably.

Probabilities

The likelihood that an event or state of nature will occur is known as its probability, and this is normally expressed in decimal form with a value between 0 and 1. A value of 0 denotes a nil likelihood of occurrence whereas a value of 1 signifies absolute certainty — a definite occurrence. A probability of 0.4 means that the event is expected to occur four times out of ten. The total of the probabilities for events which can possibly occur must add to 1.0. For example, if a tutor indicates that the probability of a student passing an examination is 0.7 then this means that the student has a 70% chance of passing the examination. Given that the pass/fail alternatives represent an exhaustive listing of all possible outcomes of the event then the probability of not passing the examination is 0.3. This information can be presented in a *probability distribution*. A probability distribution is a list of all possible outcomes for an event and the probability that each will occur. The probability distribution for the above illustration is as follows:

Outcome	Probability
Pass examination	0.7
Do not pass examination	0.3
total	1.0

Some probabilities are known as objective probabilities because they can be established mathematically or compiled from historical data. Tossing a coin and throwing a die are examples of objective probabilities. For example, the probability of heads occurring when tossing a coin logically

must be 0.5. This can be proved by tossing a coin many times and observing the results. Similarly, the probability of obtaining number 1 when a die is thrown is 0.166 (that is, one sixth). This again can be ascertained from logical reasoning or recording the results obtained from repeated throws of the dice.

It is unlikely that objective probabilities can be established for business decisions as many past observations or repeated experiments for particular decisions are not possible; the probabilities will have to be estimated based on managerial judgement. Probabilities established in this way are known as *subjective probabilities* because no two individuals will necessarily assign the same probabilities to a particular outcome. Subjective probabilities are based on an individual's expert knowledge, past experience, and observations of current variables which are likely to have an impact on future events. Such probabilities are unlikely to be estimated correctly but any estimate of a future uncertain event is bound to be subject to error. The advantage of this approach is that it provides more meaningful information than stating the most likely outcome. Consider for example a situation where a tutor is asked to state whether student A and student B will pass an examination. The tutor may reply that both students are expected to pass the examination. This is the tutor's estimate of the most likely outcome. However, the following probability distributions are preferable:

Outcome	Student A probability	Student B probability
Pass examination	0.9	0.6
Do not pass examination	0.1	0.4
	1.0	1.0

Such a probability distribution requires the tutor to specify the degree of confidence in his or her estimate of the likely outcome of a future event. This information is clearly more meaningful than a mere estimate of the most likely outcome that both students are expected to pass the examination, because it indicates that it is most unlikely that A will fail, whereas there is a possibility that B will fail. Let us now apply the principles of probability theory to business decision-making.

Probability distributions and expected value

The presentation of a probability distribution for each alternative course of action can provide useful additional information to management as the distribution indicates the degree of uncertainty which exists for each alternative course of action. Probability distributions enable management to consider not only the possible profits (that is, the payoff) from each alternative course of action but also the amount of uncertainty which applies to each alternative. Let us now consider the situation presented in Example 12.2.

EXAMPLE 12.2

A manager is considering whether to make product A or product B, but only one can be produced. The estimated sales demand for each product is uncertain, and hence the estimated profits are also uncertain. A detailed investigation of the possible sales demand for each product gives the following probability distribution of the profits for each product:

Product A probability distribution

(1) Outcome	(2) Estimated probability	(3) Weighted amount £	(Col. 1 × Col. 2)
Profits of £6,000	0.10	600	
Profits of £7,000	0.20	1,400	
Profits of £8,000	0.40	3,200	
Profits of £9,000	0.20	1,800	
Profits of £10,000	0.10	1,000	
	1.00		
Expected value		£8,000	

Product B probability distribution

(1) Outcome	(2) Estimated probability	(3) Weighted amount £	(Col. 1 × Col. 2)
Profits of £4,000	0.05	200	
Profits of £6,000	0.10	600	
Profits of £8,000	0.40	3,200	
Profits of £10,000	0.25	2,500	
Profits of £12,000	0.20	2,400	
	1.00		
Expected value		£8,900	

Which product should the company make?

From these probability distributions you will see that there is a 1 in 10 chance that profits will be

£6,000 for product A, but there is also a 4 in 10 chance that profits will be £8,000. A more useful way of reading the probability distribution is to state that there is a 7 in 10 chance that profits will be £8,000 or less. This is obtained by adding together the probabilities for profits of £6,000, £7,000 and £8,000. Similarly, there is a 3 in 10 chance that profits will be £9,000 or more.

Expected values

The expected value (sometimes called expected payoff) is calculated by weighting each of the profit levels (that is, possible outcomes) in Example 12.2 by its associated probability. The sum of these weighted amounts is called the expected value of the probability distribution. In other words, the expected value is the weighted arithmetic mean of the possible outcomes. The expected values of £8,000 and £8,900 calculated for products A and B take into account a range of possible outcomes rather than using a *single most likely estimate*. For example, the single most likely estimate is the profit level with the highest probability attached to it. For both products A and B in Example 12.1 the single most likely estimate is £8,000, which appears to indicate that we may be indifferent as to which product should be made. However, the expected value calculation takes into account the possibility that a range of different profits are possible and weights these profits by the probability of their occurrence. The weighted calculation indicates that product B is expected to produce the highest average profits in the future.

The expected value of a decision represents the longrun average outcome that is expected to occur if a particular course of action is undertaken many times. For example, if the decision to make products A and B is repeated on, say, 100 occasions in the future, then product A will be expected to give an average profit of £8,000 whereas product B would be expected to give an average profit of £8,900. The expected values are the averages of the possible outcomes based on management estimates. There is no guarantee that the *actual* outcome will equal the expected value. Indeed the expected value for product B does not appear in the probability distribution.

Measuring the amount of uncertainty

In addition to the expected values of the profits

for the various alternatives, management is also interested in the degree of uncertainty of the expected future profits. For example, let us assume that another alternative course of action, say product C, is added to the alternatives in Example 12.2 and that the probability distribution is as follows:

Product C probability distribution

Outcome	Estimated probability	Weighted amount
Loss of £4,000	0.5	(2,000)
Profit of £22,000	0.5	11,000
	Expected value	9,000

Product C has a higher expected value than either products A or product B, but it is unlikely that management will prefer product C to product B, because of the greater variability of the possible outcomes. In other words, there is a greater degree of uncertainty attached to product C.

The conventional measure of the dispersion of a probability distribution is the standard deviation. The standard deviation (θ) is the square root of the mean of the squared deviations from the expected value and is calculated from the following formula

$$\theta = \sqrt{\Sigma_{x=1}^{n}(A_x - \bar{A})^2 P_x} \qquad (12.1)$$

where A_x = each profit level observation; \bar{A} = the expected or mean value; P_x = the probability of each outcome; $\Sigma_{x=1}^{n}$ the sum of possible observations where n equals the total number of possibilities.

The square of the standard deviation θ^2 is known as the statistical variance of the distribution and should not be confused with the variance from budget or standard cost which will be discussed in subsequent chapters. The calculations of the standard deviations for products A and B in Example 12.2 are set out in Exhibit 12.1.

If we are comparing the standard deviations of two probability distributions with different expected values we cannot make a direct comparison. Can you see why this should be so? Consider the following probability distribution for another product, say product D.

Exhibit 12.1 Calculation of standard deviations

Product A

(1) Profit £	(2) Deviation from exp. value $(Ax-\bar{A})$ £	(3) Squared deviation $(Ax-\bar{A})^2$ £	(4) Probability	(5) Weighted amount £	(Col. 3 × Col. 4)
6,000	− 2,000	4,000,000	0.1	400,000	
7,000	− 1,000	1,000,000	0.2	200,000	
8,000	0	−	0.4	−	
9,000	+ 1,000	1,000,000	0.2	200,000	
10,000	+ 2,000	4,000,000	0.1	400,000	

Sum of squared deviations = 1,200,000

Standard deviation = £1095.40

Expected value = £8,000

Product B

(1) Profit £	(2) Deviation $(Ax-\bar{A})$ £	(3) Squared deviation $(Ax-\bar{A})^2$ £	(4) Probability	(5) Weighted amount £	(Col. 3 × Col. 4)
4,000	− 4,900	24,010,000	0.05	1,200,500	
6,000	− 2,900	8,410,000	0.10	841,000	
8,000	− 900	810,000	0.40	324,000	
10,000	1,100	1,210,000	0.25	302,500	
12,000	3,100	9,610,000	0.20	1,922,000	

Sum of squared deviations = 4,590,000

Standard deviation = £2,142.40

Expected value = £8,900

Product D probability distribution

Outcome	Estimated probability	Weighted amount
Profits of £40,000	0.05	2,000
Profits of £60,000	0.10	6,000
Profits of £80,000	0.40	32,000
Profits of £100,000	0.25	25,000
Profits of £120,000	0.20	24,000
Expected value		£89,000

The standard deviation for product D is £21,424 but all of the possible outcomes are ten times as large as the corresponding outcomes for product B. The outcomes for product D also have the same pattern of probabilities as product B and we might conclude that the two projects are equally

risky. Nevertheless, the standard deviation for product D is ten times as large as that for product B. This scale effect can be removed by replacing the standard deviation with a *relative measure* of dispersion. The relative amount of dispersion can be expressed by the *coefficient of variation* which is simply the standard deviation divided by the expected value. The coefficient of variation for product B is 2142.40/8,900 = 0.241 (or 24.1%) and for product D it is also 0.241 (21,424/89,000), thus indicating that the relative amount of dispersion is the same for both products.

In our discussion so far we have defined risk in terms of the spread of possible outcomes, so that risk may be large even if all the possible outcomes involve earning high profits. However, the risk attached to possible profits/losses obtained from alternative courses of action is not dispersion *per se* but the possibility of deviations *below* the

expected value of the profits. A decision maker would hardly consider large possible deviations above the expected value undesirable. Consider the following probability distributions:

Product X probability distribution

Outcome	Estimated probability	Weighted amount
Profits of £4,000	0.1	400
Profits of £6,000	0.3	1,800
Profits of £8,000	0.6	4,800
	Expected value	£7,000

Product Y probability distribution

Outcome	Estimated probability	Weighted amount
Profits of £6,000	0.2	1,200
Profits of £8,000	0.5	4,000
Profits of £12,000	0.3	3,600
		£8,800

The standard deviations are £1,342 for X and £2,227 for Y giving coefficients of variations of 0.19 for X and 0.28 for Y. These measures indicate that the estimates of product Y are subject to a greater variability, but product X appears to be the riskier product as the probability of profits being less than £7,000 (the expected value of X) is 0.4 for product X, but only 0.2 for product Y. Clearly, the standard deviation and coefficient of variation are not perfect measures of risk, but Van Horne (1977) suggests that the mathematical complexities of measuring only those deviation below the expected value are formidable for anything beyond the simplest situation.

Measures such as expected values, standard deviations or coefficient of variations are used to summarize the characteristics of alternative courses of action, but they are poor substitutes for representing the probability distributions as they do not provide the decision-maker with all the relevant information. There is an argument for presenting the entire probability distribution directly to the decision-maker. Such an approach is appropriate when management must select one from a small number of alternatives, but in situations where many alternatives need to be considered the examination of many probability distributions is likely to be difficult and time-consuming. In such situations management may have no alternative but to compare the expected values and coefficients of variation.

Attitudes to risk by individuals

How do we determine whether or not a risky course of action should be undertaken? The answer to this question depends on the decision-maker's attitude to risk. We can identify three possible attitudes: an aversion to risk, a desire for risk, and an indifference to risk. Consider two alternatives, A and B, which have the following possible outcomes depending on the state of the economy (that is, the state of nature).

	Possible returns	
	A	B
	£	£
State of the economy		
Recession	90	0
Normal	100	100
Boom	110	200

If we assume that the three states of the economy are equally likely then the expected value for each alternative is £100. A *risk-seeker* is one who, given a choice between more or less risky alternatives with identical expected values, prefers the riskier alternative (alternative B). Faced with the same choice, a *risk-averter* would select the less risky alternative (alternative A). The person who is indifferent to risk would be indifferent to both alternatives because they have the same expected values. With regard to investors in general, studies of the securities markets provide convincing evidence that the majority of investors are risk-averse (see Friend and Blume, 1975). A more detailed discussion of attitudes to risk requires that the decision-maker's utility function should be considered, but our objective in this section is to stress that different individuals may have different attitudes towards risk. For a discussion of how attitudes towards risk affect utility functions see Carsberg (1979) and Swalm (1966).

Let us now reconsider how useful expected value calculations are for choosing betwen alternative courses of action. Expected values represent a long-run average solution, but decisions should not be made on the basis of expected values alone, as they do not enable the decision-maker's attitude towards risk to be taken into account. Let us consider for example, a situation where two individuals play a coin tossing game with the loser giving the winner £5,000. The expected value to the player who calls heads is as follows:

Outcome	Cash flow	Probability	Weighted amount
Heads	+ £5,000	0.5	+ £2,500
Tails	− £5,000	0.5	− £2,500
		Expected value	0

The expected value is zero, but this will not be the actual outcome if only one game is played. The expected value calculation represents the average outcome only if the game is repeated on many occasions. However, as the game is to be played only once it is unlikely that each player will find the expected value calculation on its own to be a useful calculation for decision-making. In fact, the expected value calculation implies that each player is indifferent to playing the game but this indifference will only apply if the two players are neutral to risk. However, a risk averter will find the game most unattractive. As most business managers are unlikely to be neutral towards risk, and business decisions are rarely repeated, it is unwise for decisions to be made solely on the basis of expected values. At the very least, expected values should be supplemented with measures of dispersion and, where possible, decisions should be made after comparing the probability distributions of the various alternative courses of action.

Decision tree analysis

In the examples earlier in this chapter we have assumed that profits were uncertain because of the uncertainty of sales demand. In practice, more than one variable may be uncertain (for example sales and costs) and also the value of some variables may be dependent on the values of other variables. Many outcomes may therefore be possible and some outcomes may be dependent on previous outcomes. A useful analytical tool for clarifying the range of alternative courses of action and their possible outcomes is a decision tree.

A decision tree is a diagram which shows several possible courses of action and possible events (that is, states of nature) and the potential outcomes for each course of action. Each alternative course of action or event is represented by a branch which leads to subsidiary branches for further courses of action or possible events. Decision trees are designed to illustrate the full range of alternatives, and events which can occur, under all envisaged conditions. The value of a decision tree is that its logical analysis of a

problem enables a complete strategy to be drawn up to cover all eventualities before a firm becomes committed to a scheme. Let us now consider a simple example of how decision trees can be applied to decision-making under conditions of uncertainty.

EXAMPLE 12.3

A company is considering whether to develop and market a new product. Development costs are estimated to be £180,000 and there is a 0.75 probability that the development effort will be successful and a 0.25 probability that the development effort will be unsuccessful. If the development is successful, the product will be marketed, and it is estimated that:

(1) if the product is very successful profits will be £540,000;
(2) if the product is moderately successful profits will be £100,000;
(3) if the product is a failure, there will be a loss of £400,000.

Each of the above profit and loss calculations is after taking into account the development costs of £180,000. The estimated probabilities of each of the above events are as follows:

(1) Very successful	0.4	
(2) Moderately successful	0.3	
(3) Failure	0.3	

The decision tree for example 12.3 is set out in Fig. 12.3. The box indicates the point at which decisions have to be taken and the branches emanating from it indicate the available alternative courses of action. The circles indicate the points at which there are environmental changes which affect the consequences of prior decisions. The branches from these points indicate the possible types of environment (states of nature) which may occur.

Note that the joint probability of two events occurring together is the probability of one event times the probability of the other event. For example, the probability of the development effort succeeding and the product being very successful consists of the products of the probabilities of these two events; that is 0.75 times 0.4 giving a probability of 0.30. Similarly, the probability of the development effort being successful and the product being moderately successful is 0.225 (0.75 × 0.3). The total expected value for the decision to develop the product consists of the sum of all the items in the expected value column on the 'Develop product' branch of the decision

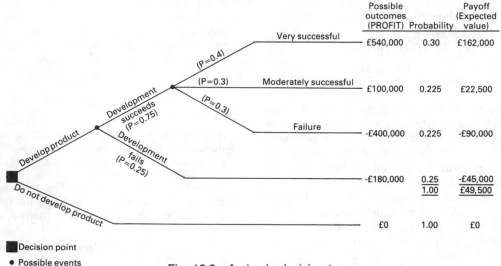

	Possible outcomes (PROFIT)	Probability	Payoff (Expected value)
Very successful	£540,000	0.30	£162,000
Moderately successful	£100,000	0.225	£22,500
Failure	-£400,000	0.225	-£90,000
	-£180,000	0.25	-£45,000
		1.00	£49,500
	£0	1.00	£0

■ Decision point
● Possible events

Fig. 12.3 A simple decision tree

tree, that is, £49,500. If we assume that there are no other alternatives available, other than the decision not to develop, the expected value of £49,500 for developing the product can be compared with the expected value of zero for not developing the product. Decision theory would suggest that the product should be developed because a positive expected value occurs. However, this does not mean that an outcome of £49,500 profit is guaranteed. The expected value calculation indicates that if the probabilities are correct and this decision was repeated on many occasions an average profit of £49,500 would result.

Unfortunately, the decision will not be repeated on many occasions and a run of repeated losses could force a company out of business before it has the chance to repeat similar decisions. Management may therefore prefer to examine the following probability distribution for developing the product:

Outcome	Probability
Loss of £400,000	0.225
Loss of £180,000	0.25
Profit of £100,000	0.225
Profit of £540,000	0.30

Management may decide that the project is too risky as there is nearly a 0.5 probability of a loss occurring.

The decision tree provides a convenient means of identifying all the possible alternative courses of action and their interdependencies. This approach is particularly useful for assisting in the construction of probability distributions when many combinations of events are possible. Note, however, that the decision tree presented in Fig. 12.3 is a simplified illustration, and for a more detailed discussion of this topic you should refer to Moore and Thomas (1978) and Magee (1978). Let us now apply the decision tree analysis procedure to a more complex problem which involves a pricing decision.

Use of cost information for pricing decisions under conditions of uncertainty

In Chapter 11 pricing decisions were based on single estimates of sales demand for different selling prices. Clearly, sales demand will be uncertain and it is preferable to incorporate uncertainty into the analysis when deciding which of several alternative selling prices to adopt. Let us now consider again Example 11.1 from the previous chapter and modify this to incorporate uncertainty. To keep things simple let us assume that only three possible selling prices are being considered and that only sales demand and variable costs are subject to uncertainty:

EXAMPLE 12.4

XYZ Ltd is introducing a new product. The company has carried out some market research studies and analysed the selling prices of similar types of competitive products which are currently

being sold. The information suggests that a selling price of £18, £19 or £20 is appropriate. The company intends to hire machinery to manufacture the product at a cost of £200,000 per annum, but if annual production is in excess of 60,000 units then additional machinery will have to be hired at a cost of £80,000 per annum. The variable cost is expected to be either £5 or £6 per unit produced depending on the outcome of future wage negotiations. The market research department has produced the following estimate of sales demand for each possible selling price. These estimates are based on pessimistic, most likely, and optimistic forecasts, and subjective probabilities have been attached to them. The estimates are as follows:

	£18		£19		£20	
	Units sold	Probability	Units sold	Probabiliy	Units sold	Probability
Pessimistic	70,000	0.3	60,000	0.1	30,000	0.4
Most likely	80,000	0.5	70,000	0.7	60,000	0.5
Optimistic	90,000	0.2	90,000	0.2	70,000	0.1

The probabilities for the unit variable cost are 0.6 for a variable cost of £5 per unit and 0.4 for a variable cost of £6 per unit. The company has also committed itself to an advertising contract of £40,000 per annum.

A decision tree for each possible outcome for each selling price is set out in Fig. 12.4. Note that for each selling price there are three possible demands and two possible variable costs giving six possible outcomes for each selling price, and eighteen possible outcomes when all three prices are considered. These eighteen possible outcomes are included in the decision tree. The expected value for each selling price is calculated by multiplying the contribution to general fixed costs column in Fig. 12.4 by the combined probability column for each possible outcome. The probability distribution for each possible selling price has been extracted from the decision tree in Fig. 12.4 and is presented in ascending order of contribution in Exhibit 12.2.

An examination of Exhibit 12.2 indicates that management would be wise not to choose a selling price of £20 as this price gives the lowest expected value. Also, the probability distribution for a selling price of £20 indicates that the probability of a contribution of £210,000 or less is 0.40 compared with zero for selling price of £18 and £19. However, it may be useful to present salient information from Exhibit 12.2 to management to assist them in deciding whether to choose a selling price of £18 or £19. The following information could be presented:

	Selling price of £18	Selling price of £19
Probability of a contribution of £590,000 or less	0.30	0.32
Probability of a contribution of £850,000 or more	0.12	0.20
Maximum possible contribution	£850,000	£940,000
Minimum possible contribution	£520,000	£540,000
Expected value	£675,400	£680,800

Exhibit 12.2 Probability distribution for each possible selling price

	Selling price of £18			Selling price of £19			Selling price of £20	
Outcome	Contribution to general fixed costs	Probability	Outcome	Contribution to general fixed costs	Probability	Outcome	Contribution to general fixed costs	Probability
	£			£			£	
2	520,000	0.12	8	540,000	0.04	14	180,000	0.16
1	590,000	0.18	10	590,000	0.28	13	210,000	0.24
4	640,000	0.20	7	600,000	0.06	16	600,000	0.20
3	720,000	0.30	9	660,000	0.42	15/18	660,000	0.34
6	760,000	0.08	12	850,000	0.08	17	730,000	0.06
5	850,000	0.12	11	940,000	0.12			
		1.00			1.00			1.00
	Expected value £675,400			Expected value £680,800			Expected value £467,400	

Fig. 12.4 Decision tree and probability distributions for various selling prices

Selling prices branch from the decision point: £18.00, £19, £20.

Demand branches:
- £18.00: 70,000 units P=0.3; 80,000 units P=0.5; 90,000 units P=0.2
- £19: 60,000 units P=0.1; 70,000 units P=0.7; 90,000 units P=0.2
- £20: 30,000 units P=0.4; 60,000 units P=0.5; 70,000 units P=0.1

(1) Selling price	(2) Demand	(3) Variable cost	(4) (Col 2 x Col 3) Combined probability	(5) Total contribution £	(6) Hire of machinery £	(7) Advertising £	(8) [Col 5 - Col 6 + 7] Contribution to general fixed costs £	(9) [Col 8 x Col 4] Expected value £	Outcome number
		P=0.6 (£5)	0.18	910,000*	280,000	40,000	590,000	106,200	
		P=0.4 (£6)	0.12	840,000	280,000	40,000	520,000	62,400	2
		P=0.6 (£5)	0.30	1,040,000	280,000	40,000	720,000	216,000	3
		P=0.4 (£6)	0.20	960,000	280,000	40,000	640,000	128,000	4
		P=0.6 (£5)	0.12	1,170,000	280,000	40,000	850,000	102,000	5
		P=0.4 (£6)	0.08	1,080,000	280,000	40,000	760,000	60,800	6
			1.00					675,400	
		P=0.6 (£5)	0.06	840,000	200,000	40,000	600,000	36,000	7
		P=0.4 (£6)	0.04	780,000	200,000	40,000	540,000	21,600	8
		P=0.6 (£5)	0.42	980,000	280,000	40,000	660,000	277,200	9
		P=0.4 (£6)	0.28	910,000	280,000	40,000	590,000	165,200	10
		P=0.6 (£5)	0.12	1,260,000	280,000	40,000	940,000	112,800	11
		P=0.4 (£6)	0.08	1,170,000	280,000	40,000	850,000	68,000	12
			1.00					680,800	
		P=0.6 (£5)	0.24	450,000	200,000	40,000	210,000	50,400	13
		P=0.4 (£6)	0.16	420,000	200,000	40,000	180,000	28,800	14
		P=0.6 (£5)	0.30	900,000	200,000	40,000	660,000	198,000	15
		P=0.4 (£6)	0.20	840,000	200,000	40,000	600,000	120,000	16
		P=0.6 (£5)	0.06	1,050,000	280,000	40,000	730,000	43,800	17
		P=0.4 (£6)	0.04	980,000	280,000	40,000	660,000	26,400	18
			1.00					467,400	

■ Decision point
● Possible events

* 70,000 units sales at a unit contribution of £13 (£18 selling price less £5 variable cost)

There would be little difference between adopting a selling price of £18 or £19 but a selling price of £19 appears to be slightly more attractive. There are strong arguments for presenting to management all the information contained in Exhibit 12.2 plus the salient information extracted above for selling prices of £18 and £19. This would enable management to choose the selling price with a probability distribution which most closely matches their attitude towards risk. It is important to note, however, that if a single value estimate approach is adopted which ignores the range of possible outcomes, management will be presented with contribution calculations based on the most likely outcomes, that is those variables which have the highest probabilities attached to them. The most likely sales demands and unit variable costs are therefore as follows:

Selling price	Sales demand	Unit variable cost
£18	80,000 units	£5
£19	70,000 units	£5
£20	60,000 units	£5

The contributions to general fixed costs for the most likely outcomes can be obtained from outcomes 3, 9 and 15 in the decision tree (Fig. 12.4) and are as follows:

Selling price of £18 — Total contribution of £720,000
Selling price of £19 — Total contribution of £660,000
Selling price of £20 — Total contribution of £660,000

You will see that a single value estimate presentation provides rather misleading results. It appears that a selling price of £20 should be seriously considered and that the highest contribution is obtained from a selling price of £18. The expected value and probability distributiuon approach provides a more revealing picture and indicates that management would be unwise to adopt a selling price of £20. Furthermore, a selling price of £19 is shown to be preferable to £18 when all the possible outcomes are considered.

You should also note that Example 12.4 contained only two variables with uncertain values — sales demand and variable cost per unit. In practice several variables may be uncertain and this can lead to a decision tree having hundreds of branches, thus causing difficulties in constructing

probability distributions on a manual basis. We shall see in Chapter 14 that this problem can be overcome by using a computer and applying simulation techniques. For a detailed discussion of pricing decisions under conditions of uncertainty see Sizer (1980) and Flower (1981).

Problems with using probability theory in decision-making

A possible objection to using the methods outlined in this chapter for decision-making is that subjective probabilities are used to quantify unforeseeable outcomes. Note, however, that the alternative of basing decisions on the most likely outcomes is just as subjective as the probability approach. The advantage of using subjective probabilities is that it forces the person providing the estimates to specify his degree of confidence in his estimates and provides better information than a single estimate of the most likely outcome.

Wooler and Gryner (1975) in a study of the major UK companies found that only 25% of the larger companies used probability theories in their decision-making models. The major argument against their use was that managers and the people providing the estimates found difficulty in working with probabilities. This is due to a lack of understanding, and the accountant therefore has an important educational role to play. If he can fully explain the meaning underlying the presentation of estimates in the form of probability distributions, the probability approach should become more widely used.

Note that the degree of uncertainty attached to various alternatives should not be viewed in isolation. For example, a firm which has a number of regular customers providing secure profits may welcome the opportunity of accepting a very risky alternative which has some chance of producing enormous profits. Alternatively, a firm whose profits are at present very volatile may prefer to choose an alternative with lower expected profits but which has only a small chance of making a loss. The important point which should be taken into account is the amount of risk which each alternative will contribute to the overall risk of the firm; the risk of each alternative should not be considered in isolation. A method of analysis which incorporates the relationship of each alternative with that of the overall risk of the firm is known as portfolio analysis, and we shall consider this later in the present chapter.

Cost–volume–profit analysis under conditions of uncertainty

In Chapter 9 we noted that cost–volume–profit analysis suffers from the disadvantage that it does not include adjustments for risk and uncertainty. A possible approach by which uncertainty can be incorporated into the analysis is to apply normal distribution theory. Consider Example 12.5.

EXAMPLE 12.5

The selling price of a product for the next accounting period is £100 and the variable cost is estimated to be £60 per unit. The budgeted fixed costs for the period are £36,000. Estimated sales for the period are 1,000 units and it is *assumed that the probability distribution for the estimated sales quantity is normal* with a standard deviation of 90 units. The selling price, variable cost and total fixed cost are assumed to be certain.

The normal probability distribution for the sales quantity is shown in Fig. 12.5. The probability that actual sales quantity will be greater than 1,060 units is shown by the shaded area to the right of 1,060 units. Alternatively, the probability that actual sales will be less than 940 units is shown by the shaded area to the left of 940 units. Because the probability distribution for sales quantity is normal with a mean of 1,000 units and a standard deviation of 90 units, and the selling price, the variable costs and the fixed costs are assumed to be certain, the probability distribution for profits will also be normal with a mean of £4,000 and standard deviation of £3,600. The calculations are as follows:

Expected profit = Expected sales volume (1,000 units) × Contribution per unit of £40 − Fixed costs (£36,000)

Standard deviation = Standard deviation of sales volume (90 units) × contribution per unit of £40[1]

Using normal distribution theory we can now answer the following questions for Example 12.5:

(1) What is the probability of a loss occurring or of profits being greater than zero?
(2) What is the probability of profits being greater than £7,600?

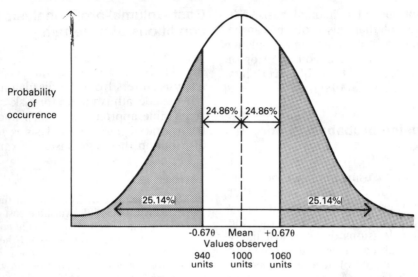

Fig. 12.5 Normal distribution for the sales quantity in
Example 12.5

(3) What is the probability of a loss in excess of £1,400?

These questions can be answered by calculating how many standard deviations each of the possible observations are from the mean:

Number of standard deviations from the mean

$$= \frac{X - \text{Mean}}{\text{Standard deviation}}$$

where X equals the outcome in which we are interested.

For a profit level of nil the calculation is:

Number of standard deviations from the mean

$$= \frac{0 - 4000}{3600} = -1.11$$

This calculation indicates that a profit of zero lies −1.11 standard deviations from the mean. To determine the probability that profit will be zero or less, we consult the normal probability distribution table in Appendix 3 at the end of this book. We find from the table that there is a 0.1335 probability that an observation will be less than −1.11 standard deviations from the mean of the distribution (see Fig. 12.6A). The shaded area

indicates that 13.35% of the observations will fall to the left of −1.11 standard deviations. Therefore the probability of a loss occurring is 13.35% (or 0.1335). The unshaded area indicates that the probability of an observation to the right of −1.11 standard deviations from the mean is 86.65% (or 0.8665). Note that the total area under the normal curve is 1.0.

The probability that profits will be in excess of £7,600 will result in an observation of one standard deviation from the mean. This is calculated as follows:

$$\frac{7,600 - 4,000}{3,600} = +1.0 \text{ standard deviation}$$

From the normal probability table in Appendix 3 you will see that the probability of an observation of +1.0 standard deviation from the mean is 0.1587, represented by the shaded area in Fig. 12.6B. The probability of profits being greater than £7,600 is therefore 15.87%.

Finally, the probability of a loss in excess of £1,400 results in an observation of −1.5 standard deviations from the mean, calculated as follows:

$$\frac{-1400 - (4000)}{3600} = -1.5 \text{ standard deviations}$$

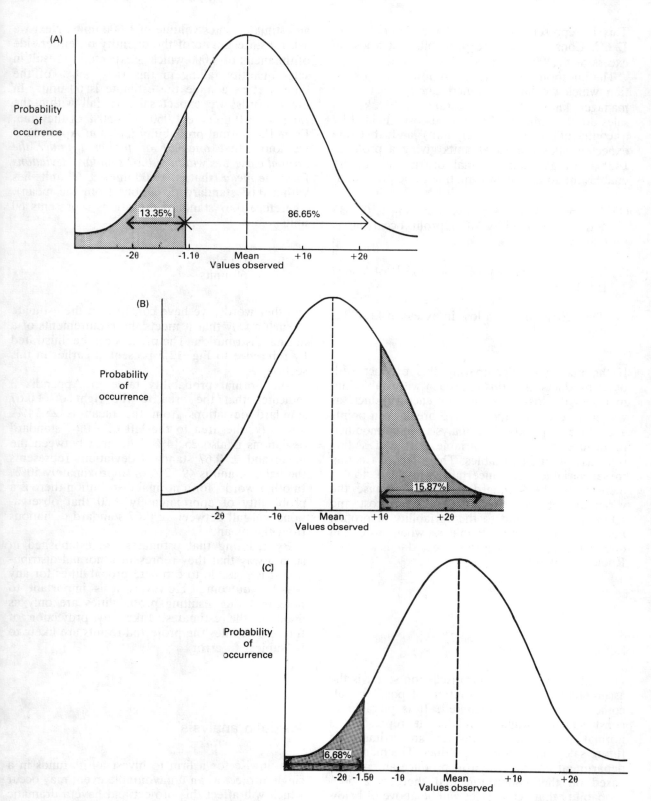

Fig. 12.6 Probability distributions for various profit levels

This is represented by the shaded area in Fig. 12.6C. Consequently, the probability of a loss in excess of £1,400 is 0.0668.

The question now arises as to how this information which we have obtained can be used. The manager knows that the estimated break-even sales are 900 units (£36,000 fixed costs divided by a contribution of £40 per unit) and that the expected sales are 1,000 units giving a profit of £4,000. In addition, normal distribution theory enables the following information to be presented:

(1) The probability of a loss occurring is 0.1335 and the probability of a profit occurring is 0.8665.

(2) The probability of profits being at least £7,600 is 0.1587.

(3) The probability of a loss in excess of £1,400 is 0.0668.

If the manager is comparing this product with other products then this approach will enable him to assess the risk involved for each product, as well as to compare the relative break-even points and expected profits. The analysis can be modified to include fixed cost, variable cost and selling price as uncertain variables. The effect of treating these variables as uncertain will lead to an increase in the standard deviation because the variability of the variable cost, fixed cost and selling price will add to the variability of profits. For a description of CVP analysis when more than one variable is uncertain see Jaedicke and Robichek (1968).

Normality assumption

Of vital importance to our discussion so far is the assumption that the distribution of possible outcomes is normally distributed. It is possible to construct an estimate so that it represents a normal distribution. Consider an estimate of future sales quantity for a product. The marketing department are requested to produce an estimate based on the assumption that there is a 50% probability that actual sales will be above or below the estimated sales. Let us assume that this gives

an estimated sales volume of 1,000 units. Next we ask for an estimate of the quantity on either side of the mean of 1,000 which is expected to result in sales quantity falling in this range 50% of the time. Let us assume the estimate is 60 units. In other words, we expect sales to fall within the range of 940 units to 1,060 units 50% of the time. From the normal probability tables in Appendix 3 we know that *one-half of the area under the normal curve lies within ± 0.67 standard deviations from the mean* (that is, 1,000 units ± 60 units lies within 0.67 standard deviations from the mean). Therefore 0.67 standard deviations represents 60 units. Thus

$$\tfrac{2}{3}\,\theta = 90 \text{ units}$$
$$\therefore\ \theta = 60 \text{ units}$$

In other words, we have constructed the estimate in such a way that it meets the requirements of a normal distribution. The process can be illustrated by reference to Fig. 12.5 presented earlier in this section.

The normal probability table in Appendix 3 indicates that the area to the right of +0.67 standard deviations from the mean is 25.14%. Similarly, the area to the left of −0.67 standard deviations is also 25.14%. The area between the mean and ± 0.67 standard deviations represents the balance and is 49.72% or approximately 50%. In other words, for a normal distribution there is a probability of approximately 0.50 that observations will fall between ± 0.67 standard deviations from the mean.

By ensuring that estimates are established in such a way that they represent a normal distribution it is possible to estimate probabilities for any possible outcome. However, it is important to note that the resulting probabilities are only as good as the estimates. Like any projection of future outcomes the projected results are likely to be subject to error.

Portfolio analysis

It is unwise for a firm to invest all its funds in a single project as an unfavourable event may occur which will affect this project and have a dramatic effect on the firm's total financial position. A

better approach would be for the firm to invest in a number of different projects. If this strategy is followed, an unfavourable event which affects one project may have relatively less effect on the remaining projects and thus have only a small impact on the firm's overall financial position. That is, a firm should not put all of its eggs in one basket, but should try to minimize risk by spreading its investments over a variety of projects. The disadvantage of this approach is that there is a danger that investing in too many separate projects may spread management and other resources too thinly and lead to a failure to compete efficiently.

The collection of investments held by an individual investor or the collection of projects in which a firm invests is known as a portfolio. The objective in selecting a portfolio is to achieve certain desirable characteristics regarding risk and expected return. Let us now consider Example 12.6.

EXAMPLE 12.6

A firm possesses £90,000 cash and has the opportunity to invest in three projects, the outcomes of which depend on two states of economic circumstances (that is, states of nature). Each outcome will last one year and the cash flows for each alternative are estimated to be as follows:

States of nature	1	2
Probability of states of nature	0.5	0.5
Cash inflows less cash outflows:		
Project A	− £40,000	+ £60,000
Project B	+ £50,000	− £50,000
Project C	+ £9,000	+ £8,000

The cash flows are arrived at *after* deducting initial outlays of £40,000 for project A, £50,000 for project B and £90,000 for project C. The following alternatives are available for an investment of £90,000.

(1) Accept project A and reject the remaining projects.
(2) Accept project B and reject the remaining projects.
(3) Accept project C and reject the remaining projects.
(4) Accept both projects A and B.

The firm has not identified any other profitable projects.

The probability distributions and expected values for each alternative are given in Exhibit 12.3.

Exhibit 12.3 Probability distributions and expected values

Project A

States of nature	Cash flow	Probability	Weighted average
1	− £40,000	0.5	− £20,000
2	+ £60,000	0.5	+ £30,000
	Expected value (\bar{R}_A)		£10,000

Project B

States of nature	Cash flow	Probability	Weighted average
1	+ £50,000	0.5	+ £25,000
2	− £50,000	0.5	− £25,000
	Expected value (\bar{R}_B)		0

Project C

States of nature	Cash flow	Probability	Weighted average
1	+ £9,000	0.5	£4,500
2	+ £8,000	0.5	£4,000
	Expected value (\bar{R}_C)		£8,500

Projects A and B

States of nature	Cash flow	Probability	Weighted average
1	+ £10,000	0.5	£5,000
2	+ £10,000	0.5	£5,000
	Expected value (\bar{R}_{AB})		£10,000

From Exhibit 12.3 it can be seen that both projects A and B are risky when considered on their own but when they are combined the risk is completely eliminated because whatever the outcome the cash inflow will be £10,000. If a decision is to be made on the basis of maximizing expected values and minimizing risk, the combination of projects A and B should be accepted.[2] Exhibit 12.3 tells us that we *should consider not only the risk of individual projects but we should take into account how the risks of the combined projects co-vary with each other*. Risk is eliminated when the cash flows of the combined projects offset each other. In other words, risk is reduced by seeking that combination of projects with the highest negative correlation coefficient of cash flows. Where returns on projects are perfectly correlated (where the correlation coefficient is +1) risk reduction

cannot be achieved when the projects are combined. However, when perfectly negative correlation exists (where the correlation coefficient is -1) risk can be eliminated completely when the projects are combined. For all other correlation values risk is reduced by seeking the combination of projects where the correlation coefficient is the closest to -1.

The correlation coefficient can be calculated by dividing the joint risk of a combination of projects (the covariance) by the product of the standard deviations of the projects. In formula terms the correlation coefficient for the cash flow returns on two projects is calculated as follows:

$$\text{Correlation } R_J R_K = \frac{\text{Covariance } R_J R_K}{\theta_J \theta_K} \quad (12.2)$$

where θ_J and θ_K represent the standard deviations of projects J and K and R_J and R_K represent the cash flow returns from projects J and K. The covariance is calculated from the following formula (12.3):

$$\text{Covariance } R_J R_K = \Sigma_{x=1}^{n} P\theta \ (R_J - \bar{R}_J)(R_K - \bar{R}_K) \quad (12.3)$$

where $P\theta$ = the probability of each state of nature, \bar{R}_J and \bar{R}_K = the expected value of cash flows on projects J and K, R_J and R_K = the cash flows of projects J and K, and $\Sigma_{x=1}^{n}$ = the sum of possible observations. Let us now illustrate this formula for the combination of projects A and B in Exhibit 12.3. The calculations are set out in Exhibit 12.4. To calculate the correlation coefficients we must first calculate the standard deviations for projects A and B (see Exhibit 12.5).

We can now calculate the correlation coefficients for the combination of projects A and B using equation (12.2).

$$\begin{aligned}\text{Correlation } R_A R_B &= \frac{\text{Covariance } R_A R_B}{\theta_A \times \theta_B} \\ &= -\frac{2{,}500 \text{ million}}{50{,}000 \times 50{,}000} \\ &= -1\end{aligned}$$

Exhibit 12.4 Covariance calculation

States of nature (θ)	R_A	R_B	$R_A - \bar{R}_A$	$R_B - \bar{R}_B$	$(R_A - \bar{R}_A)(R_B - \bar{R}_B)P\theta$
1	$-$ 40,000	$+$50,000	$-$50,000	$+$50,000	$-$ 1,250 million
2	$+$ 60,000	$-$ 50,000	$+$ 50,000	$-$ 50,000	$-$ 1,250 million
	$\bar{R}_A = 10{,}000$	$\bar{R}_B = \quad 0$		Covariance $=$	$-$ 2,500 million

Exhibit 12.5 Standard deviation calculations

Project A

States of nature (θ)	R_A	$R_A - \bar{R}_A$	$(R_A - \bar{R}_A)^2$	$P\theta$	$P\theta(R_A - \bar{R}_A)^2$
1	$-$ 40,000	$-$ 50,000	2,500 million	0.5	1,250 million
2	$+$ 60,000	$+$ 50,000	2,500 million	0.5	1,250 million
	$\bar{R}_A = 10{,}000$			Variance $(\theta^2) = $	2,500 million

Standard deviation $= \sqrt{2{,}500} \text{ million} = 50{,}000$

Project B

States of nature (θ)	R_B	$R_B - \bar{R}_B$	$(R_B - \bar{R}_B)^2$	$P\theta$	$P\theta(R_B - \bar{R}_B)^2$
1	$+$ 50,000	50,000	2,500 million	0.5	1,250 million
2	$-$ 50,000	$-$ 50,000	2,500 million	0.5	1,250 million
	$\bar{R}_B = \quad 0$			Variance $(\theta^2) = $	2,500 million

Standard deviation $= \sqrt{2{,}500} \text{ million} = 50{,}000$

You will note that the combination of returns on projects A and B are perfectly negatively correlated and risk is completely eliminated. In practice the process is more complex than our simple example suggests, as we would need to calculate the correlation coefficient for the returns on each proposed project with the returns on the firm's existing projects.

Although the measurement of risk involves a number of complex statistical calculations you should remember that it is important not to become too immersed in the calculations themselves and lose sight of one of the essential implications of portfolio analysis. Simply stated, this is that *we should not consider the risk of individual projects in isolation but should consider the overall risk from all the various selected projects*.

Summary

In this chapter we have considered some of the important methods of incorporating risk and uncertainty into the decision-making process. We have established that estimates which incorporate a range of possible outcomes with probabilities attached to each outcome are preferable to a single estimate based on the most likely outcome.

The term 'expected value' refers to the weighted average (or mean) outcome of a range of possible values which are assigned to a particular alternative course of action. Because expected values represent a long-run average solution, based on the assumption that decisions are repeated many times, and do not take risk attitudes into account, it has been suggested that decisions should not be taken solely on the basis of expected values. At the very least, expected values should be supplemented by measures of dispersion such as the standard deviation and the coefficient of variation. However, we have discovered that measures of dispersion are imperfect measures of business risk; wherever possible probability distributions for various alternatives should be compared.

Where there are many possible outcomes for various alternatives and where some outcomes are dependent on previous outcomes, decision trees are a useful tool for analysing each alternative, and we have looked at an illustration of a decision tree for a pricing problem involving two uncertain variables.

We have discovered that the degree of uncertainty attached to various alternatives should not be viewed in isolation and that we should consider the overall risk of combining projects. A method of incorporating the risk interrelationships of combining projects together, known as portfolio analysis, has been introduced, and the statistical calculations for measuring the risk reduction effects of combining projects has been illustrated.

Finally, you should note at this point that this chapter has not included all the methods of incorporating risk into decision-making, as the aim has been to introduce the *principles* involved in incorporating risk into the decision-making process. The technique described in this chapter together with other methods of incorporating risk into the analysis will be examined in Chapter 14 when we shall concentrate on capital investment decisions under uncertainty. A more detailed study of incorporating uncertainty into the decision-making process can be found in Carsberg (1979), Moore and Thomas (1978) and Bromwich (1979).

References and further reading

Borch, K. *The Economies of Uncertainty*. Princetown University Press, 1968.

Bromwich, M. *The Economics of Capital Budgeting*. Pitman, 1979, Chapters 12–15.

Carsberg, B.V. *Economics of Business Decisions*. Chapters 13-15.

Dickinson, J.P. Cost–volume–profit analysis under uncertainty. *Journal of Accounting Research* **12**(1), Spring 1974, 182-7.

Feller, W. *An Introduction to Probability Theory and its Applications* 3rd edn, Volume 1. Wiley, 1968.

Ferrara, W.L., Hayya, J.C. and Nachman, D.A. Normalcy of profit in the Jaedicke-Robichek model. *The Accounting Review* **XLII**, July 1967.

Flower, J.F. A risk analysis approach to marginal cost pricing: A comment. *Accounting and Business Research* 4, Autumn 1971, 335; also in Sizer, J. (Ed.), *Perspectives in Management Accounting*. Heinemann, 1981.

Friend, I. and Blume, M. The demand for risky assets. *The American Economic Review* December 1975, 900-22.

Grinyer, P.H. and Wooller, J. *Corporate Models Today*. Institute of Chartered Accountants in England and Wales, 1975.

Hilliard, J.E. and Leitch, R.A. Cost–volume–profit analysis under uncertainty: A log normal approach. *The Accounting Review L* January 1975, 69-80; also 'A reply', *The Accounting Review* January 1976, 168-71.

Jaedicke, R.K. and Robichek, A.A. Cost–volume–profit analysis under conditions of uncertainty. *The Accounting Review* **39**(4), October 1964, 917-26; also in Solomons, D., (Ed.), *Studies in Cost Analysis*. Sweet & Maxwell, 1968.

Johnson, G.L. and Simik, S.S. Multiproduct CVP analysis and uncertainty. *Journal of Accounting Research* **9**(2), Autumn 1971, 278-86.

Kwak, N.K. and De Lurgio, S.A. *Quantitative Models for Business Decisions*. Duxberry Press (Wadsworth), 1980.

Lau, A.H. and Hon-Shiang Lau. CVP analysis under uncertainty — A log normal approach: A comment. *The Accounting Review* **XLI** January 1976, 163-7.

Magee, J.F. Decision trees for decision-making. *Harvard Business Review* July–August 1964; also in Thomas, W.E. (Ed.), *Cost Accounting, Budgeting and Control*. South Western Publishing Company, 1978.

Moore, P.G. and Thomas, H. *The Anatomy of Decisions*. Penguin, 1978.

Sharpe, W.F. *Portfolio Theory and Capital Markets*. McGraw Hill, 1970.

Shih, W. A general decision model for cost–volume–profit analysis under uncertainty. *The Accounting Review* **LIV** October 1979, 687-706.

Sizer, J. A risk analysis approach to marginal cost pricing. *Accounting and Business Research* 1, Winter 1970, 30-38; also in Sizer, J., *Perspectives in Management Accounting*, Heinemann, 1981.

Swalm, R.O. Utility theory — Insights into risk taking. *Harvard Business Review* November–December 1966, 123-36.

Van Horne, J.C. *Financial Management and Policy*. Prentice-Hall, 1977, Chapter 2.

Problems

*Indicates that a suggested solution is to be found in the *Students' Manual*.

12.1* (a) **XY** Ltd is to quote for contract No. 1701 to supply 10,000 units of a certain product to a large group with branches throughout the country.

It knows that the group will accept the lowest bid and, from past experience and good intelligence within the industry, estimates the following probabilities of bids at various levels (in multiples of £5 only).

Price bid £	Probability of bids at that price
45	0.05
50	0.10
55	0.20
60	0.25
65	0.25
70	0.10
75	0.05
	1.00

XY Ltd's out-of-pocket costs for these items are £32 per unit.

You are required to calculate the price XY Ltd should bid for this contract if it wishes to obtain the contract and maximize its profit margin.

(b) In arriving at its out-of-pocket costs, XY Ltd has estimated an amount per unit for servicing the items for one year as required by the terms of No. 1701 contract.

If it obtains the contract there are a number of ways in which it can satisfy this servicing requirement:

1. To sub-contract to AB Ltd which is willing to undertake the work in all areas or any individual area and has quoted:

Area	No. of units to be serviced under the contract	Price quoted £
North	3,000	18,000
South	4,500	20,000
Midland	2,500	11,500

2. For South area only, to sub-contract to CD Ltd which has quoted £18,000 plus a charge for service calls above a certain level.

These charges and the assessed probability of their occurrence are:

Calls made	CD Ltd charge £	Probability of occurrence
750 or fewer	Nil	0.40
751 – 900	900	0.30
901 – 1,050	2,200	0.20
1,051 or more	3,500	0.10
		1.00

3. For Midland area only, it can use its own organization, but would need to take on extra staff.

The cost of this staff and the possibility of needing each level of extra staff are assessed as:

Cost of extra staff £	Probability of needing that level
4,500	0.20
7,000	0.35
11,000	0.45
	1.00

If sub-contractors are used, they will buy spares from XY Ltd at an average price of £2 per unit to be serviced.

The out-of-pocket costs of these spares to XY Ltd is £1.50 per unit.

You are required to calculate which combination of servicing arrangements will involve XY Ltd in the minimum cost. (Assume that the quality of all servicing is comparable and acceptable.)

(25 marks)
ICMA P3 Management Accounting
May 1981

12.2 RM Ltd is considering whether or not to make an investment in a project to improve the quality of its product, and has come to the conclusion that there are four practicable courses of action open to it:

(A) To improve the product and raise prices by 10%.
(B) To improve the product but keep prices at their present level.
(C) Not to improve the product and to keep prices at their present level.
(D) Not to improve the product but to lower prices by 15%.

The outcome of each of the above courses will, however, be affected by the actions of its major competitor XY Ltd with whom it shares about 70% of the market more or less equally. For practical purposes of decision-making, XY Ltd's choice of actions can be regarded as being identical to that of RM Ltd.

As a result of a series of project evaluation calculations, the following matrix shows the estimated annual profits over the next three years. (NB. In arriving at these profits, such capital investment as is required has been converted into a cost equivalent per annum.)

RM Ltd's potential courses of action	RM Ltd's annual profit (in (£000) if XY Ltd takes courses of action as follows:			
	A	B	C	D
A	370	350	330	305
B	350	330	360	310
C	315	285	300	270
D	335	300	390	320

You are required to recommend which course of action RM Ltd should adopt if each of the following separate conditions were to apply, and support each recommendation with brief explanations and with appropriate figures:

(a) it is known with complete confidence that XY Ltd will follow course of action C;

(b) the probabilities of XY Ltd following the various courses of action, based on extensive observation of their behaviour in comparable circumstances, are:

Course of action	Probability
A	0.15
B	0.25
C	0.40
D	0.20

(c) this is the first time that this type of situation has arisen and there is little relevant information available to RM Ltd as to how XY Ltd will behave.

(25 marks)

*ICMA P3 Management Accounting
May 1978*

12.3* For the past 20 years a charity organization has held an annual dinner and dance with the primary intention of raising funds.

This year there is concern that an economic recession may adversely affect both the number of persons attending the function and the advertising space that will be sold in the programme published for the occasion.

Based on past experience and current prices and quotations, it is expected that the following costs and revenues will apply for the function:

			£
Costs:	Dinner and dance:	Hire of premises	700
		Band and entertainers	2,800
		Raffle prizes	800
		Photographer	200
		Food at £12 per person (with a guarantee of 400 persons minimum)	
	Programme:	A fixed cost of £2,000, plus £5 per page	
Revenues:	Dinner and dance:	Price of tickets £20 per person	
		Average revenue from:	
		Raffle £5 per person	
		Photographs £1 per person	
	Programme:	Average revenue from advertising £70 per page	

A sub-committee, formed to examine more closely the likely outcome of the function, discovered the following from previous records and accounts:

No. of tickets sold	No. of past occasions
250 – 349	4
350 – 449	6
450 – 549	8
550 – 649	2
	20

No. of programme pages sold	No. of past occasions
24	4
32	8
40	6
48	2
	20

Several members of the sub-committee are in favour of using a market research consultant to carry out a quick enquiry into the likely number of tickets and the likely number of pages of advertising space that would be sold for this year's dinner and dance.

You are required to:

(a) calculate the expected value of the profit to be earned from the dinner and dance this year;

(b) recommend, with relevant supporting financial and cost data, whether or not the charity should spend £500 on the market research enquiry and indicate the possible benefits the enquiry could provide.

NB: All workings for tickets should be in steps of 100 tickets and for advertising in steps of 8 pages.

(25 marks)

*ICMA P3 Management Accounting
November 1981*

12.4 The marketing manager of an engineering company is in the process of negotiating a one year contract to supply a motor car component at a fixed price of £8 per unit. Its normal capacity for this type of component is 25,000 units a year. The estimated costs to manufacture are shown below. These costs are considered to be firm except for the direct material price.

Cost data:
 Variable costs per unit:

	£
Direct wages	1.50
Direct material	2.25
Direct expenses	0.65

Semi-variable costs per annum:

	Output levels		
	80%	100%	120%
	£	£	£
Indirect wages	15,400	16,000	23,100
Indirect materials	8,600	9,000	9,900
Indirect expenses	2,000	2,500	3,000

Fixed costs per annum:

	£
Supervisory salaries	10,000
Depreciation	4,000
Other overhead	16,000

The marketing manager is uncertain as to how many units of the car component will be required but is certain that demand will be somewhere between 20,000 and 30,000 units. The marketing manager has submitted a report to the managing director requesting him to approve the acceptance of the contract. However, the managing director is unhappy about the information he has received which was based on a demand of 25,000 units and a purchase price of £2.25 per unit for direct materials.

This concern is mainly because of the uncertainty of the expected demand and purchase price. The best estimate the purchasing officer can make for direct materials is £2.25 per unit but he thinks this could increase to a maximum of £3.25 per unit. The managing director has requested an estimate of the profit for the year based on a demand of 20,000, 25,000 and 30,000 units assuming a purchase price for direct materials of £2.25 per unit. However, he is still uncertain about the possible outcome and has requested your advice.

You ascertain from the marketing manager that the probability of the size of the order is:
 0.3 for 20,000 components
 0.6 for 25,000 components
 0.1 for 30,000 components
Similar discussions with the purchasing officer indicate the following probabilities for the unit cost of the direct materials:

0.5 for 2.25 per unit
0.3 for 2.75 per unit
0.2 for 3.25 per unit
You also ascertain that last year the company used the relevant facilities to earn a profit of £20,000 from a number of regular customers. It is expected that if the contract is not undertaken a similar profit will be obtained from these customers.
You are required to:
(a) Prepare the estimates of profit which the managing director received based on an order for the year of 20,000, 25,000 and 30,000 units assuming the direct material cost to be 2.25 per unit. (5 marks)
(b) Present a report to the managing director providing any relevant information which you think would help him to decide whether or not to accept the contract. (14 marks)
(c) Briefly outline the advantages and disadvantages of the information you have provided in (b) above compared with that which you provided in (a) above. (6 marks)

12.5* Inglestone Ltd can purchase the patent and the manufacturing rights of any one of three products. The costs of the rights are:

Product A	£130,000
Product B	£190,000
Product C	£200,000

At a meeting with three of Inglestone's directors the management accountant stated:
'We are all agreed on the facts. Each venture is a very short term project. The fixed manufacturing and advertising costs of each venture will be:

	A	B	C
	£000	£000	£000
Fixed manufacturing cost	120	20	20
Advertising costs	50	30	20

Sales and production will, once known, dovetail and there will therefore be no stock build up. The sales prices and variable costs per unit are:

	A	B	C
Sales price per unit	£340	£190	£130
Variable cost per unit	£140	£110	£70

However, the sales volume is the crunch question.
We do not know what the sales level will be but we do now the various possibilities of what the sales levels could be. Product A could be a complete flop, it could sell well, or it might sell very well. B is also quite variable whereas with C the range of outcomes is quite small. The various possible sales volumes and their associated probabilities are:

	Product				
	A		B		C

Sales volume units	Probability	Sales volume units	Probability	Sales volume units	Probability
zero	0.1	3,000	0.1	7,000	0.8
2,500	0.4	4,000	0.3	8,000	0.1
4,000	0.5	6,000	0.3	9,000	0.1
		8,000	0.3		

Based on the assumption that the above facts are all completely accurate, and we agree with this, all we need do is make the decisions as to which one product to undertake. What are your views gentlemen?'

Required:

(a) Calculate the expected money value of each product and on the basis of this advise Inglestone of the best course of action. (c. 10 marks)

(b) List and briefly comment on three other factors which may be relevant in a practical situation to the final choice between the three available courses of action. (c. 6 marks)

(c) *Consider only Product A for this Section.* The marketing manager agrees that the subjective probabilities assigned to sales levels given are as accurate as it is practical to assess; however, he suggests that if a market research study was undertaken then it would be possible to ascertain with complete accuracy exactly which of the sales levels specified would be effective, i.e. it would indicate whether the sales would be zero, 2,500 or 4,000 units. This market research would cost £20,000 and could be undertaken before deciding whether to purchase the patent and manufacturing rights. Assuming the fixed manufacturing costs are all avoidable if no production takes place then is it worthwhile to undertake the market research? (c. 4 marks)

(Total 20 marks)

Ignore tax and the cost of capital

ACCA P2 Management Accounting
June 1979

12.6 A ticket agent has an arrangement with a concert hall that holds pop concerts on 60 nights a year whereby he receives discounts as follows per concert:

For purchase of:	He receives a discount of:
200 tickets	20%
300 tickets	25%
400 tickets	30%
500 tickets or more	40%

Purchases must be in full hundreds. The average price per ticket is £3.

He must decide in advance each year the number of tickets he will purchase. If he has any tickets unsold by the afternoon of the concert he must return them to the box office. If the box office sells any of these he receives 60% of their price.

His sales records over a few years show that for a concert with extremely popular artistes he can be confident of selling 500 tickets, for one with lesser known artistes 350 tickets, and for one with relatively unknown artistes 200 tickets.

His records also show that 10% of tickets he returns are sold by the box office.

His administration costs incurred in selling tickets are the same per concert irrespective of the popularity of the artistes.

There are two possible scenarios in which his sales records can be viewed:

Scenario 1: that, on average, he can expect concerts with lesser known artistes

Scenario 2: that the frequency of concerts will be:

	%
with popular artistes	45
with lesser known artistes	30
with unknown artistes	25
	100

You are required to calculate:

A. separately for each of Scenarios 1 and 2:
 (a) the expected demand for tickets per concert;
 (b) (i) the level of his purchases of tickets per concert that will give him the largest profit over a long period of time;
 (ii) the profit per concert that this level of purchases of tickets will yield;

B. for Scenario 2 only:
 the maximum sum per annum that the ticket agent should pay to a pop concert specialist for 100% correct predictions as to the likely success of each concert.

(25 marks)

ICMA P3 Management Accounting
November 1983

12.7* (a) Allegro Finishes Ltd is about to launch an improved version of its major product — a pocket size chess computer — onto the market. Sales of the original model (at £65 per unit) have been at the rate of 50,000 per annum but it is now planned to withdraw this model and the company is now deciding on its production plans and pricing policy.

The standard variable cost of the new model will be £50 which is the same as that of the old, but the company intends to increase the selling price 'to recover the research and development expenditure that has been incurred'. The research and development costs of the improved model are estimated at £750,000 and the intention is that these should be written off over 3 years. Additionally there are annual fixed overheads of approximately £800,000 allocated to this product line.

The sales director has estimated the maximum annual demand figures that would obtain at three alternative selling prices. These are as follows:

Selling price £	Estimated maximum annual demand (physical units)
70	75,000
80	60,000
90	40,000

You are required to prepare a cost–volume–profit chart that would assist the management to choose a selling price and the level of output at which to operate. Identify the best price and the best level of output. Outline briefly any reservations that you have with this approach. (5 marks)
(b) With the facts as stated for part (a), now assume the sales director is considering a more sophisticated approach to the problem. He has estimated, for each selling price, an optimistic, a pessimistic and a most likely demand figure and associated probabilities for each of these. For the £90 price the estimates are:

	Annual demand	Probability of demand
Pessimistic	20,000	0.2
Most likely	35,000	0.7
Optimistic	40,000	0.1
		1.0

On the cost side, it is clear that the standard unit variable cost of £50 is an 'ideal' which has rarely been achieved in practice. An analysis of the past 20 months shows that the following pattern of variable cost variances (per unit of output) has arisen:

an adverse variance of around £10 arose on 4 occasions,
an adverse variance of around £5 arose on 14 occasions
and a variance of around 0 arose on 2 occasions.

There is no reason to think that the pattern for the improved model will differ significantly from this or that these variances are dependent upon the actual demand level.

From the above, calculate the expected annual profit for a selling price of £90. (6 marks)
(c) A tabular summary of the result of an analysis of the data for the other two selling prices (£70 and £80) is as follows:

	£70	£80
Probability of a loss of £500,000 or more	0.02	0
Probability of a loss of £300,000 or more	0.07	0.05
Probability of a loss of £100,000 or more	0.61	0.08
Probability of break-even or worse	0.61	0.10
Probability of break-even or better	0.39	0.91
Probability of a profit of £100,000 or more	0.33	0.52
Probability of a profit of £300,000 or more	0.03	0.04
Probability of a profit of £500,000 or more	0	0.01
Expected value of profit (loss)	(£55,750)	£68,500

You are required to compare your calculations in part (b) with the above figures and to write a short memo to the sales director outlining your advice and commenting on the use of subjective discrete probability distributions in problems of this type. (9 marks)
(d) Assume that there is a 10% increase in the fixed overheads allocated to this product line and a decision to write off the research and development costs in one year instead of over three years. Indicate the general effect that this would have on your analysis of the problem. (2 marks)
(22 marks)
ACCA Level 2 Management Accounting December 1982

12.8* In the market for one of its products, MD and its two major competitors (CN and KL) together account for 95% of total sales.

The quality of MD's products is viewed by customers as being somewhat better than that of its competitors and therefore at similar prices it has an advantage.

During the past year, however, when MD raised its price to £1.2 per litre, competitors kept their prices at £1.0 per litre and MD's sales declined even though the total market grew in volume.

MD is now considering whether to retain or reduce its price for the coming year. Its expectations about its likely volume at various prices charged by itself and its competitors are as follows:

Prices per litre			MD's expected sales
MD	CN	KL	
£	£	£	million litres
1.2	1.2	1.2	2.7
1.2	1.2	1.1	2.3
1.2	1.2	1.0	2.2
1.2	1.1	1.1	2.4
1.2	1.1	1.0	2.2
1.2	1.0	1.0	2.1
1.1	1.1	1.1	2.8
1.1	1.1	1.0	2.4
1.1	1.0	1.0	2.3
1.0	1.0	1.0	2.9

Experience has shown that CN tends to react to MD's price level and KL tends to react to CN's price level. MD therefore assesses the following probabilities:

If MD's price per litre is	there is a probability of	that CN's price per litre will be
£		£
1.2	0.2	1.2
	0.4	1.1
	0.4	1.0
	1.0	
1.1	0.3	1.1
	0.7	1.0
	1.0	
1.0	1.0	1.0

If CN's price per litre is	there is a probability of	that KL's price per litre will be
£		£
1.2	0.1	1.2
	0.6	1.1
	0.3	1.0
	1.0	
1.1	0.3	1.1
	0.7	1.0
	1.0	
1.0	1.0	1.0

Costs per litre of the product are as follows:

	£
Direct wages	0.24
Direct materials	0.12
Departmental expenses:	
Indirect wages, maintenance and supplies	16⅔% of direct wages
Supervision and depreciation	£540,000 per annum
General works expenses (allocated)	16⅔% of prime cost
Selling and administration expenses (allocated)	50% of manufacturing cost

You are required to state whether, on the basis of the data given above, it would be most advantageous for MD to fix its price per litre for the coming year at £1.2, £1.1 or £1.0.

Support your answer with relevant calculations.

(20 marks)

ICMA P3 Management Accounting
November 1982

12.9 Warren Ltd is to produce a new product in a short-term venture which will utilize some obsolete materials and expected spare capacity. The new product will be advertised in quarter I with production and sales taking place in quarter II. No further production or sales are anticipated.

Sales volumes are uncertain but will, to some extent, be a function of sales price. The possible sales volumes and the advertising costs associated with each potential sales price are as follows:

Sales price per unit	£20		£25		£40	
	Sales volume units (000s)	Probability	Sales volume units (000s)	Probability	Sales volume units (000s)	Probability
	4	0.1	2	0.1	0	0.2
	6	0.4	5	0.2	3	0.5
	8	0.5	6	0.2	10	0.2
			8	0.5	15	0.1
Advertising costs	£20,000		£50,000		£100,000	

The resources used in the production of each unit of the product are:

Production labour:	grade 1	2 hours
	grade 2	1 hour
Materials:	X	1 unit
	Y	2 units

The normal cost per hour of labour is

grade 1 £2
grade 2 £3

However, before considering the effects of the current venture, there is expected to be 4,000 hours of idle time for each grade of labour in quarter II. Idle time is paid at the normal rates.

Material X is in stock at a book value of £8 per unit, but is widely used within the firm and any usage for the purposes of this venture will require replacing. Replacement cost is £9 per unit.

Material Y is obsolete stock. There are 16,000 units in stock at a book value of £3.50 per unit and any stock not used will have to be disposed of at a cost, to Warren, of £2 per unit. Further quantities of Y can be purchased for £4 per unit.

Overhead recovery rates are

Variable overhead £2 per direct labour hour worked
Fixed overhead £3 per direct labour hour worked

Total fixed overheads will not alter as a result of the current venture.

Feedback from advertising will enable the exact demand to be determined at the end of quarter I and production in quarter II will be set to equal that demand. However, it is necessary to decide *now* on the sales price in order that it can be incorporated into the advertising campaign.

Required:
(a) Calculate the expected money value of the venture at each sales price and on the basis of this advise Warren of its best course of action. (12 marks)
(b) Briefly explain why the management of Warren might rationally reject the sales price leading to the highest expected money value and prefer one of the other sales prices. (4 marks)
(c) It will be possible, for the sales price of £40 per unit *only*, to ascertain which of the four levels of demand will eventuate. If the indications are that the demand will be low then the advertising campaign can be cancelled at a cost of £10,000 but it would then not be possible to continue the venture at another sales price. This accurate information concerning demand will cost £5,000 to obtain.
Indicate whether it is worthwhile obtaining the information and ascertain whether it would alter the advice given in (a) above. (4 marks)

(20 marks)
ACCA Level 2 Management Accounting Pilot Paper

12.10 The Central Co. Ltd has developed a new product and is currently considering the marketing and pricing policy it should employ for this. Specifically it is considering whether the sales price should be set at £15 per unit or at the higher level of £24 per unit. Sales volumes at these two prices are shown in the following table:

Sales price £15 per unit		Sales price £24 per unit	
Forecast sales volume (000)	Probability	Forecast sales volume (000)	Probability
20	0.1	8	0.1
30	0.6	16	0.3
40	0.3	20	0.3
		24	0.3

The fixed production costs of the venture will be £38,000.

The level of the advertising and publicity costs will depend on the sales price and the market aimed for. With a sales price of £15 per unit the

advertising and publicity costs will amount to £12,000. With a sales price of £24 per unit these costs will total £122,000.

Labour and variable overhead costs will amount to £5 per unit produced. Each unit produced requires 2 kg of raw material and the basic cost is expected to be £4 per kg. However, the suppliers of the raw materials are prepared to lower the price in return for a firm agreement to purchase a guaranteed minimum quantity. If Central Ltd contracts to purchase at least 40,000 kg then the price will be reduced to £3.75 per kg for *all* purchases. If Central contracts to purchase a minimum of 60,000 kg then the price will be reduced to £3.50 per kg for *all* purchases. It is only if Central Ltd guarantees either of the above minimum levels of purchases in advance that the appropriate reduced prices will be operative.

If Central Ltd were to enter into one of the agreements for the supply of raw material and was to find that it did not require to utilize the entire quantity of materials purchased then the excess could be sold. The sales price will depend upon the quantity which is offered for sale. If 16,000 kg or more are sold then the sales price will be £2.90 per kg for all sales. If less than 16,000 kg are offered the sales price will be only £2.40 per kg.

Irrespective of amount sold the costs incurred in selling the excess raw materials will be, per kg, as follows

Packaging	£0.30
Delivery	£0.45
Insurance	£0.15

Central's management team feels that losses are undesirable while high expected money values are desirable. Therefore it is considering the utilization of a formula which incorporates both aspects of the outcome to measure the desirability of each strategy. The formula to be used to measure the desirability is:

'Desirability' = L + 3E

where L = lowest outcome of the strategy and E = expected monetary value of the strategy.

The higher this measure the more desirable the strategy.

The marketing manager seeks the advice of you, the management accountant, to assist in deciding the appropriate strategy. He says 'we need to make two decisions now—
(i) which price per unit should be charged; is it £15 or £24 per unit?; and
(ii) should all purchases of raw materials be at the price of £4 per kg or should we enter into an agreement for a basic minimum quantity? If we enter into an agreement,

then what minimum level of purchases should we guarantee?
As you are the management accountant I expect you to provide me with some useful relevant figures'.
Required:
(a) Provide statements which show the various expected outcomes of each of the choices open to Central Co. Ltd. (c. 10 marks)
(b) Advise on its best choice of strategies if Central Ltd's objective is:
 (i) to maximize the expected monetary value of the outcomes;
 (ii) to minimize the harm done to the firm if the worst outcome of each choice were to eventuate;
 (iii) to maximize the score on the above mentioned measure of 'Desirability'. (c. 6 marks)
(c) Briefly comment on either
 (i) two other factors which may be relevant in reaching a decision; OR
 (ii) the decision criteria utilized in (b) above. (c. 4 marks)

<div align="right">(Total 20 marks)
ACCA P2 Management Accounting
December 1979</div>

12.11* (a) The Alternative Sustenance Company is considering introducing a new franchised product, Wholefood Waffles.

Existing ovens now used for making some of the present 'Half-Baked' range of products could be used instead for baking the Wholefood Waffles. However, new special batch mixing equipment would be needed. This cannot be purchased, but can be hired from the franchiser in three alternative specifications, for batch sizes of 200, 300 and 600 units respectively. The annual cost of hiring the mixing equipment would be £5,000, £15,000 and £21,500 respectively.

The 'Half-Baked' product which would be dropped from the range currently earns a contribution of £90,000 per annum, which it is confidently expected could be continued if the product were retained in the range.

The company's marketing manager considers that, at the market price for Wholefood Waffles of 40 pence per unit, it is equally probable that the demand for this product would be 600,000 or 1,000,000 units per annum.

The company's production manager has estimated the variable costs per unit of making Wholefood Waffles, and the probabilities of those costs being incurred, as follows:

Batch size:	200 units	300 units	600 units	600 units
	Probability if annual sales are either	Probability if annual sales are either	Probability if annual sales are 600,000 units	Probability if annual sales are 1,000,000 units
Cost per unit (pence)	600,000 or 1,000,000 units	600,000 or 1,000,000 units		
20	0.1	0.2	0.3	0.5
25	0.1	0.5	0.1	0.2
30	0.8	0.3	0.6	0.3

You are required:

(i) to draw a decision tree setting out the problem faced by the company (12 marks), and

(ii) to show in each of the following three independent situations which size of mixing machine, if any, the company should hire:

(1) to satisfy a 'maximin' (or 'minimax' criterion,

(2) to maximize the expected value of contribution per annum,

(3) to minimize the probability of earning an annual contribution of less than £100,000 (7 marks).

(b) You are required to outline briefly the strengths and limitations of the methods of analysis which you have used in part (a) above (6 marks).

(25 marks)
ICAEW Management Accounting December 1982

12.12 The Ruddle Co. Ltd had planned to install and, with effect from next April, commence operating sophisticated machinery for the production of a new product — product Zed. However, the supplier of the machinery has just announced that delivery of the machinery will be delayed by six months and this will mean that Ruddle will not now be able to undertake production using that machinery until October.

'The first six months of production' stated the commercial manager of Ruddle 'is particularly crucial as we have already contracted to supply several national supermarket groups with whatever quantities of Zed they require during that period at a price of £40 per unit. Their demand is, at this stage, uncertain but would have been well within the capacity of the permanent machinery we were to have installed. The best estimates of the total demand for the first period are thought to be:

Estimated demand — first 6 months

Quantity (units) (000)	Probability
10	0.5
14	0.3
16	0.2

'Whatever the level of demand, we are going to meet it in full even if it means operating at a loss for the first half year. Therefore I suggest we consider the possibility of hiring equipment on which temporary production can take place.' Details of the only machines which could be hired are:

	Machine		
	A	B	C
Productive capacity per six month period (units)	10,000	12,000	16,000
Variable production cost for each unit produced	£6.5	£6	£5
Other 'fixed' costs — total for six months	£320,000	£350,000	£400,000

In addition to the above costs there will be a variable material cost of £5 per unit. For purchases greater than 10,000 units a discount of 20% per unit will be given, but this only applies to the excess over 10,000 units.

Should production capacity be less than demand then Ruddle could subcontract production of up to 6,000 units but would be required to supply raw materials. Subcontracting costs are:

up to 4,000 units subcontracted — £30 per unit

any excess over 4,000 units subcontracted — £35 per unit.

These subcontracting costs relate only to the work carried out by the subcontractor and exclude the costs of raw materials.

The commercial manager makes the following further points, 'Due to the lead time required for setting up production, the choice of which machine to hire must be made before the precise demand is known. However, demand will be known in time for production to be scheduled so

that an equal number of units can be produced each month. We will, of course, only produce sufficient to meet demand.'

'We need to decide which machine to hire. However, I wonder whether it would be worthwhile seeking the assistance of a firm of market researchers? Their reputation suggests that they are very accurate and they may be able to inform us whether demand is to be 10, 14 or 16 thousand units.'

Required:

(a) For each of the three machines which could be hired show the possible monetary outcomes and, using expected values, advise Ruddle on its best course of action. (12 marks)

(b) (i) Calculate the maximum amount which it would be worthwhile to pay to the firm of market researchers to ascertain details of demand. (You are required to assume that the market researchers will produce an absolutely accurate forecast and that demand will be exactly equal to one of the three demand figures given.) (4 marks)

(ii) Comment on the view that as perfect information is never obtainable the calculation of the expected value of perfect information is not worthwhile. Briefly explain any uses such a calculation may have. (4 marks)

(20 marks)

Ignore taxation and the time value of money.

ACCA P2 Management Accounting December 1980

12.13 Butterfield Ltd manufactures a single brand of dog-food called 'Lots O' Grissle' (LOG). Sales have stabilized for several years at a level of £20 million per annum at current prices. This level is not expected to change in the foreseeable future (except as indicated below). It is well below the capacity of the plant. The managing director, Mr Rover, is considering how to stimulate growth in the company's turnover and profits. After rejecting all of the alternative possibilities that he can imagine, or that have been suggested to him, he is reviewing a proposal to introduce a new luxury dog-food product. It would be called 'Before Eight Mince' (BEM), and would have a recommended retail price of 50 p per tin. It would require no new investment, and would incur no additional fixed costs.

Mr Rover has decided that he will undertake this new development only if he can anticipate that it will at least break-even in the first year of operation.

(a) Mr Rover estimates that BEM has a 75% chance of gaining acceptance in the market-place. His best estimate is that if the product gains acceptance it will have sales in 1981 of £3.2 million at retail prices, given a contribution of £1 million after meeting the variable costs of manufacture and distribution. If, on the other hand, the product fails to gain acceptance, sales in 1981 will, he thinks, be only £800,000 at retail prices, and for various reasons there would be a negative contribution of £400,000 in that year.

You are required to show whether, on the basis of these preliminary estimates, Mr Rover should give the BEM project further consideration. (4 marks)

(b) Mr Rover discusses the new project informally with his sales director, Mr Khoo Chee Khoo, who suggests that some of the sales achieved for the new product would cause lost sales of LOG. In terms of retail values he estimates the likelihood of this as follows:

There is a 50% chance that sales of LOG will fall by half of the sales of BEM.

There is a 25% chance that sales of LOG will fall by one-quarter of the sales of BEM.

There is a 25% chance that sales of LOG will fall by three-quarters of the sales of BEM.

The contribution margin ratio of LOG is 25% at all relevant levels of sales and output. You are required to show whether, after accepting these further estimates, Mr Rover should give the BEM project further consideration. (5 marks)

(c) Mr Rover wonders also whether, before attempting to proceed any further, he should have some market research undertaken. He approaches Delphi Associates, a firm of market research consultants for whom he has a high regard. On previous occasions he has found them to be always right in their forecasts, and he considers that their advice will give him as near perfect information as it is possible to get. He decides to ask Delphi to advise him only on whether or not BEM will gain acceptance in the market-place in the sense in which he has defined it; he will back Mr Khoo Chee Khoo's judgment about the effects of the introduction of BEM on the sales of LOG. If Delphi advise him that the product will not be accepted he will not proceed further. Delphi have told him that their fee for this work would be £100,000.

You are required to show whether Mr Rover should instruct Delphi Associates to

carry out the market research proposals. (5 marks)

(d) Preliminary discussions with Delphi suggest that Delphi's forecast will not be entirely reliable. They believe that, if they indicate that BEM will gain acceptance, there is only a 90% chance that they will be right; and, if they indicate failure to gain acceptance, there is only a 70% chance that they will be right. This implies a 75% chance overall that Delphi will indicate acceptance, in line with Mr Rover's estimate.

You are required to show the maximum amount that Mr Rover should be prepared to pay Delphi to undertake the market research, given the new estimates of the reliability of their advice. (5 marks)

(e) You are required to outline briefly the strengths and limitations of your methods of analysis in (a)–(d) above. (6 marks)

ICAEW Management Accounting December 1980

13 Capital investment decisions (1)

Capital investment decisions are those decisions which involve current outlays in return for a stream of benefits in future years. It is true to say that all of the firm's expenditures are made in expectation of realizing future benefits. The distiguishing feature between short-term decisions and capital investment (long-term) decisions is time. Generally, we can classify short-term decisions as those which involve a relatively short time horizon, say one year, from the commitment of funds to the receipt of the benefits. On the other hand, capital investment decisions are those decisions where a significant period of time elapses between the outlay and the receipt of the benefits. We shall see that this commitment of funds for a significant period of time involves an interest cost which must be brought into the analysis. With short-term decisions funds are committed only for short periods of time and the interest cost is normally so small that it can be ignored.

Capital investment decisions are applicable to all sectors of society. Business firms' investment decisions include investments in plant and machinery, research and development, advertising and warehouse facilities. Investment decisions in the public sector include new roads, schools and airports. Individuals' investment decisions include house-buying and the purchase of consumer durables. In this and the following chapter we shall examine the economic evaluation of the desirability of investment proposals. We shall concentrate on the investment decisions of manufacturing firms, but the same principles, with modifications, apply to individuals, and public sector and service organizations.

To simplify the introduction to capital investment decisions we shall *assume initially that all cash inflows and outflows are known with certainty, and that sufficient funds are available to undertake all profitable investments. We will also assume a world where there are no taxes and where there is an absence of inflation.* These factors will be brought into the analysis in the next chapter.

Objectives of capital budgeting

Capital investment decisions are part of the capital budgeting process which is concerned with decision-making in the following areas:

(1) determining which specific investment projects the firm should accept;
(2) determining the total amount of capital expenditure which the firm should undertake;
(3) determining how this portfolio of projects should be financed.

Each of the above decisions should be evaluated on the basis of their estimated contribution towards the achievement of the goals of the organization. You will recall that in Chapter 1 we noted that organizations may pursue a variety of goals, for example, maximization of profits, maximization of sales, survival of the firm, achieving a satisfactory level of profits, and obtaining the largest possible share of the market.[1] The two most important goals appear to be profitability and survival of the firm. A firm which invests in risky projects takes a chance that these projects may be unsuccessful. The acceptance of risky projects thus lowers the probability that a firm will be able to survive in the future.

The theory of capital budgeting reconciles the goals of survival and profitability by assuming that management takes as its goal the maximization of the market value of the shareholders' wealth via the maximization of the market value of ordinary shares. We shall see that this is equivalent to the objective which we adopted in Chapter 1, that is, the maximization of the present value of future cash flows.

If the maximization of shareholders' funds is the firm's objective, the important goals of profitability and survival can be combined into a single measure. Let us assume that a firm is considering investing in a new product with a possibility of increasing the return on investment, but which is also risky and may be unsuccessful, and may lead to a lower return on investment or even bankruptcy. If the stock market believes that the probability of the increased return outweighs the increase in risk it is likely that the share price will rise if the investment is undertaken. Alternatively, if the stock market considers that the riskiness outweighs the increase in expected returns then one would expect the share price to fall. Therefore, defining the objectives of the firm in terms of the market value of the ordinary shares incorporates the effects made by management to seek an optimum balance between risk and profitability.

A decision-making model for capital investment decisions

To give a better understanding of capital investment decisions we will now consider how they fit into the overall framework for decision-making. In Fig. 13.1 the decision-making model presented in Chapter 12 has been adapted to incorporate capital investment decisions.

Let us now examine each of these stages more closely. Stage 1 means that the objectives or goals of the organization must be determined, and the targets which the company wishes to achieve must be established. The quantification of the objective is known as the objective function. We have noted already in this chapter that the objective function of capital budgeting is to maximize shareholders' wealth via the maximization of the market value of ordinary shares. For a review of other objectives and reasons for choosing the maximization of shareholders' wealth see Bromwich (1979) and Levy and Sarnat (1982). The empirical evidence indicates that companies have multiple objectives. A survey by Bhaskar and McNamee of the top 500 UK companies suggests that companies do have multiple corporate objectives rather than just the primary objective of profit maximization, although

Fig. 13.1 A decision-making model for capital investment decisions

the profit motive and growth were found to be dominant.

The second stage involves a creative search for investment opportunities. Potential investment projects are not just born — someone has to suggest them. Without a creative search for new investment opportunities even the most sophisticated evaluation techniques are worthless. Thus, it is important that a firm establishes a mechanism for scanning the environment for potential opportunities and which will give an early warning of future problems. For example, this scanning process may indicate that sales of the firm's major revenue-producing product are likely to decline in the future because of an expected technological change, and it is important that steps are taken immediately to respond to such a threat. A discussion of the search stage for investment projects can be found in the corporate strategy literature. Predominant texts in this area include Harvey (1982) and Johnson and Scholes (1984).

The third stage in the decision process is to gather data about the possible future environments (states of nature) which may affect the outcomes of the projects. Examples of possible states of nature include economic boom, high inflation, recession, and so on. In this chapter we shall assume that certainty prevails so that the outcome of a project is known. Only one state of nature is therefore possible. In the next chapter we shall consider capital investment decisions under conditions of uncertainty.

After the states of nature have been identified, the fourth and fifth stages are to list the possible outcomes for each state of nature, and measure the payoff of each possible outcome in terms of the objectives of the organization. When outcomes are certain there is one specific payoff. *The aim of this chapter is to examine methods of measuring payoffs based on the objective of maximizing shareholders funds*.

Stage 6 in the process is to select the investment projects which will give the maximum payoff and to include them in the firm's long-term plan. The formulation of the long-term plan is discussed in Chapter 15. When a project is included in a firm's long-term plan it does not necessarily mean that authorization has been given to implement the project. The authorization process and the procedure for reviewing capital investment decisions (stages 7 and 8) will be discussed further in the next chapter.

The arrowed lines in Fig. 13.1 which link the various stages in the process represent 'feedback loops'. They signify that the process is continuous and dynamic. In other words, capital investment decisions should be continually reviewed to see if the actual results conform with the expected results (that is, the list of possible outcomes). The potential states of nature should also be regularly monitored as this may indicate that a change is required in the search process and that the target objective function should be revised.

The theory of capital budgeting

The theory of capital budgeting is based on the economic theory of the firm by applying the principle that the firm should operate at the point where marginal cost is equal to marginal revenue. When this rule is applied to capital budgeting decisions the value of shareholders' wealth is maximized. Marginal revenue is represented by the percentage return on investment, while marginal cost is represented by this marginal cost of capital (MCC). By cost of capital we mean the cost of the funds to finance the projects. The application of this theory is illustrated in Fig. 13.2.

The horizontal axis of Fig. 13.2 measures the total funds which are invested during a year, while the vertical axis shows both the percentage rate of return on the available projects and the percentage cost of capital which is used in financing these projects. The available projects are denoted by bands. For example, project A requires an outlay of £5 million and provides a 20% rate of return; project B requires a £2 million outlay and

Fig. 13.2 Determining the total amount of capital expenditure which a firm should undertake

yields a return of 16%, and so on. You will note that the cost of capital curve is constant at 12% until the firm has raised £21 million, after which it begins to increase. This may reflect the fact that the providers of funds (such as financial institutions and banks) may perceive that the firm is less likely to find profitable investments beyond £21 million, and that there is some risk that the firm will be unable to pay the interest cost on borrowed funds beyond this level. They therefore demand an additional return on invested funds which will justify this additional risk. The effect is that the cost of capital increases when additional funds are raised beyond £21 million.

Figure 13.2 illustrates that the firm should accept projects A to D because the return on investment is in excess of the cost of capital, and that projects E and F should be rejected because the return on investment is less than the cost of raising the capital. Throughout this chapter we are assuming that the cost of capital is constant (that is, the MCC curve is constant) and that the acceptance of any project does not alter the risk of the firm as perceived by the suppliers of capital. These assumptions *enable the firm's financing decision to be held constant* so that we can concentrate on the investment decision.

Capital budgeting is a complex theoretical area which involves investment and financing decisions. *A study of financing decisions can be found in the business finance literature.* Indeed, a detailed study of capital budgeting requires a complete book on the subject. Predominant texts in this area include Bromwich (1979), Lumby (1984) and Samuels and Wilkes (1980).

The time value of money

Because capital investment decisions involve the commitment of funds for long periods of time and the receipt of funds for many years into the future it is necessary to take into account the *time value of money*. The principle is that £100 received today is not equal to £100 received one year from today. No rational person will be equally satisfied with receiving £100 a year from now as opposed to receiving it today, because money received today can be invested to earn interest over the ensuing year. Thus, one year from now an investor can have the original £100 plus one year's interest on it.

If the interest rate is 10%, £100 invested now will yield £110 one year from now. That is, £100 today is equal to £110 one year from today at 10%

interest. Alternatively, £100 one year from today is equal to £90.91 today, its *present value*, because £90.91 plus 10% interest for one year amounts to £100. The principle of the time value of money is therefore based on the fact that money can be invested to yield a return, so that any rational investor will be unwilling to exchange a given monetary amount today for the same amount in the future. He will insist upon receiving a larger amount in the future. How much larger that amount will have to be will depend upon the interest rate which is applicable and the number of years for which the money is invested. The accumulated value of £100 invested today at 10% interest, compounded annually, over a period of five years is given in Exhibit 13.1.

Exhibit 13.1 The value of £100 invested at 10%, compounded annually, for five years

	£
Year 0	100
Year 1 (£100 + 0.10 (100))	110
Year 2 (£110 + 0.10 (110))	121
Year 3 (£121 + 0.10 (121))	133.10
Year 4 (£133.10 + 0.10 (133.10))	146.41
Year 5 (£146.41 + 0.10 (146.41))	161.05

The values in Exhibit 13.1 can also be obtained by using the following formula:

$$FV_n = V_0 (1 + K)^n \qquad (13.1)$$

where FV_n denotes the future value of an investment in n years, V_0 denotes the amount invested at the beginning of the period (year 0), K denotes the rate of interest, and n denotes the number of years for which the money is invested. The calculation for £100 invested at 10% for two years is as follows:

$$FV = 100 (1 + 0.10)^2 = £121$$

In Exhibit 13.1 all of the year-end values are equal as far as the time value of money is concerned. For example, £121 received at the end of year 2 is equivalent to £100 received today and invested at 10%. Similarly, £133.10 received at the end of year 3 is equivalent to £121 received at the end of year 2 as £121 can be invested at the end of year two to accumulate to £133.10. Unfortunately, none of the amounts are directly comparable at any single moment in time as each amount is expressed at a different point in time.

When making capital investment decisions we must convert cash inflows and outflows for different years into a common value. This is achieved

by converting the cash flows into their respective values at the same point in time. Mathematically, any point in time can be chosen as all six figures in Exhibit 13.1 are equal to £100 at year 0, £110 at year 1, £121 at year 2, and so on. However, it is preferable to choose the point in time at which the decision is taken, and this is the present time or year 0. All of the values in Exhibit 13.1 can therefore be expressed in values at the present time (that is, a 'present value') of £100.

The process of converting cash to be received in the future into a value at the present time by the use of an interest rate is termed *discounting* and the resulting present value is the *discounted present value*. *Compounding* is the opposite of discounting as it is the future value of present value cash flows. Equation (13.1) for calculating future values can be rearranged to produce the following present value formula:

$$V_0 \text{ (present value)} = \frac{FV_n}{(1 + K)^n} \qquad (13.2)$$

By applying equation (13.2) the calculation for £121 received at the end of year 2 can be expressed as follows:

$$\text{Present value} = \frac{£21}{(1 + 0.10)^2} = \underline{\underline{£100}}$$

The reasoning behind the present value calculations is that if a person is given an alternative of investing money at 10%, he should not pay more than £100 to obtain £121 with certainty in two years time. If he pays more, say £110, then the present value of cash he will receive (£100) from this investment will be £10 less than the cost of the investment. To put it another way, if a person requires a 10% return on an investment a cash receipt of £121 in year 2 is not enough to repay the original investment (£110) plus a return on the investment of 10% for two years.[2]

The minimum acceptable rate of return

Business firms have to ensure that cash flows from investments will be sufficient to cover the initial investments and also to provide a return on the investment which is in excess of the minimum acceptable return. The minimum acceptable return is equal to the cost of equity capital if we

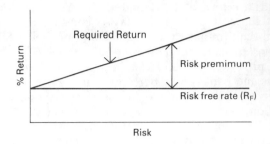

Fig. 13.3　A project's risk/return trade-off

assume that all projects are financed by raising ordinary share capital.[3] How do we establish this minimum rate of return for business organizations? Consider the situation where an investor has an investment opportunity which yields x%, and he forgoes this to invest in a project where there is equal risk. The minimum acceptable return on the project will be x%. In other words, the required rate of return on any investment opportunity is the rate which the investor has forgone on the next best alternative investment opportunity. This same rate should reflect the alternative investments of those to whom the value accrues, that is the shareholders. The minimum required rate of return which management should use in evaluating investment opportunities is therefore the next best opportunity forgone by the shareholders rather than by the firm itself. Clearly if management cannot invest in projects which yield a return in excess of the minimum acceptable return then investments should not be undertaken by the firm. This return is a market determined rate, established in the financial markets by the collective actions of investors competing against one another.

Empirical evidence (see Friend and Blume, 1975) indicates that investors are risk averse and thus *the greater the risk, the greater the compensation* required. This means that the minimum acceptable return, or the cost of capital of a project, depends on the risk of the project as illustrated in Fig. 13.3. The diagram indicates that projects with differing levels of risk must be evaluated using different minimum rates of return if shareholders' interests are to be served. Note that the minimum required rate of return or cost of capital for a project compensates investors for two things: the passage of time and risk. In symbolic terms the required rate of return (RRR) is as follows:

$$RRR = R_F + R_P$$

where R_F represents the risk free rate and R_P represents the risk premium. The risk free rate represents the return available on risk free investments such as UK Government Bonds. The risk premium is established in the financial markets by observing the excess returns demanded by investors for different degrees of risk.[4] The risk free rate represents the certain interest return for investing money which is to be repaid in the future, where the amount to be repaid is dependent on the time period for which it is invested; hence the risk free rate is also known as the *time value of money*. In this chapter we have assumed that all cash inflows and outflows can be predicted with certainty, and consequently the required rate of return used throughout this chapter is the risk free rate of interest. In Chapter 14 we shall move on to consider the required rate of return on uncertain cash flows.

Net present value

The most straightforward way of determining whether an investment will yield a return in excess of the minimum acceptable rate of return is to calculate the *net present value*. This is the difference between the present values of the forecasted cash receipts and the forecasted cash outlays which result from the investment. We shall see that if the rate of return from the investment is greater than the minimum desired return, the net present value will be positive. Alternatively, if the rate of return is lower, the net present value will be negative. A positive net present value therefore indicates that an investment should be accepted while a negative value indicates that it should be rejected. The net present value (NPV) can be calculated by applying the following formula:

$$NPV = \frac{FV_1}{1 + K} + \frac{FV_2}{(1 + K)^2} + \frac{FV_3}{(1 + K)^3}$$

$$+ \dots \frac{FV_n}{(1 + K)^n} - I_0 \qquad (13.3)$$

where I_0 represents the investment outlay and FV represents the future values received in years 1 to n. The rate of interest (i.e. K) used is the minimum desired rate of return or cost of capital.

Consider the situation in Example 13.1.

EXAMPLE 13.1

A firm has the opportunity of investing £1,000 in a project with a life of three years. The estimated cash inflows are as follows:

Year 1	£300
Year 2	£1,000
Year 3	£400

The cost of capital is 10%. You are required to calculate the net present value of the project's cash flows.

The net present value calculation is:

$$NPV = \frac{300}{(1.10)} + \frac{1000}{(1.10)^2} + \frac{400}{(1.10)^3}$$

$$- £1,000 = + £399$$

Alternatively, the net present value can be calculated by referring to a published table of present values. You will find examples of such a table if you refer to Appendix I at the end of this book. To use the table simply find the discount factors by referring to each year of the cash flows and the appropriate interest rate. For example, if you refer to year 1 in Appendix 1, and the 10% column, this will show a discount factor of 0.909. For years 2 and 3 the discount factors are 0.826 and 0.751. You then multiply the cash flows by the discount factors to find the present value of the cash flows. The calculation is as follows:

Year	Amount £	Discount factor	Present value £
1	300	0.909	273
2	1,000	0.826	826
3	400	0.751	300
			1,399
		Less Initial outlay	1,000
		Net present value	399

Note that the discount factors in the present value table are based on £1 received in n years time calculated according to the present value formula (13.2). For example, £1 received in years 1, 2 and 3 when the interest rate is 10% is calculated as follows:

Year 1 = £1/1.10 = 0.909
Year 2 = £1/(1.10)2 = 0.826
Year 3 = £1/(1.10)3 = 0.751

The positive net present value from the investment indicates the increase in the market value of the shareholders' funds which should occur once the stock market becomes aware of the acceptance of the project. The net present value also represents the potential increase in present consumption which the project makes available to the ordinary shareholders, after any funds used have been repaid with interest. For example, if we assume that the firm finances the investment in Example 13.1 by borrowing £1,000 at 10% and repays the loan and interest out of the project's proceeds as they occur, the pattern of cash outflows and receipts will be as shown in Exhibit 13.2.

The ordinary shareholders receive £120 at the end of year 2 and £400 at the end of year 3. When these receipts are discounted at 10% their present value is equal to £399.[5] Therefore, the ordinary shareholders' potential present consumption is increased by the amount of the net present value. Theoretically, *the acceptance of all available projects with a positive net present value should lead to the maximization of shareholders' wealth*.

Constant annual cash inflows

When the annual cash flows are constant the calculation of the net present value is simplified. Consider Example 13.2.

EXAMPLE 13.2

A firm has the opportunity to invest £1,000 in a project which will yield cash inflows of £600 per year for three years. The minimum desired rate of return is 10%.

The discount factors when the cash flows are the same each year are set out in Appendix II at the end of this book. We need to find the discount factor for 10% for three years. If you refer to Appendix II you will see that it is 2.487. The net present value is calculated as follows:

Annual cash inflow	Discount factor	Present value
£600	2.487	£1,492
	Less Investment cost	£1,000
	Net present value	£ 492

You will see that the total present value for the period is calculated by multiplying the cash inflow by the discount factor. It is important to note that *Appendix II can only be applied when the annual cash flows are the same each year*.

The internal rate of return

The internal rate of return is an alternative technique for use in making capital investment decisions which also takes into account the time value of money. The internal rate of return represents the true interest rate earned on an investment over the course of its economic life. This measure is sometimes referred to as the *discounted rate of return*. The internal rate of return is that interest rate (K) which, when used to discount all cash flows resulting from an investment, will equate the present value of the cash receipts to the present value of the cash outlays. In other words, it is the *discount rate which will cause the net present value of an investment to be zero*. Alternatively, the internal rate of return can be described as the maximum cost of capital which can be applied to finance a project without causing harm to the shareholders. The internal rate of return is found by solving the value of K in the following formula:

$$I_0 = \frac{FV_1}{1 + K} + \frac{FV_2}{(1 + K)^2}$$
$$+ \frac{FV_3}{(1 + K)^3} + \cdots \cdot \frac{FV_n}{(1 + K)^n} \quad (13.3)$$

Exhibit 13.2 The pattern of cash flows assuming that the loan is repaid out of the proceeds of the project

Year	Loan outstanding at start of year (1)	Interest at 10% (2)	Total amount owed before repayement (3)(= 1 + 2)	Proceeds from project (4)	Loan outstanding at year end (5) = (3 − 4)	Proceeds to to share-holders (6) = (4 − 3)
	£		£	£	£	£
1	1,000	100	1,100	300	800	–
2	800	80	880	1,000	–	120
3	–	–	–	400	–	400

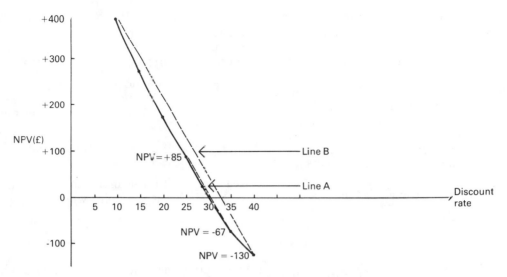

Fig. 13.4 Interpretation of the internal rate of return

It is easier, however, to use the discount tables, and Example 13.1, used for calculating the net present value, is repeated here to illustrate the internal rate of return calculation.

EXAMPLE 13.1

A firm has the opportunity of investing £1,000 in a project with a life of three years. The estimated cash inflows are as follows:

Year 1	£300
Year 2	£1,000
Year 3	£400

The minimum desired rate of return is 10%.

The internal rate of return can be found by trial and error by using a number of discount factors until the net present value equals zero. For example, if we use a 25% discount factor we get a positive net present value of £85. We must therefore try a higher figure. Applying 35% gives a negative net present value of £67. We know then that the net present value will be zero somewhere between 25% and 35%. In fact, the internal rate of return is approximately 30% as indicated in the following calculation:

Year	Net cash flow	Discount factor (30%)	Present value of cash flow
1	£300	0.769	£231
2	£1,000	0.592	£592
3	£400	0.455	£182
		Net present value	£1,005
		Less Initial outlay	£1,000
		Net present value	£ 5

It is claimed that the calculation of the internal rate of return does not require the prior specification of the cost of capital. The decision rule is that if the internal rate of return is greater than the cost of capital, the investment is profitable and will yield a positive net present value. Alternatively, if the internal rate of return is less than the cost of capital, the investment is unprofitable and will result in a negative net present value. Therefore, any interpretation of the significance of the internal rate of return will still require that we estimate the cost of capital. The calculation of the internal rate of return is illustrated in Fig. 13.4.

The dots in the graph represent the net present value at different discount rates. The point where the non-dashed line joining the dots cuts the horizontal axis indicates the internal rate of return (the point at which net present value equals zero). Figure 13.4 indicates that the internal rate of return is 30%, and you can see from this diagram that the interpolation method can be used to calculate the internal rate of return without carrying out trial and error calculations. When we use interpolation we infer the missing term (in this case the discount rate at which NPV is zero) from a known series of numbers. For example, we calculated that for a discount rate of 25% the present value is + £85 and for a discount rate of 35% the net present value is − £67. The total distance between these points is £152 (+ 85 and − 67). The calculation for the *approximate* internal rate of return is therefore

$$25\% + \frac{85}{152} \times (35\% - 25\%) = 30.59\%$$

In other words, if you move down the *dashed* line (labelled A in Fig. 13.4) from a discount rate of 25% by £85 you will reach the point at which net present value is zero. The distance between the two points on this dashed line is £152 and we are given the discount rates of 25% and 35% for these points. Therefore 85/152 represents the distance which we must move between these two points for the net present value to be zero. This distance in terms of the discount rate is 5.59% (85/152 × 10%) which when added to the starting point of 25% produces an internal rate of return of 30.59%. The formula using the interpolation method is as follows:

$$A + \frac{C}{C - D} \times (B - A) \qquad (13.4)$$

where A = discount rate of the low trial, B = discount rate of the high trial, C = net present value of cash inflow of the low trial, and D = net present value of cash inflow of the high trial. Thus:

$$25\% + \frac{85}{85 - (-67)} \times 10\%$$

$$= 25\% + \left[\frac{85}{152} \times 10\% \right]$$

$$= 30.59\%$$

Note that the interpolation method only gives an approximation of the internal rate of return. The greater the distance between any two points which have a positive and a negative net present value, the less accurate is the internal rate of return calculation. Consider the dashed line (labelled B in Fig. 13.3). The point where it cuts the horizontal axis is approximately 33% whereas the actual internal rate of return is 30.59%.

The calculation of the internal rate of return is easier when the cash flows are of a constant amount each year. Example 13.2 illustrated earlier, for the calculation of the net present value with equal annual cash flows, is repeated here to show the calculation of the internal rate of return.

EXAMPLE 13.2

A firm has the opportunity of investing £1,000 in a project which will yield cash inflows of £600 per year for three years. The minimum desired rate of return is 10%. You are required to calculate the internal rate of return.

Because the cash flows are equal each year we can use Appendix II. When the cash flows are discounted at the internal rate of return the net present value will be zero. The internal rate of return will therefore be at the point where

$$(\text{Annual cash flow}) \times \left\{ \begin{array}{l} \text{Discount factor for} \\ \text{number of years for} \\ \text{which cash flow is} \\ \text{received} \end{array} \right\}$$
$$- \left[\begin{array}{l} \text{Investment} \\ \text{cost} \end{array} \right] = 0$$

Rearranging the formula the internal rate of return will be at the point where

$$\text{Discount factor} = \frac{\text{Investment cost}}{\text{Annual cash flow}}$$

Substituting the figures from Example 13.2, then

$$\text{Discount factor} = \frac{1,000}{600} = 1.666$$

We now examine the entries for year 3 in Appendix II to find the figures closest to 1.666. They are 1.673 (entered in the 36% column) and 1.652 (entered in the 37% column). We can therefore conclude that the internal rate of return is between 36% and 37%. However, because the cost of capital is 10% an accurate calculation is unnecessary; the internal rate of return is far in excess of the cost of capital.

The calculation of the internal rate of return can be rather tedious (as the cited examples show), but the trial and error approach can be programmed for a fast and accurate solution by a computer. Indeed, small hand calculators can now be programmed to speedily calculate the internal rate of return, and the calculation problems are no longer a justification for preferring the net present value method of investment appraisal. Nevertheless, there are theoretical justifications, which we shall discuss later in this chapter, which support the net present value method.

Relevant cash flows

Investment decisions, like all other decisions, should be analysed in terms of the cash flows which can be directly attributable to them. These cash flows should include the incremental cash flows which will occur in the future following acceptance of the investment. The cash flows will

include cash inflows and outflows, or the inflows may be represented by savings in cash outflows. For example, a decision to purchase new machinery may generate cash savings in the form of reduced out-of-pocket operating costs. For all practical purposes such cost savings are equivalent to cash receipts.

It is important to note that depreciation is *not* included in the cash flow estimates for capital investment decisions as it is a non-cash expense. This is because the capital investment cost of the asset to be depreciated is included as a cash outflow at the start of the project, and depreciation is merely an accounting method for apportioning the capital costs to the relevant accounting periods. Any inclusion of depreciation will lead to double counting.

Timing of cash flows

The mathematics underlying the discount factors presented in Appendixes I and II is based on the assumption that any cash flows in future years will occur in one lump sum at the year end. Obviously, this is an unrealistic assumption as cash flows are likely to occur at various times throughout the year, and a more accurate method is to use monthly discount tables. However, the use of Appendixes I and II enables all cash flows which occur in a single year to be combined and discounted in one computation. Even though the calculations which are obtained are not strictly accurate, they are normally accurate enough for most decisions.

Comparison of the net present value and the internal rate of return

In many situations the internal rate of return method will result in the same decision as the net present value method. In the case of conventional projects (in which an initial cash outflow is followed by a series of cash inflows) which are independent of each other (that is, where the selection of a particular project does not preclude the choice of the other), both NPV and IRR rules will lead to the same accept/reject decisions. However, there are also situations where the IRR method may lead to different decisions being made from those which would follow the adoption of the NPV procedure.

Mutually exclusive projects

Where projects are *mutually exclusive* it is possible for the NPV and the IRR methods to suggest different rankings as to which project should be given priority. Mutually exclusive projects exist where the acceptance of one project excludes the acceptance of another project, for example the choice of one of several possible factory locations, or the choice of one of many different possible machines. Example 13.3 illustrates how the application of the IRR and the NPV rules can lead to different decisions:

EXAMPLE 13.3

A company has the choice of selecting one of two mutually exclusive projects. The estimated cash flows are as follows:

Initial investment outlay	Net inflow at the end of years 1–3		
£	1	2	3
Project A — 7,000	£3,430	£3,430	£3,430
Project B — 12,000	£5,520	£5,520	£5,520

The cost of capital is 10%. Which project should the company select?

The NPV and IRR calculations are as follows:

	IRR	NPV
Project A	22%	£1,530
Project B	18%	£1,728

You can see that the IRR ranks A first, but the NPV rate ranks B first. If the projects were independent this would be irrelevant as both projects would be accepted and the firm would be indifferent as to the order in which they were accepted. However, in the case of mutually exclusive projects, the ranking is crucial as only one project can be accepted and we cannot be indifferent to the outcome of applying the NPV and the IRR rules. The reasons for the different rankings are shown in Fig. 13.5.

The NPV ranking depends on the discount rate used. For a discount rate greater than 12% no contradictions arise as both the NPV and the IRR rules rank A first. However, the two methods give different ranking for discount rates which are less than 12%; project B has a higher NPV, but project A has a higher IRR. Logically such a

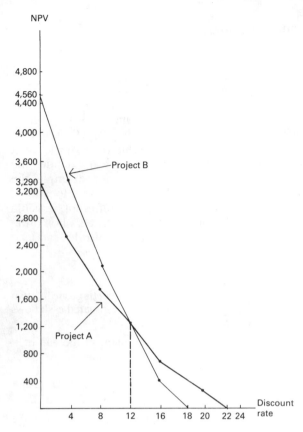

Fig. 13.5 A comparison of NPV and IRR rules for projects A and B

to the firm shifting from A to B. The IRR of the incremental investment (B−A) is 12%. As the cost of capital is 10%, the incremental project should be accepted. In other words, the IRR has indicated that we should move from project A to project B, and the superiority of the NPV method has been established by using the IRR analysis to contradict the IRR rule.

Note also that if the cost of capital is greater than 12%, it does not pay to invest in the incremental project (B−A), and the firm should not shift from project A to project B. This is exactly what the NPV method prescribes in Fig. 13.5.

Percentage returns

Another problem with the IRR rule is that it expresses the result as a percentage rather than in monetary terms. Comparison of percentage returns can be misleading; for example, compare an investment of £100 which yields a return of 50% with an investment of £1,000 which yields a return of 25%. If only one of the investments can be undertaken, the first investment will yield £50 but the second will yield £250. If we assume that the cost of capital is 10%, and that no other suitable investments are available, any surplus funds will be invested at the cost of capital. Choosing the first investment will leave a further £900 to be invested, but this can only be invested at 10%, yielding a return of £90. Adding this to the return of £50 from the £100 investment gives a total return of £140. Clearly, the second investment which yields a return of £250 is preferable.

situation should not exist, and the only explanation seems to be that one of the methods must indicate an incorrect ranking. In fact, the IRR method gives an incorrect ranking and we can prove this by considering the increments of cash flows of project B over project A. The increments are as follows:

Years	0	1	2	3
	£	£	£	£
Project B	12,000	5,520	5,520	5,520
Project A	7,000	3,430	3,430	3,430
Incremental cash flow (B−A)	5,000	2,090	2,090	2,090

If we assume that the firm adopts the IRR method and initially chooses project A, we can consider whether it is worthwhile to add the hypothetical incremental investment (B−A). The acceptance of the initial investment plus the hypothetical incremental investment is A + (B−A) and this is the equivalent of accepting project B. Therefore, if the firm is prepared to accept the incremental investment, using the IRR rule, this is equivalent

Reinvestment assumptions

The assumption concerning the reinvestment of interim cash flows from the acceptance of projects provides another reason for supporting the superiority of the NPV method. The implicit assumption if the NPV method is adopted is that the interim cash flows will be reinvested at the cost of

capital (that is, the discount rate). However, the IRR method makes a different implicit assumption about the reinvestment of the interim cash flows. It assumes that all the proceeds from a project can be reinvested to earn a return equal to the IRR of the original project. In Example 13.3 the NPV method assumes that the annual cash inflows of £3,430 for project A will be reinvested at a cost of capital of 10%, whereas the IRR method assumes that they will be reinvested at 22%. In theory, a firm will have accepted to all projects which offer a return in excess of the cost of capital, and any other funds which become available can only be reinvested at the cost of capital. This is the assumption which is implicit in the NPV rule.

Unconventional cash flows

Where a project has unconventional cash flows the IRR has a technical shortcoming. Most projects have conventional cash flows which consist of an initial negative cash flow followed by positive cash inflows in later years. In this situation the algebraic sign changes, being negative at the start and positive in all future periods. If the sign of the net cash flows changes in successive periods it is possible for the calculations to produce as many internal rates of return as there are sign changes. While multiple rates of return are mathematically possible, only one rate of return is economically significant in determining whether or not the investment is profitable. Fortunately, the majority of investment decisions consist of conventional cash flows which produce a single IRR calculation. However, the problem cannot be ignored as unconventional cash flows are possible and, if the decision-maker is unaware of the situation, serious errors may occur at the decision-making stage. Example 13.4 illustrates a situation where two internal rates of return occur.

EXAMPLE 13.4

A firm has the following series of cash flows for a specific project:

Year 0 = − 4,000
Year 1 = + 10,200
Year 2 = − 6,300

You are required to calculate the internal rate of return.

The cash flows in Example 13.4 give internal rates of return of 5% and 50%. The effect of multiple rates of return on the NPV calculations is

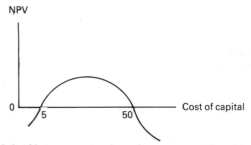

Fig. 13.6 Net present values for unconventional cash flows

illustrated in Fig. 13.6
When the cost of capital is between 5% and 50% the NPV is positive and, following the NPV rule, the project should be accepted. However, if the internal rate of return calculation of 5% is used the project may be incorrectly rejected if the cost of capital is in excess of 5%. You can see that the graph of the NPV in Fig. 13.6 indicates that this is an incorrect decision when the cost of capital is between 5% and 50%. Alternatively, if the IRR of 50% is used, this will lead to the same decision being made as if the NPV rule were adopted provided that the cost of capital is greater than 5%.

Profitability index

The profitability index is the third method of evaluating capital investment proposals which takes into account the time value of money. The method is simply a variation of the NPV method, and it is computed by dividing the present value of the cash proceeds by the initial cost of the investment. If the profitability index is less than 1, the investment should be rejected. Alternatively, if it is greater than 1 the investment should be accepted. This method is consistent with the NPV method as the index can only be less than 1 when the NPV is negative. Similarly, an index greater than 1 only arises when the NPV is positive.

In the case of independent projects and where the company is not restricted from accepting profitable projects because of the shortage of funds, the profitability index will yield the same acceptance–rejection decision as the NPV method. For mutually exclusive investments the profitability index will not always result in the same rankings as the NPV method. Consider the following situation where projects A and B are mutually exclusive.

	PV of cash flow	Initial investment outlay	Profitability index
Project A	£1,000	£ 500	2.0
Project B	£1,800	£1,000	1.8

According to the profitability index, project A is to be preferred, but given that only one of these two projects can be chosen, project B should be the one. This is because B gives the largest absolute amount. Therefore, the profitability index is a weak measure for selecting between mutually exclusive investment projects in a situation when a company can accept all investments which yield a positive net present value. However, we shall see in the next chapter that when a firm cannot accept all of those projects with positive NPVs because of the unavailability of funds, the profitability index can be a useful method for determining how the scarce funds can best be allocated.

Techniques which ignore the time value of money

In addition to those methods which take into account the time value of money, two other methods which ignore this factor are frequently used in practice (that is, the payback method and the accounting rate of return method). Methods which ignore the time value of money are theoretically weak and they will not necessary lead to the maximization of the market value of ordinary shares. Nevertheless, the fact that they are frequently used in practice means that we should be aware of their limitations.

Payback method

The payback method is one of the simplest and most frequently used methods of capital investment appraisal (see Pike, 1983). The payback period is defined as the length of time which is required for a stream of cash proceeds from an investment to recover the original cash outlay required by the investment. If the stream of cash flows from the investment is constant each year, the payback period can be calculated by dividing the total initial cash outlay by the amount of the expected annual cash proceeds. Therefore, if an investment requires an initial outlay of £60,000 and is expected to produce annual cash inflows of £20,000 per year for five years, the payback period will be £60,000 divided by £20,000, or three years. If the stream of expected proceeds is not constant from year to year, the payback period is determined by adding up the cash inflows expected in successive years until the total is equal to the original outlay. Example 13.5 illustrates two projects, A and B, which require the same initial outlay of £50,000 but which display different time profiles of benefits.

EXAMPLE 13.5

The cash flows and NPV calculations for two projects are as follows:

	Project A £		Project B £	
Initial cost		50,000		50,000
Cash inflows				
Year 1	10,000		10,000	
Year 2	20,000		10,000	
Year 3	20,000		10,000	
Year 4	20,000		20,000	
Year 5	10,000		30,000	
Year 6	–		30,000	
Year 7	–	80,000	30,000	140,000
NPV (at a 10% cost of capital)		10,500		39,460

In Example 13.5 project A pays back its initial investment cost in three years whereas project B pays back its initial cost in four years. However, project B has a higher NPV and the payback method incorrectly ranks project A in preference to project B. Two obvious deficiencies are apparent from these calculations. First, the payback method does not take into account cash flows which are earned after the payback date and, second, it fails to take into account the differences in the timing of the proceeds which are earned

prior to the payback date. Payback computations ignore the important fact that future cash receipts cannot be validly compared with an initial outlay until they are discounted to their present values.

Not only does the payback period incorrectly rank project A in preference to project B, but the method can also result in the acceptance of projects which have a negative NPV. Consider the following cash flows for project C in Example 13.6.

EXAMPLE 13.6

The cash flows and NPV calculation for project C are as follows:

Initial cost				£50,000
Cash outflows, Year	1	10,000		
	2	20,000		
	3	20,000		
	4	3,500		
	5	3,500		
	6	3,500		
	7	3,500	64,000	
NPV (at 10% cost of capital)			(−1,036)	

The payback period for project C is three years, and if this was within the time limit set by management the project would be accepted in spite of its negative NPV. Note also that the payback method would rank project C in preference to project B in Example 13.5, despite the fact that B would yield a positive NPV.

The payback period can only be a valid indicator of the time which an investment requires to pay for itself, if all cash flows are first discounted to their present values and the discounted values are then used to calculate the payback period. This adjustment gives rise to what is known as the adjusted or *discounted payback method*. Even when such an adjustment is made the adjusted payback method cannot be a complete measure of an investment's profitability. It can estimate whether an investment is likely to be profitable, but it cannot estimate how profitable that investment will be. If the adjusted payback method has any use at all it is as a supplementary indicator of the risk of an investment. For example, the longer the payback period, the greater the risk that future cash flows may not be obtained. However, this is only a rough approximation of risk as it assumes that the risk of cash flows not being realized increases as they are deferred further and further into the future. This assumption may not always be valid. Nevertheless, the payback method is frequently used in practice, and it is particularly useful for companies which have a weak cash and credit position and which require a fast repayment of investments. The payback method may also be appropriate in situations where risky investments are made in uncertain markets which are subject to fast design and product changes. If the payback method is used, it should be used in conjunction with the NPV method, and the cash flows should be discounted before the payback period is calculated. For a detailed discussion of the payback method see Boardman *et al.* (1982).

Accounting rate of return

The accounting rate of return is calculated by dividing the average annual profits from a project into the average investment cost. It differs from other methods in that profits rather than cash flows are used. The use of this method results from the wide use of the return on investment measure in financial statement analysis.

When the average annual net profits are calculated, only additional revenues and costs which follow from the investment are included in the calculation. The average annual net profit is therefore calculated by dividing the difference between incremental revenues and costs by the estimated life of the investment. The incremental costs include either the net investment cost or the total depreciation charges, these figures being identical. The average investment figure which is used in the calculation depends on the method which is used to calculate depreciation. If straight line depreciation is used it is presumed that investment will decline in a linear fashion as the asset ages. The average investment under this assumption is one-half of the amount of the initial investment less the scrap value at the end of the project's life.

For example, the three projects described in Examples 13.5 and 13.6 for which the payback period was computed required an initial outlay of £50,000. If we assume that the projects have no scrap values and that straight line depreciation is used, the average investment for each project will be £25,000. The calculation of the accounting rate of return for each of these projects is as follows:

$$\text{Accounting rate of return} = \frac{\text{Average annual profits}}{\text{Average investment}}$$

$$\text{Project A} = \frac{6,000}{25,000} = 24\%$$

$$\text{Project B} = \frac{12,857}{25,000} = 51\%$$

$$\text{Project C} = \frac{2,000}{25,000} = 8\%$$

For project A the total profit over its five-year life is £30,000, giving an average annual profit of £6,000. The average annual profits for projects B and C are calculated in a similar manner. It follows that the accounting rate of return is superior to the payback method in one respect; that is, it allows for differences in the useful lives of the assets being compared. For example, the calculations set out above reflect the high earnings of project B over the whole life of the project, and consequently it is ranked in preference to project A. Also, projects A and C have the same payback periods but the accounting rate of return correctly indicates that project A is preferable to project C.

However, the accounting rate of return suffers from the serious defect that it ignores the time value of money. When the method is used in relation to a project where the cash inflows do not occur until near the end of its life, it will show the same accounting rate of return as it would for a project where the cash inflows occur early in its life, providing that the average cash inflows are the same. For this reason the accounting rate of return cannot be recommended.

Evaluation techniques used in practice

In a comprehensive survey of 150 of the largest UK companies Pike (1983) found that payback is the most popular evaluation technique. His findings are presented in Exhibit 13.3

Exhibit 13.3 Evaluation techniques used by UK companies

	Percentage used in:	
	1975	1980
Payback period	71	79
Accounting rate of return	51	51
Internal rate of return	42	54
Net present value	32	38
Other	5	7

You will see from this table that the payback method was used by 79% of the firms in Pike's survey, but it was the sole criterion in only 11% of the firms. Most firms employ a combination of evaluation methods. This fact can be interpreted in two ways. First, it may indicate that no single appraisal technique is sufficiently simple for managers to understand, yet sufficiently complicated to embody the most important relationships holding in the real world (see Bhaskar, 1978, for a discussion of this point). Second, it may indicate that if the formal evaluation stage seeks to develop a case to justify the project which a manager believes should be accepted, then managers will select the technique which reflects the project in the best possible light (King, 1978).

Qualitative factors

Not all investment projects can be described completely in terms of monetary costs and benefits (for example, a new cafeteria for the employees, or the installation of safety equipment). Nevertheless, the procedures described in this chapter may be useful by making the value placed by management on quantitative factors explicit. For example, if the present value of the cash outlays for a project is £100,000 and the benefits from the project are difficult to quantify, management must make a value judgment as to whether or not the benefits are in excess of £100,000. In the case of capital expenditure on facilities for employees, or expenditure to avoid unpleasant environmental effects from the company's manufacturing process, one can take the view that the present value of the cash outlays represents the cost to shareholders of the pursuit of goals other than the maximization of shareholders' funds. In other words, ordinary shareholders, as a group in the bargaining coalition, should know how much the pursuit of other goals is costing them.[6]

Capital investment decisions are particularly difficult in non-profit organizations such as national and local government organizations as it is not always possible to quantify the costs and benefits of a project. *Cost–benefit analysis (CBA)*, which is an investment appraisal technique for analysing and measuring the costs and benefits to the community of capital projects, has been developed to resolve this problem and it seeks to determine the incidence of costs and benefits between different sectors of the community. CBA

attempts to take into account all the costs and benefits which accrue from a project by defining the costs and benefits in much wider terms than those which would be included in traditional accounting measures. A wider range of factors is therefore included in the analysis than those which would be incorporated in the traditional accounting investment appraisal. For example, when CBA was applied to the appraisal of the Victoria Underground Line in London attempts were made to set a monetary value on the travelling time saved. A discussion of CBA is beyond the scope of this book but if you are interested in this topic you are recommended to read Misham (1976) and Layard (1972). For a summary of a report by the Chartered Institute of Public Finance and Accountancy on project appraisal in the public sector, see Sullivan and Adair (1984).

Summary

In this chapter we have noted that capital investment decisions are of vital importance as they involve the commitment of large sums of money and they affect the whole conduct of the business for many future years. The commitment of funds for long periods of time entails a large interest cost which must be incorporated into the analysis. We have seen that the rate of return which is required by investors can be incorporated by converting future cash flows to their present values. For business firms the rate of return includes a risk free interest rate plus a risk premium to compensate for uncertainty. For certain cash flows, which we have assumed in this chapter, the required rate of return is the risk free rate.

The objective of capital budgeting is to maximize shareholders' wealth and this is achieved by the acceptance of all projects which yield positive net present values. Three alternative methods of evaluating capital investment decisions which take into account the time value of money have been examined: the net present value, the internal rate of return and the profitability index methods. We have seen that neither the internal rate of return nor the profitability index can guarantee that the correct decision will be made when there is a choice between several mutually exclusive projects. In addition, the internal rate of return is theoretically unsound regarding the reinvestment assumptions of the interim cash flows. A further point is that more than one internal rate of return is possible in situations where mid-project negative unconventional cash flows occur. The net present value method is therefore recommended where a firm can obtain sufficient funds to accept all the projects with positive net present values.

Finally we considered the payback and the accounting rate of return methods for evaluating capital investment decisions, as these are frequently used in practice, but as neither incorporates the time value of money we must conclude that they are theoretically unsound.

References and further reading

Bacon, P.W. The evaluation of mutually exclusive investments. *Financial Management* Summer 1977, 55-8.

Bhaskar, K. Linear programming and capital budgeting. *Journal of Business Finance and Accounting*, Summer 1978, 160.

Bhaskar, K. and McNamee, P. Multiple objectives in accounting and finance. *Journal of Business Finance and Accounting* Winter 1983, 595-622.

Boardman, C.M., Reinhart, W.J. and Celec, S.E. The role of the payback period in the theory and application of duration to capital budgeting. *Journal of Business Finance and Accounting* Winter 1982, 9(4), 511-22.

Bromwich, M. *The Economics of Capital Budgeting.* Pitman, 1979, Chapter 2.

Friend, I. and Blume, M.E. The demand for risky assets. *America Economic Review* 65, December 1972, 900-22.

Gordon, L.A. Accounting rate of return v. economic rate of return. *Journal of Business Finance and Accounting* 1(3), 343-56.

Harvey, D.F. *Strategic Management.* Merrill, 1982.

Johnson, G. and Scholes, K. *Exploring Corporate Strategy.* Prentice-Hall, 1984.

King, P. Is the emphasis of capital budgeting theory misplaced? *Journal of Business Finance and Accounting* Spring 1975, 69-82.

Layard, R. *Cost Benefit Analysis.* Penguin, 1972.

Lerner, E. and Rappaport, A. Limit DCF in capital budgeting. *Harvard Business Review* September/ October 1968.

Levy, H. and Sarnat, M. *Capital Investment and*

Financial Decisions. Prentice-Hall, 1982, Chapter 1.

Lumby, S. *Investment Appraisal* 2nd edn. Van Nostrand Reinhold (UK), 1984.

Misham, E.J. *Elements of Cost Benefit Analysis*. Allen & Unwin, 1976.

Pike, R.H. A review of recent trends in formal capital budgeting processes. *Accounting and Business Research* Summer 1983, 201-308. See also *Capital Budgeting in the 1980s: The Results of a Major Survey of Large Companies*. Institute of Cost and Management Accountants, 1983.

Samuels, J.M. and Wilkes, F.M. *Management of Company Finance* 3rd edn. Van Nostrand Reinhold (UK), 1980.

Sullivan, C. and Adair, R. Project appraisal in the public sector. *Public Finance and Accountancy* March 1984, 25-9.

Whittington, G. On the use of the accounting rate of return in empirical research. *Accounting and Business Research* Summer 1979, 201-8.

Wilkie, A.D. Discounting formulae used in capital budgeting — A comment. *Journal of Business Finance and Accounting* Summer 1976, **3**(2), 143-6.

Problems

*Indicates that a suggested solution is to be found in the *Students' Manual*.

13.1 The evidence of many recent studies suggests that there are major differences between current theories of investment appraisal and the methods which firms actually use in evaluating long-term investments. You are required to:
(a) present theoretical arguments for the choice of net present value as the best method of investment appraisal;
(b) explain why in practice other methods of evaluating investment projects have proved to be more popular with decision-makers than the net present value method.

13.2* A machine with a purchase price of £14,000 is estimated to eliminate manual operations costing £4,000 per year. The machine will last five years and have no residual value at the end of its life.

You are required to calculate:
(a) the discounted cash flow (DCF) rate of return;
(b) the level of annual saving necessary to achieve a 12% DCF return;
(c) the net present value if the cost of capital is 10%.

13.3 A company making motor car components uses three separate machines to undertake the turning, boring and grinding operations. The present machines are old and unreliable and the factory engineer has put forward two alternative proposals for their replacement by:
 (i) three new individual machines; or
 (ii) a combined special purpose machine.
From the data given below, you are required to:
(a) evaluate both of these proposals, and
(b) write a short appraisal of your analysis making a firm recommendation on the replacement action to be taken.

Machine type	Present machines Original capital cost	Present machines Operating expenses per year	Proposed machines Capital cost	Proposed machines Operating expenses per year
	£	£	£	£
Turning	25,000	20,000	50,000	7,000
Boring	35,000	21,000	53,000	8,000
Grinding	20,000	12,000	31,000	6,000
Multi-purpose	–	–	147,000	17,000

The economic life of all the new machines is eight years and by that time it is estimated their salvage value will be equal to their dismantling cost.

You may ignore all taxation and investment allowances in the calculations.

The company normally expects new capital investment to provide a 14% DCF return.

(30 marks)
ICMA P3 Management Accounting May 1977

13.4 Due to the financial failure of an overseas competitor, a company sees the opportunity of taking up immediately a market for its product of 325,000 tonnes per annum which is forecast to rise at 9% per annum. Sales revenue is expected to be £8 per tonne ex plant.

The company proposes to go into this market immediately and considers methods of supply involving the import from elsewhere, the hiring of plant locally, and the construction of new plant.

Details are as follows:

Import from elsewhere
It could import up to a maximum of 500,000 tonnes per annum of the product at an average

cost of £7.5 per tonne at the plant.

Hire of plant locally
It could hire plant capacity of 500,000 tonnes per annum at a nearby site. This is available immediately.

The terms of the hiring are £1.2 per tonne of capacity for a minimum of 12 years, with the plant owner being responsible for any variable operating costs. Direct material costs of £6 per tonne would be payable by the company.

Construction of new plant
It could build a plant with an effective capacity of 500,000 tonnes per annum which will be completed in three years. In the meantime, requirements may be imported.

Capital expenditure will be £1.75 million, spent at the end of each year, as follows:

June:	1980	£0.30 million
	1981	£0.45 million
	1982	£1.00 million

The expected life of the plant is 12 years and its salvage value is expected to be £0.3 million.

Direct material costs are expected to be £6 per tonne, variable operating costs £0.3 per tonne, and fixed operating costs £100,000 per annum.

The company requires a cut-off rate of 20% DCF for projects involving capital expenditure.

You are required to recommend what action the company should take to achieve its objective. Support your recommendation with relevant calculations.

Ignore taxation and inflation considerations.

(25 marks)
*ICMA P3 Management Accounting
May 1979*

13.5* Due to competition from low-priced imports a large company has decided that it must close one of its factories which is an important employer of labour in a country town. This closure will displace 600 people at present employed there.

After consultation with relevant trade unions, the board of the company is considering offering the following options to the employees at that factory:
1. To re-locate them at another of the company's factories some 100 miles away.
2. To re-train them for jobs at other plants, each some 20–25 miles away.
3. To allow early retirement for a limited category of employee.
4. To declare redundant those who do not accept, or are not eligible for, the above three options.

The board has, however, made a qualification to its offer. This is that the average cost per employee of the proposed scheme, capitalized in present value terms, should not exceed twice the average redundancy cost if all employees were to be made redundant.

The board has therefore asked you, as management accountant, to:
(a) calculate the expected average cost per employee of the proposed scheme and say whether or not it exceeds the criterion set;
(b) list what non-financial benefits might accrue to:
 (i) the company's present employees;
 (ii) the company itself;
 if the board's offer were to be accepted.

Your investigations of the situation reveal the following:

1. Re-location
It is proposed that each employee taking up this option should receive a £1,000 interest-free loan towards new housing, repayable at the end of five years, and a re-location grant of £750. The extra personnel department expenses to deal with the administration of this work will amount to £15,000 during the year following the closure.

These costs will to some extent be offset by the fact that at the new location there is a shortage of relevantly skilled labour. It is assessed that each person who re-locates will save the company recruiting costs of £50 and make available increased production (compared with unskilled employees) over the first twelve months of employment worth £120 per month in terms of contribution and a reduction in rejects of £80 per month for the first six months. However, it is expected that 10% of employees who re-locate will have left their job of their own accord by the end of the year, by which time they will all have repaid their £1,000 loans. Savings for that proportion of employees should be ignored for the whole period.

2. Re-training
Costs of a two-month re-training course payable by the company will be £180 per employee selecting this option. During this time they will each be on full salary which can be taken as an average of £350 per month. Additional administration costs of £5,000 will be incurred.

Offsetting these costs will be benefits at the plants from the work on which re-training is being done. These comprise £50 recruitment cost saving and avoidance of loss of production from labour turnover amounting to £100 per person per month in terms of contribution for the first six months. However, it is expected that after re-training only 70% of those doing the courses will take up work with the company, the balance leaving the company of their own accord.

3. Early retirement

This would offer half-pay (i.e. an average of £2,500 per annum). It can be assumed that employees in this group have, on average, five years to go before normal retirement.

4. Redundancy

This varies with the age and service of each individual employee. For calculation purposes employees may be placed into two categories. Those in category P can be regarded as averaging 12 years' service and those in category Q as averaging four years' service. The entitlement of pay for each year of service will average $1\frac{1}{4}$ weeks for the first category with an average wage of £90 per week; for the second category it is one week's pay for each year of service with an average wage of £80 per week. However, the Government will refund 41% of this cost to the company.

Employee intentions

Preliminary enquiries indicate the following intentions:

Option chosen	Number in each category choosing the option	
	P	Q
1. Re-locate	88	–
2. Re-train	198	136
3. Retire early	40	–
4. Redundancy	70	68

Other information

For purposes of this calculation the company wishes to capitalize its annual expenditures at 12% per annum.

You should work to the nearest whole number and ignore taxation. (30 marks)

ICMA P3 Management Accounting
May 1981

13.6* A holding company owns a shipbuilding subsidiary which will show a loss on its 1982 operations. At present it has no future orders on hand. The directors are considering selling the shipyard plus plant and machinery. A firm offer has been received to purchase at 31 December 1982 for £120,000.

However, since the sale discussions were started a contract has been offered to the company to build three ships. These would be for delivery at the rate of one a year commencing 31 December 1983 at a fixed price of £250,000 each. Their building would use the complete resources of the shipyard.

You are required from the data given below to:

(a) calculate whether there is a financial incentive to accept the shipbuilding contract if the cost of capital for the next three years were to be 12%, 16% or 20%.
(b) comment on the figures you have used in your calculations;
(c) state whether you consider the shipbuilding contract should be undertaken assuming that the directors assess the probability of the interest rate for the construction period to be 0.5 for 12%, 0.4 for 16% and 0.1 for 20%.

Data:

Fixed assets: The shipyard and equipment were purchased 7 years ago on a 10-year lease for £400,000. The book value at 31 December 1982 will be £120,000.

Labour: The estimated labour cost per ship is £120,000 based on forecast wage rates as at 1 January 1983. Labour rates are expected to rise by 10% per year.

If the yard closes at 31 December 1982, then pay in lieu of notice plus redundancy payments are expected to equal one year's labour cost. These payments would be spread evenly over the year. By the end of the third year, other jobs will be available to absorb the manpower.

Materials: Sufficient material is in stock to build the first ship. This was purchased two years ago for £80,000 but current replacement cost is £100,000. Prices are expected to rise by 8% per annum. Orders for further materials must be placed ahead of the year in which the material is used in construction. It is paid for on 31 December of the year of purchase. If not used the material in stock has a current scrap value of £25,000 but will deteriorate and be valueless in three years' time.

Overhead:	per year £
Variable overhead	10,000
Depreciation	4,000
Allocated head office fixed costs	5,000

Variable overhead and head office fixed costs are expected to increase by 10% per year.

Sales realizations: Realizations from the sale of the shipyard and equipment, the material stock and the new ships would be received on 31 December.

Cost of capital: The cost of capital is currently 12% per annum but the company may wish to earn up to 20% on the contract if it is taken.

Taxation: Taxation can be ignored.

Accuracy of answers: All calculations should

be made to the nearest £thousand.

(30 marks)
ICMA P3 Management Accounting
November 1982

13.7 A company occupies the following premises for its manufacturing, warehousing and office administration:

Premises P consisting of 20,000 square feet, held on a long lease at a rental of £8,500 per annum.

Premises Q consisting of 8,000 square feet, held on a lease with only three years to run. Rent is £11,000 per annum.

Premises R comprising temporary warehousing accommodation at £2,500 per annum.

Premises S are occupied by LM department of the company. This produces a product whose manufacture needs to be kept separate from the company's main production but whose warehousing does not. LM department needs a further 4,000 square feet of warehousing space.

The company's warehousing is widely and inefficiently dispersed; the management accountant has calculated that this results in lost sales whose contribution would be £12,000 per annum.

The company has found possible accommodation in buildings T or V. If it used either of these, the company could:

(a) eliminate warehousing difficulties,
(b) sublet all premises Q at £13,000 per annum,
(c) dispense with premises R, and
(d) provide total warehousing needs of LM department thus increasing manufacturing space to generate extra sales that would yield an extra net profit of £7,500 per annum.

Additional costs and benefits would be as follows:

Building T
Either
(i) 25,000 square feet would cost £1.80 per square foot. This would release 8,000 square feet of premises P for subletting at £2 per square foot. Total removal costs would be £12,000;

or
(ii) 30,000 square feet would cost £1.75 per square foot. This would release 12,000 square feet of premises P for subletting at £1.75 per square foot. Total removal costs would be £17,000.

Building V
35,000 square feet would cost £2.40 per square foot. This would enable the release of the entire premises P and its sale for a net figure of £115,000 after all expenses of sale and removal had been met.

The company's cost of capital is 12% per annum. It uses a life of 15 years for transactions of the type being considered.

You are required to calculate the comparative costs of the various configurations of premises open to the company and advise which is the most economic.

Ignore taxation and inflation, and assume that rents are payable annually in advance.

(NB: All rents given above are inclusive of rates.)

(25 marks)
ICMA P3 Management Accounting
May 1982

13.8* A meeting of the directors of the Small Company Ltd has been called to discuss the investment of surplus funds during the ensuing year. During this meeting the following conversation takes place and you are required to prepare a statement to analyse and comment on the significant features of this conversation.

Managing director —
'If you look at the budget you will see that after allowing for the replacement of equipment and distributions etc. we have got £20,000 to invest now. I am open to any suggestion as long as it does not involve more than this and provided it pays for itself within two years because as you know that is when we plan to start building our new factory and we will need all the money we can get then.'

Production director —
'I think we should invest in new automatic testing equipment. I know this would take all of the £20,000 but we are presently operating to 100% capacity and still cannot cope with all of the orders, and testing is the bottle-neck. The increased annual contribution — and that means profit — would be £12,000 over each of the next two years.'

Planning director —
'I don't like this suggestion. In two years time when we plan to move to our new premises the whole production process will be changed and this testing equipment will not be required and we won't be able to sell it for very much.'

Production director —
'I agree but the equipment will have more than paid for itself by then.'

Marketing director —
'I think we should give serious consideration to my proposal to terminate our agency agreement in Scotland. This would only cost £2,000 and

would save £1,300 per annum over the next two years. More important, however, it would give us time to get the next agency agreement sorted out properly and hopefully avoid the mess we have had in Scotland in the past.'

Production director —
'That's all very well but what do we do with the remaining £18,000?'

Marketing director —
'Surely it can be invested at 10% because after all that is our cost of capital.'

Financial director —
'Not exactly — 10% is the target rate of return we have set ourselves. It doesn't necessarily mean that is what we can earn on short term investment.'

Managing director —
'Maybe not but we must earn something.'

Planning director —
'I favour the marketing director's suggestion. It gives us a higher rate of return than the production director's suggestion and that's what matters.'

Production director —
'I know the profitability of the investment is important but so is the risk and my proposal is not so risky. After all there is no guarantee that if we spend the £2,000 we will get anything back, whereas with the testing equipment we are as certain as we can ever be that production will speed up.'

Planning director —
'Maybe not, but if your suggestion does go wrong and no matter how remote, it is still a possibility, we have lost a lot of money. I still favour the marketing director's proposal.'

Managing director —
'It is one or the other. What do you think, finance director?'

Taxation can be ignored. (25 marks)
ACCA P3 Financial Management
December 1978

13.9* The directors of Robson Ltd are considering whether to accept one of two mutually exclusive projects and, if so, which one to accept. Each project involves an immediate cash outlay of £1,000,000 and the estimates of the cash inflow from each project are as follows:

Net cash inflow at end of:	Project X £	Project Y £
Year 1	800,000	100,000
Year 2	500,000	300,000
Year 3	300,000	1,500,000

The directors of Robson Ltd do not expect capital or any other resource to be in short supply during the next three years. You are required to:
(a) prepare a graph to show the functional relationship between net present value and the discount rate for the two projects (label the vertical axis 'net present value' and the horizontal axis 'discount rate');
(b) use the graph to estimate the internal rate of return of each project;
(c) on the basis of the information given, advise the directors which project to accept if the cost of capital is (i) 10%, (ii) 20%;
(d) describe briefly any additional information you think would be useful in choosing between the two projects;
(e) discuss the relative merits of net present value and internal rate of return as methods of investment appraisal.
Ignore taxation.

13.10 Using the discounted cash flow yield (internal rate of return) for evaluating investment opportunities has the basic weakness that it does not give attention to the amount of the capital investment, in that a return of 20% on an investment of £1,000 may be given a higher ranking than a return of 15% on an investment of £10,000.

Comment in general on the above quotation and refer in particular to the problem of giving priorities to (ranking) investment proposals.

Your answers should make use of the following information.

		Project A Cash flow £	Project B Cash flow £
Year	0 (Capital investments)	1,000	10,000
	1 Cash flows	240	2,300
	2 Cash flows	288	2,640
	3 Cash flows	346	3,040
	4 Cash flows	414	3,500
	5 Cash flows	498	4,020
Cost of capital		10%	10%

Taxation can be ignored.

(20 marks)
ACCA P3 Financial Management
June 1979

13.11* Khan Ltd is an importer of novelty products. The directors are considering whether to introduce a new product, expected to have a very short economic life. Two alternative methods of promoting the new product are available, details of which are as follows:

Alternative 1 would involve heavy initial advertsing and the employment of a large number of agents. The directors expect that an

immediate cash outflow of £100,000 would be required (the cost of advertising) which would produce a net cash inflow after one year of £255,000. Agents' commission, amounting to £157,500, would have to be paid at the end of two years.

Alternative 2 would involve a lower outlay on advertising (£50,000, payable immediately), and no use of agents. It would produce net cash inflows of zero after one year and £42,000 at the end of each of the subsequent two years.

Mr Court, a director of Khan Ltd, comments, 'I generally favour the payback method for choosing between investment alternatives such as these. However, I am worried that the advertsing expenditure under the second alternative will reduce our reported profit next year by an amount not compensated by any net revenues from sale of the product in that year. For that reason I do not think we should even consider the second alternative'.

The cost of capital of Khan Ltd is 20% per annum. The directors do not expect capital or any other resource to be in short supply during the next three years.

You are required to:

(a) calculate the net present values and estimate the internal rates of return of the two methods of promoting the new product. (10 marks)

(b) advise the directors of Khan Ltd which, if either, method of promotion they should adopt, explaining the reasons for your advice and noting any additional information you think would be helpful in making the decision (8 marks), and

(c) comment on the views expressed by Mr Court. (7 marks)

Ignore taxation.

ICAEW Financial Management December 1979

13.12 Two firms for which you act as financial consultant are seeking your advice concerning the appraisal of investment projects.

Firm Exe is considering 2 independent projects. Project B is unusual and if undertaken must be continued for its whole life of 3 years; it cannot be terminated before year 3. The correctly calculated incremental after tax cash flows relating to each project, and the net present values calculated at two discount rates, are:

Project	A	B
Cash flows	(£000)	(£000)
Year 0	(500)	(900)
1	100	1,269
2	200	864
3	200	(1,305)
4	250	–
Net present values	£	£
Discount rate = 25%	(87,200)	0
Discount rate = 20%	(41,600)	1,098

Note: Brackets indicate negative figures.

Firm Wye wishes to undertake one of two mutually exclusive projects. Both projects have risk characteristics which are identical to the firm's other assets. Details of the alternative projects are:

Project	C	D
Expected cash flows	(£000)	(£000)
Year 0	(100)	(100)
1	16	110
2	44	4
3	46	6
4	42	2
5	2	2
Appraisal results		
Internal rate of return (yield)	16.05%	19.7%
Net present value (discount rate = 8%)	£21,280	£12,884

It is generally agreed that further investment opportunities available to Wye over the next decade are unlikely to promise a yield of more than Wye's cost of capital. Hence the current two proposals, each with a high promised yield, are the cause of much debate among Wye's management team.

Wye's commercial manager feels that project C should be chosen as it has the highest net present value when the expected after tax cash flows are discounted at Wye's cost of capital of 8%. The managing director insists that project D must be chosen as its internal rate of return is higher; he claims 'a yield of nearly 20% on an investment of £100,000 is clearly superior to a return of 16% on an identical outlay when both projects have equal lives'. Wye's chairman feels that project D should be chosen as its payback period is shorter and the early cash flows can then be invested in other projects to earn a further return.

Required:

(a) Calculate the net present value of projects A and B at a discount rate of 15%. Using the results of your calculations together with the figures of net present value provided, estimate, to the nearest 1%, the internal rates of return relating to projects A and B. At hurdle rates of

(i) 15%

(ii) 20%

indicate which of the two projects are acceptable using each of the two appraisal methods.

Clearly specify the range of hurdle rates for which project B is acceptable and comment on the reasons for this acceptable range. (8 marks)

(b) Explain the meaning of the 'net present value' and 'internal rate of return' measures. Outline the major comparative advantages and disadvantages of the two methods for the appraisal of *independent* projects. To what extent will the two methods give the same accept/reject signals for independent projects? (8 marks)

(c) Explain why there is an inconsistency in the ranking of mutually exclusive projects C and D, show how that inconsistency can be resolved and advise Wye on which of the two projects should be undertaken. To what extent would Wye's cost of capital have to change before the choice of project would be altered?

Comment on the views of Wye's managemet team. (6 marks)

(22 marks)
ACCA P3 Financial Management
June 1983

13.13 The trustees of a museum, which has surplus accommodation, propose to provide for visitors a cafeteria service of light meals and refreshments on a break-even basis. They further propose to use existing funds to meet initial capital costs. These funds now earn an income of 12% per annum. A condition of granting the loan for the capital costs is that the funds should be repaid over a five-year period and provide the same rate of interest as is now being earned.

It is estimated that investment in cooking equipment and furniture with a five-year life will cost £32,000. A supervisor and four other staff will be needed at an annual cost of £12,000. Selling prices of the food and refreshments will be based on a 50% uplift from direct costs. The cafeteria will be charged £2,000 at the end of each operating year to cover heating, lighting and other property expenses. It is considered that business will build up gradually and annual sales in year one will be 40% of capacity, in year two 60% of capacity and in years three, four and five each at full capacity.

You are required to:

(a) estimate the annual sales necessary in each of the five years to meet the trustees'

requirements; and

(b) write a report to the trustees commenting on their proposal, mentioning areas you consider need further investigation.

You should ignore taxation and the effects of inflation.

(30 marks)
ICMA P3 Management Accounting
November 1978

13.14 A company has two presses each capable of producing 20,000 specialized components a year selling for £6 each. Production on each press is flexible with the sole limitation that the economic batch quantity is 5,000 units.

Management anticipates that the components will only be required for a further five years and that the full 40,000 units will not be required every year.

Data:

Production level Units	Total cost per annum	
	Press A	Press B
(000)	£000	£000
0	25	35
5	60	50
10	63	55
15	70	60
20	82	98

The total cost at zero level includes for each press £5,000 for depreciation and £5,000 for apportioned production overhead. The balance is for direct labour and services which could be used elsewhere if one press were to be sold.

You are required, from the data given above, to:

(a) prepare a table to show for each 5,000 step up to 40,000 units the press or presses to use to minimize total costs;

(b) indicate the level of production which maximizes total profit;

(c) calculate whether it would be of financial benefit to sell one press for £90,000 on the assumptions that it would have a scrap value of only £10,000 in five years' time and that the average annual sales during this period would be 75% of capacity (ignore inflation and taxation and use 12% per annum as the cost of capital);

(d) comment on the main factor likely to influence the decision whether to sell or not.

(30 marks)
ICMA P3 Management Accounting
November 1981

14 Capital investment decisions (2)

In the previous chapter the major techniques which can be used for evaluating capital investment decisions were introduced and their relative merits were assessed. To simplify the discussion we made a number of assumptions: first, that cash inflows and outflows were known with certainty; second, that sufficient funds were available to enable acceptance of all those projects with positive net present values; third, that firms operated in an environment where there was no taxation and no inflation; and finally, that the cost of capital was the risk free rate. In this chapter we shall relax these assumptions and discuss how capital investment techniques can be applied to more complicated situations. In addition, we shall consider the various methods of administering and controlling capital expenditures.

A comparison of mutually exclusive investments with unequal lives

The application of the net present value method is complicated when a choice must be made between two or more projects, where the projects have unequal lives. A perfect comparison requires knowledge about future alternatives which will be available for the period of the difference in the lives of the projects which are being considered. Let us look at the situation in Example 14.1.

EXAMPLE 14.1

A company is considering whether to purchase machine X or machine Y, which perform the same task. Both machines cost £20,000 but machine X has a life of one year whereas machine Y has a life of three years.

Machine X will save £24,000 per annum for one year, whereas machine Y will save £10,000 per annum for three years. The estimated investment costs and cash savings are as follows:

	Year 0	Year 1	Year 2	Year 3
Machine X	−£20,000	+£24,000	–	–
Machine Y	−£20,000	+£10,000	+£10,000	+£10,000

The cost of capital is 10%.

The net present values are £1,818 for machine X and £4,870 for machine Y. Machine Y appears to be the most acceptable investment but the analysis is incomplete as we must consider what will happen at the end of year 1 if machine X is chosen. There are three alternative assumptions:

(1) We can assume that the firm will invest the cash proceeds in assets which will yield a return equal to the time value of money. This will give a zero net present value and the alternatives will be comparable even though their lives are unequal. This means that the computed net present values should be used when choosing between the alternatives.

(2) We can assume that the firm will reinvest the cash proceeds in assets which have

exactly the same characteristics as those which are currently being used.

(3) We can make specific assumptions about the reinvestment opportunities which may become available in the future.

If assumption 2 is appropriate, a similar machine to machine X will be purchased at the end of each of years 1 and 2 producing similar cost savings. If we ignore the problem of inflation the cash inflows and outflows over three years will be as follows:

	Year 0	Year 1	Year 2	Year 3
Project X (or similar projects)	− 20,000	− 20,000	− 20,000	
Cash inflows		+ 24,000	+ 24,000	+ 24,000

The net present value of these cash flows is £4,968 which means that project X is preferable to project Y.

If assumption 3 is adopted it is necessary to forecast how the cash proceeds from machine X will be used over the three years, and to produce a statement of cash flows similar to the schedule set out above. The net present values for the schedules of cash flows which result from each alternative machine should then be compared.

Note that each of the alternatives seeks to convert the analysis of the two projects to a common time horizon. In Example 14.1 the time horizon is three years. It is essential that the analysis considers mutually exclusive projects over equal time periods, or it will discriminate against the projects with the shortest lives. However, the conversion of alternative investments to common time horizons is not always quite so simple. Let us now consider a situation where two mutually exclusive items of equipment have the following characteristics:

Equipment	Expected life	Initial cost	Annual operating costs
A	3 years	£24,000	£4,800
B	8 years	£72,000	£3,600

We must assume that each item of equipment is replaced at the end of its useful life, and that replacements are continued for so long as is necessary to ensure a common time horizon. The common time horizon is therefore found by taking the lowest common multiple of the lives of the alternatives. In the above example, this will be a period of 24 years, with equipment A being replaced eight times and equipment B being replaced three times. This is assuming that the firm reinvests in assets of exactly the same characteristics as those currently being used with lives of three years and eight years respectively.

The conversion of the time periods to a common time horizon does neutralize the time differential but this approach makes the unlikely assumption that technology and prices will remain unchanged for the next 24 years. An alternative method of dealing with the time difference is to compare the present values for a period equivalent to the alternative with the shortest time span. In our illustration this will be equipment A with a life of three years. The estimated salvage value of the alternatives with the longer lives should be estimated and included as a cash receipt in the net present value calculation. The estimated salvage value for equipment B at the end of year 3 should therefore be included as a cash receipt in the analysis. The alternative with the lowest present value (that is, the operating cost over three years plus the initial outlay minus the salvage value after three years) should be selected. This approach requires a reasonable estimate of the salvage values at a future point in time. If such an estimate is likely to be highly uncertain and the salvage value is very significant, this method must be used with caution. For a detailed discussion of evaluating capital investments with unequal lives see Emery (1982).

Capital rationing

In our previous discussions it has been suggested that all investments with positive net present values should be undertaken. For mutually exclusive projects the project with the highest net present value should be chosen. However, situations may occur where there are insufficient funds available to enable a firm to undertake all those projects which yield a positive net present value. This situation is described as *capital rationing*.

Capital rationing occurs whenever there is a budget ceiling, or a market constraint on the amount of funds which can be invested during a specific period of time. For various reasons top management may pursue a policy of limiting the amount of funds available for investment in any

one period. Such policies may apply to firms which finance all their capital investment with internal funds. Alternatively, in a large decentralized organization top management may limit the funds which are available to the divisional managers for investment. Such restrictions on available funds may be for various reasons. For example, top management may be reluctant to issue additional share capital because they may be concerned that this will lead to outsiders gaining control of the business, or because a share issue may lead to a dilution of earnings per share. Alternatively, they may be reluctant to raise additional debt capital beyond a certain point because they do not wish to be committed to large fixed interest payments. Note that whenever a firm adopts a policy which restricts funds available

projects by net present value will favour a project which yields a net present value of £1,000, for an investment of £10,000, over two projects of £5,000 which each yield an individual net present value of £800. Clearly, if funds are restricted to £10,000 it is better to accept the two smaller projects which will yield a total net present value of £1,600. Consider the situation presented in Example 14.2.

EXAMPLE 14.2

A company which operates under the constraint of capital rationing has identified seven independent investments from which to choose. The company has £200,000 available for capital investment during the current period. Which projects should the company choose? The net present values and profitability index ratios for each of the projects are as follows:

Projects	Investment required	Present value (PV)	Net present value	Profitability index (PV/investment cost)	Ranking as per NPVs	Ranking as per profitability index
	£	£	£			
A	25,000	32,500	7,500	1.30	6	2
B	100,000	108,250	8,250	1.08	5	6
C	50,000	75,750	25,750	1.51	1	1
D	100,000	123,500	23,500	1.23	2	3
E	125,000	133,500	8,500	1.07	4	7
F	25,000	30,000	5,000	1.20	7	4
G	50,000	59,000	9,000	1.18	3	5

for investment, such a policy may be less than optimal, as the firm may reject projects with a positive net present value and forego opportunities which would have enhanced the market value of the firm.

Whenever capital rationing exists management should allocate the limited available capital in a way which maximizes the net present values, subject to the constraint of pursuing other goals which are necessary to maintain the coalition of the various interest groups.[1] Thus it is necessary to rank all investment opportunities so that the net present value can be maximized from the use of the available funds. The analytical techniques used must therefore be capable of ranking the various alternatives or of determining the optimal combination of investments which meet the constraint of limited capital. Ranking in terms of absolute net present values will normally give incorrect results, as this method leads to the selection of large projects, each having a high individual net present value but which have in total a lower net present value than a large number of smaller projects with lower individual net present values. For example, the ranking of

Our aim is to select the projects in descending order of profitability until the investment funds of £200,000 have been exhausted. If we use the net present value method of ranking, the following projects will be selected:

Projects selected in order of ranking	Investment cost (£)	Net present value (£)
C	50,000	25,750
D	100,000	23,500
G	50,000	9,000
Total net present value		58,250

If, on the other hand, we adopt the profitability index method of ranking, the selected projects will be as follows:

Projects selected in order of ranking	Investment cost (£)	Net present value (£)
C	50,000	25,750
A	25,000	7,500
D	100,000	23,500
F	25,000	5,000
Total net present value		61,750

You will see that the ranking of projects by the profitability index gives the highest net present value, but a strict application of this index will not always produce the optimum result. This is illustrated in Example 14.3.

EXAMPLE 14.3

A company which operates under the constraint of capital rationing has identified four independent projects and it has a capital expenditure limit of £600,000 for the year ending 31 December 19X1. Which projects should the company choose? The net present values and the profitability index for each of the projects are:

Projects	Investment required	Present value (PV)	Net present value	Profitability index	Ranking as per profitability index
	£	£	£		
W	400,000	460,000	60,000	1.15	1
X	250,000	282,500	32,500	1.13	2
Y	350,000	385,000	35,000	1.10	3
Z	300,000	324,000	24,000	1.08	4

If the profitability index method is strictly applied, only project W will be undertaken resulting in an investment of £400,000. The unused funds of £200,000 are insufficient for any of the remaining projects to be undertaken and the only alternative use of these funds is to invest them at the cost of capital, which will give a zero net present value. The total net present value from the available funds of £600,000 will be only £60,000. However, if we examine the schedule of projects more closely and attempt to incorporate those projects with high rankings and which will use the available funds of £600,000, an optimal solution can be found. For example, projects X and Y meet this requirement; the total investment for both projects is £600,000 which gives a total net present value of £67,500. This is the highest net present value which can be obtained when investment funds are limited to £600,000.

Note that capital rationing results in a change in the effective cost of capital which is relevant to investment decisions, as the relevant cost of capital should now be viewed in terms of opportunity cost. The relevant cost will be the internal rate of return which must be foregone on the most profitable project that is rejected because of capital rationing. For example, if a firm has calculated its cost of capital to be 12%, but because of capital rationing it has rejected investment opportunities which offer internal rates of return of 14%, 15% and 16%, the effective cost of capital will be 16%. This is the relevant cost of capital because it measures the sacrifice which the firm has had to make to use its limited capital for the investments which it was able to undertake. Nevertheless, it is important to note that the use of an opportunity cost of capital of 16% will result in a policy which is not optimal since the firm will maximize shareholders' wealth by accepting all projects down to its cost of capital of 12%.

Our discussion so far has assumed that investment funds are restricted for one period only. This is most unlikely. Also the cost of certain investment projects may be spread over several periods. In addition a one-period analysis does not take into account the intermediate cash flows which are generated by a project. Some projects may provide relatively high cash flows in the early years, and these can then be used to increase the availability of funds for investment in further projects in those early years. We should therefore consider more than just a one-period constraint in the allocation of limited capital to investment projects. To cope with such problems it is necessary to use mathematical techniques, but we shall defer our discussion of the application of mathematical techniques to multi-period capital rationing until Chapter 22.

Taxation and investment decisions

In our discussion so far we have ignored the impact of taxation. In the United Kingdom companies are subject to corporation tax on the whole of their taxable income, whether it is distributed or not, at the rates fixed by the appropriate Finance Act. From 1973 to 1983, the rate of corporation tax was 52%. There is also a 'small companies' rate of corporation tax which applies to companies with profits of less than a specified sum.[2]

Companies rarely pay tax on the profits which are disclosed in their published profit and loss accounts, as certain expenses which are deducted during the preparation of the accounts are not

allowable deductions for taxation purposes. For example, depreciation is not an allowable deduction; instead taxation legislation enables *capital allowances* to be claimed on capital expenditure which is incurred on plant and machinery and other fixed assets. This in effect means that capital allowances are standardized depreciation charges at rates specified in the latest Finance Act. In the case of plant and equipment acquired after 22 March 1972 and before 14 March 1984 companies may claim capital allowances by means of a first year allowance of 100%. From April 1986 the first year allowance will be replaced by an annual allowance of 25% on the written down value of the plant and equipment.[3] Different percentage capital allowances are also available on other assets such as industrial buildings and motor vehicles. For further information on current capital allowances you should consult the current Finance Act.

Taxation affects capital investment calculations in a number of ways. First, the cash inflows will be reduced by the amount of taxation which is paid on those cash inflows. For example, if cash inflows on a project are £50,000 per annum for five years then, assuming a taxation rate of 50%, the relevant cash flows will be the cash inflow after tax; that is, £25,000 per annum for five years. Second, the capital allowances will reduce the initial investment cost. If we assume a first year capital allowance of 100% and an investment cost of £80,000, the company will be able to deduct £80,000 from the profits which are subject to taxation. If the taxation rate is 50% then the amount of tax paid will be reduced by £40,000; the net outflow for the investment will be £40,000 (that is, £80,000 less 50% of £80,000).[4] The third impact of taxation on investment decisions is in terms of the timing of the taxation payment. In the United Kingdom taxation payments vary depending on the accounting year end but they must generally be made approximately one year after the end of the company's accounting year. This means that the taxation payments on cash inflows will normally occur about one year after the cash inflow was received. These points are illustrated in Example 14.4.

EXAMPLE 14.4

A company is considering whether to purchase some plant and machinery which will cost £100,000 but which is expected to give rise to additional cash inflows of £48,000 per annum for three years. The cost of capital is 10% and taxation is at the rate of 50%. (For the sake of simplicity here we will assume that a first year capital allowance of 100% is claimable and the taxation payments take place at the same point in time as the cash inflows and outflows occur.)

The calculations are as follows:

Year	Cash flow	Taxation	Net cash flow	Discount factor	Present value
	£	£	£		£
0	− 100,000	+ 50,000	− 50,000	1.00	− 50,000
1	+ 48,000	− 24,000	+ 24,000 ⎫		
2	+ 48,000	− 24,000	+ 24,000 ⎬	2.487	+ 59,688
3	+ 48,000	− 24,000	+ 24,000 ⎭	Net present value	+ 9,688

Let us now repeat these calculations with the more realistic assumption that taxation payment takes place exactly one year after the cash inflow or outflow. The revised calculations are:

Year	Cash flow	Taxation	Net cash flow	Discount factor	Present value
	£	£	£		£
0	− 100,000	0	− 100,000	1.00	− 100,000
1	+ 48,000	+ 50,000	+ 98,000	0.909	+ 89,082
2	+ 48,000	− 24,000	+ 24,000	0.826	+ 19,824
3	+ 48,000	− 24,000	+ 24,000	0.751	+ 18,024
4	0	− 24,000	− 24,000	0.683	− 16,392
				Net present value	+ 10,538

You can see from these figures that the taxation reduction of £50,000 arising from the 100% capital allowance will not cause a reduction in the taxation cash outflow until year 1. Similarly, the additional taxation charge of £24,000 on the cash inflow of £48,000 in year 1 will not lead to a taxation cash outflow until year 2. The objective of Example 14.4 is to provide a general understanding of the effect of taxation payment timing

ment (that is, a balancing charge) of £20,000 will therefore be required to reflect the fact that an excess capital allowance has been claimed. This will mean that an additional taxation charge of £10,000 (50% × £20,000) will be charged in year 3 and the cash payment will be due in year 4. The revised net present value calculation for Example 14.4, if we assume that the plant and machinery was sold for £20,000 in year 3, will be as follows:

Year	Cash flow	Taxation	Net cash flow	Discount factor	Present value
	£	£	£		£
0	− 100,000	0	− 100,000	1.00	− 100,000
1	+ 48,000	+ 50,000	+ 98,000	0.909	+ 89,082
2	+ 48,000	− 24,000	+ 24,000	0.826	+ 19,824
3	$\left\{\begin{array}{l} + \ 48,000 \\ + \ 20,000 \end{array}\right\}$ (1)	− 24,000	+ 44,000	0.751	+ 33,044
4	0	$\left\{\begin{array}{l} - \ 24,000 \\ - \ 10,000(2) \end{array}\right.$	− 34,000	0.683	− 23,222
				Net present value	+ 18,728

Notes
(1) Sale of plant and machinery for £20,000.
(2) Capital allowance adjustment on sale of plant and machinery (50% × £20,000).

differences. In practice the taxation payment date should be determined exactly. For example, in the calculations set out above, if the investment of £100,000 was incurred on the first day of an accounting period and the first cash inflow of £48,000 occurred within the same accounting period, the taxation charge for year 1 will be assessed on additional profits of £48,000 less a capital allowance of £100,000 giving a net reduction in the taxation payment of £26,000 (50% × £52,000). This reduction in the cash outflow will take place in year 2 and the entries in the taxation column in the schedule in our example will be nil for year 0 and year 1, and +£26,000 for year 2. In practice, the exact timing of the taxation payment must be determined but for examination purposes an assumption must be made and either of the two alternative taxation cash flows for years 0, 1 and 2 are acceptable.

A further problem occurs when an asset is sold and the capital allowances which are granted are different from the net cost of the asset. If, in Example 14.4, the plant and machinery was sold for £20,000 at the end of year 3, a capital allowance adjustment would be necessary. A first year capital allowance of 100% on £100,000 will have been claimed. However, the net capital cost of the plant after taking into account the salvage value will be £80,000. A capital allowance adjust-

The effect of inflation on capital investment appraisal

Prior to 1960 the rate of inflation in the United Kingdom was less than 5%. Low rates of inflation meant that accountants need pay little attention to it when presenting financial information to both internal and external users. The high rates of inflation experienced in the 1970s, however, made it necessary for accountants to incorporate its effects when presenting financial information.

What effect does inflation have on capital investment appraisal? To answer this question let us consider Example 14.5, which initially assumes an absence of inflation but which is then modified to take into account its effects.

EXAMPLE 14.5

A firm is considering whether to undertake a project which will cost £10,000 and which will have the following cash inflows after tax:

Year 1:	£6,000
Year 2:	£4,000
Year 3:	£10,000

The cost of capital is 10% and is based on the assumption of zero inflation.

The net present value is calculated using the following NPV formula:

$$\text{Net present value} = \frac{FV_1}{(1 + K)} + \frac{FV_2}{(1 + K)^2}$$

$$+ \frac{FV_3}{(1 + K)^3} + \cdots \cdot \frac{FV_n}{(1 + K)^n} - I_0$$

where FV = future values, K = cost of capital and I_0 = initial investment cost.

The calculation of the net present value is

$$NPV = \frac{£6,000}{1.10} + \frac{£4,000}{(1.10)^2} + \frac{£10,000}{(1.10)^3}$$

$$- £10,000 = \underline{\underline{6,273}}$$

Let us now adjust Example 14.5 and incorporate the effects of inflation. Suppose that an annual inflation rate of 8% is expected during the three years of the project. In this situation, the stock market data which is used to calculate the rate of return which is required by investors will include a premium for anticipated inflation. Hence this premium will be incorporated in the required rate of return on the project (that is, the applicable cost of capital for the project). This relationship is recognized in financial economics as the Fisher[5] effect, and is expressed in the following formula:

$$(1 + K)(1 + n)$$

where K = the cost of capital in *real* terms (that is, without inflation) and n = the anticipated inflation rate. The actual calculation is $(1 + 0.10)(1 + 0.08) = 1.188$, which represents the item $(1 + K)$ in the net present value formula. The revised required rate of return in Example 14.5 which incorporates the inflation rate of 8% will be 18.8%. This calculation can be reconciled with the 10% required rate of return when inflation was absent. Assume that an individual invests £100 and obtains (in the absence of inflation) 10% interest, or £110, at the end of the year to compensate for the time value of money. To maintain this return of £110 in real terms this sum will have to grow by 8% to £118.80 (that is, £110 + 8%). Therefore, with an inflation rate of 8% the individual will require a return of 18.8%, which consists of 10% to compensate for the time value of money plus a premium of 8.8% to maintain the purchasing power of the investment. Hence the financial market data which is used to calculate the cost of capital will include a premium for anticipated inflation. However, if the cost of capital incorporates the effect of inflation, it is also necessary to adjust the cash flow estimates for

inflation. Failure to do this will give an understatement of the net present value. If we assume that the same rate of inflation of 8% is applicable to the cash flows, the correct calculation of the net present value is

$$NPV = \frac{£6,000 \; (1.08)}{(1.10) \; (1.08)} + \frac{£4,000 \; (1.08)^2}{(1.10)^2 \; (1.08)^2}$$

$$+ \frac{£10,000 \; (1.08)^3}{(1.10)^3 \; (1.08)^3} - £10,000 = £6,273$$

Note that the inflation factors appear in both the numerator and the denominator and cancel each other out. When this adjustment is made the figures reduce to exactly the same calculation as that presented when inflation was absent. The net present values are therefore the same for both situations, which proves that the adjustment for inflation results in the net present value being expressed in *real terms*.

The net present value calculations can be adjusted in two basic ways to allow for inflation:

(1) By using a discount rate which incorporates a premium for anticipated inflation (which is the approach outlined above). If this approach is adopted it is also necessary to ensure that the cash flows are adjusted for inflation.

(2) By excluding the premium for anticipated inflation from the cost of capital calculation. It is also necessary to ensure that the cash flows are expressed in terms of *current purchasing power* as at year 0, that is, the time at which the cash payment is made for the initial investment cost. For example, if an expense is predicted to be £100,000 based on the purchasing power of a pound at year 0 and if estimated expenses are £110,000 at year 1 (based on £100,000 plus 10% for inflation), then £100,000 should be included as a cash flow in the net present value calculation.

If either of these methods are adopted the correct net present value calculation should be obtained. The most frequent error which is made is when the cost of capital calculation incorporates a premium for anticipated inflation without the estimated cash flows being adjusted for expected changes in inflation. If this incorrect approach were adopted in Example 14.5, the following *incorrect* calculation would be made:

$$NPV = \frac{£6,000}{(1.18)} + \frac{£4,000}{(1.18)^2} + \frac{£10,000}{(1.18)^3}$$

$$- £10,000 = £4,043$$

Exhibit 14.1 Procedures for handling inflation (150 largest UK firms)

	Percentage used in:	
	1975	1980
Inflation ignored	30	11
Specify rates for different costs and revenues	20	30
Specify cash flow in constant prices and apply real rate of return	29	35
Adjust for estimated changes in general level of inflation	29	39
Consider at risk analysis, sensitivity analysis stage	13	18

Fig. 14.1 Required rate of return/risk relationship

You can see that this incorrect approach results in the net present value being understated. In practice the situation may be far more complicated than is apparent from the previous illustrations. For example, differential inflation rates may exist for different cash inflows and outflows, or the anticipated rate of inflation may affect the required rates of return and cash flows differently. (See Van Horne, 1971, for a detailed discussion of the effect of differential inflation rates.)

The treatment of inflation in capital budgeting has received considerable attention in the literature (see for example Bromwich, 1969; Bagwell *et al.*, 1973 and Carsberg and Hope, 1976). Two UK surveys in the 1970s indicated that a large number of firms either ignore inflation in their capital budgeting decisions (Westwick and Shohet, 1976) or they use a money target rate of return (incorporating an inflation premium) in association with cash flows which are estimated in current prices (Carsberg and Hope, 1976). In a study of 150 of the largest UK manufacturing and retailing companies (Pike, 1983), a significant improvement was found in both the proportion of firms which incorporated inflation in project evaluations, and in the treatment which was applied. Pike's survey showed that whereas 30% of the firms surveyed ignored inflationary aspects in 1975, the proportion had fallen to only 11% in 1980. A summary of Pike's survey on the procedure for handling inflation is presented in Exhibit 14.1.

Risk and uncertainty

In the previous chapter we established that the minimum required rate of return or cost of capital which should be used in evaluating investment projects was

$$RRR = R_F + R_P$$

where R_F represents the risk free rate and R_P represents the risk premium. The risk free rate represents the return available on risk free investments such as UK Government Bonds, and the risk premium is established in the financial markets by observing the excess returns over the risk free rate demanded by investors for different degrees of risk. The required rate of return is illustrated in Fig. 14.1:

To calculate the risk premium it is necessary to determine the slope of the line in Fig. 14.1 so that we can estimate how much greater the risk premium should be for each additional increment of risk. By observing the excess returns demanded by investors for all companies listed on the stock exchange we can establish an average risk premium for each increment of risk. Clearly, the greater the risk of a proposed project the greater the required rate of return or cost of capital, so the starting point for determining the required rate of return is to measure the risk of a project's cash flows. Let us now consider some of the methods which can be used for quantifying risk. Four such methods are:

(1) standard deviations and probability distributions,
(2) simulation,
(3) sensitivity analysis,
(4) portfolio analysis.

It is important to note that none of these methods

of quantifying risk will enable us to determine the appropriate required rate of return but they will enable us to assess the risk involved for a particular investment proposal. To determine the required rate of return we must link our assessment of risk for investment proposals with the excess returns over the risk free rate which is demanded by investors in the financial markets. We shall do this by first considering some of the methods of quantifying risk, and then link the risk measure with the risk premium which investors will demand for various levels of risk. The cost of capital which we shall use for calculating the net present value for each of the methods of quantifying risk is the risk free rate. Our objective is to measure the risk of investment proposals, but if we use a discount rate which embodies a premium for risk, this would result in an adjustment for risk within the discounting process and would lead to double counting.

Standard deviations and probability distributions

If risk is recognized as a factor to be considered, a firm cannot be indifferent when it must choose between two investment proposals which have the same net present value. Consider a situation where the calculation of the net present values are based upon the expected values of the cash flows in various future periods. For example, assume that we have two investment proposals each costing £24,000 and which have expected cash inflows of £12,000 in each of the next three years.

Fig. 14.2 A comparison of probability distribution of two projects with equal expected values

So far, we have assumed that we can rank these investments equally but if we consider the probability distributions illustrated in Fig. 14.2 we can see that this is incorrect.

The dispersion of cash flows is greater for proposal X than for proposal Y, and consequently the decision-maker will not be indifferent between them as the risk for proposal X is far greater than that for proposal Y.

In Chapter 12 we discussed standard deviations, the coefficient of variation and probability distributions as methods of comparing the risk characteristics of various alternative courses of action. We shall now use these methods to compare the risk of various capital projects. Consider the situation presented in Example 14.6.

EXAMPLE 14.6

A firm is considering a capital investment proposal which requires an immediate cash outlay of £20,000. The project has an estimated life of three years and the forecasted cash flows and their estimated probabilities are as follows:

	Year 1		Year 2		Year 3
Probability	Net cash flow £	Probability	Net cash flow £	Probability	Net cash flow £
0.10	10,000	0.10	(− 5,000)	0.10	(− 10,000)
0.25	15,000	0.25	0	0.25	(− 5,000)
0.30	20,000	0.30	5,000	0.30	0
0.25	25,000	0.25	10,000	0.25	5,000
0.10	30,000	0.10	15,000	0.10	10,000
Expected value	20,000	Expected value	5,000	Expected value	0

Let us assume that the operating cash flows in any one year do not depend on the operating cash flows of previous years. The estimated cost of capital is 10%.

The expected values of the cash flows can be used to calculate each project's *expected net present value* by adding together the discounted net present values of the expected values for each year. That is:

$$\text{Expected NPV} = \frac{20,000}{(1.10)} + \frac{5,000}{(1.10)^2} + \frac{0}{(1.10)^3}$$
$$- 20,000 = £2,314$$

One method of describing the uncertainty associated with this project is to construct the entire probability distribution for the project's net present value. For example, the project has a negative NPV of £22,554 if the worst possible outcomes for each of the three years occurred together.[6] Because the cash flows are independent the probability of this occurring is 0.001 (that is, $0.10 \times 0.10 \times 0.10$). By applying this approach we can produce the complete probability distribution of the project's NPV. Probability distributions provide us with a useful indication of the risk of various projects. Unfortunately, the calculations are rather tedious as there are 125 possibilities (that is, 5^3) in Example 14.6. We could summarize the 125 possibilities in a probability distribution of several possible outcomes, but the 125 NPVs must still initially be calculated. To avoid all these calculations an indication of the risk may be obtained by calculating the standard deviation of the NPV. The formula for the calculation of the variance of the NPV is given below. The standard deviation is the square root of the variance:

$$V_p = \Sigma_{t=0}^{n} \frac{V_t}{(1 + r)^{2t}} \tag{14.1}$$

where V_p = the variance of the project's net present value, and V_t = the variance of the project's cash flow in the t year. The discount factor is squared so that it is in the same terms as the variance of the cash flows. These variances for the cash flows are identical for each of the three years, that is, £32,500,000.[7] Let us now apply equation (14.1) to calculate the variance of the project's net present value:

$$V_p = \frac{£32,500,000}{(1.10)^2} + \frac{£32,500,000}{(1.10)^4} + \frac{£32,500,000}{(1.10)^6}$$
$$= £67,402,844$$

The standard deviation is the square root of the variance, that is 8,210, so the expected value of the NPV of the project is £2,314 and the standard deviation about the expected NPV is £8,210. If a comparison of relative standard deviations of NPV, for various projects is required then the coefficient of variation may prove to be useful. This is simply the standard deviation divided by the expected value, that is 3.55. Management should then compare the expected values and risk measures of alternative projects so that they can be ranked in terms of expected NPVs and risk.

Simulation

To produce a probability distribution for the possible NPVs in Example 14.6 it is necessary to construct a decision tree with 125 different outcomes, even though the example was based on some very simple assumptions. In practice it may be necessary to produce separate probabilities for alternative sales revenue outcomes, different items of costs, and different possible life spans. Consequently, a decision tree will consist of thousands of different branches. In addition, the cash flows may be correlated over the years; for example, if a new product is successful in the early years then it is also likely to be successful in later years. When the cash flows *are* correlated over time the standard deviation calculation in equation (14.1) will not give a correct calculation of the variation of the project's NPV. For an explanation of the reasons for this statement see Van Horne (1983, pp. 153–6).

A way in which these problems can be overcome is to use Monte Carlo simulation analysis. We can use Example 14.6 to illustrate the simulation process. The first step is to construct a probability distribution for each factor which influences the capital investment decision, for example market share, selling price, operating costs and the useful life of the facilities. For Example 14.6 we shall only use probability distributions for the cash flows in each year of the project's life. The next step is to assign numbers (from 1 to 100) to the cash flows in the probability distributions to exactly match their respective

probabilities. This is achieved by working upwards cumulatively from the lowest to the highest cash flow values and assigning numbers which will correspond to probability groupings. The numbers for the cash flows in Example 14.6 for each year are as follows:

Year 1		Year 2		Year 3	
Assigned numbers	Cash flow	Assigned numbers	Cash flow	Assigned numbers	Cash flow
	£		£		£
1 – 10	10,000	1 – 10	(− 5,000)	1 – 10	(− 10,000)
11–35	15,000	11–35	0	11– 35	(− 5,000)
36 – 65	20,000	36 – 65	5,000	36 – 65	0
66 – 90	25,000	66 – 90	10,000	66 – 90	5,000
91 – 100	30,000	91 – 100	15,000	91 – 100	10,000

For year 1 the selection of a number at random between 1 and 10 obtained from between 1 and 100 has a probability of 0.1. In the above schedule this represents a cash flow of £10,000. Similarly, the selection of a number at random between 11 and 35 has a probability of 0.25 and this represents a cash flow of £15,000. *Numbers have been assigned to cash flows so that when numbers are selected at random the cash flows have exactly the same probability of being selected as is indicated in their respective probability distribution in Example 14.6.*

Simulation trials are now carried out by computer. The computer selects one number at random for each of the relevant distributions (that is, each probability distribution for years 1–3 in our example) and produces an estimated NPV. For example, if random numbers of 26, 8 and 85, respectively, are selected for each of the three distributions for each year, this will indicate cash flows of +£15,000 in year 1, −£5,000 in year 2, and +£5,000 in year 3, and the resulting net present value will be calculated. This particular NPV is only one of a particular combination of values from a computer run. The computer will select many other sets of random numbers, convert them into cash flows and compute other NPVs repeatedly, for perhaps several thousand trials. A count is kept of the number of times each NPV is computed, and when the computer run has been completed it can be programmed to produce an expected value, probability distribution and standard deviation. A graph of the probability distribution can also be plotted. If the probability distribution of NPVs for one proposal is compared with the probability distribution of NPVs for another proposal, management is able to evaluate the respective risk characteristics of different investments.

Note that computer simulation is not always feasible for risk analysis. The technique requires that probability distributions be established for a number of variables such as sales volume, selling prices, various input prices and asset lives. Therefore full scale simulation may only be appropriate for the most important projects which involve large sums of money. In such a situation a computer simulation can provide a valuable insight into the relative merits of alternative strategies. For a detailed illustration of the use of simulation techniques in making capital investment decisions see Hertz (1968).

Sensitivity analysis

For the less important decisions managers need simple methods for assessing risk. Sensitivity analysis enables managers to assess how responsive the NPV is to changes in the variables which are used to calculate it. Figure 14.3 illustrates that the NPV calculation is dependent on several independent variables, all of which are uncertain. The approach requires that the NPVs are calculated under alternative assumptions to determine how sensitive it is to changing conditions.

The application of sensitivity analysis can indicate those variables to which the NPV is most sensitive, and the extent to which these variables may change before the investment results in a negative NPV. Management should review any critical variables to assess whether or not there is a strong possibility of events occurring which will lead to a negative NPV. Management should also pay particular attention to *controlling* those variables to which NPV is particularly sensitive, once the decision has been taken to accept the investment. Sensitivity analysis is illustrated in Example 14.7.

EXAMPLE 14.7

A company is considering the purchase of a new machine and estimates of the most likely cash flows are as follows:

Years	0	1	2	3
	£	£	£	£
Initial outlay	−200,000			
Cash inflows (10,000 units at £30 per unit)		300,000	300,000	300,000
Variable costs		200,000	200,000	200,000
Net cash flows	−200,000	+100,000	+100,000	+100,000

The cost of capital is 15% and the net present value is £28,300.

Some of the variables referred to in Example 14.7 to which sensitivity analysis can be applied are:

(1) *Sales volume*: The net cash flows will have to fall to £87,604 (£200,000/2.283 discount factor) for the NPV to be zero, because it will be zero when the present value of the future cash flows is £200,000. As the cash flows are equal each year, the cumulative discount tables which you will find in Appendix II can be used. The discount factor for 15% and year 3 is 2.283. If the discount factor is divided into the required present value of £200,000 we get an annual cash flow of £87,604. Given that the most likely net cash flow is +£100,000, the net cash flow may decline by approximately £12,400 each year before the NPV becomes zero. Total sales revenue may therefore decline by £37,200 (assuming that net cash flow is $33\frac{1}{3}$% of sales). At a selling price of £30 per unit this represents 1,240 units or, alternatively, we may state that the sales volume may decline by 12.4% before the NPV becomes negative.

(2) *Selling price*: When the sales volume is 10,000 units per annum, total sales revenue can fall to £287,600 (300,000 − 12,400) before the NPV becomes negative. (Note

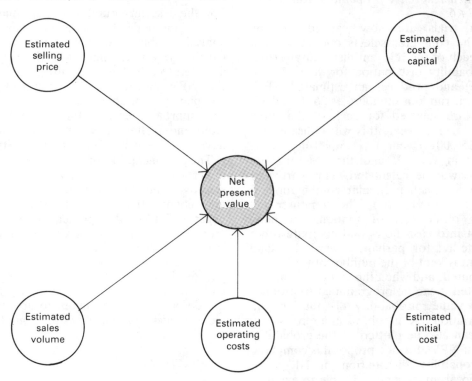

Fig. 14.3 Sensitivity of NPV to changes in independent variables

that it is assumed that total variable costs and units sold will remain unchanged.) This represents a selling price of £28.76, or a reduction of £1.24 per unit which represents a 4.1% reduction in the selling price.

(3) *Variable costs*: The total variable costs can increase by £12,400 or £1.24 per unit. This represents an increase of 6.2%.

(4) *Initial outlay*: The initial outlay can rise by the NPV before the investment breaks even. The initial outlay may therefore increase by £28,300 or 14.15%.

(5) *Cost of capital*: We calculate the internal rate of return for the project, which is 23%. Consequently, the cost of capital can increase by 53% before the NPV becomes negative.

The element to which the NPV appears to be most sensitive is the selling price followed by the variable costs, and it is important for the manager to pay particular attention to these items so that they can be carefully monitored.

Sensitivity analysis has a number of serious limitations. In particular, the method requires that changes in each key variable are isolated, but management is more interested in the combination of the effect of changes in *two or more* key variables. In addition, the method gives no indication of the probability of key variables or a probability of 0.01, then clearly the key variable change of 25% is more important.

Portfolio analysis

In Chapter 12 we noted that the degree of risk attached to various alternatives should not be viewed in isolation and that we should consider how much risk each alternative under consideration contributes to the overall risk of the firm. The principles of portfolio analysis can be applied to capital budgeting where projects can be evaluated in relation to their marginal impact on risk and NPV of the firm as a whole. Let us consider the situation in Example 14.8.

EXAMPLE 14.8

A firm has the opportunity to invest in either project B or project C. The NPVs of the projects depend on two sets of economic circumstances (known as states of nature). The NPVs for each project and the firm's existing projects are estimated to be as follows:

States of nature		1	2
Probability of state of nature		0.5	0.5
Net cash flows:			
Existing projects		− £40,000	+ £60,000
Proposed projects:	Project B	+ £50,000	− £50,000
	Project C	+ £ 9,000	+ £ 8,000

The standard deviations for each project and the correlation coefficients with existing projects are as follows:

	Project B	Project C	Existing projects
Standard deviation	£50,000	£5,000	£50,000
Correlation coefficient with existing projects	− 1.0	− 0.2	

combination of these variables occurring. For example, the sensitivity analysis may indicate that one key variable may change by 25% and another may change by 10%. This suggests that we should concentrate on the latter but, if the former has a probability of occurring of 0.5 and the latter has a When we examine the risk of each project in isolation it appears that project B is very risky whereas project C is a low-risk project. Exhibit 14.2 shows the effect on the NPV when each proposed project is combined with the existing projects.

The NPVs are calculated by adding the NPVs of each of projects B and C to the present value of the existing projects. When project B is added to the existing projects risk is completely eliminated as the NPV will be £10,000 whatever the state of the world. However, the combination of project C with the existing projects gives a large variation in the NPVs. The important point which we can learn from Exhibit 14.2 is that we should not focus on the risk of individual projects but that we should consider how much risk each project contributes to the overall risk of the firm. Although project B has the larger standard deviation, the standard deviation of the existing projects combined with project B is zero. On the other hand, project C has a low standard deviation but when this is combined with existing projects the standard deviation is higher than that which occurs when the existing projects are combined with project B.[8]

Exhibit 14.2 The combination of proposed projects with existing projects

States of nature	1	2
Existing projects plus project B NPV	+ £10,000	+ £10,000
Existing projects plus project C NPV	− £31,000	+ £68,000

The reason that project B reduces the overall risk is the perfect negative correlation with the existing projects (the correlation coefficient is −1). Alternatively, the higher the degree of positive correlation between a proposed project and the existing portfolio of projects, the higher will be the standard deviation of the NPV of the firm as a whole. Also, the greater the standard deviation of the individual projects, the greater will be the standard deviation of the NPV of the firm as a whole when the correlation coefficient is positive. The important point to note from portfolio analysis is that a negative correlation between a proposed project and the existing portfolio of projects reduces the standard deviation of the NPV of the firm as a whole.

In practice, it is extremely difficult and time consuming to apply portfolio analysis to capital investment decisions. Nevertheless, approximations of the correlation between proposed projects

and existing projects should be made, as the implications of portfolio analysis are of vital importance. *We should not focus on the risk of individual projects in isolation but should consider the overall risk from combining a proposed project with existing projects.* Note that portfolio analysis is, in practice, far more complex than the discussion here suggests, but further study of the topic is beyond the scope of this book. For a more detailed discussion of portfolio analysis see Lumby (1984) and Bromwich (1979).

Calculation of the cost of capital

We have established that the greater the risk which is attached to a proposed project, the greater will be the risk premium, which means a greater required rate of return or cost of capital. In the previous section we discussed various methods of determining the risk characteristics of proposed projects, and we are now going to consider how we can estimate the risk premium for different levels of risk.

If we observe the excess returns over the risk free rate which are required by investors for all companies listed on the stock exchange we can establish an average risk premium per unit of risk (that is, the standard deviation) which investors require. Assume that we estimate an average risk premium of 10% for all UK companies. Suppose

Fig. 14.4 The required rate of return/risk relationship

now that a company has an investment opportunity, the risk of which is considered to be identical to the average risk of all companies; investors will therefore require a risk premium of 10%. This risk/return relationship is illustrated in Fig 14.4

We can observe the risk free rate charged on government bonds, and this enables us to estimate two points on the RRR line in Fig. 14.4. If we assume a risk free rate of 9% and a risk premium of 10% for average risk investments, the required rate of return wil be 19% for average risk investments. If we join these two points we can establish the risk/return trade-off depicted in the RRR line. We also wish to estimate the risk premium for projects of above and below average risk. This is a difficult task but we can establish that the risk premium lies between 0 and 10% for investments of below average risk and above 10% for above average risk.

Ideally we should establish a quantitative measure of risk which will enable us to estimate a risk premium for projects of varying risk. Rather than using sophisticated computational techniques to estimate the risk premiums we can make informed judgements based on the risk of the project being considered relative to the average risk benchmark project. For example, a project half as risky as the average project should be charged a risk premium of 5% ($\frac{1}{2} \times 10\%$). Another project judged to be twice as risky as the average project should be charged a risk premium of 20%, and so on.

This analysis is a very simplistic presentation of how the cost of capital for investment projects can be estimated. One factor which we have ignored is the adjustments which are necessary to incorporate the effect of financing projects partly by debt finance. In addition, we have not discussed the statistical procedures which are used to estimate the cost of capital, but these procedures are based on the principles which have been outlined in this section. The theory of the relationship between the required rate of return and risk is based on the *capital asset pricing model* which was developed in the late 1960s. For a detailed explanation of this model and the adjustments which are necessary to incorporate the different methods of financing projects see Brearley and Myers (1981).

Authorization of capital investment proposals

It is essential to implement a sound system for approving capital investment proposals. Capital investment decisions frequently require the commitment of a large amount of funds for many years, and once approval has been obtained and initial outlays have been incurred, there is normally no turning back on the decision. A detailed scrutiny of capital investment proposals by top management is therefore essential. A procedure should be implemented which encourages managers to submit investment proposals as only by managers constantly reviewing future opportunities and threats can a company prosper in the long term. However, approval should not be merely a rubber-stamping of the managers' proposals, as there is a danger that a manager's favourite proposals will be implemented when they do not provide a sound financial return. It is important that top management should establish a capital investment approval procedure which both encourages managers to submit capital investment proposals and ensures that such proposals meet the long-term objectives of the company. An example of a capital investment approval procedure is illustrated in Fig. 14.5, although in practice such a procedure is likely to exist only in large firms.

Initiation of proposals

The originator of a proposal should make a request for a capital appropriation for those projects which seem to have merit. The request should include a description of the proposal, the reasons for making it, and an estimate of the costs, benefits and economic life. The originator

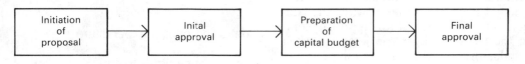

Fig. 14.5 Authorization of capital investment procedure

should obtain the assistance of the accounting department, which should provide a financial evaluation of the proposal. If the proposal does not meet the financial criteria, it will probably proceed no further, but not all desirable proposals lend themselves to financial evaluation because of the difficulty in quantifying the benefits (consider, for example, expenditure on social facilities for the employees, or pollution control devices). With these kinds of projects management will have to make a value judgement as to whether the benefits exceed the present value of the outlays.

Initial approval of the proposal

When the financial evaluation has been completed, the proposal, together with its financial evaluation, should be submitted to a top management committee consisting of the heads of various functions such as production, marketing, finance, research and development, and so on. At this stage there will be much discussion, and additional information such as sensitivity analysis or other information about the risk of the project may be requested. The committee will then either approve or reject the proposal. Minor proposals, which require only a small initial cash outlay, may not require the approval of the top management committee. The managers themselves or their superiors may be able to approve such projects. However, approval will normally be subject to the proposals meeting the company's normal profitability standards. Such projects should also be subject to *post-completion audits* (that is, a comparison of budgeted and actual cash flows). Approval by the top management team of a request indicates only that the proposal fits into the company's programme; it does not carry with it authorization to proceed immediately with the proposal.

Preparation of the annual capital budget

The accountant will normally prepare this budget but will have to work closely with the top management capital expenditure approval committee. In the capital budget, projects are often classified under the following headings:

(a) Cost reduction and replacement
(b) Expansion of existing product lines

(c) New product lines
(d) Health and safety
(e) Other

Within these classifications, individual projects may be listed in what is believed to be their order of merit, and estimated cash inflows and outflows should be analysed by years, or quarters, so that their impact on the funds of each time period can be shown. A blanket amount is normally included for the total of smaller projects which are not listed individually. The capital budget should be reviewed by a top management review committee and it will ultimately be approved, perhaps after some revision and resubmissions. When approving the capital budget an overall view should be taken; for example, the committee should consider whether the overall mix of proposed projects fits in with the required financial return and risk profile of the company.

Final approval

Approval of the capital budget will normally mean that a project is approved in principle but before a project can be undertaken it is necessary to submit a final authorization request, which spells out the proposal in more detail and includes an agreed price quotation. Final approval may be obtained from the top management approval committee or lower levels of management, depending on the cost and the importance of the project.

Review of capital investment decisions

When the capital investment decision has been made it is important to implement a sound system for revieiwng and controlling the capital expenditure. The review should consist of the following:

(1) Control over the amount of the expenditure before the project is operational.
(2) A post-completion audit of the operating cash inflows and outflows.

Controlling capital expenditure

Capital expenditure is difficult to control because each investment is usually unique, and therefore no predetermined standards or past experience

will be available for establishing what the cash outflows should be. When the actual capital expenditure costs are different from the amount originally estimated, the difference may be due to an incorrect original estimate and/or inefficiency in controlling the actual costs. Unfortunately, it is very difficult, and sometimes impossible, to isolate a variance (that is, the difference between the actual and the estimated expenditure) into a forecasting element and an efficiency element. However, the originator of a project will have prepared an estimate and defended it at the approval stage. This estimate forms a major component in determining whether or not the project should be approved, and there are sound reasons for comparing this estimate with the actual expenditures and requiring the individual responsible to explain any variances. This comparison may also indicate inefficiencies which will enable action to be taken to avoid overspending on the uncompleted part of the project. In addition, a comparison of actual costs with estimated costs will provide an incentive for the proposers of future projects to make careful estimates, and also provide an incentive to control the costs and the date of completion.

Comparisons should take place at periodic intervals during the installation and construction stage of the project. Reports should be prepared which give details of the percentage completion; over or underspending relative to the stage of completion; the estimated costs to complete compared with the original estimate; the time taken compared to the estimate for the current stage of completion; and also the estimated completion date compared with the original estimate. This information will enable management to take corrective cost-saving action such as changing the construction schedule. Every effort should be made to avoid a delay in completion because this can be expensive in terms of additional costs. Hence emphasis should be placed on the time scheduling of the project using critical path analysis. For a discussion of the methods of controlling the scheduling of projects see Shilliglaw (1982) and Anthony and Dearden (1980).

Post-completion audit of cash flows

When the investment is in operation the actual results should be compared with the estimated results which were included in the investment proposal. The comparison should be based on the same method of evaluation as was used in making the investment decision. Whenever possible, actual cash flows plus estimated cash flows for the remainder of the project's life should be compared with the cash flows which were included in the original estimate. However, the feasibility of making such a comparison will depend on the ease and cost of estimating future cash flows.

The problem is that normally no pre-set standards or past information will be available as to what the cash inflows and outflows should be, and a comparison of actual and estimated cash flows will be difficult to evaluate. Furthermore, except for the very large projects, the portion of cash flows which stem from a specific capital investment is very difficult to isolate. All one can do in such situations is to scrutinize carefully the investment at the approval stage and incorporate the estimated results into departmental operating budgets. Although the results of individual projects cannot be isolated, their combined effect can be examined as part of the conventional periodic performance review.

In situations where it is possible to make comparisons, it is important that they take place at annual or even longer intervals as capital investments are long-run decisions and cannot easily be evaluated within a short-term dimension. It is also important to assess capital investments in terms of cash flows, which are the basis for the decision, rather than with such periodic external financial reporting measures as return on investment. The reasons for this are explained in Chapter 23.

A post audit of capital investment decisions is a very difficult task and any past investment decisions which have proved to be wrong should not be interpreted in isolation. It is important to remind oneself that capital investment decisions are made under uncertainty. For example, a good decision may turn out to be unsuccessful yet still have been the correct decision in the light of the information and alternatives available at the time. We would agree that a manager should undertake a project which costs £10,000 and has a 0.9 probability of a positive net present value of £8,000 and a 0.1 probability of a negative net present value of £2,000. However, if the event with a 0.1 probability occurred a post completion audit would suggest that the investment had been undesirable.

Lister (1983) suggests that 'post-mortems' may be viewed with disfavour in industry on the

grounds that they discourage initiative and produce a policy of overcaution. This problem is likely to be reduced if managers know that their selections will be fairly judged.

In spite of all the problems a post-audit comparison *should* be undertaken. A record of past performance and mistakes is one way of improving future performance and ensuring that fewer mistakes are made. In addition, the fact that the proposers of capital investment projects are aware that their estimates will be compared with actual results encourage them to exercise restraint when making their original proposals. Over-optimistic capital investment proposals may thus be held in check. Pike (1983) in a survey of 150 of the largest UK manufacturing and retailing companies found that ex-post monitoring of capital investment decisions operates in almost all companies in one form or another. Pike found that post-completion audits were conducted on major projects in 48% of the companies surveyed, the selection of projects for investigation being random or based on size. Pike's survey also indicated that the size of companies did not influence whether post-completion audits were undertaken. This contrasts with an earlier UK study by Westwick (1976) which indicated that post-completion audits were conducted only in larger companies. Note, however, that Pike's study was restricted to the largest UK companies.

The use of post-completion audits differs substantially between the UK and the USA, according to a survey by Scapens and Sale (1981). They found that only 36% of the repsondents in the UK, compared with 84% in the USA, undertake such audits.

Summary

In this chapter we have discussed how capital investment techniques can be applied to more complicated situations. We have seen that when a choice must be made between mutually exclusive investments with unequal lives it is necessary to compare the projects over equal time periods. One method is to convert the time periods into a common time horizon and assume the replacement of identical assets. Another method is to compare the alternatives over a time span which is equal to the alternative with the shortest life and which includes the salvage values of the alternatives with the longer time spans.

Capital rationing applies to a situation where there is a constraint on the amount of funds which can be invested during a specific period of time. In this situation the net present value is maximized by adopting the profitability index method of ranking and selecting projects up to the amount of the investment funds available.

When taxation is included in the capital investment evaluation the cash flows from a project must be reduced by the amount of taxation which is paid on these cash flows. In addition, the investment cost must be reduced by the taxation saving which arises from the capital allowance. Because the timing of taxation payments does not occur at the same time as the associated cash inflows or outflows the precise timing of the taxation payment must be identified.

The net present value calculations can be adjusted in two basic ways to take inflation into account. First, a discount rate can be used, based on the market determined required rate of return which includes an allowance for inflation. Remember that cash flows must also be adjusted for inflation. Second, the anticipated rate of inflation can be excluded from the discount rate, and the cash flows can be expressed in terms of current purchasing power as at year zero.

When cash flows are subject to uncertainty, the discount rate will consist of a risk free rate plus a risk premium. The greater the risk of a project, the greater will be the risk premium. Several methods exist for quantifying the risk of projects: standard deviations, probability distribution, simulation and sensitivity analysis are some of the methods we have examined. However, using portfolio analysis, it is preferable to measure risk in terms of combining a proposed project with the existing portfolio of projects. When we have established the risk category into which a project falls, we must estimate the appropriate risk premium which should be added to the risk free rate to establish the discount rate. One approach is to estimate the risk premium which will be demanded by investors for average risk projects and use this as a benchmark for assessing the risk premium to be attached to projects with differing amounts of risk.

Finally, we have considered methods of authorizing and reviewing capital investment decisions. In spite of the difficulties involved in carrying out a post-audit review of capital investment decisions such a review is necessary so that lessons can be learned from past mistakes and to discourage the proposers of capital investment projects from submitting over-optimistic estimates.

References and further reading

Anthony, R.N. and Dearden, J. *Management Control Systems*. R.D. Irwin, 1980, Chapter 17.

Bagwell, J., Bain, N.S. and Scholefield, H.H. The effects of inflation on investment appraisal. *Journal of Business Finance* Summer 1973.

Brearly, R. and Myers, S. *Principles of Corporate Finance*. McGraw-Hill, 1981.

Bromwich, M. *The Economies of Capital Budgeting*. Pitman, 1979, Chapter 15.

Bromwich, M. Inflation and the capital budgeting process. *Journal of Business Finance* Autumn 1969.

Carsberg, B.V. and Hope, A. *Business Investment Decisions Under Inflation*. Institute of Chartered Accountants in England and Wales. 1976.

Dudley, C. A note on reinvestment assumptions in choosing between net present value and internal rate of return. *The Journal of Finance* September 1982, 907-15.

Emery, G.W. Evaluating capital investment alternatives with unequal lives. *Financial Management (USA)*, Spring 1982, 14-19.

Fama, E.F. Risk-adjusted discount rates and capital budgeting under uncertainty. *Journal of Financial Economics* **5** (1977), 3-24.

Fogler, H.R. Ranking techniques and capital rationing. *Accounting Review* January 1972, pp. 134-43.

Greer, W.R. Theory versus practice in risk analysis: An empirical study. *Accounting Review* July 1974, 496-505.

Grinyer, J.R. Inflation and capital budgeting decisions. *Journal of Business Finance and Accounting* Spring 1974, **1**(1), 149-55.

Grinyer, J.R. Relevant criterion rates in capital budgeting. *Journal of Business Finance and Accounting* Autumn 1974, **1**(3), 357-74.

Hertz, D.B. Risk analysis in capital investment. *Harvard Business Review* January–February 1968, 96-108.

Hicks, C.F. and Schmidt, L.L. Post auditing and capital investment decisions. *Management Accounting (USA)*, August 1971, 24-30.

Keane, S.M. Cost of capital and the investment decision. *Journal of Business Finance and Accounting* **4**(2), 201-17.

King, P. Strategic control of capital investment. *Journal of General Management* Autumn 1974, 17-28.

Lister, R. Appraising the value of post-audit procedures. *Accountancy Age* 20.10.83, 40.

Lumby, S. *Investment Appraisal and Related Decisions* 2nd edn. Van Nostrand Reinhold (UK), 1984, pp. 188-208.

Mao, J.C.T. Survey of capital budgeting: Theory and practice. *Journal of Finance* May 1970.

Pike, R.H. A review of recent trends in formal capital budgeting processes. *Accounting and Business Research* Summer 1983, 201-208. See also *Capital Budgeting in the 1980s: The Results of a Major Survey of Large Companies*. Institute of Cost and Management Accountants, 1983.

Pike, R.H. and Roberts, B. Investment hurdle rates and the cost of capital. *Management Accounting* June 1980, 38-40.

Salayar, R.C. and Subrata, K. A simulation model of capital budgeting under uncertainty. *Management Science* December 1968, 161-79.

Scapens, R.W. and Sale, J.T. Performance measurement and formal capital expenditure controls in divisionalised companies. *Journal of Business Finance and Accounting* **8**(3), Autumn 1981, 389-420.

Schall, L.D., Sundem, G.L. and Geigsbeek. Survey and analysis of capital budgeting methods. *The Journal of Finance* March 1978, 281-7.

Shillinglaw, G. *Managerial Cost Accounting*. R.D. Irwin, 1982, Chapter 24.

Smidt, S. A Bayesian analysis and project selection and post audit evaluations. *Journal of Finance* June 1979, 675-88.

Van Horne, J.C. A note on biases in capital budgeting introduced by inflation. *Journal of Finance and Quantitative Analysis* **6**, March 1971, 653-68.

Van Horne, J.C. *Financial Management and Policy*. Prentice-Hall, 1983, pp. 153-6.

Westwick, C.A. and Shohet. *Investment Appraisal and Inflation*. Institute of Chartered Accountants in England and Wales, Occasional Paper No. 7, 1976.

Problems

*Indicates that a suggested solution is to be found in the *Students' Manual*.

14.1 A small loss-making company is considering whether to purchase or lease a new type of fork lift truck. The truck can be leased for a four-year period, the lease payments being £12,000 per anum payable in advance. Maintenance and servicing needs are covered by the leasing agreement.

The truck could be purchased for £28,800. At the end of four years the company has been guaranteed a trade-in price of £4,800. The service and maintenance costs under a supplier's maintenance contract will be £2,400 per annum, payable at the end of each year. The truck would be depreciated both for tax and internal accounting purposes on the straight line basis over four years.

If the fork lift truck is used the company estimates it will save on the services of two employees which will save the company wage payments of approximately £14,400 per annum.

The corporation tax rate is 50%, but the company has not paid any tax for the last two years. It is anticipated that the company will not

pay any tax for the next two years because of continuing trading losses, but that large profits will be earned during year 2 of the fork lift truck's life. The company will then continue to earn profits for a number of years. Accumulated losses can be carried forward for tax purposes. The amount of profits in year 2 are expected to be well in excess of the accumulated losses.

You can assume, when appropriate, that tax is paid one year after the date of reporting profits.

The cost of capital is 12%.

You are required:

To present cost information to management indicating which alternative the company should choose.

14.2 The product development manager of Ward PLC has made a suggestion to produce and sell a range of personal computers. The machinery required to produce the personal computers would be purchased at a cost of £120,000.

His analysis, on an accounting basis, of the project's profitability is:

labour costs. Labour costs and the remaining 'other production expenses' are all incremental cash costs.

(iv) Depreciation is based on the usual 6 year life assumed for this type of machine.

(v) 'Administrative charge' is an apportionment of central fixed overheads.

(vi) If the proposal goes ahead it will enable an existing machine to be sold as its function will be performed more efficiently by the new plant in otherwise idle time with a saving of operating costs of £6,000 per annum. The machine has a book value of £30,000 and could be sold now for £10,000. It would otherwise be sold in 4 years time for £4,000. Details of the machine and the incidental savings are not included in the above analysis except that the expected disposal proceeds of the machine have been deducted from the envisaged external incremental borrowings needed to finance the project and are reflected in a reduced

Operating year	1 (£000)	2 (£000)	3 (£000)	4 (£000)
Sales	200	300	400	300
Costs				
Materials used				
Opening stock	20	40	40	30
Purchases	100	120	150	90
	120	160	190	120
Closing stock	40	40	30	—
Cost of material used	80	120	160	120
Labour	40	60	60	40
Other production expenses	40	45	46	50
Depreciation	20	20	20	20
Administrative charge	27	38	37	37
Interest	11	11	11	11
	218	294	334	278
Gross profit	(18)	6	66	22
Tax	(9)	3	33	11
Net profit	(9)	3	33	11

The following points are made in the product development manager's report to the Board:

(i) The machinery is highly specialized and is unlikely to have any residual value after meeting dismantling costs at the end of its life of at least 4 years.

(ii) Opening stock in year 1 will be purchased at the same time as the machine. All other changes in stock levels will occur at year ends.

(iii) 'Other production expenses' include apportioned fixed overhead equal to 25% of

interest charge to the project.

(vii) The accounting figures show that the average pre-tax book rate of return on initial capital outlay is nearly 16%, and this exceeds the 14% required by the Board on all capital projects.

The marketing director objects that the analysis excludes:

(a) the required advertising campaign which will cost £20,000 at the start of the project and £5,000 per annum in each of the years 1 to 3;

(b) the effect on the sales of Ward's sophisticated calculators. Sales forecasts and unit prices will need revision as follows:

| | Original forecast | | Revised forecast | |
	Units	Sales price per unit	Units	Sales price per unit
	(000)	£	(000)	£
Year 1	5	80	5	75
2	4	60	3	50
3	2	40	—	—
4	—	—	—	—

The production costs, per unit, of calculators are:

	Year 1	Year 2	Year 3
	£	£	£
Variable costs	60	45	30
Fixed costs — apportionment of general factory overheads	10	10	10
Total cost	70	55	40

The financial director suggests that the treatment of taxation in the analysis could be improved. He emphasizes:
(1) The tax rate is 50% and the tax delay is 1 year.
(2) The machinery is eligible for 100% First Year Capital Allowances and Ward has sufficient total taxable profits for this to be utilized in full at the earliest opportunity.
(3) Proceeds from the sale of the existing machinery would be subject to tax.
(4) Expenditure on advertising is tax deductible.
(5) Stock relief may be ignored.
(6) The 14% required return quoted in the Report is the after-tax discount rate applicable in a DCF appraisal.
Required:
(a) Produce a discounted cash flow appraisal of the proposed project and advise Ward on the acceptability of the proposal. Specify any assumptions made. (15 marks)
(b) Briefly discuss the other major factors which should be given further consideration, in order to enhance confidence in the decision advice specified above, if this appraisal were to be carried out as a practical exercise. (6 marks)
(c) Explain the importance in investment appraisal of the investing firm having taxable profits. Indicate the effects which a lack of taxable profits may have on investment decisions, and, briefly comment on the main possibilities open to a firm to overcome such effects. (4 marks)

(25 marks)

ACCA Level 3 Financial Mangement June 1982

14.3* Turnbull PLC is considering the possibility of manufacturing its own requirements for material Kay rather than continuing its present policy of purchasing from an external supplier.

Material Kay is purchased and paid for only at the end of each year and will be required for the next 5 years. Estimates of the demand and the purchase price per unit for Kay are:

Year	Units required	Purchase price per unit
	(000s)	£
1	20	20
2	20	24
3	20	25
4	10	30
5	10	35

Estimates of the unit costs of producing Kay are:

Estimated production costs per unit

	Years 1, 2 & 3		Years 4 & 5	
	£	£	£	£
Variable costs				
Materials	7		7	
Labour	6		7	
Variable overhead	2	15	3	17
Fixed costs				
General factory overhead	3		3	
Rates	1		2	
Depreciation	4	8	8	13
Total production costs		23		30

'General factory overhead' is an apportionment of Turnbull's total factory overheads.
'Rates' relate to rates paid on the additional land required (see (ii) below).
'Depreciation' relates only to the new machinery specifically purchased for the production of Kay (see (v) below).
The following further information is available:
 (i) All incremental cash production costs will

be paid at the end of the year to which they relate.

(ii) Turnbull would not need to acquire additional factory space for the production of Kay as it has sufficient for this purpose. This factory space has no alternative use or rental value. However, storage of the bulky raw materials used to produce Kay will necessitate the purchase of a plot of adjacent land. The land will cost £120,000 and in year 5 will have a resale value of at least £160,000. No tax allowances are available for investment in the land and it is felt that there will be no tax consequences arising from its sale.

(iii) If the proposal goes ahead then it will require the use of a piece of existing equipment. The existing equipment has a book value of £140,000 and, if not used in the production of Kay, would be sold now for its market value of £80,000. Estimated salvage value at year 5 is £10,000. The equipment has already been subject to 100% tax allowances and any sales value will be subject to assessment to tax. Depreciation of this equipment has been excluded from the cost of production specified above.

(iv) The project will save £40,000 per year in the fixed costs of material handling. This saving has been reflected in the figure of total factory overheads which has been apportioned among all cost centres as general factory overhead.

(v) The new machinery required for the production of Kay has a cost of £400,000. This machinery is expected to have no salvage value in year 5. Purchase of the machinery entitles the owner to claim 100% first year capital allowances for tax purposes. There is the possibility of entering into a non-cancellable finance lease to obtain the use of this machinery. Such a lease would require an initial payment of £60,000 at the start of the lease followed by 4 payments of £100,000 made at strictly yearly intervals. Such payments are tax deductible expenses. The alternative to leasing is to finance the purchase of the machinery by borrowing at a pre-tax interest rate of 10% per annum, the current competitive market interest rate for debt.

Turnbull is a profitable company and is able to utilize in full all tax allowances at the earliest opportunity. The tax rate is 50% and the tax delay is 1 year. If the project is accepted it will commence at the end of a tax year and the initial payments, and any lease rentals, will be included in that tax year.

It is Turnbull's policy that investment and financing decisions are appraised separately. All capital projects must be appraised by the financial controller to ascertain whether the project would be worthwhile if purchased. The normal DCF appraisal rate applied after tax cash flows is 15%. If a project is found to be acceptable, then the treasurer is required to recommend the best method of financing the project and to indicate the desirability of any leasing possibilities. To speed up the analysis of this project the details have been sent to the financial controller and the treasurer at the same time rather than sequentially.

Required:

(a) Carry out the financial controller's analysis and determine whether the project is worthwhile if purchase is the only financing option for the new machinery. (10 marks)

(b) Carry out the treasurer's analysis to determine whether purchase or leasing, on the terms specified, would be the best alternative for the new machinery. (5 marks)

(c) *Using the same discount rates utilized in (b) above*, indicate the relative merits of lease and purchase if Turnbull would produce tax losses until year 2. Year 2 would produce taxable profits after considering all accumulated losses and thereafter Turnbull will continue to produce taxable profits. Payment of tax would, when appropriate, be subject to a one year delay. (3 marks)

(d) (i) Comment on the merits and dangers of Turnbull's policy concerning the appraisal of investment and financing decisions. Indicate any improvements which could be recommended.

 (ii) Discuss the validity of using the same discount rates for the circumstances of both (b) and (c) above. Explain, without calculation, how the lease *v.* buy decision should be correctly appraised when a firm is in a temporary non-tax-paying position. (7 marks)

(25 marks)

ACCA Level 3 Financial Management
December 1983

14.4* As the financial consultant of the Bourbon Can Company, a medium sized manufacturing business, you have been asked to advise on the current year's investment proposals. The proposed projects, shown below, are not mutually exclusive.

Project A: To replace the existing data processing equipment. Initial cost £250,000. Expected life of new equipment 6 years. Expected annual after tax cash inflow £72,500.

Project B: To develop a new type of con-

tainer. Cost £70,000. All to be incurred in the current year. Expected life of product 5 years. Expected annual after tax cash inflow £30,000, the inflows to commence in one year's time.

Project C: To install safety equipment. Initial cost £110,000. Expected life 3 years. Expected annual after-tax cash inflow £45,000.

Project D: To construct a new factory building. Initial cost £210,000. Expected life 8 years. Expected annual after-tax cash inflow £57,000.

Project E: To extend the existing loading equipment. Initial cost £170,000. Expected life 4 years. Expected annual after-tax cash inflow £70,000.

Project F: To purchase patent rights to a new process. Initial cost £135,000. Expected life 7 years. Expected annual after-tax cash inflow £36,000.

You may assume that, with the exception of project B, all cash inflows would commence in the current year. For calculation purposes, you may assume that the annual cash inflows are always received on the last day of the year. Tax can be assumed to have been paid in the year in which the profits are earned.

The company's marginal cost of capital for the coming year is estimated at 16%. The company is, however, in a capital rationing situation and it estimates it will only hve £600,000 to invest on capital projects in the current year.

Required:

(a) Which projects would you recommend the company to undertake? Give the reasons for your choice. (12 marks)

(b) What factors, if any, other than those given in the question, would you advise the company to consider before making a decision? (8 marks)

(20 marks)
ACCA P3 Financial Management
June 1980

14.5* Bailey Ltd is developing a new product, the Oakman, to replace an established product, the Shepard, which the company has marketed successfully for a number of years. Production of the Shepard will cease in one year whether or not the Oakman is manufactured. Bailey Ltd has recently spent £75,000 on research and development relating to the Oakman. Production of the Oakman can start in one year's time.

Demand for the Oakman is expected to be 5,000 units per annum for the first three years of production and 2,500 units per annum for the subsequent two years. The product's total life is expected to be five years.

Estimated unit revenues and costs for the Oakman, at *current prices*, are as follows:

	£	£
Selling price per unit		35.00
Less Costs per unit:		
Materials and other consumables	8.00	
Labour (see (1) below)	6.00	
Machine depreciation and over-haul (see (2) below)	12.50	
Other overheads (see (3) below)	9.00	35.50
Loss per unit		0.50

(1) Each Oakman requires two hours of labour, paid £3 per hour at current prices. The labour force required to produce Oakman comprises six employees, who are at present employed to produce Shepards. If the Oakman is not produced, these employees will be made redundant when production of the Shepard ceases. If the Oakman is produced, three of the employees will be made redundant at the end of the third year of its life, when demand halves, but the company expects to be able to find work for the remaining three employees at the end of the Oakman's five year life. Any employee who is made redundant will receive a redundancy payment equivalent to 1,000 hours' wages, based on the most recent wage rate at the time of the redundancy.

(2) A special machine will be required to produce the Oakman. It will be purchased in one year's time (just before production begins). The current price of the machine is £190,000. It is expected to last for five years and to have no scrap or resale value at the end of that time. A major overhaul of the machine will be necessary at the end of the second year of its life. At current prices, the overhaul will cost £60,000. As the machine will not produce the same quantity of Oakmans each year, the directors of Bailey Ltd have decided to spread its original cost and the cost of the overhaul equally between all Oakmans expected to be produced (i.e. 20,000 units). Hence the combined charge per unit for depreciation and over-haul is £12.50 ([£190,000 + £60,000] ÷ 20,000 units).

(3) Other overheads at current prices comprise variable overheads of £4.00 per unit and head office fixed costs of £5.00 per unit, allotted on the basis of labour time.

All wage rates are expected to increase at an

annual compound rate of 15%. Selling price per unit and all costs other than labour are expected to increase in line with the Retail Price Index. The Retail Price Index is expected to increase in the future at an annual compound rate of 10%.

Corporation tax at 52% on net cash income is payable in full one year after the income arises. A 100% first year tax allowance is available on the machine. Bailey Ltd has a money cost of capital, net of corporation tax, of 20% per annum.

Assume that all receipts and payments will arise on the last day of the year to which they relate. Assume also that all 'current prices' given above have been operative for one year and are due to change shortly. Subsequently all prices will change annually.

You are required to:
(a) prepare calculations, with explanations, showing whether Bailey Ltd should undertake production of the Oakman (20 marks), and
(b) discuss the particular investment appraisal problems created by the existence of high rates of inflation (8 marks).

(28 marks)
ICAEW Elements of Financial Decisions July 1981

14.6 Gento Ltd has been invited to make a tender for a contract to manufacture six special processing machines. Manufacture would take a total of three years, commencing immediately (1 August 1980), and the contract price would be payable in two equal instalments, the first on 1 August 1980 and the second on 31 July 1983. The company would manufacture two machines each year.

The following estimates are available about the resources required to produce the special processing machines:

(1) Materials

Type of material	Quantity per machine tons	Amount in stock now tons	Original cost of stock per ton £	Current purchase price per ton £	Current realisable value per ton £
Gamma	20	60	700	1,000	800
Zeta	10	20	500	750	See below

Gamma is used regularly by the company on many contracts. Zeta is used rarely and if the existing stock is not applied to this contract it will have to be disposed of immediately at a net *cost* of £100 per ton. Materials required for the contract must be purchased and paid for annually in advance. Replacement costs of gamma and zeta and the realisable value of gamma are expected to increase at an annual compound rate of 20%.

(2) Labour

Each of the six machines will require 3,000 hours of skilled labour and 5,000 hours of unskilled labour. Current wage rates are £4 per hour for skilled labour and £3 per hour for unskilled labour.

Gento Ltd expects to suffer a shortage of skilled labour during the year to 31 July 1981 so that acceptance of the contract would make it necessary to give up other work on which a contribution of £7 per hour, net of skilled labour costs, would be earned. (The 'other work' would require no unskilled labour).

For the year to 31 July 1981 only, the company expects to have 20,000 surplus unskilled labour hours. Gento Ltd has an agreement with its labour force whereby it lays off employees for whom there is no work and pays them two-thirds of their normal wages during the lay off period.

All wage rates are expected to increase at an annual compound rate of 15%.

(3) Overheads

Overhead costs are currently allocated to contracts at a rate of £14 per skilled labour hour, calculated as follows:

	£
Fixed overheads (including equipment depreciation of £5)	11.00
Variable overheads	3.00
	14.00

Special equipment will be required for this contract, and will be purchased on 1 August 1980 at a cost of £200,000 payable immediately. It will be sold on 31 July 1983 for £50,000. Both fixed and variable overheads are expected to increase in line with the Retail Price Index.

Gento Ltd has a cost of capital of 20% per annum in money terms. The Retail Price Index is expected to increase in the future at an annual compound rate of 15%.

Assume that all payments will arise on the last day of the year to which they relate except where otherwise stated. Assume also that input prices will change annually at midnight on 31 July.

You are required to:
(a) calculate the *minimum* price at which Gento Ltd should be willing to undertake the contract to manufacture the six special processing machines based on the information given above (15 marks),
(b) provide brief explanations of the figures you have used (5 marks), and
(c) comment on other factors, not reflected in your calculations, which may affect the minimum acceptable price (5 marks).
Ignore taxation.

ICAEW Elements of Financial Decisions
July 1980

14.7 Gateway Ltd, a car hire firm, is considering its future cash flows. The directors of the company are interested in the period from now, that is the end of January 1981, to the end of 1986. In particular, they wish to decide on the optimal replacement cycle for the fleet of thirty hire cars. On 1 January 1981, the company purchased its existing fleet at a cost of £300,000. The vehicles are to be depreciated in the accounts over a three-year life, on a straight line basis. The resale value of a one-year-old car of the type used in the fleet is at present £7,000.

Inflation is at the rate of 10% per annum, and it is thought that it will continue at this rate for the foreseeable future. New car prices will increase in line with inflation, but second hand values are expected to remain at the present levels for a number of years. The resale value of a two-year-old fleet car is at present £4,000 and the scrap value of a three-year-old car is £500.

The revenue from operating the fleet is expected to be £250,000 in 1981. This annual revenue is expected to increase at a rate of 10% per annum irrespective of the age of the vehicles. The operating and maintenance costs for 1981 are estimated to be:

£70,000 for cars in the first year of their life,
£100,000 for cars in the second year of their life,
£160,000 for cars in the third year of their life.

The operating and maintenance costs are expected to increase at a rate of 10% per annum in line with inflation. The cars are not worth keeping for longer than three years.

The company's cost of capital is 15%.

Required:
(a) You are asked to advise the company on the optimal replacement policy for its fleet of cars for the period 1 Febaury 1981 to 31 December 1986. You can ignore taxation, and can assume that the cash flows relating to revenue and operating costs arise on the last day of the respective years. (16 marks)

(b) Comment in general terms on how taxation influences investment decisions. (4 marks)
(20 marks)

ACCA P3 Financial Management
June 1981

14.8* Butcher Ltd is considering whether to set up a divsion in order to manufacture a new product, the azam. The following statement has been prepared, showing the projected 'profitability' per unit of the new product:

	£	£
Selling price		22.00
Less Direct labour (2 hrs at £2.50 per hr)	5.00	
Material (3 kg at £1.50 per kg)	4.50	
Overheads	11.50	
		21.00
Net profit per unit		1.00

A feasibility study, recently undertaken at a cost of £50,000, suggests that a selling price of £22 per azam should be set. At this price, it is expected that 10,000 azams would be sold each year. Demand for azams is expected to cease after 5 years. Direct labour and materials costs would be incurred only for the duration of the product life.

Overheads per unit have been calculated as follows:

	£
Variable overheads	2.50
Rent (see note (1) below — £8,000 ÷ 10,000 units)	0.80
Manager's salary (see note (2) below — £7,000 ÷ 10,000 units)	0.70
Depreciation (see note (3) below — £50,000 ÷ 10,000 units)	5.00
Head office costs (see note (4) below — 2 hrs at £1.25 per hr)	2.50
	11.50

(1) Azams would be manufactured in a factory rented specially for the purpose. Annual rental would be £8,000 payable only for as long as the factory was occupied.
(2) A manager would be employed to supervise production of azams, at a salary of £7,000 per annum. The manager is at present employed by Butcher Ltd, but is due to retire in the near future on an annual pension of £2,000, payable by the company. If he continued to be employed, his pension would not be paid during the period of his employment. His subsequent pension rights would not be affected.
(3) Manufacture of the azam would require a specialized machine costing £250,000. The machine would be capable of producing azams for an indefinite

period, although due to its specialized nature it would not have any resale or scrap value when the production of azams ceased. It is the policy of Butcher Ltd to provide depreciation on all fixed assets using the straight line method. The annual charge of £50,000 for the new machine is based on a life of 5 years, equal to the period during which azams are expected to be produced.

(4) Butcher Ltd allocates its head office fixed costs to all products at the rate of £1.25 per direct labour hour. Total head office fixed costs would not be affected by the introduction of the azam to the company's range of products.

The cost of capital of Butcher Ltd is estimated at 5% per annum in real terms, and you may assume that all costs and prices given above will remain constant in real terms. All cash flows would arise at the end of each year, with the exception of the cost of the machine which would be payable immediately. The directors of Butcher Ltd are very confident about the accuracy of all the estimates given above, with the exception of those relating to product life, annual sales volume and material cost per azam.

You are required to:

(a) prepare net present value calculations, based on the estimates provided, to show whether Butcher Ltd should proceed with manufacture of the azam (10 marks),

(b) prepare a statement showing how sensitive the net present value of manufacturing azams is to errors of estimation in each of

project which will involve the investment (in 1983 money terms) of £1 million in plant, divided evenly over 1984 and 1985. This investment will yield a gross income of £800,000 per annum from 1986 to 1989 inclusive, but will incur costs of £200,000 per annum over the same period, both figures in 1983 money terms.

You are required to:

(a) Calculate for the project:
 (i) the discounted cash flow (DCF) rate (internal rate of return) in real terms to the nearest whole number;
 (ii) the net present value (NPV) if the cost of capital is 10% real.

(b) List any four tests of sensitivity analysis that could be applied to help management in its decision on this proposed investment.

(c) (i) Calculate, using a simulation method based on random numbers and working upwards cumulatively from the lowest levels of expenditure, income and costs at 00 to the highest levels at 99, the NPV of the project at 10% real if the random numbers appearing were:

	Random number
for plant	35
for income	06
for costs	93

An analysis of the possible levels of plant investment, income and costs shows the following:

Plant investment		Income		Costs	
Level in 1983 money, per annum	Probability of that level	Level in 1983 money, per annum	Probability of that level	Level in 1983 money, per annum	Probability of that level
£000		£000		£000	
450	0.10	650	0.10	170	0.10
500	0.50	700	0.15	185	0.20
550	0.30	750	0.25	200	0.40
600	0.07	800	0.35	215	0.20
650	0.03	850	0.15	230	0.10
	1.00		1.00		1.00

the three factors, product life, annual sales volume and material cost per azam (6 marks), and

(c) discuss briefly the limitations of your calculations in (a) and (b) above, and indicate any additional information that would be helpful in arriving at a decision (9 marks).

Ignore taxation.

ICAEW Elements of Financial Decisions December 1979

14.9* A company is considering an investment in a

(ii) Explain, very briefly, what advantages, if any, you see in this method of risk analysis (if a sufficiently large number of calculations were carried out) as compared with sensitivity analysis.

ICMA P3 Adapted

14.10* The Biloxi Company is considering investing in a new plant which would enable it to increase its production of floss, a fertilizer product. If the plant is constructed its operation is expected to increase the net after tax cash flow of Biloxi by £178,500 per annum. There would be no pro-

duction after the plant's tenth year of life and the plant would have zero salvage value.

The cost of constructing the plant with all its support facilities would be £750,000.

The company is unsure whether to go ahead with the investment. A crucial factor in the decision is the risk associated with the project. In the past the company has not taken risk into account when evaluating an investment proposal, but this is a major project involving a significant capital outlay and the company wishes to be thorough in its analysis. The company seek your advice on the methods of allowing for risk in investment appraisal.

The company has already been given two conflicting pieces of advice. One suggestion is that a single discount rate, reflecting the average cost of capital of the company, should be used for all investment decisions within the company. With this approach, the risk, and uncertainty can be allowed for in the probability estimates of the cash flows resulting from the project.

The other suggestion involves estimating the risk adjusted discount rate appropriate to the particular project under consideration. This approach has been formalized in the capital asset pricing model which can be used to estimate an appropriate discount rate. According to this suggestion it is the risk adjusted rate, the cost of capital appropriate to each project, that should be used to discount the returns expected to result from the project.

You are given the following information:

(i) The after tax risk free rate of interest in the economy is 10%.
(ii) The expected rate of return on a market portfolio of investments is 15%.
(iii) The revenues and expenses associated with the sales and production of floss are expected to be highly dependent on the state of the economy and industry; if the economy grows in a year by 10%, the sales and costs of floss are expected to rise by 16%; if there is a 10% downturn in the economy, the cash flow of floss is expected to suffer by 16%.
(iv) The after tax weighted average cost of capital of Biloxi Ltd is estimated to be 16%.
(v) The probability distribution of the annual net cash flows arising from the production in the new plant and the sale of floss is:

Probability	Net cash flows
0.30	0–£149,999
0.50	£150,000–£249,999
0.20	£250,000–£300,000

Required:

(a) You are asked to offer specific advice to Biloxi Ltd on the appropriate discount rate to use in the appraisal of the investment in the floss plant. Illustrate your answer by using the data given in the question. (12 marks)

(b) Advise the company on alternative methods of allowing for risk in project appraisal. (8 marks)

(20 marks)
ACCA P3 Financial Management
December 1980

14.11 The XYZ Company Ltd is considering a major investment in a new productive process. The total cost of the investment has been estimated at £2,000,000 but if this were increased to £3,000,000, productive capacity could be substantially increased. Because of the nature of the process, once the basic plant has been established, to increase capacity at some future date is exceptionally costly. One of the problems facing management is that the demand for process output is very uncertain. However, the market research and finance departments have been able to produce the following first estimates:

Investment A (£3m)

Demand probability		Annual net cash flow £m
0.3	Years 1–4	1.0
	5–10	0.7
0.5	Years 1–4	0.8
	5–10	0.4
0.2	Years 1–10	0.1
Cost of capital		10%

Investment B (£2m)

Demand probability		Annual net cash flow £m
0.4	Years 1–4	0.6
	5–10	0.5
0.4	Years 1–4	0.6
	5–10	0.2
0.2	Years 1–10	0.2
Cost of capital		10%

You are required to prepare a statement which clearly indicates the financial implications of each of the projects and comment on the other matters which management should take into consideration, referring particularly to the question of risk, before reaching a final decision.

Ignore taxation.

ACCA P3 Financial Management
June 1976

14.12 The directors of Cooper Ltd propose to install a

central heating system in an office building owned by the company. As part of the company's long-range plan, the office building is due to be sold on 31 December 1983, and the directors believe that whichever system is installed will add some £100,000 to the resale value at that time.

Three systems — gas, oil and solid fuel — are regarded as feasible. The directors estimate that the costs of installing and running the three systems are as follows:

(1) Installation costs (payable on 1 January 1981):

	£
Gas	170,000
Oil	150,000
Solid fuel	140,000

(2) Annual fuel costs (payable at the end of each year):
Annual fuel costs will depend on the severity of the weather each year, and on the rate of increase in fuel prices. At the prices expected to exist during 1981, annual fuel costs will be:

	Severe weather £	Mild weather £
Gas	40,000	24,000
Oil	53,000	37,000
Solid fuel	45,000	36,000

The directors estimate that in each year there is a 70% chance of severe weather and a 30% chance of mild weather. The chance of particular weather in any one year is independent of the weather in other years.

Fuel prices during 1982 and 1983 are expected to increase at either 15% per annum (probability equal to 0.4) or 25% per annum (probability equal to 0.6). Whichever rate of price increase obtains in 1982 will be repeated in 1983.

(3) Maintenance costs (payable at the end of the year in which they are incurred):

	£
Gas	2,500 per annum
Oil	2,000 per annum
Solid fuel	10,000 in 1982

All maintenance costs are fixed by contract when the system is installed.

The directors of Cooper Ltd feel that the systems are equivalent for heating purposes. Cooper Ltd has a cost of capital of 20% per annum in money terms.

You are required to:
(a) prepare calculations showing which central heating system should be installed; assuming that the decision will be based on the expected present values of the costs of each system (12 marks),
(b) provide brief notes of any additional factors that may affect the decision (5 marks), and
(c) discuss the limitations of using expected values as a criterion for making investment decisions under uncertainty (8 marks).
Ignore taxation.

ICAEW Elements of Financial Decisions
December 1980

14.13 Idaho Ltd designs and manufactures toys. A typical toy has a commercial life of three years. Heavy initial advertising generally leads to relatively high sales during the first two years of a toy's commercial life but there is often a substantial decline in demand during the final year. The level of demand for a toy over its life depends on product acceptance. The marketing department of Idaho Ltd has just completed an analysis of the demand for the most recent 200 types of toy marketed by the company. The analysis indicates that of the 200 types of toy, 50 enjoyed an above average demand throughout their commercial lives, 120 an average demand and 30 a below average demand.

Idaho Ltd has recently developed a new toy, the oregon. Development costs amounted to £3,500 and have just been paid. The marketing department has made the following estimates of sales for the oregon:

	Sales revenue		
	Year 1 £	Year 2 £	Year 3 £
If demand is above average	24,000	50,000	16,000
If demand is average	14,000	34,000	8,000
If demand is below average	5,000	18,000	5,000

Variable costs will amount to 30% of sales revenue. Sales revenue will be received and variable costs will be paid on the last day of the year in which they arise.

If oregons are produced, a special machine will have to be purchased at the start of year 1 at a cost of £19,000, payable at the time of purchase. The machine will have a scrap value at the end of the product's life of £1,000, receivable one year after the last year in which production takes place.

If purchased, the machine will be installed in an unused part of one of Idaho Ltd's factories.

The company has been trying to let this unused factory space at a rent of £1,600 per annum. Although there now seems no chance of letting the space during year 1, there is a 60% chance of letting it for two years at the beginning of year 2 and a 50% chance of letting it for one year at the beginning of year 3 provided that it has not been let at the beginning of year 2. Any rental receipts will be received annually in advance.

Fixed costs, which include depreciation of the special machine on a straight line basis, are expected to amount to £7,000 per annum. These costs are all specific to the production of oregons and, with the exception of depreciation, will be paid on the last day of the year in which they arise.

Advertising expenses will be paid on the first day of each year and will amount to £3,000 at the start of year 1, £2,000 at the start of year 2 and £1,000 at the start of year 3.

Idaho Ltd has a cost of capital of 20% per annum.

You are required to:

(a) prepare calculations showing whether Idaho Ltd should produce oregons, assuming that the decision will be based on expected present values (13 marks),

(b) outline the limitations of expected present values as a criterion for making investment decisions under uncertainty (5 marks), and

(c) discuss the relative merits of other criteria which might be used for making investment decisions under uncertainty (7 marks).

Ignore taxation.

ICAEW Financial Management December 1981

14.14* The Government of the Republic of Vidal have decided to sell the rights to drill for oil on a tract of land in the Republic. They have offered the rights to Santamaria Ltd, an oil exploration company, for £1.5 million, payable one year before the start of the first year of drilling. The directors of Santamaria Ltd provide the following estimates relating to the relevant tract of land in Vidal:

Quantity of oil	Probability	Annual net revenue (excluding depreciation)	
		Strong demand	Weak demand
High	0.3	£8m	£2m
Low	0.3	£4m	£1m
Zero	0.4	0	0

The selling price of oil, and hence the annual net revenue, depends on whether the demand for oil is 'strong' or 'weak'. The directors estimate that there is a 40% probability that demand will be strong and a 60% probability that it will be weak.

Exploratory drilling will be undertaken immediately after the drilling rights are acquired, and will cost £0.5 million payable at the time the drilling rights are paid for. If the existence of oil is revealed by the exploratory drilling, it will be extracted for ten years and Santamaria Ltd will purchase special drilling and other equipment at a cost of £9 million, payable at the start of the first year of drilling. It will not be necessary to purchase the equipment if no oil is discovered. If the quantity of oil is 'high' the equipment will have no resale or scrap value after ten years; if it is 'low' the equipment will have a resale value of £2 million at the end of that period.

Before deciding whether to purchase the drilling rights, Santamaria Ltd could undertake a seismographical survey to obtain information about the quantity of oil. The survey would show for certain whether or not the land contained oil and, if it did, whether the quantity was 'high' or 'low'. If the survey is undertaken it will not be necessary to incur the cost of exploratory drilling.

Santamaria Ltd has a cost of capital of 20% per annum. Annual net revenues are receivable in cash on the last day of the year.

You are required to:

(a) calculate the expected net present value of purchasing the drilling rights, assuming that the seismographical survey is not undertaken (10 marks),

(b) calculate the maximum sum that Santamaria Ltd should be willing to spend on the seismographical survey, assuming that the decision would be based on a calculation of expected net present values and that the cost of the survey would be paid one year before the start of the first year of drilling (5 marks), and

(c) discuss the limitations of expected net present values as a criterion for making investment decisions under uncertainty (10 marks).

Ignore taxation.

ICAEW Elements of Financial Decisions July 1980

14.15 Miles PLC has the opportunity to produce a new product. Expected total sales volumes together with per unit sales prices and basic variable production costs of the new product are:

Year	Sales quantities (000)	Sales price £	Per unit Basic variable production costs (*Note 1*) £
1	20	10	5
2	30	10	6
3	50	14	6
4	50	14	6

Note 1. Basic variable production costs exclude operating costs.

There are two alternative machines which Miles could purchase in order to manufacture the new product: machine A and machine B. Some details of each machine are as follows:

	Timing of cash flows Year	Machine A £000	Machine B £000
Purchase price of machine	0	300	400
Salvage value of machine	4	60	40
Cost of machine housing	0	50	30
Salvage value of machine housing	—	Nil	Nil
Fixed annual operating costs (*Note 2*)	1–4	40	30

Note 2. 'Annual operating costs' relate only to fixed cash expenses and therefore exclude depreciation of the machine and its housing. Miles depreciates on a straight line basis.

Machine A will require the installation of additional air conditioning and an existing air conditioning unit would be used for this purpose at an annual operating cash cost of £10,000. This air conditioning unit has a book value of £60,000 and if not utilized will be sold now for £25,000. Installation costs will amount to £15,000 and the salvage value of the unit at year 4 will be £10,000. The unit has previously been subject to 100% first year allowances.

Machine B utilizes some advanced technology and uses fewer raw materials, thereby reducing basic variable production costs by £1 per unit. A single routine overhaul of machine B will take place at the end of year 2 at a cost of £80,000. At this overhaul it will become apparent whether further repairs or modifications are needed. The costs of each possible level of repair or modification, together with their associated probabilities, are:

Level of further repair or modification	Cost, at year 2, of further repair or modification £000	Probability
Nil	Nil	0.5
Minor	50	0.3
Major	140	0.2

The 'major' level of repair and modification will entail reverting to traditional technology for the remainder of the product's life with a consequent loss of the saving on future variable production costs as well as a reduction of the year 4 salvage value to only £20,000. The 'minor' level of repair or modification will not entail reverting to traditional technology and will not alter the salvage value of machine B. None of the repairs will alter other operating costs. It is expected that no further overhaul or repairs will be required after year 2.

For each machine all cash operating expenses will be paid for at the end of the year to which they relate. However, sales revenues will be received as cash flows in the following manner:

70% of each year's sales received at the end of that year,

30% of each year's sales received one year later.

The corporation tax rate is 50% and there is a one year tax delay. All capital expenditure and installation costs, except those relating to machine housing, are eligible for 100% first year allowances and all salvage values are subject to tax. Expenditure on the type of machine housing to be used is not eligible for any tax relief. All other costs are tax deductible expenses. Miles can take full advantage of any tax allowances at the earliest opportunity.

An appropriate after tax discount rate is 14% per annum.

Required:

(a) Ascertain the expected net present value of producing the new product by each of the two alternative methods.

On the basis of expected net present value, advise Miles on which, if any, of the two alternative machines should be purchased. (17 marks)

(b) By paying a single lump sum now, Miles could obtain the services of a credit consultant who would ensure that all sales revenues were received in cash in the year of sale. Ascertain the maximum amount it would be worth paying to obtain the services of the credit consultant if such a payment were not a tax deductible expense. (3 marks)

(c) The managing director, who has recently

read about the capital asset pricing model, suggests that as machine B appears riskier than machine A the discount rate used in its appraisal should be higher than that used for the appraisal of machine A.

Comment on the managing director's suggestion. (5 marks)

(25 marks)

ACCA Level 3 Financial Management December 1982

14.16 The directors of Publio PLC, a UK company, are considering setting up a major project in Vitellia, a country whose national currency is the sesto. The project will begin on 1 January 1983 and will require the purchase of plant and equipment costing 65 million sestos. The plant is expected to have a five year life and no residual value. The purchase of the plant will be financed by a 5 year loan from the National Bank of Vitellia, at an annual rate of interest of 12%, payable at the end of each year. In order to provide sufficient working capital for the project, Publio PLC will provide funds of 40 million sestos on 1 January 1983.

The annual operating cash flows from the project, before interest and tax, are expected to be 25 million sestos in the first year, increasing at an annual compound rate of 10% until the fifth year, at the end of which production will cease. Corporation tax in Vitellia is charged at 50% on the annual operating cash flows less interest charges and straight line depreciation. In order to encourage foreign investment, the Vitellian tax authorities will allow a notional interest of 15% per annum, for each of the five years, on the 40 million sestos invested by Publio PLC in the project. Any taxable losses can be carried forward and set off against future taxable profits. Tax is payable twelve months after the end of each accounting period. It is expected that any additional monies received as part of the closing down of the project at the end of the fifth year will be used to cover closing down expenses. At the end of each year all cash surpluses or deficits are transferred to the UK. The tax advisors of Publio PLC believe that no additional UK corporation tax will be payable on funds remitted to the UK.

As a result of the improving political climate in Vitellia, the rate of exchange between the sesto and the pound is expected to move in the sesto's favour, and the following rates of exchange have been forecast (sestos to the pound):

1 January 1983	40
1 January 1984	38
1 January 1985	36
1 January 1986	35
1 January 1987 and subsequently	34

Publio PLC has a cost of capital of 20% for this type of project.

You are required to:

(a) calculate whether the proposed project is worthwhile on the basis of the above data (13 marks),

(b) discuss the problems, other than those related to taxation, involved in making investments in foreign countries (7 marks), and

(c) discuss how investments in foreign countries should be financed (5 marks).

(25 marks)

ICAEW Financial Management July 1982

Part IV

Information for planning and control

In Part III the objective was to consider the accounting information which should be provided to help managers to make good decisions. The objective in this section is to consider the implementation of decisions through the planning and control process. *Planning* involves systematically looking at the future, so that decisions can be made today which will bring the company its desired results. *Control* can be defined as the process of measuring and correcting actual performance to ensure that plans for implementing the chosen course of action are carried out.

Part IV contains five chapters. Chapter 15 — The Budgeting Process — considers the role of budgeting within the planning process and the relationship between the long-range plan and the budgeting process. The budgeting process in profit-oriented organizations is compared with that in non-profit organizations.

Chapters 16–19 are concerned with the control process. Chapter 16 — Control in the Organization — examines the role of management accounting in helping managers to control the activities for which they are responsible. In particular, attention is paid to the process of responsibility accounting and the role of accounting performance measures in the evaluation of managerial performance. Chapters 17 and 18 — Standard Costing Variance Analysis — describes the major features of a standard costing system: a system that enables the differences between planned and actual outcomes to be analysed in detail. Chapter 17 describes the operation of a standard costing system and explains the procedure for calculating variances. Chapter 18 examines the difficulties which arise from using standard costing and looks at some suggestions for overcoming them. You can omit this chapter if a detailed study of this topic is not required.

One of the major aims of producing accounting reports is to influence human behaviour. Chapter 19 — Behavioural Aspects of Accounting Control Systems — emphasizes that the contribution of management accounting to the planning and control process is of a behavioural nature and examines the important behavioural aspects that should be considered in the design and operation of budgetary control and standard costing systems.

15 The budgeting process

In the previous six chapters we have considered how management accounting can assist managers in making decisions. Throughout these chapters we have concentrated on individual decisions in isolation, to emphasize the important principles of decision analysis. However, the actions which follow managerial decisions normally involve several aspects of the business, such as the marketing, production, purchasing and finance functions, and it is important that management should coordinate these various interrelated aspects of decision-making. If they fail to do this, there is a danger that managers may each make decisions which they believe are in the best interests of the organization when, in fact, taken together they are not; for example, the marketing department may introduce a promotional campaign which is designed to increase sales demand to a level beyond that which the production department can handle. The various activities within a company should be coordinated by the preparation of plans of actions for future periods. These detailed plans are usually referred to as *budgets*.

Our objective in this chapter is to focus on the planning process within a business organization and to consider the role of budgeting within this process. What do we mean by planning? Ackoff (1970) states that 'Planning is the design of a desired future and of effective ways of bringing it about'. A recent development has been the emergence of *long-range planning*, alternatively known as *strategic* or *corporate* planning. How is long-range planning distinguished from other forms of planning? Sizer (1979) states that long-range planning may be defined as a systematic and formalized process for purposely directing and controlling future operations towards desired objectives for periods extending beyond one year. *Short-term planning* or *budgeting*, on the other hand, must accept the environment of today, and the physical, human and financial resources at present available to the firm. These are to a considerable extent determined by the quality of the firms' long-range planning efforts.

To help us to understand the budgetary process we will look first of all at how it fits into the overall framework for planning, decision-making and control which was introduced in Fig. 1.2 in Chapter 1. An adapted version of this model (Fig. 15.1) is used to illustrate the role of long-term and short-term planning within the overall process.

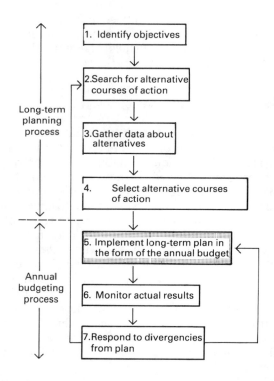

Fig. 15.1 Role of long-term and short-term planning within the planning, decision-making and control process

Stages in the planning process

Identifying objectives

Long-range planning requires the specification of objectives towards which future operations should be directed. In Chapter 1 we assumed that the primary objective of a business organization was the maximization of the present value of future cash flows. For planning purposes it is necessary that a company's objectives should specifically indicate the direction in which the resources of the organization should be pointed. Sizer (1979) suggests that objectives should answer a number of fundamental questions about the company's future growth and development. For example:

(1) What is the economic mission of the company?
(2) What kind of business should the company be in?
(3) What goods and services should be sold?
(4) What markets should be served?
(5) What share of the market is desired?
(6) What are the profit objectives?
(7) What rate of growth is required in sales, profits, assets and values of equity shareholders' investment?

Search for possible courses of action

The next stage is to search systematically and creatively for a range of possible courses of action (or strategies) which might enable the company's objectives to be achieved. If the management of a company concentrates entirely on its present product range and markets, and the company's products are allowed to enter the decline stages of their life-cycles, then the company may not be able to survive in the future. It is therefore essential that management should identify potential opportunities and threats in its current environment, and take specific steps immediately to ensure that the organization will not be taken by surprise by any developments which occur gradually in the future. In particular, the company should consider one or more of the following courses of action:

(1) developing *new* markets for existing products,
(2) developing *new* products for sale in the existing markets,

(3) developing *new* products for *new* markets.

Before selecting viable courses of action (that is, new areas of activity), management should undertake an analysis of its company's strengths and weaknesses so that it can determine what marketing, manufacturing, technical and financial know-how the company can contribute to alternative areas of activity. In particular, management must decide what resources and skills are required for each alternative new activity and which ones the company currently possesses. In addition, management should assess the capabilities of competitors in terms of managerial competence, products, access to markets and organizational and physical facilities. By comparing its own capabilities with those of its competitors, it will be possible to determine the areas where the firm is outstanding or deficient.

A creative search of new areas of activity should then be undertaken and management should try to identify the potential opportunities in the environment which will enable the company to exploit its distinctive strengths.

Gathering data about alternatives and measuring pay-offs

When the potential areas of activity have been identified, management should assess the potential growth rate of the activities, the ability of the company to establish adequate market shares, the stability of each activity in relation to possible states of nature, and the net present values. Management should choose those areas of activity which have the greatest potential for achieving the company's objectives. For a detailed discussion of the search for possible courses of action and gathering data about alternatives, see Ansoff (1968).

Select course of action

When management has selected the areas of activity which have the greatest potential for achieving the company's objectives, long-term plans should be created to implement the activities. In particular, plans for developing new products, markets and production facilities should be established. These plans must be coordinated and translated into financial terms by projecting the financial impact of current and future programmes for several years. The resulting state-

ment is known as a *long-range financial plan*. This plan shows the long-range profit, the cash flow and the balance sheet forecasts for several future years. The plan must be financed and appropriate short-, medium- and long-term finance will have to be raised before it can be implemented. For a discussion of various sources of finance and factors to be considered in raising finance see Samuels and Wilkes (1980).

The acceptance of a long-range plan does not imply that individual capital expenditure projects have been authorized. They will still be subject to the approval procedures which were outlined in the previous chapter, but the submission of capital investment proposals will normally originate from the long-term planning process. Long-term planning is a continuous process and management should constantly monitor the environment, and review and amend the existing and proposed activities whenever this is necessary.

Implementation of long-term plans

Budgeting is concerned with the implementation of the approved programme within the long-range plan and the capital budget. Programmes represent various activities such as developing new products, developing existing or new markets, and developing new distribution facilities. The budget translates the long-range plans and the capital budget into an *annual operating plan*. The long-range plan will include any revenue expenditure which will be incurred, such as the appointment of additional staff to develop new markets, but any capital expenditure, such as additional plant and machinery for manufacturing the new product, will require approval by the capital expenditure committee before it can be included in the capital budget.

The relationship between long-term planning and budgeting is illustrated in Fig. 15.2. Programmes which will also include the appropriate amount of capital expenditure which is contained in the capital expenditure budget are represented by the horizontal bars, and budgets are represented by the vertical dashed lines. You will see that the budget for year 1 includes elements of programmes 1, 2 and 3; the budget for year 2 includes elements of programmes 1, 2, 3 and 4, and so on.

Normally, when the annual budget is prepared, most of the decisions which affect the budget year will already have been made. For example, productive capacity cannot be increased significantly by decisions made in the current budget period. The only way in which plant can be expanded in the current budget period is as a consequence of decisions which were taken prior

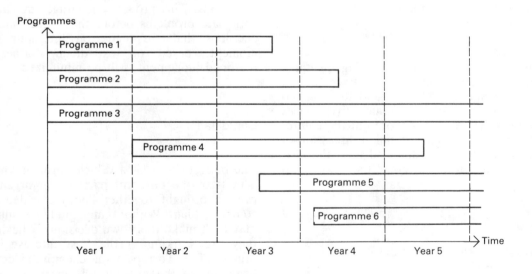

Fig. 15.2 The relationship between programming and budgeting

to the start of the budget period. Alternatively, when a new product is introduced, a considerable amount of time will have been spent prior to the budget period in developing and test marketing the product. The budget is not something which originates 'from nothing' each year; it is developed within the context of the ongoing business and is ruled by previous decisions which have been taken within the long-term planning process.

The budgeting process is not, however, one where the programmes for individual years, included in the long-term plan, are merely added together. When the programmes are initially approved for inclusion in the long-term plan they are based on uncertain estimates which are projected for several years. These programmes must be reviewed and revised in the light of more recent information. This review and revision process frequently takes place as part of the annual budgeting process and it may result in important decisions being taken on possible programme adjustments within the current period. The budgeting process cannot therefore be viewed as being purely concerned with the current year; it must be considered as an integrated part of the long-term planning process. It is influenced by decisions which have been taken in the past, and it has implications for programmes which will continue in future periods.

Monitor actual outcomes and respond to divergencies from plan

The final stages in the decision-making, planning and control process which were outlined in Fig. 15.1 are to compare the actual and the planned outcomes, and to respond to any divergencies from the plan. These stages represent the *control* process of budgeting, but a detailed discussion of budgetary control will be deferred until the next chapter. Let us now consider the short-term budgeting process in more detail.

Why do we produce budgets?

The reasons for producing budgets are as follows:

(1) to aid the *planning* of annual operations;
(2) to *coordinate* the activities of the various parts of the organization and to ensure that the parts are in harmony with each other;
(3) to *communicate* plans to the various responsibility centre managers;
(4) to *motivate* managers to strive to achieve the organizational goals;
(5) to *control* activities;
(6) to *evaluate* the performance of managers.

Let us now examine each of these six factors.

Planning

The major planning decisions will already have been made as part of the long-term planning process. However, the annual budgeting process leads to the refinement of those plans as managers must produce detailed plans for the implementation of the long-range plan. Without the annual budgeting process the pressures of day-to-day operating problems may tempt managers not to plan for future operations. The budgeting process ensures that managers do plan for future operations, and that they consider how conditions in the next year might change and what steps they should take now to respond to these changed conditions. This process encourages managers to anticipate problems before they arise, and hasty decisions that are made on the spur of the moment, based on expediency rather than reasoned judgement, will be minimized.

Coordination

The budget serves as a vehicle through which the actions of the different parts of an organization can be brought together and reconciled into a common plan. Without any guidance managers may each make their own decisions believing that they are working in the best interests of the organization. To repeat the example given at the beginning of this chapter, the marketing department may introduce a promotional campaign which is designed to increase sales demand to a

level beyond that which the production departments can handle. In some cases individual managerial interests may be in conflict: for example, the purchasing manager may prefer to place large orders so as to obtain large discounts; the production manager will be concerned with avoiding high stock levels; and the accountant will be concerned with the impact of the decision on the cash resources of the business. It is the aim of budgeting to reconcile these differences for the good of the organization as a whole, rather than for the benefit of any individual area. Budgeting therefore compels managers to examine the relationship between their own operations and those of other departments and, in the process, to identify and resolve conflicts.

It is most unlikely that the first draft of the budget will produce a perfect meshing of all the organizational activities. For example, it may specify the acquisition of raw materials in amounts or at times which make the smooth flow of production impossible. Such differences must be corrected before the final budget is agreed. A sound budgeting system helps to coordinate the separate organizational activities and ensures that all parts of the organization are in harmony with each other.

Communication

If an organization is to function effectively, there must be definite lines of communication so that all the parts will be kept fully informed of the plans and the policies, and constraints, to which the organization is expected to conform. Everyone in the organization should have a clear understanding of the part which they are expected to play in achieving the annual budget. This process will ensure that the appropriate individuals are made accountable for implementing the budget. Through the budget, top management communicates its expectations to lower-level management so that all members of the organization may understand these expectations and can coordinate their activities to attain them. It is not just the budget itself which facilitates communication; much vital information is communicated in the actual act of preparing it.

Motivation

The budget can be a useful device for influencing managerial behaviour and motivating managers to perform in line with the organizational objectives. A budget provides a standard which, under certain circumstances, a manager may be motivated to strive to achieve. However, budgets can also encourage inefficiency and conflict between managers. If individuals have actively participated in preparing the budget, and it is used as a tool to assist managers in managing their departments, it can act as a strong motivational device by providing a challenge. Alternatively, if the budget is dictated from above, and imposes a threat rather than a challenge, it may be resisted and do more harm than good. We shall discuss the dysfunctional motivational consequence of budgets in Chapter 19.

Control

A budget assists managers in managing and controlling the activities for which they are responsible. By comparing the actual results with the budgeted amounts for different categories of expenses managers can ascertain which costs do not conform to the original plan and thus require their attention. This process enables management to operate a system of *management by exception* which means that a manager's attention and effort can be concentrated on significant deviations from the expected results. By investigating the reasons for the deviations managers may be able to identify inefficiencies such as the purchase of inferior quality materials. When the reasons for the inefficiencies have been found, appropriate control action should be taken to remedy the situation.

Performance evaluation

A manager's performance is often evaluated by measuring his success in meeting the budgets. In some companies bonuses are awarded which are based on an employee's ability to achieve the targets specified in the periodic budgets, or promotion may be partly dependent upon a manager's budget record. In addition, the manager himself may wish to evaluate his own performance. The budget thus provides a useful means of informing managers of how well they are performing in meeting targets which they have previously helped to set. The use of budgets as a method of performance evaluation also influences

human behaviour and for this reason we shall consider the behavioural aspects of performance evaluation in Chapter 19.

The budget period

A detailed budget for each responsibility centre is normally prepared for one year. The annual budget may be divided into either twelve monthly or thirteen four-weekly periods. Alternatively, the annual budget may be broken down by months for the first three months, and by quarters for the remaining nine months. The quarterly budgets are then developed on a monthly basis as the year proceeds. For example, during the first quarter the monthly budgets for the second quarter will be prepared, and during the second quarter the monthly budgets for the third quarter will be prepared. The quarterly budgets may also be reviewed as the year unfolds. For example, during the first quarter the budget for the next three quarters may be changed as new information becomes available. During the second quarter the budget for the next two quarters may be revised and a new budget for the fifth quarter prepared. This process is known as *continuous* or *rolling budgeting* and ensures that a twelve-month budget is always available. For detailed planning and control, monthly or four-weekly budgets are preferable.

Administration of the annual budget

It is important that suitable administration procedures are introduced to ensure that the budget process works effectively. In practice, the procedures should be tailor-made to the requirements of the organization, but as a general rule a firm should ensure that procedures are established for approving the budgets and that the appropriate staff support is available for assisting managers in preparing their budgets.

The budget committee

The budget committee should consist of high level executives who represent the major segments of the business. Its major task is to ensure that budgets are realistically established and that they are coordinated satisfactorily. The normal procedure is for the functional heads to present their budget to the committee for approval. If the budget does not reflect a reasonable level of performance, it will not be approved and the functional head will be required to adjust the budget and resubmit it for approval. It is important that the person whose performance is being measured should agree that the revised budget can be achieved; otherwise, if it is considered to be impossible to achieve it will not act as a motivational device. If budget revisions are made the budgetees should at least feel that they were given a fair hearing by the committee. We shall discuss budget negotiation in more detail later in this chapter.

The budget committee should appoint a budget officer who will normally be the accountant. The role of the budget officer is to coordinate the individual budgets into a budget for the whole organization so that the budget committee and the budgetee can see the impact of an individual budget on the organization as a whole.

Accounting staff

The accounting staff will normally assist managers in the preparation of their budgets; they will, for example, circulate and advise on the instructions about budget preparation, provide past information which may be useful for preparing the present budget, and ensure that managers submit their budgets on time. The accounting staff do not determine the content of the various budgets but they do provide a valuable advisory and clerical service for the line managers.

Budget manual

A budget manual should be prepared by the accountant. The manual will describe the objectives and procedures involved in the budgeting process and it will provide a useful reference source for managers responsible for budget preparation. In addition, the manual may include a timetable which specifies the order in which the budgets should be prepared and the dates when they should be presented to the budget committee. The manual should be circulated to all individuals who are responsible for preparing budgets.

Stages in the budgeting process

The important stages are as follows:

(1) Communicating details of budget policy and guidelines to those people responsible for the preparation of budgets.
(2) Determining the factor which restricts output.
(3) Preparation of the sales budget.
(4) Initial preparation of various budgets.
(5) Negotiation of budgets with superiors.
(6) Coordination and review of budgets.
(7) Final acceptance of budgets.
(8) Ongoing review of budgets.

Let us now consider each of these stages in more detail.

Communicating details of the budget policy

Earlier in this chapter we asserted that many decisions affecting the budget year will have been taken previously as part of the long-term planning process. The long-range plan is therefore the starting point for the preparation of the annual budget. Thus, top management must communicate the policy effects of the long-term plan to those who are responsible for preparing the current year's budgets. Policy effects might include planned changes in sales mix, or the expansion of sales territories. In addition, other important guidelines which are to govern the preparation of the budget should be specified; for example, the allowances which are to be made for price and wage increases, and the expected changes in productivity. Also, any expected changes in industry demand and output should be communicated by top management to the managers responsible for budget preparation. It is essential that all managers are made aware of the policy of top management for implementing the long-term plan in the current year's budget so that common guidelines can be established. The process also indicates to the managers who are responsible for preparing the budgets how they should respond to any expected environmental changes.

Determining the factor which restricts performance

In every organization there is some factor which restricts performance for a given period. In the majority of organizations the factor which restricts performance is sales demand. However, it is possible for production capacity to restrict performance when sales demand is in excess of available capacity. Prior to the preparation of the budgets it is necessary for top management to determine the factor which restricts performance as this factor determines the point at which the annual budgeting process should begin.

Preparation of the sales budget

The volume of sales and the sales mix determine the level of a company's operations, when sales demand is the factor which restricts output. For this reason the sales budget is the most important plan in the annual budgeting process. This budget is also the most difficult plan to produce because total sales revenue depends on the actions of customers. In addition, sales demand may be influenced by the state of the economy or the actions of competitors.

A number of methods may be used to estimate sales demand. The simplest approach is to produce estimates which are based on the opinions of executives and sale personnel. For example, sales personnel may be asked to estimate sales of each product to their customers, or regional sales managers may estimate the total sales for each of their regions. An alternative approach is to estimate sales demand by using statistical techniques which incorporate general business and market conditions and past growth in sales. Market research may be necessary if it is intended to develop new products or new markets. A discussion of different sales forecasting procedures is beyond the scope of this book, but for a discussion of the topic see Lancaster and Lomas (1985).

Initial preparation of budgets

The managers who are responsible for meeting the budgeted perforamnce should prepare the budget for those areas for which they are responsible. The preparation of the budget should be a 'bottom-up' process. This means that the budget should originate at the lowest levels of management and be refined and coordinated at higher levels. This approach will enable managers to participate in the preparation of their budgets and

increase the probability that they will accept the budget and strive to achieve the budget targets.

There is no single way in which the appropriate quantity for a particular budget item is determined. Past data may be used as the starting point for producing the budgets, but this does not mean that budgeting is based on the assumption that what has happened in the past will occur in the future. Changes in future conditions must be taken into account, but past information may provide useful guidance for the future. In addition, managers may look to the guidelines provided by top management for determining the content of their budgets. For example, the guidelines may provide specific instructions as to the permitted changes which can be made in the prices of purchases of materials and services. For production activities standard costs may be used as the basis for costing activity volumes which are planned in the budget.

Negotiation of budgets

To implement a participative approach to budgeting, the budget should be originated at the lowest level of management. The managers at this level should submit their budget to their superiors for approval. The superior should then incorporate this budget with other budgets for which he is responsible and then submit this budget for approval to his superior. The manager who is the superior then becomes the budgetee at the next higher level. The process is illustrated in Fig. 15.3.

The lower level managers are represented by boxes 1–8. Managers 1 and 2 will prepare their budgets in accordance with the budget policy and the guidelines laid down by top management. The managers will submit their budget to their supervisor who is in charge of the whole department (department A). Once these budgets have been agreed by the manager of department A they will be combined by the departmental manager who will then present this budget to his superior (manager of Plant 1) for approval. The manager of plant 1 is also responsible for department B and will combine the agreed budgets for departments A and B before presenting the combined budget to his supervisor (the production manager). The production manager will merge the budgets for plants 1 and 2 and this final budget will represent the production budget which will be presented to the budget committee for approval.

At each of these stages the budgets will be negotiated between the budgetees and their superiors, and eventually they will be agreed by both

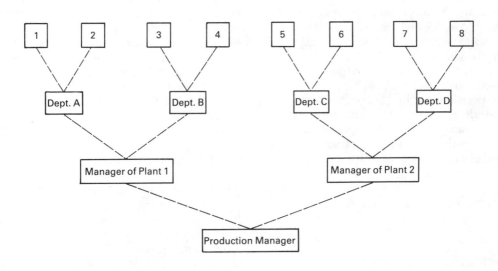

Fig. 15.3 An illustration of budgets moving up the organization hierarchy

parties. It is important that the budgetees should participate in arriving at the final budget and that the superior does not revise the budget without giving full consideration to the subordinates' arguments for including any of the budgeted items. Otherwise, real participation will not be taking place and it is unlikely that the subordinate will be motivated to achieve a budget which he did not accept. It is also necessary to be watchful that budgetees do not deliberately attempt to obtain approval for easily attainable budgets, or attempt to deliberately understate budgets in the hope that the budget which is finally agreed will represent an easily attainable target. For an illustration of budget biasing see Schiff and Lewin (1970). It is equally unsatisfactory for a superior to impose difficult targets in the hope that an authoritarian approach will produce the desired results. The desired results may be achieved in the short-term but only at the cost of a loss of morale and increased labour turnover in the future. For a discussion of how hierarchical pressure to cut costs and raise productivity can have negative effects on organizational performance see Likert and Seashore (1968).

The negotiation process is of vital importance in the budgeting process and can determine whether the budget becomes a really effective management tool or just a clerical device. If managers are successful in establishing a position of trust and confidence with their subordinates, the negotiation process will produce a meaningful improvement in the budgetary process.

Coordination and review of budgets

As the individual budgets move up the organizational hierarchy in the negotiation process they must be examined in relation to each other. This examination may indicate that some budgets are out of balance with other budgets and need modifying so that they will be compatible with other conditions, constraints and plans which are beyond a manager's knowledge or control. For example, a plant manager may include equipment replacement in his budget when funds are simply not available. The accountant must identify such inconsistencies and bring them to the attention of the appropriate manager. Any changes in the budgets should be made by the responsible managers and this may require that the budgets be

recycled from the bottom to the top for a second or even a third time until all the budgets are coordinated and are acceptable to all the parties involved. During the coordination process a budgeted profit and loss account, a balance sheet and a cash flow statement should be prepared to ensure that all the parts combine to produce an acceptable whole. Otherwise, further adjustments and budget recycling will be necessary until the budgeted profit and loss account, the balance sheet and the cash flow statement prove to be acceptable.

Final acceptance of the budgets

When all the budgets are in harmony with each other they are summarized into a master budget which consists of a budgeted profit and loss account, a balance sheet and a cash flow statement. After the master budget has been approved the budgets are then passed down through the organization to the appropriate responsibility centres. The approval of the master budget is the authority for the manager of each responsibility centre to carry out the plans contained in each budget.

Budget review

The budget process should not stop when the budgets have been agreed. Periodically the actual results should be compared with the budgeted results. These comparisons should be made on a monthly basis and a report sent to the appropriate budgetees, before the middle of the following month, so that it has the maximum motivational impact. This will enable management to identify the items which are not proceeding according to plan and to investigate the reasons for the differences. If these differences are within the control of management corrective action can be taken to avoid similar inefficiencies occurring again in the future. However, the differences may be due to the fact that the budget was unrealistic to begin with, or that the actual conditions during the budget year were different from those which were anticipated; the budget for the remainder of the year would then be invalid.

During the budget year the budget committee should periodically evaluate the actual performance and reappraise the company's future plans. If there are any changes in the actual conditions from those which were originally expected this will normally mean that the budget plans should be adjusted. This revised budget then represents a revised statement of formal operating plans for the remaining portion of the budget period. The important point to note is that the budgetary process does not end for the current year once the budget period has begun; budgeting should be seen as a continuous and dynamic process.

A detailed illustration

Let us now look at an illustration of the procedure for constructing budgets in a manufacturing company, using the information contained in Example 15.1. Note that the level of detail which is included here is much less than that which would be presented in practice. A truly realistic illustration would fill many pages, with detailed budgets being analysed in various ways. We shall consider an annual budget, whereas a realistic illustration would analyse the annual budget into twelve monthly periods. Monthly analysis would considerably increase the size of the illustration but would not give any further insight into the basic concepts or procedures. In addition, we shall assume in this example that the budgets are prepared for only two responsibility centres (that is, department 1 and department 2). In practice, many responsibility centres are likely to exist.

EXAMPLE 15.1

The Enterprise Company manufactures two products known as alpha and sigma. Alpha is produced in department 1 and sigma is produced in department 2. The following information is available for 19X1.

Standard material and labour costs:

	£
Material X	1.80 per unit
Material Y	4.00 per unit
Direct labour	3.00 per hour

Overhead is recovered on a direct labour hour basis.

The standard material and labour usage for each product is as follows:

	Model alpha	Model sigma
Material X	10 units	8 units
Material Y	5 units	9 units
Direct labour	10 hours	15 hours

The balance sheet for the previous year ending 19X0 was as follows:

Fixed assets	£	£	£
Land		42,500	
Buildings and equipment	323,000		
Less depreciation	63,750	259,250	301,750
Current assets			
Stocks, finished goods	24,769		
raw materials	47,300		
Debtors	72,250		
Cash	8,500		
	152,819		
Less current liabilities			
Creditors	62,200		90,619
Net assets			392,369
Represented by shareholders' interest 300,000 ordinary shares of			
£1 each		300,000	
Reserves		92,369	392,369

Other relevant data is as follows for the year 19X1.

	Finished product	
	Model alpha	Model sigma
Forecast sales in units	8,500	1,600
Selling price per unit	£100	£140
Ending inventory required	1,870	90
Beginning inventory is	170	85

	Direct material	
	Material X	Material Y
Beginning inventory (units)	8,500	8,000
Ending inventory required	10,200	1,700

The budgeted variable overhead rates per direct labour hour are as follows:

	Department 1 £	Department 2 £
Indirect materials	0.30	0.20
Indirect labour	0.30	0.30
Power (variable portion)	0.15	0.10
Maintenance (variable portion)	0.05	0.10

The budgeted fixed overheads are:

Depreciation	25,000	20,000
supervision	25,000	10,000
Power (fixed portion)	10,000	500
Maintenance (fixed portion)	11,400	799

The estimated non-manufacturing overheads are as follows:

	£
Stationery etc. — Administration	1,000
Salaries — Sales	18,500
Office	7,000
Commissions	15,000
Car expenses (sales)	5,500
Advertising	20,000
Miscellaneous (office)	2,000
	69,000

Budgeted cash flows are:

	Quarter 1 £	Quarter 2 £	Quarter 3 £	Quarter 4 £
Receipts from customers	250,000	300,000	280,000	246,250
Payments				
Materials	100,000	120,000	110,000	136,996
Payments for wages	100,000	110,000	120,000	161,547
Other costs and expenses	30,000	25,000	18,004	3,409

You are required to prepare a master budget for the year 19X1 and the following budgets:

1. Sales budget
2. Production budget
3. Direct materials usage budget
4. Direct materials purchase budget
5. Direct labour budget
6. Factory overhead budget
7. Selling and administration budget
8. Cash budget.

the basic data for constructing budgets for production costs, and for selling, distribution and administrative expenses. The sales budget is therefore the foundation of all other budgets as all expenditure is ultimately dependent on the volume of sales. If the sales budget is not accurate, the other budget estimates will be unreliable. We will assume that the Enterprise company has completed a marketing analysis and that the following annual sales budget is based on the results.

Schedule 1 — Sales budget for year ending 19X1

Product	Units sold	Selling price £	Total revenue £
Alpha	8,500	100	850,000
Sigma	1,600	140	224,000
			1,074,000

Schedule 1 represents the *total* sales budget for the year. In practice, the *total* sales budget will be supported by detailed *subsidiary* sales budgets where sales are analysed by areas of responsibility, such as sales territories, and into monthly periods. The detailed *subsidiary* sales budget could be set out as follows:

Sales budget

The sales budget shows the quantities of each product which the company plans to sell and the intended selling price. It provides the predictions of total revenue from which cash receipts from customers will be estimated and it also supplies

		North		South		East		West		Total	
		Units	Value	Units	Value	Units	Value	Units	Value	Units	Value
Month 1	Alpha										
	Sigma										
	Total		———		———		———		———		———
			———		———		———		———		———
Month 2											
Month 3											
Month 4											
Month 5											
Month 6											
Month 7											
Month 8											
Month 9											
Month 10											
Month 11											
Month 12											
Total months 1–12											
	Alpha	3,000	£300,000	2,500	£250,000	1,000	£100,000	2,000	£200,000	8,500	£850,000
	Sigma	500	£70,000	600	£84,000	200	£28,000	300	£42,000	1,600	£224,000
			£370,000		£334,000		£128,000		£242,000		£1,074,000

Note that the total budgeted sales of £1,074,000 is analysed by each sales territory for each month of the budget period. The detailed analysis assumes that sales are divided among the four sales territories as follows:

	Alpha	Sigma
North	3,000 units	500 units
South	2,500 units	600 units
East	1,000 units	200 units
West	2,000 units	300 units
	8,500 units	1,600 units

Production budget and budgeted stock levels

When the sales budget has been completed, the next stage is to prepare the production budget. This budget is expressed in *quantities only* and is the responsibility of the production manager. The objective is to ensure that production is sufficient to meet sales demand and that economic stock levels are maintained. The production budget (schedule 2) for the year will be as follows:

Schedule 2 — Annual production budget

	Department 1 (alpha)	Department 2 (sigma)
Units to be sold	8,500	1,600
Planned closing stock	1,870	90
Total units required for sales and stocks	10,370	1,690
Less planned opening stocks	170	85
Units to be produced	10,200	1,605

The total production for each department should also be analysed on a monthly basis.

Direct materials usage budget

The supervisors of departments 1 and 2 will prepare estimates of the materials which are required to meet the production budget. The materials usage budget (Schedule 3) for the year will be as follows:

Schedule 3 — Annual direct material usage budget

	Department 1			Department 2			Total			
	Units	Unit price £	Total £	Units	Unit price £	Total £	Total units	Unit price £		£
Material X	102,000(1)	1.80	183,600	12,840(3)	1.80	23,112	114,840	1.80		206,712
Material Y	51,000(2)	4.00	204,000	14,445(4)	4.00	57,780	65,445	4.00		261,780
			387,600			80,892				468,492

Notes
(1) 10,200 units production at 10 units per unit of production.
(2) 10,200 units production at 5 units per unit of production.
(3) 1,605 units production at 8 units per unit of production.
(4) 1,605 units production at 9 units per unit of production.

Direct materials purchase budget

The direct materials purchase budget is the responsibility of the purchasing manager as it will be he who is responsible for obtaining the planned quantities of raw materials to meet the production requirements. The objective is to purchase these materials at the right time at the planned purchase price. In addition, it is necessary to take into account the planned raw material stock levels. The annual materials purchase budget for the year will be as follows:

Schedule 4 — Direct materials purchase budget

	Material X units	Material Y units
Quantity necessary to meet production requirements as per material usage budget	114,840	65,445
Planned closing stock	10,200	1,700
	125,040	67,145
Less Planned opening stock	8,500	8,000
Total units to be purchased	116,540	59,145
Planned unit purchase price	£1.80	£4
	£209,772	£236,580

Note that this budget is a summary budget for the year but for detailed planning and control it will be necessary to analyse the annual budget on a monthly basis.

Direct labour budget

The direct labour budget is the responsibility of the respective managers of departments 1 and 2. They will prepare estimates of the departments' labour hours which will be required to meet the planned production. Where different grades of labour exist these should be specified separately in the budget. The budget rate per hour should be determined by the industrial relations department. The direct labour budget will be as follows:

Schedule 5 — Annual direct labour budget

	Department 1	Department 2	Total
Budgeted production (units)	10,200	1,605	
Hours per unit	10	15	
Total budgeted hours	102,000	24,075	126,075
Budgeted wage rate per hour	£3	£3	
Total wages	£306,000	£72,225	£378,225

Factory overhead budget

The factory overhead budget is also the responsibility of the respective production department managers. The total of the overhead budget will depend on the behaviour of the costs of the individual overhead items in relation to the anticipated level of production. The overheads must also be analysed according to whether they are controllable or non-controllable for the purpose of cost control. The factory overhead budget (Schedule 7) will be as follows:

Schedule 6 — Annual factory overhead budget

Anticipated activity — 102,000 direct labour hours (department 1)
24,075 direct labour hours (department 2)

	Variable overhead rate per direct labour hour		Overheads		
Controllable overheads	Department 1 £	Department 2 £	Department 1 £	Department 2 £	Total £
Indirect material	0.30	0.20	30,600	4,815	
Indirect labour	0.30	0.30	30,600	7,222	
Power (variable portion)	0.15	0.10	15,300	2,407	
Maintenance (variable portion)	0.05	0.10	5,100	2,407	
			81,600	16,851	98,451

Non-controllable overheads

Depreciation	25,000	20,000	
Supervision	25,000	10,000	
Power (fixed portion)	10,000	500	
Maintenance (fixed portion)	11,400	799	
	71,400	31,299	102,699
Total overhead	153,000	48,150	201,150
Budgeted departmental overhead rate	£1.50(1)	£2.00(2)	

Notes

(1) £153,000 total overheads divided by 102,000 direct labour hours.
(2) £48,150 total overheads divided by 24,075 direct labour hours.

The budgeted expenditure for the variable overhead items is determined by multiplying the budgeted direct labour hours for each department by the budgeted variable overhead rate per hour.

Selling and administration budget

The selling and administration budgets have been combined here to simplify the presentation. *In practice separate budgets should be prepared*; the sales manager will be responsible for the selling budget, the distribution manager will be responsible for the distribution expenses and the chief administrative officer will be responsible for the administration budget.

Schedule 7 — Annual selling and administration budget

Selling	£	£
Salaries	18,500	
Commission	15,000	
Car expenses	5,500	
Advertising	20,000	59,000
Administration		
Stationery	1,000	
Salaries	7,000	
Miscellaneous	2,000	
		10,000
		69,000

Departmental budgets

For cost control the direct labour budget, materials usage budget and factory overhead budget are combined into separate departmental budgets. These budgets are normally broken down into twelve separate monthly budgets and the actual monthly expenditure is compared with the budgeted amounts for each of the items concerned. This comparison is used for judging how effective managers are in controlling the expenditure for which they are responsible. The departmental budget for department 1 will be as follows:

Department 1 — Annual departmental operating budget

		Budget	Actual
Direct labour (from Schedule 5)			
102,000 hours at £3		306,000	
Direct materials (from Schedule 3)			
102,000 units of material X at £1.80 per unit	£ 183,600		
51,000 units of material Y at £4 per unit	204,000	387,600	
Controllable overheads (from Schedule 6)			
Indirect materials	30,600		
Indirect labour	30,600		
Power (variable portion)	15,300		
Maintenance (variable portion)	5,100	81,600	
Uncontrollable overheads:			
Depreciation	25,000		
Supervision	25,000		
Power (variable portion)	10,000		
Maintenance (variable portion)	11,400	71,400	
		846,600	

When all the budgets have been prepared the budgeted profit and loss account and balance sheet provide the overall picture of the planned performance for the budget period.

Budgeted profit and loss account for year ending 19X1

	£	£
Sales (Schedule 1)		1,074,000
Opening stock of raw materials (from opening balance sheet)	47,300	
Purchases (Schedule 4)	446,352(1)	
	493,652	
Less Closing stock of raw materials (Schedule 4)	25,160(2)	
Cost of raw materials consumed	468,492	
Direct labour (Schedule 5)	378,225	
Factory overheads (Schedule 6)	201,150	
Total manufacturing cost	1,047,867	
Add Opening stock of finished goods (from opening balance sheet)	24,769	
Less Closing stock of finished goods	166,496(3) (141,727)	
Cost of sales		906,140
Gross profit		167,860
Selling and administration expenses (Schedule 7)		69,000
Budgeted operating profit for the year		98,860

Notes
(1) £209,772 (X) + £236,580 (Y) from Schedule 4.
(2) 10,200 units at £1.80 plus 1,700 units at £4 from Schedule 4.
(3) 1,870 units of alpha valued at £83 per unit, 90 units of sigma valued at £125.40 per unit. The product unit costs are calculated as follows:

		Alpha units	£	Sigma units	£
Direct materials —	X	10	18.00	8	14.40
	Y	5	20.00	9	36.00
Direct labour		10	30.00	15	45.00
Factory overheads — Department 1		10	15.00	–	–
Department 2		–	–	15	30.00
			83.00		125.40

Budgeted balance sheet as at 31 December

	£	£
Fixed assets		
Land		42,500
Building and equipment	323,000	
Less depreciation(1)	108,750	214,250
		256,750

Current assets			
Raw material stock	25,160		
Finished goods stock	166,496		
Debtors(2)	70,000		
Cash(3)	49,794		
	311,450		
Current liabilities			
Creditors(4)	76,971	234,479	
		491,229	
Represented by shareholders' interest			
300,000 ordinary shares of £1 each	300,000		
Reserves	92,369		
Profit and loss account	98,860	491,229	

Notes
(1) 63,750 + 45,000 (Schedule 6) = 108,750.
(2) 72,250 opening balance + 1,074,000 sales − 1,076,250 cash.
(3) Closing balance as per cash budget.
(4) 62,200 opening balance + 446,352 purchases + 35,415 indirect materials − 466,996 cash.

Cash budgets

The objective of the cash budget is to ensure that sufficient cash is available at all times to meet the level of operations which are outlined in the various budgets. The cash budget for Example 15.1 is presented on the following page and is analysed by quarters, but in practice monthly or weekly budgets will be necessary. Because cash budgeting is subject to uncertainty it is necessary to provide for more than the minimum amount required, to allow for some margin of error in planning. Cash budgets can help a firm to avoid cash balances which are surplus to its requirements by enabling management to take steps in advance to invest the surplus cash in short-term investments. Alternatively, cash deficiencies can be identified in advance and steps can be taken to ensure that bank loans will be available to meet any temporary cash deficiencies. For example, by looking at the cash budget for the Enterprise company, management may consider

that the cash balances are higher than are necessary in the second and third quarters of the year, and they may invest part of the cash balance in short-term investments.

Cash management involves managing the cash of the firm to attain maximum cash availability and maximum interest income on any idle funds. A study of cash management is beyond the scope of this book but for a detailed discussion of the topic see Clarkson and Elliot (1983).

of maintaining current ongoing activities and then adding to those costs any further developments of the services which are considered desirable. For example, the education, health, housing and social services departments of a local authority will propose specific activities and related costs for the coming year. These budgets are coordinated by the accounting department into an overall budget proposal.

The available resources for financing the

Cash budget for year ending 19X1

| | Quarters | | | | |
	(1) £	(2) £	(3) £	(4) £	Total £
Opening balance	8,500	28,500	73,500	105,496	8,500
Receipts from debtors	250,000	300,000	280,000	246,250	1,076,250
	258,500	328,500	353,500	351,746	1,084,750
Payments					
Purchase of materials	100,000	120,000	110,000	136,996	466,996
Payment of wages	100,000	110,000	120,000	161,547	491,547
Other costs and expenses	30,000	25,000	18,004	3,409	76,413
	230,000	255,000	248,004	301,952	1,034,956
Closing balance	28,500	73,500	105,496	49,794	49,794

Final review

The budgeted profit and loss account, the balance sheet and the cash budget will be submitted by the accountant to the budget committee, together with a number of budgeted financial ratios such as the return on capital employed, working capital, liquidity and gearing ratios. If these ratios prove to be acceptable, the budgets will be approved. In Example 15.1 the return on capital employed is approximately 20%, but the working capital ratio is over 4:1, so management should consider alternative ways of reducing investment in working capital before finally approving the budgets.

The budgeting process in non-profit-making organizations

The budgeting process in a non-profit-making organization normally begins with the managers of the various activities calculating the expected costs

proposed level of public services should be sufficient to cover the total costs of such services. In the case of a local authority the resources will be raised by rates and government grants. Similar procedures are followed by churches, hospitals, charities and other non-profit-making organizations, in that they produce estimates for undertaking their activities and then find the means to finance them, or reduce the activities to realistic levels so that they can be financed from available financial resources.

One difficulty which is encountered in non-profit-making organizations is that outputs cannot be measured in monetary terms. By outputs we mean the quality and amount of the services rendered. In profit-oriented organizations output can be measured in terms of sales revenues. The effect of this is that budgets in non-profit organizations tend to be mainly concerned with the input of resources (that is, expenditure) whereas budgets in profit organizations focus on the relationships between inputs (expenditure) and outputs (sales revenue). In non-profit organizations there is not the same emphasis on what was

intended to be achieved for a given input of resources. The budgeting process tends to compare what is happening in cash input terms with the estimated cash inputs. In other words, there is little emphasis on measures of managerial performance in terms of the results which are achieved. The reason for this is that there is no clear relationship between resource inputs and the benefits which flow from the use of these resources. However, we shall see that increasing efforts have been made in recent years to overcome these deficiencies by developing measures of output which can be used to compare budgeted and actual accomplishments.

Line item budgets

The traditional format for budgets in non-profit organizations is referred to as line item budgets. A line item budget is one in which the expenditures are expressed in considerable detail, but the activities being undertaken are given little attention. A typical line item budget is illustrated in Exhibit 15.1.

The amounts in this type of budget are frequently established on the basis of historical costs which have been adjusted for anticipated changes in costs and activity levels. When they are compared with actual expenditures, line item budgets provide a basis for comparing whether or not the authorized budgeted expenditure has been exceeded or whether underspending has occurred. Note that data for the current year and for the previous year is included to indicate how the proposed budget differs from current spending

patterns. However, such line item budgets fail to identify the costs of *activities* and the *programmes* to be implemented. In addition, compliance with line item budgets provides no assurance that resources are used wisely, effectively, or efficiently, in financing the various activities in a non-profit organization.

Planning, programming budgeting systems

Non-profit organizations have found line item budgets to be unsatisfactory mainly because they fail to provide information on planned and actual accomplishments. In addition, such budgets do not provide information on the efficiency with which the organization's activities have been performed, or its effectiveness in achieving its objectives. A further deficiency with line item budgets is that they fail to provide a sound basis for deciding how the available resources should be allocated. Planning, programming budgeting systems (PPBS) is intended to overcome these deficiencies. For example Holtham (1983) states:

Advocates of such systems as PPBS pointed out that there was confusion between planning and budgeting. The essentially *short-term* financial process of annual budgeting was also being used for policy planning. There was insufficient strategic thinking and *long-term* planning. Local authorities were not clear on their objectives or local needs and had not orientated their financial information to an objective-based (pro-

Exhibit 15.1 Typical line item budget

Item of expense	Actual 19X2	Original budget 19X3	Revised budget 19X3	Proposed budget 19X4
Employees	1,292,000	1,400,000	1,441,000	1,830,000
Premises	3,239	12,000	10,800	14,200
Supplies and services	34,735	43,200	44,900	147,700
Transport	25,778	28,500	28,700	30,700
Establishment expenses	123,691	120,000	116,000	158,600
Agency charges	10,120	10,000	9,800	13,300
Financing charges	2,357	2,700	2,800	114,800
Other expenses	1,260	1,350	1,400	1,600
	1,493,180	1,617,750	1,655,400	2,310,900

gramme) format. Too little attention was given to measuring outputs and monitoring the outcomes of policies.

The aim of PPBS is to enable the management of a non-profit organization to make more-informed decisions about the allocation of resources to meet the overall objectives of the organization. PPBS is the counterpart of the long-term planning process which is operated in profit-oriented organizations. We can relate PPBS to the long-term planning process outlined in Fig. 15.1 for profit-oriented companies. The first stage in the process of PPBS is to review the organizational objectives for the activities which it performs (that is, Stage 1 in Fig. 15.1). Stage 2 involves identifying programmes which can be undertaken to achieve the organization's objectives. The third stage involves identifying and evaluating alternative methods of achieving the objectives for each specific programme. Such a comparison and evaluation will show the costs of each alternative course of action and the benefits which result. The final stage (stage 4) is to select the appropriate programmes on the basis of cost/benefit principles. At this stage it would be useful if the projects could be ranked but this is extremely difficult. It is therefore necessary for a subjective judgement to be made by the top management of the organization on the amount of resources which are to be allocated to the various programmes.

PPBS involves the preparation of a *long-term* corporate plan which clearly establishes the objectives which the organization aims to achieve. These objectives do not necessarily follow the existing organizational structure. For example, one objective of a local authority may be the care of the elderly. The following services may contribute to this objective:

(1) Provision of sheltered accommodation.
(2) Erection of aged persons dwellings.
(3) Provision of domestic health services.
(4) Provision of home nursing services.
(5) Provision of social and recreational facilities.

The provision of these activities may be undertaken by separate departments, such as housing, health and social services. However, PPBS relates the estimates of total costs to the care of the elderly programme, rather than relating costs to the various departments. A programme budget cuts across departmental barriers by providing estimates of the programme for the provision of the elderly rather than these estimates being included within the three budgets for each of the housing, health and social welfare departments.

PPBS forces management to identify the activities, functions or programmes to be provided, thereby establishing a basis for evaluating the worthiness of the programme. In addition, PPBS provides information which will enable management to assess the effectiveness of its plans; for example, is the provision of the services for the elderly as well developed as it should be for an

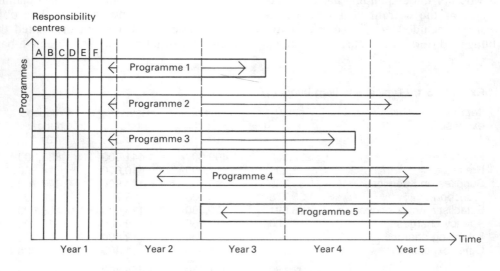

Fig. 15.4 A matrix organizational structure

expenditure of X thousand pounds? The programme structure should correspond to the principal objectives of the organization and enable management to focus on the organization's outputs (the objectives to be achieved) rather than just the inputs (the resources available to be used). Hence a more effective allocation of scarce resources can be achieved. Within the overall programme budget, apart from the main objectives of the programme, there will be a series of sub-objectives reaching down to the lower levels of management.

Because the programme structure is unlikely to match the organization's structure a particular individual must be made responsible for *controlling* and supervising the programme. Anthony and Herzlinger (1980) suggest that one possiblity is to adopt a matrix type of organizational structure, with a matrix consisting of programme managers in one dimension and functionally organized responsibility centres in the other. This process is illustrated in Fig. 15.4. The programmes are represented by horizontal bars and the budgets by vertical dashed lines. The budget for year 1 has been analysed by six responsibility centres (A to F). Such an organizational structure requires that the budgeted and the actual accomplishments are compared by programmes. In addition, information must be accumulated by department or responsibility centre (that is, responsibility centres A to F in Fig. 15.4) and line item budgets must be used for controlling expenditure. Note that the budgeting process in this illustration focuses on a single year, whereas PPBS focuses on activities which extend over a period of several years. A budget is in effect one slice of the organization's programmes where costs are related to departments or resonsibility centres, rather than programmes.

Incremental and zero-base budgeting

Before the *annual* budget is prepared a base should be determined from which the process will begin. One method is to take the current level of operating activity and the current budgeted allowances for existing activities as the starting point for preparing the next annual budget. This base is then adjusted for changes which are expected to occur during the new budget period. This approach is called *incremental budgeting* as the budget process is concerned mainly with the increment in operations or expenditure which will occur during the budget period. For example, the allowance for budgeted expenses may be based on the previous budgeted allowance plus an increase to cover higher prices caused by inflation. The big disadvantage of this approach is that it perpetuates any past inefficiencies. However, incremental budgeting may be appropriate in some cases. For example, staff salaries may be estimated on the basis of current salaries plus an increment for inflation. Similarly, a sales budget for a stable product may be prepared on the basis of existing sales plus an increase for price changes, and a minor adjustment for expected changes in sales volume.

An alternative to incremental budgeting is *zero-based budgeting*. Phyrr (1970) describes zero-base budgeting (ZBB) as follows:

> Customarily, the officials in charge of an *established* programme have to justify only the increase which they seek above last year's appropriation. In other words, what they are already spending is usually accepted as necessary, without examination. Substantial savings could undoubtedly be realised if [it were required that] every agency . . . make a case for its entire appropriation request each year, just as if its programme or programmes were entirely new. Such budgeting procedure may be difficult to achieve, partly because it will add heavily to the burdens of budget-making, and partly also because it will be resisted by those who fear that their pet programmes would be jeopardised by a system that subjects every . . . activity to annual scrutiny of its costs and results.

What is being advocated by Phyrr is that zero base budgeting rejects the traditional view of *annual* budgeting as an incremental process which takes into account current expenditure plus an estimate of next year's expenditure to arrive at the next budget. Instead, the projected expenditure for *existing* programmes should start from base zero with each year's budgets being compiled as if the programmes were being launched for the first time. The budgetees should present their requests

for appropriations in such a fashion that all funds can be allocated on the basis of cost/benefit or some similar kind of evaluative analysis. The cost/benefit approach is an attempt to ensure 'value for money'; it questions long-standing assumptions and serves as a tool for systematically examining and perhaps abandoning any unproductive projects. The type of basic question which will be asked is:

(1) Should the function be performed at all?
(2) What should the quantity level be? Are we doing too much?
(3) Should it be performed in this way?
(4) How much should it cost?

According to Stonich (1976) zero-base budgeting involves the following three stages:

(1) A description of each organizational activity in a *decision package*. For example, in local government organizations decision packages might include care of the elderly, child care, and so on.
(2) The packages are then evaluated and ranked.
(3) The resources are allocated accordingly.

A decision package represents the operation of a particular programme with incremental packages reflecting different levels of effort which may be expended on a specific function. One package — the base package — may represent a minimum level of activity, and other packages may help to identify higher activity or cost levels. For example, the base package for the care of the elderly might include provision of accommodation for aged persons and incremental packages might include home visits, meals-on-wheels services, and so on.

Once the decision packages have been completed, management is ready to start the review process. To determine how much to spend and where to spend it, management will rank all packages in order of decreasing benefits to the organization. Theoretically, once management has set the budget, the packages should be accepted down to the spending level based on cost/benefit principles. Stonich uses Fig. 15.5 to illustrate the process where A, B and C represent the existing programmes and A1, A2, A3 etc. represent the various incremental packages for programme A. The final column in Fig. 15.5 illustrates the ranking of the decision packages. The base

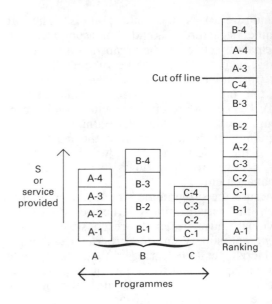

Fig. 15.5 Ranking of decision packages

packages (A1, B1 and C1) which provide the basic services are ranked first and the remaining packages are ranked in order of their decreasing benefits. All packages below the cut-off line are accepted. The cut-off line is determined by the budgeted spending level.

The benefits of this method over traditional methods of budgeting are claimed to be as follows:

(1) Traditional budgeting tends to extrapolate the past by adding a percentage increase to current year costs. This becomes very much a preservation of the status quo as the relationship between costs and benefits for a particular activity is rarely questioned and consequently costs are not necessarily allocated to uses where they are most required. Zero-base budgeting represents a move towards allocation of resources by need and benefit.

(2) Zero-base budgeting creates a questioning attitude rather than one which assumes that current practice represents value for money.

(3) Zero-base budgeting focuses attention on outputs in relation to value for money.

(4) Zero-base budgeting leads to increased staff

involvement which may lead to improved motivation and greater interest in the job.

The major problem with zero-base budgeting is that it is very time-consuming. However, it does not have to be applied throughout the organization. It can be applied selectively to those areas about which management is most concerned. For example, in a local authority it could be applied to care of the elderly in the first year, child care in the second year, health care in the third year, and so on. Also the scope of zero-base budgeting can be reduced by limiting the number of decision packages which are passed to top management. Lower level managers can approve certain amounts or percentages of the expected budget, leaving only the more controversial packages to be reviewed at higher levels.

Zero-base budgeting can be used in both profit-oriented and non-profit-making organizations. In profit-oriented organizations non-manufacturing activities such as service and support activities are prime candidates because their costs are primarily of a discretionary nature. The manufacturing activities can normally be controlled by input–output relationships. In non-profit-making organizations zero-base budgeting is particularly appropriate as quality of service is the primary function.

According to Phyrr (1976) there were 100 users of zero-base budgeting in the USA ranging from Texas Instruments to the State of Georgia, under Governor Jimmy Carter. When Carter became President he directed that all federal government agencies adopt ZBB. Suver and Brown (1977) reviewed the literature on the use of zero-base budgeting and found that in many organizations zero-base budgeting led to a considerable improvement in the budget process, but that in some organizations it had not proved successful. The reasons for the lack of success included lack of top-management support, and a failure to develop suitable output measurements. For a detailed discussion of the conditions which should be satisfied if zero-base budgeting is to lead to an improvement in the budget process see Suver and Brown (1976).

Summary

The budget process is part of a larger system which involves setting objectives, considering alternative programmes, incorporating programmes into the long-range plan, and implementing the long-range plan through the budgeting process.

Budgets are required to achieve many different aims within an organization. Not only are they an aid to planning, coordinating and communicating the activities of a business, but they are also used as a control and a motivating device. In addition, budgets are often used as a basis for evaluating a manager's performance.

Before the annual budgeting process is begun top management must communicate the policy effects of the long-term plan to those who are responsible for preparing the current year's budgets. Normally, the sales budget is the first to be prepared and this supplies the basic data for producing the remaining budgets. The managers who are responsible for meeting budgeted performance should prepare the budgets for those areas for which they are responsible and submit them to their superiors for approval. As the budgets move up the organizational hierarchy they must be examined in relation to each other to ensure that all the parts combine to produce an acceptable whole. When all the budgets are in harmony with each other they will be summarized into a master budget which will consist of a budgeted profit and loss account, a balance sheet and a cash flow statement. The approval of the master budget will constitute authority for the managers of each responsibility centre to carry out the plans which are contained in each budget. The process should not stop when all the budgets have been agreed; periodically the figures should be compared with the actual budgeted figures and remedial action taken to ensure that the results conform to plan. Budgeting is a continuous and dynamic process and should not end once the annual budget has been prepared.

In non-profit organizations the annual budgeting process compares budgeted and actual inputs but does not provide information on the efficiency with which activities have been performed, or the effectiveness in achieving objectives. PPBS attempts to overcome these deficiencies; it is a *long-term*

planning process and is the counterpart of the long-term planning process in profit-oriented companies. Incremental budgeting is a system of preparing *annual* budgets which takes the current level of operating activity as the starting point for preparing the next annual budget. This base is then adjusted for the changes which are expected to occur during the new budget period. An alternative approach is that of zero-base budgeting where the projeted expenditure for preparing the next annual budget for *existing* programmes starts from base zero.

References and further reading

Ackoff, R.L. *A Concept of Corporate Planning*. Wiley, 1970.

Amey, L.R. Budget planning: A dynamic reformulation. *Accounting and Business Research* Winter 1979, 17-25.

Ansoff, I. *Corporate Strategy*. Penguin Books, 1968.

Anthony, R.N. and Herzlinger, R.L. *Management Control in Non-Profit Organisations*. R.D. Irwin, 1980.

Clarkson, G.P.E. and Elliot, B.J. *Managing Money and Finance*. Gower Press, 1983.

Dermer, J. *Management Planning and Control Systems*. R.D. Irwin, 1977.

Henley, D., Holtham, C., Likierman, A. and Perrin, J. *Public Sector Accounting and Financial Control*. Van Nostrand Reinhold (UK), 1983, Chapter 4.

Hopwood, A.G. *Accounting and Human Behaviour*. Prentice-Hall, 1976, Chapter 3.

Lancaster, G.A. and Lomas, R.A. *Forecasting for Sales and Materials Management*. Macmillan, 1985.

Likert, R. and Seashore, S.E. Making cost control work. In Solomons, D. (Ed.), *Studies in Cost Analysis* 2nd edn. Sweet & Maxwell, 1968.

Murray, G. and Puxty, A.G. Relationships in the budgetary process. *Managerial Finance* 6(1), 9-20.

Parker, L.D. Communication in the corporate budgetary system. *Accounting and Business Research* Summer 1978, 191-207.

Phyrr, P.A. Zero-base budgeting. *Harvard Business Review* November–December 1970, 111-121.

Phyrr, P.A. Zero-base budgeting — Where to use it and how to begin. *S. A. M. Advanced Management Journal* Summer 1976, 5.

Samuels, J.M. and Wilkes, F.M. *Management of Company Finance*. 3rd edn. Van Nostrand Reinhold (UK), 1980, Chapters 7-9.

Schiff, M. and Lewin, A.V. The impact of people on budgets. *Accounting Review* April 1970, 259-68.

Sizer, J. *An Insight into Management Accounting*. Penguin Books, 1979, Chapter 7.

Sparkes, J.R. and McHugh, A.K. Forecasting techniques in British industry. *Journal of Forecasting* January/March 1984, 37-42.

Steiner, G.A. *Top Management Planning*. Macmillan, 1969.

Suver, J.D. and Brown, R.L. Where does zero-base budgeting work. *Harvard Business Review* November–December 1977, 76-84.

Welsch, G.A. *Budgeting: Profit Planning and Control*. Prentice-Hall, 1971.

Problems

*Indicates that a suggested solution is to be found in the *Students' Manual*.

15.1 R Limited manufactures three products: A, B and C.

You are required:

(a) using the information given below, to prepare budgets for the month of January for:

 (i) sales in quantity and value, including total value;

 (ii) production quantities;

 (iii) material usage in quantities;

 (iv) material purchases in quantity and value, including total value;

 (N.B. Particular attention should be paid to your layout of the budgets.)

(b) to explain the term principal budget factor and state what it was assumed to be in (a) of this question.

Data for preparation of January budgets

Sales:

Product	Quantity	Price each £
A	1,000	100
B	2,000	120
C	1,500	140

Materials used in the company's products are:

Material	M1	M2	M3
Unit cost	£4	£6	£9

Quantities used in:

		units	units	units
Product:	A	4	2	—
	B	3	3	2
	C	2	1	1

Finished stocks:

Product	A	B	C
Quantities			
1 January	1,000	1,500	500
31 January	1,100	1,650	550
Material stocks:	M1 units	M2 units	M3 units
1 January	26,000	20,000	12,000
31 January	31,200	24,000	14,400

(20 marks)
ICMA Cost Accounting 1
November 1979

15.2* You are required, from the data given below, to prepare next year's budgets for:
(a) production;
(b) purchases;
(c) production cost.
Standard cost data are as follows:

		Product	
		Aye £	Bee £
Direct materials:			
X	24 kilos at £2.0	48	
	30 kilos at £2.0		60
Y	10 kilos at £5.0	50	
	8 kilos at £5.0		40
Z	5 kilos at £6.0	30	
	10 kilos at £6.0		60
Direct wages:			
Unskilled	10 hours at £3.0 per hour	30	
	5 hours at £3.0 per hour		15
Skilled	6 hours at £5.0 per hour	30	
	5 hours at £5.0 per hour		25

Production overhead is absorbed on a basis of direct labour hours, while other overhead is recovered on the basis of 20% of production cost. Profit is calculated at 20% of sales price.
Budgeted data for the year:

		Material		
		X £	Y £	Z £
Stock at standard price				
1 January		60,000	125,000	72,000
31 December		70,000	135,000	75,000
Production overhead	£900,000			
Labour hours	75,000			

	Product	
	Aye £	Bee £
Finished goods stock at production cost		
Opening stock	152.000	256,000
Closing stock	190.000	352,000
Sales at standard sales price	1,368,000	1,536,000

(25 marks)
ICMA Cost Accounting 2
November 1983

15.3 ABC Ltd manufactures three products from three basic raw materials in three departments. The company operates a budgetary control system and values its stock of finished goods on a marginal cost basis. From the data given below, you are required to produce for the month of June 1979 the following budgets:
(a) production;
(b) materials usage;
(c) purchases;
(d) profit and loss account for each product and in total.
Budgeted data, for June 1979:

Product:	A	B	C
Sales	£1,500,000	£1,080,000	£1,680,000
Stock of finished products at 1 June 1979, in units	3,000	2,000	2,500
Department:	I	II	III
Fixed production overhead	£239,000	£201,300	£391,200
Direct labour hours	47,800	67,100	65,200
Direct material:	DM 11	DM 21	DM 31
Stock at 1 June 1979, in units	24,500	20,500	17,500

The company is introducing a new system of inventory control which should reduce stocks. The forecast is that stocks at 30 June 1979 will be reduced as follows: raw materials by 10% and finished products by 20%.

Fixed production overhead is absorbed on a direct labour hour basis. It is expected that there will be no work in progress at the beginning or end of the month.

Administration cost is absorbed by products at a rate of 20% of production cost and selling and distribution cost is absorbed by products at a rate of 40% of production cost.

Profit is budgeted as a percentage of total cost as follows: product A 25%; product B 12½% and product C 16⅔%.

Standard cost data, per unit of product:

Product:		A	B	C
Price per unit £		units	units	units
Direct material				
DM 11	2.00	5	—	12
DM 21	4.00	—	10	9
DM 31	1.00	5	5	—
Rate per hour £		hours	hours	hours
Direct wages				
Department: I	2.50	4	2	2
II	2.00	6	2	3
III	1.50	2	4	6
		£	£	£
Other variable costs		10	20	15

(35 marks)

ICMA Cost Accounting 2
May 1979

15.4* Kerryblue Ltd is a company manufacturing two products using one type of material and one grade of labour. Shown below is an extract from the company's working papers for the next period's budget.

Product	K	B
Budgeted sales	3,000 units	4,500 units
Budgeted material consumption, per product	6 kilos	2 kilos
Budgeted material cost; £3 per kilo		
Standard hours allowed, per product	5 hours	3 hours

The budgeted wage rate for the direct workers is £4 per hour for a 40 hour week, overtime premium is 50% and there are 65 direct operatives.

The target productivity ratio (or efficiency ratio) for the productive hours worked by the direct operatives in actually manufacturing the products is 90%; in addition the amount of non-productive down-time is budgeted at 20% of the productive hours worked.

There are twelve 5-day weeks in the budget period and it is anticipated that sales and production will occur evenly throughout the whole period.

At the beginning of the period it is anticipated that the stocks will be:

Product K	1,050 units
Product B	1,200 units
Raw material	3,700 kilos

The target closing stocks, expressed in terms of the anticipated activity during the budget period are:

Product K	15 days sales
Product B	20 days sales
Raw material	10 days consumption

Required:
(a) Calculate the material purchase budget and the wages budget for the direct workers, showing both quantities and values, for the next period. (16 marks)
(b) Describe the additional information required in order to calculate the weekly cash disbursements for materials and wages during the above budget period. (6 marks)

(22 marks)

ACCA Foundation Costing
June 1981

15.5 BX Ltd manufactures two products, Plain and Fancy, using one basic raw material and one grade of labour. Shown below are the actual operating results achieved for the eleven months ended November 1979.

		£	£
Sales:	Plain (£12.00 each)	48,000	
	Fancy (£20.00 each)	40,000	88,000
Actual cost of sales:	Direct material	44,000	
	Direct labour	14,000	
	Variable overhead	6,000	
	Fixed overhead	10,000	74,000
Profit			£14,000

The company operates a standard costing system and during the above period the actual material consumption was as specified in the standard, which for Plain is 3 kilos per unit, and for Fancy, 4 kilos per unit. The standard wage rate is £3 per hour. The standard labour cost of Plain is £1.50 per unit and Fancy £3 per unit. Labour achieved standard efficiency but, throughout the above period, the actual wage rate paid was higher than standard and consequently an adverse rate variance of £2,000 was incurred. Overheads were as specified in the standard, variable overheads varying directly with labour hours worked. There was no change in any stock levels during the period.

Budgeted production for 1980 is 6,000 units of Plain and 4,000 units of Fancy. Material stocks are budgeted to decrease by 2,000 kilos; there will be no change in any other stocks. The standard material consumption per unit will be as specified in 1979 and, after careful consideration, it has been agreed that the 1980 standard material price will be the actual average price paid during the eleven months ended November 1979.

The actual wage rate for 1979 will be increased by 70p per hour for 1980, 50p per hour of which is the result of a productivity agreement which will enable the company to reduce its standard time for each product by 20%. Budgeted overheads will be at the same

rate as shown for 1979 and it may be assumed there are no wages included in overheads.

Required:

(a) Calculate the material purchase budget and the wages budget, showing both quantities and values for the year ended December 1980. (16 marks)

(b) Calculate the net cost savings which the company should achieve during 1980 as a result of the productivity agreement, assuming that there is no restriction on the number of labour hours which could be made available, if required. (6 marks)

(Total 22 marks)
ACCA Foundation Costing
December 1979

15.6 A holding company established a new subsidiary company on 1 November specifically for the manufacture and selling of a new product. The holding company will inject, for working capital purposes, £30,000 cash on 1 December. Fixed capital assets are being transferred from another company in the group.

Using the data given you are required to prepare a cash budget for each of the months of December, January, February and March. Calculations are to be made to the nearest £1.

Data

The variable production cost per unit is expected to be:

	£
Direct materials	4.0
Direct wages	3.0
Variable production overhead	1.5
Variable production cost	8.5

Fixed overhead estimated at £48,000 per annum is expected to be incurred in equal amounts each month from 1 December.

Production will commence in December and sales on 1 January. The estimated sales for the first four months are:

1981	Units	Sales value £
January	6,200	65,100
February	6,800	70,720
March	5,400	59,400
April	6,000	63,000

The following information is to be taken into consideration:

1. Stocks, finished goods: 75% of each month's invoiced sales units to be produced in the month of sale and 25% of each month's invoiced sales units to be produced in the previous month.

2. Stocks, direct materials: 50% of direct mater-

ials required for each month's production to be purchased in the previous month. Direct materials to be paid for in the month following purchase.

3. Direct wages to be paid 75% in the month used and 25% in the following month.

4. Variable production overhead: 40% to be paid in the month of usage and the balance in the following month.

5. Fixed overhead: 30% to be paid in the month in which it is incurred and 40% in the following month, the balance represents depreciation of fixed assets.

6. Payments to be received from customers as follows:

	£
January	12,369
February	45,987
March	59,666

(30 marks)
ICMA Cost Accounting 1
November 1980

15.7* The management of Beck PLC have been informed that the union representing the direct production workers at one of their factories, where a standard product is produced, intends to call a strike. The accountant has been asked to advise the management of the effect the strike will have on cash flow.

The following data has been made available:

	Week 1	Week 2	Week 3
Budgeted sales	400 units	500 units	400 units
Budgeted production	600 units	400 units	Nil

The strike will commence at the beginning of week 3 and it should be assumed that it will continue for at least four weeks. Sales at 400 units per week will continue to be made during the period of the strike until stocks of finished goods are exhausted. Production will stop at the end of week 2. The current stock level of finished goods is 600 units. Stocks of work in progress are not carried.

The selling price of the product is £60 and the budgeted manufacturing cost is made up as follows:

	£
Direct materials	15
Direct wages	7
Variable overheads	8
Fixed overheads	18
Total	£48

Direct wages are regarded as a variable cost. The company operates a full absorption costing system and the fixed overhead absorption rate is

based upon a budgeted fixed overhead of £9,000 per week. Included in the total fixed overheads is £700 per week for depreciation of equipment. During the period of the strike direct wages and variable overheads would not be incurred and the cash expended on fixed overheads would be reduced by £1,500 per week.

The current stock of raw materials is worth £7,500; it is intended that this stock should increase to £11,000 by the end of week 1 and then remain at this level during the period of the strike. *All direct materials are paid for one week after they have been received. Direct wages are paid one week in arrears. It should be assumed that all relevant overheads are paid for immediately the expense is incurred.* All sales are on credit; 70% of the sales value is received in cash from the debtors at the end of the first week after the sales have been made and the balance at the end of the second week.

The current amount outstanding to material suppliers is £8,000 and direct wage accruals amount to £3,200. Both of these will be paid in week 1. The current balance owing from debtors is £31,200, of which £24,000 will be received during week 1 and the remainder during week 2. The current balance of cash at bank and in hand is £1,000.

Required:

(a) (i) Prepare a cash budget for weeks 1 to 6 showing the balance of cash at the end of each week together with a suitable analysis of the receipts and payments during each week. (13 marks)

(ii) Comment upon any matters arising from the cash budget which you consider should be brought to management's attention. (4 marks)

(b) Explain why the reported profit figure for a period does not normally represent the amount of cash generated in that period. (5 marks)

(22 marks)
ACCA Level 1 Costing
June 1983

15.8 G.T. Urnside PLC, a company which manufactures pressed steel fitments, commenced trading on 1 December 1981. Summarized below is the profit statement and balance sheet after the first year of trading.

G.T. Urnside PLC
Summarized profit statement for the year ended 30 November 1982

	£000	£000
Sales		240
Cost of sales:		
Direct materials	60	
Direct labour	48	
Variable overhead	30	
Fixed overhead	70	208
Net operating profit		£32
Proposed dividends to		
ordinary shareholders		15
Retained profit		17
		£32

G.T. Urnside PLC
Summarized balance sheet as at 30 November 1982

	£000	£000	£000
Issued share capital			
108,000 £1 ordinary			
shares			108
Reserves			
Retained profit			17
Shareholders' fund			£125
Represented by:			
Fixed assets			
Plant and machinery			
(at cost on			
1.12.1981)		120	
Less: Depreciation		24	96
Current assets			
Stocks of materials		8	
Debtors		40	
Cash		1	
		49	
Less: Current liabilities			
Creditors	5		
Dividend	15	20	
Net working capital			29
Net assets employed			£125

Shown below are relevant data extracted from the company's budget for the year ended 30 November 1983.

Sales: 1st Quarter £66,000 3rd Quarter £90,000
 2nd Quarter £78,000 4th Quarter £84,000

The weekly sales in each quarter will be constant and, on average, debtors pay eight weeks after goods have been despatched.
The selling prices and product mix will remain the same as the previous year.

Materials:

The price of materials will be 20% lower than the previous year. The weekly purchases of materials in each quarter will be constant, except for the budgeted stock increase in the third quarter shown below. Material suppliers are paid on average four weeks after the goods have been received.

Direct labour:

Wages will be paid at the 1981/82 level of £12,000 per quarter plus the following changes:

(i) All direct operatives have been awarded a 15% rate of pay increase with effect from 1 December 1982.

(ii) One additional direct operative will be recruited at the beginning of the second quarter, and another direct operative will be recruited at the beginning of the third quarter. Both operatives will be paid £100 per week and will continue to be employed for the remainder of the year.

Wages are paid at the end of the week in which they are earned.

Overheads:

Variable overheads vary directly with production activity and there will be no price increases from the previous year. Fixed overheads will increase by £12,000 p.a. and the total amount will be incurred evenly throughout the year. All relevant overheads are paid in cash immediately they are incurred.

Stocks:

Stocks of work in progress and finished goods will not be carried. However, stocks of raw materials will increase by £3,000 in the first week of the third quarter and remain at £11,000 throughout the remainder of the year.

Capital expenditure:

Additional equipment costing £20,000 will be purchased and paid for during the second quarter of the year. Depreciation on this equipment will not commence until the following year.

Dividends:

The dividends outstanding will be paid in the first quarter of the year.

Required:

Prepare the company's quarterly cash budgets for the year ended 30 November 1983.

Note: It should be assumed there are 12 weeks in each quarter and any other assumptions which you consider to be necessary should be clearly stated.

(22 marks)
ACCA Level 1 Costing
December 1982

15.9 Dyer Ltd manufactures a variety of products using a standardized process which takes one month to complete. Each production batch is started at the beginning of a month and is transferred to finished goods at the beginning of the next month. The cost structure, based on current selling prices, is:

	%	%
Sales price		100
Variable costs		
Raw materials	30	
Other variable costs	40	
Total variable cost — used for stock valuation		70
Contribution		30

Activity levels are constant throughout the year and annual sales, all of which are made on credit, are £2.4 million. Dyer is now planing to increase sales volume by 50% and unit sales price by 10%. Such expansion would not alter the fixed costs of £50,000 per month, which includes monthly depreciation of plant of £10,000. Similarly, raw material and other variable costs per unit will not alter as a result of the price rise.

In order to facilitate the envisaged increases several changes would be required in the long term. The relevant points are:

(i) The average credit period allowed to customers will increase to 70 days.

(ii) Suppliers will continue to be paid on strictly monthly terms.

(iii) Raw material stocks held will continue to be sufficient for one month's production.

(iv) Stocks of finished goods held will increase to one month's output or sales volume.

(v) There will be no change in the production period and 'other variable costs' will continue to be paid for in the month of production.

(vi) The current end of month working capital position is:

	(£000)	(£000)
Raw materials	60	
WIP	140	
Finished goods	70	270
Debtors		200
		470
Creditors		60
Net working capital — excluding cash		£410

Compliance with the long-term changes required by the expansion will be spread over several months. The relevant points concerning the transitional arrangements are:

(i) The cash balance anticipated for the end of

May is £80,000.

(ii) Up to and including June all sales will be made on one month's credit. From July all sales will be on the transitional credit terms which will mean

60% of sales will take 2 month's credit
40% of sales will take 3 month's credit.

(iii) Sales *price* increase will occur with effect from August's sales.

(iv) Production will increase by 50% with effect from July's production. Raw material purchases made in June will reflect this.

(v) Sales *volume* will increase by 50% from October's sales.

Required:

(a) Show the long-term increase in annual profit and long-term working capital requirements as a result of the plans for expansion and a price increase. (Costs of financing the extra working capital requirements may be ignored.) (6 marks)

(b) Produce a monthly cash forecast for June to December, the first seven months of the transitional period. (10 marks)

(c) Using your findings from (a) and (b) above make brief comments to the management of Dyer Ltd on the major factors concerning the financial aspects of the expansion which should be brought to their attention. (4 marks)

(20 marks)

Assume that there are 360 days in a year and each month contains 30 days.

ACCA P2 Management Accounting
June 1981

15.10* The chief accountant of Gannet Ltd is interested in developing rudimentary financial models of aspects of the company's activities. Among those ideas under consideration is the building of a simple cash budgeting model for use in forecasting the monthly cash flows from routine operations in any month.

Sales in the month of June 1979 were £100,000; the gross profit margin earned was $33\frac{1}{3}\%$ on cost of sales. It is confidently expected that the value of sales will increase by 1% per month for the foreseeable future.

20% of sales are made for cash, and the remainder on credit. Of the cash due from credit sales customers, it is expected that 20% will be collected in the month after sale, 60% in the second month after sale, and 20% in the third month after sale. No bad debts are expected.

All purchases of inventory for resale are paid for in full in the month after purchase. All inventory purchased in month t is sold in month t + 2. Similarly, all sales in month t + 2 are made from inventory purchased in month t.

Monthly expenses (other than cost of sales) are expected to be as follows:

Payroll	5% of the preceding month's sales
Utilities	£3,000
Depreciation	£1,000
Other expenses	£10,000

No expenses are accrued.

It has been decided that, at this stage, no other factors will be included in the model. The effects of dividends, taxation, capital expenditure, and any other matter not already specified may therefore be ignored.

You are required to:

(a) set out in the form of equations a model of Gannet's cash flows arising in any month from normal trading activities, suitable for use as a formula for cash budgeting. (11 marks)

(b) apply your model to produce a statement of the relevant cash flows arising in September 1979 (7 marks), and

(c) suggest how you could incorporate uncertainty into your model if the chief accountant's staff were uncertain about the rate of sales growth, the relative proportions of cash and credit sales, and the speed of payment by credit customers. (7 marks)

ICAEW Management Accounting
July 1979

15.11 The trustees of a public hall have produced the following budget for the year commencing 1 July 1981:

		£000
Income:		
Lettings at £250 a day		75
Franchise payment: bar/restaurant		10
car park		2
		87

	£000	
Expenses:		
Administrative staff	10	
Operating staff	30	
Repairs and renewals	30	
Heating and lighting	8	
General expenses	2	
Maintenance resereve	5	
Financing charges	20	105
Loss		18

Letting reservations have been made as under:

	days
Exhibitions	75
Conferences and meetings	105
Theatrical shows	60
Sporting events	60
	300

The 300 days is the maximum letting time available in the year.

Since preparing the budget the treasurer to the trustees has approached the various organizations with hall reservations and all except the theatrical shows have now agreed to an increase of 10% in the letting fee. Also, after negotiations, in addition to their franchise fees, the bar/restaurant operator has agreed to pay 1% of his gross takings and the car park operator a sliding scale fee as under:

Parking on any day	Extra fee per car pence
For the first 500 cars	Nil
For the next 500 cars	5
For the next 500 cars	6
For any additional cars	7

In the discussions, the theatrical show managers stated that they were near a point of financial balance and could not accept a higher charge. Also they considered there should be a differential charging system as their shows run for 6 days at a time and caused less work and expense than other bookings.

An investigation has shown the following facts to be relevant to the problem:

Administrative staff	50% full-time and 50% variable with attendances.
Operating staff	40% full-time and 60% variable with attendances.
Repairs and renewals	70% labour cost, of which 60% is variable with attendances; 30% material cost, all of which is fixed.
Heat and light	20% fixed and 80% variable.

All other expenses are fixed costs.

	Average attendance per day	Ratio of cars to attendance	Average bar/restaurant purchase per attendance/day £
Exhibitions	4,000	0.4	0.30
Conferences and meetings	900	0.8	8.00
Theatrical shows	1,000	0.4	1.50
Sporting events	1,500	0.5	2.00

There is a clause in the trust deed requiring that lettings to any of the four groups should be within limits of 10% and 45% of the total days available. The contracts for the bar/restaurant and car park franchises are both in the fifth year of seven-year contracts at fixed amounts.

The relative usage of the variable elements of services provided is as follows:

	Admin staff	Operating staff	Repairs & renewals	Heat and light
Exhibitions	5	5	3	7
Conferences and meetings	2	1	1	1
Theatrical shows	1	3	2.5	3
Sporting events	5	4	2	3.5

Per daily usage heads the above table.

You are required, from the information given, to:

(a) calculate a revised budget for the year distinguishing between fixed and variable items;

(b) prepare a profitability statement for each of the four letting groups;

(c) calculate a differential daily letting fee for each group based on the revised budget;

(d) comment briefly on the assertion of the theatrical show managers that their letting fees should be the lowest;

(e) state the percentage of lettings to each group, within the limitations set, which would maximize profit for the year;

(f) indicate one aspect of the present financial arrangements which you believe requires further investigation, giving reasons for your choice.

Work to nearest £100 in apportionments and to nearest £1 in daily rates.

(30 marks)
*ICMA P3 Management Accounting
May 1981*

15.12 A manufacturing company is preparing its operating budgets for the year commencing 1 July 1983 and for the machining department it is estimated a total of 48,000 hours of standard output wil be required. The company operates on a 13 × 4-weekly control cycle and the spread of production in the year is as under:

Period	Standard hours of production as a % of the annual total
1	7.2
2	7.4
3	7.9
4	7.2
5	7.7
6	7.8
7	7.3
8	8.4
9	8.5
10	8.8
11	7.2
12	7.6
13	7.0

This department produces an average of 0.8 standard hours of output for each attendance hour; the balance of time is lost through production delays.

Paid absence for holidays and sickness is expected to occur on the following scale:

Periods	% paid absence
1, 8, 9 and 10	10
2, 3, 4, 12 and 13	15
5, 6, 7 and 11	20

The basic week is 40 hours and the forecast wage rate is £2.40 per hour. Overtime is paid at time and one-half but, by a trade union agreement, must not exceed 10% of basic paid hours in any period. All 'non-productive' hours are paid at the flat rate as operatives are expected to undertake clean-up work at these times. Employee benefits and employer's insurance contributions amount to £12 per week for each employee.

You are required:
(a) to prepare a manpower budget for the year, on the basis of maintaining a static labour force throughout and using overtime within the agreed limitations, so as to minimize total labour costs;
(b) to evaluate *separately* the following proposals and make a recommendation to management on their viability:
 (i) to initiate a safety campaign costing £2,000 to reduce accidents and thereby reduce the paid absence given above from 10%, 15% and 20% to 9%, 14% and 19% respectively;
 (ii) to undertake additional preventive maintenance at a cost of £5,000 to reduce machine breakdowns and thereby eliminate 25% of the time lost through production delays;
(c) to outline briefly *three* other areas where you think an investigation might lead to a

reduction in labour costs.

(35 marks)
ICMA P3 Management Accounting
May 1983

15.13* What is zero-base budgeting and how does it differ from other, more traditional forms of budgeting? Discuss the applicability of zero-base budgeting to profit-orientated organizations.
ACCA Level 2 Management Accounting
June 1983

15.14* The chief executive of your organization has recently seen a reference to zero-base budgeting. He has asked for more details of the technique.

You are required to prepare a report for him, explaining:
(a) what zero-base budgeting is and to which areas it can best be applied;
(b) what advantages the technique has over traditional-type budgeting systems; and
(c) how the organization might introduce such a technique.

(20 marks)
ICMA P3 Management Accounting
May 1979

15.15* Prepare brief notes about zero-base budgeting covering the following topics:
(a) what zero-base budgeting means;
(b) how zero-base budgeting would operate;
(c) what problems might be met in introducing zero-base budgeting;
(d) what special advantages could be expected from zero-base budgeting, as compared with more traditional budgeting methods, for an organization operating in an economic recession.

(20 marks)
ICMA P3 Management Accounting
November 1982

15.16* (a) '. . . corporate planning and budgeting are complementary, rather than the former superseding the latter.'

You are required to compare the aims and main features of 'corporate planning' and 'budgeting' systems (12 marks).
(b) The aims of zero-base budgeting have been described recently in the following terms:

Zero-base budgeting is a general management tool that can provide a systematic way to evaluate all operations and programmes; a means of establishing a working structure to recognise priorities and performance measures for current and future plans; in essence, a methodology for the continual redirection of resources into the highest priority programmes, and to identify explicitly trade-offs among

long-term growth, current operations, and profit needs.

You are required to explain how a system of zero-base budgeting works, and to assess its likely success in attaining the aims set out above (13 marks).

ICAEW Management Accounting
December 1980

15.17* 'A budgetary planning and control system may include many individual budgets which are integrated into a "master budget".'

You are required to outline and briefly explain with reasons the steps which should normally be taken in the preparation of master budgets in a manufacturing company, indicating the main budgets which you think should normally be prepared (12 marks).

ICAEW Management Accounting
July 1980

15.18* A company that has hitherto prepared its operating budgets on a single target level of performance is considering changing to one of the following:

(a) a three-level budget;
(b) a decision tree analysis leading to a calculation of joint probabilities of budget levels;
(c) a simulation of probabilities of budget levels (probably computer-based).

You are required to:

(i) explain briefly the method of constructing budgets for (a), (b) and (c) above;
(ii) comment briefly on the advantages that would result from choosing:

method (a) over the existing method;
method (b) over method (a);
method (c) over method (b).

(20 marks)

ICMA P3 Management Accounting
May 1982

16 Control in the organization

Control is the process of ensuring that a firm's activities conform to its plans and that its objectives are achieved. There can be no control without objectives and plans as these predetermine and specify the desirable behaviour and set out the procedure which should be followed by members of the organization to ensure that the firm is operated in the desired manner.

Drucker (1964) distinguishes between 'controls' and 'control'. 'Controls' are measurement and information, whereas 'control' means direction. In other words 'controls' are purely a means to an end; the end is control. 'Control' is the function which makes sure that actual work is done to fulfil the original intention, and 'controls' are used to provide information to assist in determining the control action to be taken. For example, material costs may be greater than budget. 'Controls' will indicate that costs exceed budget and that this may be because the purchase of inferior quality materials causes excessive wastage. 'Control' is the *action which is taken* to purchase the correct quality materials in the future to reduce excessive wastage.

'Controls' encompasses all the methods and procedures which direct employees towards achiev-ing the organizational objectives, for example job descriptions, operating manuals, training proced-ures, budgets, and so on. Such controls are called *administrative* controls. There are also *social* controls, which are exercised by individuals over one another. For example, procedures used by small groups within an organization to regulate the performance of their own members and to bring them into line when they deviate from the group norms. These are often more effective in controlling behaviour than any of the administrative controls. Hopwood (1976a) states:

> Control, in whatever direction, is not only achieved by formal means but also by pressures exerted by individuals over one another. For in any situation, the controllers and the potentially controlled have a social relationship with one another. The motiv-ations, expectations and personal relationships of all the members of the enterprise therefore exert a significant effect on the outcome of the control process. The personalities of the managers and subordinates, their approach to their job and the subordinates' acceptance of the ligitimacy of managerial roles are also important influences.

Administrative and social controls cannot be considered independently of each other. If both types of controls are not working in harmony, the potential power of each will be considerably reduced. For example, administrative controls may be designed to reward productivity increases but they are unlikely to have any effect if the employees have developed their own social controls which place restrictions on productivity. An effective control system must therefore ensure that administrative and social controls are working in the same direction so that control may be effectively exercised. In this chapter and the following two we shall focus on budgetary control and standard costing systems, which are administrative controls. In Chapter 19 we shall consider the impact of social controls on budgetary control and standard costing systems.

Control systems

A control system is a communications network that monitors activities within the organization and provides the basis for corrective action in the future. The control system can best be illustrated in terms of a mechanical model such as a thermostat (see Fig. 16.1).

Fig. 16.1 A mechanical control system

Note that the control system consists of the following elements:

(1) The process (the room's temperature) is continually monitored by an automatic regulator (the thermostat).

(2) Deviations from a predetermined level (the desired temperature) are identified by the automatic regulator.

(3) Corrective actions are started if the output is not equal to the predetermined level. The automatic regulator causes the input to be adjusted by turning the heater on if the temperature falls below a predetermined level. The heater is turned off when the output (temperature) corresponds with the predetermined level.

The output of the process is monitored and whenever it varies from the predetermined level the input is automatically adjusted. For a detailed description of a mechanical control model and its similarity to a management control system see Anthony and Dearden (1980).

The elements of a mechanical control system

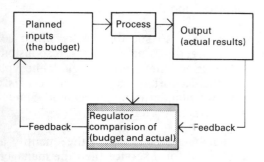

Fig. 16.2 The budgetary control process

also apply to a budgetary control system (see Fig. 16.2).

From this illustration you can see that planned inputs as reflected in the budgets are compared with the actual results (that is, the output) and the deviations from the desired inputs are identified. Control reports are issued by the accountant to the managers responsible for controlling the inputs. Effective control requires that corrective *action* is taken so that the actual outputs conform to the planned inputs in the future. Alternatively, the planned inputs may require modifications if the comparisons indicate that the budget can no longer be attained. Just as the thermostat compared actual and desired temperatures, the budgetary control system must compare actual and planned performance to isolate deviations and to enable corrective action to be taken.

At the end of the year the actual results should be compared with those envisaged in the long-term plan. This comparison should result in a review of the long-term plan and an assessment of what progress has been made towards the realization of the organization's objectives. This process is illustrated in Fig. 15.1 in the previous chapter. In addition, the comparison enables management to review the long-range objectives in the light of new circumstances which may have rendered those objectives unrealistic. This aspect of control is exercised by top management, normally on an annual basis.

The control of day-to-day operations is exercised by lower level managers. To control short-term operations it is essential that lower level managers are provided at frequent intervals with detailed comparisons of actual performance with budgeted performance. Such comparisons cannot lead to actions which will rectify past events, but isolating past inefficiencies and the reasons for them will enable managers to take action which will avoid the same inefficiencies being repeated in the future. The system which provides reports that compare budget performance with actual performance is known as 'responsibility accounting'.

Responsibility accounting

Responsibility accounting is based on the recognition of individual areas of responsibility as specified in a firm's organization structure. These areas of responsibility are known as responsibility

centres. A responsibility centre may be defined as a segment of an organization where an individual manager is held responsible for the segment's performance. Remember from Chapter 2 that there are three types of responsibility centre:

(1) A *cost centre* where managers are accountable for the expenses which are under their control.
(2) A *profit centre* where managers are accountable for sales revenue and expenses; for example, a division of a company which is responsible for the manufacture and selling of a product.
(3) An *investment centre* where managers are normally accountable for sales revenue and expenses but in addition are responsible for capital investment decisions and are thus able to influence the size of the investment.

In this chapter we shall concentrate mainly on cost centres but the same principles apply to profit centres and investment centres, and we shall consider these in Chapter 23.

The objective of responsibility accounting is to accumulate costs and revenue for each individual responsibility centre so that deviations from budgets can be attributed to the person in charge. Responsibility accounting is implemented by issuing performance reports at frequent intervals which inform responsibility centre managers of the deviations from the budget for various items of expense. An example of a performance report issued to a departmental head is presented in the lower section of Exhibit 16.1.

Controllable and uncontrollable costs

Responsibility accounting is based on the principle that it is appropriate to charge to an area of responsibility only those costs which are significantly influenced by the manager of that responsibility centre. It is not always easy to decide whether a particular item of expense is controllable or uncontrollable. Controllability of costs depends on two factors: first, on the level and scope of management authority, and second, on the time span involved. For example, the cost of insuring machinery may not be controllable by the manager of the producing department but it may be controllable by the manager of the insurance department. When the organization is viewed as a whole, all costs are controllable. For any item of expense there will be someone in the organization who can influence it. Theoretically, the costs of any department can be reduced to zero by closing the department down, so the question is not what costs are controllable, but what costs are controllable by a specific responsibility centre?

The time period involved also has an important influence on determining which costs are controllable. For example, the monthly rental of machinery may not be controllable on a monthly basis by a production manager if the contract is renewed annually for a fixed period of one year. However, if the time period for evaluation is changed from one month to one year, the cost will become controllable.

The problem of dual responsibility

Frequently, the responsibility for a particular item of expense may be shared. For example, the quantity of raw materials used will be the responsibility of the manager of a production department, but the purchasing officer will be responsible for the price which is paid for these materials. Wastage provides a further illustration of how responsibility may be difficult to pinpoint. Excessive wastage may be due to careless handling of materials by a production department or it may be due to the purchase of inferior quality materials by the purchasing officer. Difficult though the task may be, it is essential that all differences between actual costs and budgeted costs are reported so that causes can be brought to light, responsibility placed, and remedial action taken. The system will break down if individuals who lack authority to control expenditure are incorrectly charged with the responsibility for its incurrence.

Guidelines for reporting

It is not possible to specify exactly which costs should be charged to a manager of a responsibility centre. However, the following guidelines published by the Report of the Committee of Cost Concepts and Standards in the United States in 1956 still prove to be useful:

(1) If a manager can control the quantity and price paid for a service then the manager is responsible for all the expenditure incurred for the service.

(2) If the manager can control the quantity of the service but not the price paid for the service then only that amount of difference between actual and budgeted expenditure which is due to usage should be identified with the manager.

(3) If the manager cannot control either the quantity or the price paid for the service then the expenditure is uncontrollable and should not be identified with the manager.

An example of the latter situation is when the costs of an industrial relations department are apportioned to a department on some arbitrary basis; such arbitrary apportionments are uncontrollable by managers of responsibility centres. There is an argument that arbitrary apportionments should be allocated to managers to draw their attention to those costs which the company incurs to support their activities. This is because the manager may be able indirectly to influence these costs and should therefore be made aware of the sums which are involved. If this approach is adopted, it is essential to distinguish between controllable and uncontrollable costs in the performance report. The arguments for using this approach apply to a situation such as the apportionment of personnel department costs to production departments. This reporting procedure may discourage managers from making unnecessary requests to the personnel department when they are made aware of the costs which are apportioned to them.

Levels of reporting

Another problem which arises when operating a system of responsibility accounting is that of determining the lowest levels of responsibility for reporting purposes. This depends on the delegation of authority and the assignment of responsibility. Note, however, that the lower down the organization one goes with responsibility reporting, the greater will be the number of responsibility centres and the greater the cost of responsibility reporting. It may not therefore be worthwhile to produce reports for many small reponsibility centres.

If this view is adopted it will be necessary to combine small responsibility centres, such as work groups, into larger responsibility centres such as departments. The foremen of the work groups can then control by observation and direct supervision instead of relying on formal reports, and within a department the foremen of the various work groups will be responsible to the head of the department for the activities of their groups. Formal control reports which show the difference between the budgeted and the actual expenditure will only be issued at departmental level and above. The various departmental heads will then be responsible for these costs to the plant manager who in turn will be responsible to the works manager.

The information which is reported and the frequency of reports

No hard and fast rules can be laid down for determining the accounting and statistical information that managers need, but a vast amount of information is now available from computerized information systems. According to Ackoff (1978) the problem is not providing more information, but providing the appropriate information. It is essential that the managers concerned should be heavily involved in discussions with the accountant as to what information should be reported to them. A monthly report which contains a large amount of detail may increase the accounting costs out of proportion to the value of the data provided, and may overwhelm the unfortunate manager who receives a mass of indigestible figures.

When the nature of the required information has been determined, some thought must be given to the frequency of reporting the information, the amount of detail to be presented, and the format. Reports for control may be issued at monthly, weekly or even daily intervals. The frequency of reporting and the amount of detail included in performance reports will vary according to the level of management. At successively higher levels of management less time is devoted to control and more time is devoted to planning. Departmental heads may therefore need considerable detail and frequent reports which might also include items expressed in physical terms. For example, labour hours, materials used and machine efficiency may be reported. On the other hand, reports to senior management will not be so frequent, and will be in a condensed form which summarizes the results of lower level management. This process is illustrated in the performance reports included in Exhibit 16.1.

Great care is necessary in determining the

Exhibit 16.1 Responsibility accounting monthly performance reports

Performance report to managing director

| | Budget | | Variance* F(A) | |
	Current month £	Year to date £	This month £	Year to date £
Factory A	453,900	6,386,640	(80,000)	(98,000)
Factory B	X	X	X	X
Factory C	X	X	X	X
Administration costs	X	X	X	X
Selling costs	X	X	X	X
Distribution costs	X	X	X	X
	2,500,000	30,000,000	(400,000)	(600,000)

Performance report to production manager of factory A

	Current month £	Year to date £	This month £	Year to date £
Works manager's office				
Machining department 1	165,600	717,600	(32,760)	(89,180)
Machining department 2	X	X	X	X
Assembly department	X	X	X	X
Finishing department	X	X	X	X
	453,900	6,386,640	(80,000)	(98,000)

Performance report to head of machining department 1

	Current month £	Year to date £	This month £	Year to date £
Direct materials	X	X	X	X
Direct labour	X	X	X	X
Indirect labour	X	X	X	X
Indirect materials	X	X	X	X
Power	X	X	X	X
Maintenance	X	X	X	X
Idle time	X	X	X	X
Other	X	X	X	X
	165,600	717,600	(32,760)	(89,180)

Managing director → Factory A (performance report to managing director)

Production manager → Machining department 1 (performance report to production manager of factory A)

Head of department (performance report to head of machining department 1)

*F indicates a favourable variance (actual cost less than budgeted cost) and A indicates an adverse budget (actual cost greater than budget cost). Note that at the lowest level of reporting, the *departmental head's* performance report contains *detailed* information on operating costs. At successively higher levels of management less detail is reported. For example, the *managing director's* information on the control of activities consists of examining those variances which represent significant departures from the budget for each factory and functional area of the business and requesting explanations from the appropriate managers.

frequency of reporting. Reports at too-frequent intervals make it difficult to judge managerial performance, whereas a longer reporting period means that there will be a long delay in reporting to management significant deviations from plan. It is important to achieve the correct balance. Dearden (1978) expresses a concern that the development of computer information systems may result in performance reports being issued at too-frequent intervals. He states:

Since the primary purpose of a financial control system is to provide the manager with informa-

tion to help evaluate the performance of his subordinates, it follows that the time period covered by each report should be no shorter than the time span of the job. Consequently, we must stop thinking in terms of traditional accounting periods when we develop financial control systems. Rather we must think in terms of developing feedback time cycles that are consistent with the minimum time span of the job for which the system is being developed. In particular, we should not shorten the time periods covered by a report simply because the computer has made it economically feasible.

Motivational impact of performance reports

Performance reports should not be used to 'pinpoint the blame' on managers. If the reports are used as a punitive post mortem device there is a danger that managers may resort to such activities as trying to obtain over-generous budgets at the planning stage, deliberately producing lower performance to ensure that easily attainable budgets are obtained in the future, and the establishment of groups that are in conflict with top management. For a detailed discussion of the motivational impact of performance reports see Hopwood (1976b).

Performance reports should help to monitor activities and identify those items which are not proceeding according to plan. The reports themselves, however, do not provide answers, and when each responsibility unit receives a report a narrative commentary should be prepared by the departmental head which explains the reasons for the important variations from the budget and *the action which is being taken* to remedy the situation. The accountant will provide clues by identifying a variance between the actual and the budgeted costs. For example, he might identify that a direct materials variance was due to excessive usage of a certain chemical in a particular process. The responsibility centre manager must then investigate the process and identify the reasons for the excessive usage.

Incorporation of other variables

There is a danger that, if performance reports include only those items which can be expressed in monetary terms, managers will concentrate on only these variables and ignore other important variables which cannot easily be quantified in monetary terms. For example, Likert and Seashore (1968) illustrate that it is always possible to obtain short-term improvements in cost control by hierarchical pressure to cut costs and raise productivity but this will eventually have negative effects on managerial performance in the form of adverse motivational changes, increased labour turnover and reduced product quality. The problem is that reductions in costs are measured and included in performance reports but the state of the morale of a department cannot easily be measured. Performance reports should therefore be broadened to incorporate other variables besides costs and revenues. Unfortunately, performance reports which are based only on costs

and revenues do not give a sufficient indication of the future results which can be expected from present actions.

One possible improvement is for performance reports to be supplemented by non-financial measures. Ferrara (1978) suggests that the following additional measures should be included:

Manufacturing activities
Labour turnover
Plant efficiency
Units produced per hour
Percentage of units rejected to good units
Hours available for production and hours used in production

Distribution activities
Sales, gross profit and/or contribution per order received
Percentage of orders to calls
Percentage of orders to customers
Percentage of calls to customers
Miles travelled per call
Miles travelled per day on the road
Number of new customers

In addition, performance reports should be accompanied by a written explanation from the responsibility head giving reasons why their performance is above or below some pre-set level and how it has been obtained.

Flexible budgeting

Because some costs vary with changes in the level of activity it is essential when preparing performance reports for cost centres to take into account the variability of costs. For example, if the actual level of activity is greater than the budgeted level of activity then those costs which vary with activity will be greater than the budgeted costs purely because of changes in activity. Let us consider the simplified situation presented in Example 16.1.

EXAMPLE 16.1

An item of expense included in the budget for department X is estimated to vary directly in relation to activity at £1 per unit of output. The budgeted monthly level of activity is 1,000 units but the actual level of activity was 1,200 units at a cost of £1,150.

It is clearly incorrect to compare actual costs of £1,150 from an activity level of 1,200 units with budgeted costs of £1,000 from an activity level of 1,000 units. This would incorrectly suggest an

overspending of £150. If managers are to be made responsible for their costs, it is essential that they are responsible for performance under the conditions in which they worked, and not for a performance which is based on conditions when the budget was drawn up. In other words, it is *misleading to compare actual costs at one level of activity with budgeted costs at another level of activity*. The original budget must be adjusted to the actual level of activity. This procedure is called flexible budgeting. In Example 16.1 the performance report should be as follows:

Budgeted expenditure (flexed to 1,200 units)	Actual expenditure (1,200 units)
£1,200	£1,150

The budget is adjusted to reflect what the costs should have been for an actual activity of 1,200 units. This indicates that the manager has incurred £50 less expenditure that would have been expected for the actual level of activity, and a favourable variance of £50 should be recorded on the performance report, not an adverse variance of £150, which would have been recorded if the original budget had not been adjusted. Example 16.1 assumed only one variable item of expense but in practice the budget will include fixed, semi-fixed and variable expenses.

Budget formula

The flexible budget approach is based on an adequate knowledge of cost behaviour patterns. The techniques available for ascertaining the relationship between costs and activity are discussed in Chapter 20. A budget formula must be constructed for each item of expense to calculate a flexible budget allowance. For example, a purely variable item will be a specific amount per unit activity. Alternatively, some items of expense may consist of a fixed and a variable element. These items are called *semi-variable costs*. Expenditure on maintenance may consist of an element of planned maintenance which will not change in relation to activity, and a variable element which will depend on the level of activity. If the fixed element is estimated at £1,000 and the variable cost is estimated at £1 per unit of output, the budget formula would be described as £1,000 fixed cost (FC) + £1 per unit of output. When the budget formulas have been estimated flexible budgets can be produced for various levels of activity. Exhibit 16.2 illustrates a series of flexible budgets for a machining department. Note that fixed costs are not adjusted for changes in activity.

Performance reports

If we assume in Exhibit 16.2 that the original *fixed budget* is for an output level of 10,000 units for a particular month, and the actual output is 9,000 units, then the costs for an output level of 9,000 units will be extracted from the flexible budgets and compared with the actual costs.[1] A performance report similar to Exhibit 16.3 should then be presented.

The performance report indicates that the scheduled production of 10,000 units was not

Exhibit 16.2 Machining department flexible budgets

Item of expense	Budget formula	Activity levels (units of output)				
		8,000 £	9,000 £	10,000 £	11,000 £	12,000 £
Direct labour	£6 per unit of output	48,000	54,000	60,000	66,000	72,000
Direct materials	£5 per unit of output	40,000	45,000	50,000	55,000	60,000
Overheads						
Indirect labour	£40,000 FC + £4 per unit of output	72,000	76,000	80,000	84,000	88,000
Lighting and heating	£6,000 FC	6,000	6,000	6,000	6,000	6,000
Power	Zero FC + £1 per unit of output	8,000	9,000	10,000	11,000	12,000
Maintenance	£5,000 FC + £2 per unit of output	21,000	23,000	25,000	27,000	29,000
Indirect materials	Zero FC + £0.50 per unit of output	4,000	4,500	5,000	5,500	6,000
Depreciation of machinery	£10,000 FC	10,000	10,000	10,000	10,000	10,000
		209,000	227,500	246,000	264,500	283,000

Exhibit 16.3 Machining department monthly performance report

	Budget based on 9,000 units	Original budget 10,000 units Actual output 9,000 units Actual	Variance
	£	£	£
Controllable costs			
Direct labour	54,000	60,000	6,000 A*
Direct materials	45,000	43,000	2,000 F*
Indirect labour	76,000	80,000	4,000 A
Power	9,000	8,800	200 F
Maintenance	23,000	24,000	1,000 A
Indirect materials	4,500	5,000	500 A
	211,500	220,800	9,300 A
Uncontrollable costs			
Lighting and heating	6,000	6,500	500 A
Depreciation	10,000	10,000	–
	16,000	16,500	500 A

*A = Adverse variance
F = Favourable variance

achieved. This may be because the manager was not effective in attaining the output level or it may be due to a failure to meet the budgeted sales demand. Alternatively, the original budget may be incorrect. In addition, the performance report indicates how efficient the manager is in controlling the costs by comparing actual costs for 9,000 units with budgeted costs for 9,000 units.

Variable costs vary with input

It is unlikely that all items in a flexible budget will vary with the same activity base. The majority of costs are likely to vary with an *input* based activity level such as direct labour hours or machine hours. For example, if it normally takes 100 direct labour hours to produce 25 units, but because of inefficiency only 25 units are produced in 200 direct labour hours, it is unlikely that such variable items as indirect labour, power or maintenance will remain unchanged. The cost of these items is likely to double because direct labour hours of *input* have doubled even though output has remained unchanged.

Some variable overheads such as indirect materials may vary in relation to *output* rather than *input*, but the majority of costs will vary with *input*, and it is therefore *normally assumed that all variable overheads vary with input*. Variable overhead rates based on machine hours or direct labour hours of *input* are normally used to estimate flexible budget allowances; we should select the measures which exert the most influence on costs using the techniques which will be explained in Chapter 20.

Allowance based on output

Even though it is assumed that costs vary with hours of input it is *essential that the flexible budget allowance is based on an output-based activity measure*. This is illustrated in Example 16.2.

EXAMPLE 16.2

The variable overhead for a department varies in relation to the direct labour hours of input and is estimated to be £2 per direct labour hours. From past experience it has been established that it should take three direct labour hours to produce one unit of output. Production for the month of April was 100 units and this required five hundred direct labour hours.

If the manager is given a flexible budgt allowance based on 500 direct labour hours of input, the allowance will be £1,000. Alternatively, if the 100 units were produced in the time it should have taken, that is 300 direct labour hours, the budget allowance will be £600. Therefore, a flexible budget allowance based on direct labour hours of *input* enables managers to obtain higher budget allowances when they are inefficient. In

this example a flexible budget allowance based on direct labour hours of *input* results in an allowance of £1,000, whereas if the department was efficient and completed the work in 250 hours, the allowance will be reduced to £500. It is clearly incorrect to base flexible budget allowances on input hours as this will encourage managers to be inefficient in an attempt to obtain a higher budgeted allowance. The correct procedure is to base the flexible budget allowance on *output*. The manager should be given a flexible budget allowance of £600 based on an output of 100 units. This output should take 300 hours to produce at a variable overhead rate of £2 per direct labour hour of input. The important point to note is that *variable overheads are assumed to vary in relation to input, but the flexible budget allowance is calculated on output to avoid managers getting larger allowances for being inefficient.*

Standard hours produced

It is not possible to measure *output* in terms of units produced for a department which produces several different products or operations. For example, if a department produces 100 units of product X, 200 units of product Y and 300 units of product Z, it is not possible to add the production of these items together because they are not homogeneous. This problem can be overcome by ascertaining the amount of time, working under efficient conditions, it should take to make each product. This time calculation is called *standard hours produced*. In other words, *standard hours* are an *output* measure which can act as a common denominator for adding together the production of unlike items. Let us assume that the following *standard times* are established for the production of one unit of each product:

Product X	5 standard hours
Product Y	2 standard hours
Product Z	3 standard hours

This means that it should take 5 hours to produce one unit of product X under efficient production conditions. Similar comments apply to products Y and Z. The production for the department will be calculated in standard hours as follows:

Remember that standard hours produced is an output measure and flexible budget allowances should be based on this. In the illustration we would expect the *output* of 1,800 standard hours to take 1,800 direct labour hours of *input* if the department works at the prescribed level of efficiency. The department will be inefficient if 1,800 standard hours of output are produced using, say, 2,000 direct labour hours of input. The flexible budget allowance should therefore be based on 1,800 standard hours produced to ensure that no extra allowance is given for the 200 excess hours of input. Otherwise, a manager will obtain a higher budget allowance through being inefficient.

Analysis of variances into price and quantity effects

Flexible budgets are used to ascertain the costs which should be incurred for the output which has been achieved. These calculations are then compared with the actual costs to calculate the variances. Departmental managers may not, however, be responsible for the total amount of the variance. In most situations they will be responsible for only that part of the variance which was due to using a greater *quantity* of input hours than should have been used. This will lead to the actual expenditure being greater than the flexible budget allowance if the expense item varies with direct labour hours of input.

Part of the total variance may, however, be due to the fact that the actual *price* paid for the various resources was greater than the budgeted price. It is unlikely that the departmental manager will be responsible for these price effects as other managers will be involved. For example, the personnel manager will be responsible for the wage rates paid, and the purchasing officer will be responsible for the material prices. The variance should therefore be analysed into the *quantity effects*, which are likely to be controllable by the departmental manager, and the *price effects* which are unlikely to be controllable by the departmental manager. Generally, price variances are not controllable by the departmental manager although there are some situations where he may

Product	Standard time per unit produced	Actual output	Standard hours produced
X	5 hours	100 units	500 hours
Y	2 hours	200 units	400 hours
Z	3 hours	300 units	900 hours
			1,800 standard hours

be responsible. For example, the departmental manager may employ more expensive grades of labour than are necessary. Example 16.3 illustrates how the variance can be analysed into the price and quantity effects.

EXAMPLE 16.3

The budget for department Y of ABC Ltd is as follows:

Activity		Expenditure
Product X	2,000 units	Direct labour (12,500 hours at £2 per hour) £25,000
Product Y	1,000 units	Variable overheads (12,500 hours at £3 per hour) £37,500
Product Z	500 units	

Engineering studies have shown that the standard times for making products X, Y and Z are as follows:

Product X = 3 hours
Product Y = 4 hours
Product Z = 5 hours

At the end of the period you discover that the *actual production* was:

Product X 1,800 units
Product Y 800 units
Product Z 400 units

The total direct labour hours worked were 12,000 hours and the costs incurred were:

Direct labour £26,000
Variable overheads £40,000

You are required to prepare a flexible budget and analyse the variances between price and quantity.

The departmental flexible budget is set out in Exhibit 16.4.

We have calculated the total variance by comparing a flexible budget allowance based on *output* (measured in standard hours produced) with actual expenditure. This variance is further analysed to identify the price and quantity effects. The price variance is calculated by comparing the actual costs from 12,000 actual input hours (column 2) with the budgeted costs which were based on 12,000 input hours (column 3).[2] Actual input hours are used for both columns (2) and (3). By doing this, the quantity effects are excluded, so that any difference is due to the actual prices being different from the budgeted prices.

The quantity or efficiency variance is calculated by comparing columns (1) and (3). In column (1) the budgeted costs have been calculated for the actual output produced, measured in standard hours produced. In column (3) the budgeted costs have been calculated for the actual input hours. The difference between columns (1) and (3) is because the output should have required 10,600 input hours, but 12,000 hours were actually required. 1,400 additional hours have been used

Exhibit 16.4 Departmental flexible budget

Budgeted production — 12,500 standard hours produced (See note 1)
Actual production — 10,600 standard hours produced (See note 2)

Item of expense	Budget formula	(1) Flexible budget based on 10,600 standard hours produced £	(2) Actual costs £	(3) Budget based on 12,000 input direct labour hours £	(4) Total variance (1–2)	(5) Price variance (3–2)	(6) Quantity/ efficiency variance (1–3)
Direct labour	£2 per DLH	21,200	26,000	24,000	4,800A	2,000A	2,800A
Variable overheads	£3 per DLH	31,800	40,000	36,000	8,200A	4,000A	4,200A
		53,000	66,000	60,000	13,000A	6,000A	7,000A

(1) Budgeted production: 2,000 units of X at 3 hours per unit
 1,000 units of Y at 4 hours per unit
 500 units of Z at 5 hours per unit
(2) Actual production: 1,800 units of X at 3 hours per unit
 800 units of Y at 4 hours per unit
 400 units of Z at 5 hours per unit

which should cost £2 per hour for direct labour, and £3 per direct labour hour for variable overheads. This gives £2,800 excess costs for direct labour, and £4,200 for variable overheads. Note that both columns (1) and (3) are based on budgeted costs. This ensures that the price effects are removed from the comparison and that the difference is due entirely to the quantity effects. When the departmental performance report is produced the total variance should be analysed into price and quantity effects. In addition, the comparisons between budgeted and actual costs for overheads should be analysed by the *individual* items rather than comparing budgeted and actual *total* expenditure. An illustration of this is presented in Exhibit 17.6 in Chapter 17.

Influence of other factors

Flexible budgeting assumes that changes in costs result solely from changes in activity, but in practice it is likely that other factors besides activity will influence costs. For example, changes in production methods, length of production runs and the composition of each individual batch produced will influence the costs for a particular period. In addition, some costs will vary with hours of *input* and other costs will vary with *output*. Because of this it is important to note that the budget formulas which are used to construct flexible budgets are likely to represent approximations rather than accurate cost calculations.

Statistical applications can provide useful indications about the accuracy of flexible budget calculations and more sophisticated procedures can also be used to produce flexible budgets. These techniques are outlined in Chapter 20. At this stage, however, it is important to note that flexible budget calculations represent approximations and should be used with care when evaluating managerial performance. A small adverse variance may be due to the fact that flexible budget allowances are based on approximations, rather than to inefficient managerial performance.

Control of non-manufacturing costs

In the earlier part of this chapter we focused mainly on the procedures for the effective control of manufacturing costs. However, the costs of distributing goods and services, of administering large and complex organizations, of financing organizations and of conducting research and development represent a large share of the total costs of a profit-oriented organization. Such costs are too large to be ignored. To the extent that non-manufacturing costs are similar in nature to manufacturing costs, similar control techniques may be used; to the extent that they are dissimilar, special techniques must be devised to control them.

Alternative activity measures

Non-manufacturing costs cannot normally be related to the units of the product being made. Some costs, however, may be a function of other measures of operating volume. For example, some selling expenses may be related to the number of customer enquiries received, some of the costs of the purchasing department may be related to the number of purchase orders issued, and the number of documents typed may be taken as a measure of the volume of work in a typing pool. In these situations costs should be controlled in relation to the appropriate volume measure.

When a relevant measure has been selected for a particular non-manufacturing department, the flexible budget can be constructed in the manner described earlier in this chapter. Actual departmental costs may then be compared with the flexible budget adjusted to actual volume using the same procedure as that described for the control of manufacturing costs.

Many non-manufacturing costs are unrelated to any useful volume measure, and must be controlled by other methods. Costs which fall into this category are *committed fixed costs* and *discretionary costs*. The task of controlling these costs is more complex because activities are neither routine nor repetitive.

Committed fixed costs

Committed fixed costs may be defined as those fixed costs which are incurred each period as a consequence of a major decision made some time in the past. For example, a contract to rent a warehouse for a three-year period represents a committed cost for years 1, 2 and 3 once the rental has been incurred. The major characteristic of a

committed cost is that its amount is predetermined and can be altered only by another major decision to reverse or amend the earlier commitment. A committed cost is therefore one whose amount must be planned and controlled at the point in time when the major commitment is made. The capital expenditure budget is normally the principal accounting technique for the control of such costs. Once a commitment has been made the fixed costs are difficult to influence by short-run actions. Hence, careful long-term planning rather than short-term control is the key to managing committed fixed costs. A decision which leads to committed fixed costs should be evaluated by means of a capital expenditure post-evaluation audit following the approach outlined in Chapter 14. You will recall that it was argued that the results of this evaluation should improve the quality of future decisions.

Discretionary costs

A large proportion of non-manufacturing costs are of a discretionary nature. In respect of such costs management has some significant range of discretion as to the amount it will budget for the particular activity in question. Examples of discretionary costs (sometimes called managed or programmed costs) include advertising, research and development and training costs. There is no optimum relationship between inputs (as measured by the costs) and outputs (as measured by revenues or some other objective function) for these costs. Furthermore, they are not predetermined by some previous commitment. In effect, management can determine what quantity of service it wishes to purchase. For example, it can choose to spend small or large amounts on research and development or advertising. The great difficulty in controlling such costs is that there is no established method for determining the appropriate amount to be spent in particular periods.

One approach to this problem is to compare amounts spent on the various discretionary items with that of similar organizations or with past periods. However, past periods may represent excessive or deficient budget allocations and therefore are a weak base for comparison purposes. Another approach is to allow the spending of an amount which management believes it can afford. For example, some firms budget discretionary expenses as a percentage of sales. The weakness of this approach is that future sales may be determined by such items as research and development and advertising expenditure, but when the sales revenue declines, the budgeted expenditure on research and development and advertising will be similarly reduced. This may be an incorrect approach as it may be more appropriate in the circumstances to increase expenditure on research and development and advertising to stimulate future sales.

The major argument for selecting sales as a basis for determining the amount of budgeted expenditure on discretionary items is not because there is any presumed casual relationship with sales, but because sales represents a useful indication of how much the company can afford to spend.

It is essential that fixed budgets are used for the control of discretionary expenses. At the budget stage management will have determined the amount to be spent. This will normally be a policy decision which should be implemented and the costs will then be regarded as fixed for the appropriate budget period. Flexible budgets based on the adjustment of expenditure because of changes in activity are therefore inappropriate for the control of discretionary expenses. Note also that any underspending may not necessarily be a good thing as this may result in a lower level of service than that which was originally planned by management. For example, underspending on research and development may indicate that the policy on the amount to be spent on research and development has not been followed.

Measuring effectiveness

One of the major problems that arises in controlling non-manufacturing expenditure is the difficulty of measuring the effectiveness of the expenditure. For example, an advertising budget of £500,000 may not have been exceeded but this does not necessarily mean that the advertising expenditure has been effective. The advertising may have been incorrectly timed, it may have been directed to the wrong audience, or it may have contained the wrong message. Determining the effectiveness and efficiency of non-manufacturing operations is one of the most difficult tasks facing management accountants as there is frequently no way of measuring the output from expenditure on non-manufacturing activities.

To overcome these difficulties a number of

additional control measures should be used. Such measures include a greater reliance on physical measures such as the number of purchase orders processed, the numbers of the workforce who use training facilities, the number of calls made by salesmen, and so on. In addition, comparison of unit costs, management audits and management by objectives may be used to facilitate control. These techniques are discussed in the next section when we consider management control in non-profit organizations.

Control in non-profit organizations

Control in non-profit organizations is particularly difficult because it is not always possible to state the objectives in quantitative terms or to measure the output of services. If it is not possible to produce a statement of a particular objective in measurable terms, the objective should be stated with sufficient clarity so that there is some way of judging whether or not it has been achieved.

A comparison of the planned objectives with the actual objectives which are accomplished may take the form of a subjective judgement by a person or group of persons, or it may be derived from information which is not directly based on human judgement. A judgement by a qualified person or group of qualified people may provide a better measure of the quality of performance than an objective measure as humans incorporate judgement factors which no set of objective measures can take into account. Subjective judgements can also be expressed in quantitative terms. For example, performances in ice skating, diving and gymnastic competitions consist of subjective judgements which are represented in quantitative terms.

In a non-profit organization performance measures should attempt to measure both the *quantity* and the *quality* of outputs. It is usually much easier to measure quantity than quality. For example, in an educational establishment the quantity measure of the number of students who graduated in the previous year is much easier to measure than the quality measure of how well the students were educated. Nevertheless, the quality measure should not be overlooked. In some cases the quantity indicator may provide an approximate measure of quality. For example, the number of students who have graduated in the previous year, analysed according to degree clas-

sification, may provide an approximation of the quality of the education.

Frequently in non-profit organizations input measures are used as proxy measures for output. If no satisfactory output measures can be formulated, input measures are a better measure of output than no measure at all. For example, it may not be feasible to construct output measures reflecting the quality of health care in a community. In the absence of such measures, the amount spent on health care may provide a useful clue to output. If, in the extreme, nothing was spent, we can conclude that nothing was accomplished. When inputs are used as proxy output measures, care must be exercised to avoid undue reliance on them, and every attempt should be made to try to develop useful measures of output. For example, the number of elderly people housed in aged persons flats in the previous year and the number requiring flats and residential accommodation provides a useful indication of the quantity of service offered.

A comparison of unit costs may also provide useful information for cost control. Comparing unit costs with historical trends or similar cost data with other activities and organizations highlights those costs which are excessive. For example, unit cost measurements per mile of road resurfaced, per resident day in hospitals, per swimmer in baths, and per student in an educational establishment provide useful information when compared over time and with similar data for other organizations and activities.

Unit cost calculations also create a climate of cost consciousness. When unit cost calculations are published the general public are made aware of the cost of public services and are thus likely to expose inefficiency and support corrective action. In addition, organizations with higher than average unit costs are often penalized when funds are allocated by central government. Therefore, the knowledge that unit costs will be subject to public exposure is likely to encourage the participants in non-profit organizations to control costs efficiently.

The management accountant should present information about the performance of responsibility centres. This usually involves a comparison of budgeted outputs and costs with actual outputs and costs. We have seen that the construction of performance measures in non-profit organizations is far more difficult than in profit-oriented organizations. However, performance measures may provide useful indicators of various aspects of

performance. For example, the ratio of academic staff to students analysed by various departments in a college, the cost per student, and an analysis of students' examination performance, may provide useful indicators of the performance of various departments in an educational institution. In addition, line item budgets ensure that the budgeted costs for each item of expense are not exceeded without prior top management approval.

Management audits

Management audits can be used to facilitate control in both profit and non-profit organizations. Management or performance audits are intended to help management to do a better job by identifying waste and inefficiency and recommending corrective action. Management audits investigate the entire management control system and focus on the following aspects of an organization's performance:

(1) the nature and functioning of the organization's managerial systems and procedures;
(2) the economy and efficiency with which the organization's services are provided;
(3) the effectiveness of the organization's performance in achieving its objectives.

There are a number of different ways in which a management audit can be carried out. However, Fielden and Robertson (1980) suggest, on the basis of their own experience of undertaking management audits in non-profit organizations in the United Kingdom, that a management audit should consist of the following:

(1) **An initial analysis of financial statistics, unit costs and other performance indicators:** This analysis should involve a comparison with past statistics and other organizations of a similar character. The auditors should seek an explanation of trends and major differences from other similar organizations. The results of this initial analysis should give some guidance to those areas requiring further study.
(2) **Management and systems review:** The purpose of this is to investigate the ways in which objectives are established, policies implemented and results monitored. The emphasis is on how efficiently this process is carried out rather than reviewing the object-

ives and policies themselves.
(3) **Analysis of planning and control processes:** This involves exploring questions on the ways of comparing the objectives with the needs of the population, methods of identifying activities which are not meeting objectives, the use of investment appraisal techniques and the methods of monitoring projects against the initial appraisal. In addition methods of reviewing operating results should be studied by analysing control and reporting systems and the extent to which they alert members and officers of the need for action.
(4) **Efficiency assessment:** This is extremely difficult to assess but suggestions include the use of checklists of good practice whereby the reviewers build up a detailed knowledge of cost effective practices and, based on this, a checklist is developed and debated by the auditors with service managers. Another suggestion is for a small number of specific investigations to be carried out into activities with high unit costs, poor performance measures or suspected poor management in order to try and determine the reasons for adverse performance measures and identify the appropriate remedial action.
(5) **Effectiveness review:** This involves a study to determine whether or not the activities are achieving their stated aims. This will involve discussions with service managers and committee members on the details of particular services, and requires answers to such questions as to why a service is provided, the reasons for the service being organized in the way it is, what alternatives have been considered and why have they been rejected, and how performance is to be measured? The interpretation of the answers to such questions may involve some element of judgement but all the reviewer can do is to report as factually as possible his conclusions.
(6) **Reporting:** The draft report should be discussed in detail with members and officers before it is finalized and presented. Management audits can be performed by internal auditors as well as by independent outsiders. Some internal auditing staffs of non-profit organizations have performed management audits for many years and have developed sophisticated procedures for conducting them. Alternatively, management

audits may be undertaken by outside audit firms or management consultants. In the United Kingdom a number of large audit firms have developed audit teams which specialize in management audits in non-profit organizations.

Management by objectives

Management by objectives is a system of control whereby managers are required to state, as specifically as possible, the objectives that they expect to attain during the budget year. These statements of objectives should represent outputs and be a substitute for the profitability objective which is a key part of the budget process in a profit-orientated organization. The process encourages members of an organization, by working with each other, to identify appropriate individual objectives, to coordinate their efforts towards the achievement of those objectives, and then to evaluate their progress.

In a management-by-objectives programme, each subordinate initially develops his or her own objective and then, after discussions with the supervisor, a final set of objectives are agreed. From this set of mutually agreed objectives, they develop measures of performance to be used as a basis of evaluation. Management by objectives provides all the benefits of subordinate participation. It produces the motivational benefits of individual goal setting as well as the positive effects of feedback. In addition, individuals clearly understand what they are expected to accomplish because well-defined task responsibility has been accomplished.

The results are measured against objectives and this normally involves the use of periodic performance appraisal interviews in which the supervisor and subordinate jointly discuss the results and consider the implications for the future. The performance appraisal interview is essentially a discussion between the manager and the subordinate about their objectives and their achievement. The process is particularly applicable to non-profit organizations and the control of non-manufacturing activities in profit-oriented organizations where control by means of formal reports of planned input and outputs is difficult when outputs cannot easily be measured.

Summary

Control is ensuring that a firm's activities conform to its plans. This is achieved by comparing actual performance with planned performance and taking the appropriate remedial action for those items which are not proceeding according to plan. Comparisons should be made annually with the *long-term* plan to assess what progress has been made towards achieving the specified objectives. At this stage the long-term plan should be reviewed. Responsibility accounting is the process of presenting detailed control information on short-term operating activities. The accountant presents performance reports, normally at monthly intervals, which compare the actual and the budgeted costs. It is important to distiguish in the performance reports between controllable and uncontrollable costs. The system will break down if individuals who lack authority to control expenditure are incorrectly charged with responsibility for its incurrence. When operating a system of responsibility accounting it is important to determine the lowest levels of responsibility for reporting purposes, the information to be reported, and the frequency of reporting. These problems should be resolved on a cost versus benefits basis.

If performance reports are used as a basis for attempting to 'pinpoint the blame', a number of dysfunctional behavioural consequences are likely to arise. It is therefore important that managers see performance reports as a device to help them and not as a device for undertaking recriminatory post mortems. There is also a danger that if performance reports include only monetary items, managers will ignore other important variables which cannot be quantified; performance reports should thus be supplemented with data on non-financial variables.

Because some costs vary with activity the costs in the original budget must be adjusted to the actual level of activity. This procedure is termed flexible budgeting. The budgeted allowance should be based on actual *output* and the difference between the budgeted allowance and the actual costs should be analysed into the price and quantity effects. The departmental manager is unlikely to be responsible for the price element of the variance.

The control of non-manufacturing costs is difficult because many of the tasks are non-repetitive. Hence it is not possible to observe past or repeated operations to determine input–output relationships. To the extent that costs are related to various methods of operating volume they should be controlled by a system of flexible budgets. Committed fixed costs should be controlled when they are incurred whereas discretionary costs should be controlled by a system of fixed budgets supplemented by various comparisons of physical measures.

Control in non-profit organizations is particularly difficult because it is not always possible to state objectives in quantitative terms or measure the output of services. Frequently input measures are used as proxy measures of output but such measures should be interpreted with care. Ideally, we should measure both the quantity and the quality of outputs, but the latter is extremely difficult to measure. A comparison of unit costs may also be used to measure the efficiency of a service. Other techniques which can be used for measuring performance in both non-profit and profit organizations include management audits and management by objectives.

References and further reading

Ackoff, R.L. Management misinformation systems. In Anton, H.R., Firmin, P.A. and Grove, H.D. (Eds.) *Contemporary Issues in Cost and Management Accounting*. Houghton Mifflin Company, 1978.

Amey, L. Towards a new perspective on accounting control. *Accounting, Organisations and Society* 4(4), 1979, 247-58.

Amigoni, F. Planning management control systems. *Journal of Business Finance and Accounting* 5(3), Autumn 1978, 279-92.

Anthony, R.N. and Dearden, J. *Management Control Systems* 4th edn. R.D. Irwin, 1980, Chapter 1.

Anthony, R.N. and Herzlinger, R.E. *Management Control in Non-Profit Organisations*. R.D. Irwin, 1980.

Dearden, J. Time span in management control. In Thomas, W.E. (Ed.), *Readings in Cost Accounting Budgeting and Control* 5th edn. South Western Publishing Company, 1978.

Dermer, J. *Management Planning and Control Systems*. R.D. Irwin, 1977.

Dew, R.. and Gee, K.P. Frequency of performance reporting. *Accounting and Business Research* Summer 1972(a), 234-6.

Dew, R.B. and Gee, K.P. Control information needs of middle management. *Management Accounting* April 1972(b), 89-92.

Drucker, P.F. Controls, control and management, In Bonini, C.P., Jaedicke, R. and Wagner, H. (eds), *Management Controls: New Directions in Basic Research*. McGraw Hill, 1964.

Ferrara, W.F. Responsibility accounting — A basic control concept. In Thomas, W.E. (Ed.), *Readings in Cost Accounting Budgeting and Control* 5th edn. South Western Publishing Company, 1978.

Fielden, J. and Robertson, J. The content of a value for money review or performance audit. *Public Finance and Accounting* November 1980, 23-5.

Hopwood, A.G. *Accounting and Human Behaviour*. Prentice-Hall, 1976(a), Chapter 2.

Hopwood, A.G. *Accounting and Human Behaviour*. Prentice-Hall, 1976(b), Chapter 5.

Koehler, R.W. and Neyhart, C.A. Difficulties in flexible budgeting. *Managerial Planning* May–June 1972.

Likert, R. and Seashore, S.E. Making cost control work. In Solomons, D. (Ed.), *Studies in Cost Analysis* 2nd edn, Sweet & Maxwell, 1968.

McCosh, A. Planning and control systems and their evolution during inflation. in Cooper, D., Scapens, R. and Arnold, J. (Eds), *Management Accounting Research and Practice*. Institute of Cost and Management Accountants, 1983.

McNally, G.M. Responsibility accounting and organisational control. *Journal of Business Finance and Accounting* Summer 1980, 165-82.

Parker, L. A reassessment of the role of control in corporate budgeting. *Accounting and Business Research* Spring 1977, 135-43.

Patz, A.L. and Rowe. A.J. *Management Control and Decision Systems*. Wiley, 1977.

Report of the Committee on Cost Concepts and Standards. *The Accounting Review* 1956, 189.

Problems

*Indicates that a suggested solution is to be formed in the *Student's Manual*.

16.1* The Victoria Hospital is located in a holiday resort which attracts visitors to such an extent that the population of the area is trebled for the summer months of June, July and August. From past experience this influx of visitors doubles the

activity of the hospital during these months. The annual budget for the hospital's laundry department is broken down into four quarters, i.e. April/June, July/September, October/December and January/March, by dividing the annual budgeted figures by four. This budgeting work has been done for the current year by the secretary of the hospital using the previous year's figures and adding 16%. It is realized by the Hospital Authority that management information for control purposes needs to be improved and you have been recruited to help to introduce a system of responsibility accounting.

You are required, from the information given, to:

(a) comment on the way in which the quarterly budgets have been prepared and to suggest improvements which could be introduced when preparing the budgets for 1979/80;
(b) state what information you would like to flow from the actual against budget comparison (NB: calculated figures are *not* required);
(c) state the amendments that would be needed to the current practice of budgeting and reporting to enable the report shown below to be used as a measure of the efficiency of the laundry manager.

Victoria Hospital — Laundry Department
Report for quarter ended 30th September, 1978

	Budget	Actual
Patient days	9,000	12,000
Weight processed, in lbs.	180,000	240,000
Costs:	£	£
Wages:	8,800	12,320
Overtime premium	1,400	2,100
Detergents and other supplies	1,800	2,700
Water, water softening and heating	2,000	2,500
Maintenance	1,000	1,500
Depreciation of plant	2,000	2,000
Manager's salary	1,250	1,500
Overhead, apportioned:		
for Occupancy	4,000	4,250
for Administration	5,000	5,750

(15 marks)
ICMA Cost Accounting 1
November 1978

16.2* The budget for department X of XYZ Manufacturing Company is as follows:

Product	Activity	Expenditure	
A	2,500 units	Direct labour	= £40,000
B	5,000 units	Variable overheads	= £20,000
			£60,000

Engineering studies have shown that the standard times for producing one unit of A and B are as follows:

Product A = 4 hours
Product B = 2 hours

At the end of the period you discover that the actual results were as follows:

Product A — produced 2,000 units
Product B — produced 4,500 units

The total direct labour hours worked was 19,000 hours and the costs incurred were:

Direct labour = £39,000
Variable overheads = £24,000

You are required to prepare a flexible budget and analyse the variances between price and quantity.

16.3 Gray Ltd will commence operations at the beginning of the year and the budgets for activity and costs for the first 3 quarters of operation are shown below.

Budgets — Quarters I–III

	QI	QII	QIII
Period covered, months	1–3	4–6	7–9
Activity	(000)	(000)	(000)
Sales, units	9	17	15
Production, units	10	20	15
Costs	(£000)	(£000)	(£000)
Direct materials, A	50	100	75
B	40	80	60
Production labour	180	285	230
Factory overheads, excluding depreciation	80	110	95
Depreciation of production machinery	14	14	14
Administration expenses	30	30	30
Selling and distribution expenses	29	37	35
Total costs	423	656	539

The figures in the budgets for quarters I to III reflect Gray's cost structures which have the following major features:
(i) the fixed element of any cost is completely independent of activity levels;
(ii) any variable element of each cost displays a simple linear relationship to volume except

that the variable labour costs become 50% higher for activity in excess of 19,000 units per quarter due to the necessity for over-time working;
(iii) the variable element of selling and distribution expenses is a function of sales; *all* other costs with a variable element are a function of production volume.

In quarter IV the sales volume could range from an extreme low volume of 15,000 units to an extreme high volume of 21,000 units but with a most likely volume of 18,000 units. In month 9 it will be possible to estimate accurately sales for quarter IV and the production level for that quarter will be set equal to the sales volume. Activity for each quarter is spread evenly throughout that quarter. Cost structures will remain the same in quarters I to III but are expected to differ in quarter IV *only* in the following respects:
(i) Material A will rise in price by 20%.
(ii) All production labour wage rates will rise by $12\frac{1}{2}\%$.
(iii) Variable labour input per unit of output will decrease, due to the learning curve effect, such that only 80% of the previous labour input per unit of output is required in quarter IV. The threshold for overtime working remains at 19,000 units per quarter.
(iv) Fixed factory overheads and the fixed element of selling and distribution costs will each rise by 20%. (The variable element of selling and distribution costs will be unaltered.)

The effect of these changes is considered too small to require a change in the standard cost per unit of £30 which is used for stock valuation.

Sales price in quarter IV, £40 will be identical to the price charged in the previous three quarters. All sales are made on terms which are strictly net and allow two months credit. However, the actual payment pattern expected will lead to —

70% of all sales being paid in accordance with the credit terms.
100% of all sales being paid for within 3 months.

All cash expenses relating to production are paid for in the month in which production takes place and similarly expenses relating to selling and distribution are paid for in the month of sale.

Required:
(a) Produce a statement which analyses, under each cost classification given in the budgets, the variable cost per unit and the fixed costs which will be effective in quarter IV. (c. 6

marks)
(b) Prepare a flexible budget of estimated production costs for quarter IV. The budget should be drawn up with step points which will facilitate simple interpolation of costs for production levels between those presented in the budget and will also show expected costs for the most likely production level. (c. 4 marks)
(c) (i) Prepare statements showing the profit and the cash flow to be derived during quarter IV at the expected, extreme high and extreme low levels of activity. (c. 8 marks)
(ii) Briefly comment on the reasons for any differences between the behaviour of cash flow and profit at the three levels of activity. (c. 2 marks)

(Total 20 marks)
ACCA P2 Management Accounting
July 1980

16.4 A company sells a large number of products that are accessories for a certain class of machine. For the United Kingdom it has nine salesmen, each of whom is responsible for sales in a separate territory.
Estimates of total market potential are £6.0 million and £7.1 million for 1981 and 1982 respectively.
Data for two individual salesmen and for the company as a whole are:

	Territory		Total UK (including territories 1 and 2)
	1	2	
Territory area (000 sq km)	7.30	15.40	230.90
Number of machines in territory (millions)	1.65	0.83	12.80
Potential number of accounts	6.99	423	5,965
Salesmen	Abbott	Bartram	
1981:			
Sales (£000)	97	101	1,211
Customers (number of accounts)	412	323	3,318
Gross margin (£000)	34	39	426
Calls made	1,410	1.163	10,901
1982:			
Sales (£000)	112	123	1,460
customers (number of accounts)	398	364	3,271
Gross margin (£000)	39	47	498
Calls made	1,450	1,220	11,030
Salary (£)	7,100	6,000	60,800
Commission (£)	1,680	1,845	21,585
Total remuneration (£)	8,780	7,845	82,385
Expenses (£)	1,940	3,200	28,060

You are required:
(A) for the average of all nine salesmen and for

each of salesmen Abbot and Bartram for 1982, to calculate:

- (a) (i) sales potential;
 - (ii) sales penetration percentages;
 - (iii) sales potential per account.
- (b) eight relevant indices that would help assess the performance of each salesman. These indices should be developed from the data given under the following five headings:
 - (i) customers;
 - (ii) gross margin;
 - (iii) calls made;
 - (iv) remuneration;
 - (v) expenses.

At least one index should be calculated for each heading.

(B) to assess the performance of Bartram for 1982 based on a combination of the data in (A) above plus any other data that you may consider relevant.

(25 marks)
ICMA P3 Management Accounting
November 1983

16.5 Maxcafe Ltd sold its own brand of coffee throughout the United Kingdom. Sales policies, purchasing and the direction of the company was handled from head office in London. The company operated three roasting plants in Glasgow, Hull and Bristol. Each plant had profit and loss responsibility and the plant manager was paid a bonus on the basis of a percentage on gross margin. Monthly operating statements were prepared for each plant by head office and the following statement is a monthly report for the Glasgow plant:

Operating statement
Glasgow plant
April

	£	£
Net sales		1,489,240
Less: Cost of sales		
Special coffee — at contract cost		747,320
Roasting and grinding:		
Labour	76,440	
Fuel	49,560	
Maufacturing expenses	67,240	
		193,240
Packaging:		
Container	169,240	
Packing carton	18,280	
Labour	24,520	
Manufacturing expenses	50,880	
		262,920
Total manufacturing cost		1,203,480
Gross margin on sales		285,760

Each month the plant manager was given a production schedule for the current month and a tentative schedule for the next month. Credit collection and payment was done by Head Office. The procurement of special coffee for roasting operations was also handled by the purchasing department at Head Office. The objective of the purchasing department was to ensure that any one of forty grades of special coffee was available for the roasting plants.

Based on estimated sales budgets, purchase commitments were made that would provide for delivery in 3 to 15 months from the date that contracts for purchases were made. While it was possible to purchase from local brokers for immediate delivery, such purchases were more costly than purchases made for delivery in the country of origin and hence these 'spot' purchases were kept to a minimum. A most important factor was the market 'know-how' of the purchasing department, who must judge whether the market trend was up or down and make commitments accordingly.

The result was that the purchasing department was buying a range of coffees for advance delivery at special dates. At the time of actual delivery, the sales of the company's coffee might not be going as anticipated when the purchase commitment was made. The difference between actual deliveries and current requirements was handled through either 'spot' sales of surplus special grades or 'spot' purchases when actual sales demand of the completed coffee brands was greater than the estimated sales.

In accounting for coffee purchases a separate record was maintained for each purchase contract. This record was charged with coffee purchased and import and transport expenses, with the result that a net cost per bag was developed for each purchase. The established policy was to treat each contract on an individual basis. When special coffee was delivered to a plant, a charge was made for the cost represented by the contracts which covered that particular delivery of coffee, with no element of profit or loss. When special coffee was sold to outsiders, the sales were likewise costed on a specific contract basis with a resulting profit or loss on these transactions.

For the past several years there has been some dissatisfaction on the part of plant managers with the method of computing gross margins subject to bonuses. This had finally led to a request from the managing director to the accountant to study the whole method of reporting on results of *plant operations* and the *purchasing operation*.

Required:
An explanation to the managing director

indicating any weaknesses of the current control system,

and

an explanation of what changes you consider should be made in the present reporting and control system.

16.6* Outline the main features of a responsibility accounting system. (6 marks)

ACCA Level 2 Management Accounting
December 1982

16.7* In the context of budgetary control, certain costs are not amenable to the use of flexible budgets. These include some costs which are often called 'discretionary' (or 'programmed').

You are required to explain:

(a) the nature of discretionary (or programmed) costs and give *two* examples;

(b) how the treatment of these costs differs from that of other types of cost in the process of preparing and using budgets for control purposes.

(20 marks)

ICMA P3 Management Accounting
November 1983

16.8* A local government authority is organized so that some operating departments (e.g. building, transport, printing, catering) supply services to several functional departments (e.g. education, recreational facilities, road works, fire service). At present the total cost of each service department is allocated on a simple proportional basis to user departments.

As an aid to cost control the authority has decided to charge the user departments for these services on the basis of cost or market price

whichever is the lower.

You are required to:

(a) indicate the benefits likely to arise from this decision;

(b) outline the problems you expect may be encountered in putting the decision into practice;

(c) state how these problems might be overcome.

(20 marks)

ICMA P3 Management Accounting
November 1983

16.9* One of the major practical difficulties of applying a financial reporting and control system based on flexible budgeting to a service or overhead department is in identifying and measuring an appropriate unit of activity with which to 'flex' the budget.

Required:

(a) Describe and comment on the desirable attributes of such a measure in the context of a valid application of flexible budgeting to a service centre or to a cost centre where standard costing is not applicable. (c. 8 marks)

(b) Explain the difficulties in obtaining such a measure. (c. 6 marks)

(c) List three suitable measures of activity, indicating the circumstances in which each would be suitable and the circumstances in which each of them would be misleading or unsuitable. (c. 6 marks)

(Total 20 marks)

ACCA P2 Management Accounting
June 1979

17 Standard costing and variance analyses

In the previous chapter we noted that responsibility accounting accumulates costs and revenues for each responsibility centre so that deviations from budgets for various items of expense can be allocated to the person in charge. In this chapter we shall consider a control system which enables the deviations from budget to be analysed in detail thus enabling costs to be controlled more effectively. This system of control is called standard costing. In particular, we shall examine how a standard costing system operates and how the variances are calculated. In the next chapter we shall consider some of the criticisms which are made against standard costing variance analysis, and look at various ways of overcoming the problems which arise.

Standard costs are predetermined costs; they are target costs which should be incurred under efficient operating conditions. They are not the same as budgeted costs. A budget relates to an entire activity or operation; a standard presents the same information on a per unit basis. A standard therefore provides cost expectations *per unit* of activity and a budget provides the cost expectation for the *total activity*. If the budget is for 10,000 units and the budgeted cost is £30,000, the standard cost will be £3 per unit. We shall see that establishing standard costs for each unit produced enables a detailed analysis to be made of the difference between the budgeted cost and the actual cost so that costs can be controlled more effectively.

Establishing cost standards

To establish standard costs for a product it is necessary to determine the costs which will be incurred for labour, materials and overheads. Consequently, a detailed study of the operations which are involved in the manufacture of each product should be undertaken. The standard costs for labour, materials and overhead are then added together to establish the product standard cost.

Material standards

Material standards are based on product specifications which are set up after an intensive study has been made of the input quantity which is neces-

sary for each unit of output. This study should establish the most suitable materials for the product based on design and quality policy, and also the correct quantity which should be used after taking into account the normal losses which are inevitable in the production process.[1] The standard material cost is then found by multiplying the standard quantities by the appropriate standard prices.

The standard prices are obtained from the purchasing department. The standard material prices are based on the assumption that the purchasing department has carried out a suitable search of alternative suppliers and has selected a supplier who can supply the required quantity of sound quality materials at the best price. Standard prices should be based on the economic order quantities after taking into account quantity dis-

counts. Standard material prices then provide a suitable base against which actual prices paid for materials can be evaluated.

Labour standards

To set labour standards, activities should be analysed by the different operations. Each operation is studied and an allowed time is computed, usually after carrying out a time and motion study. The normal procedure for a time and motion study is to analyse each operation to eliminate any unnecessary elements and to determine the most efficient production method. The most efficient methods of production, equipment and operating conditions are then standardized. This is followed by time measurements which are made to determine the number of standard hours which are required by an average worker to complete the job. Delays that seem unavoidable are included in the standard time. Wage rate standards are normally either a matter of company policy or the result of negotiations between management and unions. The agreed wage rates are applied to the standard time allowed to determine the standard labour cost for each operation.

Overhead standards

The procedure for establishing standard manufacturing overhead rates for a standard costing system is the same as that which is used for establishing predetermined overhead rates as outlined in Chapter 4. Separate rates for fixed and variable overheads are essential for planning and control. Normally the standard overhead rate will be based on a rate per direct labour hour or machine hour of input.

The main difference with the treatment of overheads under a standard costing system as opposed to a non-standard costing system is that the product overhead cost is based on the hourly overhead rates multiplied by the *standard hours* (that is, hours which should have been used) rather than the *actual hours* used.

Review of standards

Standards should be continuously reviewed because changes in production methods and input prices may lead to more efficient methods of production. The expectation that standards should improve over time can also be justified in terms of a learning process, as operations can be performed more effectively as they become more familiar. We shall discuss how the learning curve can be applied to standard setting in Chapter 20. For a detailed discussion of this topic see Harvey and Soliman (1983).

Types of cost standards

The determination of standard costs raises the problem of how demanding the standard should be. Should they represent ideal or faultless performance or should they represent easily attainable performance? Standards are normally classified into three broad categories:

(1) basic cost standards,
(2) ideal standards,
(3) currently attainable standards.

Basic cost standards

Standards of this type represent constant standards which are left unchanged over long periods. The main advantage of basic standards is that a base is provided for a comparison with actual costs through a period of years with the same standard, and efficiency trends can be established over time. When changes occur in methods of production, price levels or other relevant factors, basic standards are not very useful because they do not represent *current* target costs. For this reason basic cost standards are seldom used.

Ideal standards

These standards represent perfect performance. Ideal standard costs are the minimum costs which are possible under the most efficient operating conditions. In practice, ideal standards are unlikely to be achieved but such standards may be used by management if it is considered that they provide the best motivation. Evidence appears to indicate that such standards are considered impossible to achieve and therefore cease to represent a target. For this reason ideal standards are rarely used. We shall discuss the relationship between

the type of standards set and their impact on performance in Chapter 19.

Currently attainable standard costs

These standards represent those costs which should be incurred under efficient operating conditions. They are standards which are difficult, but not impossible to achieve. Attainable standards are easier to achieve than ideal standards because allowances are made for normal spoilage, machine breakdowns and lost time. In practice, currently attainable standards are the most frequently used as they provide a fair base from which to measure deviations from targets for which employees are held responsible. The fact that these standards represent a target which can be achieved under efficient conditions, but which is also viewed as being neither too easy to achieve nor impossible to achieve, provides the best norm to which actual costs should be compared.

In addition, attainable standards can be used for planning as they represent standards which *should* be achieved. It is preferable to prepare the master budget and the cash budget using these standards. Clearly, it is inappropriate to use ideal standards, which are unlikely to be achieved, in formulating these budgets. Hence, attainable standards lead to economies as they can be used for both planning and control.

Motivational effect of standards

A standard will only motivate desired behaviour when it is accepted by an employee, and it is therefore important to be aware of the factors which affect the motivational power of standards. For a detailed discussion of these factors see Chapter 19.

Operation of a standard costing system

Standard costing is most suited to an organization whose activities consist of a series of *common* or *repetitive* operations. It is therefore relevant in manufacturing organizations as the processes involved are often of a repetitive nature. Standard costing procedures can also be applied to non-manufacturing activities where the operations are of a repetitive nature but it cannot easily be applied to activities of a non-repetitive nature, as there is no basis for observing repetitive operations and consequently standards cannot be set. For an illustration of standard costing applied to the distribution function see Barnes and Targett (1984).

A standard costing system can be applied to organizations which produce many different products so long as production consists of a series of common operations. For example, if the output from a factory is the result of five common operations it is possible to produce many different product variations from these operations. It is therefore possible that a large product range may result from a small number of common operations. The standard product costs can be obtained by simply combining the standard costs from the operations which are necessary to make the

Exhibit 17.1 Standard costs analysed by operations and products

Responsibility centre	Operation No. and standard cost		Products 100	101	102	103	104	105	106	Total standard cost	Actual cost
	No.	Standard Cost								£	
A	1	£20	✓	✓		✓	✓	✓	✓	120	
B	2	£30		✓		✓		✓		90	
C	3	£40	✓		✓	✓				120	
D	4	£50	✓	✓	✓				✓	200	
Standard product cost			£110	£100	£90	£50	£60	£50	£70	530	

product. The process is illustrated in Exhibit 17.1. We have assumed that the standard costs are £20, £30, £40 and £50 for each of the operations 1 to 4. The standard cost for *product* 100 is therefore £110, which consists of £20 for operation 1, plus £40 and £50 for operations 3 and 4. The standard costs for each of the other products are calculated in a similar manner. In addition the total standard cost for the total output of each *operation* has been calculated. For example, six items of operation number 1 have been completed giving a total standard cost of £120 for this operation (six items at £20 each). Three items of operation 2 have been completed giving a total standard cost of £90, and so on.

Variances allocated to responsibility centres

You can see from Exhibit 17.1 that different responsibility centres are responsible for each operation. Consequently, there is no point in comparing the actual cost of *product* 100 with the standard cost of £110 for the purposes of control, as responsibility centres A, C and D are responsible for the variance. None of the responsibility centres is solely answerable for the variance. Cost control requires that responsibility centres are identified with the standard cost for the output achieved. Therefore, if the actual costs for *responsibility centre A* are compared with the standard cost of £120 for the production of the six items, the manager of this responsibility centre will be answerable for the full amount of the variance. *Only by comparing total actual costs with total standard costs for each operation or responsibility centre for a period can control be effectively achieved.* A comparison of standard product costs with actual costs which involves several different responsibility centres is clearly inappropriate.

Actual product costs not required

It is questionable whether the allocation of actual costs to products serves any useful purpose. Because standard costs represent *future* target costs they are preferable to actual *past* costs for decision-making. Also, the statement of standard accounting practice on stocks and work in progress (Accounting Standards Committee, SSAP 9) indicates that if standard product costs provide a reasonable approximation of actual product costs, they are acceptable for stock valuation calcula-

tions for external reporting.

There are therefore strong arguments for not producing actual *product* costs when a standard costing system exists, as this will lead to large clerical savings. However, it must be stressed that actual costs mut be accumulated periodically for each operation or responsibility centre so that comparisons can be made with standard costs. Nevertheless, there will be considerably fewer responsibility centres than products and the accumulation of actual costs is therefore much less time consuming.

Detailed analysis of variances

The use of a standard costing system also enables a detailed analysis of the variances to be presented. For example, variances for each responsibility centre can be identified by each element of cost and analysed according to the price and quantity content. The accountant assists managers by pinpointing where the variances have arisen and the responsibility managers can undertake to carry out the appropriate investigations to identify the reasons for the variance. For example, the accountant might identify the reason for a direct materials variance as being excessive usage of a certain material in a particular process, but the responsibility centre manager must investigate this process and identify the reasons for the excessive usage. Such an investigation should result in appropriate remedial action being taken or, if it is found that the variance is due to a permanent change in the standard, the standard should be changed.

Comparisons after the event

It may be argued that there is little point in comparing actual performance with standard performance because such comparisons can only be made after the event. Nevertheless, if people know in advance that their performance is going to be judged, they are likely to act differently from the way they would have done if they were aware that their performance was not going to be measured. Furthermore, even though it is not possible for a manager to change his performance after the event, an analysis of how well a person has performed in the past may indicate, both to the person concerned and his superior, ways of obtaining better performance in the future.

Variance analysis

It is possible to compute variances simply by committing to memory a series of variance formulas. If you adopt this approach, however, it will not help you to understand what a variance is intended to depict and what the relevent variables represent. In our discussion of each variance we will therefore concentrate on the fundamental meaning of the variance so that you can logically deduce the variance formulas as we go along.

All of the variances presented in this chapter are illustrated from the information contained in Example 17.1.

EXAMPLE 17.1

Alpha manufacturing company produces a single

Overheads:		
Variable — 3 hours at £2 per direct labour hour	6.00	
Fixed — 3 hours at £4 per direct labour hour	12.00	18.00
Total standard cost		32.00
Standard profit margin (25% on cost)		8.00
Standard selling price		40.00

Alpha Ltd plan to produce 10,000 units of sigma in the month of April and the budgeted costs based on the information contained in the standard cost card are as follows:

Budget based on the above standard costs and an output of 10,000 units

			£
Sales (10,000 units of Sigma at £40 per unit)			400,000
Direct materials: A 20,000 kilos at £1 per kilo	20,000		
B 10,000 kilos at £3 per kilo	30,000	50,000	
Direct labour: 30,000 hours at £3 per hour		90,000	
Variable overheads: 30,000 hours at £2 per direct labour hour		60,000	
Fixed overheads		120,000*	320,000
Budgeted profit			80,000

*Budgeted fixed overheads are £120,000 per month and are charged on the basis of direct labour hours, giving a fixed overhead rate of £4 per direct labour hour (£120,000 ÷ 30,000 direct labour hours).

The actual results for April are:

			£
Sales (9,000 units at £42)			378,000
Direct materials: A 19,000 kilos at £1.10 per kilo	20,900		
B 10,100 kilos at £2.80 per kilo	28,280		
Direct labour 28,500 hours at £3.20 per hour	91,200		
Variable overheads	52,000		
Fixed overheads	116,000	308,380	
Profit		69,620	

Manufacturing overheads are charged to production on the basis of direct labour hours. Actual production and sales for the period were 9,000 units.

Figure 17.1 shows the breakdown of the profit variance (the difference between budgeted and actual profit) into the component cost and revenue variances which can be calculated for Example 17.1. Let us now use the information contained in Example 17.1 to calculate each of these variances for a standard absorption costing variance system. In the latter part of this chapter we shall compare this with standard variable costing.

product which is known as sigma. The product requires a single operation and the standard cost for this operation is presented in the following standard cost card:

Standard cost card for product sigma

	£
Direct materials	
2 kilos of A at £1 per kilo	2.00
1 kilo of B at £3 per kilo	3.00
Direct labour	
3 hours at £3 per hour	9.00

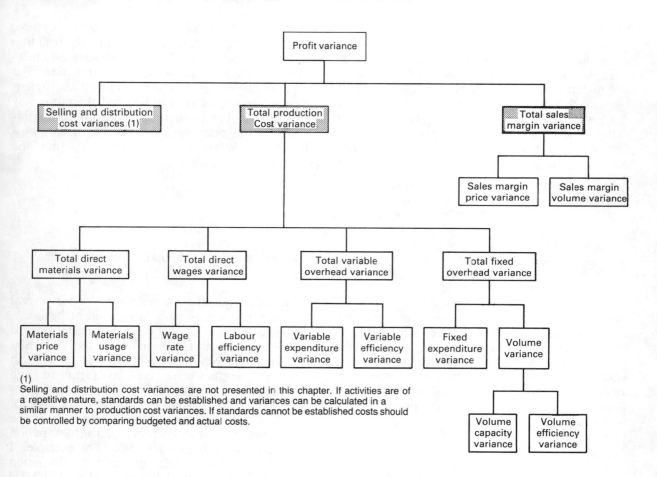

Fig. 17.1 Absorption costing variance analysis

Material variances

The cost of the materials which are used in a manufactured product is determined by two basic factors: the price which was paid for the materials, and the quantity of materials which were used in production. This gives rise to the possibility that the actual cost will differ from the standard cost because the actual *quantity* of materials used will be different from the standard *quantity* and/or that the actual *price* paid will be different from the standard *price*. We can then calculate a material usage and a material price variance.

Material price variances

The starting point for calculating this variance is simply to compare the standard price per unit of materials with the actual price per unit. In Example 17.1 the standard price for material A was £1 per kilo but the actual price paid was £1.10 per kilo. The price variance is 10p per kilo. This is of little consequence if the excess purchase price has been paid only for a small number of units of purchases. But the consequences are important if the excess purchase price has been paid for a large number of units as the effect of the variance will

be greater.

The difference between the standard material price and the actual price per unit should be multiplied by the quantity of materials purchased. For material A the price variance is 10p per unit, but as 19,000 kilos were purchased the excess price was paid out 19,000 times. Hence the total material price variance is £1,900 adverse. The formula for the material price variance now follows logically:

The material price variance is equal to the difference between the standard price (SP) and the actual price (AP) per unit of materials multiplied by the quantity of materials purchased (QP), or

$$(SP - AP) \times QP$$

For material B the standard price is £3.00 compared with an actual price of £2.80 giving a 20p saving per kilo. As 10,100 kilos were purchased the total price variance will be £2,020 (10,100 kilos at 20p). The variance for material B is favourable and the variance for material A is adverse. The normal procedure is to present the amount of the variances followed by symbols A or F to indicate either adverse or favourable variances.

Possible causes

It is incorrect to assume that the material price variance will always indicate the efficiency of the purchasing department. Actual prices may exceed standard prices because of a change in market conditions which cause a general price increase for the type of materials used. The price variance might therefore be beyond the control of the purchasing department. Alternatively, an adverse price variance may reflect a failure by the purchasing department to seek the most advantageous sources of supply. A favourable price variance might be due to the purchase of inferior quality materials which may lead to inferior production or more wastage. For example, the price variance for material B is favourable but we shall see in the next section that this is offset by excess usage. If the reason for this excess usage is due to the purchase of inferior quality materials then the material usage variance should be charged to the purchasing department.

It is also possible that another department may be responsible for all or part of the price variance. For example, a shortage of materials resulting from bad stock control may necessitate an emergency purchase being made at short notice. The supplier may incur additional handling and freight charges on special rush orders and therefore may charge a higher price for the materials. In this situation the price variance will be the responsibility of the stores department and not the purchasing department.

Calculation on quantity purchased or quantity used

In practice the price variance may be for several different reasons, some of which will be beyond a company's control, but others may be due to inefficiencies. It is therefore important that variances are reported as quickly as possible so that any inefficiencies can be identified and remedial action taken. A problem occurs, however, with material purchases in that the time of purchase and the time of usage may not be the same: materials may be purchased in one period and used in a subsequent period. For example, if 10,000 units of a material are purchased in period 1 at a price of £1 per unit over standard and 2,000 units are used in each of periods 1 to 5, the following alternatives are available for calculating the price variance:

(1) The full amount of the price variance of £10,000 is reported in *period 1* with quantity being defined as the *quantity purchased*.
(2) The price variance is calculated with quantity being defined as the *quantity used*. The unit price variance of £1 is multiplied by the quantity used (that is, 2,000 units) which means that a price variance of £2,000 will be reported for each of *periods 1 to 5*.

Method (1) is recommended because the price variance can be reported in the period in which it is incurred, and reporting of the total variance is not delayed until months later when the materials are used. For the sake of simplicity let us assume in Example 17.1 that the actual purchases are identical to the material used.

Material usage variance

The starting point for calculating this variance is simply to compare the standard quantity which should have been used with the actual quantity which has been used. In Example 17.1 the standard usage for the production of one unit of Sigma is two kilos for material A. As 9,000 units of Sigma are produced, 18,000 kilos of material A should have been used; however, 19,000 kilos are actually used, which means there has been an excess usage of 1,000 kilos.

The importance of this excess usage depends on the price of the materials. For example, if the price is 1p per kilo, an excess usage of 1,000 kilos will not be very significant, but if the price is £10 per unit, an excess usage of 1,000 kilos will be very significant. It follows that to assess the importance of the excess usage the variance should be expressed in monetary terms.

Calculation based on standard price or actual price

Should the standard material price per kilo or the actual material price per kilo be used to calculate the variance? The answer is the standard price. If the *actual* material price is used the usage variance will be affected by the efficiency of the purchasing department as any excess purchase price will be assigned to the excess usage.

It is therefore necessary to remove the price effects from the usage variance calculation and this is achieved by valuing the variance at the standard price. Hence, the 1,000 kilos excess usage of material A is multiplied by the standard price of £1 per unit, which gives an adverse usage variance of £1,000. The formula for the variance is as follows:

> The material usage variance is equal to the difference between the standard quantity (SQ) required for actual production and the actual quantity (AQ) used multiplied by the standard material price (SP), or

$$(SQ - AQ) \times SP$$

For material B the standard quantity is 9,000 kilos but 10,100 kilos have been used. The excess usage of 1,100 kilos is multiplied by the standard price of £3 per kilo which gives an adverse variance of £3,300. Note that the principles of flexible budgeting also apply here with *standard quantity being based on actual production and not budgeted production*. This ensures that a manager is evaluated under the conditions in which he actually worked and not those which were envisaged at the time the budget was prepared.

Possible causes

The material usage variance is normally controllable by the production foreman. Common causes of material usage variances include the careless handling of materials by production personnel, the purchase of inferior quality materials, pilferage, changes in quality control requirements, or changes in methods of production. Separate material usage variances should be calculated for each type of material used and allocated to each responsibility centre.

Reporting

To ensure speedy reporting of variances, stores requisitions should be issued by the production planning department for the standard quantity of material which is required for each production order. This is obtained by referring to the output specified on the production order and multiplying by the material requirements per unit of output which are listed on the standard cost card. If the production department requires additional materials it will be necessary to issue a supplementary requisition. This should be a different colour, with a distinctive code designation so that the variance is highlighted when the excess materials are issued. The stores requisition should contain a statement of the reasons for the excess usage and should be signed by the person who is responsible for the materials usage variance. If this procedure is followed the person responsible will quickly be made aware of any excess usage.

Joint price usage variance

Note that the analysis of the material variance into the price and usage elements is not theoretically correct as there may be a small joint mutual price/quantity effect. The following information is extracted from Example 17.1 for material A:

(1) 18,000 kilos of material A are required at a standard price of £1 per kilo.

(2) 19,000 kilos are used at a price of £1.10.

The purchasing officer might readily accept responsibility for the price variance of 10p per kilo for 18,000 kilos but may claim that the extra 1,000 kilos at 10p is more the responsibility of the production foreman. It may be argued that if the foreman had produced in accordance with the standard, the extra 1,000 kilos would not have been needed.

The foreman, on the other hand, will accept responsibility for the 1,000 kilos excess usage at a standard price of £1 but will argue that he should not be held accountable for the additional purchase price of 10p per unit.

One possible way of dealing with this would be to report the joint price/quantity variance of £100 (1,000 units at 10p) separately and not charge it to either manager. However, conventional variance analysis includes this joint price/quantity variance of £100 as part of the price variance. The reason for this is that the usage variance is considered to be far more important than the price variance because management can exert a more direct influence over the usage variance. It is argued that the joint price/quantity variance is less likely to cause arguments if it is included in the price variance rather than in the quantity variance.

Total material variance

From Figure 17.1 you will see that this variance is the total variance before it is analysed into the price and usage elements. The formula for the variance is as follows:

> The total material variance is the difference between the standard material cost (SC) for the actual production and the actual cost (AC), or

$$SC - AC$$

For material A the standard material cost is £2 per unit giving a total standard material cost of £18,000. The actual cost is £20,900 and therefore the variance is £2,900 adverse. The price variance of £1,900 plus the usage variance of £1,000 agrees with the total materials variance. Similarly, the total materials variance for material B is £1,280 consisting of a favourable price variance of £2,020 and an adverse usage variance of £3,300. Note that if the price variance is calculated on the actual quantity *purchased* instead of the actual quantity *used*, the price variance plus the usage variance will agree with the total variance only when the quantity purchased is equal to the quantity which is used in the particular accounting period. Reconciling the price and usage variance with the total variance is merely a reconciliation exercise and you should not be concerned if reconciliation of the sub-variances with the total variances is not possible.

Labour variances

The cost of labour is determined by the price which is paid for labour and the quantity of labour which is used. Thus a price and quantity variance will also arise for labour. Unlike materials, labour cannot be stored because the purchase and usage of labour normally takes place at the same time. Hence ther actual quantity of hours *purchased* will be equal to the actual quantity of hours *used* for each period. For this reason the price variance plus the quantity variance should agree with the total labour variance.

Wage rate variance

This variance is calculated by comparing the standard price per hour with the actual price paid per hour. In Example 17.1 the standard wage rate per hour is £3 and the actual wage rate is £3.20 per hour giving a wage rate variance of 20p per hour. To determine the importance of the variance it is necessary to ascertain how many times the excess payment of 20p per hour is paid.

As 28,500 labour hours are used we multiply 28,500 hours by 20p. This gives an adverse wage rate variance of £5,700. The formula for the wage rate variance is as follows:

> The wage rate variance is equal to the difference between the standard wage rate per hour (SR) and the actual wage rate (AR) multiplied by the actual number of hours worked (AH), or

$$(SR - AR) \times AH$$

Possible causes

The wage rate variance may be due to a negotiated increase in wage rates not yet having been reflected in the standard wage rate. In a situation such as this the variance cannot be regarded as controllable. However, part or all of the variance may be due to the assignment of skilled labour to work which is normally performed by unskilled labour. The variance may then be regarded as the responsibility of the foreman because he should have matched the appropriate grade of labour to the task at hand. Nevertheless, the wage rate variance is probably the one that is least subject to control by management. In most cases the variance is due to wage rate standards not being kept in line with changes in actual wage rates and for this reason it is not normally controllable by departmental managers.

Labour efficiency variance

The labour efficiency variance represents the quantity variance for direct labour. The quantity of labour which should be used for the actual output is expressed in terms of *standard hours produced*. In Example 17.1 the standard time for the production of one unit of sigma is 3 hours. Thus a production level of 9,000 units results in an output of 27,000 standard hours. In other words, working at the prescribed level of efficiency, it should take 27,000 hours to produce 9,000 units. However, 28,500 direct labour hours are actually required to produce this output which means that 1,500 excess direct labour hours are used. We multiply the excess direct labour hours by the *standard* wage rate to calculate the variance. This gives an adverse variance of £4,500. The formula for calculating the labour efficiency variance is as

follows:

> The labour efficiency variance is equal to the difference between the standard labour hours for actual production (SH) and the actual labour hours worked (AH) during the period multiplied by the standard wage rate per hour (SR), or

$$(SH - AH) \times SR$$

Possible causes

The labour efficiency variance is normally controllable by the production foreman and may be due to a variety of reasons. For example, the use of inferior quality materials, different grades of labour, failure to maintain machinery in proper condition, the introduction of new equipment or tools, and changes in the production processes will all result in changes in the efficiency of labour. An efficiency variance may not always be controllable by the production foreman; it may be due, for example, to poor production scheduling by the planning department, or to a change in quality control standards.

Recording procedure

The most suitable procedure for identifying the labour efficiency variance is for the job card to include the standard labour time for the particular operation. When the operation is completed the actual labour time is recorded and the foreman can be made aware immediately of the variance.

Total labour variance

From Fig. 17.1 you will see that this variance represents the total variance before analysis into the price and quantity elements. The formula for the variance is as follows:

> The total labour variance is the difference between the standard labour cost (SC) for the actual production and the actual labour cost (AC), or

$$SC - AC$$

In Example 17.1 the actual production was 9,000 units and with a standard labour cost of £9 per unit the standard cost is £81,000. The actual cost is

£91,200 which gives an adverse variance of £10,200. This consists of a wage rate variance of £5,700 and a labour efficiency variance of £4,500.

Overhead variances

The analysis of overhead variances explains the difference between the actual amount of production overhead incurred and the amount which is charged to production through previously determined overhead absorption rates. It is easier to understand the analysis if the actual overheads which are incurred and the amounts which are charged to production are divided into their fixed and variable components. The variances for the fixed and the variable overheads may then be computed individually as illustrated in Fig. 17.1.

To help you to understand overhead variances the appropriate information from Example 17.1 is summarized in Exhibit 17.2.

Note that the budgeted direct laboor hours are based on a budgeted output of 10,000 units of sigma with a standard time of 3 hours per unit. Hence the company plans an *output* in terms of standard hours produced of 30,000. At the planning stage an *input* of 30,000 direct labour hours will also be planned as the company will budget at the level of efficiency specified in the calculation of the product standard cost. Thus the budgeted hours of *input* and the budgeted hours of *output* (that is, standard hours produced) will be the same at the planning stage.

The actual production is 9,000 units and with a standard time of 3 hours per unit of output the *actual production* is 27,000 standard hours. How-

ever, 28,500 direct labour hours of *input* were required to achieve this output. The budgeted fixed overheads are £120,000 per month and planned monthly production is 10,000 units or 30,000 hours when measured in standard hours produced. This will give a budgeted fixed overhead rate of £4 per standard hour produced.

Let us now calculate the fixed overhead variances outlined in Fig. 17.1 from the information contained in Exhibit 17.1.

Total fixed overhead variance

The *total* labour and material variances were calculated by comparing the standard cost for actual production with the actual cost. The total fixed overhead variance is calculated in the same way. The actual production is 27,000 standard hours. The standard fixed overhead is therefore £108,000 for an output of 27,000 standard hours (27,000 hours at £4). The actual fixed overhead which is incurred is £116,000 giving an adverse variance of £8,000. The formula for the variance is as follows:

> The total fixed overhead variance is the difference between the standard fixed overhead charged to production (SC) and the actual fixed overhead incurred (AC), or

> SC – AC

The effect of charging fixed overheads to production at £4 per standard hour produced is that fixed costs will be treated as if they were variable costs. This is necessary for calculating product costs for stock valuation, but for cost control the procedure is questionable.

You may have realized that the total fixed overhead variance is equivalent to the under or over recovery of fixed overheads which we discussed in Chapter 4. In that chapter we noted that the under or over recovery may be for one of two reasons:

(1) that the actual expenditure is different from the budgeted expenditure;
(2) that actual production is different from budgeted production.

These two reasons relate to the two sub-variances of the total fixed overhead variance presented in Fig. 17.1 — that is, the fixed overhead expenditure variance and the volume variance.

Exhibit 17.2 Comparison of budget and actual overhead expenditure

	Budget	Actual
Monthly fixed overheads	£120,000	£116,000
Monthly variable overheads	£ 60,000	£ 52,000
Direct labour hours of input (input hours)	30,000 hrs	28,500 hrs
Direct labour hours of output (standard hours produced)	30,000 hrs	27,000 hrs
Standard fixed overhead rate per standard hour	£4	
Standard variable overhead rate per standard hour	£2	

Fixed overhead expenditure or spending variance

This variance seeks to identify that portion of the total fixed overhead variance which is due to *actual fixed overhead expenditure* differing from the *budgeted fixed overhead expenditure*. The standard fixed overhead rate is calculated on the basis of budgeted fixed overhead expenditure of £120,000 but actual fixed overhead expenditure is £116,000. An over recovery of £4,000 will arise because actual fixed overhead expenditure is less than the budgeted expenditure. This under or over recovery of fixed overheads which occurs because actual overheads are different from budgeted overheads is called an expenditure variance. The formula for the variance is as follows:

The fixed overhead expenditure variance is the difference between the budgeted fixed overheads (BFO) and the actual fixed overheads incurred (AFO), or

$$BFO - AFO$$

Whenever the actual fixed overheads are less than the budgeted fixed overheads the variance will be favourable. The total of the fixed overhead expenditure variance on its own is not particularly informative. Any meaningful analysis of this variance requires a comparison of the actual expenditure for each individual item of fixed overhead expenditure against the budget. The difference may be due to a variety of causes such as changes in salaries paid to supervisors, or the appointment of additional supervisors. Only by comparing individual items of expenditure and ascertaining the reasons for the variances can one determine whether the variance is controllable or uncontrollable. Generally, this variance is likely to be uncontrollable.

Volume variance

This variance seeks to identify that portion of the total fixed overhead variance which is due to *actual production* being different from *budgeted production*. In Exhibit 17.2 the standard fixed overhead rate of £4 per hour is calculated on the basis of a normal activity of 30,000 standard hours per month. Only when actual standard hours produced are 30,000 will the budgeted monthly fixed overheads of £120,000 be exactly recovered. Actual output, however, is only 27,000 standard hours. The fact that the actual production is 3,000 standard hours less than the budgeted hours will lead to a failure to recover £12,000 fixed overheads (3,000 hours at £4 fixed overhead rate per hour). The formula for the variance is as follows:

The volume variance is the difference between actual production (AP) and budgeted production (BP) for a period multiplied by the standard fixed overhead rate (SR), or

$$(AP - BP) \times SR$$

The volume variance reflects the fact that fixed overheads do not fluctuate in relation to output in the short term. Whenever actual production is less than budgeted production, the fixed overhead charged to production will be less than the budgeted cost and the volume variance will be adverse. Conversely, if the actual production is greater than the budgeted production the volume variance will be favourable.

Sunk cost

Information which indicates that actual production is 3,000 standard hours less than budgeted production is useful to management but to attach a fixed overhead rate to this figure is of little value for control because fixed costs represent sunk costs. The volume variance of £12,000 does not reflect the cost of the facilities which remain idle as the fixed overhead cost will not change if production declines, at least in the short term. A cost of lost output only occurs if a firm has a demand for the lost output. In this situation it is more meaningful to measure the cost of the lost output in terms of the lost contribution from a failure to produce the budgeted output (see Horngren, 1978). We shall consider this approach in the next chapter.

Possible causes

Changes in production volume from the amount budgeted may be caused by shifts in demand for products, labour disputes, material shortages, poor production scheduling, machine breakdowns, labour efficiency and poor production quality. Some of these factors may be controllable by production or sales management while others may

not.

When the adverse volume variance of £12,000 is netted with the favourable expenditure variance of £4,000 the result is equal to the total fixed overhead adverse variance of £8,000. Figure 17.1 illustrates that *it is also possible to analyse the volume variance into two further sub-variances — the volume efficiency variance and the capacity variance*.

Volume efficiency variance

If we wish to identify the reasons for the volume variance we may ask why the actual production was different from the budgeted production. One possible reason may be that the labour force worked at a different level of efficiency from that which was anticipated in the budget.

The actual number of direct labour hours of input was 28,500. Hence one would have expected 28,500 hours of output (that is, standard hours produced) from this input, but only 27,000 standard hours were actually produced. Thus one reason for the failure to meet the budgeted output was that output in standard hours was 1,500 hours less than it should have been. If the labour force had worked at the prescribed level of efficiency an additional 1,500 standard hours would have been produced and this would have led to a total of £6,000 (1,500 hours at £4 per standard hour) fixed overheads being absorbed. The inefficiency of labour is therefore one of the reasons why the actual production was less than the budgeted production and this gives an adverse variance of £6,000. The formula for the variance is as follows:

The volume efficiency variance is the difference between the standard hours of output (SH) and the actual hours of input (AH) for the period multiplied by the standard fixed overhead rate (SR), or

$$(SH - AH) \times SR$$

You may have noted that the physical content of this variance is a measure of labour efficiency and is identical to the labour efficiency variance. Consequently, the reasons for this variance will be identical to those previously decribed for the labour efficiency variance. Note also that as this variance is a sub-variance of the volume variance the same comments apply as to the usefulness of attaching a value for fixed overheads, because

fixed overheads represent sunk costs. Total fixed overhead will not change because of the efficiency of labour. Again it would be better to measure this variance in terms of the lost contribution arising from lost sales.

Volume capacity variance

This variance indicates the second reason why the actual production might be different from the budgeted production. The budget is based on the assumption that the direct labour hours of input will be 30,000 hours, but the actual hours of input are 28,500 hours. The difference of 1,500 hours reflects the fact that the company has failed to utilize the planned capacity. If we assume that the 1,500 hours would have been worked at the prescribed level of efficiency, an additional 1,500 standard hours could have been produced and an additional £6,000 fixed overhead could have been absorbed. Hence the capacity variance is £6,000 adverse.

Whereas the volume efficiency variance indicates a failure to utilize capacity *efficiently*, the volume capacity variance indicates a failure to utilize capacity *at all*. The formula is as follows:

The volume capacity variance is the difference between the actual hours of input (AH) and the budgeted hours of input (BH) for the period multiplied by the standard fixed overhead rate (SR), or

$$(AH - BH) \times SR$$

A failure to achieve the budgeted capacity may be for a variety of reasons. Machine breakdowns, material shortages, poor production scheduling, labour disputes and a reduction in sales demand are all possible causes of an adverse volume capacity variance. Again, it is better to express this variance in terms of lost contribution from lost sales caused by a failure to utilize the capacity. It is not very meaningful to attach fixed costs to the variance as the total fixed costs will not be affected by a failure to utilize capacity.

Summary of fixed overhead variances

The volume efficiency variance is £6,000 adverse, and the volume capacity variance is also £6,000 adverse. When these two variances are added

Exhibit 17.3 Analysis of the volume variance

(1) Budgeted hours of output and input	(2) Actual hours of input	(3) Actual hours of output
30,000	28,500	27,000

Capacity = 1,500 hrs Efficiency = 1,500 hrs
(1–2) (2–3)

Volume 3,000 hrs
(1–3)

together they agree with the fixed overhead volume variance of £12,000. Exhibit 17.3 summarizes how the volume variance is analysed according to capacity and efficiency.

The actual output was 3,000 hours less than the budget giving an adverse volume variance. The capacity variance indicates that one reason for failing to meet the budgeted output was that 1,500 hours of *capacity* were not utilized. In addition, those 28,500 hours which were utilized only led to 27,000 hours of output. An *inefficient* use of the capacity therefore provides a second explanation as to why the budgeted output was not achieved. A fixed overhead rate of £4 per hour is applied to the physical quantity of the variances so that fixed overhead variances may be presented in monetary terms. Exhibit 17.4 summarizes the variances which we have calculated in this section.

Variable overhead variances

A total variable overhead variance is calculated in the same way as the total fixed overhead variance. In Example 17.1 the output is 9,000 units and the standard variable overhead cost is £6 *per unit* produced. The standard cost of production for variable overheads is £54,000. Alternatively, the standard cost can be calculated by measuring the production in standard hours. Reference to Exhibit 17.2 indicates that actual output is 27,000 standard hours and the variable overhead rate is £2 *per standard hour* which also gives a standard cost of £54,000. The actual variable overheads incurred are £52,000, giving a favourable variance of £2,000. The formula for the variance is as follows:

Exhibit 17.4 Diagram of fixed overhead variances

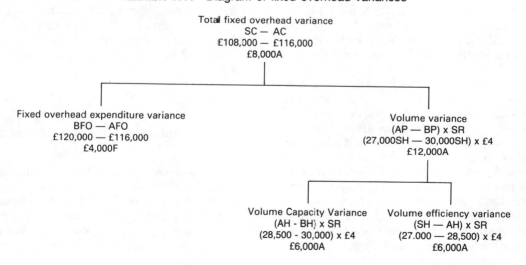

Total fixed overhead variance
SC — AC
£108,000 — £116,000
£8,000A

Fixed overhead expenditure variance
BFO — AFO
£120,000 — £116,000
£4,000F

Volume variance
(AP — BP) x SR
(27,000SH — 30,000SH) x £4
£12,000A

Volume Capacity Variance
(AH - BH) x SR
(28,500 - 30,000) x £4
£6,000A

Volume efficiency variance
(SH — AH) x SR
(27.000 — 28,500) x £4
£6,000A

The total variable overhead variance is the difference between the standard variable overheads charged to production (SC) and the actual variable overheads incurred (AC), or

$$SC - AC$$

It is normally assumed that variable overheads vary with direct labour hours of *input* and the total variable overhead variance will therefore be due to one or both of the following:

(1) Actual expenditure may be different from budgeted expenditure.

(2) The actual direct labour hours of input may be different from the direct labour hours of input which should have been used.

These reasons give rise to the two sub-variances which are shown in Fig. 17.1 — the variable overhead expenditure variance and the variable overhead efficiency variance.

Variable overhead expenditure variance

To compare the actual overhead expenditure with the budgeted expenditure it is necessary to flex the budget. Because it is assumed that variable overheads will vary with direct labour hours of *input* the budget is flexed on this basis. (For a more refined approach which flexes the budget on the basis of *input* and *output*, see Solomons, 1972.) Actual variable overhead expenditure is £52,000 resulting from 28,500 direct labour hours of input. For this level of activity variable overheads of £57,000, which consist of 28,500 input hours at £2 per hour, should have been spent. Spending was £5,000 less than it should have been and the result is a favourable variance.

If we compare the budgeted and the actual overhead costs for 28,500 direct labour hours of input we will ensure that any efficiency content is removed from the variance. This means that any difference must be due to the actual variable overhead spending being different from the budgeted variable overhead spending. The formula for the variance is as follows:

The variable overhead expenditure variance is equal to the difference between the budgeted flexed variable overheads (BFVO) for the actual direct labour hours of input and the actual variable overhead costs incurred (AVO), or

$$(BFVO - AVO)$$

Possible causes

The variable overhead expenditure variance on its own is not very meaningful. Any meaningful analysis of this variance requires a comparison of the actual expenditure for each individual item of variable overhead expenditure against the budget. The budgeted amounts are based upon expected prices and consumption rates for each variable cost item. It is possible for any combination of these items to change. For example, if indirect material costs are greater than budgeted costs, the difference may be due to an increase in the price of indirect materials, or to an increase in the rate of usage of these items, or a combination of both. Similarly, variable indirect labour costs may be different from the budget because of changes in wage rates or the rate of usage. These price and quantity differences may be traced to the same types of causes as those discussed earlier in this chapter in connection with direct labour and materials. Also, maintenance costs, power costs and other utilities may change because of rate changes or variations in consumption. Consequently, any meaningful interpretation of the expenditure variance must focus on individual cost items. If you refer to the performance report presented in Exhibit 17.6 you can see how the £5,000 variable overhead expenditure variance can be analysed by individual items of expenditure.

Variable overhead efficiency variance

The variable overhead efficiency variance arises because 28,500 direct labour hours of input were required to produce 27,000 standard hours. Thus 1,500 excess direct labour hours of input were required. Because variable overheads are assumed to vary with direct labour hours of input an

additional £3,000 (1,500 hours at £2) variable overheads will be incurred. The formula for the variance is as follows:

> The variable overhead efficiency variance is the difference between the standard hours of output (SH) and the actual hours of input (AH) for the period multiplied by the standard variable overhead rate (SR), or

$$(SH - AH) \times SR$$

Note that this variance arises from the efficiency of labour. Consequently, the reasons for the variance are the same as those which have been described previously for the labour efficiency variance. If you refer again to Fig. 17.1 you will see that the variable overhead expenditure variance (£5,000 favourable) plus the variable efficiency variance (£3,000 adverse) add up to the total variable overhead variance of £2,000 favourable.

Sales variances

Sales variances can be used to analyse the performance of the sales function on broadly similar terms to those for manufacturing costs. The most significant feature of sales variance calculations is that they are calculated in terms of *profit margins* rather than *sales values*.

EXAMPLE 17.2

> The budgeted sales for a company are 100 units at £11 per unit. The standard cost per unit is £7. Actual sales are 120 units at £10 per unit and the actual cost per unit is £7.

Reference to Example 17.2 indicates that when the variances are calculated on the basis of sales *value* it is necessary to compare the budgeted sales *value* of £1,100 with the actual sales of £1,200. This gives a favourable variance of £100. This calculation, however, ignores the impact of the sales effort on profit. The budgeted profit is £400 which consists of 100 units at £4 per unit, but the actual impact of the sales effort in terms of profit margins indicates a profit of £360, which consists of 120 units at £3 per unit, indicating an adverse variance of £40. If we examine Example 17.2 we can see that the selling prices have been reduced,

and that this has led to an increase in the total sales revenue but to a reduction in total profit. If we assume that the objective of the selling function is to influence favourably total profits, *a more meaningful performance measure will be obtained by comparing the results of the sales function in terms of profit margins rather than sales revenues.*

Let us now calculate the sales variances from the information contained in Example 17.1.

Total sales margin variance

The total sales *margin* variance seeks to identify the influence which the sales function has on the difference between budget and actual profit. In Example 17.1 the budgeted profit is £80,000 which consists of budgeted sales of 10,000 units at a profit of £8 per unit. This is compared with the profit from the actual sales volume of 9,000 units. Because the sales function is responsible for the sales volume and the unit selling price but *not* the unit manufacturing costs, *the standard cost of sales and not the actual cost of sales is deducted* from the actual sales revenue. The calculation of actual profit for ascertaining the total sales margin variance will therefore be as follows:

Actual sales revenue (9,000 units at £42)	£378,000
Standard cost of sales for actual sales volume (9,000 units at £32)	288,000
Actual profit margin	90,000

To calculate the total sales margin variance we compare the budgeted profit of £80,000 with the actual profit of £90,000. This gives a favourable variance of £10,000 because the actual profit margin exceeds the budgeted profit margin.

The formula for calculating the variance is as follows:

> The total sales margin variance is the difference between the actual profit (AP) and the budgeted profit (BP) (both based on standard unit costs), or

$$AP - BP$$

Using the standard cost to calculate both the budgeted and the actual profit ensures that the production variances do not distort the calculation of the sales variances. The effect of using standard costs throughout the profit margin calculations

means that the sales variances arise because of changes in those variables which are controlled by the sales function, that is, selling prices and sales quantity. Consequently, Fig. 17.1 indicates that it is possible to analyse the total sales margin variance into two sub-variances — a sales margin price variance and a sales margin volume variance.

Sales margin price variance

In Example 17.1 the actual selling price is £42 but the budgeted selling price is £40. With a standard unit cost of £32, the change in selling price has led to an increase in the profit margin from £8 per unit to £10 per unit. Because the actual sales volume is 9,000 units, the increase in the selling price means that an increased profit margin is obtained 9,000 times, giving a favourable sales margin price variance of £18,000. The formula for calculating the variance is as follows:

The sales margin price variance is the difference between the actual margin (AM) and the standard margin (SM) (both based on standard unit costs) multiplied by the actual sales volume (AV), or

$$(AM - SM) \times AV$$

Sales margin volume variance

To ascertain the effect of changes in the sales volume on the difference between the budgeted and the actual profits we must compare the budgeted sales volume with the actual sales volume. The budgeted sales are 10,000 units but the actual sales are 9,000 units, and to enable us to determine the impact of this reduction in sales volume on profit, we must multiply the 1,000 units by the standard profit margin of £8. This gives an adverse variance of £8,000.

The use of the standard margin (standard selling price less standard cost) ensures that the standard selling price is used in the calculation, and the volume variance will not be affected by any *changes* in the actual selling prices. The formula for calculating the variance is as follows:

The sales margin volume variance is the difference between the actual sales volume (AV) and

the budgeted volume (BV) multiplied by the standard profit margin (SM), or

$$(AV - BV) \times SM$$

Difficulties in interpreting sales margin variances

The favourable sales margin price variance of £18,000 plus the adverse volume variance of £8,000 adds up to the total sales margin variance of £10,000. It may be argued that it is not very meaningful to analyse the total sales margin variance into price and volume components because changes in selling prices are likely to affect sales volume. Consequently, a favourable price variance will tend to be associated with an adverse volume variance and vice versa. It may be unrealistic to sell more than the budgeted volume when selling prices have increased.

A further problem with sales variances is that the variances may arise from external factors and may not be controllable by management. For example, changes in selling prices may be the result of a response to changes in selling prices of competitors. Alternatively, a reduction in both selling prices and sales volume may be the result of an economic recession which was not foreseen when the budget was prepared. Manufacturing variances are not influenced as much by external factors and for this reason management are likely to focus most of their attention on the control of the manufacturing variances. Nevertheless, sales margin variances provide useful information which enables the budgeted profit to be reconciled with the actual profit.

Reconcilation of budgeted profit and actual profit

Top management will be interested in the reasons for the actual profit being different from the budgeted profit. By adding the favourable production and sales variances to the budgeted profit and deducting the adverse variances the reconciliation of budgeted and actual profit shown in Exhibit 17.5 can be presented in respect of Example 17.1.

Example 17.1 assumes that Alpha Ltd produces a single produce and that the activities are per-

Exhibit 17.5 Reconciliation of budgeted and actual profit for April

					£
Budgeted net profit					80,000
Sales variances:					
Sales margin price		18,000 F			
Sales margin volume		8,000 A	10,000 F		
Direct cost variances					
Material — Price: Material A	1,900 A				
Material B	2,020 F	120 F			
Usage:Material A	1,000 A				
Material B	3,300 A	4,300 A	4,180 A		
Labour — Rate		5,700 A			
Efficiency		4,500 A	10,200 A		
Manufacturing overhead variances					
Fixed — Expenditure	4,000 F				
Volume capacity	6,000 A				
Volume efficiency	6,000 A	8,000 A			
Variable — Expenditure	5,000 F				
Efficiency	3,000 A	2,000 F	6,000 A		10,380 A
Actual profit					69,620

formed by one responsibility centre. In practice, most companies make many products which require operations to be carried out in different responsibility centres. A reconciliation statement such as that presented in Exhibit 17.5 will therefore normally represent a summary of the variances for many responsibility centres. The reconciliation statement thus represents a broad picture to top management which explains the major reasons for any difference between the budgeted and the actual profit.

Performance reports

The managers of responsibility centres will require a more detailed analysis of the variances to enable them to exercise effective control, and detailed performance reports should be prepared at monthly or weekly intervals to bring to their attention any significant variances. A typical performance report based on the information contained in Example 17.1 is presented in Exhibit 17.6. A departmental performance report should include only those items which the responsibility manager can control or influence. The material price variances and the monetary amount of the volume variance are *not* presented as these are not considered to be within the control of the manager

of the responsibility centre. However, the physical quantity of the volume variance can be obtained from the report by comparing actual production in standard hours with budgeted hours of production. In addition the report will show the physical quantity for the capacity and efficiency variance.

A comparison of current variances with those of previous periods and/or with those of the year to date is presented in the summary of the performance report. This information is often useful in establishing a framework within which current variances can be evaluated. In addition to monthly performance reports the manager of a responsibility centre may receive daily reports on those variances which are controllable on a daily basis. This normally applies to material usage and labour efficiency. For these variances the monthly performance reports will provide a summary of the information that has previously been reported on a daily basis.

Standard variable costing

We considered a variable costing system in Chapter 8. In a standard variable costing system the fixed overheads for the period are charged to the profit and loss account and are not included in the accumulation of product costs. Consequently,

Exhibit 17.6 A typical departmental performance report

DEPARTMENTAL PERFORMANCE REPORT

Department
Period April 19..

Actual production 27,000 standard hours
Actual working hours 28,500 hours
Budgeted hours 30,000 hours

Control ratios: Efficiency 94.7% Capacity 95% Volume 90%

DIRECT MATERIALS

Type	Standard quantity	Actual quantity	Difference	Standard price	Usage variance	Reason
A	18,000 kilos	19,000	1,000	£1.00	£1,000 A	
B	9,000 kilos	10,100	1,100	£3.00	£3,300 A	

DIRECT LABOUR

Grade	Standard hours	Actual hours	Difference	Standard cost	Actual cost	Total variance	Analysis Efficiency	Rate	Reason
	27,000	28,500	1,500	£81,000	£91,200	£10,200	£4,500A	£5,700A	

OVERHEADS

	Allowed cost	Actual cost	Expenditure variance	Reason	Variable overhead efficiency variance	
Controllable costs (variable) Indirect labour Power Maintenance Indirect materials					Difference between standard hours and actual hours at £2 per hour	Hours 1500 £ 3000A
Total	£57,000	£52,000	£5,000F			1500 3000A
Uncontrollable costs (fixed) Lighting and heating Depreciation Supervision						
	£120,000	116,000	4,000F			

SUMMARY

	Variances This month	Cumulative	Comments
	£		
Direct materials	4,300 A		
Direct labour:			
Efficiency	4,500 A		
Wage rate	5,700 A		
Controllable overheads			
Expenditure	5,000 F		
Variable overhead efficiency	3,000 A		
Total	12,500 A		

a volume variance will not arise because fixed overhead will not be absorbed on the basis of production. In Example 17.1 the £116,000 actual fixed overheads will be chargd as a period cost rather than beging included as part of the cost of production. The difference between the actual fixed overheads of £116,000 and the budgeted fixed overheads of £120,000 represents the fixed

Exhibit 17.7 Reconciliation of budgeted and actual profit for a standard variab e costing system

			£
Budgeted net profit			80,000
Sales variances:			
Sales margin price	18,000 F		
Sales margin volume	20,000 A	2,000 A	
Direct cost variances:			
Material: Price	120 F		
Usage	4,300 A	4,180 A	
Labour: Rate	5,700 A		
Efficiency	4,500 A	10,200 A	
Manufacturing overhead variances:			
Fixed overhead expenditure	4,000 F		
Variable overhead expenditure	5,000 F		
Variable overhead efficiency	3,000 A	6,000 F	10,380 A
Actual profit			69,620

overhead expenditure variance and this should be entered in the reconciliation statement to reconcile the budgeted and actual profits. With a variable absorption costing system the fixed overhead volume variance is not considered to be of economic significance as fixed overheads are a sunk cost. The fixed overhead expenditure variance, however, should still be calculated, as spending on fixed overheads may be controllable in the short term.

The only other change to the procedure which was outlined earlier in this chapter for a standard absorption costing system is that the sales margin variances are calculated in terms of contribution margins rather than profit margins. The budgeted profit is reconciled with the actual profit by adding or subtracting the *variable* cost variances, fixed overhead expenditure variance, and the revised sales margin variances. The reconciliation of the budgeted and the actual profit for the variances in Example 17.1 is set out in Exhibit 17.7.

If we compare the absorption cost reconciliation statement presented in Exhibit 17.5 with the variable costing reconciliation statement we can see that the sales volume variance of 100 units is expressed in terms of a unit contribution of £20 rather than a profit margin of £8 per unit, giving a revised variance of £20,000. In addition, the volume variance consisting of the capacity and efficiency variances do not appear in the variable costing reconciliation statement as fixed overhead costs are not absorbed as product costs but are written off as period costs.

Summary of variance formulas

To enable you to review your understanding of variance calculations the formulas for the variances which we have considered in this chapter are summarized below. In each case, the formula is arranged so that a positive variance is favourable and an adverse variance is unfavourable.

Materials and labour

(1) Material price variance = (Standard price per unit of material − actual price) × quantity of materials purchased

(2) Material usage variance = (Standard quantity of materials for actual production − actual quantity used) × standard price per unit

(3) Total materials cost variance = (Actual production × standard cost per unit of production) − actual materials cost

(4) Wage rate variance = (Standard wage rate per hour − actual wage rate) × actual labour hours worked

(5) Labour efficiency variance = (Standard quantity of labour hours for actual production − actual labour hours worked) × standard wage rate per hour

(6) Total labour cost variance = (Actual production × standard cost per unit of production) − actual labour cost

Fixed production overhead

(7) Fixed overhead expenditure variance = Budgeted fixed overheads − actual fixed overheads

(8) Fixed overhead volume variance = (Actual production − budgeted production) × standard fixed overhead rate

(9) Volume efficiency variance = (Standard quantity of input hours for actual production − actual input hours) × standard fixed overhead rate

(10) Volume capacity variance = (Actual hours of input − budgeted hours of input) × standard fixed overhead rate

(11) Total fixed overhead variance = (Actual production × standard fixed overhead rate per unit) − actual fixed overhead cost

Variable production overhead

(12) Variable overhead expenditure variance = (Budgeted variable overheads for actual input volume − actual variable overhead cost)

(13) Variable overhead efficiency variance = (Standard quantity of input hours for actual production − actual input hours) × variable overhead rate

(14) Total variable overhead variance = (Actual production × standard variable overhead rate per unit) − actual variable overhead cost

Sales margins

(15) Sales margin price variance = (Actual unit profit margin* − standard unit profit margin) × actual sales volume

(16) Sales margin volume variance = (Actual sales volume − budgeted sales volume) × standard profit margin

(17) Total sales margin variance = Total actual profit* − total budgeted profit

*Note that actual profit margins are based on actual selling price less *standard cost* of sales.

References and further reading

Accounting Standards Committee. *Accounting for Stocks and Work in Progress* (SSAP 9), 1977.

Barnes, K. and Targett, P. Standard costing in distribution. *Management Accounting* May 1984, 26-7.

Clark, J. A new approach to labour variances. *Management Accounting (USA)* December 1982, 36-40.

Greer, W.R. Standard costing in non-manufacturing activities. *Cost and Management (Canada)* November–December 1975, 12-16.

Harvey, D.W. and Soliman, S.Y. Standard cost variance analysis in a learning environment. *Accounting and Business Research* Summer 1983, 181-9.

Horngren, C.T. A contribution margin approach to the analysis of capacity utilization. In Anton, H.R., Firmin, P.A. and Grove, H.D. (Eds), *Contemporary Issues in Cost and Managerial Accounting*, Houghton Mifflin Company, 1978.

Solomons, D. An analysis of standard cost variances. In Solomons, D. (Ed.), *Studies in Cost Analysis* 2nd edn. Sweet & Maxwell, 1968.

Solomons, D. Flexible budgets and the analysis of overhead variances. In Anton, H.R. and Firmin, P.A. (Eds), *Contemporary Issues in Cost and Managerial Accounting*. Houghton Mifflin Company, 1972.

Problems

*Indicates that a solution is to be found in the *Students' Manual*.

17.1 For a product the following data are given:

Standards per unit of product

Direct material 4 kilos at £0.75 per kilo
Direct labour 2 hours at £1.60 per hour

Actual details for given financial period:

Output produced in units		38,000
Direct materials:		£
Purchased	180,000 kilos for	126,000
Issued to production	154,000 kilos	
Direct labour	78,000 hours worked for	136,500

There was no work in progress at the beginning or end of the period.

You are required to:

(a) calculate the following variances:
 (i) direct materials cost;
 (ii) direct materials price, based on issues to production;
 (iii) direct materials usage;
 (iv) direct wages cost;
 (v) direct wages rate;
 (vi) direct labour efficiency;

(b) state whether, in each of the following cases, the comment given and suggested as the possible reason for the variance, is *consistent* or *inconsistent* with the variance you have calculated in your answer to (a) above, supporting each of your conclusions with a brief explanatory comment.

Item in (a):
 (ii) direct materials price variance: the procurement manager has ignored the economic order quantity and, by obtaining bulk quantities, has purchased material at less than the standard price;
 (iii) direct materials usage variance: material losses in production were less than had been allowed for in the standard;
 (v) direct wages rate variance: the union negotiated wage increase was £0.15 per hour lower than expected;
 (vi) direct labour efficiency variance: the efficiency of labour was commendable.

(25 marks)
ICMA Cost Accounting 1
May 1980

17.2* Shown below is the standard prime cost of a tube of industrial adhesive, which is the only product manufactured in one department of Gum PLC.

Industrial adhesive

	£ per tube	£ per tube
Materials: Powder	1.50	
Chemicals	0.60	
Tube	0.30	2.40
Labour — Mixing and pouring		1.80
Total standard prime cost		£4.20

The standard material allowance for each tube of adhesive is 2 lbs of powder, $\frac{1}{4}$ litre of chemical and one tube. The standard wage rate for mixing and pouring is £4.50 per hour.

During the previous month 4,500 tubes of adhesive were produced, there were no work-in-progress stocks at the beginning or end of the month, and the receipts and issues of materials during the month are shown below:

	Powder	Chemicals	Tubes
Opening stock	1,500 lbs	200 litres	100 tubes
Purchases:	10,000 lbs at 70p per lb	600 litres at £2.30 per litre	200 tubes at 40p each
		600 litres at £2.50 per litre	5,000 tubes at 30p each
Issues:	9,800 lbs	1,050 litres	4,520 tubes

The above materials are used exclusively in the production of the adhesive and it is the policy of the company to calculate any price variance when the materials are purchased.

The direct employees operating the mixing and pouring plant worked a total of 2,050 hours during the previous month and earned gross wages of £8,910.

Required:
(a) Calculate for the previous month the following variances from standard cost:
 Materials price variance, analysed as you consider appropriate.
 Materials usage variance, analysed as you consider appropriate.
 Direct labour efficiency variance.
 Direct wages rate variance. (12 marks)
(b) Discuss the possible causes of the material variances and the direct labour efficiency variance. (10 marks)

(22 marks)
ACCA Level 1 Costing
December 1983

17.3 A business manufactures a single product which has the following specifications:

Component No.	Standard quantity	Standard price, each £
345	5	20
789	6	25

Number of standard direct labour hours	20
Standard wage rate per hour	£3.50
Budgeted production overhead (all fixed) per month	£14,000
Budgeted production per month, in units	200

A summary profit statement for the month of October is stated below:

	£	£
Sales		90,000
Materials used	47,480	
Direct wages	12,480	
Production overhead	14,200	
		74,160
Gross profit		15,840
Administration costs	3,000	
Selling and distribution costs	5,500	
		8,500
Net profit		£7,340

Additional information: 180 units were produced and sold during October, at the standard selling price.

It should be assumed that work in progress stocks at the end of the month were the same as at the beginning of October.

Component No.	Stock at 1 Oct.	Stock at 31 Oct.	Purchase during October Quantity	Purchase during October Price each £
345	200	250	1,000	19
789	240	150	1,000	27

Direct labour — actual hours worked during the month were 3,900.

You are required:
(a) to calculate the following variances for the month of October:
 (i) direct materials price for each component and in total, based on usage;
 (ii) direct materials usage for each component and in total;
 (iii) direct wages rate;
 (iv) direct labour efficiency;
 (v) fixed production overhead expenditure;
 (vi) fixed production overhead volume.
(b) utilizing the variances you have calculated, to present a statement for management reconciling the standard gross profit with the actual gross profit;
(c) to explain the meaning of the term 'fixed production overhead volume variance' and its significance to management.

(25 marks)
ICMA Cost Accounting 1
November 1981

17.4* Shown below is the previous month's overhead expenditure and activity, both budget and actual, for one department in a manufacturing company.

	Month's budget	Month's actual
Activity:		
Standard hours	8,000	8,400
Fixed overheads:	£	£
Salaries	6,750	6,400
Maintenance	3,250	3,315
Variable overheads:		
Power	17,600	20,140
Consumable materials	6,000	5,960
Indirect labour	4,400	4,480
Total overheads	£38,000	£40,295

The budgeted overheads shown above are based upon the anticipated activity of 8,000 standard hours and it should be assumed that the department's budgeted overhead expenditure and activity occur evenly throughout the year. Variable overheads vary with standard hours produced.

The company operates a standard costing system and the department's total overheads are absorbed into production using a standard hour rate.

Required:
(a) Calculate the following variances incurred by the department during the previous month:
 Fixed overhead volume variance
 Fixed overhead expenditure variance
 Variable overhead expenditure variance
 (9 marks)
(b) Draft a suitable operating statement which will assist management in controlling the department's overheads. (9 marks)
(c) Carefully explain why the difference between budgeted and actual activity will cause a change in the anticipated profit by the amount of the volume variance calculated in (a) above. (4 marks)

(22 marks)
ACCA Foundation Costing
June 1981

17.5* You are required:
(a) to comment on the statement that 'for most

managerial purposes the sales margin variances (operating profit variances) are more informative than sales variances'.

(b) using the data given in the table below, to calculate for each product and in total, the operating profit variances:
 (i) due to sales;
 (ii) due to selling prices;
 (iii) due to sales volume.

| Product | Per unit | | | | Totals | |
	Selling price £	Cost £	Profit £	Quantity units	Profit £	Sales £
Budget						
A	30	16	14	1,500		
B	10	9	1	3,500		
C	20	18	2	1,000		
Actual						
A			15	1,100	16,500	34,100
B			1	5,200	5,200	52,000
C			4	1,100	4,400	24,200
Total					26,100	110,300

ICMA Cost Accounting 1
November 1982

17.6* The summarized profit statements for A Ltd for each of two years ended 30 June, after the effects of inflation have been eliminated, are given below:

Year ended:	30 June 1980 £000	30 June 1981 £000
Sales	6,000	7,700
Direct material	3,000	3,240
Direct wages and variable overhead	1,800	2,060
Marginal cost	4,800	5,300
Contribution	1,200	2,400
Fixed overhead	800	1,500
Profit	400	900

Before 30 June 1980 the management in planning its tactics for the next year decided to reorganize the production methods, increase substantially the advertising expenditure and increase selling prices by 10%. All these plans became effective from 1 July 1980.

In the year to 30 June 1980, 24,000 units of material were used and 360,000 hours of labour were employed. In the year to 30 June 1981, the corresponding figures were 27,000 units of material and 400,000 hours of labour.

You are required to:
(a) use the information given for year ended 30 June 1980 as the base year, to analyse the results for the year ended 30 June 1981 and to show in a form helpful to management the amount each factor has contributed to the change in profit;
(b) calculate for the year ended 30 June 1980 the margin of safety.

(20 marks)
ICMA Cost Accounting 2
November 1981

17.7 Mr Flower is a baker specializing in the production of his famous individual meat pies which he sells to shops, throughout the area. Shown below is a summary of the previous year's budgeted and actual trading results, which Mr Flower has just received from his accountant.

	Budget £	Budget £	Actual £	Actual £
Sales		50,000		54,000
Operating costs:				
Materials	20,000		26,000	
Power	5,000		5,500	
Fixed overheads	15,000	40,000	17,000	48,500
Profit		£10,000		£5,500

Mr Flower is extremely worried by the above results, as at the beginning of the year, after the budget specified above had been prepared, he had decided to make several changes which he had anticipated would have increased the profitability of his business. The changes which he had made were:

(i) In order to increase the number of pies sold he reduced the selling price per pie from the budgeted 25p each to 22½p each.

(ii) In order to reduce operating costs he changed his supplier of materials and obtained a 20% price reduction compared with that budgeted. Mr Flower was aware that the materials from the new supplier were of a lower quality and there would be a little more waste.

(iii) In an attempt to reduce power costs, which he regards as variable, he changed his method of working from that implied in the budget.

Required:

(a) Analyse the effect of the above changes on the year's profit, and produce a statement reconciling budgeted and actual profit in a manner which you consider would be most helpful to Mr Flower.
It should be assumed that the original budget shown above was an accurate estimate of the likely results based on the original assumption. (16 marks)

(b) Briefly comment on your analysis in (a) above. (3 marks)

(c) Explain how you would measure the profitability of Mr Flower's business and identify any additional information which would be required in order to make the appropriate calculations. (3 marks)

(22 marks)
ACCA Level 1 Costing
June 1983

17.8 K Ltd uses standard costs and flexible budgets for control purposes. The following information is given:

Standard and budgeted data:
The standard material allowed per unit is 4 kilograms at a standard price of £0.75 per kilogram.
Budgeted direct labour hours for a four-week period were 80,000 hours at a budgeted cost

of £152,000.
Budgeted variable production overhead for 80,000 hours was £96,000.

Details for four-week period ended 29 April 1978 were:

Incurred:	£	
Direct wages	163,800	
Variances:		
Direct wages rate, £0.20 per hour adverse.		
Direct materials price (calculated on purchases at time of receipt at £0.05 per kilogram)	9,000	favourable
Direct materials usage	1,500	adverse
Variable production overhead	2,200	favourable
Variable production overhead efficiency	2,400	adverse

Production, 38,000 units.

There were no stocks at beginning of period, but there were 26,000 kilograms of direct materials in stock at 29 April 1978.
You are required to state for the period:
(a) the number of kilograms of direct material purchased;
(b) the number of kilograms of direct material used above the standard allowed;
(c) the variable production overhead expenditure variance;
(d) the actual hours worked;
(e) the number of standard hours allowed for the production achieved.

(20 marks)
ICMA Cost Accounting 1
May 1978

17.9* (a) The management accountant of S Ltd has prepared the following profit and loss statement.

Profit and loss statement			October	
	£	£	£	
Budgeted profit			50,000	
Variances	Favourable	Adverse		
Direct materials: Price		4,960		
Usage		3,200		
Direct wages: Rate		3,600		
Efficiency	1,800			
Fixed overhead: Expenditure	1,400			
Productivity	1,200			
Capacity		2,000		
Sales: Price	4,800			
Volume		2,000	6,560	
Actual profit			43,440	

Note: Administration and selling overhead may be ignored.

Budgeted data are as follows:

Output for the year 60,000 units
Fixed overhead for the year £240,000

Standard cost of one unit of product is:

Direct materials: 5 kilos at £4 per kilo
Direct wages: 2 hours at £3 per hour
Fixed overhead absorbed as a labour hour rate
Profit is 25% of sales price.

You are required to prepare the financial profit and loss account for the month of October.
(b) Describe briefly three different types of standard which may be used as the basis for a standard costing system.

(25 marks)
ICMA Cost Accounting 2
May 1982

17.10 Summarized below are the actual results and cost variances for period 10 for Joanna PLC, a company which manufactures two products.

The total cost variances for each element of cost are the only variances omitted from the above schedule.

The company uses only one grade of direct material and, throughout period 10, the actual price paid was £0.40 per kilo *above* standard price. The standard material cost of Product A is £36 per unit.

The company employs only one grade of direct labour. During period 10 the actual wage rate paid was £3.40 per hour. Three standard hours are required to produce one unit of Product A.

Fixed and variable overhead absorption rates are based upon standard hours produced.

There were no stocks of materials, work in progress or finished goods held at either the beginning or end of the period.

Required:
(a) Calculate for period 10:
 (i) the actual quantity of direct material consumed, in kilos;
 (ii) the actual price, per kilo, paid for the material;

	Product A	Product B	£	
Production	5,000 units	6,200 units		
Actual cost of direct material purchased			285,600	
Actual direct wages paid			204,000	
Variable overheads incurred			31,500	
Fixed overheads incurred			240,000	
The variances from standard cost were:				
Direct material usage variance			7.200	Fav*
Direct material price variance			13,600	Adv
Direct wages efficiency variance			5,600	Adv
Direct wages rate variance			6,000	Fav
Variable overhead expenditure variance			2,300	Adv
Fixed overhead volume variance			11,600	Fav
Fixed overhead expenditure variance			18,000	Adv

*Fav indicates a favourable variance; Adv an adverse variance.

(iii) the actual direct labour hours worked;
(iv) the direct labour hours worked in excess of standard. (8 marks)

(b) Construct the total standard cost per unit for each product. (14 marks)

(22 marks)
*ACCA Foundation Costing
December 1981*

17.11* (a) Explain what you understand by the term 'a standard hour'. (3 marks)
(b) The budgeted production for period 7 in the finishing department of a pottery manufacturer is 4,500 cups, 4,000 saucers and 6,250 plates. In one standard hour a direct operative is expected to be able to finish either, 30 cups, or 40 saucers, or 25 plates. During period 7 400 direct labour hours were worked and actual production was 4,260 cups, 6,400 saucers and 3,950 plates.

Required:

Using the above information calculate for period 7:

(i) the productivity of the direct operatives,

(ii) an appropriate ratio expressing the department's actual production relative to that budgeted,

(iii) another ratio which you consider may be useful to management and explain the meaning of the ratio you have calculated. (7 marks)

(c) Critically examine the validity of the following statement made by the personnel manager of the above pottery company.
'If the productivity of our direct operatives increase, then the company's profitability will also increase'. (7 marks)

(17 marks)
*ACCA Level 1 Costing
December 1982*

17.12 (a) Explain, briefly, what is meant by each of the following terms:

(i) standard hour;

(ii) productivity (or efficiency) ratio;

(iii) production volume ratio.

(b) Using the information given below, you are required to calculate the productivity ratio and the production volume ratio for each of the two production departments X and Y.

Department X	Product D	Product G
Budgeted production, in units	18,000	4,000
Standard minutes required to produce one unit:	20	30
Actual units produced	15,000	10,000
Total actual hours worked on both products: 11,111.		

Department Y		
Budgeted standard hours		10,000
Actual hours worked		9,000
Standard hours produced		9,450

(15 marks)
*ICMA Cost Accounting 1
May 1980*

17.13 An engineering company planned to manufacture 5,000 components in the month of September. Each component requires four standard hours to complete. For the 22 working days in the month 120 workers were allocated to the job. The factory operates an 8-hour day. The labour allocation included a margin for absenteeism and idle time.

When the actual results were analysed it was revealed that absenteeism had averaged 5%; an average of 5 hours overtime had been worked by those present and 4,800 components had been completed at an average of 3.8 standard hours each.

During October, 120 of the completed components have been scrapped because of defective material.

It is planned in November to produce another 5,000 components plus the shortfall from September.

From the information given, you are required to:

(a) calculate the following ratios for September:
(i) the production volume ratio;
(ii) the capacity ratio;
(iii) the productivity (or efficiency) ratio;

(b) explain the significance of these results;

(c) estimate the manpower needed for the planned November production using 21 working days with one hour overtime per man per day, working at the budgeted efficiency level and the same percentage of absenteeism, idle time and rejects as occurred in the September production;

(d) calculate for November the bonus, on a 50:50 profit sharing basis, which could be paid as an addition to the wage rate if the September production efficiency was achieved, idle time reduced to 5% but all other features were the same as in (c) above.

(30 marks)
ICMA P3 Management Accounting
November 1982

17.14 BS Ltd manufactures one standard product and operates a system of variance accounting using a fixed budget. As assistant management accountant you are responsible for preparing the monthly operating statements. Data from the budget, the standard product cost and for the month ended 31 October 1982 are given below.

Using the data given you are required to prepare the operating statement for the month ended 31 October 1982 to show the budgeted profit; the variances for direct materials, direct wages, overhead and sales, each analysed into causes; and actual profit.

Budgeted and standard cost data:

Budgeted sales and production for the month 10,000 units
Standard cost for each unit of product:
Direct material: X 10 kilos @ £1 per kilo
 Y 5 kilos @ £5 per kilo
Direct wages 5 hours @ £3 per hour
Fixed production overhead is absorbed @ 200% of direct wages
Budgeted sales price has been calculated to give a profit of 20% of sales price.

Actual data for month ended 31 October, 1982:
Production, 9,500 units sold at a price of 10% higher than that budgeted
Direct materials consumed:
 X 96,000 kilos @ £1.20 per kilo
 Y 48,000 kilos @ £4.70 per kilo
Direct wages wages incurred 46,000 hours @ £3.20 per hour
Fixed production overhead incurred £290,000

(30 marks)
ICMA Cost Accounting 2
November 1982

17.15* The Britten Co. Ltd manufactures a variety of products of basically similar composition. Production is carried out by subjecting the various raw materials to a number of standardized operations, each major series of operations being carried out in a different department. All products are subjected to the same initial processing which is carried out in departments A, B and C, the order and extent of further processing then depending upon the type of end product to be produced.

It has been decided that a standard costing system could be usefully employed within Britten and a pilot scheme is to be operated for six months based initially only on department B, the second department in the initial common series of operations. If the pilot scheme produces useful results then a management accountant will be employed and the system would be incorporated as appropriate throughout the whole firm.

The standard cost per unit of output of department B is:

	£	£
Direct labour (14 hours at £2 per hour)		28
Direct materials		
(i) Output of department A (3 kg at £9 per kg)	27	
(ii) Acquired by and directly input to department B		
Material X (4 kg at £5 per kg)	20	47
Variable overhead (at £1 per direct labour hour worked)		14
Fixed production overheads		
(i) Directly incurred by department B (note 1)		
Manufacturing overhead (per unit)	3	
(ii) Allocated to department B General factory overhead (per unit)	8	11
Standard cost per unit		£100

Note 1 — Based on normal monthly production of 400 units.

In the first month of operation of the pilot study (month 7 of the financial year), department B had no work in progress at the beginning and the end of the month. The actual costs allocated to department B in the first month of operation were:

	£	£
Direct labour (6,500 hours)		14,000
Direct materials		
(i) Output of department		
A (1,400 kg) — (note 2)	21,000	
(ii) Material X (1,900 kg)	11,500	32,500
Variable overhead		8,000
Fixed overhead		
(i) Directly incurred		
manufacturing over-		
head	1,600	
(ii) Allocated to depart-		
ment B — (note 3)	2,900	4,500
		£59,000

Note 2 — Actual cost of output of department A.

Note 3 — Based on the actual expenditure on joint manufacturing overheads and allocated to departments in accordance with labour hours worked.

The production manager feels that the actual costs of £59,000 for production of 500 units indicates considerable inefficiency on the part of department B. He says, 'I was right to request that the pilot standard costing system be carried out in department B as I have suspected that they are inefficient and careless — this overspending of £9,000 proves I am right.'

Required:

(a) Prepare a brief statement which clearly indicates the reasons for the performance of department B and the extent to which that performance is attributable to department B. The statement should utilize variance analysis to the extent it is applicable and relevant. (14 marks)

(b) Comment on the way the pilot standard costing system is currently being operated and suggest how its operation might be improved during the study period. (6 marks)

ACCA P2 Management Accounting
December 1981

17.16 Before entering the market for the manufacture and sale of shower cubicle units the managing director and major shareholder of Home Showers Ltd, Roy Simpson, had carried out forecasting carefully to arrive at the following figures:

	£	£
Expected selling price (per cubicle)		140
Expected costs (per cubicle)		
Direct labour (10 hours at £3 per hour)	30	
Direct materials (20 kg at £1.25)	25	
Variable overheads (at £1.50 per direct labour hour)	15	
Variable selling and delivery costs (per cubicle sold)	20	
Total variable costs (per cubicle)		£90

Expected fixed costs (per month)	£	
Manufacturing overheads	40,000	
Selling and delivery	5,000	
Administration	5,000	
		£50,000

'Normal production and sales levels once the company is established' states Roy Simpson 'will be 2,000 units per month; but for the first few months the company will obviously have to plan to produce and sell fewer units. With a contribution of £50 per unit it will need only 1,000 units to break even. Therefore the company shall never operate at a loss as even the planned production and sales of the first month is exactly 1,000 units — and it is planned to increase production and sales monthly until the normal 2,000 units figure is reached.'

After the firm had completed its first month's activities the part time accountant produced statements reporting on those activities. The statements were:

Statement of manufacturing costs — Month 1

	£
Direct labour (15,500 hours)	45,500
Direct materials (28,400 kg)	35,200
Variable overheads	21,400
Fixed manufacturing overheads	40,000
Total manufacturing costs	£142,100
No. of units produced	1,400
Cost per unit	£101.50

Profit statement — Month 1

	£	£
Sales 900 units at £150		135,000
Less: Manufacturing costs of sales 900 at £101.50		91,350
Gross profit		43,650
Selling and delivery costs	25,500	
Administration	5,500	31,000
Profit		£12,650

Roy Simpson was extremely pleased by the figures and stated 'I thought that the company would make a loss as sales were below our budget of 1,000 and this was, of course, the break even expectation. But with a profit of more than £12,000 I am not complaining. I think the reasons for the company's success are the increase in sales price and the fact that labour standards are tight and known to be tight. The men know that 10 hours per cubicle will be difficult to achieve, this motivates them and obviously they have achieved it. However, it would be interesting to see the exact causes of the profit being higher than expected'.

Required:

(a) Prepare a budgeted profit statement, based on long term standard costs, which uses Mr Simpson's prior estimates of the first month's activity. (c. 3 marks)

(b) Prepare a statement based on the first month's results which will be useful to Mr Simpson in highlighting deviations from the prior plan and displays the reasons for any variances from the plan. (c. 12 marks)

(c) Show how the results for the first month's activities derived in (b) above can be reconciled with the profit of £12,650 produced by the part time accountant. (c. 2 marks)

(d) List the three most important points to which you would draw Mr Simpson's attention concerning standards and variances in (b) above. Very briefly, producing no more than one short sentence each, give the reasons why each item is deserving of his attention. (c. 3 marks)

(Total 20 marks)
ACCA P2 Management Accounting
June 1979

17.17 Amalgamated Processors PLC is a divisionalized organization which operates a standard costing and budgetary planning and control system in which the preparation of detailed operating budgets is undertaken by the divisions them-selves after centrally determined profit targets have been communicated to them.

The Penbrock Division of the company produces and sells a standardized component which is sold externally at £10 per unit and internally, to other divisions, at a transfer price of £9 per unit. The standard specification for this product is as follows:

	£
Standard specification	
2 m² of material A at £0.20 per m²	0.40
5 units of component B at £0.37 per unit	1.85
15 minutes of labour at £2.00 per hour	0.50
Variable manufacturing overhead — 150% of direct labour cost	0.75
Fixed maufacturing overhead	1.50
Standard unit manufacturing cost	5.00
Central office charge	1.00
Selling and distributive overhead	1.00
Standard unit cost	£7.00

The fixed manufacturing overhead is absorbed on the basis of the 'normal' monthly output of 15,000 units. The selling and distributive overhead relates solely to external sales and the monthly divisional budget for this comprises a fixed element of £9,600 and a variable element of £0.20 for each unit of budgeted external sales. The fixed selling and distributive overhead has been unitized assuming a 'normal' monthly external sales level of 12,000 units. The 'central office charge' element of the standard specification relates to a charge made by the 'head office' for central services provided — this has also been unitized assuming the normal monthly activity level of 15,000 units. Unsold stock is carried at standard manufacturing cost.

The details on p. 416 apply to the Penbrock Division for April 1982:

Profit and loss account
April 1982

	Actual Units	£	Budget Units	£
Sales — External	10,000	100,000	12,000	120,000
Internal	4,000	36,000	3,000	27,000
	14,000	£136,000	15,000	£147,000
Cost of goods manufactured	16,000	85,000	15,000	75,000
Less: Stock adjustment	2,000	10,000	—	—
	14,000	75,000	15,000	75,000
Selling and distributive overhead		13,000		12,000
Central office charges		15,000		15,000
Profit		33,000		45,000
		£136,000		£147,000

The 'actual' cost of goods manufactured can be analysed as follows:

	£
Material A	6,500
Component B	31,745
4,250 labour hours at £2.10	8,925
Variable manufacturing overhead	12,325
Fixed manufacturing overhead	25,505
	£85,000

The stores records of the Penbrock Division are kept at standard cost so that the material cost figures include both the cost of the actual direct materials used (priced at their standard cost) and the price variance on materials purchased during April. The details of usage and purchases are as follows:

Material A:	Usage	34,000 m²
	Purchases	30,000 m² at £0.19 per m²
Component B:	Usage	78,500 units
	Purchases	90,000 units at £0.40 unit.

The workstaff have complained that the quality of the most recently purchased batch of Material A is inferior to the regular grade, that it gives rise to more waste and that it requires more time to process.

You are required:

(a) To prepare a statement, for the general manager of the Penbrock Division, analysing the reasons for the profit shortfall of £12,000 and to provide a commentary on this statement. (16 marks)

(b) To comment on the practice of isolating material price variances at the time of the material's purchase. (3 marks)

(c) To comment on the transfer pricing method used by the Penbrock Division. (3 marks)

(22 marks)

ACCA Level 2 Management Accounting
June 1982

18 Standard costing (2): Further aspects

In the previous chapter we examined the principles of standard costing variance analysis. We are now going to consider how the material usage and the sales margin volume variance can be further analysed, and look at the accounting entries which are necessary to record the variances. We shall then turn our attention to some of the criticisms of standard costing variance analysis and consider some suggestions which may provide a more meaningful approach to variance analysis. Finally, we will consider some factors which should be taken into account in deciding whether or not it is worthwhile investigating variances. Let us begin by looking at material mix and yield variances.

Direct materials mix and yield variances

In a number of industries, particularly of the process type, materials mix and yield have an important effect on the product cost. In such a situation, it is possible to analyse the material usage variance into mix and yield variances. In some production processes standards can be established by combining two or more raw materials, thus making it possible to vary the mix of materials used and still produce an acceptable product. Laboratory and engineering studies are therefore necessary to determine the mix of materials which is acceptable to provide the desired product quality. The costs of the different material mixes are estimated, and a standard mix is determined based on that mix of materials which best minimizes costs but still meets the quality requirements. Deviations from the standard mix can be established and a mix variance calculated.

The material mix variance arises when a different mix of materials is used from the predetermined mix which is included in the calculation of the standard cost of a product. If the mixture is varied so that a larger than standard proportion of more expensive materials is used, there will be an unfavourable variance. When a larger proportion of cheaper materials are included in the mixture, there will be a favourable variance. Consider Example 18.1.

EXAMPLE 18.1

A company has established the following standard mix for producing seven gallons of chemical Z:

5 gallons of A at £5 per gallon — £25
3 gallons of B at £3 per gallon — £ 9

£34

A standard loss of $12\frac{1}{2}\%$ on input is expected to occur. Actual input was 42,000 gallons of A and 22,000 gallons of B giving an output of 55,000 gallons of chemical Z. The purchase price of both inputs was identical to the standard costs.

The total input is 64,000 gallons and, using the

standard mix, an input of 40,000 gallons of A ($\frac{5}{8}$ × 64,000) and 24,000 gallons of B ($\frac{3}{8}$ × 64,000) should have been used. However, 42,000 gallons of A and 22,000 gallons of B were used, which means that 2,000 additional gallons of A at a standard cost of £5 per gallon were substituted for 2,000 gallons of B at a standard cost of £3 per gallon. The overall effect of not using the standard mix is that additional costs of £4,000 were incurred. The formula for the direct materials mix variance is as follows:

The direct materials mix variance is the difference between the actual usage in standard proportions less the actual usage multiplied by the standard price of the materials

If we apply this formula the calculation is as follows:

Actual usage in standard proportions:
A = 40,000 gallons ($\frac{5}{8}$ × 64,000) at £5 standard cost :	£200,000
B = 24,000 gallons ($\frac{3}{8}$ × 64,000) at £3 standard cost :	£ 72,000
	£272,000

Actual usage in actual proportions:
A = 42,000 gallons at £5 standard cost :	£210,000
B = 22,000 gallons at £3 standard cost :	£ 66,000
	£276,000
Variance =	£4,000 Adverse

Note that standard prices are used to calculate the mix variance to ensure that the price effects are removed from the calculation. A favourable mix variance will result from substituting cheaper materials for more expensive materials but this may not always be in a company's best interests as the quality of the product may suffer or output might be reduced.

Generally, the use of a less expensive mix of inputs will mean the production of fewer units of output than standard. This may be because of excessive evaporation of the input units, an increase in rejects due to imperfections in the lower quality inputs, or other similar factors. To analyse the effect of changes in the quantity of outputs from a given mix of inputs, a yield variance can be calculated. It is important that the standard mix is continuously reviewed and adjusted where necessary since price changes may lead to a revised standard mix. For an illustration of this approach see Wolk and Hillman (1972).

Direct materials yield variance

The yield variance arises because there is a difference between the standard output for a given level of inputs and the actual output which is attained. In Example 18.1 an input of 64,000 gallons should have given an output of 56,000 gallons of chemical Z. (Every eight gallons of input should produce seven gallons of output.) In fact, only 55,000 gallons were produced which means that the output was 1,000 gallons less than standard. This output is valued at the average standard cost per unit of *output* which is calculated as follows:

Each eight gallons of *input* is expected to yield seven gallons of *output*.
The standard cost for this output is £34.
Therefore standard cost for one gallon of *output*
$$= \frac{£34}{7}$$
$$= £4.857$$

The yield variance will be £4.857 × 1000 = £4,857A. The formula is as follows:

$$\left[\text{Actual yield (55,000 gallons)} \right] - \left[\begin{array}{l} \text{Standard yield from} \\ \text{actual input of material} \\ \text{(56,000 gallons)} \end{array} \right]$$
$$\times$$
$$[\text{Standard cost per unit of output (£4.857)}]$$

The yield variance may arise from a failure to follow standard procedures. For example, in the steel industry a yield variance may indicate that the practice which was followed for pouring molten metal may have been different from that which was determined as being the most efficient when the standard yield was calculated. Alternatively, the use of inferior quality materials may be responsible for an adverse yield variance.

Material usage variance

The material usage variance consists of the mix variance and the yield variance. The material usage variance is therefore an adverse variance of £8,857 which consists of a mix variance of £4,000 and a yield variance of £4,857. To calculate the material usage variance we compare the standard quantity of materials for the actual production with the actual quantity of materials used and multiply by the standard material prices in the normal way. The calculations are as follows:

Standard quantity for actual production at standard prices

Actual production of 55,000 gallons requires an input of 62,857 gallons $(55,000 \times {}^8/_7)$ consisting of:

39,286 gallons of A $(62,857 \times \frac{5}{8})$ at £5 per gallon = £196,430
23,571 gallons of B $(62,857 \times \frac{3}{8})$ at £3 per gallon = £ 70,713

£267,143 (i)

Actual quantity at standard prices

42,000 gallons of A at £5 per gallon = £210,000
22,000 gallons of B at £3 per gallon = £ 66,000

£276,000 (ii)

Material usage variance (i − ii) = £ 8,857 Adverse

Sales mix variances

When a company sells several products which have different profit margins, the total profit will be influenced by the relative proportions or mix of high margin to low margin products sold. The difference in profits which is caused by the difference between the proportions assumed in the budgeted sales mix and the proportions actually sold represents the sales margin mix variance. Consider the situation in Example 18.2.

EXAMPLE 18.2

The budgeted sales for a period were as follows:

Product	Units	Selling price £	Standard cost £	Profit margin £
X	200	20	10	10
Y	300	15	9	6
Z	500	10	6	4
	1,000			

and the actual sales were:

Product	Units	Selling price £	Standard cost £	Profit margin £
X	150	22	10	12
Y	350	15	9	6
Z	600	9	6	3
	1,100			

You are required to calculate the sales margin variance.

The budgeted sales mix consists of 20% (200/1,000) for product X, 30% for product Y and 50% for product Z. The formula for calculating the sales mix variance is as follows:

(Actual sales quantity − Actual sales quantity in budgeted proportions)
×
Standard margin

If we apply this formula we will obtain the following calculation:

Product	Actual sales quantity	Actual sales in budgeted proportions	Difference	Standard margin £	Sales margin mix variance £
X	150 units	1,100 × 20% = 220 units	− 70 units	10	700A
Y	350 units	1,100 × 30% = 330 units	+ 20 units	6	120F
Z	600 units	1,100 × 50% = 550 units	+ 50 units	4	200F
					380A

The sales *volume* margin variance is calculated according to the procedure outlined in the preceding chapter, that is the difference between the actual sales volume and the budgeted sales volume multiplied by the standard margin. The calculation is as follows:

Product	Actual sales (units)	Budgeted sales (units)	Difference (units)	Standard margin £	Sales volume margin variance £
X	150	200	− 50	10	500A
Y	350	300	+ 50	6	300F
Z	600	500	+ 100	4	400F
					200F

The sales volume margin variance indicates that because actual sales exceeded budgeted sales, a favourable variance of £200 will arise. However, because the actual sales mix was not in accordance with the budgeted sales mix an adverse sales mix variance of £380 occurred. In other words, if the actual sales volume had been sold in the budgeted proportions the volume variance would have been £580 favourable instead of £200 favourable. To complete the analysis of the sales margin variances we must calculate the sales margin *price* variance. You should remember from Chapter 17 that the formula for this is as follows:

(Actual margin − Budgeted margin) × Actual sales quantity

The sales margin price variance in Example 18.2 is therefore:

Product	Actual margin	Budgeted margin	Difference	Actual sales quantity units	Sales margin price variance
	£	£	£		£
X	12	10	+ 2	150	300F
Y	6	6	0	350	0
Z	3	4	− 1	600	600A
					300A

We can now summarize the sales margin variances as follows:

Sales margin price variance	£300A	
Sales margin volume variance	£200F	(which consists of a £380 adverse mix variance)
Sales margin total variance	£100A	

Standard cost accounting

By substituting standard costs for actual costs in the cost accounting records a saving in clerical time and accounting costs can be made. For example, if raw material stocks are valued at standard cost, the stock records may be maintained in terms of physical quantities only. The value of raw materials stock may be obtained simply by multiplying the physical quantity of raw materials in stock by the standard cost per unit. This avoids the need to record stocks on a first-in, first-out or average cost basis. Stock valuations based on standard costs may be included in

externally published financial statements provided that the standard costs used are current and attainable (Accounting Standards Committee — SSAP 9, 1977).

Variations exist in the data accumulation methods which are adopted for standard costs, but these variations are merely procedural and the actual stock valuations and profit calculations will be the same whichever method is adopted. In this chapter we shall be looking at a system which values all stocks at standard cost, and any amounts which are debited and credited to raw materials, work in progress and finished goods stocks will therefore be at *standard prices*. Any differences between standard costs and actual costs are debited or credited to variance accounts. Adverse variances will appear as debit balances as they are additional costs in excess of standard.

Conversely, favourable variances will appear as credit balances. Only production variances are recorded and sales variances are not entered in the accounts.

Let us now consider the cost accounting records for Example 17.1 which was presented in the previous chapter. Basically, the accounting entries will be the same as those illustrated in Chapter 5 for an actual cost system. The variances recorded in the accounts will be those which we calculated in the previous chapter and we need not therefore explain them again here, but if you cannot remember the points we made then, please turn back now to Chapter 17 and refresh your memory. To keep things simple and to avoid confusion we will now repeat Example 17.1 and the reconciliation of budgeted and actual profits for this example (which was Exhibit 17.5 in the previous chapter).

EXAMPLE 17.1

Alpha manufacturing company produces a single product which is known as sigma. The product requires a single operation and the standard cost for this operation is presented in the following standrd cost card:

Standard cost card for product sigma

		£
Direct materials		
2 kilos of A at £1 per kilo		2.00
1 kilo of B at £3 per kilo		3.00
Direct labour		
3 hours at £3 per hour		9.00
Overheads:		
Variable — 3 hours at £2 per direct labour hour	6.00	
Fixed — 3 hours at £4 per direct labour hour	12.00	18.00
Total standard cost		32.00
Standard profit margin		8.00
Standard selling price		40.00

Alpha Ltd plan to produce 10,000 units of sigma in the month of April and the budgeted costs based on the information contained in the standard cost card are as follows:

Budget based on the above standard costs and an output of 10,000 units

			£
Sales (10,000 units of sigma at £40 per unit)			400,000
Direct materials: A 20,000 kilos at £1 per kilo	20,000		
B 10,000 kilos at £3 per kilo	30,000	50,000	
Direct labour: 30,000 hours at £3 per hour		90,000	
Variable overheads: 30,000 hours at £2 per direct labour hour		60,000	
Fixed overheads		120,000*	320,000
Budgeted profit			80,000

*Budgeted fixed overheads are £120,000 per month and are charged on the basis of direct labour hours, giving a fixed overhead rate of £4 per direct labour hour (£120,000 ÷ 30,000 direct labour hours).

The actual results for April are:

		£
Sales (9,000 units at £42)		378,000
Direct materials: A 19,000 kilos at £1.10 per kilo	20,900	
B 10,100 kilos at £2.80 per kilo	28,280	
Direct labour 28,500 hours at £3.20 per hour	91,200	
Variable overheads	52,000	
Fixed overheads	116,000	308,380
Profit		69,620

Manufacturing overheads are charged to production on the basis of direct labour hours. Actual production and sales for the period were 9,000 units.

The reconciliation of budgeted and actual profits is as shown in Exhibit 17.5:

Let us now consider the accounting entries for Example 17.1 The appropriate ledger entries are presented in Exhibit 18.1. Each ledger entry and journal entry has been labelled with numbers from 1 to 13 to try to give you a clear understanding of each accounting entry.

Purchase of materials

19,000 kilos of raw material A at £1.10 per kilo and 10,100 kilos of raw material B at £2.80 per kilo were purchased. This gives a total purchase cost of £20,900 for A and £28,280 for B. The standard prices were £1 per kilo for A and £3 per kilo for B. The accounting entries for material A are:

(1) Dr Stores ledger control account (AQ × SP) 19,000
(1) Dr Material price variance account 1,900
 (1) Cr Creditor's control account (AQ × AP) 20,900

You will see that the stores ledger control account is debited with the standard price (SP) for the actual quantity purchased (AQ), and the actual price (AP) to be paid is credited to the creditor's control account. The difference is the material price variance. The accounting entries for material B are:

(2) Dr Stores ledger control account (AQ × SP) 30,300
 (2) Cr Material price variance account 2,020
 (2) Cr Creditors (AQ × AP) 28,280

Exhibit 17.5 Reconciliation of budgeted and actual profit for April

				£
Budgeted net profit				80,000
Sales variances:				
Sales margin price	18,000 F			
Sales margin volume	8,000 A	10,000 F		
Direct cost variances				
Material — Price: Material A	1,900 A			
Material B	2,020 F	120 F		
Usage:Material A	1,000 A			
Material B	3,300 A	4,300 A	4,180 A	
Labour — Rate		5,700 A		
Efficiency		4,500 A	10,200 A	
Manufacturing overhead variances				
Fixed — Expenditure	4,000 F			
Volume capacity	6,000 A			
Volume efficiency	6,000 A	8,000 A		
Variable — Expenditure	5,000 F			
Efficiency	3,000 A	2,000 F	6,000 A	10,380 A
Actual profit				69,620

Usage of materials

19,000 kilos of A and 10,100 kilos of B were actually issued and the standard usage (SQ) was 18,000 and 9,000 kilos at standard prices of £1 and £3. The accounting entries for material A are:

(3) Dr Work in progress (SQ × SP) 18,000
(3) Dr Material usage variance 1,000
 (3) Cr Stores ledger control account (AQ × SP) 19,000

Work in progress is debited with the standard quantity of materials at the standard price and the stores ledger account is credited with the actual quantity issued at the standard price. The difference is the material usage variance. The accounting entries for material B are:

(4) Dr work in progress (SQ × SP) 27,000
(4) Dr material usage variance 3,300
 (4) Cr Stores ledger control account (AQ × SP) 30,300

Direct wages

The actual hours worked were 28,500 hours for the month. The standard hours produced were 27,000. The actual wage rate paid was £3.20 per hour, compared with a standard rate of £3 per hour. The actual wages cost is recorded in the same way in a standard costing system as in an actual costing system. The accounting entry for the actual wages paid is:

(5) Dr wages control account 91,200
(5) Cr Wages accrued account 91,200

The wages control account is then cleared as follows:

(6) Dr Work in progress (SQ × SP) 81,000
 (6) Cr Wages control account 81,000
(6) Dr Wage rate variance 5,700
(6) Dr Labour efficiency variance 4,500
 (6) Cr Wages control account 10,200

The wages control account is credited and the work in progress account is debited with the standard cost (that is, standard hours produced times the standard wage rate). The wage rate and labour efficiency variance accounts are debited as they are both adverse variances and account for the difference between the actual wages cost (recorded as a debit in the wages control account) and the standard wages cost (recorded as a credit in the wages control account).

Manufacturing overhead costs incurred

The actual manufacturing overhead incurred is £52,000 for variable overheads and £116,000 for fixed overheads. The accounting entries for actual overhead *incurred* are recorded in the same way in a standard costing system as in an actual costing system. That is:

(7) Dr Factory variable overhead control account 52,000
(7) Dr factory fixed overhead control account 116,000
 (7) Cr Expense creditors 168,000

Absorption of manufacturing overheads and recording the variances

Work in progress is debited with the standard manufacturing overhead cost for the output produced. The standard overhead rates were £4 per standard hour for fixed overhead and £2 per standard hour for variable overheads. The actual output was 27,000 standard hours. The standard fixed overhead cost is therefore £108,000 (27,000 standard hours at £4 per hour) and the variable overhead cost is £54,000. The accounting entries for fixed overheads are:

(8) Dr Work in progress (SQ × SP) 108,000
(8) Dr Volume variance 12,000
 (8) Cr Factory fixed overhead control account 120,000
(8) Dr Factory fixed overhead control account 4,000
 (8) Cr Fixed overhead expenditure variance 4,000

You will see that the debit of £108,000 to the work in progress account and the corresponding credit to the factory fixed overhead control account represents the standard fixed overhead cost of production. The difference between the debit entry of £116,000 in the factory fixed overhead control account in Exhibit 18.1 for the *actual* fixed overheads incurred, and the credit entry of £108,000 for the *standard* fixed overhead cost of production is the total fixed overhead variance, which consists of an adverse volume variance of £12,000 and a favourable expenditure variance of £4,000. This is recorded as a debit to the volume variance account and a credit to the expenditure variance account. The accounting entries for variable overheads are:

(9) Dr Work in progress account (SQ × SP) 54,000
(9) Dr Variable overhead efficiency variance 3,000
 (9) Cr Factory variable overhead control account 57,000
(9) Dr Factory variable overhead control account 5,000
 (9) Cr Variable overhead expenditure variance
 account 5,000

The same principles apply with variable overheads. The debit to work in progress account and the corresponding credit to the factory variable overhead control account of £54,000 is the standard variable overhead cost of production. The difference between the debit entry of £52,000 in the factory variable overhead account in Exhibit 18.1 for the *actual* variable overheads incurred and the credit entry of £54,000 for the *standard* variable overhead cost of production is the total variable overhead variance, which consists of an adverse efficiency variance of £3,000 and a favourable expenditure variance of £5,000.

Completion of production

In Exhibit 18.1 the total amount which is recorded on the debit side of the work in progress account is £288,000. As there are no opening or closing stocks this represents the total standard cost of production for the period which consists of 9,000 units at £32 per unit. When the completed production is transferred from work in progress to finished goods stock the accounting entries will be as follows:

(10) Dr Finished stock account 288,000
 (10) Cr Work in progress account 288,000

Because there are no opening or closing stocks both the work in progress account and the stores ledger account will show a nil balance.

Sales

Sales variances are not recorded in the accounts, so actual sales of £378,000 for 9,000 units will be recorded as:

(11) Dr Debtors 378,000
 (11) Cr Sales 378,000

As all the production for the period has been sold there will be no closing stock of finished goods and the standard cost of production for the 9,000 units will be transferred from the finished goods account to the cost of sales account:

(12) Dr Cost of sales account 288,000
 (12) Cr Finished goods account 288,000

Finally, the cost of sales account and the variance accounts will be closed by a transfer to the costing profit and loss account (the item labelled (13) in Exhibit 18.1). The balance of the costing profit and loss account will be the *actual* profit for the period.

Calculation of profit

To calculate the profit we must add the adverse variances and deduct the favourable variances from the standard cost of sales which is obtained

Exhibit 18.1 Accounting entries for a standard costing system

Stores ledger control account

(1) Creditors (material A)	19,000		(3) Work in progress (material A)		18,000
(2) Creditors (material B)	30,300		(3) Material usage variance (material A)		1,000
			(4) Work in progress (material B)		27,000
			(4) Material usage variance (material B)		3,300
	49,300				49,300

Work in progress account

(3) Stores ledger (material A)	18,000		(10) Finished goods stock account	288,000
(4) Stores ledger (material B)	27,000			
(6) Wages control	81,000			
(8) Fixed factory overhead	108,000			
(9) Variable factory overhead	54,000			
	288,000			288,000

Variance accounts

(1) Creditors (material A)	1,900		(2) Creditors (material price B)	2,020
(3) Stores ledger control (material A usage)	1,000		(8) Fixed factory overhead (expenditure)	4,000
(4) Stores ledger control (material B usage)	3,300		(9) Variable factory overhead (expenditure)	5,000
(6) Wages control (wage rate)	5,700			11,020
(6) Wages control (lab. effic'y)	4,500		(13) Costing P + L A/c (bal.)	20,380
(8) Fixed factory overhead (volume)	12,000			
(9) Variable factory overhead (effic'y)	3,000			
	31,400			31,400

Wages control account

(5) Wages accrued account	91,200		(6) WIP	81,000
			(6) Wage rate variance	5,700
			(6) Lab. effic'y variance	4,500
	91,200			91,200

Fixed factory overhead account

(7) Expense creditors	116,000		(8) WIP	108,000
(8) Expenditure variance	4,000		(8) Volume variance	12,000
	120,000			120,000

Variable factory overhead account

(7) Expense creditors	52,000		(9) WIP	54,000
(9) Expenditure	5,000		(9) Efficiency variance	3,000
	57,000			57,000

Costing P + L account

(x) Cost of sales at standard cost	288,000		(11) Sales	378,000
(x) Variance account (net variances)	20,380			
Profit for period	69,620			
	378,000			378,000

Finished goods stock account

(10) WIP	288,000		(12) Cost of sales	288,000

Cost of sales account

(12) Finished goods stock	288,000		(13) Costing P + L A/c	288,000

from the cost of sales account. This calculation gives the actual production cost for the period which is then deducted from the actual sales to produce the actual profit for the period. The calculations are as follows:

Sales		378,000
Less Standard cost of sales	288,000	
Plus Adverse variances:		
Material A price variance	1,900	
Material usage variance	4,300	
Wage rate variance	5,700	
Labour efficiency variance	4,500	
Volume variance	12,000	
Variable overhead efficiency variance	3,000	31,400
		319,400

Less Favourable variances:		
Material B price variance	2,020	
Fixed overhead expenditure variance	4,000	
Variable overhead expenditure variance	5,000	11,020
Actual cost of sales		308,380
Actual profit		69,620

Accounting disposition of variances

At the end of an accounting period a decision must be made as to how the variances which have arisen during the period should be treated in the accounts. Should a portion of the variance be recorded as a gain or expense in the calculation of

profit for the period? If standards are current and attainable then debiting or crediting the total amount of the variances for the period to the profit and loss account appears to be theoretically sound as the variances are likely to represent efficiencies or inefficiencies. It can be argued that the cost of an inefficient operation should not be included in the stock valuation but that it should be charged to the period in which the inefficiency occurred; that is, the full amount of the *quantity* variances should be included in the profit calculation.[1] On the other hand, as *price* variances are frequently not controllable by a firm because they can arise following changes in the external market, it can be argued that they do not represent inefficiencies and they should affect the current period's product costs. There is therefore a good argument for apportioning the price variances between the stock accounts and the profit and loss account depending on the particular circumstances as to how the variances occurred and whether or not they were due to inefficiencies. For an illustration of the accounting disposition of variances see the answer to question 18.10 in the Students' Manual to this book.

Criticisms of standard costing variance analysis

Standard costing variance analysis has some recognized disadvantages. Most of the problems centre around the comparison of actual performance with the standard. If the standard is weak, then the comparison is also likely to be weak. Standards or plans are normally based on the environment which is anticipated when the targets are set. However, Demski (1977) has argued that if the environment is different from that which was anticipated, actual performance should be compared with a standard which reflects these changed conditions (that is, an ex-post variance analysis approach). Clearly, to measure managerial performance we should compare like with like and compare actual results with adjusted standards based on the conditions which managers actually operated during the period. Let us now apply this principle to a selection of cost variances. For a more detailed discussion of the items covered in the foregoing section see Bromwich (1980) and answer to question 18.11 in the Students' Manual to this book.

EXAMPLE 18.3

The standard cost per unit of raw material was estimated to be £5 per unit. The general market price at the time of purchase was £5.20 per unit and the actual price paid was £5.18 per unit. 10,000 units of the raw materials were purchased during the period.

The traditional material price variance is £1,800 adverse (10,000 units at 18 p). However, this variance consists of an adverse planning variance of £2,000 which is due to incorrect estimates of the target buying price and a favourable purchasing efficiency variance of £200. The planning variance is calculated as follows:

Purchasing planning variance

$$= \begin{bmatrix} \text{Original} \\ \text{target} & - & \text{General} \\ \text{price} & & \text{market} \\ & & \text{price} \end{bmatrix} \times \begin{bmatrix} \text{Quality} \\ \text{purchased} \end{bmatrix}$$

$$\begin{array}{ccc} (£5 & - & £5.20) & \times & 10,000 \\ = & £2,000 \text{ Adverse} \end{array}$$

This planning variance is not controllable but it provides useful feedback information to management on how successful they are in forecasting material prices, thus helping managers to improve their future estimates of material prices.

The efficiency of the purchasing department is assessed by a purchasing efficiency variance which is calculated as follows:

Purchasing planning variance

$$= \begin{bmatrix} \text{General} \\ \text{market} & - & \text{Actual} \\ \text{price} & & \text{price} \\ & & \text{paid} \end{bmatrix} \times \begin{bmatrix} \text{Quality} \\ \text{purchased} \end{bmatrix}$$

$$\begin{array}{ccc} (£5.20 & - & £5.18) & \times & 10,000 \\ = & £200 \text{ Favourable} \end{array}$$

Hence the traditional price variance of £1,800 adverse can be divided into an *uncontrollable* adverse material planning variance of £2,000 and a *controllable* favourable purchasing efficiency variance of £200. This analysis gives a clearer indication of the *efficiency* of the purchasing function and avoids including an adverse uncontrollable planning variance in performance reports. If an adverse price variance of £1,800 is reported, this is likely to lead to dysfunctional motivation effects if the purchasing department have performed the purchasing function efficiently but adverse variances appear on their performance reports.

Material usage variance

Part of the material usage variance may also be

due to uncontrollable environmental changes. For example, materials may be in short supply and it may be necessary to purchase inferior substitute materials. The material usage variance should therefore be based on a comparison of actual usage with an adjusted standard which takes account of the change in environmental conditions. The difference between the original standard and the adjusted standard represents an uncontrollable planning variance. Example 18.4 illustrates the analysis of the material usage variance.

EXAMPLE 18.4

The standard quantity of materials per unit of production for a product is 5 kilos. Actual production for the period was 250 units and actual material usage was 1,450 kilos. The standard cost per kilo of materials was £1. Because of a shortage of skilled labour it has been necessary to use unskilled labour and it is estimated that this will increase the material usage by 20%.

An adverse material usage variance of £200 (200 kilos at £1) would be reported to management but this is misleading if all or part of this variance is due to uncontrollable environmental changes. When the standard is adjusted to take into account the changed conditions, the standard quantity is 6 kilos per unit which gives a *revised* standard of 1,500 kilos for an output of 250 units. The difference between this revised standard and the original standard quantity of 1,250 kilos (250 units at 5 kilos per unit) represents the *uncontrollable planning variance* due to environmental changes. The uncontrollable planning variance is therefore £250 adverse and is calculated as follows:

$$\begin{bmatrix} \text{Original} \\ \text{standard} \\ \text{quantity} \end{bmatrix} - \begin{bmatrix} \text{Revised} \\ \text{standard} \\ \text{quantity} \end{bmatrix} \times \begin{bmatrix} \text{Standard} \\ \text{price} \end{bmatrix}$$

$$(1,250 \quad - \quad 1500) \quad \times \quad £1$$

The *revised controllable usage variance* is the difference between the standard quantity of 1,500 kilos based on the revised standard usage, and the actual usage of 1,450 kilos. Hence the controllable usage variance will be £50 favourable.

You will see that the original material usage variance of £200 adverse has been divided into an uncontrollable adverse planning variance of £250 and a revised controllable usage variance of £50 favourable. This approach produces variance calculations which provide a truer representation of a manager's performance and avoids any uncontrol-

lable elements being included in the material usage variance.

Labour variances

The criticisms which we have identified for the material variances are also applicable to the labour variances. For example, the labour efficiency variance should be adjusted to reflect changes in the environmental conditions which prevailed during the period. A situation where this might occur is when unskilled labour is substituted for skilled labour because of conditions in the labour market. It is necessary in these circumstances to adjust the standard and analyse the labour efficiency variance into the following variances:

(A) Uncontrollable planning variance due to environmental changes.
(B) Controllable efficiency variance.

The variance should be calculated in a similar manner to that described for material variances.

Overhead variances

Traditional fixed overhead variance analysis treats fixed costs as being variable with production by using fixed overhead absorption rates per unit of output in the volume variance calculation. This results in the calculation of a volume variance whenever actual production is different from the activity level used to establish the standard overhead rate. The value of this variance can be very misleading as total fixed overhead expenditure will not change because actual production was different from budgeted production. It may be more appropriate to report the difference between the actual and the budgeted production in physical terms rather than attaching fixed costs to the physical variance. A more meaningful approach may be to ascertain whether sales or production were responsible for the actual output being different from the budget. The variance, expressed in terms of lost contribution, should be charged to the appropriate responsibility centre. This process is illustrated in the next section.

A relevant cost approach to variance analysis

The traditional approach to variance analysis is to

calculate variances based on *acquisition costs* — the standard prices for the acquisition of the resources. This is misleading when scarce resources exist as a failure to use scarce resources efficiently leads not only to increased acquisition costs but also to a lost contribution. A more meaningful approach would be to incorporate the lost contribution in the variance calculations. For example, if materials are a scarce factor, any excess usage will cause material costs to be greater than necessary in addition to there being a loss of contribution because of inefficient usage of the materials. The lost contribution and the acquisition cost should therefore be attached to the material usage variance. Inefficient use of those resources which are not in scarce supply will *not* lead to a lost contribution because additional resources can be obtained. In these circumstances only the acquisition cost should be attached to the variance calculations. Let us now look at an illustration of the application of this approach in Example 18.5.

EXAMPLE 18.5

XYZ Ltd manufactures a single product, the standards of which are as follows:

		£
Standards per unit		
Standard selling price		52
Less		
Standard cost		
Materials — 5 kilos at £2 per kilo	10	
Labour — 4 hours at £4 per hour	16	
*Variable overheads — 4 hours at £1.50 per hour	6	
*Fixed overheads — 4 hours at £1.50 per hour	6	38
Standard profit		14

*Overheads are allocated on the basis of direct labour hours.

The following information relates to the previous month's activities:

	Budget	Actual
Production and sales	2,000 units	1,800 units
Direct materials	10,000 kilos at £2 per kilo	10,000 kilos at £2 per kilo
Direct labour	8,000 hours at £4 per hour	7,400 hours at £4 per hour
Variable overheads	£12,000	£11,100
Fixed overheads	£12,000	£12,000

The actual selling price was identical to the budgeted selling price and there were no opening or closing stocks during the period.

You are required to calculate the variances and reconcile the budgeted and actual profit for each of the following methods:
(1) The traditional (or conventional) method.
(2) The relevant cost method assuming *materials* are the limiting factor and materials are restricted to 10,000 kilos for the period.
(3) The relevant cost method assuming *labour hours* are the limiting factor and labour hours are restricted to 8,000 hours for the period.
(4) The relevant cost method assuming there are no *scarce inputs*.

An analysis of the variances and a reconciliation of the budgeted and actual profits is presented in Exhibit 18.2. Note that the price or spending variances are unaffected when scarce resources exist because *only the quantity variances are affected by how efficiently scarce resources are being used*. For this reason Example 18.6 has been designed so that *all the price variances are zero*. This will enable us to concentrate on the quantity variances. Let us now consider each of the columns in Exhibit 18.2.

Column (1): Conventional method

The variances in column (1) are calculated according to the methods outlined in the previous chapter. Please turn back to Chapter 17 if you need to refresh your memory on how these calculations are made.

Column (2): Scarce materials

The material usage variance in column (2) is £6,000 adverse compared with £2,000 adverse using the conventional method. The conventional method values the 1,000 kilos excess usage at the standard acquisition cost of £2 per unit.[2] However, because materials are scarce the relevant cost method includes the lost contribution which arises from the excess usage because the scarce resources were not used efficiently. The product contribution is £20 and each unit produced requires 5 scarce kilos of materials, giving a planned contribution of £4 per kilo. The excess usage of 1,000 kilos leads to a lost contribution of £4,000. This contribution is added to the acquisition cost for the excess materials giving a total variance of £6,000.

Exhibit 18.2 Variance analysis using a conventional and relevant cost approach

	(1) Conventional method	(2) Scarce materials	(3) Scarce labour hours	(4) Sales = limiting factor
Budgeted profit	28,000	28,000	28,000	28,000
Direct material usage variance	2,000A	6,000A	2,000A	2,000A
Labour efficiency variance	800A	800A	1,800A	800A
Variable overhead efficiency	300A	300A	300A	300A
Volume efficiency	300A	Nil	Nil	Nil
Volume capacity	900A	Nil	3,000A	Nil
Sales margin volume	2,800A	Nil	Nil	4,000A
Actual profit	20,900	20,900	20,900	20,900

Because labour hours are not scarce the labour variances are identical to the conventional method. Volume capacity and efficiency variances are zero because fixed overheads are sunk costs, and the total amount of fixed overhead expenditure will not change if the actual production is different from the budgeted production. The relevant fixed overhead cost is therefore zero. The sales margin volume variance is also different from the conventional method because the failure to achieve budgeted sales is due to a failure to use efficiently the scarce materials. Hence the cost should be charged to the responsible production manager and not to the sales manager.

Column (3): Scarce labour

Because it is assumed that materials are no longer scarce the materials usage variance in column (3) is identical to the conventional method calculation in column (1). Because labour hours are scarce the acquisition cost will not reflect the true economic cost for the labour efficiency variance. The conventional approach values the 200 excess hours at the standard acquisition cost of £4 per hour, but the relevant cost method in column (3) adds the lost contribution from the excess usage of 200 scarce labour hours.[3] The product contribution is £20 and each unit produced requires 4 scarce labour hours, so each labour hour is planned to yield a £5 contribution. Thus the 200 excess labour hours lead to a £1,000 lost contribution. This lost contribution of £1,000 is added to the acquisition cost for the excess labour hours giving a total relevant cost variance of £1,800.

With the conventional approach the volume efficiency variance consists of the excess labour

hours multiplied by the fixed overhead rate. Because fixed overheads are a sunk cost the relevant volume efficiency variance is zero. The lost contribution for labour efficiency has already been charged to the labour efficiency variance. The capacity variance for the conventional method consists of a failure to use 600 of the available 8,000 scarce labour hours. The fixed overhead rate of £1.50 is multiplied by 600 hours resulting in an adverse variance of £900 if the conventional approach is adopted. However, fixed overheads are not a relevant cost for the reasons we have previously described. The correct economic cost for failing to use *scarce* labour hours is the lost contribution per labour hour of £5. Consequently, the relevant cost approach allocates £3,000 (600 hours at £5) to the volume capacity variance *when labour hours are scarce*. For a detailed discussion of the volume capacity variance see Horngren (1978). The sales margin volume variance is again zero, the reasons being the same as those which were described previously when we were considering scarce materials.

Column (4): No scarce inputs

The labour and material variances in column (4) are the same as the conventional method as these resources are not scarce. The volume capacity and efficiency variances are zero, the reasons being the same as those explained in relation to scarce materials. Because there are no scarce production inputs the failure to achieve the budgeted sales volume is the responsibility of the sales manager. The lost sales volume of 200 units will mean a loss of profits equivalent to the lost product contribution of £20 per unit, giving an adverse variance of

£4,000. The conventional approach attaches the profit per unit of £14 to the lost sales volume of 200 units. This is incorrect because changes in the sales volume affect profits by changing the contribution per unit sold and not the profit per unit sold.

Conclusion

There are strong arguments for valuing variances at relevant cost and not acquisition cost. This approach requires that scarce resources are identified in advance of production but this is not easy to do in practice. In addition, the approach must rely on linear programming techniques when more than one scarce resource exists. The important points that you should note from this discussion are, first, that if quantity variances are valued at the acquisition cost of resources, this may not be a true reflection of the correct economic cost. Second, standard costing variance analysis must not be viewed as a mechanical procedure but as an intelligent approach to charging the controllable *economic* cost of the difference between actual and target performance to responsible individuals.

The investigation of variances

When a standard costing system is implemented it is possible to produce a vast amount of information for a wide range of variances which will indicate any likely areas requiring further investigation in respect of items not proceeding according to plan. However, it is unwise to investigate all the variances which occur in an accounting period because many may be insignificant or may have been caused by random uncontrollable factors.

Random uncontrollable factors

These factors exist when a particular process is performed by the same worker under the same conditions, yet performance varies. When no known cause is present to account for this variability, it is said to be due to random uncontrollable factors. A standard is determined from a series of observations of a particular operation. It is most unlikely that repeated observations of this operation will yield the same result even if the operation consists of the same worker repeating the same task under identical conditions. The correct approach is to choose a representative reading from these observations to determine a standard. Frequently, the representative reading which is chosen is the average or some other measure of central tendency. The important point to note is that one summary reading has been chosen to represent the standard when in reality a range of outcomes is possible when the process is *under control*. Any observation which differs from the chosen standard *when the process is under control* can be described as a random uncontrollable variation around the standard.

Any investigation of variances due to random uncontrollable factors will involve a cost and will not yield any benefits because no assignable cause for the variance is present. In addition, those variances where assignable causes are present (which means that the process is out of control) do not necessarily warrant investigation. For example, such variances may only be worthy of investigation if the benefits expected from the investigation exceed the costs of searching for and correcting the sources of the variance.

Variances may therefore be due to the following causes:

(1) Random uncontrollable factors when the operation is under control.
(2) Assignable causes but the costs of investigation exceed the benefits.
(3) Assignable causes but the benefits from investigation exceed the cost of investigation.

A number of articles have appeared in the accounting literature which use statistical theory to determine the probability that a process is in or out of control and whether or not further investigation is justified. For a summary of this literature see Kaplan (1978). One approach advocated in the literature is the use of normal distribution theory.

Application of normal distribution theory

Consider a situation where the standard cost for a particular operation for a period is £5,000 with the standard cost representing the average outcome for the possible observations when the operation is under control. Assume that the distribution of possible outcomes is normal and that the standard

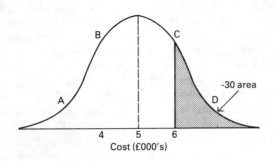

Fig. 18.1

deviation for the possible observations about the mean is £1,923. We can ascertain the probability of an observation of £6,000 or more *when the process is under control* by applying normal distribution theory. An observation of £6,000 is 0.52 standard deviations from the mean based on the following formula:

$$\frac{\text{Actual cost (£6,000)} - \text{Mean cost (£5,000)}}{\text{Standard deviation (£1,923)}}$$

$$= \underline{\underline{0.52}}$$

The normal probability table in Appendix III at the end of this book indicates that the probability of an observation greater than 0.52 standard deviations from the mean is 0.3015. This is illustrated in Fig. 18.1. The shaded area indicates that 30.15% of the area under the curve falls to the right of 0.52 standard deviations from the mean. Thus the probability of actual cost being £6,000 or more when the operation is under control is approximately 30%. Management might subjectively determine whether an investigation is worthwhile by considering whether the costs and benefits of an investigation are justified when the probability that the operation is under control is 30%. Alternatively, rather than making subjective decisions as to whether further investigation is justified we can formulate a model which considers the costs and the benefits of an investigation.

Incorporation of costs and benefits

Decision theory can be used to ascertain whether

variances should be investigated. The decision to investigate depends on whether or not the variance is due to random uncontrollable variations from the standard, or whether the variation is due to assignable causes. When the variance is due to random uncontrollable factors, an investigation will not yield any benefits. However, when the variance is due to an assignable cause the investigation will lead to a future cost saving. Bierman, Fouraker and Jaedicke (1977) have developed a model based on these principles using C to represent the cost of an investigation and L to represent the present value of the future cost savings from the investigation. It is assumed that L is greater than C, otherwise an investigation will never be undertaken. In addition, the probability of the variance resulting from a *random uncontrollable cause* is represented by P. Hence the probability of the variance being due to an *assignable cause* is represented by (1 − P).

We can now establish a decision rule by stating that if the expected cost of investigation is greater than the expected benefits from an investigation the investigation should not be undertaken. This can be represented as follows:

$$C < L(1 - P) \quad \text{investigate}$$
$$C > L(1 - P) \quad \text{do not investigate}$$

Let us now apply this decision rule to a situation where the standard cost is £1,000, the standard deviation is £90 and the cost of investigating a variance is £10. In addition, let us assume that the benefits from investigation are exactly equal to the amount of the variance. Assuming a variance of £90 should we investigate? If we use the formula:

$$\frac{\text{Actual cost} - \text{Mean cost}}{\text{Standard deviation}}$$

we can determine that a favourable variance is −1 standard deviation [(910 −1,000)/90] and an adverse variance is +1 standard deviation [(1,090 − 1,000)/90] from the mean. From the normal probability table the probability of an observation in excess of one standard deviation from the mean is approximately 0.16. The situation is presented in Fig. 18.2.

You will see that the probability of a favourable *or* adverse variance of £90 or more is 0.32 (represented by the area of 0.16 in both tails of the distribution) when the reason is random non-controllable factors. Hence the value of P is 0.32. We can now apply the decision rule by calculating:

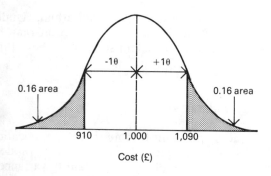

Fig. 18.2

$$L(1 - P) = 90 (1 - 0.32) = 61.2$$
$$\therefore C(10) < 61.2$$

In other words, we should investigate because the cost of the investigation will definitely be £10 and the expected cost savings are £61.20.

Let us now consider whether or not a variance of £30 should be investigated. If we apply the above procedure we find that £30 is ± 0.33 standard deviations from the mean.[4] From the normal probability table in Appendix III the probability of an observation in excess of 0.33 standard deviations from the mean is 0.37; the area in *both* tails of the distribution is therefore 0.74. Consequently, there is a 0.74 probability of a variance of £30 or more; the value for P is 0.74 and L(1 − P) equals 30(1 − 0.74) or £7.80. Because the cost of investigation is £10 the variance should not be investigated.

Normality assumption

Clearly the application of the model described in the previous paragraph depends on the assumption that the standard or budgeted cost can be represented by a normal distribution. This may be an unrealistic assumption. However, for new operations we might be able to estimate the standard cost in such a way that a normal distribution is a reasonable assumption. You should refer back to Chapter 12 for a description of this procedure.

It may be argued that a standard or budgeted cost should be represented by a measure different from the mean. For example, in Chapter 19 we will see that tighter standards with a possibility of failure may be more appropriate to motivate personnel. Therefore, it is possible that standards which are difficult to achieve will make the assumption of normality unrealistic. Nevertheless, there is no reason why the analysis cannot be modified to accommodte some probability distribution other than the normal distribution.

The problem of estimating costs and benefits

A major problem with the model outlined by Bierman, Fouraker and Jaedicke concerns the difficulty in determining the costs of investigation (C) and the benefits of investigation (L). Note that L is defined as the present value of the costs which will be incurred if an investigation is not made now. In situations where the inefficiency will be repeated, there will be many opportunities in the future to correct the process, and the discounted future costs, assuming no future investigation, will be an overestimate of L. In addition, the cost of an investigation will vary depending upon the cause of the variance. Some assignable causes will be detected before others, depending upon the ordering of the stages in the investigation procedure. If the variance is not due to an assignable cause, the cost of investigation will be higher because the investigation must eliminate all other causes before it can be established that the variance is not due to an assignable cause. Also, *additional* costs of carrying out the investigation may not be incurred as they may be carried out by existing staff at no extra cost to the organization. However, some opportunity cost is likely to be involved because of alternative work foregone while the investigation is being undertaken.

Because of the practical problems involved it appears that a model which includes the costs and benefits of investigation is unlikely to find wide acceptance in business enterprises at the present time. However, recognizing that a standard represents a range of possible outcomes rather than a specific figure and applying statistical techniques to determine the probability that an operation is under control appears to warrant further application to budgetary control and standard costing variance analysis.

Behavioural advantages

The application of statistical techniques to determine the probability of variances being due to random uncontrollable factors should result in a number of improvements in the behavioural

consequences of variance analysis. (For a discussion of the behavioural effects see Miles and Vergin, 1969.) There is a danger with non-statistical methods that the standard will be interpreted as a norm, with a performance better than the standard being considered as good, and a performance worse than the standard being considered as bad. If the latter situation occurs the individual may be spotlighted in a position of failure which might lead to dysfunctional behavioural consequences. (We shall discuss these behavioural consequences in Chapter 19.)

In addition, managers must examine extensive variance reports and react to those variances which may be interpreted as bad. The recognition of a standard as a range determined statistically by management should avoid some of these problems. Also, the acceptance of variability within the standards enables individuals to establish their own performance goals rather than being forced to equal or exceed a figure to avoid failure. Statistical techniques take into account normal variations in the individual's performance by establishing a zone or range of satisfactory performance. However, when performance does fall beyond the limits of normal variation, the variance is considered to be abnormal. Under these circumstances, management action may be viewed more as problem-solving rather than punitive.

Quantity variances

Finally, it is important to note that the application of statistical techniques which incorporate random variations is only applicable to quantity variances, that is, labour and overhead efficiency, material usage and overhead volume variances. There is a fundamental difference between these variances and price variances. Efficiency cannot be pre-determined in the same way as material prices and wage rates, first, because of the random variations inherent in the human element and, second, because the resulting non-uniformity is more pronounced. One does not expect actual results to be equal to standard where the human element is involved, as some variances may be expected to occur even when no assignable cause is present. For this reason statistical techniques are likely to be most useful when applied to the analysis of quantity variances.

Summary

In some production processes it is possible to vary the mix of materials which are used to make the final product. We have seen in this chapter that any deviations from the standard mix will lead to a mix variance. A favourable mix variance will result when cheaper materials are substituted for more expensive materials. This may not always be in the company's best interest as product quality may suffer or output may be reduced leading to an adverse yield variance. The yield variance arises because there is a difference between the standard output for a given level of input and the actual output attained.

Part of the sales margin volume variance may be accounted for because the actual sales mix differs from the budgeted sales mix. This element can be isolated by calculating a sales margin mix variance.

One of the criticisms of standard costing is that standards are normally based on the environment which was anticipated when the targets were set. To overcome this problem, whenever the actual environment is different from the anticipated environment, performance should be compared with a standard which reflects the changed conditions. One possible solution is to analyse the variance so that a planning or forecasting variance is extracted. This variance provides management with useful feedback information on how successful management are in predicting target costs. The price or usage variance should then be calculated based on a revised target for the conditions under which the managers operated during a period.

Another criticism of standard costing is that the variances are calculated using standard acquisition costs, and in some cases acquisition costs do not represent the economic cost for the excess usage of resources. In such situations it is preferable to value the quantity variances at the relevant cost of resources.

The decision to investigate a variance should depend on whether the expected benefits are likely to exceed the costs of carrying out the investigation. Variances may be due to the following causes:

(1) Random uncontrollable variances when the variance is under control.
(2) Assignable causes but the costs of investigation exceed the benefits.
(3) Assignable causes but the benefits from investigation exceed the costs of investigation.

We should aim to investigate only those variances which fall into the final category.

References and further reading

Accounting Standards Committee. *Accounting for Stocks and Work in Progress* (SSAP 9), 1977.

Barnes, P. Which variances are worth investigating? *Accountancy* December 1979, 80-83.

Bierman, H., Fouraker, L.E. and Jaedicke, R.K. A use of probability and statistics in performance evaluation. In Benston, G.J. (Ed.) *Contemporary Cost Accounting and Control.* Dickenson Publishing Company, 1977.

Bromwich, M. Standard costing for planning and control. In Arnold, J., Carsberg, B. and Scapens, R. (Eds), *Topics in Management Accounting.* Philip Allan, 1980.

Buzby, S.L. Extending the applicability of probabilistic management planning and control methods *The Accounting Review* January 1974, 35-41.

Chumachenko, N.G. Once again: The volume–mix–price/cost budget variance analysis. *The Accounting Review* **XLIII**(4), October 1968, 753-62.

Demski, J.S. Analysing the effectiveness of the traditional standard costing variance model. In Benston, G.J. (Ed.), *Contemporary Cost Accounting and Control.* Dickenson Publishing Company, 1977.

Demski, J.S. Variance analysis using a constrained linear model. In Solomons, D. (Ed.), *Studies in Cost Analysis* 2nd edn. Sweet & Maxwell.

Dopuch, N., Birnberg, J.E. and Demski, J. An extension of standard cost variance analysis. *The Accounting Review* **XLII**(3), July 1967, 526-36.

Dyckman, T. The investigation of cost variances. *Journal of Accounting Research* **7**(2), Autumn 1969, 215-44.

Harvey, M. and Thompson, T. Planning and operational variances. *Accountancy* February 1978, 84-6.

Hasseldine, C.R. Mix and yield variances. *The Accounting Review* **XLII**(3), July 1967, 497-515.

Horngren, C.T. A contribution margin approach to the analysis of capacity utilization. In Anton, H.R., Firmin, P.A. and Grove, H.D. (Eds), *Contemporary Issues in Cost and Managerial Accounting.* Houghton Mifflin Company, 1978.

Kaplan, R.S. The significance and investigation of cost variances: Survey and extensions. *Journal of Accounting Research* **13**(2), Autumn 1975, pp. 311-37; also in Anton, H.R., Firmin, P.A. and Grove, H.D. (Eds), *Contemporary Issues in Cost and Managerial Accounting.* Houghton Mifflin, 1978.

Kennedy, A. Mixes in variance analysis. *Management Accounting* February 1982, 29-31.

Koehler, R.W. The relevance of probability statistics to accounting variance control. *Management Accounting (USA)* October 1968, 35-41.

Luh, F.S. Controlled cost: An operation concept and statistical approach for standard costing. *Accounting Review* January 1968, 123-32; also in Rappaport, A. (Ed.), *Information for Decision-Making.* Prentice-Hall, 1975.

Magee, R.P. Cost variance investigation models. *Accounting Review* July 1976, 529-45.

Manes, R.P. The expense of expected idle capacity. *Management Accounting (USA)*, March 1969, 37-41.

Martindale, A. Stirring the variances mix. *Management Accounting* November 1982, 40-2.

Miles, R.E. and Vergin, R.C. Behavioural properties of variance controls. In Bruns, W.J. and De Coster, D.T. (Eds), *Accounting and its Behavioural Implications.* McGraw Hill, 1969.

Ronen, J. Capacity and operating variances: An expost approach. *Journal of Accounting Research* **8**(1), Autumn 1970, 232-52.

Shank, J. and Churchill, N. Variance analysis: A management orientated approach. *Accounting Review* **XLII**(4), October 1977, 950-7.

Solomons, D. Flexible budgets and the analysis of overhead variances. In Anton, H.R. and Firmin, P.A. (Eds), *Contemporary Issues in Cost Accounting.* Houghton Mifflin, 1972.

Solomons, D. An analysis of standard cost variances. In Solomons, D. (Ed.), *Studies in Cost Analysis* 2nd edn. Sweet & Maxwell, 1968.

Wolk, H.I. and Hillman, D.A. Material mix and yield variances: A suggested improvement. *The Accounting Review* **XLVII**(3), July 1972, 549-55.

Problems

*Indicates that a suggested solution is to be found in the *Students' Manual*.

18.1* A material price variance may be calculated and entered in the accounts of a business at either the time of receipt of the stock, or the time of issue from stores to production.

(a) State which of the methods is usually regarded as the better and why.

In your answer, to save writing the description of each method in full, you may refer to Method 1 (indicating calculation at time of receipt) and Method 2 (indicating calculation at time of issue).

(b) Draw up two sets of ledger accounts and record in them the transactions shown below, when:
 (i) method 1 is used (calculation and entry at time of receipt); and
 (ii) method 2 is used (calculation and entry at time of issue to production).

There was no opening stock of component number 53623 and its standard price has been fixed at £4 each.

1 April 400 components number 53623 were received from and invoiced by AB Ltd at a total cost of £1,720.

14 April 150 of these components were issued from stores to production and included in goods sold in April.

(c) State the value of the closing stock for the balance sheet at 30 April.

(d) Write brief notes to show that you understand the meaning of each of the following terms:
 (i) forecast;
 (ii) master budget;
 (iii) fixed budget;
 (iv) flexible budget;
 (v) budget manual.

(30 marks)
ICMA Cost Accounting 1
May 1981

18.2* Exe PLC manufactures one standard product and operates a standard costing system. From the data given below, you are required to prepared accounts for the following:

material stores,
wages,
production overhead,
work in progress,
finished goods,
cost of sales,
profit and loss.

Standard/budgeted data:
The standard price of a tonne of material is £400, and from each tonne it is expected that 50 units will be produced. A 40-hour week is operated by 20 employees, who receive a standard rate of pay of £4 per hour. The standard performance is 40 units to be produced per hour. Budgeted fixed production overhead

for the year is £480,000 and it is expected that 50 weeks will be worked.

Actual data:
During the first week of October the actual materials bought and consumed were 35 tonnes at a price of £390 per tonne. No abnormal time resulted, but 5 employees were paid at £4.2 per hour. Production was 1,660 units and the overhead incurred amounted to £9,700. Sales were valued at £33,200. There were no opening or closing stocks.

(30 marks)
ICMA Cost Accounting 2
November 1983

18.3 SC Ltd operates a system of cost control accounts and standard costing. From the data given below for the first week in November 1980 you are required to prepare the following accounts:
(a) work in progress;
(b) finished goods;
(c) profit and loss.

In a particular process in the company, ten employees are paid at a standard rate of £3 per hour. The standard rate of output is 2 units of product per employee-hour. An eight-hour day is worked, five days per week. The product is manufactured from a material called Stancost. This material costs £200 per tonne and from each tonne of material input, a standard output of 50 units is obtained. Production overhead is absorbed at 300% of the cost of direct wages.

In calculating the selling price of the product, administration overhead is included at 25% of production cost, selling and distribution overhead at 35% of production cost and profit at 20% of selling price.

During the first week in November 1980, 18 tonnes of Stancost were issued to production. There were no differences in material prices, in wage rates or in overhead expenditure when actual was compared with standard. A power failure caused a complete stoppage of production for two hours. The actual output for the week was 840 units. There was no work in process at the beginning or end of the week. Finished goods stock at the beginning of the week was 60 units and at the end of the week was 80 units. Administration overhead and selling and distribution overhead are not absorbed into the cost of goods produced and amounted to £2,050 and £2,870 respectively.

(30 marks)
ICMA Cost Accounting 2
November 1980

18.4 B Ltd operates an integral accounting system. From the data given below you are required to:
(a) show the ledger accounts for the month of

April, 1981;
(b) prepare:
 (i) the cumulative profit and loss account for the period ended 30 April 1981;
 (ii) the balance sheet as at 30 April 1981.
On 31 March 1981 the balances in the ledger were as follows:

	£000	£000
Issued share capital		500
Reserves		220
10% Debentures		480
Buildings	650	
Plant and machinery	600	
Provision for depreciation of plant and machinery		220
Raw material stock, at standard cost	300	
Work in progress, at standard cost	50	
Finished goods stock, at standard cost	80	
Debtors	100	
Creditors		60
Expense creditors		20
Debenture interest	8	
Wages payable		40
Bank	52	
Administrative overhead	25	
Selling and distribution overhead	15	
Direct material: price variance		20
Usage variance	5	
Direct labour: Rate variance	25	
Efficiency variance		15
Production overhead: Expenditure variance		5
Volume variance		30
Cost of sales	400	
Sales		700
	2,310	2,310

	£000
Relevant budgeted data	
Production overhead (including depreciation per annum)	2,160

Output, per annum 72,000 units
Standard cost per unit of product:
 Direct material 5 kg at £2 per kg
 Direct wages 10 hours at £4 per hour
 Production overhead 10 hours at £3 per hour

Actual data for April 1981

		£000
Direct material:		
Purchased from suppliers 30,000 kg·		66
Issued to production 29,500 kg		
Direct wages:		
Incurred	60,000 hours	252
Paid		238
Production overhead		185
Administration overhead		20

	£000
Selling and distribution overhead	15
Creditors paid	76
Expense creditors paid	205
Finished goods stock, at 30 April	120
Sales	742
Debtors, cash received	767

Depreciation of plant and machinery is 20% per annum on cost
Output 5,800 units

(30 marks)
ICMA Cost Accounting 2
May 1981

18.5* SC Ltd manufactures a special floor tile which measures $\frac{1}{2}$m × $\frac{1}{4}$m × 0.01m. The tiles are manufactured in a process which requires the following standard mix:

Material	Quantity kg	Price £	Amount £
A	40	1.5	60
B	30	1.2	36
C	10	1.4	14
D	20	0.5	10
			£120

Each mix should produce 100 square metres of floor tiles of 0.01m thickness. During April, 60 mixes were processed and the actual output was 46,400 tiles from an input of:

Material	Quantity kg	Price £	Amount £
A	2,200	1.6	3,520
B	2,000	1.1	2,200
C	500	1.5	750
D	1,400	0.5	700
			£7,170

For the month of April, you are required to:
(i) calculate for each material:
 (a) cost variance;
 (b) price variance;
 (c) usage variance; and
 (d) mix variance;
(ii) calculate the yield variance.

(25 marks)
ICMA Cost Accounting 2
May 1981

18.6 A company operates a standard cost system. All material, labour, overhead, work in progress and finished goods are accounted for at standard. Variances are extracted at the earliest identifiable point.
 Data are given below for Product A for the month of October 1983.
 You are required to:
(a) show in a diagrammatical form the flow of

financial data and the control points at which the variances may be extracted;

(b) (i) calculate the actual profit achieved for the month against the standard profit expected, with the variances identified;

(ii) state the quantity and value of materials and goods in stock at the month-end;

(iii) give a brief management report on the results achieved in the month compared with the standard planned.

Data
Standard cost

Production	Requirement per item of product
Direct material	20 units at £1.50 per unit
Direct wages	30 hours at £2.10 per hour

	per month
Overhead — fixed	£40,000
variable (based on units)	£160,000
Normal capacity	120,00 hours

Marketing

	per month
Sales	4,000 items at £175 each

Actual for the month of October 1983		Cost £000
Production		
Direct material — purchased	80,000 units	£128
issued	78,000 units	
Direct wages	116,000 hours	232
Overhead — fixed		42
variable		150
Output	3,800 items	

Marketing		Value £000
Sales	3,500 items	623

There was no stock at the beginning of the month.

(30 marks)
ICMA P3 Management Accounting
November 1983

18.7 From the data given below, relating to the manufacture of a special lubricant you are required to:

(a) calculate the operating profit variance for the month of October 1980;

(b) analyse this difference into its sub-variances covering sales and production changes; and

(c) explain briefly what you consider to be the main problem indicated by the figures and how this could be overcome.

Budget — operations for one month.
Input, 20 batches of 500 litres each

Direct materials	% of quantity	Price per litre £
X	30	0.60
Y	20	0.30
Z	50	0.45

Direct labour	% of hours	Rate per hour £
Blending	60	2.50
Filtering	30	2.25
Packing	10	2.00

Total labour hours		8,000
Overhead cost: Variable		£0.06 per litre
Fixed		£5,750
Output		10,000 litres
Selling price		£3.55 per litre

Actual results for the month of October 1980.

Direct materials used	Litres	Price per litre £
X	2,200	0.80
Y	2,500	0.35
Z	4,800	0.65

Direct labour	Hours	Rate per hour £
Blending	5,000	2.60
Filtering	2,000	2.20
Packing	700	2.00

	£
Overhead cost: Variable	655
Fixed	5,800

The output of 9,500 litres from 19 batches processed was all sold at an average price of £3.71 per litre.

(30 marks)
ICMA P3 Management Accounting
November 1980

18.8* Darms Ltd manufactures only a single type of product which it sells both to independent retailers under its own brand name and also to several national groups of multiple retailers for them to retail under their own brand names. Although the products sold in these two markets are physically identical, except for the brand name, Darms has a two-tiered price structure with a different price for each of the two markets and for invoicing purposes the products are known as Ds (Darms' brand name) and Rs (retailer's own brand name).

The budgeted costs for the first half of the year were based on production and sales levels of 1,000 units. The budgeted figures were:

	Per Unit	£	Total (£000)
Production costs			
Direct labour	10 hours at £3 per hour	30	30
Direct materials	20 kg at £2 per kg	40	40
Variable overheads	£1 per labour hour worked	10	10
Fixed overheads	per unit produced	20	20
	Standard production cost	100	100
Delivery costs	per unit delivered	10	10
			110

	(£000)	
Other costs		
Fixed sales costs	40	
Fixed administrative costs of the purchasing department	20	60
Total budget cost		£170

The figures for the budgeted sales and the sale mix for the first half of the year were:

		£ (000s)
Ds (Darm's own brand name)	500 units at £210	105
Rs (Retailer's brand name)	500 units at £200	100
Total budgeted sales revenues		£205

The actual results for the first half of the year were:

Detailed profit statement, months I–VI

	£000	£000	£000
Sales revenues			
Ds 600 units at £230		138	
Rs 400 units at £210		84	222
Cost of goods sold			
Opening stock of finished goods			
200 units at standard cost of £100		20	
Manufacturing costs for 900 units produced			
Direct labour hours paid, 8,000	28		
Direct materials 20,000 kg	35		
Variable overhead	10		
Fixed overhead	23	96	
		116	
Less: Closing stock of finished goods 100 units at standard cost of £100		10	106
Delivery costs			12
Sales costs			48
Administrative costs of the purchasing department			21
Total costs			187
Profit			£35

Douglas Armstrong, the managing director, was quite pleased with the results and made the following further points:

(i) Each of the four major operating departments within the firm — selling, purchasing, production and delivery — are largely free to decide how the operations within their own functions are carried out. As the profit achieved equals that planned, each department can feel satisfied with its own performance.

(ii) Although production, at 900 units, was less than planned all orders were met, even though to do so required reducing the levels of finished goods held in stock. There were no stocks of raw materials or work in progress at the beginning or the end of the period.

(iii) Output was less than planned due to the temporary closure of production facilities during the period following the failure of the purchasing department to provide an adequate supply of raw materials. Included in the figures of direct labour hours paid are exactly 1,000 hours which were due to idle time payments which resulted from the factory closure caused by the failure in raw materials supply.

Required:

(a) Produce a statement which will be useful to Mr Armstrong in highlighting the reasons for the performance of Darms Ltd for the first half year. The statement should analyse the performance of each of the four major operating departments and should use variance analysis to the extent it is applicable and useful. (c. 14 marks)

(b) Briefly:
(i) comment on the performance of Darms Ltd and its four major operating departments, (c. 4 marks), and
(ii) describe two of the major difficulties inherent in such an analysis of the performance. (c. 2 marks)

(Total 20 marks)

ACCA P2 Management Accounting June 1980

18.9 In view of the highly specialized skills needed in the production of Wyes, the management of Richardson have delegated considerable authority to the Wye department to control its own activities. The department is, for example, responsible for its own purchasing function and for determining its own wage rates. However, the management team require frequent, and detailed, reports on the performance of the Wye department.

The standard cost of production of each unit of Wye, based on normal monthly production of 2,000 units, is

Standard cost per unit of Wye

	£	£
Labour — 4 hours at £3 per hour		12
Materials — Aye 2 litres at £4 per litre	8	
Bee 3 litres at £5 per litre	15	23
Variable production overheads — £1 per standard labour hour		4
Fixed production overheads — £2 per standard labour hour		8
		£47

The actual expenses recorded for month 4 were:

	£	£	
Labour 9,000 hours		30,000	
Materials used in production			
Aye 6,000 litres	25,000		
Bee 6,000 litres	27,000	52,000	(Note 1)
Variable production overheads		8,500	
Fixed production overheads		27,500	(Note 2)
		£118,000	

Note 1: Material costs are based on the weighted average method of stock valuation with a new average recalculated after each purchase.

Note 2: This figure includes a payment of £12,000 which applies to the six months from month 4 to month 9. The original budget for this amount was £10,800 and was expected to be paid in month 4.

There were no stocks of raw materials or work in progress at the beginning of month 4.
Activity during month 4 was

2,000 units fully completed,
500 units partly completed and carried forward to month 5.

The partly completed units were fully complete with respect to material inputs but only 40% complete in terms of labour and overhead inputs.
In month 4 the following raw materials were purchased:

Aye — Purchase 1	7,000 litres at £4 per litre
Purchase 2	8,000 litres at £5 per litre
Bee — Purchase 1	10,000 litres at £4.5 per litre

The management of Richardson require a monthly control report which reflects for the Wye department all deviations from budgeted performance at the earliest possible time. Management is particularly interested in learning whether the materials are used in the correct proportions and whether the materials are of

sufficient quality to yield the expected output.

Required:

(a) Produce a statement which shows to management how the performance of the Wye department in period 4 compared with the expected efficiency and which identifies all deviations from plans at the earliest possible time. (14 marks)

(b) Produce a brief written report to management which explains and outlines the advantages of your treatment of
 (i) materials price variance,
 (ii) other reported variances relating to production materials,
 (iii) fixed overhead variances. (6 marks)

(20 marks)

ACCA P2 Management Accounting
December 1980

18.10* Mingus Ltd produces granoids. It revises its cost standards annually in September for the year commencing 1 December.

At a normal annual volume of output of 40,000 granoids its standard costs, including overheads, for the year to 30 November 1981 were:

Cost	Standard	Per unit (£)	Total (£000)
Direct materials	5 kg at £10 per kg	50	2,000
Direct labour	2 hrs at £5 per hr	10	400
Variable overheads	£1 per kg of direct material	5	200
Fixed overheads	£5 per hr of direct labour	10	400
		75	3,000

The actual expenditure incurred in that year to produce an actual output of 50,000 granoids was:

Cost	Total expenditure (£000)	Further details
Direct materials	2,880	320,000 kg at £9 per kg
Direct labour	540	90,000 hrs at £6 per hr
Variable overheads	280	
Fixed overheads	380	
	4,080	

Due to an industrial dispute in 1980 there was no stock-holding of materials, work in progress, or completed granoids at 1 December 1980. At 30 November 1981 there was an inventory of 10,000 completed granoids, but no work in progress, and no raw materials inventory.

(a) You are required to calculate in each case the balance which would remain in the finished goods inventory account if each of the following six costing systems were used:

(i) actual absorption costing,

(ii) standard absorption costing with variances written off,

(iii) standard absorption costing with variances pro-rated between cost of sales and inventory,

(iv) actual direct costing,

(v) standard direct costing with variances written off,

(vi) standard direct costing with variances pro-rated between cost of sales and inventory (10 marks).

(b) You are required to comment briefly in general terms on the main effects of applying to inventory valuation the various costing systems set out above, referring to your calculations in part (a) if you wish (5 marks).

(c) Overhead cost absorption may be used in connection with various other matters.

You are required to discuss the use of overhead cost absorption procedures for either
 (i) pricing, or
 (ii) control of costs (10 marks).

(25 marks)

ICAEW Management Accounting
December 1981

18.11* A year ago Kenp Ltd entered the market for the manufacture and sale of a revolutionary insulating material. The budgeted production and sales volumes were 1,000 units. The originally estimated sales price and standard costs for this new product were:

	£	£
Standard sales price, per unit		100
Standard costs, per unit		
Raw materials, Aye 10 lbs at £5	50	
Labour, 6 hours at £4	24	74
Standard contribution, per unit		£26

Actual results were:

First year's results

	(£000)	(£000)
Sales, 1,000 units		158
Production costs, 1,000 units		
Raw materials, Aye 10,800	97.2	
Labour, 5,800 hours	34.8	132
Actual contribution		£26

'Throughout the year we attempted to operate as efficiently as possible, given the prevailing conditions' stated the managing director. 'Although in total the performance agreed with budget, in every detailed respect, except volume, there were large differences. These were due, mainly, to the tremendous success of the new insulating material which created increased demand both for the product itself and all the manufacturing resources used in its production. This then resulted in price rises all round.'

'Sales were made at what was felt to be the highest feasible price but, it was later discovered, our competitors sold for £165 per unit and we could have equalled this price. Labour costs rose dramatically with increased demand for the specialist skills required to produce the product and the general market rate was £6.25 per hour — although Kenp always paid below the general market rate whenever possible.'

'Raw material Aye was chosen as it appeared cheaper than the alternative material Bee which could have been used. The costs which were expected at the time the budget was prepared were, per lb, Aye, £5 and Bee, £6. However the market prices relating to efficient purchases of the materials during the year were:

Aye £8.50 per lb, and
Bee £7.00 per lb.

Therefore it would have been more appropriate to use Bee, but as production plans were based on Aye it was Aye that was used.'

'It is not proposed to request a variance analysis for the first year's results as most of the deviations from budget were caused by the new product's great success and this could not have been fully anticipated and planned for. In any event the final contribution was equal to that originally budgeted so operations must have been fully efficient.'

Required:

(a) Compute the traditional variances for the first year's operations. (5 marks)

(b) Prepare an analysis of variances for the first year's operations which will be useful in the circumstances of Kenp Ltd. The analysis

should indicate the extent to which the variances were due to operational efficiency or planning causes. (10 marks)

(c) Using, for illustration, a comparison of the raw material variances computed in (a) and (b) above, briefly outline two major advantages and two major disadvantages of the approach applied in part (b) over the traditional approach. (5 marks)

(20 marks)

ACCA P2 Management Accounting
June 1981

18.12 The management team of Thorpe Ltd feel that standard costing and variance analysis have little to offer in the reporting of some of the activities of their firm.

'Although we produce a range of fairly standardized products', states the accountant of Thorpe Ltd, 'prices of many of our raw materials are apt to change suddenly and comparison of actual prices with a pre-determined, and often unrealistic, standard piece is of little use. For some of our products we can utilize one of several equally suitable raw materials and we always plan to utilize the raw material which will, in our opinion, lead to the cheapest total production costs. However, we are frequently caught out by price changes and the material actually used often proves, after the event, to have been more expensive than the alternative which was originally rejected.

'For example, consider the experience over the last accounting period of two of our products, Alpha and Beta. To produce a unit of Alpha we can use either 5 kg of gamma of 5 kg of delta. We planned to use gamma as it appeared it would be the cheaper of the two and our plans were based on a cost of gamma of £3 per kg. Due to market movements the actual prices changed and if we had purchased efficiently the costs would have been

gamma	£4.50 per kg
delta	£4.00 per kg

'Production of Alpha was 2,000 units and usage of gamma amounted to 10.800 kg at a total cost of £51,840.

'Product Beta uses only one raw material, epsilon, but again the price of this can change rapidly. It was thought that epsilon would cost £30 per tonne but in fact we only paid £25 per tonne and if we had purchased correctly the cost would have been less as it was freely available at only £23 per tonne. It usually takes 1.5 tonnes of epsilon to produce 1 tonne of Beta but our production of 500 tonnes of Beta used only 700 tonnes of epsilon.

'So you can see that with our particular

circumstances the traditional approach to variance analysis is of little use and we don't use it for materials although we do use it for reporting on labour and variable overhead costs.'

Required:

(a) Analyse the material variances for both Alpha and Beta utilizing
 (i) traditional variance analysis; and
 (ii) an approach which distinguishes between planning and operational variances. (c. 12 marks)
(b) Write brief notes which
 (i) explain the approach to variance analysis which distinguishes between planning and operational variances;
 (ii) indicate the extent to which this approach is useful for firms in general and for Thorpe Ltd in particular;
 (iii) highlight the main difficulty in the application of this approach. (c. 8 marks)

(Total 20 marks)

ACCA P2 Management Accounting
December 1979

18.13 (a) If standard cost variances are to be interpreted meaningfully it is obviously important that the nature of the standards themselves is clearly understood.

 You are required to suggest alternative bases on which standards might be set, and to discuss the nature and significance of variances arising from the use of each basis (12 marks).

(b) (i) McPartland Ltd manufactures and sells a single product. In the quarter to 30 November 1980 sales of 10,000 units were budgeted at a unit selling price of £5 and a unit contribution of £1 (after charging variable costs). The budget had been prepared in the previous spring, and proved to be inaccurate. Actual sales for the November quarter were 7,000 units at a unit selling price of £8, giving a unit contribution of £3.

 You are required to calculate appropriate sales margin variances on the basis of this information (3 marks).

(ii) When reviewing the results for the quarter to 30 November the sales manager ascertained several additional facts.

 The total market for the product nationally had been only 45,000 units during the quarter, and not 50,000 units as McPartland had originally anticipated. McPartland had previously maintained a 20% share of the market for many years, adopting a policy of

matching the market price. An index of the selling price levels of competitors' products had risen to 140, instead of remaining at the level of 100 as originally budgeted. McPartland's variable costs (all materials) had risen in line with the change in the appropriate commodity price index, which had gone up from the expected level of 100 to an actual level of 125.

 You are required to calculate a set of variances to take appropriate notice of this additional information, and to discuss their significance (10 marks).

ICAEW Management Accounting
December 1980

18.14 The Original Jellyroll Company PLC makes a single product, the rodmason. It operates a standard costing system in respect of labour and materials, but not overheads (which are all fixed).

The standards per unit of output in the first half of 1982 were as follows:

Material	4 kg at £60 per kg
Direct labour	50 hours at £2.50 per hour

In the six months January–June 1982 the company produced and sold 23,000 units of rodmason, having no work in progress at either the start or the end of the period, and no opening stock of raw material. The following data also relate to that half-year:

Direct labour costs	1,200,000 hours, costing £2,880,000
Material purchased	120,000 kg, costing £6,960,000
Material used in production	96,000 kg
Material in stock at 30 June 1982	24,000 kg

When reviewing the results for the first half of 1982 the company's operations manager came to the conclusion that the standard for materials had been inappropriately set. He considered that, with the benefit of hindsight, for each unit of output they should have been 5 kg at £55 per kg.

You are required:

(a) to set out the alternative bases which might have been used in setting the original standards, and to compare these alternatives in terms of the significance of variances arising from the use of each of them respectively (7 marks),
(b) to set out the methods of calculating respectively a two-way and a three-way variance analysis of fixed overheads, and to advise the operations manager of the Original Jellyroll Company PLC whether he should introduce either of these systems of

variance analysis for the company's fixed overheads (8 marks),
(c) to write a memorandum to the operations manager which explains briefly what you understand by the terms 'operating' and 'planning' variances, shows calculation of suitable such variances for materials for the Original Jellyroll Company PLC for the period January–June 1982, and interprets them for him (6 marks), and
(d) to answer a criticism by the operations manager that, given time and usage standards, in hours and kg respectively, he could control the business satisfactorily without the use of any cost standards (4 marks).
Note: it is not necessary to make calculations in answering parts (a), (b) and (d) of this question.

(25 marks)
ICAEW Management Accounting July 1982

18.15* Blue Ltd manufactures a single product, the standards of which are as follows:

	£
Standards per unit	
Standard selling price	268
Less	

Standard cost:	£	
Materials 16 units at £4	64	
Labour 4 hours at £3	12	
*Overheads 4 hours at £24	96	172
Standard profit		96

*Total overhead costs are allocated on the basis of budgeted direct labour hours.

The following information relates to last month's activities:

	Budgeted	Actual
Production and sales	600 units	500 units
Direct labour	2,400 hours at £3	2,300 hours at £3
Fixed overheads	£19,200	£20,000
Variable overheads	£38,400	£40,400
Materials	9,600 units at £4 per unit	9,600 units at £4 per unit

The actual selling price was identical to the budgeted selling price and there was no opening or closing stocks during the period.
(a) You are required to calculate the variances and reconcile the budgeted and actual profit for each of the following methods:
 (i) the traditional method;
 (ii) the relevant cost method assuming *materials* are the limiting factor and materials are restricted to 9,600 units for the period;
 (iii) the relevant cost method assuming *labour hours* are the limiting factor and labour hours are restricted to 2,400 hours for the period;
 (iv) the relevant cost method assuming there are *no scarce inputs*.
(b) Briefly explain and comment on any differences between your answers to (a)(i) to (a)(iv) above.

18.16 XYZ Ltd manufactures a single product, the standards of which are as follows:

	£
Standards per unit	
Standard selling price	54
Less	

Standard cost:		
Materials 4 units at £4	16	
Labour 2 hours at £5	10	
*Overheads 2 hours at £6	12	38
Standard profit		16

*Total overhead costs are allocated on the basis of budgeted labour hours.

The following information relates to last month's activities:

	Budgeted	Actual
Production and sales	1,200 units at £54	1,000 units at £54
Direct materials	4,800 units at £4 per unit	4,800 units at £4 per unit
Direct labour	2,400 hours at £5 per hour	2,100 hours at £3 per hour
Fixed overheads	£4,800	£5,000
Variable overheads	£9,600	£10,100

The actual selling price was identical to the budgeted selling price and there were no opening or closing stocks during the period.

You are required to calculate the variances and reconcile the budgeted and actual profit for each of the following methods:
(i) the traditional method;
(ii) the relevant cost method assuming *materials* are the limiting factor and materials are restricted to 4,800 units for the period;
(iii) the relevant cost method assuming *labour hours* are the limiting factor and labour hours are restricted to 2,400 hours for the period;
(iv) the relevant cost method assuming there are *no scarce inputs*.

18.17* (a) The Secure Locke Company operates a system of standard costing, which it uses amongst other things as the basis for calculating certain management bonuses.

In September 1979 the Company's production of 100,000 keys was in accordance with budget. The standard quality of material used in each key is one unit; the standard price is £0.05 per unit. In September 105,000 units of material were used, at an actual purchase price of £45 per thousand units (which was also the replacement cost).

The materials buyer is given a bonus of 10% of any favourable materials price variance. The production manager is given a bonus of 10% of any favourable materials quantity variance.

You are required:
(i) to calculate the materials cost variances for September 1979; (4 marks)
(ii) to record all relevant bookkeeping entries in journal form; (2 marks)
(iii) to evaluate the bonus system from the viewpoints of the buyer, the production manager and the company. (6 marks)
(b) In October 1979 there was an adverse materials quantity variance of £500. A decision has to be made as to whether to investigate the key-making process to determine whether it is out of control.

On the basis of past experience the cost of an invstigation is estimated at £50. The cost of correcting the process if it is found to be out of control is estimated at £100. The probability that the process is out of control is estimated at .50.

You are required:
(i) to calculate the minimum present value of the expected savings that would have to be made in future months in order to justify making an investigation; (6 marks)
(ii) to suggest why the monthly cost savings arising from a systematic investigation are unlikely to be as great as the

adverse materials variance of £500 which was experienced in the month of October 1979; (3 marks)
(iii) to calculate, if the expected present value of cost savings were *first* £600 and *second* £250, the respective levels of probability that the process was out of control, at which the management would be indifferent about whether to conduct an investigation. (4 marks)

ICAEW Management Accounting December 1979

18.18 Blake Ltd has been operating a standard costing system for several years and now wishes to consider whether or not it is worthwhile investigating variances that are disclosed in its monthly performance reports. The performance reports for the past several years have been analysed and variances have been identified into the following classes:

Class X: Those that continue over a period of time as a result of such inefficiencies as slow workmanship or bad materials.

Class Y: Those tha arise from similar causes as in Class X, but which do not continue as they are either random or easily recognized and quickly corrected by the relevant manager.

Class Z: Those that continue over a period of time because the process has some inherent inadequacy which would be too expensive to correct in the short term, or where the original budget was incorrect.

Past experience has indicated that in the past the frequency of these variances has been as follows:

Class X	30%
Class Y	60%
Class Z	10%

Past information also indicated that investigations of class Y and class Z variances has yielded no benefits to the company but on 80% of the occasions investigations of class X variances has resulted in successful elimination of the variance, but the remaining 20% did not.

You ascertain that the cost of investigation variances is £60 and the cost to correct the process if you discover it is out of control is £100. The cost savings resulting from the investigation have an average estimated present value of £400.

You are required to:
(a) Calculate whether or not it is profitable for the company to investigate the variances as a matter of routine.

(b) Calculate the maximum investigation costs the company should be prepared to pay before investigation becomes unprofitable.

(c) Calculate the percentage level of class X variances resulting in succssful elimination of the variances that would need to occur for the benefits of investigation to be equal to the costs of investigation.

(d) Briefly discuss the difficulties in using probability statistics and decision theory in determining whether or not to investigate variances.

18.19* (a) Specify and explain the factors to be considered in determining whether to investigate a variance which has been routinely reported as part of a standard costing system. (12 marks)

(b) Describe how accumulated production variances should be treated at the end of an accounting period. (8 marks)

(20 marks)
ACCA P2 Management Accounting
December 1980

18.20* (a) Outline the factors a management account-ant should consider when deciding whether or not to investigate variances revealed in standard costing and budgetary control systems.

(b) Indicate briefly what action the management accountant can take to improve the chances of achieving positive results from investigating variances.

(20 marks)
ICMA P3 Management Accounting
May 1983

18.21* Explain:
(a) the problems concerning control of operations that a manufacturing company can be expected to experience in using a standard costing system during periods of rapid inflation;

(b) three methods by which the company could try to overcome the problems to which you have referred in answer to (a) above, indicating the shortcomings of each method.

(20 marks)
ICMA Management Accounting
November 1981

19 Behavioural aspects of accounting control systems

Budgetary control and standard costing systems play an important role in influencing behaviour during the various stages of the management process. Aspects of planning and control systems which influence human behaviour include the setting of goals, informing individuals what they must do to contribute to the accomplishment of these goals, motivating desirable performance, evaluating performance and suggesting when corrective actions must be taken. The contribution of management accounting to this process is of a behavioural nature and for this reason management accountants must be concerned with behavioural science.

In the past behavioural scientists have complained that accountants have not given sufficient consideration to the impact of their control systems on human behaviour. Indeed, they have argued that this inattention to behavioural consequences may lead to the application of management accounting techniques which frequently do not achieve improved performance, and which may even hinder the accomplishment of the organizational objectives. Furthermore, behavioural scientists have argued that accountants are far more concerned with the technical excellence and sophistication of their systems than with their implications for human behaviour. A classic study on the human problems of producing budgets was published over thirty years ago by Argyris (1953). The following human relations problems were identified:

(1) Budget pressure tends to unite the employees against management, and tends to place the factory supervisor under tension. This tension may lead to inefficiency and aggression, and perhaps to a complete breakdown of the supervisor. Argyris suggested that constant pressure from top management for greater production may lead to long-term negative results. People living under these conditions tend to be suspicious of every new move management makes to increase production, particularly budgets. One method people use to reduce the effect of pressure is to join

groups. This may help to absorb and combat much of the management pressure, but may lead to the development of new cohesive anti-management groups.

(2) The finance staff may feel that success can only be achieved by finding fault with factory people. Feelings of failure among factory supervisors can lead to many human relations problems. Argyris states that the success of the finance man derives from finding errors, weaknesses and faults which exist in the plant. But when the finance staff discover such conditions they are in effect singling out a guilty party and placing him in a position of failure. This has a number of adverse effects such as making the foreman feel deficient, causing him to lose confidence and interest in his work, and to expect failure in the future. To make matters worse the entire incident will be made public by being placed in some budget report and distributed through many top channels.

(3) Supervisors frequently use budgets as a way of expressing their own patterns of leadership. If this leads to people getting hurt, the budget, which is in itself a neutral thing, will often get the blame.

Since Argyris's study a wealth of evidence has been presented in the behavioural literature on the dysfunctional effects of accounting control systems. For a detailed summary of this literature see Buckley and McKenna (1978). Our objective in the present chapter is to consider some of these research findings. In particular, we shall examine the following behavioural aspects of accounting control systems:

(1) the use of budgets as targets;
(2) the use of accounting control techniques for performance evaluation;
(3) participation in the budgeting and standard setting process;
(4) bias in the budget process;
(5) management use of budgets.

The use of budgets as targets

The research studies provide substantial evidence that the existence of a defined, quantitative goal or target is likely to motivate higher levels of performance than would be achieved if no such target was set. French, Kay and Meyer (1965) conducted performance appraisal inteviews at the General Electric Corporation and found that the conscious setting of objectives resulted in superior performance. The researchers concluded that:

> Appreciable improvements were realised only when specific objectives were established with time measures set and result measures agreed upon. Regardless of how much emphasis the manager gave to an improvement need in the appraisal discussion, if this did not get translated into a specific goal, very little performance improvement was achieved.

If we accept that the setting of targets can increase motivation, we must then consider at what level of difficulty the targets should be set. The research evidence indicates that when individuals are set very difficult targets they are unlikely to be accepted. They may perceive the target to be impossible to attain and give up, thus producing a performance which is worse than if a less demanding goal had been set. Alternatively, if very easy targets are set it is likely that the target will be achieved but individuals will not be motivated to achieve their full potential.

The research evidence indicates that the highest level of performance is likely to be achieved by setting the most difficult specific goals which will be accepted by managers and which will be internalized and accepted as their own personal goals (see Hofstede, 1968). The fact that a budget represents a specific quantitative goal gives it a strong motivational potential, but the targets which are set must be accepted if managers are to be motivated to achieve higher levels of performance. Unfortunately, it is not possible to specify the optimal degree of budget difficulty as cultural, organizational and personality factors all affect an individual manager's reaction to a budget standard.

Aspiration levels

One of the most important studies on targets within a budgeting context was conducted by Stedry (1960). The study was intended to be a simulation of the budgetary situation and it was found that the formulation of a specific target improved performance, although the precise effect was determined by how the target influenced the participant's own prsonal goal or 'level of aspiration'. In the study the participants were given different budget target levels, and various procedures were used to ascertain their levels of aspiration. Four different types of budgets were used:

(1) an implicit budget, where the participants were not told the goals they should attain;
(2) a low budget;
(3) a medium budget;
(4) a high budget.

Before the tasks were undertaken by the participants they were asked to state the level of performance which they hoped to attain (that is, their level of aspiration). This was ascertained in the following ways:

(a) no question asked;
(b) question asked before subjects received their budget;
(c) question asked after subjects received their budget.

The results of the experiment are presented in Exhibit 19.1. The figures in the table represent the performance score.

You will see that the implicit budget gave the best overall results but in nearly all cases the explicit formulation of a personal aspirational level improved performance. An interesting feature of the results occurs in situations (b4) where participants were given an explicit budget above the level of aspiration which they had just stated. In this situation performance declined dramatically. The best performance was achieved when the participants stated their aspiration level after receiving the most difficult budget (c4).

The results suggest that a significant interrelationship exists between budget levels, aspiration levels and performance. For example, the best performance was in the high budget group which set its aspiration levels *after* receiving the budget (c4). However, the high budget group which set its aspiration levels *before* receiving the budget showed the poorest performance of all the groups (b4). One possible interpretation of these findings is that when the subjects established their aspiration levels *after* they had received their

Exhibit 19.1 Results of Stedry's budget experiment

	Aspiration levels			
	(a) Not asked for	(b) Stated before receiving budget	(c) Stated after receiving budget	Average
Budget				
(1) Implicit	4.6	5.4	5.6	5.2
(2) Explicit — Low	4.1	4.7	4.6	4.5
(3) Explicit — Medium	4.4	5.5	5.5	5.1
(4) Explicit — High	5.1	4.0	5.9	5.0
Average	4.5	4.9	5.4	4.9

budgets, the aspiration levels tended to reflect the performance objectives contained in the budget. This suggests that the budget goals were internalized by the participants. Alternatively, when the aspiration levels were set *first*, the budget goals represented a conflict which the participants were unwilling to accept. Note that low budgets were usually associated with very low performance.

The effect of budget levels on performance

Hofstede's research (1968) provides a useful outline of the effect of budget levels on aspiration levels and peformance. He uses the diagram reproduced in Fig. 19.1 to illustrate the effects. This diagram illustrates an expense budget where the level of expense is shown on the vertical axis and the degree of tightness of the budget is shown on the horizontal axis, going from very loose on the left to very tight on the right. The budget, aspiration levels and actual results are denoted by the letters, b, a and r. In the absence of a budget (Stedry's implicit budget situation) the expense level is assumed to be N, and the diagram shows what will happen if we consider various alternative budget levels from very loose (case 1) to very tight (case 6). In case 1 the budget is too loose (that is, above level N). The budgetee (that is, the person who is responsible for the budget) will not find the budget very challenging and will set a higher aspiration level (lower than the budgeted cost) but still above N. The result r will be equal to the aspiration level.

In Case 2, the budget is equal to N, and the aspiration level and the result coincide with the

budget; the budget will not influence performance. In case 3, the budget is below N and the budgetee responds by altering his aspiration level to below N but not to the budgeted level of expenditure. Because the aspiration level is not too difficult the actual result will be equal to the aspiration level. In case 4, the budget is tighter still and this results in an improvement in the aspiration level. However, since the budget and aspiration level are so tight, there is a strong possibility that the actual result will not be as good as the aspiration level. Therefore r is shown to be above a, but the highest level of performance will be achieved at this point.

In case 5 the budget is very tight. The budgetee sees this as almost impossible and sets an aspiration level which is easier than case 4. In this situation the actual result will be equal to the

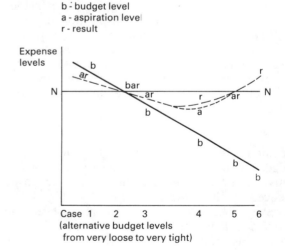

Fig. 19.1 The effect of budget levels on aspiration

aspiration level. In case 6 the budget is so tight that the budgetee will regard it as impossible. He will stop trying and will not attempt to set an aspiration level. The effect of this approach is that the actual result will be worse than that which would have been achieved had no budget been set.

A close examination of Fig. 19.1 indicates that budgets do not always lead to improved performance. In cases 1 and 6 the budgets do more harm than good, and improvements occur only in cases 3, 4 and 5. The problem is further complicated by the fact that failure to achieve the budget is likely to lead to a lowering of aspiration levels. Therefore, in case 4, where the actual result is worse than the aspiration level, the budgetee might respond by setting a less ambitious aspiration level next time. The effect may be that case 4 will shift to case 5. Becker and Green (1962) suggest the following budget changes when actual performance and aspiration levels are compared:

(1) If the performances meet or slightly exceed expectation, then levels of aspiration will rise and budgets can and should be revised; otherwise employees will perform at the budget level when they could be performing at higher than budget level.
(2) If performances are just slightly below budget expectations, budget changes are not necessary, but feedback is, so that budgetees will strive for the budget goals.
(3) If performances are well below the budget, it may be advisable to revise the budget downwards. If such a revision is not made, the employees' level of aspiration will fall. The danger here is that levels of aspiration and output will fall much more than is necessary. If the budget is revised downward only enough so that it is perceived as being attainable, then maximum output will be achieved again.

An interesting implication of the findings on budget targets is that the budget level which motivates the best perforamnce is unlikely to be achieved much of the time (case 4 in Fig. 19.1). However, a budget which is usually achieved will motivate a lower level of performance (cases 1 and 2 in Fig. 19.1). Therefore, if budgets are to be set at a level which will motivate individuals to achieve maximum performance, adverse budget variances are to be expected. In such a situation it is essential that adverse budget variances are not used by management as a punitive device, as this is likely to encourage budgetees to attempt to obtain looser budgets by either underperforming or deliberately negotiating easily attainable budgets. This may lead to fewer adverse variances, but also to poorer overall performance.

Conflicting roles of budgets

It appears from our previous discussion that tight budgets should be established to motivate maximum performance, although it may mean that the budget will not be achieved. However, it is most unlikely that tight budgets can be used for planning purposes. For example, tight budgets *which are unlikely to be achieved* are most unsuitable for cash budgeting and for harmonizing the company plans in the form of a master budget. Because of this conflict Stedry (1960) suggests that separate budgets should be used for planning and for motivation purposes. The counter argument to this is that budgetees may react unfavourably to a situation where they believe that one budget is used to evaluate their perforamnce and a second looser budget is used by top management. But it must nevertheless be recognized that if separate budgets are not used it is unlikely that one set of budgets can, at the same time, meet both the planning and the motivational requirements. For a discussion of the planning and motivational conflicts of budgeting see Barrett and Fraser (1977).

The use of accounting control techniques for performance evaluation

Managers are frequently encouraged to achieve organizational goals by having rewards linked to the level of performance which they achieve. The rewards are frequently based on a manager's budget record. Organizational rewards might include the payment of a bonus to sales managers when a budget sales quota is exceeded. Alternatively, promotion may be partly dependent upon a manager's budget record, or a subordinate may consider it important to meet his budget to gain approval from his superior. To encourage behaviour which is appropriate to the acheivement of organizational goals, performance measures must

A = Behaviour neccessary to achieve organizational goals
B = Behaviour actually engaged in by individual manager
C = Behaviour formally measured by control systems

Fig. 19.2 The measurement reward process with imperfect measures

be constructed which represent the desired levels and it must be ensured that successful achievement of these performance measures is rewarded. Otley (1977) uses Fig. 19.2 to illustrate this process.

Note that the aspects of behaviour on which subordinates are likely to concentrate to achieve their personal goals (circle B) do not necessarily correspond with those which are necessary for achieving the wider organizational goals (circle A). In an ideal system the measured behaviour (represented by circle C) should completely cover the area of desired behaviour (represented by circle A). Therefore, if a manager maximizes the performance measure, he will also maximize his contribution to the goals of the organization. In other words the performance measures encourage *goal congruence*. In practice, it is unlikely that perfect performance measures can be constructed which measure all desirable organizational behaviour, and so it is unlikely that all of circle C will cover circle A. Assuming that managers desire the rewards offered by circle C, their actual behaviour (represented by circle B) will be altered to include more of circle C and, to the extent that C coincides with A, more of circle A.

The introduction of a system of performance measures, backed up by an appropriate reward structure, should therefore motivate actions which will improve the performance measure. However, organizational performance will be improved only

to the extent that the performance measure is a good indicator of what is desirable to achieve the organization's goals. Unfortunately, performance measures are not perfect. Some measures may encourage goal congruence or organizationally desirable behaviour (that part of circle C which coincides with A) but other measures will not encourage goal congruence (that part of circle C which does not coincide with A). Consequently, there is a danger that subordinates will concentrate only on what is measured regardless of whether or not it is organizationally desirable.

The dysfunctional consequences of performance measures

Dysfunctional consequences of performance measures arise when performance measures motivate managers to engage in behaviour which is not organizationally desirable. In this situation performance measures are said to lead to a *lack of goal congruence*. The behavioural literature provides a wealth of evidence of performance measures, which have dysfunctional behavioural consequences. For example, Dearden (1962) outlines examples of situations where managers were reluctant to replace equipment and make new investments even when these actions were in the

company's economic interests, because of the heavy book losses which would be unfavourably reflected in current performance reports. Managers who are evaluated on return on investment may be reluctant to invest if the proposed investment will lower their overall average return. For example, a manager whose performance is evaluated on the basis of return on investment and who has a current return of 30% may refuse an investment which will yield 25% as this would lower his average rate of return; but do you remember that in Chapter 13 we saw that it is desirable for the organization as a whole to accept the investment if the cost of capital is less than the return on investment? We shall discuss ways of resolving this problem in Chapter 23.

In a study of the response of government administrators to evaluation on the basis of statistical perforamnce indices, Blau (1955) found that the administrators behaved so as to increase their performance on the basis of the indices even if this was not in the best interests of the organization. A further problem is that the main emphasis of accounting reports is on short-term performance measures while the evaluation of managerial performance should be concerned with more long-term considerations. Likert and Seashore (1968) have outlined a number of adverse long-term consequences which have resulted from short-term performance measures. They found that people strived to obtain the desired cost reductions to meet the required performance measure but that this process led to greater pressure and tension and this in turn caused increased absenteeism and a higher turnover of labour. The cost implications of such dysfunctional consequences were either not reflected in the accounting reports of the responsible manager or they were reflected with a delay.

A number of technical improvements have been suggested to avoid the dysfunctional consequences of accounting measures of performance. Ridgway (1975) suggests that it is preferable to use several measures of performance rather than a single accounting measure. However, he states that the individual is forced to rely on his judgement to determine whether increased effort on one criterion improves overall perforamnce, or whether there may be a reduction in performance on some other criterion which will outweigh the increase in the first. Ridgway suggests that this problem can be overcome by weighting each performance measure, thus making it an easy task to combine the measures of the various subgoals into a composite score of overall performance.

Managerial use of accounting information in performance evaluations

Some of the dysfunctional consequences which occur with accounting measures of performance may not be due to the inadequacy of the performance measures but may result from the way in which the accounting measures are used. The information provided by an accounting system must be interpreted and used with care when evaluations are made from it. Many accountants realize this and some act accordingly, but accounting information is also used by other managers who may not use the information in an appropriate manner. If accounting information is to lead to organizationally desirable behaviour it is essential that it is interpreted correctly.

A number of studies have been undertaken on the use of accounting information in performance evaluation. Hofstede (1968) found that stress on the actual results in performance evaluation led to more extensive use of budgetary information, and this made the budget more relevant. However, this stress was also associated with a feeling that the performance appraisal was unjust, and to overcome this problem the correct balance must be established when the budget performance is evaluated. Too much stress on the results leads to a feeling of injustice, but too little stress on the results leads to a budget being of little relevance and a poor motivation device. Hofstede suggests that a balance may be obtained by good upwards communication from one's subordinates, and by using the budget in a supportive and flexible manner; this will allow the subordinate adequate scope for creativity.

A more detailed study on how budgets are used in performance evaluation was undertaken by Hopwood (1976) based on observations in a manufacturing division of a large US company. Three distinct styles of using budget and actual cost information in performance evaluation were observed and were described as follows:

(1) *Budget-constrained style*. Despite the many problems in using accounting data as comprehensive measures of managerial performance, the evaluation is based primarily upon the cost centre

head's ability continually to meet the budget on a short-term basis. This criterion of performance is stressed at the expense of other valued and important criteria and a cost centre head will tend to receive an unfavourable evaluation if his actual costs exceed the budgeted costs, regardless of other considerations.

(2) *Profit-conscious style.* The performance of the cost centre head is evaluated on the basis of his ability to increase the general effectiveness of his unit's operations in relation to the long-term goals of the organization. One important aspect of this at the cost centre level is his concern with the minimization of long-run costs. The accounting data must be used with some care and in a rather flexible manner.

(3) *Non-accounting style.* Accounting data plays a relatively unimportant part in the supervisor's evaluation of the cost centre head's performance.

Hopwood observed that while the accounting data clearly indicated whether a person had been successful in meeting the budget, the data did not necessarily indicate whether a manager was behaving so as to minimize long-term costs. To assess this ability, the data has to be used with discretion, and where necessary supplemented with information from other sources. Hopwood identified such an approach as consistent with a *profit-conscious style* which emphasizes the wider use of accounting information rather than just a rigid analysis of the reported variances.

The evidence from Hopwood's study indicated that both the budget-constrained and the profit-conscious styles of evaluation led to higher degree of involvement with costs than the non-accounting style. Only the profit conscious style, however, succeeded in attaining this involvement without incurring either emotional costs for the managers in charge of the cost centres or defensive behaviour which was undesirable from the company's point of view. The budget-constrained style gave rise to a belief that the evaluation was unjust, and widespread worry and tension on the job. Hopwood provides evidence of manipulation and undesirable decision behaviour as methods of relieving tension when a budget-constrained style of evaluation is used. In addition, the manager's relationships with the budget-constrained supervisors were allowed to deteriorate and the rigid emphasis on the short-term budget results also highlighted the interdependent nature of their tasks, so that the immediate instrumental concerns permeated the pattern of social relationships among colleagues. For example, managers went out to improve their own reports regardless of the detrimental effects on the organization and then tried to pass on the responsibility by blaming their colleagues. In contrast, Hopwood found that the profit conscious style avoided these problems, while at the same time it ensured that there was an active involvement with the financial aspects of the operations.

A summary of the effect of the three styles of evaluation is given in Exhibit 19.2.

The educational role of the accountant

The evidence indicates that a major reason for some of the dysfunctional effects of accounting control systems appears to be due to the incorrect managerial use of the accounting information rather than to the defects of the system itself. Nevertheless, the accountant cannot complacently sit back and blame others. It is essential that

Exhibit 19.2 Hopwood's findings on the effect of different styles of evaluating budget performance

	Style of evaluation		
	Budget-constrained	Profit-conscious	Non-accounting
Involvement with costs	High	high	Low
Job-related tension	High	Medium	Medium
Manipulation of accounting information	Extensive	Little	Little
Relations with superior	Poor	Good	Good
Relations with colleagues	Poor	Good	Good

accountants are fully aware of the behavioural implications of their own systems. In addition, it is necessary to go one stage further and educate managers and employees in the appropriate use of accounting information as it is unreasonable to expect them to use the information in the appropriate manner when they have not had adequate education and training. They need to understand fully the assumptions and approximations which are incorporated into accounting control systems, and also the inadequacies of the information and the consequences of attaching too much importance to it. In particular, it is vital that accountants should educate managers so that they realize that the accounting control information is intended to assist them in managing their departments more efficiently and that it should not be used in a recriminatory manner to evaluate their subordinates; otherwise, the full benefits will not be obtained from accounting information. If managers see the accounting control system as being there to assist them, rather than to judge them, the dysfunctional behavioural effects should be minimized.

Participation in the budgeting and standard setting process

Participation has been advocated by many writers as a means of making tasks more challenging and giving individuals a greater sense of responsibility. However, the empirical studies have presented conflicting evidence on the usefulness of participation in the management process. For every study which indicates that participation leads to better attitudes and improved performance, an alternative frequently exists which suggests the opposite. For example, Coch and French (1958) studied the effect of participation in the introduction of change in an American pyjama factory. They found that a change in the production programme with participation led to an increase in performance without any of the employees leaving, instead of the performance drop and high labour turnover which was usual on such occasions. This study was repeated by French and Israel (1960) in Norway but here there was no difference in productivity between workers who did, and those who did not, participate in the design of the change programme. This finding was attributed by the authors to the different cultural values in Norway. To further complicate the issue

Bryan and Locke (1967) found a negative association between participation and performance, and Stedry (1960) produced similar results showing that a more authoritarian structure led to higher productivity. Rather than try to prove whether or not participation is associated with improved performance, we shall here consider the factors which may have been responsible for the conflicting outcomes of the empirical studies.

Factors influencing participation

Several studies have identified a number of important factors which influence the effectiveness of participation. For example, one explanation offered for the conflicting results between the Coch and French study and the replicated study by French and Israel is the different cultural setting in which the studies were undertaken. In a classic study Vroom (1960) demonstrated that personality variables can have an important influence on the effectiveness of participation. He identified that authoritarianism is an important factor which conditions the relationship between participation and performance. Vroom found that highly authoritarian people with a low need for independence were unaffected by participative approaches and that high participation was effective only for individuals who were low on the authoritarianism measure. Hopwood (1977) suggests that greater satisfaction might therefore be obtained when both superior and subordinate expectations are identical with authoritarian supervisors in charge of subordinates with authoritarian expectations, and more participative supervisors in charge of subordinates who are more appreciative of participative approaches.

Hopwood (1977) identifies the importance of the work situation in determining the appropriateness of participation. He states:

In highly programmed, environmentally and technologically constrained areas, where speed and detailed control are essential for efficiency, participative approaches may have much less to offer from the point of view of the more economic aspects of organizational effectiveness. . . . In contrast, in areas where flexibility, innovation and the capacity to deal with unanticipated problems are important, participation in decision-making may offer a more immediate and more narrowly economic payoff than more authoritarian styles.

The influence of participation in the budget process

Participation within the budget and standard setting process may be defined as the extent by which responsible managers are able to influence the figures which make up their budgets. It is important that participation is perceived by the budgetee if it is to increase motivation and performance. Unfortunately, a number of researchers have observed that some firms which profess to use participative budgeting are not really using it at all. Instead, they are involved in what has been termed 'pseudoparticipation'. For example, Argyris (1953) found that the managers which he interviewed claimed to encourage participation, but this proved to be acceptance under pressure of management budgets. True participation means that people can be spontaneous and free in their discussion and influence the budgets rather than being pressurized into budget acceptance. Hofstede (1968) presents the diagram shown in Fig. 19.3 to illustrate the relationship between participation in standard setting and performance.

The diagram indicates that participation is seen as affecting performance in three ways. First, allowing a manager to participate in budget setting improves his attitude towards the budget system and this should reduce some of the dysfunctional behavioural consequences. Second, a manager who has had an influence on setting a standard is likely to see the standard as more relevant than one that has been imposed upon him. This should

increase the likelihood of the budget being accepted by the subordinate and therefore becomes a target. Third, performance is also affected by the potential for improved communication and control which stems from the use of participative methods. This should also lead to better and more relevant standards. Note that both relevance and attitude affect motivation, and this in turn should lead to improved performance.

A number of studies on the role of participation within the budgeting context have been undertaken. Here, also, the findings appear to be in conflict. In a study of foremen of a large industrial company, Milani (1975) showed that participation was positively associated with attitudes towards both job and company, and Collins (1978) found a similar association with attitude towards the budgetary system. Kenis (1979), in a survey study of department managers and supervisors, found participation positively and significantly associated with performance. However, Milani (1975) found only a weak positive association between participation and performance.

Conditions for effective participation in the budgeting process

The differences in the research findings and the limitations identified of the effects of budgetary participation on performance led to a number of studies being made which attempt to specify the

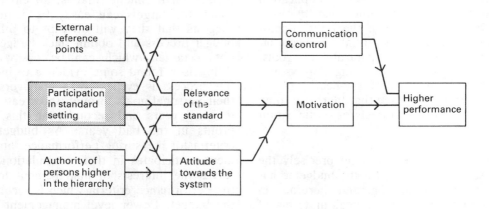

Fig. 19.3 Hofstede's model of the relationship between participation in standard setting and performance

conditions under which participation appears to be effective. For example, Bruns and Waterhouse (1975) found that managers in decentralized organizations perceived themselves as having more influence, as participating more in budget planning, and as appearing more satisfied with budget-related activities than their counterparts in centralized organizations where the relative lack of emphasis on participation in the budget process was viewed as being more appropriate. This suggests that organizational structure may be an important factor which influences the effectiveness of participation.

Brownell (1981) examined the role of the personality variable, locus of control (that is, the degree to which individuals feel they have control over their own destiny), and its effect on the participation–performance relationship. Budgetary participation was found to have a positive effect on those individuals who felt they had a large degree of control over their destiny, but it had a negative effect on those individuals who felt that their destinies were controlled by luck, chance or fate. Brownell suggests that when an organization has discretion over the level of budgetary participation which is afforded to its members, role descriptions should be modified (specifically in regard to participation) to suit the individual characteristics of the role occupants.

The evidence indicates that participative styles of management will not necessarily be more effective than other styles, and that participative methods should be used with care. It is therefore necessary to identify those situations where there is evidence that participative methods are effective, rather than to introduce universal application into organizations. Participation must be used selectively, but if it is used in the right circumstances it has an enormous potential for encouraging the commitment to organizational goals, improving attitudes towards the budgeting system, and increasing subsequent performance.

Note, however, at this stage that there are some limitations on the positive effects of participation in standard setting:

(1) Performance is measured by precisely the same standard with which the budgetee has been involved in setting, and therefore an improvement in performance, in terms of comparison with the budget, may result merely by lowering the standard. It will be useful if external reference points are available as this can provide an indication as to

whether the participation process leads to low performance because of loose standards.

(2) Personality traits of the participants may limit the benefits of participation. For example, the evidence appears to indicate that authoritarians and persons of weak independence needs may well perform better on standards set by a higher authority.

(3) Participation by itself is not adequate in ensuring commitment to standards. The manager must also believe that he can significantly influence the results and be given the necessary feedback about them.

Bias in the budget process

When managers are able to influence their budget standard there is a possibility that they will bias the information to gain the greatest personal benefit. For example, Williamson (1964) has emphasized that managers are motivated to achieve two sets of goals — the firm's goals and their own personal goals. He concludes that managers can best achieve their personal goals in a slack environment (that is, an environment in which the targets can easily be achieved), and suggests that they will attempt to influence the budget process and obtain slack budgets (that is, obtain targets which can be easily achieved). Williamson found some evidence to indicate that this process is cyclical with managers satisfying their personal goals through the creation of slack in good years and reconverting this slack into profits in the bad years. As budgets are the criteria for measuring performance, and management participates in their formulation, it clearly serves the interests of management to influence the performance criteria which is incorporated in the budget. Lower level management can therefore be expected to strive for a budget which it feels is attainable and, at the same time, meets the requirement of management for a desirable net profit. Schiff and Lewin (1970) also found evi-

dence that managers will create slack in their budgets through a process of understating revenues and overstating costs, and this process was more than sufficient in accommodating expected top management requests for higher profits at budget review sessions.

One of the most detailed studies of the motivations which give rise to budget bias was undertaken by Lowe and Shaw (1968) in a study of the sales budgeting process in a chain of retail shops in the United Kingdom. Bias was defined as the extent to which forecasters adjust their forecasts according to their own personal interests and independently of factors which might influence the actual result. Three main reasons for its occurrence were identified:

(1) The reward system of the company which involved salary increments, bonuses and promotions based on sales achievements. For example, a league table of sales areas according to the percentage achievement of budget was widely circulated and believed by shop managers to have a substantial influence on the distribution of rewards. Thus managers would be motivated to seek lower rather than higher budgets so that their actual performance would subsequently appear in a more favourable light.

(2) The influence of company practice which had involved an implicit norm that sales would continue to grow. Managers had a desire to please head office and thus tended to submit optimistic forecasts. This was found particularly at shops which were faced with declining sales.

(3) The insecurity of certain managers because their recent past performance had been poor also led to optimistic forecasts. Managers whose performance, according to company standards, had been unsatisfactory, may feel that by promising improvement they can continue to obtain the approval of their superiors and thus keep their jobs longer.

Lowe and Shaw also found that managers could choose whether to introduce upward or downward bias into their forecasts. A conservative forecast increases the likelihood of future success, but at the cost of disappointing senior management at the time of the forecast; an optimistic forecast may initially please senior management, but carries the risk of increased future disapproval. Lowe and Shaw concluded that biasing may be a common phenomenon in industry wherever the information provided by managers is later converted into standards against which their performance is judged.

Cyert and March (1961) also conducted an interesting experiment on the bias introduced when individuals formulate estimates. In their experiment subjects who were given a set of figures and informed that they represented sales, tended to be conservative in making their own forecasts, but when they were told that the figures represented costs they produced considerably higher forecasts. It may well be that the individuals perceive that less harm is done by conservative sales forecasts and over-generous forecasts of costs. Finally, Read (1962) found that managers tend consistently to distort the information which they pass to their superiors which means that senior managers are not informed about unfavourable items. Managers may hope that they will have been promoted or rewarded before the true situation has been revealed. This effect is moderated by the trust which exists between the manager and his superior, as a high degree of trust will minimize the distortion of information.

In view of the overwhelming empirical evidence which indicates that bias is prevalent in the budget process, what steps can be taken to reduce budget bias? It appears that if budgets are strictly adhered to and a budget-constrained style of evaluation is used, substantial bias in the budget process is likely to occur. However, if the budget standard is used in a more flexible profit-conscious style of evaluation, it is probable that budget biasing will be substantially reduced.

Schiff and Lewin (1970) also suggest a number of approaches for dealing with the problem of slack creation. First, the evaluation and review of the budget should be shifted from the termination of the process to points during the process. They state that to influence the budget process at its critical formative stages, top management (consisting of special task groups) must question the information base underlying the formulation of specific estimates. The objective of this process is to force the budgetee to rethink their previous unquestioned assumptions and long-standing standard operating procedures. Such constant probing of basic assumptions should lead to a minimal slack environment and approach conditions of optimal performance. Nevertheless, it appears that such suggestions are unlikely to lead to perfect solutions and some bias is likely to be a

fact of organizational life.

A more radical approach for removing slack from the budget process is to apply a zero-budgeting approach (see Chapter 15) rather than an incremental budgeting approach.

Management use of budgets

Budgeting is part of a management information system and should provide managers with useful scorekeeping and attention-directing information to enable them to manage their responsibility centres more effectively.[1] Thus it is essential that the accountant is concerned with ensuring that the budget information meets these requirements and is seen as being useful and meaningful to managers. Unfortunately, few research studies have been undertaken about the ways in which managers make use of budget information. A disturbing feature of one study (Dew and Gee, 1973) indicated that many managers considered that the budgetary information with which they were provided was not very useful, and it was frequently ignored. Dew and Gee found that managers appeared to pay little attention to their predetermined standards of performance, or to the examination of achievement as depicted in the performance reports.

To account for this situation Dew and Gee tested the following conditions which were considered necessary for an effective system of budgetary control.

(1) Management's authority and responsibility must be clear

Dew and Gee included 406 middle managers in their study who were thought by their senior managers to know their jobs, their limits of authority, and the nature of their responsibility. However, 186 of these managers gave definitions of their authority which were substantially at variance with the definitions provided by the senior managers. Dew and Gee conclude that if senior and middle managers do not agree closely as to who is responsible for different middle management tasks, they can hardly be expected to be in agreement about the nature of the information required for these tasks to be undertaken effectively. They stress that it is also essential for those who produce and prepare the control information for managers to be equally clear on the limits of authority and the nature of the responsibility of the various managers.

(2) The managers must accept their budgets and consider them to be attainable

Dew and Gee found that the following situations existed in the budget systems which were operated by the companies included in their research:

(1) *Participation*: the middle managers prepared their own budgets and submitted them for approval by higher management.
(2) *Consultation*: the budgets were draw up by higher management and agreed with the middle manager after consultation.
(3) *Non-consultation*: either no consultation of any kind or only a nominal consultation, so that in effect, the budgets remained as they had been originally.

The findings indicated that managers who participated also used their budgetary control information to the greatest extent. Next in order came the managers who were consulted. The managers who used their information the least were those who did not enter the budget process at all — where central mandatory budgets had been issued to them. Dew and Gee's findings indicate that participation improves the attitude of middle management towards control information and also improves their willingness to be involved in the budgetary control function.

(3) Budgetary control information must be understood by the managers

The study also indicated that managers did not like the form in which their information was presented; it was not in the language in which they personally thought and worked, for example, in terms of weights, or yards, or volumes, or hours. They did not appreciate information presented in the language of the accountant in terms of costs and standards of output. Dew and Gee suggest that instead of trying to persuade the managers to think in the same terms as the accountants, perhaps accountants should be more ready to lend their experience to interpreting the significance of what they have to tell, by translating it into a variety of 'languages' which would be familiar to many different managers of different disciplines.

For example, greater use might be made of physical measures of performance such as the number of units *actually* produced, compared with the number of units which *should have been produced*.

(4) Training in budgetary control must be effective

The study indicated that what managers wanted was not so much formal training as an interpretation service aimed at showing the implications of the cost control information, and the significance of alternative consequential courses of action. The vast majority of the managers blamed infrequent personal contact for failures to appreciate cost information, and it was argued that accountants would greatly increase their effectiveness if they became more involved with operations at shop floor level.

(5) Managers must understand the aim of budgetary information

Dew and Gee's investigation suggested that many senior managers considered that cost information was required to judge them rather than to help them. This led many of these managers to have an enormous in-built emotional resistance to the whole idea of the budgetary system, which nevertheless they were expected to use for control.

Conclusion

The research evidence which we have considered indicates that some of the behavioural problems which arise from budgeting and standard costing systems may result not from the incorrect design of the systems, but rather from the way in which the accounting information is used. We have seen that accountants have an important role to play in educating managers in the benefits which are available from the correct use of the accounting information. In particular, we have stressed the supportive role of the accounting system and noted the importance of educating managers not to use the system as additional ammunition for applying a system of punitive control. Managers should be encouraged to adopt a profit-conscious style of evaluation.

Budget and standard costing systems should also be used in such a way that they convey freedom to fail. Individuals may need assurance that they will not be spotlighted in a position of failure if they do not meet their budgets. The evidence suggests that performance is maximized when tight budgets are introduced and adverse variances are a fact of organizational life. You will remember from the previous chapter that budgets or standards may be based on estimated *average* performance and that some deviation from the average is inevitable even when the costs are under control. Statistical control theory could therefore be usefully applied to accounting control sytems by presenting the standard or budget as a *range* of acceptable costs rather than as a single figure. This would mean that any results which were in excess of average costs but which fell within the acceptable range would not lead to the manager being spotlighted in a position of failure. This may reduce the psychological effects of failure and avoid some of the dysfunctional effects which we have outlined in this chapter. In addition, repeated reporting of unfavourable results at the upper end of the range could still be investigated.

Accounting reports should also be broadened to incorporate other variables besides cost. Empirical evidence on single measures of performance indicates tha employees place emphasis on this single factor and neglect other factors which are important in the overall results. For example, Likert and Seashore (1968) assert that it is always possible to obtain short-term improvements in cost control by hierarchical pressure to cut costs and raise productivity, but this will eventually have negative effects on managerial performance in the form of adverse motivational changes, increased labour turnover and reduced product quality. Unfortunately, performance reports which are based on costs alone do not give sufficient indication of the future results which can be expected from present actions. One possible improvement is for performance reports to be supplemented by non-financial measures such as production quantity and quality, employees' dependability and loyalty, training, labour turnover, plant efficiency, and so on. In addition, performance reports could be accompanied by written explanations from the budgetees in which they explain why their performance is above or below some pre-set level and how it has been obtained.

Management should identify *critical success*

factors which are critical in the sense that failure in any one of these factors might prevent the advancement of the company. For example, Lewis (1980) in a case study of management planning and control in the General Electric Company outlines a management reporting system which provides management with control reports on the following 'critical success factors':

(1) Profitability
(2) Market position (that is, share of the market)
(3) Productivity (efficiency with which inputs to the production process are converted into outputs)
(4) Product leadership (how does the company's products compare with competition?)
(5) Personnel development (ability of managers to fill present and future posts)
(6) Employee attitudes
(7) Public responsibility
(8) Balance between short-range and long-range goals.

In recent years a contingency approach to management accounting has dominated the behavioural literature. Otley (1980), states:

> The contingency approach to management accounting is based on the premise that there is no universally appropriate accounting system which can be applied to all organisations in all circumstances. Rather it is suggested that the particular features of an appropriate accounting system will depend upon the specific circumstances in which an organisation finds itself.

In other words, a contingency theory of budgeting will suggest a different type and mode of operation for a budget system for different sets of circumstances, rather than a universal theory which applies to all circumstances (Otley, 1977). For example, a budget system is influenced by the technology and environment in which the organ-

ization operates, the objectives of the organization, and the organization structure within which the budget system is implemented. The technological and environmental factors may result in stable, rapidly changing, certain or uncertain technologies and environments, all of which may lead to differences in the budget systems. Alternatively, the objectives of the organization may be profit maximizing or satisficing, which may also result in differences in the design and use of a budget system. Also, how an organization structures itself and the degree to which it centralizes or decentralizes the decision-making process will influence the accounting control system. A contingency approach to the design of budgetary control systems may therefore provide a framework for improving the design of budgetary control systems by identifying the circumstances which are most suited to the operation of different types of budget systems. For example, we have already noted that participation in the budget process is effective in some circumstances but ineffective in other circumstances. For a discussion of contingency theory see Dermer (1977). Research in the future may suggest which type and mode of operation for a budget system is most appropriate for different sets of circumstances. It may then be possible to prescribe a more appropriate behavioural approach to budgeting and standard cost systems and to avoid some of the dysfunctional behavioural consequences which have been identified in this chapter. Nevertheless, you should remember that individual behaviour is too diverse and changeable for even the most soundly designed accounting control systems to ensure that the dysfunctional behavioural effects are completely eliminated. It is therefore essential that the designers and users of accounting control systems are aware of the limitations of the accounting data and that they use the results with care to ensure that the dysfunctional behavioural effects are minimized.

Summary

Budgetary control and standard costing control systems are introduced with the intention of influencing human behaviour and motivating managers to achieve organizational goals. However, it is argued that accountants do not give sufficient attention to human behaviour when designing and operating their control systems.

It appears that there is a significant relationship between budget levels, aspiration levels and performance, and that the highest performance is likely to be achieved by setting the most difficult

budgets which will be accepted by managers. If difficult budgets are set, adverse variances are likely to occur and it is important that the performance reports are not used as a punitive control device by management. A conflict arises if tight budgets are used as a basis for motivating improved performance because such budgets may not be achieved. Tight budgets are therefore unsatisfactory for planning purposes.

Some of the dysfunctional consequences which occur with accounting measures of performance may not be due to the inadequacy of the performance measures but may result from the way in which the accounting measures are used. We have identified three distinct styles of using budget and actual cost information in performance evaluation: a budget-constrained, a profit-conscious, and a non-accounting style of evaluation. Only the profit-conscious style of evaluation appears to encourage managers to use budgets to control costs without any dysfunctional behavioural effects.

The conclusions derived from the empirical studies on the effect of participation on subsequent performance are in conflict. We have seen that the factors which appear to influence whether or not participation will improve performance include the personality of the supervisor and the budgetee, the organizational structure, and the technology and environment in which the organization operates. Where managers are able to influence their budget, the empirical evidence indicates that budgetees create slack, and bias the information which is presented to management. However, if a profit-conscious style of evaluation is used it is probable that budget biasing will be substantially reduced. Finally, we have examined a study which was based on the management use of budgets. This indicates that many managers find budgetary information not very useful and a number of possible reasons for this have been considered.

References and further reading

Argyris, C. Human problems with budgets. *Harvard Business Review* January–February 1953, 97-110; also in Solomons, D. *Studies in Cost Analysis*. Sweet & Maxwell, 1968.

Barrett, M.E. and Fraser, L.B. Conflicting roles in budgeting operations. *Harvard Business Review* July–August 1977, 137-59.

Becker, S.W. and Green, D. Budgeting and employee behaviour. *Journal of Business* 35(4), October 1962, 392-402.

Belkaoui, A. Judgement related issues in performance evaluation. *Journal of Business Finance and Accounting* 9(4), Winter 1982, 489-500.

Blau, P.M. *The Dynamics of Bureaucracy*. University of Chicago Press, 1955.

Brownell, P. Participation in budgeting, locus of control and organisational effectiveness. *The Accounting Review* October 1981, 944-58.

Bruns, W.J. and Waterhouse, J.H. Budegtary control and organisation structure. *Journal of Accounting Research* Autumn 1975, 177-203.

Bryan, J.F. and Lock, E.A. Goal setting as a means of increasing motivation. *Journal of Applied Psychology* June 1967, 264-7.

Buckley, A. and McKenna, E. Budgetary control and business behaviour. In Parker, R.H. (ed.), *Readings in Accounting and Business Research, 1970-77. Accounting and Business Research*, 1978.

Burchell, S., Clubb, C., Hopwood, A., Hughes, J. and Nahapiet, J. The role of accounting in organizations and society. *Accounting Organisations and Society* 5(1), 1980, 5-28.

Caplan, E.H. *Management accounting and behavioural science*. Addison-Wesley, 1971.

Chenhall, R.H., Harrison, C.L. and Watson, D.J.H. (Eds). *The Organizational Context of Management Accounting*. Pitman, 1981.

Cherrington, D.J. and J.O. Appropriate reinforcement contingencies in the budget process. *Journal of Accounting Research* Selected Studies, 1973 (Supplement to Vol. 11), 225-66.

Coch, L. and French J.R.P. Overcoming resistance to change. *Human Relations* 1, 1948, 512-32.

Collins, F. The interaction of budget characteristics and personality variables with budget response attitudes. *The Accounting Review*, April 1978, 324-35.

Cooper, D. A social and organizational view of management accounting. In Bromwich, M. and Hopwood, A.G. (Eds), *Essays in British Accounting Research*, Pitman, 1981.

Cyert, R.M., March, J.G. and Starbuck, W.H. Two experiments on bias and conflict in organisational estimation. *Management Science* 1961, 254-64.

Dearden, J. Limits on decentralised profit responsibility. *Harvard Business Review* July–August 1962, 81-9.

Dermer, J. *Management Planning and control Systems*. R.D. Irwin, 1977.

Dew, R.B. and Gee, K.P. *Management Control and Information*. Macmillan, 1973.

Flamholtz, E.G. Accounting, budgeting and control

systems. *Accounting, Organizations and Society* **8**(2/3), 153-70.

French, J.R.P. and Israel, J. D. An experiment on participation in a Norwegian factory. *Human Relations* **13**, 1960, 3.

French, J.R.P., Kay, E. and Meyer, H. Split roles in performance appraisal. *Harvard Business Review* January–February 1965, 123-9.

Gordon, L.A. and Miller, D. A contingency framework for the design of accounting information systems. *Accounting, Organisations and Society* **1**(1), June 1976, 59-69.

Hayes, D. The contingency theory of management accounting. *Accounting Review* **LIII**(1), January 1977, 22-39.

Hofstede, G.H. *The Game of Budget Control*. Tavistock, 1968.

Hopwood, A.G. *Accountancy and Human Behaviour*. Prentice-Hall, 1976.

Hopwood, A.G. Towards an organisational perspective for the study of accounting and information systems. *Accounting, Organisations and Society* **3**(1), 1978, 3-14.

Kenis, I. The effects of budgetary goal characteristics on managerial attitudes and performance. *The Accounting Review* October 1979, 707-21.

Livingstone, J.L. (ed.). *Managerial Accounting: The Behavioural Foundations*. Grid Inc., 1975.

Lowe, E.A. and Shaw, R.W. An analysis of managerial biasing: Evidence from a company's budgeting process. *Journal of Management Studies* October 1968, 304-15.

Lewis, R.W. Measuring, reporting and appraising results in operations with reference to goals, plans and budgets, A case study of management planning and control at General Electric Company. New York Controller Foundation Inc., 1955; also in Anthony, R.N. and Dearden, J. *Management Control Systems*. Irwin, 1980.

Likert, R. and Seashore, S.E. Making cost control work. *Harvard Business Review* November–December 1963, 96-108; also in Solomons, D. (Ed.), *Studies in Cost Analysis*. Sweet & Maxwell, 1968.

Machin, J.L.J. A contingent methodology of management control. *Journal of Management Studies* **16**(1), 1-30.

Madsen, V. and Polesie, T. *Human Factors in Budgeting: Judgement and Evaluation*. Pitman, 1981.

Magee, R.P. Equilibria in budget participation. *Journal of Accounting Research* **18**(2), Autumn 1980, 551-73.

McRae, T.W. The behavioural critique of accounting. *Accounting and Business Research* Spring 1971, 83-93.

Merchant, K.A. The design of the corporate budgeting system: Influences on managerial behaviour and performance. *Accounting Review* **LVI**(4), October 1981, 813-29.

Milani, K. The relationship of participation in budget setting to industrial supervisor performance and attitudes: A field study. *The Accounting Review* April 1975, 274-84.

Otley, D.T. Behavioural aspects of budgeting. *Accountants Digest* No. 49, 1977.

Otley, D.T. Budget use and managerial performance. *Journal of Accounting Research* **16**(1), Spring 1978, 122-49.

Otley, D.T. The contingency theory of management accounting: Achievement and prognosis. *Accounting, Organisations and Society* **5**(4), 1980, 413-28.

Otley, D.T. Budgets and managerial motivation. *Journal of General Management*, Autumn 1982, 26-43.

Otley, D.T. and Berry, A.J. Control, organisation and accounting. *Accounting, Organisations and Society* **5**(2), 1980, 231-46.

Parker, L.D. Communication in the budget process. *Accounting and Business Research* Summer 1978, 191-208.

Parker, L.D. Participation in budget planning: The prospects surveyed. *Accounting and Business Research* **9**(34), Spring 1979, 123-38.

Parker, L.D. Goal congruence: A misguided concept. *Abacus* **12**(1), 3-14.

Read, W.H. Upward communication in industrial hierarchies. *Human Relations* **15**, 1962, 3-16.

Ridgway, V.G. Dysfunctional consequences of performance measurement. In Rappaport, A. (Ed.), *Information for Decision Making*. Prentice-Hall, 1975.

Ronen, J. and Livingstone, J.L. Motivation and budgets. *The Accounting Review* October 1975, 671-86.

Ronen, J. and Livingstone, J.L. An Expectancy Theory Approach to the Motivational Impacts of Budgets *Accountancy Review* **L**(4), October 1975, 671-85.

Schiff, M. and Lewin, A.Y. The impact of people on budgets. *The Accounting Review* April 1970, 259-68.

Stedry, A.C. *Budget Control and Cost Behaviour*. Prentice-Hall, 1960.

Vroom, V.H. *Some Personality Determinants of the Effects of Participation*. Prentice Hall, 1960.

Williamson, O.E. *The Economics of Discretionary Behaviour*. Prentice-Hall, 1964.

Problems

*Indicates that a suggested solution is to be found in the *Students' Manual*.

19.1* What are the behavioural aspects which should be borne in mind by those who are designing and operating standard costing and budgetary control systems?

(20 marks)
ICMA Cost Accounting 2
May 1979

19.2* One purpose of management accounting is to influence managers' behaviour so that their resulting actions will yield a maximum benefit to the employing organisation.

In the context of this objective, you are required to discuss:
(a) how budgets can cause behavioural conflict;
(b) how this behavioural conflict may be overcome;
(c) the importance of the feedback of information; and
(d) the purpose of goal congruence.

(20 marks)
ICMA P3 Management Accounting
November 1982

19.3* In his study of *The Impact of Budgets on People*, published in 1952, C. Argyris reported *inter alia* the following comment by a financial controller on the practice of participation in the setting of budgets in his company:

'We bring in the supervisors of budget areas, we tell them that we want their frank opinion, but most of them just sit there and nod their heads. We know they're not coming out with exactly how they feel. I guess budgets scare them.'

You are required to suggest reasons why managers may be reluctant to participate fully in setting budgets, and to suggest also unwanted side effects which may arise from the imposition of budgets by senior management. (13 marks)
ICAEW Management Accounting
July 1980

19.4* Several assumptions are commonly made by accountants when preparing or interpreting budgetary information.

You are required to explain why each of the following five assumptions might be made by accountants when designing a system of budgeting, and to set out in each case also any arguments which, in your view, raise legitimate doubts about their validity:
(a) budgeted performance should be reasonably attainable but not too loose (5 marks),
(b) participation by managers in the budget-setting process leads to better performance (5 marks),
(c) management by exception is the most effective system of routine reporting (5 marks),
(d) a manager's budget reports should exclude all matters which are not completely under his control (5 marks), and
(e) budget statements should include only matters which can be easily and accurately measured in monetary terms (5 marks).

(25 marks)
ICAEW Management Accounting
December 1981

19.5* The level of efficiency assumed in the setting of standards has important motivational implications — Discuss. (8 marks)
ACCA Level 2 Management Accounting
June 1983

19.6* In discussing the standard setting process for use within budgetary control and/or standard costing systems, the following has been written: 'The level of standards appears to play a role in achievement motivation . . .'

Required:
(a) Briefly distinguish between the motivational and managerial reporting objectives of both budgetary control and standard costing. Describe the extent to which these two objectives place conflicting demands on the standard of performance utilized in such systems. (6 marks)
(b) Describe three levels of efficiency which may be incorporated in the standards used in budgetary control and/or standard costing systems. Outline the main advantages and disadvantages of each of the three levels described. (6 marks)
(c) Discuss the advantages and disadvantages of involving employees in the standard setting process. (8 marks)

(Total 20 marks)
ACCA P2 Management Accounting
December 1981

19.7* You are required to:
(i) discuss the factors that are likely to cause managers to submit budget estimates of sales and costs that do not represent their best estimates or expectations of what will actually occur (8 marks), and
(ii) suggest, as a budget accountant, what procedures you would advise in order to minimize the likelihood of such biassed estimates arising (4 marks).
ICAEW Management Accounting
July 1983

19.8 'Budgeting is too often looked upon from a purely mechanistic viewpoint. The human factors in budgeting are more important than the accounting techniques. The success of a budgetary system depends upon its acceptance by the company members who are affected by the budgets.'

Discuss the validity of the above statement from the viewpoint of both the planning and the control aspects of budgeting. In the course of your discussion present at least one practical illustration to support your conclusions.

(20 marks)
ACCA P2 Management Accounting
December 1980

19.9 'The major reason for introducing budegtary control and standard costing systems is to influence human behaviour and to motivate the managers to achieve the goals of the organization. However, the accounting literature provides many illustrations of accounting control systems that fail to give sufficient attention to influencing human behaviour towards the achievement of organization goals.'

You are required:
(a) to identify and discuss four situations where accounting control systems might not motivate desirable behaviour;
(b) to discuss briefly the improvements you would suggest in order to ensure that some of the dysfunctional behavioural consequences of accounting control systems are avoided.

19.10 'The final impact which any accounting system has on managerial and employee behaviour is dependent not only upon its design and technical characteristics but also in the precise manner in which the resulting information is used' (A. Hopwood, *Accounting and Human Behaviour*).

Discuss this statement in relation to budgeting and standard costing.

19.11 'Motivation is the over-riding consideration that should influence management in formulating and using performance measures, and in designing management control systems.'

Discuss this statement in relation to the design and implementation of budgetary control systems.

The application of quantitative methods to management accounting

In this Part we examine the application of quantitative methods to various aspects of management accounting. In Chapters 12 and 18 we considered how probability theory and normal distribution theory were applied to decision-making and the investigation of variances; Chapters 20–22 now look at the further applications of quantitative methods to management accounting. These chapters are included in Part V because they relate to topics which were covered in Parts III and IV and you should therefore read Parts III and IV before you proceed to read Chapters 20–22.

Chapter 20 — Mathematical Approaches to Cost Estimation — examines the contribution of mathematical and statistical techniques in determining cost behaviour patterns for cost–volume–profit analysis and the planning and control of costs and revenues. Chapter 21 — Quantitative Models for the Planning and Control of Stocks — examines the application of quantitative models to determine the optimum investment in stocks. We also consider in this chapter how the performance evaluation system conflicts with the optimum quantitative decision models. Chapter 22 — The Application of Linear Programming to Management Accounting — looks at the application of linear programming to decision-making, planning and control activities.

20 Mathematical approaches to cost estimation

Determining how costs will change with output or other measurable factors of activity is of vital importance for decision-making, planning and control. The preparation of budgets, the production of performance reports, the calculation of standard costs and the provision of relevant costs for pricing and other decisions all depend on reliable estimtes of costs at different output levels. Unfortunately, costs are not easy to predict as they behave differently under different circumstances. For example, costs may behave differently when they are tightly controlled compared with a situation where control is relaxed or removed. Direct labour which is generally presumed to be variable may be non-variable (that is, a fixed cost) in companies which employ a fixed number of people and maintain this number even when output declines. Depreciation is often quoted as a non-variable cost but it may well be variable if asset value declines in direct proportion to usage. We cannot therefore generalize by categorizing direct labour as a variable cost and depreciation as a non-variable cost.

The importance of accurately estimating costs and the complexity of cost behaviour means that accountants must use increasingly sophisticated techniques. The introduction of the microcomputer, with its supporting software, has made it possible for more sophisticated techniques to be used for estimating costs, even by small businesses. These developments have led to an increasing awareness of the important potential which mathematical and statistical techniques can play in estimating costs, and it is the aim of this chapter to provide an understanding of these techniques. Some non-mathematical techniques will also be explained so that we can assess the additional benefits which can be obtained from using the more sophisticted techniques. We shall then examine the effect of experience on cost, which is normally referred to as the learning curve. The emphasis in this chapter will be on manufacturing costs and we shall consider various techniques for estimating how these costs change with activity; similar techniques, however, can be applied to non-manufacturing costs which change with activity.

Non-mathematical techniques

Engineering methods

These methods of analysing cost behaviour are based on the use of engineering analyses of technological relationships; for example, methods study, work sampling and time and motion studies. The procedure involved for such a study is to make an analysis of the underlying physical quantities which are required for an activity and then to convert the final results into cost estimates. Engineers, who are familiar with the technical requirements, estimate the quantities of materials and the labour and machine hours which will be required for various operations, and prices and rates are applied to the physical measures to obtain the cost estimates. The method is usually satisfactory for estimating costs which are associated with direct materials, labour and

machine time, because these items can be directly observed and measured.

The engineering method is not restricted to manufacturing activities; time and motion studies can also be applied to well-structured administrative and selling activities such as typing, invoicing and purchasing. It is not generally appropriate, however, for estimating costs which are difficult to associate directly with individual units of output, such as costs of maintenance, cleaning up and supervision, as these items cannot easily be directly observed and measured.

One disadvantage of the engineering method is that methods study, work sampling and time and motion study techniques can be expensive to apply in practice. The use of these methods is most appropriate when direct costs form a large part of the total costs and when input–output relationships are fairly stable over time. Engineering methods may also be applied in situations where there is no historical data to analyse past cost relationships.

Inspection of the accounts

This method requires that the departmental manager and the accountant inspect each item of expenditure within the accounts for some output level, and then classify each item of expense as wholly fixed, wholly variable or as a semi-variable cost. A single average *unit* cost figure is selected for the items which are categorized as variable, whereas a single *total* cost for the period is used for the items which are categorized as fixed. For semi-variable items the departmental manager and the accountant agree on a cost formula which appears to best describe the cost behaviour. The process is illustrated in Example 20.1.

EXAMPLE 20.1

The following cost information has been obtained from the accounts for an output level of 10,000 units.

	£
Direct materials	100,000
Direct labour	140,000
Indirect labour	30,000
Depreciation	15,000
Repairs and maintenance	10,000
	295,000

The departmental manager and the accountant will examine each item of expense and analyse the expenses into their variable and non-variable elements. The analysis might be as follows:

	Unit variable cost £	Total non-variable cost £
Direct materials	10.00	
Direct labour	14.00	
Indirect labour		30,000
Depreciation		15,000
Repairs and maintenance	0.50	5,000
	24.50	50,000

Note that repairs and maintenance have been classified as a semi-variable cost which consists of a variable element of £0.50 per unit of output plus £5,000 non-variable cost. A check on the calculation indicates that the estimate of a unit variable cost of £24.50 will give a *total* variable cost of £245,000 at an output level of 10,000 units. The non-variable costs of £50,000 are added to this to produce an estimated *total* cost of £295,000. These cost estimates are then used for estimating costs at other output levels for each of the individual items of expense.

You will see from this example that the analysis of costs into their variable and non-variable elements is very subjective. Also, the latest cost details which are available from the accounts will normally be used, and this may not be typical of either past or future cost behaviour. Whenever possible, cost estimates should be based on a series of observations. Cost estimates which are based on this method involve individual and often arbitrary judgements and estimates may therefore lack the precision which is necessary when they are to be used in making decisions which involve large sums of money and which are sensitive to measurement errors. This method is also inappropriate for calculating flexible budget allowances to be included in performance reports.

High–low method

The high–low method consists of selecting the periods of highest and lowest activity levels and comparing the changes in costs which result from the two levels.

EXAMPLE 20.2

	Volume of production (units)	Indirect costs (£)
Lowest activity	5,000	22.000
Highest activity	10,000	32,000

The variable cost per unit is calculated as follows:

$$\frac{\text{Difference in cost}}{\text{Difference in activity}} = \frac{£10{,}000}{5{,}000}$$

= £2 variable cost per unit of output

The non-variable cost can be estimated at any level of activity (assuming a constant unit variable cost) by subtracting the variable cost portion from the total cost. At an activity level of 5,000 units the total cost is £22,000 and the total variable cost is £10,000 (5,000 units at £2 per unit). The balance of £12,000 is therefore assumed to represent the non-variable cost. The method is illustrated in Fig. 20.1.

Points X and Y represent the lowest and highest output levels, and TC1 and TC2 represent the total cost for each of these levels. The other crosses represent past cost observations for other output levels. The straight line joining the observations for the lowest and highest activity levels represents the costs which would be estimated for each activity level when the high–low method is used.

You will see from this illustration that the method ignores all cost observations other than the observations for the lowest and highest activity levels. Unfortunately, cost observations at the extreme ranges of activity levels are not always typical of normal operating conditions and therefore may reflect abnormal rather than normal cost relationships. Figure 20.1 indicates how the method can give inaccurate cost estimates when they are obtained by observing only the highest and lowest output levels. It would obviously be more appropriate to incorporate all of the available observations into the cost estimate, rather than to use only two extreme observations. For this reason the high–low method is not recommended.

Mathematical techniques

Before we consider the various mathematical methods which are appropriate for estimating costs, we need to look at some of the terms which will be used. A regression equation identifies an estimated relationship between a dependent variable (cost) and one or more independent variables (activity, air temperature and so on) based on past observations. When the equation includes only one independent variable it is referred to as simple regression and it is possible in this situation to plot the regression equation on a graph as a regression line. When the equation includes two or more independent variables it is referred to as multiple regression. If there is only one independent variable and the relationship is linear, the regression line can be described by the equation for a straight line:

$$Y = a + bx$$

Assuming that we wish to express the relationship between the dependent variable (cost) and the independent variable (activity), then:

Y = total cost for the period at an activity level of x
a = total non-variable cost for the period
b = average variable cost per unit of activity
x = activity level for the unit

If non-variable costs for a particular period are £5,000, the average unit variable cost is £1, and activity is measured in direct labour hours, then:

Total cost = £5,000 + [£1 × direct labour hours (x)]

or (Y) = (a) + (bx)

Graphical or scattergraph method

You will recall that when we considered the high–low method we concluded that there was a need to consider all of the available observations when drawing a line to establish a cost estimate. The graphical method recognizes this and uses all the available observations in arriving at the cost

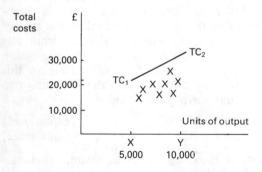

Fig. 20.1 High–low method

estimate; the total costs are plotted on a graph for each activity level. The total cost is represented on the vertical axis and the activity levels are recorded on the horizontal axis. A straight line is fitted to this scatter of points by visual approximation. Figure 20.2 illustrates the procedure using the data contained in Example 20.3.

EXAMPLE 20.3

The total maintenance costs and the direct labour hours for the past ten five-weekly accounting periods were as follows:

Period	Hours (x)	Maintenance cost (Y)
1	400	960
2	240	880
3	80	480
4	400	1,200
5	320	800
6	240	640
7	160	560
8	480	1,200
9	320	880
10	160	400

Fig. 20.2 Graph of maintenance costs at different activity levels

The maintenance costs are plotted on a graph (Fig. 20.2) and a straight line is drawn through the middle of the data points as closely as possible so that the distances of observations above the line are equal to the distances of observations below the line.

The point where the straight line in Fig. 20.2 cuts the vertical axis (that is, £240) represents the non-variable costs or item a in the regression formula y = a + bx. The unit variable cost or b in the regression formula is found by observing the differences between two points on the line and completing the following calculations:

$$\frac{\text{Difference in cost}}{\text{Difference in activity}} = \frac{£720 - £560}{240 \text{ hours} - 160 \text{ hours}}$$
$$= £2 \text{ per hour}$$

This calculation is based on a comparison of the changes in costs on the straight line between activity levels of 160 and 240 hours. This gives a regression formula of Y = 240 + 2x.

If x is assigned a value of 100 hours then

$$Y = 240 + 2(100) = £440$$

The graphical method is simple to use and it provides a useful visual indication of any lack of correlation or erratic behaviour of costs. However, the method suffers from the disadvantage that the determination of exactly where the straight line should fall is subjective, and different people will draw different lines with different slopes giving different cost estimates. To overcome this difficulty it is preferable to determine the line of best fit mathematically.

The least squares method

This method determines mathematically the regression line of best fit. It is based on the principle that the sum of the squares of the vertical deviations from the line which is established by using the method is less than the sum of the squares of the vertical deviations from any other line which might be drawn. The regression equation for a straight line which meets this requirement can be found from the following two equations and solving for a and b:

$$\Sigma Y = Na + b\Sigma x \qquad \text{(Equation 1)}$$
$$\Sigma xY = \Sigma x\, a + b\Sigma x^2 \qquad \text{(Equation 2)}$$

To illustrate the method let us assume that past observations of maintenance costs and hours of activity have been recorded and computations

Exhibit 20.1 Past observations of maintenance costs

Hours (x)	Maintenance cost (Y) £	x^2	xY
90	1,500	8,100	135,000
150	1,950	22,500	292,500
60	900	3,600	54,000
30	900	900	27,000
180	2,700	32,400	486,000
150	2,250	22,500	337,500
120	1,950	14,400	234,000
180	2,100	32,400	378,000
90	1,350	8,100	121,500
30	1,050	900	31,500
120	1,800	14,400	216,000
60	1,350	3,600	81,000
$\Sigma x = 1,260$	$\Sigma Y = 19,800$	$\Sigma x^2 = 163,800$	$\Sigma xY = 2,394,000$

have been made as shown in Exhibit 20.1. The past obervations are listed in the first two columns.

We can now insert the computations into the formulas (note that n represents the number of observations) as follows:

$$19,800 = 12a + 1260b \qquad \text{(Equation 1)}$$
$$2,394,000 = 1260a + 163,800b \qquad \text{(Equation 2)}$$

We can now solve the above two simulataneous equations.

To solve for b multiply equation 1 by 105 (1260 ÷ 12) to provide

$$2,079,000 = 1,260a + 132,300b \qquad \text{(Equation 3)}$$

Subtracting equation 3 from equation 2 the a values will cancel out to yield 315,000 = 31,500b.

$$\therefore b = \pounds 10$$

Substituting the value of b in equation 1 and solving for a we have:

$$19,800 = 12a + 1260 (10)$$
$$\therefore a = 600$$

The regression line can now be described by the following equation:

$$Y = a + bx$$
$$\therefore Y = 600 + 10x$$

We can now use this formula to predict the cost which will be incurred at different activity levels, including those for which we have no past observations. For example, at an activity level of 90 hours the cost should be £600 non-variable cost, plus £900 variable cost (£90 × 10). This agrees with the actual observation in Exhibit 20.1. However, as the cost equation represents the average costs it is unlikely that the estimated costs will always be equal to past observations. For example, the estimated cost for an activity level of 150 hours is £2,100 but reference to the actual observations in Exhibit 20.1 indicates that costs

Fig. 20.3 Regression line Y = 600 + 10x compared with actual observations

were £1,950 and £2,250 for this activity level.

The regression line and actual observations (represented by the dots) are recorded in Fig. 20.3. You will see from the actual observations that different costs may be recorded for the same activity levels, so it is not possible to produce a simple regression which will exactly match past costs. A manager, however, will wish to establish that a regression equation provides a close approximation to actual past observations, and so it is important to carry out tests to check how reliable the regression equation is when compared with past observations.

Tests of reliability

In Example 20.3 the regression equation was calculated on the assumption that costs varied with hours of activity. However, a number of different activity measures exist. For example, costs may vary with different measures of activity such as direct labour hours of input, machine hours of input, number of units of output, direct labour cost, and amount of material used. Various tests of reliability can be applied to see how reliable each of these activity measures are in predicting specific costs. Three such tests are as follows:

(1) The coefficient of determination
(2) The standard error of the estimate

(3) The standard error of the coefficient.

The coefficient determination

If the regression line calculated by the least squares method were to fit the actual observations perfectly, all of the observed points would lie on the regression line in Fig. 20.3. You will see from this diagram that reliability is based on the size of the deviations of the actual observations (Ya) from the estimated values on the regression line (Ye). The size of these deviations can be ascertained by squaring the difference between the estimated and the actual values. (The sums of the deviations will always add to zero, and it is therefore necessary to square the deviations.) The average of these squared deviations is defined as the residual variation. In statistical terms this represents the variance of the actual observations from the regression line and is denoted by θ^2. The calculation of the residual variation for the information presented in Exhibit 20.1 is shown in Exhibit 20.2.

In formula terms the residual variation is calculated as follows:

$$\theta^2 = \frac{\Sigma (Ya - Ye)^2}{n} = \frac{405,000}{12} = 33,750$$

To determine how reliable the activity base chosen is in predicting costs we must determine the total dispersion of the observations and compare this with the dispersion which occurs when hours of activity are used in predicting costs.

Exhibit 20.2 Calculation of residual variation

Hours (x)	Actual cost (Ya)	Estimated cost (Ye) (Y = 600 + 10x)	Deviations (Ya − Ye)	Deviations squared (Ya − Ye)2
90	1,500	1,500	0	0
150	1,950	2,100	−150	22,500
60	900	1,200	−300	90,000
30	900	900	0	0
180	2,700	2,400	300	90,000
150	2,250	2,100	150	22,500
120	1,950	1,800	150	22,500
180	2,100	2,400	−300	90,000
90	1,350	1,500	−150	22,500
30	1,050	900	150	22,500
120	1,800	1,800	0	0
60	1,350	1,200	150	22,500
	19,800			405,000

Exhibit 20.3 Dispersion of observations around the average

Actual cost (Ya)	Average (Ȳa)	Deviation (Ya − Ȳa)	Deviation squared (Ya − Ȳa)²
1,500	1,650	−150	22,500
1,950	1,650	300	90,000
900	1,650	−750	562,500
900	1,650	−750	562,500
2,700	1,650	1,050	1,102,500
2,250	1,650	600	360,000
1,950	1,650	300	90,000
2,100	1,650	450	202,500
1,350	1,650	−300	90,000
1,050	1,650	−600	360,000
1,800	1,650	150	22,500
1,350	1,650	−300	90,000
			3,555,000

The total dispersion of the cost observations can be found by removing volume from the cost equation and working out what the dispersion would be if volume is ignored. Any estimate of cost would then be based on a simple calculation of the average of all the actual cost observations. In Exhibit 20.2 there are twelve observations of actual cost which add up to £19,800, the average being £1,650 (£19,800 ÷ 12). Let us now calculate the dispersion of the actual observations around the average (see Exhibit 20.3).

The dispersion from the average (that is, θ^2) is calculated from the following formula:

$$\theta^2 = \frac{\Sigma\,(Ya - Ȳa)^2}{n} = \frac{3,555,000}{12} = 296,250$$

The total dispersion is £296,250 but, by introducing hours into the regression equation as a possible way of predicting variations in cost, we have accounted for all but £33,750 of the total variation of £296,250. In percentage terms the means that the activity base used has failed to account for 11.39% (that is (33,750/296,250) × 100) of the variation of cost. In other words, 88.61% of the variation in total cost is explained by variations in the activity base, and the remaining 11.39% is explained by either entirely random variation or random variation plus the combined effect that other (omitted variables) have on the dependent variable — total cost. The term used for describing the calculation of 88.61% is the *coefficient of determination* (that is, r^2). In

formula terms the coefficient of determination is calculated as follows:

$$r^2 = 1 - \frac{\Sigma\,(Ya - Ye)^2/n}{\Sigma\,(Ya - Ȳa)^2/n} = 1 - \frac{33,750}{296,250}$$
$$= 0.8861$$

The degree of association between two variables such as cost and activity is normally referred to as *correlation*. The *correlation coefficient (r) is the square root of the coefficient of determination*. If the degree of association between the two variables is very close, it will be almost possible to plot the obervations on a straight line and r and r^2 will be very near to 1. In this situation a high correlation between costs and activity exists as illustrated in Fig. 20.4.

At the other extreme, costs may be so randomly distributed that there is little or no correlation between costs and the activity base selected. The r^2 calculation will be near to zero. An illustration of the situation where no correlation exists is given in Fig. 20.5.

Standard error of the estimate

The coefficient of determination gives us an indication of the reliability of the estimate of total cost based on the regression equation but it does not give us an indication of the absolute size of the probable deviations from the line. This information can be obtained by calculating the standard

Fig. 20.4 High correlation

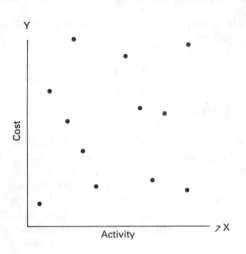

Fig. 20.5 No correlation

error (Se) of the estimate based on the following formula:

$$Se = \sqrt{\frac{\Sigma (Ya - Ye)^2}{n - 2}} = \sqrt{\frac{405,000}{10}} = 201.25$$

The sample size (n) is reduced by 2 because two variables (a and b) in the regression equation had to be estimated from the sample of observations. Note that the calculation for $\Sigma (Ya - Ye)^2$ has been obtained from Exhibit 20.2.

The calculation of the standard error is necessary because the least squares line was calculated from sample data. Other samples would probably result in different estimates. Obtaining the least squares calculation over all the possible observations which might occur for the maintenance cost would result in a calculation of the true least squares line. The question is, how close does the sample estimate of the least squares line (Y = 600 + 10x) come to the true least squares line. The standard error enables us to establish a range of values of the dependent variable (Y) within which we may have some degree of confidence that the true value lies. Different ranges can be calculated for different degrees of confidence. Thus the standard error of the estimate is quite similar to a standard deviation in normal probability analysis. It is a measure of variability around the regression line.

Statistical theory indicates that for least squares analysis the points are t-distributed about the regression line and that the distribution becomes normal as the number of observations reaches 30. As our estimate of the regression line was based on twelve observations we shall assume that the points are t-distributed about the regression line. An important characteristic of this distribution is that there is a 0.9 probability that the true cost lies within ± 1.812 standard errors from the estimated cost. (An explanation of this is presented in the Appendix to this chapter.) If you refer back to Exhibit 20.2 you will see that the estimated cost for 180 hours of activity is £2,400. This means that there is a 0.90 probability that the true cost will fall within the range:

$$£2,400 ± 1.812 (201.25) = £2,035 \text{ to } £2,765$$

If a narrower range is required, the probability that the true cost will fall within this narrower range will be less than 0.9. For example, the t-distribution indicates that there is a probability of 0.80 that the true cost will fall within 1.372 standard errors from the estimated cost. This means that there is a 0.80 probability that the true cost will fall within the following range:

$$£2,400 ± 1.372 (201.25) = £2,124 \text{ to } £2,676$$

Alternatively, if a greater degree of confidence is required, a probability higher than 0.90 can be obtained, but this will give a wider range within which the true cost lies. The tighter the observations around the regression line, the lower the value of Se. When observations of costs and output are widely distributed around the regression line.we can expect a high Se, as we need a much larger range to describe our estimate of true costs.

These principles can usefully be applied to flexible budgeting by presenting a flexible budget which portrays a range of possible costs for each level of activity. For a detailed illustration of this approach see Koehler and Neyhart (1972). A flexible budget based on a 0.9 probability for activity levels of 150 and 180 hours is presented in Exhibit 20.4.

We would expect costs to fall within the given range for 90% of the time. Alternatively, we would expect costs to fall outside the range for 10% of the time when they are from the same population from which the least squares estimate was derived. Therefore, for any actual cost observations which are outside the range, there is a high probability that the costs are out of control.

Exhibit 20.4 Flexible budgets

Activity	150 hours			180 hours		
	Lower limit	Mean	Upper limit	Lower limit	Mean	Upper limit
	£1,735	£2,100	£2,465	£2,035	£2,400	£2,765

We discussed this principle in Chapter 18 when we considered the investigation of variances.

Standard error of the coefficient

We have previously computed the standard error of the estimate to measure the reliability of the estimates of *total cost*. However, we may also be interested in the reliability of the estimate of the regression coefficient b (that is, the *variable cost*). This is because the analyst often focuses on the rate of variability rather than on the absolute level of the prediction. The formula for the standard error of the b coefficient (Sb) can be expressed as follows:

$$Sb = \frac{Se}{\sqrt{\Sigma (x - \bar{x})^2}}$$

This equation can be simplified to:

$$Sb = \frac{Se}{\sqrt{\Sigma x^2 - \bar{x}\Sigma x}}$$

If we use the standard error which we have calculated and the data which we used for calculating the regression equation in Exhibit 20.1, the calculation is as follows:

$$Sb = \frac{201.25}{\sqrt{163,800 - \frac{1260}{12}(1260)}} = \frac{201.25}{\sqrt{31,500}}$$

$$= 1.134$$

We can now use the t-distribution, again noting that there is a 0.9 probability that the true variable cost lies within ± 1.812 standard errors from the estimated cost. Using the regression equation Y = 600 + 10x, we can state that we are 90% confident that the true variable cost lies within the following range:

£10 ± 1.812 (1.134) = £7.95 to £12.05

We can calculate different ranges of variable costs based on different probability levels. For example, the t-distribution indicates that there is a 0.8 probability that the true variable cost lies within 1.372 standard errors from the mean. Therefore we can be 80% confident that the true variable cost lies within the following range:

£10 ± 1.372 sb

A partial table of t-values is set out in the Appendix to this chapter to show how the t-values of 1.812 and 1.372 have been calculated.

Multiple regression analysis

The least squares regression equation was based on the assumption that total cost was determined by one activity based variable only. However, other variables besides activity are likely to influence total cost. A certain cost may vary not only with changes in the hours of operation but also with the weight of the product being made, temperature changes or other factors. With simple least squares regression only one factor is taken into consideration, but with multiple regression several factors are considered in combination. As far as possible all the factors which are related to cost behaviour should be brought into the analysis so that costs can be predicted and controlled more effectively.

The equation for simple regression can be expanded to include more than one independent variable. If there are two independent variables and the relationship is assumed to be linear, the regression equation will be as follows:

$$Y = a + b_1x_1 + b_2x_2$$

Item a represents the non-variable cost item. Item b_1 represents the average change in Y which results from a unit change in x_1, assuming that x_2 and all the unidentified items remain constant; similarly, b_2 represents the average change in Y

which results from a unit change in x_2, assuming that x_1 remains constant. The normal equations for a regression equation with two independent variables are as follows:

$$\Sigma Y = an + b_1 \Sigma x_1 + b_2 \Sigma x_2$$
$$\Sigma x_1 Y = a \Sigma x_1 + b_1 \Sigma(x_1^2) + b_2 \Sigma x_1 x_2$$
$$\Sigma x_2 Y = a\Sigma x_2 + b_1 \Sigma x_1 x_2 + b_2 \Sigma(x_2^2)$$

The value of Y can be determined by solving these equations but the calculations are very tedious. Fortunately, standard computer programs are available which can generate the value of Y together with details of standard errors of the individual regression coefficients. We shall therefore now concentrate on the principles and the application of multiple regression analysis and ignore the tedious arithmetical calculations.

Consider a plant which generates its own steam and uses this steam both for heating and for motive power. A simple least squares regression based on machine hours is likely to provide a poor estimate of the total cost of steam generation and will produce a relatively low coefficient of determination. The cost of steam generation is likely to be determined by both temperature and machine hours, and a multiple regression equation is therefore likely to produce a more accurate estimate of the total costs. The equation could take the following form:

$$Y = a + b_1 x_1 + b_2 x_2$$

where Y = total cost, a = total non-variable cost, x_1 = number of machine hours, b_1 = regression coefficient for machine hours, x_2 = number of days per month in which the temperature is less than 15°C, b_2 = regression coefficient for temperature. The equations for this formula can be developed by using past monthly observations of the number of machine hours, the days on which the temperature was below 15°C and the total cost. This information is imputed into the equations and the result will be an output similar to the following format:

$$Y = 20 + 4x_1 + 12x_2$$

Estimates of total steam cost can now be developed based on the estimated machine hours and the temperature for future periods. For example, if the number of estimated machine hours for a particular month are 1,000, and past experience indicates that the temperature is likely to be below 15°C for the full month of 30 days, the estimated cost will be:

$$Y = 20 + 4(1,000) + 12(30) = £4,380$$

The value of the coefficients b_1 and b_2 enables us to determine the marginal cost which is associated with each of the determining factors. For example, the value of the coefficient of b_1 is £4 which indicates the marginal change in the total cost for each additional machine hour with the effects of temperature accounted for.

The coefficient of multiple determination and the standard errors of the individual regression coefficients can be calculated with the aid of formulas which are similar to those which we used for simple least squares regression. For a detailed description of the application, the use and limitations of multiple regression analysis, and the procedures which accountants should follow in recording data which will be used as inputs for the analysis, see Benston (1977).

Multicollinearity

Multiple regression analysis is based on the assumption that the independent variables *are not* correlated with each other. When the independent variables *are* highly correlated with each other, it is very difficult, and sometimes impossible, to separate the effects of each of these variables on the dependent variable. This occurs when there is a simultaneous movement of two or more independent variables in the same direction and at approximately the same rate. This condition is called 'multicollinearity'. An example of multicollinearity is where several complementary products are manufactured and the output of each product is treated as an independent variable. If the demand for each of these products is highly correlated, the output of all the products will be the same, all being high in one period and low in another period. In this situation the regression coefficients have no meaning; they cannot estimate the likely changes in cost which will arise from a unit change in given independent variables while the other dependent variables are held constant. This is because there is a lack of independence among the independent variables which prevents the availability of sufficient information to enable the regression coefficients to be determined. However, multicollinearity does not affect the validity of the predictions of the total cost if the past relationships between the independent variables are maintained. Multicollinearity can be found in a variety of ways. One way is to measure the correlation between the

independent variables. Kaplan (1982) makes the following comment on the effect of multi-collinearity and the accounting implications:

> The collinearity problem is most severe when we are trying to obtain accurate coefficient estimates for product planning, pricing, and a cost–volume–profit analysis. If we are mainly interested in using the regression equation to predict cost behaviour in a period (i.e. as a flexible budget), then we are not concerned with the individual coefficient estimates. The standard error of the regression and of the forecasts from the regression are not affected by collinearity among subsets of the independent variables. Therefore, if the analyst feels that the correlated variables are all necessary for predicting overall costs, they can remain in the regression equation.

Requirements for using mathematical techniques

Several requirements are necessary to ensure that a sound system is developed for estimating costs. If these requirements are not met, there is a danger that less accurate cost estimates will be produced, and there will be an increased probability that the quality of the information system will be impaired. Let us now consider some of these requirements.

Review of various activity bases

There are often several activity measures which can be used to measure the independent variables. The total cost of an activity may be a function of the number of units produced, the direct labour hours of input, the machine hours of input, the direct labour cost incurred, the quantities of materials used, and so on. The objective is to find the activity base which has the greatest effect on cost. In theory, it is necessary to calculate the coefficient of determination and the standard errors of each activity base for each item of expense to determine which activity base should be used for estimating each individual item of expense. In practice, this process is only likely to be carried out for significant expense items. For those items of expense which are not very large the inspection of accounts method may be appropriate. For other items, like direct materials,

where it is possible to specify optimum amounts of input, the engineering methods are likely to be the most appropriate.

The cost data and activity should be related to the same period

It is not uncommon for some costs to lag behind the associated activity. For example. wages paid in one period may be calculated by reference to the output from a previous period. Let us consider the following situation where a piecework system is in operation and where wages are paid on the basis of £1 per unit produced:

	Activity (x)	Wages paid (y)
Week 10	5,000 units	£3,000 (output for week 9
Week 11	2,500 units	£5,000 was 3,000 units)
Week 12	4,000 units	£2,500

In this example the firm follows a policy of paying the labour force for the output which was achieved in the previous week. It is clearly incorrect to relate costs to output for each week when calculating the cost estimation equation. It is therefore necessary to correct the bias in the data by relating the costs in period t to the output in period $t-1$ before the cost equation is calculated.

Number of observations

If acceptable cost estimates are to be produced a sufficient number of observations must be obtained. If figures are used only from recent periods there may be insufficient observations. However, if observation other than those from previous periods are used some adjustment of the data will be required. If insufficient observations are obtained the standard error is likely to be large and the confidence intervals or ranges of costs will be quite large for each activity level.

Accounting policies

The data must be examined to ensure that the accounting policies are not significantly biased. For example, if *fixed* maintenance costs are allocated to production departments on the basis of the number of maintenance hours, this accounting allocation may make the fixed costs appear to be variable. If the objective is to determine the cost behaviour pattern in a single production

department, only those costs which are incurred within the department should be included. Allocated costs should be excluded from the analysis.

Adjustments for past changes

An analysis of past data will yield estimates of future costs which are based on the cost relationships of previous periods. The appropriateness of using past data depends on the extent to which the future will correspond with the past. Any changes of circumstances in the future will require past data to be adjusted in line with future data. For example, if it is estimated that future costs will increase by 10%, all past data should be adjusted by a price index to future price levels before the cost estimation equation is established.

It is also possible that technological changes in the production process may have taken place, and past data must then be adjusted to reflect the circumstances which will apply in the future. Conversely, any observations from past periods which represent abnormal situations which are not expected to occur again in the future should be excluded from the analysis. The major problem is one of ensuring that a correct balance is maintained between obtaining sufficient observations to produce a reliable cost estimate, and keeping the time span short enough so that the data is appropriate to the circumstances in the future.

Problems which may arise when using mathematical cost equations

It may be very misleading to use a cost estimation equation to estimate the total costs for ranges of activities which had not been observed when the cost equation was established. This is because a cost equation is normally only valid within the range of the actual observations which were used to establish the equation. In fact, the equation gives no information about the costs relating to activity levels which are outside the range of observations (see Fig. 20.6).

You will see from this illustration that in the past the company has operated only between activity levels X_1 and X_2, as the dots represent the

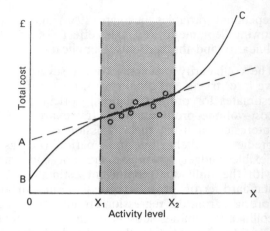

Fig. 20.6 Effect of extrapolation of costs

actual observations. A cost equation developed from this information may provide satisfactory cost estimates for activity levels between X_1 and X_2, but it may not do so for activity levels which are outside this range of observations. For example, the dashed line which meets the vertical axis at A might represent a cost equation which has been developed from these observations; the dashed line will represent a satisfactory estimate of total cost between activity levels X_1 and X_2. However, any extrapolation of the dashed line outside the range of observations may result in an unsatisfactory estimate of total cost.

Do you remember that in Chapter 9 we discovered that linear cost functions may only apply over the relevant production range, and that over a very wide range of activity a curvilinear relationship may exist, similar to the curved line BC in Fig. 20.6? It follows, therefore, that the extrapolation of the dashed line represents an unsatisfactory estimate outside the relevant range if a curvilinear relationship exists. Also, the non-variable item (that is, a in the equation $y = a + bx$) is unlikely to represent the total non-variable cost at zero activity. The cost equation in Fig. 20.6 gives an estimated non-variable cost of 0A compared with an actual non-variable cost of 0B. Hence the value of the constant term (a) in the cost equation is not the costs which would be expected if there was zero output; it is only the value which is calculated as a result of the regression line computed from the available data.

In practice, the problem of extrapolation may not occur as the majority of decisions are normally

taken within the relevant operating range over which the firm has had experience of operating in the past. However, if decisions are to be based on cost information which is projected beyond the relevant range, the cost estimates must be used with care.

A further problem may occur when the least squares method is used. This method minimizes the sum of the squares of the deviations of actual cost observations from their estimates, and there is a danger that the method may impute a disproportionately large weight to the influence of larger deviations compared to smaller ones. This will cause the least squares line to tilt upwards or downwards. If the observations represent abnormal or unusual occurrences there may be an argument for excluding such observations from the analysis because our objective is to establish normal relationships between cost and activity.

Care must be taken when unusual observations are excluded at both ends of the range of activity which is used in the analysis as this may reflect the fact that a curvilinear cost relationship exists. We should not throw out observations just to get a nice fit of the regression line, but we would be justified in omitting observations which were not representative of normal operating conditions. To determine whether such a relationship exists it is a good idea to plot the observations on a graph, so that a subsequent examination of the graph may indicate that a curvilinear cost–volume relationship exists over the anticipated operating range. It may be appropriate in this sort of situation to develop non-linear cost equations, but a description of such techniques is beyond the scope of this book. You will find a detailed description of non-linear cost equations in Draper and Smith (1966). To ensure that some of the important requirements of regression analysis are not violated it is always a good idea to prepare graphs and look carefully at the data; blind reliance on mathematical techniques can be very dangerous.

Cost estimation when the learning effect is present

Difficulties occur in estimating costs when technological changes take place in the production process; past data is not then very useful for estimating costs. For example, changes in the efficiency of the labour force may render past information unsuitable for predicting future labour costs. A situation like this may occur when workers become more familiar with the tasks which they perform so that less labour time is required for the production of each unit. This phenomenon has been observed in a number of manufacturing situations and is known as the *learning curve* effect. From the experience of aircraft production during World War II, aircraft manufacturers found that the rate of improvement was so regular that it could be reduced to a formula and the labour hours required could be predicted with a high degree of accuracy from a *learning curve*. Based on this information experiments have been undertaken in other industries with learning curves, and these experiments also indicate some regularity in the pattern of a worker's ability to learn a new task.

The first time a new operation is performed both the workers and the operating procedures are untried. As the operation is repeated the workers become more familiar with the work, labour efficiency increases and the labour cost per unit declines. This process continues for some time and a regular rate of decline in cost per unit can be established at the outset. This rate of decline can then be used in predicting future labour costs. The learning process starts from the point when the first unit comes off the production line. From then on each time cumulative production is doubled, the average time taken to produce each unit of cumulative produciton will be a certain percentage of the average time per unit of the previous cumulative production.

An application of the 80% learning curve is presented in Exhibit 20.5 which shows the labour hours required on a sequence of six orders where the cumulative number of units is doubled for each order. The first unit was completed on the first order in 2,000 hours; for each subsequent order the cumulative production was doubled, so that the average hours per unit were 80% of the average hours per unit of the previous cumulative production. For example, the cumulative average time shown in column (4) of Exhibit 20.5 for each unit of output is calculated as follows:

Order number 1 = 2,000 hours
2 = 1,600 hours (80% × 2,000)
3 = 1,280 hours (80% × 1,600)
4 = 1,024 hours (80% × 1,280)
5 = 819 hours (80% × 1,024)
6 = 655 hours (80% × 819)

Exhibit 20.5 Labour hours for 80% learning curve

	Number of units			Cumulative hours		Hours for each order	
Order no. (1)	Per order (2)	Cumulative production (3)	Per unit (4)	Total (5) (3 × 4)		Total (6)	Per unit (7) (6 ÷ 2)
1	1	1	2,000	2,000		2,000	2,000
2	1	2	1,600	3,200		1,200	1,200
3	2	4	1,280	5,120		1,920	960
4	4	8	1,024	8,192		3,072	768
5	8	16	819	13,104		4,912	614
6	16	32	655	20,960		7,856	491

Information is provided for specific quantities only. No information is available for other quantities such as 10, 20 or 30 units, although such information could be obtained either graphically or mathematically.

Graphical method

The quantities for the average time per unit of cumulative production (column (4) of Exhibit 20.5) are presented in graphical form in Fig. 20.7.

The graph shows that the average time per unit declines rapidly at first and then more slowly until eventually the decline is so small that it can be ignored. When no further improvement is expected and the regular efficiency level is reached the situation is referred to as the *steady state production level*. The cumulative average hours per unit is 953 hours for 10 units and 762 hours for 20 units. To obtain the total number of hours we merely multiply the average number of hours by the cumulative quantity produced, which gives 9,530 total hours for 10 units and 15,240 total hours for 20 units.

Mathematical method

The learning curve can be expressed in equation form as:

$$Y_x = aX^b$$

where Y_x is defined as the cumulative average

Fig. 20.7 80% learning curve

time which is required to produce x units, a is the time required to produce the first unit of output and X is the number of units of output under consideration. The exponent b is defined by the ratio of the logarithm of the learning curve improvement rate (for example, 0.8 for an 80% learning curve) divided by the logarithm of the number 2. The improvement exponent can take on any value between −1 and zero. The exponent for an 80% learning curve, for example, is −0.322. Using the formula we can calculate the cumulative average time taken to produce 10 and 20 units. The calculations are as follows:

$$Y_{10} = 2,000 \times 10^{-0.322}$$
$$= 2,000 \times 0.476431$$
$$= 953$$

and
$$Y_{20} = 2,000 \times 20^{-0.322}$$
$$= 2,000 \times 0.381126$$
$$= 762$$

A computation of the exponent values may be made by using either logarithms or a calculator with exponent functions.

Estimating incremental hours and incremental cost

Incremental hours cannot be determined directly from the learning curve graph or formula as the results are expressed in terms of cumulative average hours. It is possible, however, to obtain incremental hours by examining the differences between total hours for various combinations of cumulative hours. For example, assume that for Exhibit 20.5 the company has completed orders such that cumulative production is 4 units and that an enquiry has been received for an order of 6 units. We can calculate the incremental hours for these 6 units as follows:

	Hours
Total hours if an additional 6 units are produced (cumulative production will be ten units)	= 9,530 (10 × 953)
Total hours for the first 4 units (4 × 1,280)	= 5,120
Hours required for 6 units after completion of 4 units	= 4,410

Note that the total hours are calculated by taking the average hours for cumulative production and multiplying by the cumulative production. The incremental hours for 6 units are obtained by taking the difference between the time required for 10 units and the time required for 4 units.

Let us assume that the company completes the order for the 6 units and then receives a new order for an additional 10 units. How many labour hours will be needed? The cumulative quantity is now 20 units (10 already completed plus 10 now on order). The estimated hours for the 10 new units are calculated as follows:

	Hours
Total hours for first 20 units (20 × 762)	15,240
Total hours for first 10 units (10 × 953)	9,530
Hours required for ten units after completion of ten units	5,710

The learning curve can be used to estimate labour costs and those other costs which vary in direct proportion to labour costs. Note that the learning effect only applies to direct labour costs and those variable overheads which are a direct function of labour hours of input. It does not apply to material costs, non-variable costs or items which vary with output.

Let us now assume that a company has just completed the first two units of production of a new product which is subject to an 80% learning curve at a labour cost of £10,000. Assuming that the company now receives an enquiry for the production of two further units, what is the estimated labour cost and variable overhead cost if the variable overheads amount to 20% of direct labour cost? As the cumulative production will be doubled if the two units are produced, the incremental labour and variable overhead costs for the two units can be calculated as follows:

A. Cumulative average labour cost for first two units was £5,000 (£10,000 ÷ 2)
B. Cumulative average labour cost for first four units will be £4,000 (80% × £5,000)

C. The labour cost for the enquiry for the two units will be calculated as follows:

Labour cost for four units (£4,000 × 4)	£16,000
Labour cost for two units	£10,000
Cost for new order of two units	£ 6,000

D. The estimated labour and variable overhead costs for the two additional units are as follows:

Direct labour cost	£6,000
Variable overheads (20% of 6,000)	£1,200

Learning curve applications

The learning curve generally applies to those situations where the labour input for an activity is large and where the activity is complex. Andress (1954) suggests that conditions conducive to learning are ideal in the electronics, home appliances, construction and shipbuilding areas, but he suggests that industries which are capital intensive, such as petroleum refining, would find the learning curve to be of little value.

Learning curves are not theoretical abstractions but are based on observations of past events. When new products have been made in previous periods, the learning curve principles can be applied from the experience which has been gained. In new situations where there is no historical data, the curves for previous products or processes with known improvement factors can be used if management can identify similarities with the new situation. We have considered in this chapter an 80% learning curve, but this percentage may vary depending on the technology. In the aircraft industry studies indicated that a learning curve of 80% was appropriate but other industries may suggest that other percentages should be applied to take account of the learning factor. Generally, the figures vary between 70% and 90%.

Unfortunately, the true nature of the learning curve which is associated with a new product or process will never be known. However, a reasonable assumption of its shape is better than an assumption of no learning curve at all. The learning curve may be applied to the following situations:

(1) Pricing decisions

The main impact of the learning curve is likely to be in providing better cost predictions to enable price quotations to be prepared for potential orders. An ability to forecast cost reductions and consequent selling price reductions may make the difference between landing and losing profitable orders. Simmonds (1981) suggests that early experience with a *new* product could confer an unbeatable lead over competition, and that the leading competitor should be able to reduce his selling price (through the learning curve effect), which would further increase his volume and market share and eventually force some lagging competitors out of the industry.

(2) Work scheduling

Learning curves enable firms to predict their required inputs more effectively and this enables them to produce more accurate delivery schedules. This in turn can lead to improved customer relationships and possibly result in increased future sales.

(3) Standard setting

If budgets and standards are set without considering the learning effect, meaningless variances are likely to occur. If management creates a climate where learning is encouraged and expected then improvements in efficiency are more likely to occur (see Harvey and Saliman, 1983, for a discussion of the application of learning curves to standard costing). For a more general review of the literature on learning curves and a discussion on the accounting implications of product start-ups see Baloff and Kennelly (1977).

Summary

Total costs for a particular expense may be a function of the number of units produced, direct labours of input, machine hours of input, quantities of materials used and so on. The objective is to find the activity measure which exerts the major influence on cost. Various tests of reliability can be applied to see how reliable each of these activity measures are in predicting specific costs. Such tests include the coefficient of determination, the standard error of the estimate, or the standard error of the coefficient. If a single activity measure is found to be sufficiently reliable a regression equation should be established using the least squares method.

If the tests of reliability suggests unreliable cost estimates and it is considered that total cost is a function of more than one variable, estimates based on multiple regression should be established for the important cost items.

A number of requirements are necessary before statistical cost estimation techniques can be used. The time period should be long enough to enable meaningful information to be collected, the cost data and activity must be related to the same period, the analysis should consist of a sufficient number of observations and past data should be adjusted to reflect future expectations. A further problem is that the cost equation is only valid within the range of actual observations which were used to establish the equation. Incorrect cost estimates will result if the estimates are projected outside this activity level as curvilinear relationships might exist. Some of the problems can be spotted by plotting a graph and looking carefully at the data.

When technological changes occur in the production process, past costs cannot be used to predict future costs. If the labour content per unit is expected to decline as workers become more familiar with the process, learning curve principles can be applied.

References and further reading

Abernathy, W.J. and Wayne, K. Limits of the learning curve. *Harvard Business Review* September–October 1974, 109-19.

Andress, F.J. The learning curve as a production tool. *The Harvard Business Review* January–February 1954, 87-97.

Baloff, N. and Kennelly, J.W. Accounting implications of product and process start-ups. In Benston, G. (Ed.), *Contemporary Issues in Cost Accounting and Control*. Dickenson Publishing Company, 1977.

Benston, G. Multiple regression analysis and cost behaviour. In Benston, G. (Ed.), *Contemporary Issues in Cost Accounting and Control*. Dickenson Publishing Company, 1977.

Bump, E.A. Effects of learning on cost projections. *Management Accounting (USA)* April 1971, 352-65.

Chan, K.H., Sbrocchi, F.L. and Van Zante, N.R. Forecasting methods and the management accountant. *Cost and Management (Canada)* January–February 1980, 40-45.

Draper, N.R. and Smith, H. *Applied Regression Analysis*. Wiley, 1966.

Gillespie, J.F. An application of learning curves to standard costing. *Management Accounting (USA)*, 63-6.

Harris, L.B.C. and Stephens, W.L. The learning curve in accountancy. *Management Accounting (USA)*, February 1978, 78-84.

Harvey, D.W. Financial planning information for production start-ups. *The Accounting Review* October 1976, 838-46.

Harvey, D.W. and Saliman, S.Y. Standard costing variance analysis in a learning environment. *Accounting and Business Research* Summer 1983. 181-200.

Hirschmann, W.B. Profit from the learning curve. *Harvard Business Review* January–February 1964, 125-39.

Jensen, R. Multiple regression models for cost control — Assumptions and limitations. *The Accounting Review* XLIII, April 1967, 265-72.

Johnston, J. *Statistical Cost Analysis*. McGraw Hill, 1972, Chapters 3 and 4.

Koehler, R.W. and Neyhart, C.A. Difficulties in flexible budgeting. *Managerial Planning* May–June 1972, 21-8; also in DeCoster, D.T. *et. al* (Eds), *Accounting for Managerial Decision Making*. Wiley, 1978.

Liao, W.M. Simulating learning curve parameters for managerial planning and control. *Accounting and Business Research* 12, No. 46, Spring 1982, 141-7.

Malpas, R. Planning product/processing technology. *Harvard Business Review (USA)*, July–August 1983, 122-31.

Morse, W.J. Reporting production costs that follow the learning curve phenomenon. *The Accounting Review* October 1972, 761-73.

Simmonds, K. Strategic management accounting. *Management Accounting* April 1981, 26-9.

Simmonds, K. *The fundamentals of strategic management accounting. ICMA Occasional Paper, Institute of Cost and Management Accountants,* 1981.

Summers, E.L. *and Welsh, G.A. How learning curve models can be applied to profit planning. Management Services* March/April 1970, 45-50.

Wood, D. and Fildes, R. *Forecasting for Business Methods and Applications.* Longman, 1976.

Problems

*Indicates that a suggested solution is to be found in the *Students' Manual.*

20.1* The transport department of the Norwest Council operates a large fleet of assorted vehicles. These vehicles are used as the need

Year	Month	Machine hours (000)	Fuel oil expense ($)
1978	July	34	640
	August	30	620
	September	34	620
	October	39	590
	November	42	500
	December	32	530

arises by the various departments of the Council. Each month a statement is prepared for the transport department comparing actual results with budget.

One of the items in the transport department's monthly statement is the cost of vehicle maintenance. This maintenance is carried out by the employees of the department.

To facilitate his control the transport manager has asked that future statements should show vehicle maintenance costs analysed into fixed and variable costs.

Data for the six months from January to June 1982 inclusive are given below:

1982	Vehicle maintenance cost £	Vehicle running hours
January	13,600	2,100
February	15,800	2,800
March	14,500	2,200
April	16,200	3,000
May	14,900	2,600
June	15,000	2,500

You are required to:
(a) (i) analyse the vehicle maintenance costs into fixed and variable costs, by means of a graph, based on the data given;
 (ii) prove your results by utilizing the least squares method;
(b) discuss briefly how you would propose to calculate rates for charging out the total costs incurred to the user departments.

(20 marks)
ICMA Cost Accounting 2
November 1982

20.2 Albatross Pty, the Australian subsidiary of a British packaging company, is preparing its budget for the year to 30 June 1980. In respect of fuel oil consumption it is desired to estimate an equation of the form $y = a + bx$, where y is the total expense at an activity level x, a is the fixed expense, and b is the rate of variable cost.

The following data relate to the year to 30 June 1979:

Year	Month	Machine hours (000)	Fuel oil expense ($)
1979	January	26	500
	February	26	500
	March	31	530
	April	35	550
	May	43	580
	June	48	680

The annual total and monthly average figures for 1978/79 were as follows:

	Machine hours (000)	Fuel oil expense ($)
Annual total	420	6,840
Monthly average	35	570

You are required to:
(a) estimate fixed and variable elements of fuel oil expense from the above data by both of the following methods:
 (i) high and low points (4 marks)
 (ii) least squares regression analysis (8 marks);
(b) compare briefly the methods used in (a) above in relation to the task of estimating fixed and variable elements of a semi-variable cost (7 marks);
(c) accepting that the coefficient of determination (r^2) arising from the data given in the question is approximately 0.25, interpret the significance of this fact. (6 marks)

ICAEW Management Accounting
July 1979

20.3* Savitt Ltd manufactures a variety of products at its industrial site in Wales. One of the products, the LT, is produced in a specially equipped factory in which no other production takes place. For technical reasons the company keeps no stocks of either LTs or the raw material used in their manufacture. The costs of producing LTs in the special factory during the past four years have been as follows:

	1977	1978	1979	1980 (estimated)
	£	£	£	£
Raw materials	70,000	100,000	130,000	132,000
Skilled labour	40,000	71,000	96,000	115,000
Unskilled labour	132,000	173,000	235,000	230,000
Power	25,000	33,000	47,000	44,000
Factory overheads	168,000	206,000	246,000	265,000
Total production costs	£435,000	£583,000	£754,000	£786,000
Output (units)	160,000	190,000	220,000	180,000

The costs of raw materials and skilled and unskilled labour have increased steadily during the past four years at an annual compound rate of 20%, and the costs of factory overheads have increased at an annual compound rate of 15% during the same period. Power prices increased by 10% on 1 January 1978 and by 25% on 1 January of each subsequent year. All costs except power are expected to increase by a further 20% during 1981. Power prices are due to rise by 25% on 1 January 1981.

The directors of Savitt Ltd are now formulating the company's production plan for 1981 and wish to estimate the costs of manufacturing the product LT. The finance director has expressed the view that 'the full relevant cost of producing LTs can be determined only if a fair share of general company overheads is allocated to them.' No such allocation is included in the table of costs above.

You are required to:
(a) use linear regression analysis to estimate the relationship of total production costs to volume for the product LT for 1981 (ignore general company overheads and do *not* undertake a separate regression calculation for each item of cost) (12 marks),
(b) discuss the advantages and limitations of linear regression analysis for the estimation of cost–volume relationships (8 marks), and
(c) comment on the view expressed by the finance director (5 marks).
Ignore taxation.

ICAEW Elements of Financial Decisions December 1980

20.4* A company is considering investing in a project with the following characteristics:

Equipment is to be purchased costing £70,000, payable at once and having a life of five years with no residual value. The equipment is used to produce one type of product whose sales are budgeted as follows:

Year to 30 June	Number of units
1983	20
1984	40
1985	50
1986	30
1987	10
Total	150

The selling price of the units is to be £4,000 each.
Costs of units are:

Direct materials	£1,200 each
Variable production overhead	50% of direct wages
Variable selling and administration overhead	10% of selling price

Direct wages are paid at £3 per hour. The first unit to be produced is budgeted to take 1505.3 man-hours of work and an 80% learning curve applies to direct wages.

Fixed overhead relating to this projet is £12,000 per annum.

The company requires a 12% DCF return on its investments.

You are required to:
(a) calculate whether or not the project meets the company's investment criterion, based on:
 (i) the average direct wages rate for the whole quantity of units budgeted to be sold;
 (ii) the direct labour times expected to be

required in each individual year;
(b) comment briefly on the relative merits of bases (a) (i) and (a) (ii) above.

Ignore the effects of tax and inflation.

NB: An 80% learning curve on ordinary graph paper would show the following relationship between the x axis (volume) and y axis (cumulative average cost of elements subject to the learning curve):

x	y%	x	y%
1	100	70	25.48
2	80	80	24.40
10	47.65	90	23.50
20	38.13	100	22.71
30	33.46	110	22.03
40	30.50	120	21.41
50	28.39	130	20.86
60	26.77	140	20.38
		150	19.93

(25 marks)

ICMA P3 Management Accounting
May 1982

20.5* AB Ltd, which has a fairly full order book, is approached by a customer with the offer of a contract for a model that is a variant, in terms of dimensions and materials used, of one of its existing products.

Though the customer expects to pay a normal price for the model, he wants AB Ltd to take account of an 80% learning curve in its price calculations; this level has been shown to be reasonable in AB Ltd's industry for relevant work.

The prospective contract is for a total of 464 units made up of an initial order of 160 units, two subsequent orders of 80 units each, and three subsequent orders of 48 units each.

AB Ltd estimates the following average costs per unit for the initial order:

Direct materials: £

P	8 metres	at 3.50 per metre
Q	12 kg	at 1.00 per kg.

Direct wages: £

Department:	1	4 hours	at 1.25 per hour
	2	50 hours	at 1.50 per hour
	3	15 hours	at 1.00 per hour

Variable overhead: 20% of direct wages

Fixed overhead rates, per hour £

Department:	1	2.0
	2	1.00
	3	0.80

The nature of the work in the three production departments is as follows:

Department 1 uses highly automatic machines. Although the operators on these machines need to be fairly skilled, their efficiency only affects the quality of the work but can have little impact on the quantity of this department's output which is largely machine-controlled.

Department 2 is partially mechanized.
Department 3 is an assembly department.
In both departments 2 and 3 the skill of operators is a major determinant of the volume of output.

The terms of the contract price allow for:

Direct materials cost plus 2½% profit margin
Conversion cost plus 12½% profit margin.

You are required to:
(a) calculate the price per unit for:
 (i) the initial order of 160 units;
 (ii) the second, third and fourth orders, if given successively but without guarantee of further orders;
 (iii) the whole contract of six orders if given from the start but on the same basis of production and delivery.
(b) discuss what factors should be considered in deciding whether the learning curve should be taken into account when setting standards for a standard costing system.

[NB: An 80% learning curve on ordinary graph paper would show the following relationship between the x axis (volume) and y axis (cumulative average price of elements subject to the learning curve):

x	y %	x	y %
1.0	100	2.1	78.9
1.1	96.9	2.2	77.8
1.2	93.3	2.3	76.8
1.3	91.7	2.4	76.0
1.4	89.5	2.5	74.9
1.5	87.6	2.6	74.0
1.6	86.1	2.7	73.2
1.7	84.4	2.8	72.3
1.8	83.0	2.9	71.5
1.9	81.5	3.0	70.7
2.0	80.0	3.1	70.0]

(35 marks)

ICMA P3 Management Accounting
May 1977

20.6 A company is asked to quote for a special order to be delivered ex works.

Direct material costs per unit of output are:

For a total of:

	£
100	18 each
200	18 less 10% discount each
400	18 less 20% discount each

The work would be done in two departments:

Department F employs highly skilled operators paid at £2.50 per hour. Each unit of output requires 6 direct labour hours of work for the first 100 units. However, experience has shown that an 80% learning curve can be expected to operate.

Department G employs skilled operators paid at £2.00 per hour. Each unit of output requires 3 direct labour hours of work for the first 100 units. Here, too, an 80% learning curve is expected.

Overtime in either department is paid at time and a half. No premium for overtime is included in standard manufacturing overhead.

Standard manufacturing overhead per direct labour hour is as follows:

	Department F £	Department G £
Variable	1.00	1.00
Fixed	3.50 (a)	2.00 (b)

(a) based on a budgeted level of 3,000 direct labour hours per period;
(b) based on a budgeted level of 2,000 direct labour hours per period;

The special order will require special tooling of £300 which is chargeable to the customer.

If the order received is for 100 or 200 units, the work will have to be done in period No. 8 which, for department F, is already loaded with 2,200 direct labour hours of work. Department G however, will be working at only around 55% of capacity.

On special orders of this type, it is the company's practice to add the following margins on cost in arriving at selling prices:

	%
Department F	20
Department G	10
Direct materials	2
Sub-contractor's work (when used)	2

An outside sub-contractor has offered, irrespective of the size of the order, to do the work of department G on this order for a price of £8 per unit, including collection from and delivery to the works.

You are required to calculate:

(a) the price per unit for an order of 100 units if made entirely in the company;
(b) the price per unit for an order of 200 units if made entirely in the company;
(c) a separate price per unit for an extra 200 units subsequent to the order for 200 in (b) above, thus bringing the total order to 400 units; (N.B. You are to assume that:
 (i) this additional order for the extra 200 units could be done when there are no capacity limitations in either department;
 (ii) the materials supplier would give the full discount for the 400 units.)
(d) the change in unit selling price that would result from using the outside sub-contractor instead of department G for an order of:
 (i) 100 units
 (ii) 200 units
 (iii) 400 units.

(25 marks)
ICMA P3 Management Accounting
November 1979

20.7 In some kinds of specialized manufacturing operations, involving for example difficult or even unique design or production problems, it is suggested that production costs may follow what is known as the 'learning curve phenomenon' as more units of the same kind are produced.
You are required:
(a) to explain the following two statements, to discuss their possible implications, and to assess their significance:
 (1) when the production costs of a product follow the learning curve phenomenon the ratio of actual production costs to units produced declines over the product's life cycle, the production process having two joint products — one physical and the other intangible (5 marks), and
 (2) with constant selling prices, attaching actual production costs to individual units for a firm whose production costs follow the learning curve phenomenon means that the firm's reported earnings will depend on the current stage of the product's life cycle (5 marks), and
(b) to present a table of production times showing the following columns for E. Condon Ltd, which produces up to 16 units while experiencing a 90% learning curve, the first unit requiring 1,000 hours of production time:
 (1) Units produced,
 (2) Total production time (hrs),
 (3) Average production time per unit in each successive lot (hrs),

(4) Cumulative average production time per unit (hrs), and

(5) Percentage decline in (4) (10 marks).

ICAEW Management Accounting
July 1981

20.8 An engineering company employs 30 people on repair and maintenance work on its own plant and equipment. The total cost of labour and materials for this work is £1,200,000 a year.

A study has been undertaken to see if additional preventive maintenance would reduce this overall cost. It is not intended to employ any more people. The extra preventive maintenance would be achieved by reducing manpower on repair work. The study showed that:

(i) Maintenance work at present incurs one-third of the total cost. For each additional man (M) transferred from repair work the maintenance cost would increase by M^2 (£000). The expanding effect results from the need to replace ever-larger units ahead of their deterioration.

(ii) Repair work at present incurs the remaining two-thirds of total costs. For each man (M) transferred to maintenance work the repair cost would reduce by 10M (£000).

You are required:

(a) to calculate the maximum number of extra men it would be financially beneficial to re-allocate to preventive maintenance;

(b) to illustrate your answer to part (a) in a graphical form;

(c) to state the percentage saving in total repair and maintenance costs at the optimal level;

(d) to describe a problem likely to be encountered in trying to achieve this saving.

(25 marks)

ICMA P3 Management Accounting
May 1983

20.9* Explain the 'learning curve' and discuss its relevance to setting standards. (5 marks)

ACCA Level 2 Management Accounting
June 1982

20.10* Discuss the conditions that should apply if linear regression analysis is to be used to analyse cost behaviour. (6 marks)

ACCA Level 2 Management Accounting
December 1982

20.11* (a) Briefly discuss the problems that occur in constructing cost estimation equations for estimating costs at different output levels. (7 marks)

(b) Describe four different cost estimation methods and for each method discuss the limitations and circumstances in which you would recommend their use. (18 marks)

Appendix 20.1: Partial table of t-values

Exhibit 20.A1 Maximum values of t consistent with confidence interval with probability of:

Degrees of freedom	0.80	0.90	0.95	0.98	0.99
1	3.078	6.314	12.706	31.821	63.657
2	1.886	2.920	4.303	6.965	9.925
3	1.638	2.353	3.182	4.541	5.841
4	1.533	2.132	2.776	3.747	4.604
5	1.476	2.015	2.571	3.365	4.032
6	1.440	1.943	2.447	3.143	3.707
7	1.415	1.895	2.365	2.998	3.499
8	1.397	1.860	2.306	2.896	3.355
9	1.383	1.833	2.262	2.821	3.250
10	1.372	1.812	2.228	2.764	3.169
11	1.363	1.796	2.201	2.718	3.106
12	1.356	1.782	2.179	2.681	3.055
13	1.350	1.771	2.160	2.650	3.012
14	1.345	1.761	2.145	2.624	2.977
15	1.341	1.753	2.131	2.602	2.947
Infinite	1.282	1.645	1.960	2.326	2.576

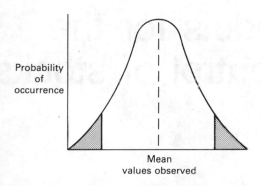

Fig. 20.A1 A t-distribution

The relevant numbers for the probabilities of 0.80 and 0.90 quoted in this chapter are 1.372 and 1.812. These items are obtained from the appropriate columns for the line representing 10 degrees of freedom. The number of degrees of freedom are obtained from the number of observations (that is, 12) reduced by the number of variables in the simple regression equation which had to be estimated from the sample observations (that is, two for regression coefficients a and b in the equation $y = a + bx$).

Note that the headings of t-tables usually identify the probabilities of values falling in one tail of the t-distribution. However, to simplify the situation, the normal presentation has been reversed for the sake of greater clarity and the probabilities of the value falling in the main body of the distribution, and not the tail, are presented. For example, the entries in Exhibit 20.A1 indicate the probability of an observation falling in the unshaded area of Fig. 20.A1.

Assuming that the shaded area in each tail of the distribution represents $t = 0.025$ then 0.05 of the area under the curve falls in the tails of the distribution. Consequently, 0.95 of the area under the curve falls in the unshaded area. Therefore the entries in Exhibit 20.A1 are for 0.95 and not 0.025 which is the normal presentation.

21 Quantitative models for the planning and control of stocks

Investment in stocks represents a major asset of most industrial and commercial organizations, and it is essential that stocks are managed efficiently so that such investments do not become unnecessarily large. A firm should determine its optimum level of investment in stocks, and to do this two conflicting requirements must be met. First, it must ensure that stocks are sufficient to meet the requirements of production and sales; and second it must avoid holding surplus stocks which are unnecessary and which increase the risk of obsolescence. The optimal stock level lies somewhere between these two extremes. Our objective in this chapter is to examine the application of quantitative models for determining the optimum investment in stocks. We shall also consider the economic order quantity and the level at which stocks should be replenished. We shall concentrate here on manufacturing firms but the same basic analysis can also be applied to merchandizing companies and non-profit organizations.

Why do firms hold stocks?

Amey and Egginton (1973) suggest three general reasons for holding stocks; the *transactions motive*, the *precautionary motive* and the *speculative motive*. The transactions motive occurs whenever there is a need to hold stocks to meet production and sales requirements, and it is not possible to meet these requirements instantaneously. A firm might also decide to hold additional amounts of stocks to cover the possibility that it may have underestimated its future production and sales requirements. This represents a *precautionary motive* which applies only when future demand is uncertain.

When it is expected that future input prices may change, a firm might maintain higher or lower stock levels to *speculate* on the expected increase or decrease in future prices. In general, quantitative models do not take into account this speculative motive. Nevertheless, management should be aware that optimum stock levels do depend to a certain extent on expected price movements. For example, if prices of input factors are expected to rise significantly, a firm should consider increasing its stocks to take advantage of a lower purchase price. However, this decision should be based on a comparison of future cost savings with the increased costs from holding additional stocks.

Where a firm is able to predict the demand for its inputs and outputs with perfect certainty and where it knows with certainty that the prices of inputs will remain constant for some reasonable length of time, it will have to consider only the transactions motive for holding stocks. To simplify the introduction to the use of models for determining the optimum investment in stocks we shall

begin by considering some quantitative models which incorporate only the transactions motive for holding stocks.

Relevant costs for quantitative models under conditions of certainty

The relevant costs for use in quantitative models normally consist of *holding* costs and *ordering* costs. *Holding costs* usually consist of the following:

opportunity cost of investment in stocks,
incremental insurance costs,
incremental warehouse and storage costs,
incremental material handling costs,
costs of obsolescence and deterioration of stocks.

The relevant holding costs for use in quantitative models should include only those items which will vary with the levels of stocks. Costs which will not be affected by changes in stock levels are not relevant costs. For example, in the case of warehousing and storage, only those costs should be included which will vary with changes in the number of units ordered. Salaries of storekeepers, depreciation of equipment and fixed rental of equipment and buildings are often irrelevant because they are unaffected by changes in stock levels. On the other hand, if storage space is owned and can be used for other productive purposes or be used to obtain rent income then the opportunity cost must be included in the analysis. Insurance costs should be included only when premiums are charged on the fluctuating value of stocks. A fixed annual insurance cost will not vary with different levels of stocks and is therefore not a relevant holding cost.

To the extent that funds are invested in stocks, there is an opportunity cost of holding them. This opportunity cost is reflected by the return which is lost from investing in stocks rather than some alternative investment. What required rate of return should we use to determine the lost return on funds which are invested in stocks? The answer is that the rate of return should be determined in the manner described in Chapter 14, with investments in stocks being treated as an asset to which capital is committed, as in any capital budgeting project (see Van Horne, 1983 for a discussion of this topic). In particular, the opportunity cost of capital should be applied only to those costs which

vary with the number of units purchased and which are incurred at the time the units are received (see Horngren, 1982). The relevant holding costs for other items such as material handling, obsolescence and deterioration are difficult to estimate but we shall see that these costs are unlikely to be critical to the investment decision. Normally holding costs are expressed as a percentage rate per pound of average investment.

Ordering costs usually consist of the clerical costs of preparing a purchase order, receiving deliveries and paying invoices. Ordering costs which are common to all stock decisions are not relevant and only the incremental costs of placing an order are used in formulating the quantitative models. In practice, it is extremely difficult to distinguish between variable and non-variable ordering costs but this problem can be resolved by developing a cost equation as described in Chapter 20 where the number of orders placed represents the independent variable.

The costs of acquiring stocks through buying or manufacturing are not a relevant cost to be included in the quantitative models as the acquisition costs remain unchanged irrespective of the order size or stock levels, unless quantity discounts are available. (We shall discuss the effect of quantity discounts later in this chapter.) For example, it does not matter in terms of acquisition cost whether total annual requirements of 1,000 units at £10 each are purchased in a 1,000 unit batch, ten 100 unit batches or one-hundred 10 unit batches; the acquisition cost of £10,000 will remain unchanged. The acquisition cost is not therefore a relevant cost, but the ordering and holding costs will change in relation to the order size and these *will* be relevant for decision-making models.

Determining the economic order quantity

If we assume certainty, the optimum order quantity will be determined by those costs which are affected by either the quantity of stocks held or the number of orders placed. If more units are ordered at one time, fewer orders will be required per year. This will mean a reduction in the ordering costs. However, when fewer orders are placed, larger average stocks must be maintained, which leads to an increase in holding costs. The problem is therefore one of trading off the costs of

carrying large stocks against the costs of placing more orders. The optimum order size is the order quantity which will result in the total amount of the ordering and holding costs being minimized. This optimum order size is known as the *economic order quantity* (EOQ); it can be determined by tabulating the total costs for various order quantities, by a graphical presentation or by using a formula. All three methods are illustrated with the aid of Example 21.1.

EXAMPLE 21.1

A company purchases a raw material from an outside supplier at a cost of £9 per unit. The total annual demand for this product is 40,000 units, and the following additional information is available.

Required annual return on investment in stocks (10% × £9)	£0.90
Other holding costs per unit	£0.10
Holding costs per unit	£1.00
Cost per purchase order:	
Clerical costs, stationery, postage, telephone etc.	£2.00

You are required to determine the optimal order quantity.

Tabulation method

The annual relevant costs for various order quantities are set out in Exhibit 21.1.

You will see that the economic order quantity is 400 units. At this point the total annual relevant costs are at a minimum.

Graphical method

The information tabulated in Exhibit 21.1 is presented in graphical form in Fig. 21.1 for every order size up to 800 units. The vertical axis represents the relevant annual costs for the investment in stocks, and the horizontal axis can be used to represent either the various order quantities or the average stock levels; two scales are actually shown on the horizontal axis so that both items can be incorporated. You will see from the graph that as the average stock level or the order quantity increases, the holding cost also increases. Alternatively, the ordering costs decline as stock levels and order quantities are increased. The total cost line represents the summation of both the holding and the ordering costs.

Note that the total cost line is at a minimum for an order quantity of 400 units and occurs at the point where the ordering cost and holding cost curves intersect. That is, the economic order quantity is found at the point where the holding costs equal the ordering costs. It is also interesting to note from the graph that the total relevant costs are not particularly sensitive to changes in the order quantity. For example, a 25% change in the order quantity from 400 units to either 300 or 500 units leads to an increase in annual costs from £400 to £410 or £416, an increase of 2.5% or 4%. Alternatively, an increase of 50% in the order quantity from 400 units to 600 units leads to an increase in annual costs from £400 to £434 or 8.5%.

Formula method

The economic order quantity can be found by

Exhibit 21.1 Relevant costs for various order quantities

Order quantity	100	200	300	400	500	600	800	10,000
Average stock in units (1)	50	100	150	200	250	300	400	5,000
Number of purchase orders (2)	400	200	133	100	80	67	50	4
Annual holding cost (3)	£50	£100	£150	£200	£250	£300	£400	£5,000
Annual ordering cost	£800	£400	£266	£200	£160	£134	£100	£ 8
Total relevant cost	£850	£500	£416	£400	£410	£434	£500	£5,008

Notes
(1) If there are no stocks when the order is received and the units received are used at a constant rate, the average stock will be one-half of the quantity ordered. Even if a minimum safety stock is held, the average stock relevant to the decision will still be one-half of the quantity ordered because the minimum stock will remain unchanged for each alternative order quantity.
(2) The number of purchase orders is ascertained by dividing the total annual demand of 40,000 units by the order quantity.
(3) The annual holding cost is ascertained by multiplying the average stock by the holding cost of £1 per unit.

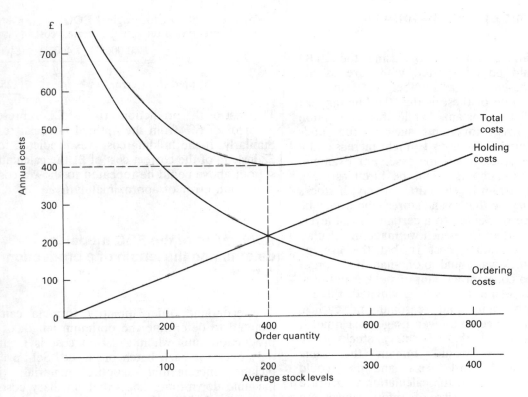

Fig. 21.1 Economic order quantity graph

applying a formula which incorporates the basic relationships between holding and ordering costs and order quantities. These relationships can be stated as follows: the number of orders for a period is the total demand for that item of stock for the period (represented by d) divided by the quantity ordered in units (represented by Q). The total ordering cost is obtained by multiplying the number of orders for a period by the ordering cost per order (represented by O). In formula terms the total ordering cost will be:

$$\frac{\text{Total demand for period}}{\text{Quantity ordered}} \times \text{Ordering cost per order} = \frac{DO}{Q}$$

Assuming that holding costs are constant per unit, the total holding cost for a period will be equal to the average stock for the period, which is represented by the quantity ordered divided by two (represented by Q/2) multiplied by the holding cost per unit (represented by H). In formula terms the total holding cost will be:

$$\frac{\text{Quantity ordered}}{2} \times \text{Holding cost per unit} = \frac{QH}{2}$$

The total relevant cost (TC) for any order quantity can now be expressed as follows:

$$TC = \frac{DO}{Q} + \frac{QH}{2}$$

We can determine a minimum for this total cost function by differentiating the above formula with respect to Q and setting the derivative equal to zero.[1] We then get the economic order quantity (Q):

$$Q = \sqrt{\frac{2DO}{H}}$$

or

$$Q = \sqrt{\frac{2 \times \text{Total demand for period} \times \text{Cost per order}}{\text{Holding cost per unit}}}$$

If we apply this formula to Example 21.1 we have:

$$Q = \sqrt{\frac{2 \times 40,000 \times 2}{1}}$$
$$= 400 \text{ units}$$

Assumptions of the EOQ formula

The calculations obtained by using the EOQ model should be interpreted with care as the model is based on a number of important assumptions; one of these is that the holding cost per unit will be constant. While this assumption might be correct for items such as the funds invested in stocks, other costs might increase on a step basis as stock levels increase. For example, additional storekeepers might be hired as stock levels reach certain levels. Alternatively, if stocks decline, it may be that casual stores labour may be released once stocks fall to a certain critical level.

Another assumption which we made in calculating the total holding cost is that the average balance in stock was equal to one-half of the order quantity. If a constant amount of stock is not used per day, this assumption will be violated; there is a distinct possibility that seasonal and cyclical factors will produce an uneven usage over time. It was also assumed that if safety stocks were maintained, they would remain the same irrespective of the order size, and they could therefore be ignored in the calculation of average stock. However, the size of safety stocks are probably not independent of order quantity as relatively larger safety stocks are likely to be associated with smaller order quantities.

Effect of approximations

Despite the fact that much of the data used in the model represents rough approximations, calculation of the EOQ is still likely to be useful. If you examine Fig. 21.1 you will see that the total cost curve tends to flatten out so that total costs may be affected very little if the underlying assumptions are violated or the costs are incorrectly estimated. For example, assume that the cost per order in Example 21.1 was predicted to be £4 instead of the correct cost of, say, £2. The cost of this error would be as follows:

$$\text{Revised EOQ} = \sqrt{\frac{2DO}{H}} = \sqrt{\frac{2 \times 40,000 \times 4}{1}} = 565$$

Total relevant cost for revised EOQ $= \dfrac{DO}{Q} + \dfrac{QH}{2}$
but using the correct ordering cost

$$= \frac{40,000(2)}{565} + \frac{565(1)}{2} = £425$$

Total relevant cost for original EOQ of 400 units based on actual ordering cost

$$= \frac{40,000(2)}{400} + \frac{400(1)}{2} = \frac{£400}{}$$

Cost of prediction error \qquad £25

The cost of the prediction error of £25 represents an error of 6% from the optimal financial result. Similarly, if the holding cost was predicted to be £2 instead of the correct cost of £1 the calculations set out above could be repeated to show a cost of prediction error of approximately 6%.

Application of the EOQ model in determining the length of a production run

The economic order quantity formula can be adapted to determine the optimum length of the production runs when a set-up cost is incurred only once for each batch produced. Set-up costs include incremental labour, material, jigs, machine down-time, and other ancillary costs of setting up facilities for production. The objective is to find the optimum number of units which should be manufactured in each production run and this involves balancing set-up costs against stock holding costs. To apply the EOQ formula to a production run problem we merely substitute set-up costs for the production runs in place of the purchase ordering costs.

To illustrate the formula let us assume that the annual sales demand (D) for a product is 9,000 units. Labour and other expenditure in making adjustments in preparation for a production run require a set-up cost (S) of £90. The holding cost is £2 per unit per year. The EOQ model can be used for determining how many units should be scheduled for each production run to secure the lowest annual cost. The EOQ formula is modified in terms of symbols to reflect the circumstances; the symbol O (ordering costs) is replaced by the symbol S (set-up costs). Using the formula

$$Q = \sqrt{\frac{2DS}{H}}$$

$$= \sqrt{\frac{2 \times 9,000 \times 90}{2}}$$

$$= \quad 900$$

With an annual demand of 9,000 units and an optimum production run of 900 units, 10 production runs will be required throughout the year. If we assume there are 250 working days throughout the course of the year, this will mean that production runs are undertaken at 25 day intervals. If demand is uniform throughout the year 36 units will be demanded per working day (that is, 9,000 units annual demand divided by 250 working days). To determine the point when the production run should be started we need to ascertain the number of days which are required for a production run. Let us assume it is five days. So during this period 180 units (five days at 36 units per day) will be demanded before any of the production run is available to meet demand. If we assume that no safety stock is required, we can establish that a production run should be started when the stock level reaches 180 units. This situation should occur 25 days after the start of the previous production run. The process is illustrated in Fig. 21.2.

Quantity discounts

Circumstances frequently occur where firms are able to obtain quantity discounts for large pur-chase orders. Because the price paid per unit will not be the same for different order sizes this must be taken into account when the economic order quantity is determined. However, the basic EOQ formula can still be used as a starting point for determining the optimum quantity to order. Buying in larger consignments to take advantage of quantity discounts will lead to the following savings:

(1) A saving in purchase price, which consists of the total amount of discount for the period.
(2) A reduction in the total ordering cost because fewer orders are placed to take advantage of the discounts.

These cost savings must, however, be balanced against the increased holding cost which arises from higher stock levels when larger quantities are purchased. To determine whether or not a discount is worthwhile, the benefits must be compared with the additional holding costs (see Example 21.2).

EXAMPLE 21.2

A company purchases a raw material from an outside supplier at a cost of £7 per unit. The total annual demand for this product is 9,000 units. The holding

Assumptions: EOQ = 900 units; length of production run = 5 days;
point where production run started = 180 units;
usage per day = 36 units; length of production run = 5 days
Production run started on days 20, 45, 70, 95 etc.

Fig. 21.2 EOQ model and length of production run

cost is £4 per unit and the ordering cost is £5 per order. A quantity discount of 3% of the purchase price is available for orders in excess of 1,000 units. Should the company order in batches of 1,000 units and take advantage of quantity discounts?

The starting point to determine this is to calculate the economic order quantity and then to decide whether the benefits exceed the costs if the company moves from the EOQ point and purchases larger quantities to obtain the discounts. The procedure would be as follows:

$$EOQ = \sqrt{\frac{2 \times 9,000 \times 5}{4}} = 150 \text{ units}$$

The savings available to the firm if it purchases in batches of 1,000 units instead of batches of 150 units are:

(1) Saving in purchase price = £1,890
 (3% of annual purchase cost of
 £63,000)
(2) Saving in ordering cost
 $\dfrac{DO}{Q^d} - \dfrac{DO}{Q} = \dfrac{9,000(5)}{1,000} - \dfrac{9,000(5)}{150}$ = £ 255
 (Note that Q^d represents the quantity
 ordered to obtain the discount and Q
 represents EOQ)

 Total savings $\underline{£2,145}$

The additional holding cost if the larger quantity is purchased is calculated as follows:

$$\frac{(Q^d - Q)H}{2} = \frac{(1,000 - 150)4}{2} = £1,700$$

The additional savings of £2,145 exceed the additional costs, and the firm should adopt the order quantity of 1,000 units. If larger discounts are available, for example, purchasing in batches of 2,000 units, a similar analysis should be applied which compares the savings from purchasing in batches of 2,000 units against purchasing in batches of 1,000 units. The amount of the savings should then be compared with the additional holding costs. Note that the EOQ formula serves as a starting point for balancing the savings against the costs of a change in order size.

Determining when to place the order

To determine the point at which the order should be placed to obtain additional stocks (that is, the *reorder point*) we must ascertain the time which will elapse between placing the order and actual delivery of the stocks. This time period is referred to as the *lead time*. In a world of certainty the reorder point will be the number of days/weeks lead time multiplied by the daily/weekly usage during the period. For materials, components and supplies the reorder point is the point in time when the purchase requisition is initiated, and the order is sent to the supplier. For the finished goods stock of a manufacturer the reorder point is the level of finished goods stock at which the production order should be issued.

If we assume that an annual usage of a raw material is 6,000 units, and the weekly usage is constant, then if there are 50 working weeks in a year the weekly usage will be 120 units. If the lead time is two weeks the order should be placed when stocks fall to 240 units. The economic order quantity can indicate how frequently the stocks should be purchased. For example, if the EOQ is 600 units then, with an annual demand of 6,000 units, ten orders will be placed during a year. On the basis of 50 working weeks an order will be placed every five weeks. However, with a lead time of two weeks the firm will place an order three weeks after the first delivery when the stock will have fallen to 240 units (600 units EOQ less three weeks usage at 120 units per week). The order will then be repeated at five-weekly intervals. The EOQ model therefore also gives us a *rule for deciding when to replenish stocks and the amount to replenish*. This process is illustrated in Fig. 21.3A.

Uncertainty and safety stocks

In practice, demand or usage of stocks is not known with certainty. In addition there is usually a degree of uncertainty associated with the placement of an order and delivery of the stocks. To protect itself from conditions of uncertainty a firm will maintain a level of *safety stocks* for raw materials, work in progress and finished goods stocks. Thus safety stocks are the amount of stocks which are carried in excess of the expected use during the lead time to provide a cushion against running out of stocks. For example, a firm which sets its reorder point on the assumption that the average lead time will be two weeks with an average weekly usage of 120 units will reorder

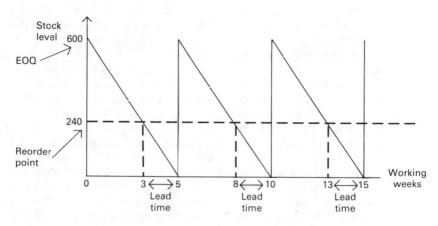

Part A: Demand known with certainty

Assumption:
EOQ = 600 units; Lead time = 2 weeks; Usage per week = 120 units;
Reorder point 240 units; Order placed at end of weeks 3,8,13 etc

Part B: Demand not known with certainty and role of safety stocks

Fig. 21.3 Behaviour of stocks under conditions of
certainty and uncertainty

when stocks fall to 240 units. However, the firm will run out of stock if actual demand increases to 140 units per week or if the lead time is three weeks. A firm might respond to this possibility by setting a reorder point of 420 units based on a *maximum usage* of 140 units per week and a lead time of three weeks. This will consist of a reorder point based on *expected* usage and lead time of 240 units (two weeks at 120 units) plus the balance of 180 units *safety stocks* to cover the possibility that lead time and expected usage will be greater than expected. Thus when demand and lead time

are uncertain *the reorder point is computed by adding the safety stock to the average usage during the average lead time*.

In this illustration the safety stock was calculated on the basis of maximum demand and delivery time. It may well be that the probability of both these events occurring at the same time is extremely low. Under such circumstances the managers of the company are adopting a very risk-averse approach and taking no chances of running out of stock. Maintaining high safety stocks may not be in the company's best interests if the cost of

holding the excessive stocks exceeds the costs that will be incurred if the company runs out of stock. It is therefore desirable to establish a sound quantitative procedure for determining an acceptable level of safety stocks. The level should be set where the cost of a stockout plus the cost of holding the safety stocks are minimized.

Stockout costs are the opportunity costs of running out of stock. In the case of finished goods the opportunity cost will consist of a loss of contribution if customers take their business elsewhere because orders cannot be met when requested. In the case of regular customers who are permanently lost because of a failure to meet delivery, this will be the discounted value of the lost contribution on future sales. When a stockout occurs for raw materials and work in progress stocks, the cost of being out of stock is a stoppage in production and the resulting inefficiencies which occur. This may be reflected by an estimate of the labour cost of idle time assuming that sales are *not* lost because of the stockout. Clearly, stockout costs are very difficult to estimate and there are strong arguments for applying sensitivity tests to any analysis which uses estimated stockout costs. In practice, the lost contribution resulting from failure to meet demand may provide a reasonable approximation.

Once the stockout costs have been estimated the costs of holding safety stocks should be compared for various demand levels. However, it is preferable to attach probabilities to different potential demand levels and to decide on the appropriate quantity of safety stocks by comparing the *expected cost values* or probability distributions for various levels of safety stocks. Let us now illustrate this process.

The use of probability theory for determining safety stocks

By constructing probability distributions for future demand and lead time it is possible to calculate the expected values for various safety stock levels. Suppose, for example, the total usage for an item of stock over a two-week lead time is expected to be as follows:

Usage in units	60	120	180	240	300	360	420
Probability	0.07	0.08	0.20	0.30	0.20	0.08	0.07

The average usage during the two-week lead time is 240 units and it is assumed that the lead time is known with certainty. If the firm carries no safety stock, the reorder level will be set at 240 units (that is, average usage during the lead time) and there will be no stockouts if actual usage is 240 units or less. However, if usage during the lead time period proves to be 300 units instead of 240 units there will be a stockout of 60 units, and the probability of this occurring is 0.20. Alternatively, if usage is 360 or 420 units there will be stockouts of 120 units and 180 units respectively. By maintaining a safety stock of 180 units the firm ensures that a stockout will *not* occur.

Assuming we estimate stockout costs of £5 per unit and a holding cost of £1 per unit for the period, we can calculate the expected stockout cost, holding cost and total cost for various levels of safety stock. This information is presented in Exhibit 21.2.

A safety stock of 60 units represents the level at which total expected costs are at their lowest. Hence a reorder point of 300 units will be set consisting of the average usage during the lead time of 240 units plus a safety stock of 60 units.

A reorder point of 300 units with an uncertain demand is illustrated in Fig. 21.3B for a demand of 240, 300 and over 300 units during the lead time period. Note that the declines in stock do not fall on a straight line when demand is uncertain. If the probability distributions for each two weekly period are expected to remain unchanged throughout the year, this safety stock should be maintained. However, if demand is expected to vary throughout the year the calculations presented in Exhibit 21.2 must be repeated for the probability distributions for each period in which the probability distribution changes. The safety stock should then be adjusted prior to the commencement of each period.

In Exhibit 21.2 it was assumed that the lead time was known with certainty, but that demand was uncertain. In practice, both the lead time and demand are likely to be uncertain. In this situation the analysis becomes more complex but the expected value method may still be applied. However, a decision tree will be required to determine the various combinations of delivery times and demand. A discussion of decision trees was presented in Chapter 12. The expected costs for various levels of safety stocks based on various combinations of lead time and demand can then be ascertained, and the safety stock which results

Exhibit 21.2 Expected costs for various safety stocks

Average usage (units)	Safety stock (units)	Reorder point (units)	Stockout (units)	Stockout cost (£5 per unit) £	Probability	Expected stockout cost £	Holding cost (1) £	Total expected cost £
240	180	420	0	0	0	0	180	180
240	120	360	60	300	0.07	21	120	141
240	60	300	120	600	0.07	42		
			60	300	0.08	24		
						66	60	126
240	0	240	180	900	0.07	63		
			120	600	0.08	48		
			60	300	0.20	60		
						171	0	171

Note
(1) To simplify the analysis it is assumed that a safety stock is maintained throughout the period. The average safety stock will therefore be equal to the total of the safety stock.

in the lowest expected total cost should be adopted. When estimates of demand and lead times vary over a wide range and the probability distributions include a larger number of possible events, it may be extremely difficult to construct a decision tree because of the large number of possible observations. The problem can be resolved, however, by the use of Monte Carlo simulation analysis using random numbers to represent the cumulative probability distributions for demand and lead time.[2] For an illustration of simulation applied to determining stock levels see Flower (1973).

Because of the difficulty in estimating the cost of a stockout some firms might prefer not to use quantitative methods to determine the level of safety stocks. Instead, they might specify a maximum probability of running out of stock. If the firm in our illustration does not wish the probability of a stockout to exceed 10%, it will maintain a safety stock of 120 units and maintain a reorder point of 360 units. A stockout will then occur only if demand is in excess of 360 units; the probability of such an occurrence is 7%.

Control of stocks through classification

In large firms it is quite possible for tens of thousands of different items to be stored. It is

clearly impossible to apply the techniques outlined in this chapter to all of these items. It is therefore essential that stocks are classified into categories of importance so that a firm can apply the most elaborate procedures of controlling stocks only to the most important items. The commonest procedure is known as the ABC classification method. This is illustrated in Exhibit 21.3. The ABC method requires that an estimate is made of the total purchase cost for each item of stock for the period. The sales forecast is the basis which is used for estimating the quantities of each item of stock to be purchased during the period. Each item is then grouped in decreasing order of annual purchase cost. The top 10% of items in stock in terms of annual purchase cost are categorized as A items, the next 20% are categorized as B items and the final 70% are categorized as C items. If we assume there are 10,000 stock items then the top 1,000 items in terms of annual purchase costs will be classified as A items, and so on. In practice, it will be unnecessary to estimate the value of many of the 7,000 C items as their annual purchase cost will be so small it will be obvious that they will fall into the C category.

You will see from Exhibit 21.3 that 10% of all stock items (that is, the A items) represent 73% of the total cost, 20% of the items (B items) represent 19% of the total cost and 70% of the items (C items) represent 8% of the total cost. It follows that the greatest degree of control should be exerted over the A items which account for the

Exhibit 21.3 ABC classification of stocks

Stage 1. For each item in stock multiply the estimated average usage for a period by the estimated unit price to obtain the total purchase cost:

Item	Estimated usage	Unit price £	Total purchase cost £
1	60,000	1.00	60,000
2	20,000	0.05	1,000
3	1,000	0.10	100
4	10,000	0.02	200
5	100,000	0.01	1,000
6	80,000	2.00	160,000

(This list is continued until all items in stock are included.)

Stage 2. Group all the above items in descending order of purchase price and then divide into class A (top 10%), class B (next 20%) and then class C (bottom 70%). The analysis might be as follows:

	Number of items in stock		Total cost	
	No.	%	Amount	%
Class A	1,000	10	£730,000	73
Class B	2,000	20	190,000	19
Class C	7,000	70	80,000	8
	10,000	100	1,000,000	100

high investment costs and it is the A category items which are most appropriate for the application of the quantitative techniques which we have discussed in this chapter. For these items an attempt should be made to maintain low safety stocks consistent with avoiding high stockout costs. Larger orders and safety stocks are likely to be a feature of the C category items. Normally, reorder points for these items will be determined on a subjective basis rather than using quantitative methods, the objective being to minimize the expense in controlling these items. The control of B category items is likely to be based on quantitative methods but they are unlikely to be as sophisticated as for the A category items.

The percentage value of total cost for the A, B and C categories in Exhibit 21.3 is typical of most manufacturing companies. In practice, it is normal for between 10 and 15% of the items in stock to account for between 70 and 80% of the total value of purchases. At the other extreme, between 70 and 80% of the items in stock account for approximately 10% of the total value. The control of stock levels is eased considerably if it is

concentrated on that small proportion of stock items which account for most of the total cost.

Other considerations

Shortage of future supplies

For various reasons a firm may depart from quantitative models which provide estimates of the economic order quantity and the reorder point. A company may not always be able to rely on future supplies being available if the major suppliers are in danger of experiencing a strike. Alternatively, future supplies may be restricted because of import problems or transportation difficulties. In anticipation of such circumstances a firm may over-order so that stocks on hand will be sufficient to meet production while future supplies are restricted.

Future price increases

When a supplier announces a price increase which will be effective at some future date, it may be in a firm's interest to buy in excess of its immediate requirements before the increase becomes effective. Indeed, in times of rapid inflation firms might have an incentive to maintain larger stocks than would otherwise be necessary.

Obsolescence

Certain types of stocks are subject to obsolescence. For example, a change in technology may make a particular component worthless. Alternatively, a change in fashion may cause a clothes retailer to sell stocks at considerably reduced prices. Where the probability of obsolescence is high or goods are of a perishable nature, frequent purchases of small quantities and the maintenance of low stocks may be appropriate even when the EOQ formula may suggest purchasing larger quantities and maintaining higher stock levels.

Steps to reduce safety stocks

When demand is uncertain, higher safety stocks are likely to be maintained. However, safety

stocks may be reduced if the purchasing depart-
ment can find new suppliers who will promise
quicker and more reliable delivery. Alternatively,
pressure may be placed on existing suppliers for
faster delivery. The lower the average delivery
time, the lower will be the safety stock which a
firm needs to hold and the total investment in
stocks will be reduced.

Performance reporting

Formal performance reports may not record all
the relevant costs which are used in the decision
models for calculating the economic order
quantity or optimum stock levels. In Chapter 19
we noted that a manager is likely to concentrate
only on those variables which are measured and
ignore other important variables which are not
measured. Indeed, a manager is likely to take
action which will improve his performance rating,
as indicated on the performance report, even if
this is not always in the best interests of the
company. For example, if annual holding costs are
not allocated in a performance report to each
manager, a manager may be induced to obtain
larger order sizes even though this may not be the
correct policy for the company as a whole. This
may occur when a production manager engages in

longer, but less frequent production runs, as this is
likely to reduce the total annual costs which are
charged to him, although larger stocks (with large
holding costs) will be required to meet demand
between the production runs.

This type of situation can be avoided by
charging holding costs to the appropriate
manager. One way of doing this is to charge an
imputed interest charge on the stocks for which a
manager is responsible. (See the answer to
question 21.8 in the *Students' Manual* to this book
for an illustration.)

Advanced quantitative models

With the increasing use of computers it is now
possible to use more advanced quantitative
models for determining optimum stock levels. A
review of these models is beyond the scope of this
book, but the models presented in this chapter
provide an appropriate framework for approx-
imating the optimum level of stocks, indicating
how much should be ordered and when. However,
such models normally require some elaboration to
overcome the complex stock control problems
which are encountered in practice. For a descrip-
tion of the more advanced models see Starr and
Miller (1961).

Summary

The objective of stock control models is to determine the order quantity which minimizes the cost of
holding stocks. The costs of maintaining stocks consist of ordering costs and holding costs. Ordering
costs decline and holding costs increase when the order quantity is increased. The economic order
quantity is at the point where ordering costs are equal to holding costs. This point can be derived by the
EOQ formula. This formula can also be used to determine the optimum length of a production run, and it
can be used as the starting point for determining whether a firm should increase the order quantity so as
to take advantage of quantity discounts.

When uncertainty of demand and lead times are incorporated into the analysis firms must hold safety
stocks to cover the possibility that demand and lead time may be different from that used in the EOQ
formula. Safety stocks should be determined using probability analysis.

In practice, approximately 20% of the total quantity of stocks may account for about 80% of its value.
This principle is known as Pareto analysis, and is based on observations by Pareto (1848–1923) that a
very small proportion of items usually accounts for the majroity of value. By concentrating on the small
proportion of stock items which jointly account for 80% of the total value, a firm may well be able to
control most of its monetary investment in stocks.

References and further reading

Amey, L.R. and Egginton, D.A. *Management Accounting — A Conceptual Approach*. Longman, 1973, Chapter 19.

Amey, L.R. and Egginton, D.A. Stock control models. In Arnold, J., Carsberg, B. and Scapens, R. (Eds), *Topics in Management Accounting*. Philip Allan, 1980.

Beranek, W. Financial implications of lot-size inventory models. *Management Science* 13(8), April 1967, B401-B408; also in Smith, K.V. *Management of Working Capital*. South Western Publishing Company, 1974.

Biddle, G.C. Accounting methods and management decision: The case of inventory costing and inventory policy. *Journal of Accounting Research Studies on Economic Consequences of Financial and Managerial Accounting* 1981, 235-78.

Bierman, E., Bonini, C.P. and Hausman, W.H. *Quantitative Analysis for Business Decisions* 5th edn. Irwin, 1977, Chapters 17–19.

Brown, R.G. *Statistical Forecasting for Inventory Control*. McGraw Hill, 1959.

Firth, M.A. *The Management of Working Capital*. Macmillan, 1976.

Flower, J. *Computer Models for Accountants*. Haymarket, 1973, Chapters 4, 5.

Gregory, G. and Piper, J. A study of the raw material reorder decisions in small batch manufacturing companies. In Cooper, D., Scapens, R. and Arnold J. (Eds), *Management Accounting Research and Practice*. Institute of Cost and Management Accountants, 1983.

Horngren, C.T. *Cost Accounting: A Managerial Emphasis*. Prentice-Hall, 1982, p. 762.

Jagetia, L.C. Inventory control as simple as ABC. *Management Accounting (UK) September 1976*, 305-6.

Khoury, N.T. The optimum level of safety stocks. In Smith, K.V. *Management of Working Capital*. West Publishing Company, 1974.

La Londe, B.J. and Lambert, D.M. Calculating inventory carrying costs. *International Journal of Physical Distribution (UK)* No. 4/77, 195-232.

Magee, J.F. Guides to inventory policy. *Harvard Business Review* January–February 1956, 103-16 and May–June 1956, 57-70.

Morse, W. and Scheiner, J. Cost minimisation, return on investment, residual income: Alternative criteria for inventory models. *Accounting and Business Research* Autumn 1979, 320-24.

Smith, K.V. *Guide to Working Capital Management*. McGraw Hill, 1979, Chapter 6.

Snyder, A. Principles of inventory management. *Financial Executive Col. 32* No. 4, April 1964, 13-21; also in Smith, K.V. *Management of Working Capital*. West Publishing Company, 1974.

Starr, M.K. and Miller, D.W. *Inventory Control: Theory and Practice*. Prentice-Hall, 1962.

Van Horne, J.C. *Financial Management and Policy*. Prentice-Hall, 1983, p. 426.

Problems

*Indicates that a suggested solution is to be found in the *Students' Manual*.

21.1 (a) Explain what is meant by the term 'economic order quantity'. Your explanation should be supported by a sketch or graph, which need not be on graph paper.

(b) Using the information stated below, you are required to prepare a schedule showing the associated costs if 1, 2, 3, 4, 5 or 6 orders were placed during a year for a single product.

From your schedule, state the number of orders to be placed each year and the economic order quantity.

Annual usage of product	600 units
Unit cost of product	£2.4
Cost of placing an order	£6.0
Stock holding cost as a percentage of average stock value	20%

(c) Comment briefly on three problems met in determining the economic order quantity.

(20 marks)
ICMA Cost Accounting 1
November 1978

21.2* A large local government authority places orders for various stationery items at quarterly intervals.

In respect of an item of stock coded A32, data are:

annual usage 5,000 boxes
minimum order quantity 500 boxes
cost per box £2

Usage of material is on a regular basis and, on average, half of the amount purchased is held in inventory. The cost of storage is considered to be 25% of the inventory value. The average cost of placing an order is estimated at £12.5.

The chief executive of the authority has asked you to review the present situation and to consider possible ways of effecting cost savings.

You are required to:
(a) tabulate the costs of storage and ordering item A32 for each level of orders from four to twelve placed per year;
(b) ascertain from the tabulation the number of orders which should be placed in a year to minimize these costs;
(c) produce a formula to calculate the order

level which would minimize these costs — your formula should explain each constituent part of the formula and their relationships;
(d) give an example of the use of the formula to confirm the calculation in (b) above;
(e) calculate the percentage saving on the annual cost which could be made by using the economic order quantity system;
(f) suggest *two* other approaches which could be introduced in order to reduce the present cost of storage and ordering of stationery.

(25 marks)
ICMA Cost Accounting 2
November 1983

21.3* XYZ Ltd produces a product which has a constant monthly demand of 4,000 units. The product requires a component which XYZ Ltd purchases from a supplier at £10 per unit. The component requires a three day lead time from the date of order to the date of delivery. The ordering cost is £0.60 per order and the holding cost is 10% per annum.
(a) You are required to calculate:
 (i) the economic order quantity,
 (ii) the number of orders required per year,
 (iii) the total cost of ordering and holding the components for the year.
(b) Assuming that there is no safety stock and that the present stock level is 400 components, when should the next order be placed (assume a 360 day year)?
(c) Discuss the problems which most firms would have in attempting to apply the EOQ formula.

21.4 Sandy Lands Ltd carries an item of inventory in respect of which the following data apply:

the fixed cost of ordering per batch is £10
the expected steady quarterly volume of sales

Usage (in units)	1800	1900	2000	2100	2200	2300	2400	2500
Probability	0.06	0.14	0.30	0.16	0.13	0.10	0.07	0.04

is 3,125 units
the cost of holding one unit in stock for one year is £1

You are required to:
(i) calculate the minimum annual cost of ordering and stocking the item (4 marks),
(ii) calculate to the nearest whole number of units the optimal batch size if the expected steady quarterly volume of sales
 first falls to 781 units
 and *second* rises to 6,250 units
 and to state the relationship between the rates of change of sales and the optimal batch size (4 marks).

(iii) explain the basis of the derivation of the formula for the optimal batch size which is given in the table of formulas (4 marks).
ICAEW Management Accounting
July 1979

21.5* A company uses 50,000 units of material per annum to service a steady demand for its products. Order costs are £100 per order and holding costs are £0.40 per unit.
(a) Determine the optimal order quantity.
(b) The supplier now offers a quantity discount of £0.02 per unit if it buys in batches of 10,000 units. Should the company take advantage of the quantity discount?

21.6 A company is considering the possibility of purchasing from a supplier a component it now makes. The supplier will provide the components in the necessary quantities at a unit price of £9. Transportation and storage costs would be negligible.
 The company produces the component from a single raw material in economic lots of 2,000 units at a cost of £2 per unit. Average annual demand is 20,000 units. The annual holding cost is £0.25 per unit and the minimum stock level is set at 400 units. Direct labour costs for the component are £6 per unit, fixed manufacturing overhead is charged at a rate of £3 per unit based on a normal activity of 20,000 units. The company also hires the machine on which the components are produced at a rate of £200 per month.
 Should the company make the component?

21.7* A company has determined that the EOQ for its only raw material is 2,000 units every thirty days. The company knows with certainty that a four day lead time is required for ordering. The following is the probability distribution of estimated usage of the raw material for the month:

Stockouts will cost the company £10 per unit, and the average monthly holding cost is £1 per unit.
(a) Determine the optimal safety stock.
(b) What is the probability of being out of stock?

21.8* The annual demand for an item of raw material is 4,000 units and the purchase price is expected to be £90 per unit. The incremental cost of processing an order is £135 and the cost of storage is estimated to be £12 per unit.
(a) What is the optimal order quantity and the total relevant cost of this order quantity?

(b) Suppose that the £135 estimate of the incremental cost of processing an order is incorrect and should have been £80. Assume that all other estimates are correct. What is the cost of this prediction error assuming that the solution to part (a) is implemented for one year?

(c) Assume at the start of the period a supplier offers 4,000 units at a price of £86. The materials will be delivered immediately and placed in the stores. Assume that the incremental cost of placing this order is zero and the original estimate of £135 for placing an order for the economic batch size is correct. Should the order be accepted?

(d) Present a performance report for the purchasing officer assuming that the budget was based on the information presented in (a) and the purchasing officer accepted the special order outlined in (c).

21.9 Mr Evans is a wholesaler who buys and sells a wide range of products, one of which is the Laker. Mr Evans sells 24,000 units of the Laker each year at a unit price of £20. Sales of the Laker normally follow an even pattern throughout the year but to protect himself against possible deviations Mr Evans keeps a minimum stock of 1,000 units. Further supplies of the Laker are ordered whenever the stock falls to this minimum level and the time lag between ordering and delivery is small enough to be ignored.

At present, Mr Evans buys all his supplies of Lakers from May Ltd, and usually purchases them in batches of 5,000 units. His most recent invoice from May Ltd was as follows:

	£
Basic price: 5,000 Lakers at £15 per unit	75,000
Delivery charge: Transport at 50p per unit	2,500
Fixed shipment charge per order	1,000
	78,500

In addition, Mr Evans estimates that each order he places costs him £500, comprising administrative costs and the cost of sample checks. This cost does not vary with the size of the order.

Mr Evans stores Lakers in a warehouse which he rents on a long lease for £5 per square foot per annum. Warehouse space available exceeds current requirements and, as the lease cannot be cancelled, spare capacity is sub-let on annual contracts at £4 per square foot per annum. Each

unit of Laker in stock requires 2 square feet of space. Mr Evans estimates that other holding costs amount to £10 per Laker per annum.

Mr Evans has recently learnt that another supplier of Lakers, Richardson Ltd, is willing, unlike May Ltd, to offer discounts on large orders. Richardson Ltd sells Lakers at the following prices:

Order size	price per unit £
1–2,999	15.25
3,000–4,999	14.50
5,000 and over	14.25

In other respects (i.e. delivery charges and the time between ordering and delivery) Richardson Ltd's terms are identical to those of May Ltd.

You are required to:

(a) calculate the optimal re-order quantity for Lakers and the associated annual profit Mr Evans can expect from their purchase and sale, assuming that he continues to buy from May Ltd (10 marks),

(b) prepare calculations to show whether Mr Evans should buy Lakers from Richardson Ltd rather than from May Ltd and, if so, in what batch sizes (8 marks), and

(c) explain the limitations of the methods of analysis you have used (7 marks).

Ignore taxation.

(25 marks)

ICAEW Elements of Financial Decisions July 1981

21.10* Pink Ltd is experiencing some slight problems concerning two stock items sold by the company.

The first of these items is product Exe which is manufactured by Pink. The annual demand for Exe of 4,000 units, which is evenly spread throughout the year, is usually met by production taking place four times per year in batches of 1,000 units. One of the raw material inputs to product Exe is product Dee which is also manufactured by Pink. Product Dee is the firm's major product and is produced in large quantities throughout the year. Production capacity is sufficient to meet in full *all* demands for the production of Dees.

The standard costs of products Exe and Dee are:

Standard costs, per unit

	Product	
	Exe	Dee
	£	£
Raw materials — purchased from external suppliers	13	8
Dee standard cost	22	—
Labour — unskilled	7	4
skilled	9	5
Variable overheads	5	3
Fixed overheads	4	2
Standard cost	£60	£22

Included in the fixed overheads for Exe are the set up costs for each production run. The costs of each set up, which apply irrespective of the size of the production run, are:

Costs per set up

	£
(i) Labour costs — skilled labour	66
(ii) Machine parts	70
Total	£136

The 'machine parts' relate to the cost of parts required for modifications carried out to the machine on which Exe is produced. The parts can be used for only one run, irrespective of run length, and are destroyed by replacement on re-instatement of the machine. There are no set up costs associated with Dee. The cost of financing stocks of Exe is 15% p.a. Each unit of Exe in stock requires 0.40 square metres of storage space and units *cannot* be stacked on top of each other to reduce costs. Warehouse rent is £20 p.a. per square metre and Pink is only required to pay for storage space actually used.

Pink is not working to full capacity and idle time payments are being made to all grades of labour except unskilled workers. Unskilled labour is not guaranteed a minimum weekly wage and is paid only for work carried out.

The second stock item causing concern is product Wye. Product Wye is purchased by Pink for resale and the 10,000 unit annual demand is again spread evenly throughout the year. Incremental ordering costs are £100 per order and the normal unit cost is £20. However, the suppliers of Wye are now offering quantity discounts for large orders. The details of these are:

Quantity ordered	Unit price £
Up to 999	20.00
1,000 to 1,999	19.80
2,000 and over	19.60

The purchasing manager feels that full advantage should be taken of discounts and purchases should be made at £19.60 per unit using orders for 2,000 units or more. Holding costs for Wye are calculated at £8.00 per unit per year and this figure will not be altered by any change in the purchase price per unit.

Required:

(a) Show the optimum batch size for the production of Exes. If this differs from the present policy, calculate the annual savings to be made by Pink Ltd from pursuing the optimal policy. Briefly explain the figures incorporated in your calculations. (The time taken to carry out a production run may be ignored.) (10 marks)

(b) Advise Pink Ltd on the correct size of order for the purchase of Wyes. (6 marks)

(c) Briefly describe two major limitations, or difficulties inherent in the practical application, of the model used in (a) to determine the optimum batch size. (4 marks)

(20 marks)

ACCA P2 Management Accounting
June 1981

21.11* B Ltd, a young, fast-growing company, is planning to develop a new factory. The managing director of the company has discussed various aspects of the plan with functional heads and has now asked you, as management accountant, to provide him with a report on certain aspects of inventory control. He is interested particularly in the contribution which the following could make to a raw materials stock control system.

(a) ABC inventory analysis;

(b) setting of stock levels;

(c) economic order quantity.

Prepare a report to your managing director, discussing briefly the important points of each of the above. (20 marks)

ICMA Cost Accounting 2
November 1979

21.12* Explain briefly the rationale behind economic order quantity (EOQ) models and discuss the extent to which the principles on which they are based can be used by a management accountant to help an organization to decide the most appropriate levels of service that it should offer its customers. (20 marks)

ICMA P3 Management Accounting
May 1980

22 The application of linear programming to management accounting

In the previous chapters we have seen that there is an opportunity cost for scarce resources which should be included in the relevant cost calculation for decision-making and variance calculations in a standard costing system. Our previous discussions, however, have assumed that output is limited by one scarce resource but in practice several resources may be scarce. The opportunity costs of these scarce resources can be determined by the use of linear programming techniques. Our objective in this chapter is to examine linear programming techniques and to consider how they can be applied to some specific types of decisions which a firm may have to make.

Single resource constraints

In Chapter 10 we considered how accounting information should be used to ensure that scarce resources are efficiently allocated. We established that where a scarce resource exists, which has alternative uses, the contribution per unit should be calculated for each of these uses. The available capacity for this resource is then allocated to the alternative uses on the basis of contribution per scarce resource. A typical problem is presented in Exhibit 22.1.

Exhibit 22.1 A single resource constraint problem

LP Ltd is a manufacturing company which currently produces two products. The standards per unit of product are as follows:

Product Y	£	£	Product Z	£	£
Standard selling price		38	Standard selling price		42
Less:			Less:		
Standard cost:	£		Standard cost:	£	
Materials			Materials		
8 units @ £1	8		4 units @ £1	4	
Labour			Labour		
6 hours @ £2	12		8 hours @ £2	16	
Variable overhead			Variable overhead		
4 machine hours @ £1	4	24	6 machine hours @ £1	6	26
Contribution		14	Contribution		16

During the next accounting period it is expected that the availability of labour hours will be restricted to 2,880 hours. The remaining production inputs are not scarce but the marketing manager estimates that the maximum sales potential for product Y is 420 units. There is no sales limitation for product Z.

If we follow the procedure which was suggested in Chapter 10 we can ascertain the contribution per unit of the scarce resource. Product Y yields a contribution of £14 and uses 6 scarce labour hours. This is a contribution of £2.33 per labour hour. Similarly, the contribution per labour hour for product Z is £2. The company should therefore allocate scarce labour hours to the manufacture of product Y. Sales of product Y, however, are limited to 420 units which means that 2,520 labour hours (420 units at 6 hours per unit) will be used. The remaining 360 hours will then be allocated to product Z. As one unit of product Z requires 8 labour hours, the total output of product Z will be 45 units.

Profits will be maximized when the firm manufactures 420 units of product Y and 45 units of product Z. This will give a total contribution of £6,600, which is calculated as follows:

420 units of Y at a contribution of £14 per unit = £5,880
45 units of Z at a contribution of £16 per unit = £ 720
‾‾‾‾‾‾
£6,600

Two resource constraints

Where more than one scarce resource exists the optimum production programme cannot easily be established by the process previously outlined. Consider the situation in Exhibit 22.1 where there is an additional scarce resource besides labour. Let us assume that both products Y and Z use a common item of material and that the supply of this material in the next accounting period is restricted to 3,440 units. There are now two scarce resources — labour and materials. If we apply the procedure outlined above the contributions per unit of scarce resource would be as follows:

	Product Y	Product Z
Labour	£2.33	£2.00
Material	£1.75 (£14/8)	£4.00 (£16/4)

This analysis shows that product Y yields the largest contribution per labour hour, and product Z yields the largest contribution per unit of scarce

materials, but there is no clear indication of how the quantity of scarce resources should be allocated to each product. In such circumstances there is a need to resort to higher powered mathematical techniques to establish the optimal output programme.

Linear programming

Linear programming is a powerful mathematical technique which can be applied to the problem of rationing limited facilities and resources among many alternative uses in such a way that the optimum benefit can be derived from their utilization. It seeks to find a feasible combination of output which will maximize or minimize the *objective function*. The objective function refers to the quantification of an objective and usually takes the form of maximizing profits or minimizing costs. Linear programming may be used when relationships can be assumed to be linear and where an optimal solution does in fact exist.

To comply with the linearity assumption it must be assumed that the contribution per unit for each product and the utilization of resources per unit are the same whatever quantity of output is produced and sold within the output range being considered. It must also be assumed that units produced and resources allocated are infinitely divisible. This means that an optimal plan which suggests we should produce 94.38 units is possible. However, it will be necessary to interpret the plan as a production of 94 units.

Let us now apply this technique to the problem outlined in Exhibit 22.1 where there is a labour restriction plus a limitation on the availability of materials and machine hours. The revised problem is presented in Exhibit 22.2.

The procedure which we should follow to solve this problem is, first, to formulate the problem algebraically with Y representing the number of units of product Y, and Z representing the number of units of product Z which are manufactured by the company. Second, we must specify the objective function, which in this example is to maximize contribution, followed by the input constraints. We can now formulate the linear programming model as follows:

Maximize $C = 14Y + 16Z$ (that is, maximize total contribution) subject to
$8Y + 4Z \leqslant 3,440$ (material constraint)

Exhibit 22.2 Multiple resource constraint

LP Ltd is a manufacturing company which currently makes two products. The standards per unit of product are as follows:

Product Y		£	Product Z		£
Standard selling price		38	Standard selling price		42
Less:			Less:		
Standard cost:	£		Standard cost:	£	
Materials			Materials		
8 units @ £1	8		4 units @ £1	4	
Labour			Labour		
6 hours @ £2	12		8 hours @ £2	16	
Variable overhead			Variable overhead		
4 machine hours @ £1	4	24	6 machine hours @ £1	6	26
Contribution		14	Contribution		16

During the next accounting period the availability of resources are expected to be subject to the following limitations:

Labour	2,880 hours
Materials	3,440 units
Machine capacity	2,760 hours

The marketing manager estimates that the maximum sales potential of product Y is limited to 420 units. There is no sales limitation for product Z. You are asked to advise how these limited facilities and resources can best be used so as to gain the optimum benefit from them.

$$6Y + 8Z \leq 2,880 \text{ (labour constraint)}$$
$$4Y + 6Z \leq 2,760 \text{ (machine capacity constraint)}$$
$$0 \leq Y \leq 420 \text{ (maximum sales limitation)}$$
$$Z \geq 0 \text{ (minimum sales limitation)}$$

In this model, 'maximize C' indicates that we wish to maximize contribution with an unknown number of units of Y produced, each yielding a contribution of £14 per unit, and an unknown number of units of Z produced, each yielding a contribution of £16. The labour constraint indicates that 6 hours of labour are required for each unit of product Y which is made, and 8 hours for each unit of product Z. Thus, (6 hours × Y) + (8 hours × Z) cannot exceed 2,880 hours. Similar reasoning applies to the other inputs and the model also indicates that sales of product Y cannot be less than zero or greater than 420.

Because linear programming is nothing more than a mathematical tool for solving constrained optimization problems, nothing in the technique itself ensures that an answer will 'make sense'. For example, in a production problem, for some very unprofitable product, the optimal output level may be a negative quantity, which is clearly an impossible solution. To prevent such nonsensical results, we must include a non-negative requirement, which is a statement that all variables in the problem must be equal to or greater than zero.

We must therefore add to the model in our example the constraint that Y and Z must be greater than zero, that is, $Z \geq 0$ and $0 \leq Y \leq 420$.

The model can be solved graphically, or by the Simplex method. When not more than two products are manufactured, the graphical method can be used, but it becomes impracticable where *more* than two products are involved, and it is necessary then to resort to the Simplex method.

Graphical method

Taking the first constraint for the *materials* input $8Y + 4Z \leq 3,440$ means that we can make a maximum of 860 units of product Z when production of product Y is zero. The 860 units is arrived at by dividing the 3,440 units of materials by the four units of material which are required for each unit of product Z. Alternatively, a maximum of 430 units of product Y can be made (3,440 units divided by eight units of materials) if no materials are allocated to product Z. We can therefore state:

When Y = 0, Z = 860
When Z = 0, Y = 430

These items are plotted in Fig. 22.1 with a straight line running from Z = 0, Y = 430 to Y = 0, Z = 860. Note that the vertical axis represents the

Fig. 22.1 Constraint imposed by limitations of materials

number of units of Y produced and the horizontal axis represents the number of units of Z produced.

The area to the left of the line $8Y + 4Z \leq 3{,}440$ contains all possible solutions for Y and Z in this particular situation, and any point along the line which connects these two outputs represents the maximum combination of Y and Z which can be produced with not more than 3,440 units of materials. Every point to the right of the line violates the material constraint.

The *labour constraint* $6Y + 8Z \leq 2{,}880$ indicates that if production of product Z is zero, a maximum of 480 units of product Y can be produced (2,880/6), and if the output of Y is zero 360 units of Z (2,880/8) can be produced. We can now draw a second line Y = 480, Z = 0 to Y = 0, Z = 360 and this is illustrated in Fig. 22.2. The area to the left of line $6Y + 8Z \leq 2{,}880$ in Fig.

22.2 represents all the possible solutions which will meet the labour constraint.

The *machine input constraint* is represented by Z = 0, Y = 690 and Y = 0, Z = 460 and the line indicating this constraint is illustrated in Fig. 22.3. The area to the left of line $4Y + 6Z \leq 2{,}760$ in Fig. 22.3 represents all the possible solutions which will meet the machine capacity constraint.

The final constraint is that the *sales output* of product Y cannot exceed 420 units. This is represented by the line Y ≤ 420 in Fig. 22.4 and all the items below this line represent all the possible solutions which will meet this sales limitation.

It is clear that any solution which is to fit all the constraints must occur in the area ABCDE in Fig. 22.5 which represents Figs 22.1 to 22.4 combined together. The point must now be found within the area ABCDE where the contribution (C) is the

Fig. 22.3 Constraint imposed by machine capacity

Fig. 22.2 Constraint imposed by limitation of labour

Fig. 22.4 Constraint imposed by sales limitation of product Y

greatest. The maximum will occur at one of the corner points ABCDE. The objective function is C = 14Y + 16Z and a random value is chosen which will result in a line for the objective function falling within the area ABCDE.

If we assume that the total contribution is equal to £2,240, this could be obtained from producing 160 units of Y at £14 contribution per units or 140 units of Z at a contribution of £16 per unit. We can therefore draw a line Z = 0, Y = 160 to Y = 0, Z = 140 and this is represented by the dashed line in Fig. 22.5. Each point on the dashed line represents all the output combinations of Z and Y which will yield a total contribution of £2,240. The dashed line is extended to the right until it touches the last corner of the boundary ABCDE. This is the optimal solution and is at point C which indicates an output of 400 units of Y (contribution £5,600) and 60 units of Z (contribution £960), giving a total contribution of £6,560.

The logic in the previous paragraph is illustrated in Fig. 22.6. The shaded area represents the feasible production area ABCDE which is outlined in Fig. 22.5, and parallel lines represent possible contributions which take on higher values as we move to the right. If we assume that the firm's objective is to maximize total contribution, it should operate on the highest contribution curve obtainable. At the same time, it is necessary to satisfy the production constraints which are indicated by the shaded area in Fig. 22.6. You will see that point C indicates the solution to the problem as no other point within the feasible area touches

Quantity of Y produced

Fig. 22.6 Solution to the problem

such a high contribution line.

Simplex method

Where more than two products can be manufactured using the scarce resources available, the optimum solution cannot easily be established from the graphical method. An alternative is a non-graphical solution known as the Simplex method. This method also provides additional information on opportunity costs and marginal rates of substitution which is particularly useful for decision-making, and also for planning and control.

The Simplex method involves making many tedious calculations, but there are in existence standard computer programs which will complete the task within a few minutes. The aim of this chapter is not therefore to delve into these tedious calculations but to provide an understanding of their nature and their implications for management accounting. Nevertheless, to provide a basic understanding of the method the procedure for completing the calculations must be outlined, and we shall do this by applying the procedure to the problem set out in Exhibit 22.2.

To apply the Simplex method we must first formulate a model which does not include any inequalities. This is done by introducing what are called *slack variables* to the model. Slack variables are added to a linear programming problem to account for any constraint which is unused at the point of optimality, and one slack variable is introduced for each constraint. In our example, LP Ltd is faced with constraints on materials, labour, machine capacity and maximum sales for

Quantity of Y produced

Fig. 22.5 Combination of Figs 22.1 to 22.4

product Y. Therefore, S_1 is introduced to represent unused material resources, S_2 represents unused labour hours, S_3 represents unused machine capacity and S_4 represents unused potential sales output. We can now express the model for Exhibit 22.2 in terms of equalities:

Maximize $C = 14Y + 16Z$
subject to the following constraints:
$8Y + 4Z + S_1 = 3,440$ (materials constraint)
$6Y + 8Z + S_2 = 2,880$ (labour constraint)
$4Y + 6Z + S_3 = 2,760$ (machine capacity constraint)
$1Y + S_4 \quad = \quad 420$ (sales constraint for product Y)

For labour (6 hours × Y) + (8 hours × Z) plus any unused labour hours (S_2) will equal 2,880 hours when the optimum solution is reached. Similar reasoning applies to the other production constraints. The sales limitation indicates that the number of units of Y sold plus any shortfall on maximum demand will equal 420 units. We shall now express all the above equations in matrix form with the slack variables on the left-hand side:

First matrix

Quantity	Y	Z		
$S_1 = 3,440$	−8	−4	(1)	(materials constraint)
$S_2 = 2,880$	−6	−8	(2)	(labour constraint)
$S_3 = 2,760$	−4	−6	(3)	(machine hours constraint)
$S_4 = \quad 420$	−1	0	(4)	(sales constraint)
$C = 0$	+14	+16	(5)	

Note that the quantity column in the matrix indicates the resources available or the slack which is not taken up when production is zero. For example, the S_1 row of the matrix indicates that 3,440 units of materials are available when production is zero. Column Y indicates that 8 units of materials, 6 labour hours and 4 machine hours are required to produce 1 unit of product Y, and this will reduce the potential sales of Y by 1. You will also see from column Y that the production of 1 unit of Y will yield £14 contribution. Similar reasoning applies to column Z. Note that the entry in the contribution row (that is, C row) for the quantity column is zero because this first matrix is based on nil production, which gives a contribution of zero.

Choosing the product

The next stage is to examine the matrix to determine which product we should choose. As product Z yields the highest contribution we

should choose this, but our production is limited because of the input constraints. Materials limit us to a maximum production of 860 units (3,440 units ÷ 4 per unit), labour to a maximum production of 360 units (2,880 hours ÷ 8 per hour) and machine capacity to a maximum production of 460 units (2,760 hours ÷ 6 per hour). We are therefore restricted to a maximum production of 360 units of product Z because of a labour constraint. The procedure which we should follow is to *rearrange the equation which results in the constraint (that is S_2) in terms of the product we have chosen to make (that is, product Z)*.

\therefore Equation (2) which is $S_2 = 2,880 − 6Y − 8Z$
becomes $8Z = 2,880 − 6Y − S_2$
$\therefore Z = \quad 360 − \tfrac{3}{4}Y − \tfrac{1}{8}S_2$

We now substitute this value for Z into each of the other equations which appear in the first matrix. The calculations are as follows:

$$S_1 = 3,440 − 8Y − 4 (360 − \tfrac{3}{4}Y − \tfrac{1}{8}S_2) \qquad (1)$$
$$= 3,440 − 8Y − 1,440 + 3Y + \tfrac{1}{2}S_2$$
$$= 2,000 − 5Y + \tfrac{1}{2}S_2$$

$$S_3 = 2,760 − 4Y − 6 \quad (360 − \tfrac{3}{4}Y − \tfrac{1}{8}S_2) \qquad (3)$$
$$= 2,760 − 4Y − 2,160 + 4\tfrac{1}{2}Y + \tfrac{3}{4}S_2$$
$$= \quad 600 + \tfrac{1}{2}Y + \tfrac{3}{4}S_2$$

$$C = \quad 0 + 14Y + 16 (360 − \tfrac{3}{4}Y − \tfrac{1}{8}S_2) \qquad (5)$$
$$= \quad 0 + 14Y + 5,760 − 12Y − 2S_2$$
$$= 5,760 + 2Y − 2S_2$$

Note that equation (4) in the first matrix remains unchanged because Z is not included. We can now restate the revised five equations in a second matrix:

Second matrix

Quantity	Y	S_2		
$S_1 = 2,000$	−5	$+\tfrac{1}{2}$	(1)	(materials constraint)
$Z = \quad 360$	$−\tfrac{3}{4}$	$−\tfrac{1}{8}$	(2)	
$S_3 = \quad 600$	$+\tfrac{1}{2}$	$+\tfrac{3}{4}$	(3)	(machine hours constraint)
$S_4 = \quad 420$	−1	0	(4)	(sales constraint)
$C = 5,760$	+2	−2	(5)	

The substitution process outlined for the second matrix has become more complex but the logical basis still remains. For example, *the quantity column of the second matrix indicates that 2,000 units of material are unused, 360 units of Z are to be made, 600 machine hours are still unused and sales of product Y can still be increased by another 420 units before the sales limitation is reached. The contribution row indicates that a contribution of £5,760 will be obtained from the production and sale of 360 units of product Z. Column Y indicates that production of 1 unit of

product Y uses up 5 units of the stock of materials, but, because no labour hours are available, $\frac{3}{4}$ units of product Z must be released. This will release three units of materials ($\frac{3}{4} \times 4$), 6 labour hours ($\frac{3}{4} \times 8$ hours) and $4\frac{1}{2}$ machine hours ($\frac{3}{4} \times 6$). From this substitution process we now have 8 units of materials (5 units + 3 units), 6 labour hours and $4\frac{1}{2}$ machine hours.[1]

From the standard cost details in Exhibit 22.2 you can see that one unit of Y requires 8 units of materials, 6 labour hours and 4 machine hours. This substitution process thus provides the necessary resources for producing 1 unit of product Y as well as providing an additional half hour of machine capacity. This is because production of 1 unit of product Y requires that production of item Z is reduced by $\frac{3}{4}$ units which releases $4\frac{1}{2}$ machine hours. However, product Y only requires 4 machine hours, so production of 1 unit of Y will increase the available machine capacity by half an hour. This agrees with the entry in column Y of the second matrix for machine capacity. Column Y also indicates that production of 1 unit of Y reduces the potential sales of product Y (S_4) by 1 unit.

The optimum solution is achieved when the contribution row contains only negative or zero values. Because row C contains a positive item, our current solution can be improved by choosing the product with the highest positive contribution. Thus we should choose to manufacture product Y, as this is the only positive item in the contribution row. The second matrix indicates that the contribution can be increased by £2 by substituting 1 unit of Y for $\frac{3}{4}$ units of Z. We therefore obtain an additional contribution of £14 from Y but lose a £12 contribution from Z ($\frac{3}{4} \times 16$) by this substitution process. The overall result is an increased contribution of £2 by adopting this substitution process.

The procedure is then repeated to formulate the third matrix. Column Y of the second matrix indicates that we should use 5 units of materials and release $\frac{3}{4}$ units of Z to obtain an additional unit of Y, but there are limitations in adopting this plan. The unused materials are 2,000 units, and each unit of Y will require 5 units, giving a maximum production of 400 units of Y. We have 360 units of Z allocated to production, and each unit of Y requires us to release $\frac{3}{4}$ units of Z. A maximum production of 480 units of Y ($360 \div \frac{3}{4}$) can therefore be obtained from this substitution process. There is no limitation on machine hours, as the second matrix indicates that the substitution

process increases machine hours by half an hour for each unit of Y produced. The sales limitation of Y indicates that a maximum of 420 units of Y can be produced. The following is a summary of the limitations in producing product Y:

S_1 (materials) = 400 units ($2,000 \div 5$)
Z (substitution of product Z) = 480 units
($360 \div \frac{3}{4}$)
S_4 (max. sales of Y) = 420 units ($420 \div 1$)

In other words, we merely divide the negative items in column Y into the quantity column. The first limitation we reach is 400 units and this will be the maximum production of Y because of the impact of the materials constraint. The procedure which we applied in formulating the second matrix is then repeated; that is, we rearrange the equation which results in the constraint (S_1) in terms of the product we have chosen to make (that is, product Y):

\therefore Equation (1) which is $S_1 = 2,000 - 5Y + \frac{1}{2}S_2$
becomes $5Y = 2,000 - S_1 + \frac{1}{2}S_2$
$\therefore Y = \underline{400 - \frac{1}{5}S_1 + \frac{1}{10}S_2}$

Substituting for Y in each of the other equations in the second matrix we get in the following revised equations:

$$Z = 360 - \frac{3}{4}(400 - \frac{1}{5}S_1 + \frac{1}{10}S_2) - \frac{1}{8}S_2 \quad (2)$$
$$= 360 - 300 + \frac{3}{20}S_1 - \frac{3}{40}S_2 - \frac{1}{8}S_2$$
$$= \underline{60 + \frac{3}{20}S_1 - \frac{1}{5}S_2}$$

$$S_3 = 600 + \frac{1}{2}(400 - \frac{1}{5}S_1 + \frac{1}{10}S_2) + \frac{3}{4}S_2 \quad (3)$$
$$= 600 + 200 - \frac{1}{10}S_1 + \frac{1}{20}S_2 + \frac{3}{4}S_2$$
$$= \underline{800 - \frac{1}{10}S_1 + \frac{4}{5}S_2}$$

$$S_4 = 420 - 1(400 - \frac{1}{5}S_1 + \frac{1}{10}S_2) \quad (4)$$
$$= \underline{20 + \frac{1}{5}S_1 - \frac{1}{10}S_2}$$

$$C = 5,760 + 2(400 - \frac{1}{5}S_1 + \frac{1}{10}S_2) - 2S_2 \quad (5)$$
$$= 5,760 + 800 - \frac{2}{5}S_1 + \frac{1}{5}S_2 - 2S_2$$
$$= \underline{6,560 - \frac{2}{5}S_1 - 1\frac{4}{5}S_2}$$

We now restate the revised five equations in a third marix.

Third matrix

	Quantity	S_1	S_2	
Y =	400	$-\frac{1}{5}$	$+\frac{1}{10}$	(1)
Z =	60	$+3/20$	$-\frac{1}{5}$	(2)
S_3 =	800	$-\frac{1}{10}$	$+\frac{4}{5}$	(3)
S_4 =	20	$+\frac{1}{5}$	$-\frac{1}{10}$	(4)
C =	6,560	$-\frac{2}{5}$	$-1\frac{4}{5}$	(5)

The contribution row (equation 5) contains only negative items which signifies that the optimal

solution has been reached. The quantity column for any products listed on the left-hand side of the matrix indicates the number of units of the product which should be manufactured when the optimum solution is reached. 400 units of Y and 60 units of Z should therefore be produced, giving a total contribution of £6,560. This agrees with the results we obtained using the graphical method. *When an equation appears for a slack variable, this indicates that unused resources exist.* The third matrix therefore indicates that the optimal plan will result in 800 unused machine hours (S_3) and an unused sales potential of 20 units for product Y (S_4). The fact that there is no equation for S_1 and S_2 means that these are the inputs which are fully utilized and which limit further increases in output and profit.

Interpreting the final matrix

The S_1 column (materials) of the third matrix indicates that the materials are fully utilized. (Whenever *resources* appear as column headings in the final matrix this indicates that they are fully utilized.) So to obtain a unit of materials, the column for S_1 indicates that we must increase production of product Z by 3/20 of a unit and decrease production of product Y by 1/5 of a unit. The effect of removing one scarce unit of material from the production process is summarized in Exhibit 22.3.

Let us focus on the machine capacity column of Exhibit 22.3. If we increase production of product Z by 3/20 of a unit then more machine hours will be required, leading to the available capacity being reduced by 9/10 of an hour. Each unit of product Z requires six machine hours, so 3/20 of a unit will require 9/10 of an hour (3/20 × 6). Decreasing production of product Y by 1/5 unit will release 4/5 of a machine hour, given that 1 unit of product Y requires 4 machine hours. The

overall effect of this process is to reduce the available machine capacity by 1/10 of a machine hour. Similar principles apply to the other calculations which are presented in Exhibit 22.3.

Let us now reconcile the information set out in Exhibit 22.3 with the materials column (S_1) of the third matrix. The S_1 column indicates that to release 1 unit of materials from the optimum production programme we should increase the output of product Z by 3/20, and decrease product Y by 1/5 of a unit. This substitution process will lead to the unused machine capacity being reduced by 1/10 of a machine hour, an increase in the unfulfilled sales demand of product Y (S_4) by 1/5 of a unit and a reduction in contribution of £$^2/_5$. All this information is obtained from column S_1 of the third matrix, and Exhibit 22.3 provides the proof. Note that Exhibit 22.3 also proves that the substitution process which is required to obtain an additional unit of materials releases exactly 1 unit. In addition, Exhibit 22.3 indicates that the substitution process for labour gives a net effect of zero, and so no entries appear in the S_1 column of the third matrix in respect of the labour row (that is, S_2).

Opportunity cost

The contribution row of the final matrix contains some vital information for the accountant. The figures in this row represent opportunity costs for the scarce factors of materials and labour. For example, the reduction in contribution from the loss of 1 unit of materials is £2/5 (40 p) and from the loss of one labour hour is £$1^4/_5$ (£1.80). Our earlier studies have indicated that this information is vital for decision-making, and we shall use this information again shortly to establish the relevant costs of the resources.

The proof of the opportunity costs can be found in Exhibit 22.3. From the contribution column we

Exhibit 22.3 The effect of removing 1 unit of material from the optimum production programme

	S_3 Machine capacity	S_4 Sales of Y	S_1 Materials	S_2 Labour	Contribution (£)
Increase product Z by 3/20 of a unit	$-^9/_{10}(^3/_{20} \times 6)$	–	$-^3/_5(^3/_{20} \times 4)$	$-1^1/_5(^3/_{20} \times 8)$	$+2^2/_5(^3/_{20} \times 16)$
Decrease product Y by 1/5 of a unit	$+^4/_5(^1/_5 \times 4)$	$+^1/_5$	$+1^3/_5(^1/_5 \times 8)$	$+1^1/_5(^1/_5 \times 6)$	$-2^4/_5(^1/_5 \times 14)$
Net effect	$-^1/_{10}$	$+^1/_5$	$+1$	Nil	$-^2/_5$

can see that the loss of one unit of materials leads to a loss of contribution of 40 p.

Substitution process when additional resources are obtained

Management may be able to act to remove a constraint which is imposed by the shortage of a scarce resource. For example, LP Ltd might obtain substitute materials or they may purchase the materials from an overseas supplier. A situation may therefore occur where resources additional to those included in the model used to derive the optimum solution are available. In such circumstances the marginal rates of substitution specified in the final matrix can indicate the optimum use of the *additional* resources. However, when additional resources are available it is necessary to *reverse the signs* in the final matrix. Can you see why this should be so? The reason is that the removal of one unit of materials from the optimum production programme requires that product Z be increased by 3/20 of a unit and product Y be decreased by 1/5 of a unit. If we then decide to return released materials to the optimum production programme we must reverse this process, that is increase product Y by 1/5 of a unit and reduce product Z by 3/20 of a unit. The important point to remember is that when considering the response to obtaining *additional resources* over and above those specified in the initial model *the signs of all the items in the final matrix must be reversed*.

We can now establish how we should best use an additional unit of scarce materials. Inspection of the third matrix indicates that product Y should be increased by 1/5 of a unit and product Z reduced by 3/20 giving an additional contribution of £0.40.

Note that this process will lead to an increase in machine hours of 1/10 hour (S_3) and a decrease in potential sales of product Y by 1/5 (S_4). Similarly, if we were to obtain an additional labour hour we should increase production of Z by 1/5 of a unit and decrease production of product Y by 1/10 of a unit which would yield an additional contribution of £1.80. These are the most efficient uses which can be obtained from additional labour and material resources. From a practical point of view, decisions will not involve the use of fractions, for example LP Ltd might be able to obtain 200 additional labour hours; the final matrix indicates

that optimal production should be altered by increasing production of product Z by 40 units ($200 \times 1/5$ of a unit) and decreasing production of product Y by 20 units. This process will lead to machine capacity being reduced by 160 hours and potential sales of product Y being increased by 20 units.

Uses of linear programming

Calculation of relevant costs

The calculation of relevant costs is essential for decision-making. When a resource is scarce alternative uses exist which provide a contribution. An opportunity cost is therefore incurred whenever the resource is used. The relevant cost for a scarce resource is calculated as

Acquisition cost of resource + opportunity cost

When more than one scarce resource exists the opportunity cost should be established by using linear programming techniques. Let us now calculate the relevant costs for the resources used by LP Ltd. The costs are as follows:

Materials = £1.40 (£1 acquisition cost plus 40 p opportunity cost)
Labour = £3.80 (£2 acquisition cost plus £1.80 opportunity cost)
Variable overheads = £1.00 (£1 acquisition cost plus zero opportunity cost)
Fixed overheads = Nil

Because variable overheads are assumed to vary in proportion to machine hours, and as machine hours are not scarce, no opportunity costs arise for variable overheads. Fixed overheads have not been included in the model since they do not vary with changes in activity. The relevant cost for fixed overheads is therefore zero.

Introduction of a new product

Let us now assume that the company is contemplating marketing a new product which requires 10 units of each input, and the market price is expected to be £50. Should this product be manufactured? Conventional accounting information does not provide us with the information necessary to make this decision. The new product

can be made only by restricting output of Y or Z because of the input constraints, and we need to know the opportunity costs of releasing the scarce resources to this new product. Opportunity costs were incorporated in our calculation of the relevant costs for each of the resources and so the relevant information for the decision is as follows:

		£
Selling price of new product		50
Less Relevant costs:		
Materials (10 × 1.40)	14	
Labour (10 × 3.80)	38	
Variable overhead (10 × 1.00)	10	
		62
Contribution		(−12)

The introduction of the new product will reduce the total contribution by £12 for each item produced.

Maximum payment for additional scarce resources

Opportunity costs provide important information in situations where a company can obtain additional scarce resources, but only at a premium. How much should the company be prepared to pay? For example, the company may be able to remove the labour constraint by paying overtime. The matrix indicates that the company can pay up to an additional £1.80 over and above the standard wage rate for each hour worked in excess of 2,880 hours and still obtain a contribution from the use of this labour hour. The total contribution will therefore be improved by any additional payment below £1.80 per hour. Similarly, LP Ltd will improve the total contribution by paying up to 40 p in excess of the standard material cost for units obtained in excess of 3,440 units. Hence the company will increase short-term profits by paying up to £3.80 for each additional labour hour in excess of 2,880 hours and up to £1.40 for units of material which are acquired in excess of 3,440 units.

Control

Opportunity costs are also important for cost control. In Chapter 18 we saw that standard costing could be improved by incorporating opportunity costs into the variance calculations. For example, material wastage is reflected in an adverse material usage variance. The responsibility centre should therefore be identified not only with the acquisition cost of £1 per unit, but also with the opportunity cost of 40 p from the loss of one scarce unit of materials. This process highlights the true cost of the inefficient usage of scarce resources and encourages responsibility heads to pay special attention to the control of scarce factors of production.

Transfer pricing

Linear programming can be used to determine the correct transfer price when goods are transferred within the divisions of a company. However, we shall not discuss the application of linear programming to transfer pricing until we have considered the principles necessary for establishing a sound transfer pricing system as this would be inappropriate. Our discussion of how linear programming can be used in setting transfer prices will be deferred to Chapter 24.

Sensitivity analysis

Opportunity costs are of vital importance in making management decisions, but production constraints do not exist permanently and, therefore, opportunity costs cannot be regarded as permanent. There is a need to ascertain the range over which the opportunity cost applies for each input. This information can be obtained from the final matrix. For materials, we merely examine the negative items for column S_1 in the final matrix and divide each item into the quantity column as follows:

$$Y = 400 \div -\tfrac{1}{5} = -2,000$$
$$S_3 = 800 \div \tfrac{1}{10} = -8,000$$

The number closest to zero in this calculation (that is, 2,000) indicates by how much the availability of materials used in the model can be reduced. Given that the model was established using 3,440 units of materials, the lower limit of the range is 1,440 units (3,440 units − 2,000). The upper limit is determined in a similar way. We divide the positive items in column S_1 into the quantity column as follows:

$$Z = 60 \div \tfrac{3}{20} = 400$$
$$S_4 = 20 \div \tfrac{1}{5} = 100$$

The lower number in the calculation (that is, 100)

indicates by how much the materials can be increased. Adding this to the 3,440 units of materials indicates that the upper limit of the range is 3,540 units. The opporuunity cost and marginal rates of substitution for materials therefore apply over the range of 1,440 to 3,540 units.

Let us now consider the logic on which these calculations are based. The lower limit is determined by removing materials from the optimum production programme. We have previously established from the final matrix and Exhibit 22.3 that removing one unit of material from the optimum production programme means that product Y will be reduced by 1/5 and machine capacity will be reduced by 1/10 of an hour. Since the final matrix indicates an output of 400 units of product Y, this reduction can only be carried out 2,000 times (400 ÷ 1/5) before the process must stop. Similarly, 800 hours of machine capacity are still unused and the reduction process can only be carried out 8,000 times (800 ÷ 1/10) before the process must stop. Given the two constraints on reducing materials, the first constraint that is reached is the reduction of product Y. The planned stock of materials can therefore be reduced by 2,000 units before the substitution process must stop. The same reasoning applies (with the signs reversed) in understanding the principles for establishing the upper limit of the range.

Similar reasoning can be applied to establish that the opportunity cost and marginal rates of substitution apply for labour hours over a range of 2,680 to 3,880 hours. For any decisions based on scarce inputs outside the ranges specified a revised model must be formulated and a revised final matrix produced. From this matrix, revised opportunity costs and marginal rates of substitution can be established.

The use of linear programming in capital budgeting

In Chapter 14 we discussed capital rationing and identified this as being a situation where there is a budget ceiling or constraint on the amount of funds which can be invested during a specific period of time. In such a situation we should select the combination of investment proposals which provide the highest net present value, subject to the budget constraint for the period. In Chapter 14 we assumed that investment funds were restricted to one period only, but it was suggested that in practice more than a one period constraint must be considered. Where there is multi period capital rationing we should use linear programming techniquies to maximize the net present value. Let us consider the example set out in Exhibit 22.4 to illustrate the application of linear programming to capital rationing where there are budget constraints for three periods.[2]

We can formulate the linear programming model by representing each of the proejcts numbered 1 to 6 by X_j (where $j = 1 \ldots 6$); X_1 represents investment number 1, X_2 represents investment number 2, and so on. Our objective is to maximize the net present value subject to the

Exhibit 22.4 Multi-period capital rationing

Investment project	Present value of outlay in period 1 £000	Present value of outlay in period 2 £000	Present value of outlay in period 3 £000	Net present value of investment £000
1	12	3	5	14
2	54	10	4	30
3	6	6	6	17
4	6	2	5	15
5	30	35	10	40
6	6	10	4	6

The present value of the outlays for the budget constraints for each of periods 1 to 3 are as follows:

	£000
Period 1	35
Period 2	20
Period 3	20

You are required to formulate the linear programming model which will maximize net present value.

budget constraints for each of the three periods. The model is as follows:

Maximize $14X_1 + 30X_2 + 17X_3 + 15X_4 + 40X_5 + 6X_6$

subject to $12X_1 + 54X_2 + 6X_3 + 6X_4 + 30X_5 + 6X_6 + S_1 = 35$

(period 1 constraint)

$3X_1 + 10X_2 + 6X_3 + 2X_4 + 35X_5 + 10X_6 + S_2 = 20$

(period 2 constraint)

$5X_1 + 4X_2 + 6X_3 + 5X_4 + 10X_5 + 4X_6 + S_3 = 20$

(period 3 constraint)

$0 \leqslant X_j \leqslant 1, (X_j = 1 \ldots .6)$

The final term in the model indicates that X_j may take any value from zero to 1. This ensures that a project cannot be undertaken more than once but allows for a project to be partially accepted. The terms S_1, S_2 and S_3 represent the slack variables (that is, unused funds) for each of the three periods. It is assumed that the budgeted capital constraints are absolute and cannot be removed by project generated cash flows. (For an illustration of a model where capital constraints can be eased by project generated cash flows see the answer to question 22.10 in the accompanying *Students' Manual* to this book.) The solution to the problem is presented in Exhibit 22.5.

You can see from these figures that we should fully accept projects X_1, X_3 and X_4, 7% of project 2, 23.5% of project 5 and zero of project 6. Substituting these values into the equations for the objective function gives a net present value of £57.50 (in 000s).

The slack variables indicate the opportunity costs of the budget constraints for the various future periods. These variables indicate the present value that can be gained if a budget constraint is relaxed by £1. For example, the slack variable of £0.408 for period 1 indicates that the present value can be increased by £0.408 if the budget of funds available for investment in period 1 is increased by £1, while the slack variable of £0.792 indicates that present value can be increased by £0.792 if the budget is also increased by £1 in period 2. If the budget is increased by £1,000 in period 1, the present value will increase by £408.

The slack variables can also indicate how much it is worth paying over and above the market price of funds which are used in the net present value calculation for additional funds in each period. A further use of the opportunity costs is to help in appraising any investment projects which might be suggested as substitutes for projects 1 to 6. For example, assume that a new project whose cash inflows are all received in year 3 is expected to yield a net present value of £4 for an investment of £5 for each of years 1 and 2; this project should be rejected because the opportunity cost of the scarce funds will be £6 ($5 \times 0.408 + 5 \times 0.792$) and this is in excess of the net present value.

Note that in formulating the model we have assumed that the investment projects were divisible in the sense that a partial acceptance of an investment proposal was possible. In the optimal solution both projects 2 and 5 were fractional. However, in practice investment projects are unlikely to be divisible; acceptance will involve acceptance of the full amount of the investment and rejection will involve zero investment. To overcome this problem it is possible to use an integer programming model by requiring that X_j be an integer of either 0 or 1. This process excludes fractional investments. For an illustration of integer programming see Carsberg (1969a).

The model can also be modified to take account of mutually exclusive projects. For example, if projects 1, 3 and 6 are mutually exclusive, we can simply add the constraint $X_1 + X_3 + X_6 \leqslant 1$. When this constraint is used with integer programming we are assured that only one of these projects will appear in the final solution. Also, if project 2 is contingent upon the acceptance of project 1, the constraint $X_2 \leqslant X_1$ ensures that the contingency is recognized in the final solution.

The major problem with the application of linear programming to the capital budgeting process is that it is based on the assumption that future investment opportunities are known. However, management may be aware of future investment opportunities for the earliest years only. Budget constraints for later years are likely to be utilized only as new investment proposals are generated and they are unlikely to be binding. To overcome this problem the selection process must be revised continually. For a more detailed

Exhibit 22.5 Optimum values for multi-period capital rationing problem

$x_1 = 1.0$	$X_2 = 0.07$	$X_3 = 1.0$	$X_4 = 1.0$	$X_5 = 0.235$	$X_6 = 0.0$
$S_1 = 0.408$	$S_2 = 0.792$	$S_3 = 0.0$	Objective function = £57.50		

discussion of the application of linear programming to capital investment decisions see Weingartner (1963).

Practical problems in applying linear programming

In practice linear programming models are likely to be far more complex than the models which have been presented in this chapter. Practical linear programming models can be very large, having at least a few hundred constraints and variables. However, these models can be quickly solved using a computer. For an example of a linear programming model developed for BP Ltd see Deam, Bennett and Leather (1975).

A further problem with the application of linear programming is that the objective function assumes a constant contribution per unit of output regardless of the level of activity. The implications of this is that the selling price and the variable cost per unit remain constant. It is therefore assumed that a constant quantity of resources is used per unit for all levels of output and that there will be no savings in the usage of inputs per unit of output when producing large output levels or large batches instead of small ones. In practice labour may be more efficient when working on large production runs or savings may be made with long production runs because there is less starting and stopping of machines. Another assumption is that fixed costs remain the same at all levels of output from zero to the maximum shown in the optimum solution. In practice, fixed costs are likely to increase in steps; for example, an additional supervisor may be appointed to cope with an increased level of activity.

Dev (1980) states:

. . . where the data for a particular business problem involves non-linear relationships, a modified version of linear programming may yield assumptions which are sufficiently accurate for many purposes. For example, if the expected selling price is dependent on the volume sold, the total revenue function may be approximated by a number of linear segments of different slopes. Each segment may be represented by a linear equation and an algebraic expression obtained for the total revenue function for use in the linear programming model. In cases where such approximations are inappropriate, we may need to employ the techniques of non-linear programming.

For a discussion of mathematical programming where there are non-linear relationships see Carsberg (1975) and Baumol (1977).

In the linear programming models presented in this chapter it has been assumed that output and use of resources are perfectly divisible. For example, the marginal rates of substitution for input resources and the output of products included fractions. We can avoid this problem by using integer programming. Here suitable constraints are added to the linear programming model to permit acquisition of whole numbers of a resource or the production of a complete product. In addition integer programming can also handle step fixed costs. Most of the problems with applying linear programming stem from the linearity assumption, but note that a number of statistical studies suggest that, within a fairly wide relevant range, cost functions can be reasonably approximated by linear expressions (for examples see Johnston, 1972).

Application to other business problems

In this chapter we have illustrated the use of linear programming as a method of establishing the optimum output level which maximizes profit. However, for other business problems such as transport routeing, or choosing an appropriate production process, the objective function of the linear programming model will be to minimize costs. Alternatively, management may have an objective to achieve a number of goals concurrently. In this type of situation there is no single function to be optimized; instead we must attempt to achieve a series of goals simultaneously within specified constraints. The problem can be resolved by using a special kind of linear programming procedure known as goal programming. (For a discussion of goal programming see Salkin and Kornbluth, 1973.)

With goal programming, the decision-makers must either rank or weight the quantitatively expressed goals in terms of their subjective opinion of their relative importance. An objective function is then formulated which incorporates this ranking or weighting. For example, we could incorporate in the model that goal 1 is of overriding importance and must be satisfied as far as possible, irrespective of other goals included in

the model. Alternatively, it is possible to specify in the model that the profit goal is twice as important as a second goal.

Linear programming is not just a thoeretical tool; a number of firms have found it to be a useful technique for planning their activities. See Wooler and Grinyer (1975) and Moore and Hodges (1970) for evidence on the use of linear programming models. Furthermore, the reduction in the relative costs of computers has enabled the smaller firms to purchase sophisticated computer equipment. Software linear programming packages are also available which are extremely simple to operate and which can provide a solution within a few minutes. Consequently, there is a strong possibility that linear programming may be applied increasingly to business problems in the future.

Summary

When there is more than one scarce input factor, linear programming can be used to determine the production programme which maximizes total contribution. This information can be obtained by using either a graphical approach or the Simplex method. The graphical approach, however, is inappropriate where more than two products can be produced from the scarce inputs and in such a situation the Simplex method should be used. This latter method has the added advantage that it provides details of the opportunity costs and the marginal rates of substitutions for the scarce resources.

Linear programming can be applied to a variety of management accounting problems. In particular, the technique enables the relevant costs of production inputs to be computed. This information can be used for decision-making, standard costing variance analysis and the setting of transfer prices in divisionalized companies. It can also be applied to capital budgeting in multi-period capital rationing situations.

Linear programming has a number of limitations when applied to real world situations but some of these problems can be overcome by establishing more complex models and using integer progrmaming techniques.

References and further reading

Barron, M.J. Linear programming dual prices in management accounting. *Journal of Business Finance* Spring 1972, 51-70.

Baumol, W.J. *Economic Theory and Operation Analysis*. Prentice-Hall, 1977.

Bernhard, R.N. Some problems in applying mathematical programming to opportunity costing. *Journal of Accounting Research* 6(1), Spring 1968, 143-8.

Bhaskar, K.N. Borrowing and lending in a mathematical programming model of capital budgeting. *Journal of Business Finance and Accounting* 1(2), Summer 1974, 267-94.

Bhaskar, K.N. Linear programming and capital budgeting: A reappraisal. *Journal of Business Finance and Accounting* 3(3), Autumn 1976, 29-40.

Bhaskar, K.N. Linear programming and capital budgeting: The financing problem. *Journal of Business Finance and Accounting* 5(2), Summer 1978, 159-94.

Carsberg, B. *An Introduction to Mathematical Programming for Accountants*. Allen & Unwin, pp. 92-9.

Carsberg, B. On the linear programming approach to asset valuation. *Journal of Accounting Research* 7(2), Autumn 1969, 165-82.

Carsberg, B. *Economics of Business Decisions*. Penguin, 1975, pp. 187-202.

Deam, R.J., Bennett, J.W. and Leather, J. Firm: A computer model for financial planning. Institute of Chartered Accountants in England and Wales Research Committee Occasional Paper No. 5, 1975.

Dev. S, Linear programming dual prices in management accounting and their interpretation. *Accounting and Business Research* 9(33), Winter 1978, 11-18.

Dev, S. Linear programming and production planning. In Arnold, J., Carsberg, B. and Scapens, R. (Eds), *Topics in Management Accounting*. Philip Allan, 1980.

Drury, J.C. Linear programming for decision-making and control. *Accountancy* Part I, January 1979, 95-8; Part II, February 1979, 109-12.

Grinyer, P.H. and Wooller, J. *Corporate Models Today*. Institute of Chartered Accountants in England and Wales, 1975.

Hughes, J.S. and Lewellen, W.G. Programming solu-

tions to capital rationing problems. *Journal of Business Finance and Accounting* **1**(1), 55-74, Spring 1974.

Ijiri, Y., Levy, F.K. and Lyon, R.C. A linear programming model for budgeting and financial planning. *Journal of Accounting Research* **1**(2), Autumn 1963, 198-212.

Jensen, R.E. Sensitivity analysis and integer linear programming. *The Accounting Review* July 1968, 425-46.

Johnston, J. *Statistical Cost Analysis*. McGraw Hill, 1972.

Kaplan, R.S. *Advanced Management Accounting*. Prentice-Hall, 1983, Chapters 5, 8, 12, 13, 14.

Lin, W.T. Applications of goal programming to accounting. *Journal of Business Finance and Accounting* **6**(4), Winter 1979, 559-78.

Moores, P.G. and Hodges, S.D. *Programming for Optional Decisions*. Penguin, 1970.

Salkin, G. and Kornbluth, J. *Linear Programming in Financial Planning*. Prentice-Hall, 1973, Chapter 7.

Samuels, J.M. Opportunity costing: An application of mathematical programming. *Journal of Accounting Research* **3**(2), Autumn 1965, 182-91; also in Solomons, D. (Ed.),. *Studies in Cost Analysis*. Sweet & Maxwell, 1968.

Weingartner, H.M. *Mathematical Programming and the Analysis of Capital Budgeting Problems*. Prentice-Hall, 1963.

Problems

* Indicates that a suggested solution is to be found in the *Students' Manual*.

22.1 (A) Discuss the importance of key factors or limiting factors in an organization.

(B) E Ltd manufactures two products, K and L, the selling prices of which are £48 and £72 respectively. Standard cost data are as follows:

	Product K	Product L
Per article	£	£
Direct material	10	12
Direct wages, £4 per hour:		
Department: 1	8	12
2	4	8
3	12	–
4	–	16
Variable overhead	2	6
Per annum		
Fixed overhead £50,000		

E Ltd operates a 40-hour week for 50 weeks each year. Currently the employees in each department are:

Department: 1	15
2	8
3	9
4	12

You are required to state if one product only were to be made:

(i) which product would give maximum profit and the problems that you envisage could arise;

(ii) which product should be made and the amount of profit per annum resulting, assuming that products K and L use the same direct material and that there is a shortage of the material with supply limited at current price to a maximum of £200,000 per annum;

(iii) which product should be made and the amount of profit per annum resulting, assuming that there is a shortage of persons possessing the skills required in department 2, with the result that the number of employees there cannot be increased;

(C) How many of each product should be made and the amount of profit resulting, assuming that the number of employees cannot be increased or transferred from one department to another. (30 marks)

ICMA Cost Accounting 2
November 1981

22.2 A company manufactures plastic-covered steel fencing in two qualities: standard and heavy gauge. Both products pass through the same processes involving steel-forming and plastic-bonding.

The standard gauge sells at £15 a roll and the heavy gauge at £20 a roll. There is an unlimited market for the standard gauge but outlets for the heavy gauge are limited to 13,000 rolls per year. However, the factory operations of each process are limited to 2,400 hours each per year.

Other relevant data are given below:
Variable costs per roll:

Gauge	Direct material £	Direct wages £	Direct expense £
Standard	5	7	1
Heavy	7	8	2

Processing hours per 100 rolls:

Gauge	Steel-forming	Plastic-bonding
Standard	6	4
Heavy	8	12

Agreement has been reached on revised working methods that will increase output of all processes by 10%. This could be achieved without additional manpower or longer working

hours.

You are required to calculate:

(a) the production mix which will maximize total contribution:
 (i) at present output levels; and
 (ii) assuming the 10% production improvement is achieved;
(b) the total amount of productivity bonus which will be paid to employees under (a) (ii) on the basis of their receiving 40% of the additional contribution.

(20 marks)

ICMA P3 Management Accounting
November 1979

22.3* LP Ltd is a manufacturing company which currently produces three products. The standards per unit of product are as follows:

	Product X		Product Y		Product Z	
	£		£		£	
Standard selling price	9		8		7	
Less Standard costs (1)						
Materials 2 units at £1 =	2		3 units at £1 = 3		4 units at £1 = 4	
Labour 4 hours at £1 =	4		1 hour at £1 = 1		1 hour at £1 = 1	
Machine time 1 hour at £1 = 1	7		5 hours at £1 = 5	9	1 hour at £1 = 1	6
Standard profit per unit		2		(−1)		1

Note

(1) The charge for materials and labour is based on their cost of acquisition. The charge for machine time is based on the allocation of £8,000 overheads (all of which are fixed costs) over an estimated capacity of 8,000 hours.

During the next cost period, the availability of resources is expected to be subject to the following limitations:

Materials	9,000 units
Labour	9,200 hours
Machinery	8,000 hours

Furthermore, the output of the products is limited because of a marketing constraint. The marketing manager estimates the maximum sales of the three products to be as follows:

Product X	2,100 units
Product Y	1,400 units
Product Z	380 units

During the next period the standard costs and selling prices are expected to remain unchanged.

The managing director is aware that a rival company uses mathematical programming to plan its production and has asked you to apply the same technique to the above data. You have used a computer package and the following final linear programming model has just been received from the computer.

		Slack 1 L (labour)	Slack 2 M/c (Machinery)	Slack 3 SZ (Sales of Z)
M (Materials)	220	7/19	10/19	3.2/19
SY (Sales of Y)	260	−1/19	4/19	−3/19
X (Product X)	1,920	−5/19	1/19	4/19
SX (Sales of X)	180	5/19	−1/19	−4/19
Y (Product Y)	1,140	1/19	−4/19	3/19
Z (Product Z)	380	0	0	−1
	11,080	−11/19	−13/19	−14/19

Required:
(a) Prepare the first tableau of the linear programming model to which the solution is given. (5 marks)
(b) The managing director has requested an explanation of the meaning of the final tableau. You are required to provide an explanation of the meaning of each of the terms in the final tableau and provide any other information which would be of use that can be derived from the final tableau. (14 marks)

(c) Discuss briefly the possible uses of linear programming for short-term planning and indicate whether there are any limitations in using a model of this kind. (6 marks)

22.4* (a) Corpach Ltd manufactures three products for which the sales maxima, for the forthcoming year, are estimated to be:

Product 1	Product 2	Product 3
£57,500	£96,000	£125,000

Summarized unit cost data are as follows:

	Product 1 £	Product 2 £	Product 3 £
Direct material cost	10.00	9.00	7.00
Variable processing costs	8.00	16.00	10.00
Fixed processing costs	2.50	5.00	4.00
	£20.50	£30.00	£21.00

The allocation of fixed processing costs has been derived from last year's production levels and the figures may need revision if current output plans are different.
The established selling prices are:

Product 1	Product 2	Product 3
£23.00	£32.00	£25.00

The products are processed on machinery housed in three buildings:
Building A contains type A machines on which 9,800 machine hours are estimated to be available in the forthcoming year. The fixed overheads for this building are £9,800 p.a.

Building B1 contains type B machines on which 10,500 machine hours are estimated to be available in the forthcoming year.
Building B2 also contains type B machines and again 10,500 machine hours are estimated to be available in the forthcoming year.
The fixed overheads for the B1 and B2 buildings are, in total, £11,200 p.a. The times required for one unit of output for each product on each type of machine, are as follows:

	Product 1	Product 2	Product 3
Type A machines	1 hour	2 hours	3 hours
Type B machines	1.5 hours	3 hours	1 hour

Assuming that Corpach Ltd wishes to maximize its profits for the ensuing year, you are required to determine the optimal production plan and the profit that this should produce. (9 marks)
(b) Assume that, before the plan that you have prepared in part (a) is implemented, Corpach Ltd suffers a major fire which completely destroys building B2. The fire thus reduces the availability of type B machine time to 10,500 hours p.a. and the estimated fixed overhead for such machines to £8,200. In all other respects the conditions set out in part (a) to this question continue to apply.
In his efforts to obtain a revised production plan, the company's accountant makes use of a linear programming computer package. This package produces the following optimal tableau:

Z	X1	X2	X3	S1	S2	S3	S4	S5	
0	0	0	0	0.5	1	0	0.143	−0.429	1,150
0	0	1	0	−0.5	0	0	−0.143	0.429	1,850
0	0	0	0	0	0	1	−0.429	0.286	3,800
0	0	0	1	0	0	0	0.429	−0.286	1,200
0	1	0	0	1	0	0	0	0	2,500
1	0	0	0	1.5	0	0	2.429	0.714	35,050

In the above:
Z is the total contribution,
X1 is the budgeted output of product 1,
X2 is the budgeted output of product 2,
X3 is the budgeted output of product 3,
S1 is the unsatisfied demand for product 1,
S2 is the unsatisfied demand for product 2,
S3 is the unsatisfied demand for product 3,
S4 is the unutilized type A machine time,
S5 is the unutilized type B machine time.

The tableau is interpreted as follows:

Optimal plan — Make 2,500 units of product 1, 1,850 units of product 2 and 1,200 units of product 3.

Shadow prices — Product 1 £1.50 per unit,
Type A machine time £2,429 per hour
Type B machine time £0.714 per hour.

Explain the meaning of the shadow prices and consider how the accountant might make use of them. Calculate the profit anticipated from the revised plan and comment on its variation from the profit that you calculated in your answer to part (a). (9 marks)
(c) Explain why linear programming was not necessary for the facts as set out in part (a) whereas it was required for part (b). (4 marks)
(22 marks)

ACCA Level 2 Management Accounting
June 1983

22.5 Bronx Ltd is in the process of preparing its budget for the coming year. The information from the marketing department indicates that sales demand is in excess of present plant capacity. Because equipment is specialized and made to order, a lead time in excess of one year is necessary on all plant additions.

Bronx Ltd produces three products and the estimated demand is as follows:

Product X	90,000 units
Product Y	34,000 units
Product Z	46,000 units

Production of these quantities is immediately recognized as being impossible. Practical capacity is 41,000 machine hours in department 1 and 48,000 machine hours in department 2. Work study estimates of machine time for each product are as follows:

	X	Y	Z
Department 1	30 mins	15 mins	15 mins
Department 2	15 mins	7½ mins	45 mins

Standard costs and profits for the three products are as follows:

	X £	Y £	Z £
Direct materials	6.00	4.00	17.25
Direct labour	2.00	1.00	3.50
Factory overheads	5.00	2.50	8.75
Selling and administrative overheads	3.00	1.50	4.50
Profit (loss)	4.00	1.00	(4.00)
Selling price	20.00	10.00	30.00

Factory overhead is absorbed on the basis of direct labour cost at a rate of 250%; approximately 20% of the overheads are variable and vary with direct labour costs. Selling and administrative costs are allocated on the basis of sales at the rate of 15%; approximately one-half of this is variable and varies with sales value. The estimated overhead for the period is £525,000 for factory overhead and £250,000 for selling and administrative overhead.

The managing director has suggested that product Z should be eliminated from the product line and that the facilities be used to produce product X and Y. The sales manager objects to this solution because of the need to provide a full product line. In addition he maintains that the firm's regular customers provide, and will continue to provide, a solid base for the firm's activities and that these customers' needs must be met. He has provided a list of these customers and their estimated purchases are as follows:

Product X	40,000 units
Product Y	16,000 units
Product Z	8,000 units

The managing director has reluctantly agreed to this proposal but has asked you, as the newly appointed accountant, to provide him with information of the maximum profit that can be obtained from the *remaining* capacity. You decide to use mathematical programming to determine the optimal results from the *uncommitted* capacity and the final tableau of the linear programming model is as follows:

	Y (product Y)	Slack 1 (department 1)	Slack 2 (department 2)	
X (product X)	12,000	−0.5	−2.4	+0.8

Let me format properly:

		Y (product Y)	Slack 1 (department 1)	Slack 2 (department 2)
X (product X)	12,000	−0.5	−2.4	+0.8
Z (product Z)	36,000		+0.8	−1.6
Slack X (sales of X)	38,000	+0.5	+2.4	−0.8
Slack Y (sales of Y)	18,000	−1.0		
Slack Z (sales of Z)	2,000		−0.8	+1.6
	303,000	−1.0	−18.6	−0.8

Required:

(a) Prepare the first tableau of the linear programming model to which the solution is given. (8 marks)

(b) What is the maximum profit for the period? Also, explain how you would obtain information of how much profit is lost as a result of the imposition of the minimum sales constraints and indicate why this information would be useful for product mix decisions. (7 marks)

(c) The managing director has requested an explanation of the meaning of the final tableau. You are required to provide an explanation of the meaning of each of the terms in the final tableau and provide any other information which would be of use that can be derived from the final tableau. (10 marks)

(25 marks)

22.6* Brass Ltd produces two products, the Masso and the Russo. Budgeted data relating to these products on a unit basis for August 1980 are as follows:

	Masso £	Russo £
Selling price	150	100
Materials	80	30
Salesmen's commission	30	20

Each unit of product incurs costs of machining and assembly. The total capacity available in August 1980 is budgeted to be 700 hours of machining and 1,000 hours of assembly, the cost of this capacity being fixed at £7,000 and £10,000 respectively for the month, whatever the level of usage made of it.

The number of hours required in each of these departments to complete one unit of output is as follows:

	Masso	Russo
Machining	1.0	2.0
Assembly	2.5	2.0

Under the terms of special controls recently introduced by the Government in accordance with EEC requirements, selling prices are fixed and the maximum permitted output of either product in August is 400 units (i.e. Brass Ltd may produce a maximum of 800 units of product). At the present controlled selling prices the demand for the products exceeds this considerably.

You are required:

(a) to calculate Brass Ltd's optimal production plan for August 1980, and the profit earned (10 marks),

(b) to calculate the value to Brass Ltd of an independent marginal increase in the available capacity for each of machining and assembly, assuming that the capacity of the other department is not altered and the output maxima continue to apply (10 marks),

(c) to state the principal assumptions underlying your calculations in (a) and (b) above, and to assess their general significance (5 marks).

ICAEW Management Accounting July 1980

22.7 Goode, Billings and Prosper PLC manufactures two products, Razzle and Dazzle. Unit selling prices and variable costs, and daily fixed costs are:

	Razzle £	Dazzle £
Selling price per unit	20	30
Variable costs per unit	8	20
Contribution margin per unit	12	10
Joint fixed costs per day		£60

Production of the two products is restricted by limited supplies of three essential inputs: raz, ma, and taz. All other inputs are available at prevailing prices without any restriction. The quantities of raz, ma, and taz necessary to

produce single units of Razzle and Dazzle, together with the total supplies available each day, are:

	lbs per unit required		Total available
	Razzle	Dazzle	(lbs per day)
Raz	5	12.5	75
Ma	8	10	80
Taz	2	0	15

William Billings, the sales director, advises that any combination of Razzle and/or Dazzle can be sold without affecting their market prices. He also argues very strongly that the company should seek to maximize its sales revenues subject to a minimum acceptable profit of £44 per day in total from these two products.

In contrast, the financial director, Silas Prosper, has told the managing director, Henry Goode, that he believes in a policy of profit maximization at all times.

You are required to:

(a) calculate:

(i) the profit and total sales revenue per day, assuming a policy of profit maximization (10 marks),

(ii) the total sales revenue per day, assuming a policy of sales revenue maximization subject to a minimum acceptable profit of £44 per day (10 marks), and

(b) suggest why businessmen might choose to follow an objective of maximizing sales revenue subject to a minimum profit constraint (5 marks).

(25 marks)

ICAEW Management Accounting July 1983

22.8 (a) Blanton Ltd manufactures two enriched powder products known as Yin and Zee. After charging all direct costs, including the variable element of labour time and machine time, the products make a contribution per kilogram of output of £22 for Yin and £15 for Zee.

The total fixed manufacturing capacity available in the first week of 1982 is 1,200 hours of labour and 1,000 hours of machine time. The number of hours of each of these resources required to produce a kilogram of output is as follows:

	Yin	Zee
Labour	4	2
Machine time	2	5

Any fraction of a kilogram can be produced for either product.

You are required:

(i) to calculate Blanton Ltd's optimal production plan for the first week of 1982, and the contribution earned from this plan (5 marks),

(ii) to calculate the related shadow price per hour of labour time and of machine time respectively (5 marks),

(iii) to state clearly and concisely the significance of the shadow price of resources (5 marks).

(b) Hinton Ltd also has the capacity to manufacture Yin and Zee. Until recently Hinton earned the same contribution per kilogram of output as Blanton, and required the same amount of resources as Blanton to produce a kilogram of output. However, its weekly capacity was 800 hours of labour and 2,450 hours of machine time. Its optimal production plan was to produce 400 kg of Zee and no Yin, giving a contribution of £6,000.

Hinton's engineering superintendent has recently made some irreversible adjustments to the machines to try to reduce the amount of machine time needed to make Zee. In addition to the fixed costs of the machines, the variable cost of machine time actually used was £4 per machine-hour. As this variable cost was charged before arriving at the contribution per kilogram of output, any reduction in the machine time required would directly increase the contribution per unit of output of Zee. These engineering adjustments would have no effect on the production of Yin, if that were to be undertaken.

The adjustments have had only limited success. A small sample of observations taken at different times has led to the estimate that the average machine time per kilogram of output of Zee is still expected to be 5 hours, but that due to the wide variation of machining times in the sample the standard error of this estimate is 1 hour.

You are required:

(i) to calculate the range within which there is a 95.4% probability that Hinton Ltd's weekly contribution will lie under the above conditions, and also the expected value of the contribution, if it continues to produce as much Zee as possible per week and no Yin (5 marks), and

(ii) to calculate Hinton Ltd's optimal production plan for both Yin and Zee if the machine time required per kg of Zee produced were to be assumed to be 7 hours for certain, all other matters remaining unchanged (5 marks).

(25 marks)

ICAEW Management Accounting December 1981

22.9 Riverside Processors PLC recycles by-products

from nearby industrial sites. It produces two products, Ackney and Boylle. The current level of production is 100 tonnes of each product per week, but there remains some unused production capacity.

Due to restrictions on the availability of an essential ingredient, Zalium, the maximum weekly output of Ackney is 150 tonnes. Furthermore, the effluent from the production of Ackney is acid, but is neutralized by effluent from the production of Boylle; as a matter of policy, Riverside restricts the production of Ackney to not more than twice the production of Boylle.

The production process of each of the products requires heat, fuelled by gas. However, Riverside is restricted in the quantity of gas it can use, the maximum being 30,000 therms per week. The production of one tonne of either product requires 100 therms of gas. The production process of both Ackney and Boylle incorporates filtration, and the capacity of the filtration plant is limited to 1,750 labour hours per week in normal operation. The production of one tonne of Ackney requires 7 labour hours of filtration, and one tonne of Boylle requires 5 labour hours.

The company is test marketing a new product, Spotz; this requires neither additional process heat nor filtration, although it incorporates the scarce material, Zalium, which is also used in the production of Ackney. The following cost and revenue data are available concerning the three products (in £ per tonne):

	Ackney (actual)	Boylle (actual)	Spotz (estimated)
Variable costs:			
Input materials			
Zalium (one unit)	27	–	27
Other	10	48	25
Labour			
Filtration plant	28	20	–
Other	30	29	40
Process heat	20	20	–
Total variable costs	115	117	92
Selling price	171	137	130

The company's fixed costs are £10,000 per week.

You are required

(a) assuming that the new product, Spotz, is *not* produced, to:
 (i) show the feasible outputs of Ackney and Boylle, and to calculate the optimal production plan for Riverside Processors PLC (9 marks),
 (ii) calculate the shadow prices of Zalium, filtration plant labour, and process heat for the optimal production plan which you have calculated in (i) above (5 marks),
 (iii) calculate the maximum extra quantity of Zalium (in addition to the 150 units which are available at £27 per unit) which the company should be willing to buy if it could be imported at a price of £50 per unit and if filtration plant throughput cannot be increased (6 marks),

(b) assuming that the test marketing campaign for Spotz is successful in demonstrating a sufficient demand at the proposed selling price, and also assuming that no imported Zalium is obtainable, to:
 (i) calculate the shadow price of Zalium (2 marks),
 (ii) calculate the optimum contribution which Riverside Processors PLC can then earn (3 marks).

(25 marks)
ICAEW Management Accounting July 1982

22.10* Coasters Ltd is considering its capital investment programme for 1980 and 1981. The company is financed entirely by ordinary shares and has a cost of capital of 15% per annum. The directors of Coasters Ltd have reduced their initial list of projects to five, the expected cash flows of which are as follows:

Project	Cash flows			
1 January:	1980 £	1981 £	1982 £	1983 £
A	−60,000	+30,000	+25,000	+25,000
B	−30,000	−20,000	+25,000	+45,000
C	−40,000	−50,000	+60,000	+70,000
D	0	−80,000	+45,000	+55,000
E	−50,000	+10,000	+30,000	+40,000

None of the above projects can be delayed. All the projects are divisible; outlays may be reduced by any proportion and net inflows will then be reduced in the same proportion. No project can be undertaken more than once. Coasters Ltd is able to invest surplus funds in a bank deposit account yielding an annual return of 10%.

You are required to:
(a) prepare calculations showing which projects Coasters Ltd should undertake, if capital is expected to be available in indefinitely large amounts at 15% per annum, during all future periods (5 marks),
(b) show how your answer to (a) would vary if capital available for investment was limited to £100,000 at 1 January 1980, but was not limited thereafter (5 marks),
(c) provide a mathematical programming formulation which would assist the directors of Coasters Ltd in choosing investment projects if capital available at 1 January 1980 was limited to £100,000, capital available at 1 January 1981 was limited to £90,000, capital was available thereafter without limit at 15% per annum, and shareholders' required return from the company was 15% per annum at all relevant times (8 marks),
(d) comment on any limitations of the formulation you have provided in (c) (7 marks).
Ignore taxation.

ICAEW Elements of Financial Decisions July 1979

22.11* Details of projects available to Glaser Ltd, a wholly owned subsidiary of a publicly quoted company, are:

Project	Cash Flows at Time				NPV	IRR
	0 (£M)	1 (£M)	2 (£M)	3 (£M)	(£M)	%
A	(7)	1.5	2.0	2.0	1.0	19
B	(6)	2.0	1.0	1.0	0.8	21
C	(2)	4.0	(0.5)	(2.0)	(0.6)	—
D		(8.0)	(2.0)	(1.0)	3.0	17
E			(3.0)	1.0	0.7	25

Each of the projects have cash flows which extend beyond time 3 and this has been reflected in the NPV and IRR calculations. The investment shown is the maximum possible for each project but partial investment in a project is possible and this would result in strictly proportional cash flows, accounting profits and NPV figures. The timing of the start of each project cannot be altered and, if started, a project must run for its whole life.

External funds available for investment are:

Time 0 — up to £12M, of which £5M is a loan to be repaid with interest at 10% at time 1.
Time 1 — a new equity injection from Glaser's holding company of £7.5M.
Time 2 and 3— nil.

Funds generated from investment in the five available projects will also be available for further investment by Glaser. None of the funds generated by Glaser's existing activities are available for investment in projects A to E or for the payment of interest, or principal, relating to the loan.

At time 0, Glaser's holding company will require the surrender of any cash not used for investment. With effect from time 1 confiscation of surplus cash will cease and excess funds can be put on deposit to earn the competitive risk free interest rate of 8% per year, the gross amount then being available for investment. After time 3 Glaser will be free to seek funds from the capital market.

The holding company requires Glaser to produce accounting profits from projects (i.e. ignoring interest payments or receipts) which are always at least 10% higher than those of the previous year. Existing projects will produce profits of

Year to time	Profits £M
0	10
1	10
2	12
3	11

	Accounting Profit in year to time		
	1 (£M)	2 (£M)	3 (£M)
A	0.6	0.6	1.4
B	0.8	0.3	0.8
C	(0.1)	(0.2)	(0.3)
D		(0.3)	(0.2)
E			1.5

Required:
(a) Provide an appropriate linear programming formulation which is capable of assisting in, or indicating the impossibility of, deriving a solution to the problem of selecting an optimum mix of projects within the constraints imposed on Glaser.

Glaser's objective is to maximize the economic wellbeing of the shareholders of the holding company. Clearly specify how this objective is to be incorporated in the

programming formulation.

Specify the meaning of each variable and describe the purpose of every constraint used.

You are required to formulate the problem, you are not required to attempt a solution. Ignore tax. (10 marks)

(b) Briefly explain the circumstances under which it may be rational for a firm to undertake a project with a negative NPV, such as project C. (3 marks)

(c) Outline the main merits and deficiencies of mathematical programming and mathematical modelling in practical financial planning. (7 marks)

(20 marks)

ACCA P3 Financial Management
December 1983

22.12 Raiders Ltd is a private limited company which is financed entirely by ordinary shares. Its effective cost of capital, net of tax, is 10% per annum. The directors of Raiders Ltd are considering the company's capital investment programme for the next two years, and have reduced their initial list of projects to four. Details of the projects are as follows:

be undertaken more than once. Raiders Ltd is able to invest surplus funds in a bank deposit account yielding a return of 7% per annum, net of tax.

You are required to:

(a) prepare calculations showing which projects Raiders Ltd should undertake if capital for immediate investment is limited to £500,000, but is expected to be available without limit at a cost of 10% per annum thereafter (5 marks),

(b) provide a mathematical programming formulation to assist the directors of Raiders Ltd in choosing investment projects if capital available immediately is limited to £500,000, capital available after one year is limited to £300,000, and capital is available thereafter without limit at a cost of 10% per annum (8 marks),

(c) outline the limitations of the formulation you have provided in (b) (6 marks),

(d) comment briefly on the view that in practice capital is rarely limited absolutely, provided that the borrower is willing to pay a sufficiently high price, and in consequence a technique for selecting investment projects

| | Cash flows (net of tax) | | | | | |
Project	Immediately £000	After one year £000	After two years £000	After three years £000	Net present value (at 10%) £000	Internal rate of return (to nearest 1%)
A	−400	+50	+300	+350	+157.0	26%
B	−300	−200	+400	+400	+150.0	25%
C	−300	+150	+150	+150	+73.5	23%
D	0	−300	+250	+300	+159.5	50%

None of the projects can be delayed. All projects are divisible; outlays may be reduced by any proportion and net inflows will then be reduced in the same proportion. No project can

which assumes that capital is limited absolutely is of no use (6 marks).

(25 marks)

ICAEW Financial Management
July 1983

Divisional performance evaluation

This Part examines the special problems which are associated with measuring the performance of managers in divisionalized companies. There are two chapters: Chapter 23 — Performance Measures and Control in Divisionalized Companies — considers how a financial control system might be devised, which will motivate divisional managers to pursue goals which are in the best interests of the company as a whole. Chapter 24 — Transfer Pricing — focuses on various approaches which can be adopted to arrive at transfer prices between divisions which will motivate divisional managers to make sound decisions and which will at the same time lead to a divisional profit calculation that is a fair reflection of the manager's performance.

23 Performance measures and control in divisionalized companies

Large companies such as ICI produce and sell a wide variety of products throughout the world. Because of the complexity of their operations it is difficult for head office directly to control operations. It is therefore appropriate to divide the company into separate self-contained segments or divisions and to allow divisional managers to operate with a great deal of independence. The danger in creating autonomous divisions is that divisional managers might not pursue goals which are in the best interests of the company as a whole. The objective of this chapter is to devise performance measures which will motivate managers to pursue those goals which will best benefit the company as a whole. In other words the objective is to develop performance measures which will achieve goal congruence.[1]

Functional and divisionalized organizational structure

A *functional* organizational structure is one in which all activities of a similar type within a company are placed under the control of the appropriate departmental head. A simplified organizational chart for a functional organizational structure is illustrated in Fig. 21.1A. It is assumed that the company illustrated consists of five separate departments — production, marketing, financial administration, purchasing and research and development. None of the managers of the five departments is responsible for more than a part of the process of acquiring the raw materials, converting them into finished products, selling to customers, and administering the financial aspects of this process. For example, the production department is responsible for the manufacture of all products at a minimum cost, and of satisfactory quality, and to meet the delivery dates requested by the marketing department. The marketing department is responsible for the total sales revenue and any costs which are associated with selling and distributing the products, but not for the total profit. The purchasing department is responsible for purchasing supplies at a minimum cost and of satisfactory quality so that the production requirements can be met. Let us now consider Fig. 23.1B which shows a *divisionalized* organizational structure which is split up into divisions in accordance with the products which are made. You will see from the diagram that each divisional manager is responsible for all of the operations which relate to his particular product. Note also that a functional structure is applied to each division. Figure 23.1B shows a simplified illustration of a divisionalized organizational structure. In practice, however,

(A) A functional structure

Chief Executive

Production | Marketing | Financial and Administration | Purchasing | Research and Development

(B) A divisionalized structure

Chief executive

Product X division | Product Y division | Product Z division

Functional structure | Functional structure | Functional structure

Fig. 23.1 A functional and divisionalized organization structure

only part of a company may be divisionalized. For example, activities such as research and development, industrial relations and general administration may be structured centrally on a functional basis with a responsibility for providing services to *all* of the divisions.

Generally, a divisionalized organizational structure will lead to a decentralization of the decision-making process. For example, divisional managers may be free to set selling prices, make product mix and output decisions, and select suppliers (this may include buying from other divisions within the company or buying from other companies). In a functional organizational structure, pricing, product mix and output decisions will be made by central management. Consequently, the functional managers in a centralized organization will have far less independence than divisional managers. One way to express the difference between the two organizational structures is to say that the divisional managers have profit responsibility. They are responsible for generating revenues, controlling costs and earning a satisfactory return on the capital which is invested in their operations. The managers of the functional organizational structure do not have profit responsibility. For example, in Fig. 23.1A the production manager has no control over sources of supply, selling prices or product mix and output decisions.

Profit centres and investment centres

The creation of separate divisions may lead to the delegation of different degrees of authority; for example, in some organizations a divisional manager may be responsible for capital investment decisions. Where this situation occurs the division is known as an *investment centre*. Alternatively, where a manager is responsible only for the profits obtained from operating the fixed assets which are assigned to him by the head office, the segment is referred to as a *profit centre*. In contrast, a *cost centre* manager in a functional organizational structure is responsible for controlling costs but *not* profits.

As far as we are concerned here the most important factor relating to the delegation of authority is the effect which performance measures have on influencing managerial performance. The managers of highly autonomous divisions may be evaluated by many measures, including profits and return on investment; altern-

atively managers of divisions with less autonomy will be evaluated on different measures. Some examples include meeting planned production goals, sales quotas and target profits. Standard costs and variance analysis might be used to evaluate the performance of cost centre managers.

Advantages of divisionalization

Divisionalization can improve the decision-making process both from the point of view of the quality of the decision and the speed of the decision. The quality of the decisions should be improved because decisions can be made by the person who is familiar with the situation and who should therefore be able to make more informed judgements. Speedier decisions should also occur because information does not have to pass along the chain of command to and from top management. Decisions can be made on the spot by those who are familiar with the product lines and production processes and who can react to changes in local conditions in a speecy and efficient manner.

In addition, delegation of responsibility to divisional managers provides managers with greater freedom thus making their activities more challenging and providing the opportunity to achieve self-fulfilment. This process should mean that motivation and efficiency will be increased not just at the divisional manager level but throughout the whole division. A study by Dittman and Ferris (1978) of the attitudes of managers in companies in the USA found that those managers in charge of profit centres have greater job satisfaction than the managers of cost centres. They conclude that wherever possible system designers ought to try to construct profit centres for organizational units.

Another important reason for adopting a divisionalized structure is that the distribution of decision-making responsibility to divisions frees top management from detailed involvement in day-to-day operations and enables them to devote more effort to strategic planning. It is also claimed that divisions can provide an excellent training ground for future members of top management by enabling trainee managers to acquire the basic managerial skills and experience in an environment which is less complex than managing the company as a whole. Finally, it is argued that divisions provide a far more effective measure of

divisional profit performance because a manager will be responsible for both revenues and costs, and this will improve accountability within the company.

Disadvantage of divisionalization

If a company is divisionalized there is a danger that divisions may compete with each other excessively and that divisional managers may be encouraged to take action which will increase their own profits at the expense of the profits of other divisions. This may adversely affect cooperation between the divisions and lead to a lack of harmony in achieving the overall organizational goals of the company. This in turn may lead to a reduction in total company profits.

It is also claimed that the costs of activities which are common to all divisions may be greater for a divisionalized structure than for a centralized structure. For example, a large central accounting department in a centralized organizational structure may be less costly to operate than separate accounting departments for each division within a divisionalized structure. If top management are contemplating a divisionalized structure it is important that they should assess whether the additional benefits will exceed the additional costs.

A further argument against divisionalization is that top management loses some control by delegating decision-making to divisional managers. It is argued that a series of control reports is not as effective as a detailed knowledge of a company's activities. However, with a good system of performance evaluation together with appropriate control information, top management should be able to control operations just as effectively.

Prerequisites for successful divisionalization

A divisionalized structure is most suited to companies which are engaged in several dissimilar activities. The reason is that it is difficult for top management to be intimately acquainted with all the diverse activities of the various segments of the business. On the other hand, when the major activities of a company are closely related these

activities should be carefully coordinated, and this coordination is more easily achieved in a centralized organizational structure.

For successful divisionalization it is important that the activities of a division are as independent as possible of other activities. However, Solomons (1965) argues that even though substantial independence of divisions from each other is a necessary condition for divisionalization, if carried to the limit it would destroy the very idea that such divisions are an integral part of any single business. Divisions should be more than investments; they should contribute not only to the success of the company but to the success of each other.

According to Solomons, a further condition for the success of divisionalization is that the relation between divisions should be regulated so that no one division, by seeking its own profit, can reduce that of the company as a whole. He states that this is not the same as seeking profit at the expense of other divisions, but the amount which a division adds to its own profit must exceed the loss which it inflicts on another division. Unfortunately conflicts between divisions do arise and one of the important tasks of the accountant is to design an accounting control system which will discourage a division from improving is own profit at the expense of the company as a whole.

For a theoretical framework explaining why companies decentralize decision-making to divisions, and a survey of the extent and success of divisionalization in the UK, see Ezzamel and Hilton (1980).

Measuring divisional performance

Because our definition of a division is based on a segment of a business which produces and markets its own product or range of products, it is possible to measure performance in terms of profitability. Before we consider which profitability measures are most appropriate we should note that there are two alternative measures of divisional performance. First, there is a measure of the *personal* performance in which the focus is on how successful the divisional manager is in controlling the activities of the division; and second there is the measure of *economic* performance in which the focus is on how successful the division is as an economic entity. The messages transmitted from

these two measures may be quite different. For example, the economic performance of the most successful divisional manager may be the worst in the group. However, he may have produced a remarkable performance considering the difficult environment within which the division has operated. Alternatively, a manager of a division operating in a favourable economic environment may have produced high profits, which are nevertheless most unsatisfactory when the favourable economic environment is taken into account.

In this chapter we shall concentrate on measuring the performance of the divisional manager and not the performance of the division as an economic entity. Personal performance is measured at frequent intervals whereas economic performance is normally measured at less frequently, such as when expansion or contraction decisions are being contemplated, so the personal performance measure normally determines the design of the performance measurement system. Measures of economic performance normally consist of special studies at infrequent intervals where the emphasis is on expected future results rather than past results, and it is therefore inappropriate to design a system which produces routine information to meet this requirement.

Factors to be considered in designing managerial perforamnce measures

The major challenge facing the accountant is to devise performance measures which do not encourage a division to make a profit at the expense of the company as a whole. Shillinglaw (1982) suggests that there are three rules with which divisional profit measures must comply before they can be regarded as acceptable. They are:

(1) Divisional profit should not be increased by any action which reduces total company profit.
(2) Each division's profit should be as independent as possible of performance efficiency and managerial decisions elsewhere in the company.
(3) Each division's profit should reflect all items which are subject to any substantial degree of control by the divisional manager or his subordinates.

Divisional profit should not be increased by any action which reduces total company profits

This rule may be broken when transfer prices are set on the basis of total absorption cost plus a profit margin. Assume, for example, that the internal transfer price for a component produced by division A is £200 and the variable production cost is £150. Another division within the company, division B, uses this component in its production process. If the market price from an outside supplier is £180 then division B will increase its profits by purchasing the component from the outside supplier. However, if division A has spare capacity, the *relevant* internal production cost within the company is £150, but a transfer price of £200 will motivate the manager of division B to purchase from an outside supplier at £180. In this situation the accounting system has encouraged a manager to increase his own division's profit at the expense of total company profit.

Another example of a division increasing its own profit at the expense of total company profit is where fixed overheads are included in the stock valuations which are used for measuring managerial profit performance. Here there is a real danger that divisional managers will attempt to increase their profits by producing for inventory when they cannot produce for sale. By doing so, a proportion of the fixed overhead is carried forward into the cost of inventory, thus increasing current profits. The division will show a higher profit than would otherwise be the case, even though this may mean that some of the company's capital is unnecessarily tied up in stocks.[2]

Profit independence of divisions

Full independence is impossible because divisions contribute to each other's performance and it is not always possible to isolate such inter-dependencies. For example, inter-divisional transfers might prevent a division's profits from being independent of the performance of the other parts of the company if there is no market for the intermediate product. In this situation the transfer price will be cost-based. However, if the inter-mediate product is transferred at a transfer price which is based on actual cost, the supplying division will be able to pass on its inefficiencies to the receiving division. It is more appropriate in such circumstances to base the transfer price on standard cost and not on actual cost, thus ensuring

that cost inefficiencies are not passed on. We shall discuss the transfer pricing problem in the next chapter.

Profits should reflect items which are controllable

This raises the question as to whether we should use net profit, contribution margin or controllable profit as the measure of divisional performance. *Net profit* is not acceptable for measuring managerial performance because it will include arbitrary allocations of corporate overheads. *Contribution margin* appears to be a more attractive measure, as by excluding fixed expenses one is excluding many arbitrary overhead apportionments. However, contribution margin can only be a satisfactory measure when the divisional managers are prevented from determining the amount of capital which is invested in their divisions (that is, profit centres exist). If managers can influence the amount of the capital investment, and they are evaluated on the contribution which is obtained, they may be motivated to substitute capital equipment for labour even when this is not in the best interests of the company. This is because contribution is calculated by deducting variable costs, including direct labour, from sales, whereas depreciation is not included in the contribution calculation. By substituting capital equipment for labour, managers can therefore increase their contribution as labour costs are reduced but the resulting increase in the depreciation charge does not form part of the contribution calculation.

In situations where the divisional manager has responsibility for some capital investment decisions, he should be evaluated on the basis of *controllable operating profit*. This calculation is based on contribution less a deduction for depreciation on controllable investment and a further deduction for other controllable overheads. Item (1) in Exhibit 23.1 provides an illustration of the calculation of controllable operating profit.

Evaluating the economic performance of the division

When measuring managerial performance every effort should be made to concentrate on a measure which is free of all cost elements which are beyond the control of the divisional manager. For other company decisions, such as new invest-

ment or withdrawal of funds from the division, the important factor is the success or failure of the segment, and not the performance of the divisional manager. Thus all information relating to the division, whether it refers to matters within the control of the division or matters handled by the head office, should be taken into account for economic decisions. The *net* residual income calculation (item (iii) in Exhibit 23.1), which includes items beyond the control of the divisional manager, should therefore be the starting point for appraising the success of the division rather than the manager. (A detailed explanation of residual income is presented later in this chapter.) In addition, special studies will be required based on the future impact of expansion and contraction decisions. However, the routine generation of a *net* residual income calculation similar to Exhibit

Exhibit 23.1 Calculation of controllable profit[3]

		£
Sales to outside customers	xxx	
Transfers to other divisions	xxx	xxx
Less:		
Variable cost of goods sold and transferred	xxx	
Other variable divisional expenses	xxx	xxx
Contribution		xxx
Less:		
Controllable divisional overhead	xxx	
Depreciation on controllable fixed assets	xxx	xxx
(i) *Controllable operating profit*		xxx
Less:		
Interest on controllable investment		xxx
(ii) *Controllable residual income before taxes*		xxx
Less:		
Non-controllable divisional overhead	xxx	
Incremental central administration expenses chargeable to division	xxx	
Interest on non-controllable investment	xxx	xxx
(iii) *Net residual income before taxes*		xxx

23.1 will normally provide the stimulus for such studies.

Controllable and non-controllable expenses

To calculate *controllable operating profit* we must distinguish between controllable and non-controllable expenses. It is often difficult to distinguish between these items in practice. However, three situations can be identified which will assist us in overcoming this problem.

Where a division is completely free to shop around for a service and there is no rule requiring the division to obtain the service from within the company, the expense is clearly controllable. Alternatively, a division may not be free to choose an outside source of supply for the service in question, but it may be able to decide how much of this service is utilized. In this latter situation the quantity is controllable by the division but the price is not. An appropriate solution here is for the division to be charged with the actual quantity at the standard cost for the service which has been obtained. Finally, the division may not be free to decide on either the quantity of the service it utilizes or the price it will be charged. Industrial relations costs may fall into this category. Here the divisions have no choice but to accept an apportioned cost for the benefits they have obtained. (Such apportionments may be made for external reporting purposes.) In situations like this, the costs charged to the division for the service can only be regarded as a non-controllable item of divisional overhead.

Note that the depreciation charge for an investment centre should be regarded as a controllable expense; otherwise a situation could occur where a division progressively substitutes capital equipment for labour, thus showing a steady rise in controllable profit when this is not due to a reduction in costs. This would occur because the reduction in labour costs would increase the controllable profit, but the compensating increase in depreciation would show up only below the controllable profit line in Exhibit 23.1. So if depreciation on controllable investment is not recorded as a controllable expense it is possible for a divisional manager to show an improvement when no real improvement has taken place simply by substituting non-controllable production inputs for controllable production inputs.

Return on investment and residual income

Return on controllable investment

Having argued in favour of controllable profit for evaluating managerial performance, you should note that, like any profit measure, this measure is misleading if it is considered in isolation. To overcome this problem we can calculate the return on controllable investment as follows:

$$\text{Percentage return on controllable investment} = \frac{\text{Controllable profit}}{\text{Controllable investment}} \times 100$$

The return on controllable investment (ROI) will enable us to make valid comparisons with different accounting periods or different divisions. ROI, however, is not a good measure of a divisional manager's performance because if managers are assessed on this basis they may make divisional decisions which are not in the best interests of the company. Consider the following example:

	Division X	Division Y
Investment project available	£100,000	£100,000
Net annual return (controllable profit)	£16,000	£11,000
ROI of divisions at present	18%	9%

We will assume that the overall cost of capital for the company is 13%. The manager of division X would be reluctant to invest the additional £100,000 because the return on the proposed project is 16% and this would reduce his overall ROI. On the other hand, the manager of division Y would wish to invest the £100,000 because the return on the proposed project of 11% is in excess of his present return of 9%, and it would increase his overall ROI. Consequently, the managers of both divisions would make decisions which would not be in the best interests of the company. The company should accept only those projects where the return would be in excess of the cost of capital of 13%, but the manager of division X would reject a potential return of 16% and the manager of division Y would accept a potential return of 11%. ROI can therefore lead to a lack of goal congruence.

Residual income

To avoid situations where managers are unwilling to expand investment when this will lower their overall return, even though the incremental return is still in excess of the cost of capital, the controllable residual income measure of evaluation should be used. *Residual income can be defined as controllable profit less a cost of capital charge on controllable investment.* (The calculation is illustrated in item (ii) of Exhibit 23.1.) When applying this measure we shall see that managers are encouraged, when acting in their own interest, to also act in the best interests of the company. In other words, residual income encourages *goal congruence*. The residual income calculation in respect of the previous illustration is as follows:

	Division X	Division Y
Proposed investment	£100,000	£100,000
Interest on proposed investment (i.e. 13% cost of capital)	£13,000	£13,000
Controllable profit on proposed investment	£16,000	£11,000
Residual income	£3,000	(−£2,000)

This calculation indicates that the manager of division X would invest and the manager of division Y would not invest. These actions are in the best interests of the company. In the case of profit centres, where the division manager is not authorized to make capital investment decisions or where he cannot influence the investment in working capital, ROI may be a satisfactory performance measure, because if the return on investment is maximized on a fixed quantity of capital, the absolute return itself will also be maximized. However, in the case of investment centres, or profit centres where managers can significantly influence the investment in working capital, ROI appears to be an unsatisfactory method of measuring managerial performance and in these circumstances the residual income method should be used.

Controllable and non-controllable investment

When the residual income measure is used only that investment which is controllable by the manager should be used to calculate the controllable investment. The controllable investment

consists of all those assets, less liabilities, which can be influenced by the manager. Assets which are managed by central headquarters should *not* be included in the calculation. For example, if debtors and cash are administered centrally they should not be included as part of the controllable investment. On the other hand, if a divisional manager *can* influence these amounts they should be included in the investment base. If they were not included a manager could improve his profits by granting over-generous credit terms to customers; he would obtain the rewards of the additional sales without being charged with any cost for the additional capital which would be tied up in debtors.

To determine 'controllable investment' any liabilities which are within the control of the division must be deducted. For example, a division may finance its investment in stocks by the use of trade creditors; this liability for creditors should therefore be deducted in the calculation of the controllable investment. Our overall aims in analysing controllable and non-controllable investment are to produce performance measures which will encourage a manager to behave in the best interests of the organization and also to provide a good approximation of managerial performance. It is therefore appropriate to include in the investment base only those assets which a manager can influence and any arbitrary apportionments should be excluded.

Valuation of controllable investment

It is common to find fixed assets valued at either their original cost or their written down value for the purpose of calculating return on investment and residual income, but both of these valuation methods are weak. Consider, for example, an investment in an asset of £100,000 with a life of five years and annual cash flows of £29,000. If the straight line method of depreciation is used the annual profit will be £9,000. If the asset is valued at original cost there will be a return of 9% per annum for five years. This will understate the true return because the economic valuation is unlikely to remain at £100,000 each year for five years and then immediately fall to zero. If, instead of original cost, we use the written down value, the investment base will decline each year, and with constant profits the effect will be to show a steady increase in return on investment. For example, in

year 5 the asset will have a written down value of £20,000 and the return on investment will be 45% (£9,000/20,000 × 100). This steady increase in return on investment will suggest an improvement in managerial performance when the economic facts indicate that performance has remained unchanged over the five-year period.

Similar inconsistencies can be found when using the residual income method. The problem arises because historical cost is very misleading when it is used as a basis for performance measurement. Later in this chapter we shall see that the problem can be overcome either by using unconventional depreciation methods or by valuing assets at the present value of future cash flows, but unfortunately, both of these suggestions present serious practical difficulties. An appropriate solution to the practical problems is to value assets at replacement cost (see Lee, 1980, for a discussion of this topic). Although this method is conceptually distinct from the present value method of valuation, it may provide answers which are reasonable approximations of what would be obtained using a present value approach. In addition, replacement cost is conceptually superior to the historical cost method of asset valuation. It follows that the depreciation charge on controllable investment based on replacement cost is preferable to a charge based on historical cost. The return on investment and residual income would then be calculated on controllable investment valued at replacement cost.

However, a judgement of the most appropriate method of calculating depreciation and valuing assets for evaluating the performance of divisional managers can only be made when we have established a sound theoretical model. Such a model requires asset valuations and depreciation calculations which are consistent with decision-making techniques which maximize the long-term benefits to the company as a whole. We shall now consider whether or not alternative methods of depreciation and valuing assets will motivate managers towards this goal.

The effect of performance measurement on capital investment decisions

Capital investment decisions are the most important decisions which a divisional manager will have to make. We noted in Chapter 13 that these decisions should be taken on the basis of the net

Exhibit 23.2 Mutually exclusive capital projects[4]

	X £	Y £	Z £
Machine cost initial outlay (time zero)	£861	£861	£861
Estimated net cash flow (year 1)	250	390	50
Estimated net cash flow (year 2)	370	250	50
Estimated net cash flow (year 3)	540	330	1,100
Estimated net present value at 10% cost of capital	77	(52)	52
Ranking	1	3	2

Exhibit 23.3 Estimated profit and ROI from mutually exclusive projects

Profits	X £	Y £	Z £
Year 1	(37)	103	(237)
Year 2	83	(37)	(237)
Year 3	253	43	813
Total profits	299	109	339
PV of future profits	225	96	199
ROI (%)	X %	Y %	Z %
Year 1	(4.3)	11.9	(27.5)
Year 2	14.5	(6.4)	(41,3)
Year 3	88.1	15.0	283.2
Average	32.8	6.8	71.5

present value decision (NPV) rule. The way in which the performance of the divisional manager is measured, however, is likely to have a profound effect on the decisions which he will make. There is a danger that, because of the way in which divisional performance is measured, the manager may be motivated to take the wrong decision and not follow the NPV rule. We noted in an earlier example (see page 535) that the residual income method of evaluation appeared to encourage a divisional manager to make capital investment decisions which are consistent with the NPV rule, but there is no guarantee that this or any other profit measure will in fact motivate the manager to act in this way. Consider the information presented in Exhibit 23.2 which relates to three mutually exclusive projects X, Y and Z.

Applying the NPV rule the manager should choose project X in preference to project Z, and he should reject project Y.

Profits and return on investment

If a manager is evaluated on the amount of profits that are earned it is by no means certain which project he will choose. The estimated profits for projects X, Y and Z are presented in Exhibit 23.3. The estimated profit calculations in Exhibit 23.3 are based on the net cash flows for each year presented in Exhibit 23.2 less straight line depreciation of £287 per year. The ROI is calculated on the *opening* written down value at the start of the year. From the calculation in Exhibit 23.3 you will see that a manager who is anxious to improve his *short-term* performance will choose project Y if he is evaluated on total profits or return on investment as project Y earns the largest profits and

ROI in Year 1; but project Y has a negative net present value and should be rejected. Alternatively, a manager who assesses the impact of the projects on his performance measure *over the three years* will choose project Z because this yields the highest total profits and average ROI.

Only the present value of future profits will encourage a manager to take the correct decision and select project X. However, if the projects are not mutually exclusive the present value of future profits will incorrectly suggest acceptance of project Y, which has a negative NPV. The present value of future profits is not therefore consistent with the net present value of future cash flows and will not lead to the correct accept/reject capital investment decision, because the discounted acquisition cost of the machine is £861 at time zero. The present value of future profits takes the acquisition cost into account by making an annual depreciation charge of £287 which is discounted in each of years 1, 2 and 3. This process does not take into account the correct timing of the cash outflows. Hence the present value of estimated future profits may not encourage a manager to accept all positive, and reject all negative NPV projects.

Residual income

Let us now consider whether the residual income calculations are consistent with the NPV calculations. Exhibit 23.4 presents the estimated residual income calculations for project X.

The *total* present value of residual income for project X is £77, and this is identical to the NPV of project X which was calculated in Exhibit 23.2. This supports Solomons' (1965) claim that residual

Exhibit 23.4 Estimated residual income calculations

	Year 1 £	Year 2 £	Year 3 £	Total £
Profit before interest	(37)	83	253	
10% interest on opening WDV	86	57	29	
Residual income	(123)	26	224	
PV of residual income	(112)	21	168	77

income is the long-term counterpart of the discounted NPV. Consequently, if a manager is evaluated on the basis of his long-run present value of residual income his capital investment decisions should be consistent with the decisions which would be taken using the NPV rule. However, there is no guarantee that the *short-run* residual income measure will be consistent with the *longer-run* measure. For example, the residual income for year 1 for each of the projects is as follows:

Project X = (−£123)
Project Y = £17
Project Z = (−£323)

The *short-term* measure of residual income may lead to acceptance of project Y. In addition, if a manager is concerned about a possible deterioration in his expected residual income he may reject project X even when he is aware that acceptance will mean an increase in long-term residual income.

Let us now repeat the facts which we have established in our discussion so far. Decisions taken on the basis of a project's impact on divisional profit and return on investment are not consistent with the NPV rule. If a manager's performance is evaluated on the basis of either of these two measures, there is a danger that he will make decisions which will improve his own performance measure, even if such decisions are not in the best interests of the organization. The present value of residual income is the long-run counterpart of the discounted NPV, but the short-run measure may not signal the same decision as the long-run measure. Hence there is a need to establish a short-term measure of residual income which signals the same decision as the long-run measure. If this can be achieved and managers are evaluated on this basis, decisions which are based on improving their own short-term performance

will be consistent with decisions taken using the NPV rule. In the next section we shall examine some alternative theoretical models of asset valuations which ensure that the short-term residual income measure does not conflict with the long-term measure and which are therefore consistent with the NPV rule, but there are some practical problems with operating these models, and it is unlikely that they will be adopted. We will see that *a comparison of budgeted and actual cash flows is the most appropriate method of measuring divisional performance* but, for various reasons, accounting methods based on the accruals concept may be preferred.

If you do not wish to refer to a discussion of these alternative theoretical models you should note the comments in the previous paragraph and continue reading from page 542 onwards.

Reconciling short-term and long-term residual income measures

Valuing assets at NPV of future cash flows

It is not easy to design a short-term measure of performance which does not conflict with decisions based on the NPV rule. One approach is to value the assets at the present value of the future cash flows. This is illustrated in Exhibit 23.5 for project A.

You will see that the asset is valued at £938 at the start and, because the asset is purchased for £861, an immediate profit of £77 is recognized. This is identical to the NPV which was calculated in Exhibit 23.2. A residual income of zero will then be recorded for the next three years. This approach recognizes that the firm will be better off at the time of the acquisition by £77. However, because of the difficulty of valuing an asset at the present value of future cash flows, and writing the asset up in value above cost at the start, it is unlikely that this approach will be acceptable to accountants and managers.

Annuity depreciation

When the cash inflows are constant and the annuity method of depreciation is used the short-term residual income will also be constant. In addition, the total present value of the residual

Exhibit 23.5 Effect of valuing assets at NPV of future cash flows

Value of asset at start	$(250 \times 0.909) + (370 \times 0.826) + (540 \times 0.751) = £938$
Value at end of year 1	$(370 \times 0.909) + (540 \times 0.826)$ = £782
Value at end of year 2	(540×0.909) = £491
Value at end of year 3	= Nil

	Year 1	Year 2	Year 3
Cash inflow	250	370	540
Depreciation	156(1)	291	491
Profit before interest	94	79	49
Interest (10%)	94(2)	79	49
Residual income	–	–	–

(1) Value at start (938) less value at end of year 1 (782)
(2) Calculated on opening written down value (10% of £938)

income will be equal to the NPV calculation. In other words, decisions taken on the basis of the short-term measure will be consistent with decisions taken on the basis of the long-term measure or the NPV rule. Let us illustrate the procedure using the annuity method of depreciation.

EXAMPLE 23.1

A division has the opportunity to acquire a new machine for £100,000. The machine is expected to produce cash savings of £29,000 per year for five years. The cost of capital is 10%.

The net present value for the new machine is £9,939 and is calculated as follows:

	£
Investment cost	100,000
Present value of cash savings (29,000 × 3.791)	109,939
Net present value	9,939

It is important to note that the residual income for year 1 using the straight line method of depreciation will be:

		£29,000
Annual cash inflow		£29,000
Less Depreciation	20,000	
Interest on capital (10% of £100,000)	10,000	30,000
Residual income		(1,000)

There is a danger that this project will be rejected on the basis of the first year's residual income calculation if the straight line method of depreciation is used.

If we use the annuity method of depreciation, the annual amount of the depreciation will be equivalent to the capital element of an annuity required to redeem £100,000 borrowed at 10% over five years. If you refer to Appendix IV at the end of this book you will see that the capital recovery factory for five years at 10% is 0.2638 for £1; look at the entry in the five year row and the 10% column. A repayment of £26,380 per annum is therefore required to repay £100,000 borrowed for five years. The repayment schedule is set out in Exhibit 23.6.

The £100,000 will be repaid with interest and

Exhibit 23.6 Capital repayment schedule

Year	Annual repayment 1 £	10% interest on capital outstanding 2 £	Capital repayment 3 (1−2) £	Capital outstanding 4 (4−3) £
0				£100,000
1	£26,380	10,000	16,380	83,620
2	26,380	8,362	18,018	65,602
3	26,380	6,560	19,820	45,782
4	26,380	4,578	21,802	23,980
5	26,380	2,398	23,982	(2)

Exhibit 23.7 Residual income calculation

Year	Opening WDV 1	Cash inflow 2	Depreciation 3	Interest on capital (10%) 4	Residual income (2−(3+4)) 5
1	£100,000	£29,000	£16,380	£10,000	£2,620
2	83,620	29,000	18,018	8,362	2,620
3	65,602	29,000	19,820	6,560	2,620
4	45,782	29,000	21,802	4,578	2,620
5	23,980	29,000	23,982	2,398	2,620

the capital repayment column represents the annual depreciation charge. The residual income calculation using this depreciation charge is shown in Exhibit 23.7.

The annual cash inflow is constant and the residual income is also constant at £2,620 per annum for five years. The present value of £2,620 which is received annually for five years is equal to the net present value calculation of £9,939. The short-term measure should therefore lead to decisions being made which are consistent with decisions which would be taken on the basis of NPV calculations, when the cash inflows are constant and the annuity method of depreciation is used. Also, a manager will undertake the machinery purchase, even if he places great emphasis on the impact of the purchase on the first year's performance. He may, however, reject the purchase if residual income is calculated using the straight line method of depreciation.

Uneven cash flows

Unfortunately, the annuity method of depreciation only produces a short-term measure which will lead to decisions that are consistent with the NPV rule when the net cash inflows are equal each year. Example 23.1 has been amended so that the total net cash inflows of £145,000 fluctuate between years. All other items remain unchanged.

The revised problem is presented in Example 23.2.

EXAMPLE 23.2

A division has the opportunity to acquire a new machine for £100,000. The machine has expected cash savings of £145,000 over five years. The timing of the expected cash savings is as follows:

Year 1	£20,000
Year 2	£25,000
Year 3	£50,000
Year 4	£40,000
Year 5	£10,000

The cost of capital is ten per cent and the NPV is £9,938.

The residual income for this example, using the annuity method of depreciation which was calculated in Exhibit 23.6, is presented in Exhibit 23.8.

The present value of the residual income in Exhibit 23.8 is £9,938 and this is identical to the NPV calculation. There is, however, a danger that the manager may reject the investment because of the negative residual income calculations in years 1 and 2. This means that the short-term residual income measure may be in conflict with the NPV rule when the annuity method of depreciation is used and *unequal cash flows occur*. Tomkins (1975) shows that it is possible to construct a depreciation schedule which avoids negative residual income calculations and which will motiv-

Exhibit 23.8 Residual income with unequal cash flows

Year	Opening written down value	Cash inflow	Depreciation	Interest on capital	Residual income
1	£100,000	£20,000	£16,380	£10,000	(£6,380)
2	83,620	25,000	18,018	8,362	(1,380)
3	65,602	50,000	19,820	6,560	23,620
4	45,782	40,000	21,802	4,578	13,620
5	23,980	10,000	23,982	2,398	(16,380)

Exhibit 23.9 Depreciation based on interest deducted from cash flows

Year	Cash inflow 1	Capital outstanding (written down value) 2	Interest (10%) 3	Depreciation 4 (1−3)	Residual income 5 [1−(3+4)]
0		£100,000			
1	£20,000	90,000	£10,000	£10,000	0
2	25,000	74,000	9,000	16,000	0
3	50,000	31,400	7,400	42,600	0
4	40,000	0	3,140	31,400	5,460
5	10,000	0	0	0	10,000

ate managers to accept projects which yield positive NPVs. He suggests that instead of using the annuity method of depreciation, a depreciation figure should be calculated by deducting the interest on the written down value of the asset from the expected cash inflows for the year, instead of deducting it from the annuity which is required to redeem the loan. This procedure is illustrated in Exhibit 23.9.

You will see that the interest is calculated on the opening written down value. For example, the £9,000 interest charge for year 2 is based on 10% of the opening written down value for year 2 of £90,000. (This is represented by the written down value at the end of year 1.) Depreciation is then calculated by deducting interest from the cash inflow. In year 4 the depreciation charge is limited to the written down value of £31,400. The effect of the depreciation charge being based on a deduction of interest from the cash flow means that residual income is zero each year until the asset is completely written off. Any cash inflows which are received after this point will result in a positive residual income calculation. The present value of the residual income in years 4 and 5 is £9,931 compared with the capital investment net present value calculation of £9,938.

If a divisional manager is evaluated with residual income calculated in the manner illustrated in Exhibit 23.9 he will recognize that in the short term residual income will remain unchanged, and that by years 4 and 5 the benefits will be reflected in the performance measure; he will be motivated to accept the project. It remains doubtful, though whether widespread adoption of this method can be achieved as the depreciation is merely a balancing figure which does not conform to any of the usual notions of depreciation. Also, the calculations indicate that the residual income does not become positive until the initial investment cost topped up with interest cost has been recovered. Tomkins suggests that a better description of this concept would be capital surplus rather than residual income.

Comparison of actual with budget

When considering performance evaluation the *actual* residual income must be compared with a *pre-determined* standard such as budgeted residual income. If we use the procedure suggested in Exhibit 23.9, however, we will obtain a zero residual income calculation in the early years of a project's life for both the actual and the budgeted results. Consequently, there are no benefits to be derived from making such a comparison between budgeted and actual residual income. Tomkins suggests that the relevant yardstick of performance in this situation is a comparison between the budgeted capital outstanding at the end of the year and the actual capital outstanding. Any difference, though, between budgeted and actual capital outstanding can only result from actual cash flows being different from budgeted cash flows, as both interest and depreciation charges will be dependent on actual cash flows.[5] Tomkins therefore concludes that calculating residual income and comparing budgeted and actual capital outstanding is only an elaborate way of achieving what can be attained far more simply merely by comparing actual cash flows with those budgeted in the capital investment proposals.

Which method?

In this chapter we have established that evaluating a divisional manager on the basis of profits or return on investment will not motivate him to make decisions which are consistent with the net

present value rule. It is interesting to note that Example 23.1 requires an investment of £100,000 with a net cash inflow of £29,000. If straight line depreciation of £20,000 is charged the return on investment will be 9%. If we assume that the current return on investment for the division is greater than 9%, the manager of the division will incorrectly reject the project.

We have also seen that in the long-run the residual income method produces a calculation which is consistent with the NPV rule. The short-term residual income calculation may not, however, motivate managers to select projects which are consistent with applying the NPV rule. In the case of constant cash flows the problem can be resolved by using the annuity method of depreciation, but when annual cash flows fluctuate this method of depreciation does not ensure that the short-term residual income measure is consistent with the NPV rule. This problem can be resolved by making depreciation a balancing figure but this approach is unlikely to be acceptable. The most suitable approach is to compare budgeted and actual cash flows which is equivalent to comparing budget and actual residual incomes.

It appears that the choice is between using an accounting method based on the accruals concept which will lead to the correct decision more often than other methods or comparing budgeted and actual cash flows. If the former method is preferred residual income is the most appropriate method of measuring the performance of divisional managers.[6]

Determining the divisional cost of capital

To calculate NPV and residual income we must ascertain the cost of capital for each division. Should the same cost of capital figure be used for all divisions? Alternatively, should we not recognize that, if the divisions were separate businesses, they would not all have to pay the same price for the capital they have raised? Solomons (1965) argues that divisions cannot be considered as separate businesses for determining the riskiness of the undertakings:

Just as an insurance company reduces the uncertainty of its loss experience by increasing the spread of the risk it insures, just as an investor reduces the uncertainty of his investment income by increasing the size and variety of his portfolio, so diversification in a division-alized business aims to reduce the risk borne by the corporation. It does this by offsetting the risks associated with the separate divisions. Thus the addition of a divisional activity which in itself is quite risky might actually reduce the riskiness for the whole corporate enterprise. For this reason, the riskiness of a division is not to be assessed by looking at it in isolation from the rest of the business. For this reason, also, a single corporate cost of capital can quite appropriately be used throughout the company without regard to the supposed riskiness of any division considered as a separate entity.

The use of a single corporate cost of capital appears to be common. For example, a study by Mauriel and Anthony (1966) indicated an overwhelming tendency to use the same cost of capital for all divisions. The use of a uniform cost of capital is probably due to the fact that divisional managers consider this to be a fairer method of comparing their results with other divisions. In addition, it is claimed that the use of uniform rates avoids friction and has a more favourable impact on the morale of managers.

It appears, however, that the use of a uniform cost of capital may lead to incorrect decisions. The theory of business finance supports the use of a different cost of capital being used for different divisions (see Van Horne, 1983). The various divisions of a company can be viewed as a collection of different investments whose income streams results from different risks. The cost of capital is a function of risk and as various divisions face different risks, a different cost of capital should therefore be used for each division, based on the relative investment risk of each division.

To establish the cost of capital to be used for each division, Van Horne (1983) suggests that quoted companies should be identified which are engaged solely in the same line of business as the division. The cost of capital of the identified companies can then be used as an approximation of the division's cost of capital.

Van Horne also provides an illustration of how the use of a uniform cost of capital for each division can lead to incorrect decisions. He shows, for example, how safe projects with little risk may be rejected because they do not provide a return in excess of the company's *overall* cost of capital. Some of these projects, however, provided a return in excess of that which was required by the capital market for the risk involved and should

have been accepted. Similarly, some risky projects were incorrectly accepted which provided a return in excess of the overall cost of capital but below the return required by the market for the risk involved.

A full discussion of what is the appropriate cost of capital that should be used is beyond the scope of this book but for a detailed discussion of this topic see Van Horne (1983). The important point to note when measuring managerial performance is that we have attempted to establish a measure which is consistent with the NPV rule. If the measure which is chosen requires that a manager is charged with the cost of capital on the divisional investment (that is, residual income), the cost of capital which is used in this calculation should be the same rate as that which is used for capital investment decisions. Only by using the same cost of capital can the success of a manager's past investment decisions be truly established.

Use of non-accounting measures

It is important to note that any financial measure is subject to weaknesses when evaluating short-term profit performance as it is virtually impossible to capture in one financial measure all the variables which measure the success of a division. For example, two divisional managers using exactly the same investment may produce exactly the same residual income or ROI but this does not necessarily mean that their performances are the same. One manager may have built up customer goodwill by offering excellent customer service, but the other manager may have done the opposite and skimped on customer service. Simi-

larly, one manager may have paid great attention to training, education, research and development etc. while another manager may not have given these items any consideration. Differences such as these would not be shown in short-term financial reports, so the performance reports should be supplemented by non-financial measures and written explanations by the managers pointing out why their performance is above or below some pre-set level and how it has been achieved.

ROI and residual income cannot stand alone as a measure of divisional performance. Short-run profitability is only one of the factors which contributes to a company's long-run objectives. Return on investment and residual income are short-run concepts which deal only with the past year, whereas managerial performance must include future results that can be expected because of present actions. Other measures which could be added to financial reports to judge managerial performance include plant efficiency, share of the market, employee turnover, sales volume, discovery of new products, public relations, employee attitudes and so on. For a discussion of the quantitative and qualitative measures that might be used to evaluate divisional performance, see Parker (1979). Evaluation of managerial performance is a complex area and one summary financial measure should not be used to measure all the variables which influence managerial performance. It is therefore essential that accountants broaden their reporting systems to include additional variables in their performance reports. For an illustration of additional variables which were used by General Electric Company to evaluate the performance of their divisional managers, see Lewis (1980).

Summary

The major organizational device to maximize decentralization is the creation of divisions. Divisions may consist of investment centres or profit centres. In an investment centre a divisional manager can significantly influence the size of the investment whereas in a profit centre managers are only responsible for obtaining profits from the assets which are assigned to them. The major challenge to the accountant is to design a performance measure which creates a situation where managers acting in their own best interests also act in the best interests of the company as a whole.

The two most common methods of measuring divisional performance are controllable profit expressed as a percentage of controllable investment (ROI), and controllable residual income. ROI suffers from the disadvantage that the managers of those divisions with an existing ROI investment in excess of the cost of capital may incorrectly reject projects with positive NPVs. Similarly, managers with an existing ROI

which is lower than the cost of capital may accept projects with returns which are less than the cost of capital. ROI is therefore an unsatisfactory method of measuring managerial performance in investment centres or those profit centres where a manager can significantly influence the amount which is invested in working capital.

In the long run the residual income method leads to a calculation which is consistent with the net present value rule but, if conventional accounting methods of depreciation are used, the short-term residual income calculation may not motivate a decision which is consistent with the NPV rule. This problem can be resolved by using the annuity method of depreciation if the project's annual cash flows are constant. When the annual cash flows fluctuate this method does not ensure that the short-term measure is consistent with the NPV rule. This problem can be overcome by making depreciation a balancing figure but such an approach is unlikely to be acceptable. One possible solution is to compare the budgeted and the actual cash flows, which is equivalent to comparing budgeted and actual residual incomes.

The choice is between using accounting methods which will lead to decisions which maximize NPV more often than other methods, or comparing budgeted and actual cash flows. If the former approach is chosen it appears that residual income is the most appropriate accounting measure. It is recommended, however, that accounting measures of performance should also be supplemented by non-financial measures. For a survey of performance measures used in the UK and USA see Tomkins (1973).

References and further reading

Amey, L.R. Tomkins on residual income. *Journal of Business Finance and Accounting* 2(1), Spring 1975, 55-68.

Amey, L.R. Interest on equity capital as an ex-post cost. *Journal of Business Finance and Accounting* Autumn 1980, 347-65.

Bierman, H. ROI as a measure of managerial performance. *Financial Executive (USA)*, March 1973, 40-45.

Bromwich, M. Measurement of divisional performance: A comment and extension. *Readings in Accounting and Business Research* 1977, 131-40.

Coates, J.B., Smith, J.E. and Stacey, R.J. Results of a preliminary survey into the structure of divisionalized companies, divisionalized performance appraisal and the associated role of management accounting. In Cooper, D., Scapens, R. and Arnold, J. (Eds), *Management Accounting Research and Practice*. Institute of Cost and Management Accountants, 1983.

Dearden, J. The case against ROI control. *Harvard Business Review* May–June 1969, 124-35.

Dittman, D.A. and Ferris, K.R. Profit centre: A satisfaction generating concept. *Accounting and Business Research* 8(32), Autumn 1978, 242-45.

Emmanual, C.R. and Otley, D. The usefulness of residual income. *Journal of Business Finance and Accounting* 13(4), Winter 1976, 43-52.

Ezzamel, M.A. and Hilton, K. Divisionalisation in British industry: A preliminary study. *Accounting and Business Research* Summer 1980, 197-214.

Gup, B.E. and Norwood, S.W. Divisional cost of capital. *Financial Management (USA)* Spring 1982, 20-6.

Hamermesh, R.G. Responding to divisional profit crises. *Harvard Business Review* March/April 1977, 124-31.

Lee, T.A. *Income and Value Measurement* 3rd edn. Van Nostrand Reinhold (UK), 1985.

Lewis, R.W. Measuring, reporting and appraising results in operation with reference to goals, plan and budgets, A case study of management planning and control at General Electric Company, New York Controller Foundation Inc. 1955; also in Anthony, R.N. and Dearden, J. *Management Control Systems*. Irwin, 1980.

Mauriel, J. and Anthony, R.N. Mis-evaluation of investment centre performance. *Harvard Business Review* March–April 1966.

Morse, W.J. and Scheiner, J.H. Cost minimisation, return on investment, residual income: Alternative criteria. *Accounting and Business Research* Autumn 1979, 320-24.

Parker, L.D. Divisional profit performance: Beyond an exclusive profit test. *Accounting and Business Research* Autumn 1979, 309-19.

Reece, J.S. and Cool, W.R. Measuring investment centre performance. *Harvard Business Review* May–June 1978, 29-49.

Scapens, R.W. and Sale, J.T. Performance measurement and formal capital expenditure controls in divisionalised companies. *Journal of Business Finance and Accounting* 8(3), Autumn 1981, 389-420.

Solomons, D. *Divisional Performance: Measurement and Control*. R.D. Irwin, 1965.

Shillinglaw, G.D. *Cost Accounting: Analysis and Control*. R.D. Irwin, 1982. See also his articles: Guides to internal profit measurement. *Harvard*

Business Review **35**(2), March–April 1957, 22-29; Towards a theory of divisional income measurement. *Accounting Review* No. 2, April 1962, 208-16.

Tomkins, C. Another look at residual income. *Journal of Business Finance and Accounting* Spring 1975a, **2**(1), 39-54.

Tomkins, C. Residual income — A rebuttal of Professor Amey's arguments. *Journal of Business Finance and Accounting* No. 2, Summer 1975b, 161-8.

Tomkins, C. *Financial Planning in Divisionalised Companies*. Haymarket Publishing Company, 1973 (particularly Chapter 8 for a review of company practices in UK and USA).

Van Horne, J.C. *Financial Management and Policy*. Prentice-Hall, 1983, Chapter 8.

Problems

* Indicates that a suggested solution is to be found in the *Students' Manual*.

23.1* A large company is organized into divisions which are operationally autonomous. The performance of these divisions is compared by means of return on capital employed (ROCE).

Existing basis of calculation

The existing basis of calculating ROCE is:

Profits	These are net of depreciation which is calculated on a straight-line basis. Any loss on sale of an asset is charged fully against profits in the year in which it is incurred.
Capital employed	Current assets (excluding cash) are at average value throughout the year. Fixed assets are at original cost.

Proposed basis of calculation

The company is proposing to retain its bases of calculating profits and current assets, but to change its basis of valuing fixed assets in divisonal ROCE calculations to net book value (original cost less accumulated depreciation) at the end of the year.

As company management accountant you have been asked to compare the expected results under the two systems in respect of certain likely typical separate transactions.

These transactions are:

Transaction No. 1: The proposed scrapping of equipment reference J472 on 1 January 1978. This equipment was put into service on 1 January 1974 at an original cost of £80,000 with an expected life of five years. It is currently earning profits of £8,800 per annum before depreciation and has no scrap value (after deducting removal costs).

Transaction No. 2: The proposed purchase of an additional process control plant on 1 January 1978 at a cost of £59,500 with an expected life of seven years, at the end of which it would have no scrap value. This plant would give rise to savings of £15,000 per annum.

Transaction No. 3: The offer to customers of a discount for speedier payment of their accounts. This would cost £3,000 per annum but would reduce debtors by £20,000 on average throughout the year.

Transaction No. 4: The increase of an average of £30,000 worth of stock of finished goods throughout the year. This is budgeted to increase profit by £5,000 per annum.

These transactions are to be considered in respect of either or both divisions A and B (as specified in detail below and in the answer sheet), for which budgeted data for 1978, exclusive of any of the transactions, are:

Budgeted	Division A £	Division B £
Profit 1978	90,000	55,000
Current assets 1978	100,000	200,000
Fixed assets:		
Original cost	400,000	400,000
Net book value as at 31 December 1978	210,000	160,000

The company's DCF cut-off rate for investment projects is 12%.

You are required to:

1. Insert the results of your ROCE calculation in the boxes, shown in the table given below:

<div align="center">1978</div>

	Existing basis		Proposed basis	
	Div'n A %	Div'n B %	Div'n A %	Div'n B %
(a) Budgeted ROCE (ignoring any of the transactions)	☐	☐	☐	☐
(b) ROCE resulting from transaction No. 1	☐	—	☐	—
(c) ROCE resulting from transaction No. 2	☐	—	☐	—
(d) ROCE resulting from transaction No. 3	☐	☐	—	—
(e) ROCE resulting from transaction No. 4	—	—	☐	☐

2. Calculate the budgeted DCF return to the whole company from transaction No. 2. Work to the nearest whole number. Ignore all tax and investment allowances.
3. Explain whether there would be any lack of goal congruence between the divisions and the company as a whole.

<div align="right">ICMA P3 Adapted
Management Accounting
November 1977</div>

23.2 Theta Ltd compares the performance of its subsidiaries by return on capital employed (ROCE) using the following formula:

Profit:	Depreciation is calculated on a straight-line basis. Losses on sale of assets are charged against profit in the year of the sale.
Capital employed:	Net current assets — at the average value throughout the year. Fixed assets — at original cost less accumulated depreciation as at the end of the year.

Theta Ltd whose cost of capital is 14% per annum is considering acquiring Alpha Ltd whose performance has been calculated on a similar basis to that shown above except that fixed assets are valued at original cost.

During the past year, apart from normal trading, Alpha Ltd was involved in the following separate transactions:

A. It bought equipment on 1 November 1980 (the start of its financial year) at a cost of £120,000. Resulting savings were £35,000 for the year; these are expected to continue at that level throughout the six years expected life of the asset after which it will have no scrap value.

B. On 1 November 1980 it sold a piece of equipment that had cost £200,000 when bought exactly three years earlier. The expected life was four years, with no scrap value. This equipment had been making a contribution to profit of £30,000 per annum before depreciation and realized £20,000 on sale.

C. It negotiated a bank overdraft of £20,000 for the year to take advantage of quick payment discounts offered by creditors; this reduced costs by £4,000 per annum.

D. To improve liquidity, it reduced stocks by an average of £25,000 throughout the year. This resulted in reduced sales with a reduction of £6,000 per annum contribution.

The financial position of Alpha Ltd for the year from 1 November 1980 to 31 October 1981 *excluding the outcomes of transactions A to D above*, was:

	£000
Profit for the year	225
Fixed assets:	
Original cost	1,000
Accumulated depreciation	475
Net current assets (average for the year)	250

You are required to:
(a) Calculate the ROCE of Alpha Ltd using its present basis of calculation:
 (i) if none of the transactions A to D had taken place;

(ii) if transaction A had taken place but not B, C or D;

(iii) if transaction B had taken place but not A, C or D;

(iv) if transaction C had taken place but not A, B or D;

(v) if transaction D had taken place but not A, B or C.

(b) Calculate the ROCE as in (a)(i) to (a)(v) above using Theta Ltd's basis of calculation.

(c) Explain briefly whether there would have been any lack of goal congruence as between Theta Ltd and the management of Alpha Ltd (assuming that Alpha Ltd had been acquired by Theta Ltd on 1 November 1980 and that Theta Ltd's basis of calculation was used) in respect of:

(i) transaction A;
(ii) transaction B.

Taxation is to be ignored.

(25 marks)
ICMA P3 Management Accounting
November 1981

23.3 A group of companies is divided into ten operating divisions, each of which is autonomous. The cost of capital for the group is 12% per annum and it is currently earning 15% on its capital employed.

In the ROCE calculation, return is equated with net profit and capital employed is the figure at the beginning of the financial year. All fixed assets are depreciated on a straight-line basis. Investments in new projects include incremental working capital. Projects sold or withdrawn from operation are treated as consisting of fixed assets only.

If no new capital expenditure transactions take place the position of four of the divisions would be:

Division	Capital employed as at 1 January 1980	Budgeted for 1980 Net profit	Sales
	£000	£000	£000
P	320	80	800
Q	450	150	1,400
R	280	84	700
S	200	26	200

The following transactions are proposed:

Division P: Investment of £100,000 to yield sales of £150,000 per annum and net profit of £20,000 per annum.

Division Q: Sale for £75,000 of a project that is budgeted to yield a net profit of £15,000 in 1980. The original equipment cost £600,000 seven years ago with an expected life of eight years.

Division R: (i) Sale of product line at book value. The original equipment cost £60,000 two years ago with an expected life of three years. This line is budgeted to yield a net profit of £20,000 in 1980; combined with

(ii) replacement of (i) above by investing £100,000 in a new product to yield £30,000 per annum.

Division S: Investment of £80,000 in a project to yield sales of £36,000 per annum and a net profit of £11,200 per annum.

N.B. In connection with each of the above transactions, you are to assume that the sale and/or investment would be completed by 1 January 1980 so as to be included in the relevant ROCE calculations for the year 1980. Ignore taxation and inflation considerations and assume that actual results are as budgeted.

You are required to:

(a) On the assumption that each transaction goes ahead:

(i) calculate the new ROCE for each division for the year ending 31 December 1980;

(ii) identify those divisional managers whose bonuses will be higher if they receive annual bonuses directly related to the level of their respective ROCE;

(iii) state, in respect of each division, whether the group's interests will be favourably or adversely affected by the proposed transactions. Explain briefly why in each case.

(b) Identify, with brief reasons, which proposals the group would approve if its new capital expenditure were limited to £200,000 for the four divisions.

(c) (i) Compare the old results of division P and division S, both of which are in the same type of business, and briefly advise the divisional manager of division S how he might improve his performance based on the data concering division P;

(ii) comment briefly on how the new project for division S fits in with the advise given in (c) (i) above.

(d) Calculate the lowest price at which the equipment should be sold by division Q if the transaction proposed is to break even financially for the group.

(e) (i) Explain briefly the concept of 'residual income' in the context of performance evaluation;

(ii) calculate the residual income for each division for 1980 on the assumption that

each transaction goes ahead.

(35 marks)
ICMA P3 Management Accounting
November 1979

23.4 You are the highly-trusted chief accountant of Ragwort Ltd, a manufacturer of sports equipment, and you have strong private hopes of joining the Board in the next year or two in a newly-created post of Finance Director.

Ragwort is organized into three divisions, each of which is formed as a separate subsidiary company; you have a seat on the Board of each of them. The three divisions and their general managers are North-West (Christopher Perkins), Home Counties (Geoffrey Gilmore) and Eastern Counties (Morton Jackson). The Group Executive Committee consists of the three general managers, under the chairmanship of group chairman and chief executive Thomas Ragwort. It meets monthly, and the meeting usually lasts two days.

At the end of the first day of this month's meeting Ragwort calls you to his office, and tells you that he has a problem. 'You know', he says, 'that for some time now I've been concerned about what is the best measure for us to use to compare the performance of the divisions. You know what I mean — what is the right sort of target to set for them? It's no good if I impose something without agreement, and we simply didn't manage to get it today. I'm going to re-open the discussion tomorrow, and I want a decision but first I want some advice from you'.

You ask him what has happened.

'Well', he says, 'you know that we've been working out a divisional return on investment. We find pre-tax profits for each division, after charging out Group Head Office costs in proportion to divisional turnover. We set that against a base of written down net assets, excluding cash.

Gilmore is satisfied with that, but Perkins came up with something he called residual income — he argued that we have to make absolute profits, not just a return on investment. And then Jackson said that what we really want

is growth, and that the only way to get that in the long-run is to set the target as percentage sales growth.

They were obviously split, so I let it run on.

To cut a long story short, Gilmore said he could certainly accept that residual income was a better measure than looking just at growth. Jackson wouldn't accept that, and still wanted the growth measure, but he agreed with Gilmore's view that it was better to stick with our present ROI than to change to this new residual income idea.

Perkins stuck to his guns over residual income. He's smart. He told Jackson that he could see at least some merit in the growth idea, because in the end it would probably correlate with residual income. But he still thought that the ROI figure should be dropped. I tried a compromise approach then. I suggested that we took the measures in pairs, starting with ROI and residual income. After all, they sound pretty similar. Gilmore and Jackson voted for ROI, and only Perkins supported residual income. So I had them compare ROI with growth, thinking I was home and dry and we needn't change anything. And Perkins joined Jackson in supporting the growth idea! I had to admit that he'd said as much.

But Gilmore is pretty smart too, you know. He whispered something to Perkins. Then he reminded us that Perkins wanted us to try out residual income, and that he had already told the meeting that in his view residual income was a better control measure than percentage sales growth. So if we were going to make a change the majority obviously preferred residual income to growth.

By then, I felt that it was time to adjourn!

You'd better keep all this under your hat. But give me a short report summarizing the pros and cons of these three possibilities, and giving me your view on which one would be best in principle for us to use in future. If I eventually have to lay the law down I want to get it right. But make sure you keep it short — not more than about four pages'.

On returning to your office you cancel your previous arrangements for the evening, and then quickly work out the following table, showing the average annual performance of the divisions over the last three years in historic cost terms:

Division	Manager	ROI %	Residual income (£)	Sales growth %
Home Counties	Geoffrey Gilmore	10	80,000	15
Eastern Counties	Morton Jackson	8	60,000	25
North-West	Christopher Perkins	6	100,000	20

You send a copy of the table to Mr Ragwort with a note commenting that it may help to explain the attitudes being taken in the meeting. You then settle down to think about the three measures proposed as means of controlling divisional performance.

You are required to write a report for Mr Ragwort about the proposed methods of measuring divisional performance, to comply with the terms of his instruction.

ICAEW Management Accounting
July 1978

23.5* The executive directors and the seven divisional managers of Kant Ltd spent a long weekend at a country house debating the company's goals. They concluded that Kant had multiple goals, and that the performance of senior managers should be assessed in terms of all of them.

The goals identified were:
(i) to generate a reasonable financial return for shareholders;
(ii) to maintain a high market share;
(iii) to increase productivity annually;
(iv) to offer an up-to-date product range of high quality and proven reliability;
(v) to be known as responsible employers;
(vi) to acknowledge social responsibilities;
(vii) to grow and survive autonomously.

The finance director was asked to prepare a follow-up paper, setting-out some of the implications of these ideas. He has asked you, as his personal assistant, to prepare comments on certain issues for his consideration.

You are required to set out briefly, with reasons:
(a) suitable measures of performance for each of the stated goals for which you consider this to be possible; (18 marks)
(b) an outline of your view as to whether any of the stated goals can be considered to be sufficiently general to incorporate all of the others. (7 marks)

ICAEW Management Accounting
December 1979

23.6* (a) 'Because of the possibility of goal incongruence, an optimal plan can only be achieved if divisional budgets are constructed by a central planning department, but this means that divisional independence is a pseudo-independence.'

Discuss the problems of establishing divisional budgets in the light of this quotation. (9 marks)
(b) 'Head Office' will require a division to submit regular reports of its performance.

Describe, discuss and compare three measures of divisional operating performance that might feature in such reports. (8 marks)

(17 marks)
ACCA Level 2 Management Accounting
December 1983

23.7* From an accounting perspective an organizational unit of an accounting entity may be a cost centre or a profit centre or an investment centre. Explain these categories, describe the strengths and weaknesses of each and the

conditions in which each would be most appropriate if the aim is to develop efficient planning and control procedures. (7 marks)

ACCA Level 2 Management Accounting
June 1983

23.8* A long-established, highly centralized, company has grown to the extent that its chief executive, despite having a good supporting team, is finding difficulty in keeping up with the many decisions of importance in the company.

Consideration is therefore being given to reorganizing the company into profit centres. These would be product divisions, headed by a divisional managing director, who would be responsible for all the division's activities relating to its products.

You are required to explain, in outline:
(a) the types of decision areas that should be transferred to the new divisional managing directors if such a reorganization is to achieve its objectives;
(b) the types of decision areas that might reasonably be retained at company head office;
(c) the management accounting problems that might be expected to arise in introducing effective profit centre control.

(20 marks)
ICMA P3 Management Accounting
November 1979

23.9* Divisionalization is a common form of organizational arrangement but there is some diversity of opinion as to the best measure of divisional performance.

Discuss this topic and describe and compare the main performance measures that have been suggested. (17 marks)

ACCA Level 2 Management Accounting
June 1982

23.10* 'The most suitable income figure for use in appraising the performance of divisional management, and also for use by divisional executives in guiding their decisions, is controllable residual income.' (Solomons).

Discuss.

23.11* Critically discuss the methods of evaluating the performance of managers of divisionalized companies. What factors should be considered in designing control systems for evaluating divisional profit performances?

23.12* 'In the control of divisional operations within a large company, conflicts often arise between the aims of the organization as a whole and the aspirations of the individual divisions.'

What forms may these conflicts take, and how would you expect the finance function to assist in the relation of such conflicts?

23.13* 'Profit, return on investment and residual income are all imperfect measures for the purpose of evaluating the performance of a divisional manager and may indeed have some dysfunctional effects, and yet these measures have stood the test of time and are widely used.'

Discuss the strengths and weaknesses of these measures of performance.

24 Transfer pricing in divisionalized companies

In Chapter 23 divisional return on investment, residual income and a comparison of budgeted and actual cash flows were suggested as methods which could be used to evaluate the performance of divisional managers. However, problems will arise whichever of these measures is adopted when the divisions transfer goods and services to each other. The established transfer price is a cost to the receiving division and revenue to the supplying division, which means that whatever transfer price is set it will affect the performance measure of each division. In addition, this transfer price will also significantly influence each division's input and output decisions and thus the total company profits.

In this chapter we shall discuss the various approaches which can be adopted to arrive at transfer prices for transactions between divisions. In particular, we shall consider setting transfer prices when the market for the intermediate product (that is, the product transferred) is perfect. We shall then look at the implications for setting transfer prices when the market is imperfect, and consider the application of linear programming to setting transfer prices where demand is in excess of supply. Finally, we shall identify the conflicts in transfer pricing and discuss the methods by which these conflicts might be resolved. A more rigorous economic analysis of transfer pricing is illustrated graphically in the appendix at the end of this chapter.

Objectives of transfer pricing

Anthony and Dearden (1980) suggest that a sound transfer pricing system should accomplish the following objectives:

(1) It should motivate the divisional manager to make *sound decisions*, and it should communicate information which provides a reliable basis for such decisions. This will happen when actions that divisional managers take to improve the reported profit of their divisions also improve the profit of the company as a whole.

(2) It should result in a report of divisional profits that is a reasonable measure of the *managerial performance* of the division.

(3) It should ensure that divisional *autonomy* is not undermined.

Sound decisions

Goods which are transferred from the supplying division to the receiving division are known as *intermediate products*. The products which are sold by the receiving division to the outside world are known as *final products*. The objective of the receiving division is to subject the intermediate product to further processing before it is sold as a final product in the outside market. The transfer price of the intermediate product establishes part of the receiving divisions costs and therefore influences the price and output decisions of the receiving division.

In a centralized company the decision as to whether an intermediate product should be sold or processed further is determined by comparing the incremental costs of, and the revenues from, further processing. In a divisionalized organization

structure, however, the manager of the receiving division will treat the price at which the intermediate product is transferred as an incremental cost, and this may lead to incorrect decisions being made. For example, let us assume that the incremental cost of the intermediate product is £100, and the additional further processing costs of the receiving division are £60. The incremental cost of producing the final product will therefore be £160. Let us also assume that the supplying division is not operating at full capacity and that the market price of the final product is £200. To simplify the illustration we assume there is no market for the intermediate product. The correct decision would be to convert the intermediate product into the final product. In a centralized company this decision would be taken, but in a divisionalized organization structure where the transfer price for the intermediate product is based on a full cost of, say, £150, the incremental cost of the *receiving* division will be £210 (150 + 60). The divisional manager would, therefore, incorrectly decide not to purchase the intermediate product for further processing. This problem can be overcome if the transfer price is set at the incremental cost of the supplying division, which in this example is £100.

Evaluating managerial performance

When goods are transferred from one division to another, a portion of the revenue of the supplying division becomes a portion of the cost of the receiving division. Consequently, the prices at which goods are transferred can influence each division's performance measure, and there is a danger than an unsound transfer price will result in a misleading performance measure which may cause divisional managers to believe that the transfer price is affecting their performance rating unfairly. This may lead to disagreement and negative motivational consequences.

Conflict of objectives

We shall see that in some situations the decision-making and the performance evaluation objectives which are required for establishing a transfer pricing system may conflict with each other. For example, a transfer price which is equal to incremental cost may be appropriate for motivating a manager to make sound decisions, but the manager of the supplying division may have no incentive to transfer the goods to the receiving division at the incremental cost because his divisional performance measure will not be improved. Furthermore, if a transfer price equal to incremental cost is imposed on the manager of the supplying division, the concept of *divisional autonomy* is undermined.

Market prices

In most circumstances, where there is a competitive market price for an intermediate product, the current market price is the most suitable basis for setting the transfer price. When transfers are recorded at market prices divisional performance is more likely to represent the real economic contribution of the division to total company profits. If the supplying division did not exist, the intermediate product would have to be purchased on the outside market at the current market price. Alternatively, if the receiving division did not exist, the intermediate product would have to be sold on the outside market at the current market price. Divisional profits are therefore likely to be similar to the profits which would be calculated if the divisions were separate organizations. Consequently, divisional profitability can be compared directly with the profitablity of similar companies which operate in the same type of business.

In a *perfectly competitive* market the supplying division should supply as much as the receiving division requires at the current market price so long as the incremental cost is lower than the market price. If this supply is insufficient to meet the receiving division's demand it must obtain additional supplies by purchasing from an outside supplier at the current market price. Alternatively, if the supplying division produces more of the intermediate product than the receiving division requires, the excess can be sold to the outside market at the current market price.

Where the selling costs for internal transfers of the intermediate product are identical to those which arise from sales in the outside market, it will not matter whether the supplying division's output is sold internally or externally. Let us assume initially that the output of the supplying division is sold *externally* and that the receiving division purchases its requirements *externally*. Now consider a situation where the output of the intermediate product is transferred *internally* at the market price and is not sold on the outside

Exhibit 24.1

(A) Purchase and sale of intermediate product in the external market

(B) Purchase and sale of intermediate product internally

market. Exhibit 24.1 shows that divisional and total profits are not affected, whatever alternative is chosen.

The diagram illustrates a situation where the receiving division sells 1,000 units of the final product in the external market. The incremental costs for the production of 1,000 units of the *intermediate* product are £5,000 with a market price for the output of £8,000. The incremental costs of the receiving division for the additional processing of the 1,000 units of the intermediate product are £4,000. This output can be sold for £18,000. You will see that it does not matter whether the intermediate product is transferred internally or sold externally; the profits of each division and total company profits remain unchanged.

The effect of selling expenses

In practice it is unlikely that total company profits will remain unchanged. The supplying division will incur selling expenses when selling the intermediate product on the external market but such expenses will not be incurred on interdivisional transfers. If the transfer price is set at the current market price, the receiving division will be indifferent between obtaining internal or external supplies of the intermediate product. However, if the receiving division purchases the intermediate product externally, the company will be worse off to the extent of the selling expenses which are incurred by the supplying division in disposing of its output on the external market. (For a more detailed discussion of the impact of selling

expenses on transfer prices see Gould, 1977 and the appendix to this chapter.) In practice, many companies modify the market price rule for pricing interdivisional transfers and deduct a margin to take account of the savings in selling and collection expenses.

Other market imperfections

One of the major problems with using market prices is that markets may not be perfectly competitive. In addition, the transferred product may have special characteristics which differentiate it from other varieties of the same product. The market price for the intermediate product is appropriate only when quality, delivery, discounts and back-up services are identical. Furthermore, it may be possible to purchase the intermediate product in the external market from suppliers who are selling at a temporary distress price which is below total cost but above variable cost. If the supplying division has excess capacity, incorrect decisions may arise because of strict adherence to the market price rule. For example, suppose that the supplying division has spare capacity and produces an intermediate product at an incremental cost of £1,000; the transfer price for this product is set at the external market price of £1,600. Now suppose that a supplier of the intermediate product is selling at a temporary distress price of £1,500. Given this situation the manager of the receiving division will prefer to purchase the intermediate product from the external supplier at £1,500 than from the supplying division at a cost of £1,600. Because the supplying division has spare capacity, the relevant cost of making the product internally is £1,000, and strict adherence to the market price rule can therefore motivate managers to take decisions which are not in the best interests of the company.

Implications for perfect markets

The complications indicated in the previous paragraph arise because the market for the intermediate product is not perfectly competitive. It is important, therefore, to ascertain whether market conditions do approximate closely to those of perfect competition. If they do, the transfer price should be set at the market price of the intermediate product, and any excess of interdivisional demand over supply, or supply over demand, can

be resolved by the purchase or sale of the intermediate product on the external market. Overall company profits will then be optimized. If, however, conditions approximating to a perfect market are not met, the use of a market price for internal transfers may mean that the supplying division will be induced to supply less, or the receiving division may be induced to take less, than the quantity which will optimize company profits. Let us now consider the setting of transfer prices when the market for the intermediate product is imperfect.

Transfer pricing in imperfect markets

In a perfect market a going market price exists which a firm will accept. There will be no advantage in selling output at a reduced price, and marginal revenue will be equal to the selling price. In an imperfect market, however, the firm will face a downward sloping demand curve which will enable sales volume to be expanded if the selling price is reduced, and marginal revenue will then be less than the previous selling price.[1] This implies that the market price rule must be modified as a basis for establishing transfer prices.

To illustrate how optimal transfer prices might be determined for imperfect markets we shall assume initially that there is no market for the intermediate product and that the market for the final product is imperfect. We shall see that the principles established for setting transfer prices when there is no market for the intermediate product can also be applied to situations where there is an imperfect market.

Imperfect market for the final product but no market for the intermediate product

Where there is an imperfect market for the *final* product, the correct transfer price for decision-making is the one which will motivate the divisions to maximize the profits of the company. The transfer price which meets this objective is the *marginal or incremental cost of the supplying division for that output at which the marginal cost equals the receiving divisions net marginal revenue from processing the intermediate product.* Net marginal revenue can be defined as the marginal revenue from the sale of an additional unit by the receiving division less the incremental costs of

Exhibit 24.2 Optimum transfer price for an imperfect final market and no market for the intermediate product

	Supplying division			Receiving division	
Units produced	Total cost (£)	Marginal cost (£)	Units produced	Total *net* revenue (£)	Net marginal revenue (£)
1	4	4	1	10	10
2	7	3	2	19	9
3	10	3	3	27	8
4	11	1	4	34	7
5	13	2	5	40	6
6	15	2	6	45	5
7	19	[4]	7	49	[4]
8	24	5	8	52	3
9	31	7	9	54	2
10	39	8	10	55	1
11	48	9	11	55	0
12	58	10	12	54	−1

converting the intermediate product into the final product; so *net marginal revenue excludes the transfer price*. This transfer pricing rule is illustrated in Exhibit 24.2.[2] The marginal cost of the supplying division and the net marginal revenue of the receiving division are the same at an output level of seven units; this gives a transfer price of £4. The receiving division will compare this transfer price with its net marginal revenue and select an output level of seven units. The transfer price of £4 will also induce the supplying division to produce exactly seven units. At an output level below seven units the supplying division will be motivated to expand output because the transfer price will be in excess of its marginal cost. However, the supplying division will not be motivated to produce beyond seven units as the marginal cost will be in excess of the transfer price. A graphical illustration of a situation where

no market exists for the intermediate product is presented in the appendix to this chapter.

Imperfect market for intermediate and final product

In Exhibit 24.2 we have not included the possibility of the supplying and receiving divisions selling or buying the intermediate product in the external market. Figure 24A.4 in the appendix to this chapter shows in a graphical form that *the correct transfer price where there is an imperfect market for the intermediate product is where the marginal cost of the supplying division is equal to the sum of the net marginal revenue of the receiving division and the marginal revenue from the sale of the intermediate product.* Consider now Exhibit 24.3

Exhibit 24.3 Optimum transfer price for an imperfect intermediate market

	Supplying division			Receiving division	
Units produced	Total cost (£)	Marginal cost (£)	Marginal revenue (£)	Units produced	Net marginal revenue (£)
1	19	19	40 (1)	1	35.00 (3)
2	37	18	37 (2)	2	33.50 (5)
3	54	17	34 (4)	3	32.00 (6)
4	69	15	31 (7)	4	30.50 (8)
5	83	14	28 (10)	5	29.00 (9)
6	98	15	25 (13)	6	27.50 (11)
7	114	16	22	7	26.00 (12)
8	132	18	19	8	24.50
9	152	20	16	9	23.00
10	175	23	13	10	21.50
11	202	27	10	11	20.00
12	234	32	7	12	18.50
13	271	37	4	13	17.00

where the intermediate product can be sold on the external market.

The numbers in parentheses refer to the ranking of the sale of the intermediate product on the basis of marginal revenue/net marginal revenue. You will see that the sale of the first unit in the intermediate external market gives a marginal revenue of £40 compared with a net marginal revenue of £35 if the first unit is tranferred to the receiving division and sold as a final product. Consequently the first unit of output of the supplying division should be sold in the intermediate external market. The rankings indicate that the second unit of output should also be sold in the intermediate market, the third unit sold in the final market, and so on.

The allocation of the output of the supplying division based on these rankings is shown in Exhibit 24.4.

You will see that the optimum output for the company as a whole is at the point where the marginal cost of the supplying division is equal to the sum of the marginal revenue schedule of the supplying division and net marginal revenue schedule of the receiving divisions (the sum of these schedules is shown in the final column of Exhibit 24.4). This occurs when the eleventh unit is sold. The twelfth unit should not be made because the marginal cost of the supplying division is in excess of the marginal revenue/net marginal revenue.

Applying the transfer price rule, the marginal cost of the supplying division will be equal to the sum of the net marginal revenue of the receiving division from the sale of the final product and the marginal revenue from the sale of the intermediate product at just below £27.50. In fact a transfer price of £27 will induce the managers of the supplying and receiving divisions to make the correct output decisions.

If you refer to Exhibit 24.3 you will see that if the transfer price is set at £27 the manager of the supplying division will choose to sell the first five units of the intermediate product on the external market (this is because marginal revenue is in excess of the transfer price) and transfer the remaining output to the receiving division (this is because the transfer price is in excess of marginal revenue). You will also see that the manager of the supplying division will select an output level of eleven units based on the principle that he will not manufacture any units when the marginal cost is in excess of the transfer price.

At a transfer price of £27 the manager of the receiving division will choose to sell six units (see Exhibit 24.3) because net marginal revenue is in excess of the transfer price. The transfer price of £27 will therefore induce the supplying division to produce eleven units, sell five units to the external market and transfer six units to the receiving division; the receiving division will also wish to purchase six units from the supplying division. This is identical to the optimal output schedule for the company as a whole shown in Exhibit 24.4.

What would be the correct transfer price if the variable cost per unit of the intermediate product was constant (that is, marginal cost equals variable cost)? The answer is that applying the marginal cost rule *will result in the transfer price being set at the variable cost per unit of the supplying division.*

Exhibit 24.4 Allocation of output of supplying division between intermediate and external market

Output (units)	Marginal cost of supplying division £	Allocation per ranking in Exhibit 24.3	Marginal revenue/ net marginal revenue £
1	19	Intermediate market	40.00
2	18	Intermediate market	37.00
3	17	Final market	35.00
4	15	Intermediate market	34.00
5	14	Final market	33.50
6	15	Final market	32.00
7	16	Intermediate market	31.00
8	18	Final market	30.50
9	20	Final market	29.00
10	23	Intermediate market	28.00
11	27	Final market	27.50
12	32	No allocation	26.00

Can you see that if the variable/marginal cost of the supplying division was £30 throughout the entire output schedule in Exhibits 24.3 and 24.4, then applying the above procedure would result in the transfer price being set at £30?

Capacity constraint

When there is a capacity constraint, a transfer price based on the marginal cost rule will not ensure that the optimum output levels are achieved. For example, let us assume that in Exhibits 24.3 and 24.4 capacity of the supplying division is restricted to six units. You will see from the ranking (see Exhibit 24.3) that the scarce capacity of six units should be allocated so that three units are transfered to the receiving division and three units are sold on the intermediate external market. However, Exhibit 24.3 indicates that at a transfer price of £27 the supplying division will maximize its own profits by selling five units of the intermediate product in the external market and transferring one unit to the receiving division. Alternatively, the receiving division will maximize its own profits by taking the entire output of six units from the supplying division and selling them as a final product.[3]

Both divisions pursuing their own best interests in isolation will not therefore arrive at the optimal company solution, that is, the sale of three units of the intermediate product and three units of the final product. A conflict occurs because what is in the best interests of a specific division s not in the best interests of the company as a whole. One way of ensuring that the optimal solution is achieved is for central headquarters to obtain information from the supplying and the receiving divisions and to work out the optimal production programme for each division. However, such an approach strikes at the very heart of the transfer price problem because the optimal production programme has been achieved by an infringement of divisional autonomy. We shall return to this theme later in the chapter.

Summary

Let us now summarize our findings where there is an imperfect market for the intermediate product. Where the supplying division has no capacity constraints *the correct transfer price is the marginal cost of the supplying division for that output at which marginal cost equals the sum of the receiving division's net marginal revenue from using the intermediate product and the marginal revenue from the sale of the intermediate product*. Where unit variable cost is constant and fixed costs remain unchanged this rule will give a transfer price which is equal to the variable cost per unit of the supplying division. However, when capacity constraints apply and the profit maximizing ouput cannot be achieved, transfer prices which are based on marginal cost will not ensure that optimal output is achieved and in this situation it may be necessary for staff at the central headquarters to establish the optimum production programme for each division.

Effect of cost-plus transfer prices

We have established that where there are no capacity constraints the transfer price should be set at the variable cost per unit of producing the intermediate product if variable cost is constant per unit of output. However, surveys by Tomkins (1973) and Rook (1971) indicate that many firms use cost-plus transfer prices such as 'variable cost plus' or 'total cost plus' *when there is no market for the intermediate product*. There is a serious danger that cost-plus based transfer prices will motivate the manager of the receiving division to restrict output below that of the optimal output level for the company as a whole. This situation is illustrated in Exhibit 24.5.

You will note that the optimum output level is eleven units, this being the point where the

Exhibit 24.5 Effect of cost-plus based transfer prices

Supplying division		Receiving division	
Units produced	Variable (marginal) cost £	Units produced	Net marginal revenue £
1	10	1	20
2	10	2	19
3	10	3	18
4	10	4	17
5	10	5	16
6	10	6	15
7	10	7	14
8	10	8	13
9	10	9	12
10	10	10	11
11	10	11	10
12	10	12	9

marginal cost of the supplying division is equal to the net marginal revenue of the receiving division. Let us assume that a transfer price is set at variable cost plus 40%. This will give a transfer price of £14. At this transfer price the receiving division will restrict its output to seven units and the optimal output for the company will not be achieved.

Note that transfers should be at standard marginal cost and not at actual cost as this approach will avoid any inefficiencies of the supplying division being passed on to the receiving division. Any difference between the transferred-out costs and the actual costs incurred will mean either adverse or favourable variances, which will encourage the managers of the supplying divisions to minimize their costs.

The use of linear programming in establishing optimum transfer prices

When the supplying division cannot meet the profit maximizing output it should use linear programming to establish the optimum production programme. This topic was dealt with in Chapter 22, and you are recommended at this stage to re-read that chapter to ensure a thorough understanding of linear programming before proceeding further.

Let us consider a situation where a company has two divisions, a supplying division and a receiving division. The supplying division produces two intermediate products I_1 and I_2. There is no external market for the intermediate product I_1, but I_2 can be sold externally. The receiving division produces two products F_1 and F_2 for which it requires I_1 and I_2. There are capacity constraints in the supplying division such that the total output of I_1 and I_2 is restricted. Information appropriate to the supplying and receiving division is presented in Exhibit 24.6.

The problem we have is to determine how much of the intermediate products I_1 and I_2 should be produced, the quantity of the intermediate products which should be transferred to the receiving division, and the quantity of the intermediate and the final products which should be sold externally. We also wish to establish a transfer price for the intermediate products so that each divisional manager can maximize divisional profits having regard only to the transfer price and not to the cost and revenue functions of the other divisions. The transfer price should also motivate managers to maximize total company profits.

To formulate the linear programming model we must first calculate the product contributions:

		F_1	F_2
Supplying divisions variable costs:	I_1	£16	£16
	I_2	8	16
Receiving divisions variable costs		3	2
Total variable cost		27	34
Selling price		37	48
Contribution per unit		10	14

We can now formulate the problem:

Maximize contribution = $0.5I_2 + 10F_1 + 14F_2$
Subject to
$4F_1 + 4F_2 \leq 80,000$ (I_1 capacity constraint)
$1I_2 + 4F_1 + 8F_2 \leq 120,000$ (I_2 capacity constraint)
$I_2, F_1, F_2 \geq 0$

The optimal solution to this problem is to produce 10,000 units of F_1, 10,000 units of F_2 and zero units of I_2 for sale in the external market. The maximum quantity of I_1 and I_2 should be produced but all of the output should be passed to the receiving division for further processing; this will yield a total contribution of £240,000. A production programme such as this could be dictated to the divisions by the management at central headquarters but this would be interfering with divisional affairs. However, Solomons (1968) suggests that a transfer price can be established using the output from the linear programming problem which will motivate the managers to produce the optimum output. This transfer price is calculated by adding together opportunity costs and the variable costs of the intermediate product. The opportunity costs are obtained from the

Exhibit 24.6 Data from the supplying and the receiving divisions

Supplying division	Product I_1	Product I_2
Variable cost per unit	£4	£2
Selling price per unit in the external market	—	£2.50
Contribution per unit	—	£0.50
Maximum production	80,000 units	120,000 units

Receiving division	Product F_1	Product F_2
Variable cost per unit of processing in receiving division	£3	£2
Selling prices	£37	£48
Required input of I_1	4 units	4 units
Required input of I_2	4 units	8 units

solution to the linear programming problem and are £1.50 for I_1 and £1 for I_2. The transfer prices will therefore be calculated as follows:

	I_1	I_2
Variable cost	£4.00	£2.00
Opportunity cost	1.50	1.00
Relevant cost (transfer price)	5.50	3.00

Using these transfer prices the manager of the supplying division can calculate the following contributions:

	Transfer of I_1	Transfer I_2	Sale of I_2 on external market
Transfer price/external selling price	£5.50	£3.00	£2.50
Variable cost	4.00	2.00	2.00
Contribution	1.50	1.00	0.50

The manager of the supplying division can maximize divisional profits by formulating a linear programming model where I_1 and I_2 represent transfers of the intermediate product and I_2^e represents the sale on the external market of intermediate product I_2. The linear programming problem is as follows:

$$\text{Maximize contribution} = 1.50I_1 + 1.00\,I_2 + 0.5\,I_2^e$$
$$\text{subject to}\quad I_1 \leqslant 80,000$$
$$I_2 + I_2^e \leqslant 120,000$$
$$I_1, I_2, I_2^e \geqslant 0$$

The optimal solution for the *supplying division* is to produce 80,000 units of I_1 and 120,000 units of I_2 with all of the output being transferred to the receiving division. This is the optimal solution for the *whole company*, and gives a total contribution for the supplying division of £240,000 which is equal to the total contribution for the company as a whole.

Let us now consider how the manager of the receiving department will react to the suggested transfer prices of £5.50 and £3. He will calculate the unit contributions of products F_1 and F_2 as follows:

		F_1
Selling price		£37
Receiving division's variable costs:		
Purchases from supplying division		
I_1, 4 units at £5.50	22	
I_2, 4 units at £3.00	12	
Receiving division's variable costs	3	37
Contribution per unit		0

The manager of the receiving division will be indifferent about making products F_1 and F_2, because each product yields a zero contribution but the company as a whole will be worse off if outputs of products F_1 and F_2 are zero. This means that we can only be sure that divisional managers will arrive at the optimal solution if head office instructs the receiving division to convert all the output which the supplying division is prepared to transfer at the transfer prices which are obtained from the linear programming solution.

Tomkins (1973) provides an illustration of a situation where transfer prices based on the solution from a linear programming model will not lead to an optimal solution even when the receiving division is requested to convert all output which the supplying division is prepared to supply. Assume that the linear programming model for Exhibit 24.6 is altered as follows:

$$\text{Maximize contribution} = 10F_1 + 14F_2$$
Subject to
$$4F_1 + 4F_2 \leqslant 80,000 \ (I_1 \text{ capacity constraint})$$
$$4F_1 + 8F_2 \leqslant 120,000 \ (I_2 \text{ capacity constraint})$$
$$F_1 \leqslant 6,000 \ (F_1 \text{ capacity})$$
$$F_2 \leqslant 20,000 \ (F_2 \text{ capacity})$$
$$F_1, F_2 \geqslant 0$$

We are now assuming that the supplying division cannot sell the intermediate product externally. In addition, constraints are introduced on the output of the final products F_1 and F_2. The optimal solution is to produce 6,000 units of F_1 and 12,000 units of F_2 giving a maximum total contribution of £228,000. The opportunity costs are zero for I_1 capacity constraint, £1.75 for I_2 capacity constraint, £1.50 for F_1 capacity constraint and zero for F_2 capacity constraint. We can now apply the procedure which was outlined earlier to arrive at a transfer price of £4 for I_1 (£4 variable cost + zero opportunity cost) and £3.75 for I_2 (£2 variable cost + £1.75 opportunity cost). Hence the manager of the supplying division will want to maximize transfers of I_2 rather than transferring I_1 at

		F_2
		48
4 units at £5.50	22	
8 units at £3.00	24	
	2	48
		0

variable cost which yields a zero contribution. The

calculation of the product contributions for the receiving division indicates that the manager will wish to maximize production of F_1 and will be indifferent about F_2.[4] This is not consistent with the optimal solution for the company as a whole. Therefore, transfer prices calculated from this linear programming solution cannot necessarily be guaranteed to motivate managers to achieve the optimum output level.

The linear programming model, however, is required to determine the optimal production programme for each division. This approach will lead to a loss of divisional autonomy because the production schedule is determined by central headquarters. There are also additional problems associated with the application of linear programming in setting transfer prices; if you are interested in this topic you should refer to Manes (1970) for a detailed discussion of these problems. Note also that a number of writers have suggested methods for overcoming the problems which are identified with using opportunity costs as a basis for setting transfer prices (see, for example, Tomkins, 1973, and Ronen and McKinney, 1970).

Transfer pricing conflicts

In this chapter we have established that in certain situations a theoretically correct transfer price can be determined which will lead to the activities of a receiving and a supplying division, taken together, being the same as if they had been jointly organized as a single profit centre. In the absence of a competitive market for the intermediate product the theoretically correct transfer price can be established only when the information for all the divisions is gathered together to give a composite picture. This is likely to result in staff at the central headquarters gathering together the information and setting the transfer prices.

When transfer prices are set by central headquarters there is a loss of divisional autonomy. It can be argued that if divisions are not free to set their own transfer prices, central headquarters might just as well dictate the types and volumes of products to be transferred instead of dictating the prices at which transfers are to pass between them. However, even though imposed transfer prices from central headquarters are likely to be an infringement of divisional autonomy, they are likely to be less objectionable to divisions than direct interference with production and marketing plans.

Earlier in this chapter transfer prices based on marginal costs were recommended when the market for the intermediate product was imperfect. The transfer price will be set at the variable cost per unit of the intermediate product if unit variable cost is constant. In this situation the supplying divisions will not obtain any contribution towards fixed costs for the transfer of intermediate products to the receiving division. A conflict then arises because the transfer price which is correct for *decision-making* will give a *performance measure* which shows a zero contribution for the supplying division. The manager of the supplying division might argue that production of the intermediate product is essential to overall company profit and that he should be entitled to a share of this profit. Thus a transfer price which is based on variable cost may be the most suitable method for decision-making but it is unlikely that the supplying division will be motivated to transfer intermediate products at variable cost unless the division is instructed to do so by central headquarters. This will mean a loss of divisional autonomy and a performance report which does not reflect the true picture of the economic contribution which the supplying divison has made to total company profits.

The conflict between establishing a transfer price which is correct for sound decisions, maintaining divisional autonomy and producing an acceptable performance measure may also apply to the *receiving* division. For example, we have established that when the supplying division does not have sufficient capacity to meet all the demands which are placed upon it, the linear programming solution suggests a transfer price which will result in the supplying division being credited with total company contribution. In this situation the receiving division will earn a zero contribution. Again the transfer price will mean a loss of divisional autonomy and a performance report which does not reflect the economic performance of the division.

Resolving transfer price conflicts

Lump sum payments

How can we resolve the problem when the total contribution is allocated to one division only? One

Exhibit 24.7 Projected statement of company budgeted costs and revenues

Sale of finished product:		
100,000 units at £10		1,000,000
Variable costs:		
Supplying division 100,000		
units at £2	200,000	
Receiving division 100,000		
units at £6	600,000	800,000
Contribution		200,000

solution is to apportion the total contribution between the supplying and the receiving divisions. You will recall that where there is no competitive market for the intermediate product, a transfer price based on marginal cost was recommended. This will give a transfer price equal to the variable cost of the intermediate product when variable cost per unit is constant. Consider now the statement of budgeted variable costs and revenues presented in Exhibit 24.7.

A transfer price set at a variable cost of £2 per unit for the intermediate product would mean a zero contribution for the supplying division, and £200,000 for the receiving division. The apportionment of the total contribution might consist of a lump sum payment from the receiving division to the supplying division for the franchise of handling the product. For example, the contribution of £200,000 could be apportioned on the basis of standard variable cost for the budgeted transfers. The receiving division would be charged with £50,000 cost for the privilege of handling the intermediate product, and the supplying division would be credited with this amount.[5] The effect of

variable cost of the supplying division into his output decisions. For a demonstration of a transfer pricing system where the lost contribution charge is levied on the selling division together with an internal trading discount, see Emmanuel and Gee (1982).

Dual transfer pricing

Another solution which has been proposed for avoiding the situation where the total contribution is assigned to either the supplying or the receiving division is to recognize that there is no necessity to have a single transfer price. There is no reason why one transfer price cannot be used for decision-making and another transfer price be used for measuring performance. In Exhibit 24.7 the receiving division could be charged with the variable cost of £2 per unit and the supplying division credited with an amount in excess of variable cost. To keep things simple here, let us assume that this is variable cost plus 50%. If the receiving division is charged with the variable cost per unit, the manager will be induced to take the correct decisions for the organization as a whole. The performance of the manager of the supplying division would also be enhanced by supplying sufficient goods to meet the requirements of the receiving division because each unit transferred will be at a price of £3 and provide a contribution towards the total fixed costs. Let us now consider the situation in Exhibit 24.7 where the total transfers are 100,000 units. The results for each division will be as follows:

Supplying division		Receiving division		
Transfers to supplying division		Sales of finished product		
at £3	£300,000	at £10		£1,000,000
(100,000 units at £2 plus		Variable costs		
50%)		Supplying division transfers		
Variable costs (100,000 × £2)	£200,000	(100,000 × £2)	200,000	
		Conversion costs		
		(100,000 × £6)	600,000	800,000
Contribution	100,000	Contribution		200,000

such a lump sum payment would be that the manager of the supplying division would be willing to transfer at variable cost because he would be compensated for items transferred to the receiving division in the form of a lump sum payment. By basing the lump sum payment on budgeted transfers, the manager of the receiving division would regard this charge as a fixed cost and would correctly incorporate only the transfers at the

Note that the contribution for the company as a whole will be less than the sum of the divisional profits by £100,000, but this can easily be resolved by a simple accounting adjustment.

Negotiated transfer prices

The difficulties which have been encountered in

establishing a sound system of transfer pricing have led to suggestions that negotiated transfer prices should be used. Negotiated transfer prices are most appropriate in situations where some market imperfections exist for the intermediate product, particularly when there are different selling costs for internal and external sales, or where there are in existence several different market prices. When there are such imperfections in the market, the respective divisional managers must have the freedom to buy and sell outside the company to enable them to engage in a bargaining process. It is claimed that if this is the case the friction and bad feeling which may arise from a centrally controlled market transfer price will be eliminated without incurring a misallocation of resources.

There are strong arguments for believing that in certain situations, if divisions are allowed to bargain freely with each other, they will usually make decisions which will maximize total company profits — this is of course assuming that managers are competent and know how to use the accounting information.

The behavioural literature also supports the use of negotiated transfer prices. Watson and Baumler (1975) advocate that negotiated transfer prices can help to resolve conflicts between organizational sub-units. They argue that mathematically elegant solutions to the transfer pricing problem may be less than ideal in behavioural terms because decentralization is sacrificed to optimize a numerical solution. Lawrence and Lorsch's (1967) research evidence indicated that successful firms facing uncertain environments were able effectively to resolve interdepartmental conflict, and the most important means of resolving this conflict was by confrontation, that is, negotiation. Watson and Baumler therefore argue that if the appropriate conflict resolution process is negotiation, the transfer price should be the one which is arrived at in this way. In particular, they argue that if the requisite degree of decentralization is achievable and there is a problem in obtaining adequate integration between the divisions then one integrative tool which is available is a system of negotiated transfer prices.

The situation may arise where divisional managers cannot agree on a mutually satisfactory transfer price, or where one division refuses to deal with another division. Central headquarters may then have to resolve the dispute, but the difficulty here is that the managers involved can no longer be said to have complete responsibility

for the activities of their divisions. This not only raises immediate behavioural problems with respect to morale and motivation, but it also means that when divisional performance is evaluated the managers will be held responsible for the results of decisions which they did not make. The overall effect is a breakdown in decentralized profit responsibility and a move towards centralized decision-making.

It is important to note that negotiated transfer prices are inappropriate where there is a perfect market for the intermediate product, as in a perfect market situation transfer prices can be based on the competitive market price without the need for the managers to engage in a negotiating process. At the other extreme, where there is no market for the intermediate product it is most unlikely that managers can engage in meaningful negotiation. Consequently, the supplying and the receiving divisions have no alternative other than to buy and sell from each other, and the negotiating process may mean that an unrealistic transfer price is agreed upon which bears no relationship to the theoretically correct transfer price. This might lead to the divisions operating at non-optimal output levels.

Negotiated transfer prices are therefore best suited to situations where there is a competitive market but where some imperfections exist, such as different selling costs on outside sales and inter-company transfers. Where there is no market for the intermediate product and where variable cost is equal to marginal cost, the correct transfer price is variable cost. It is most unlikely that the manager of the supplying division will be prepared to negotiate such a price. However, if a lump sum payment is negotiated and transfers are made at the variable cost of the intermediate product, the managers should be able to find a satisfactory solution.

Even if negotiated prices do not result in an optimum output level, the motivational advantages of giving managers full independence over their input and output decisions may lead to increased profits which outweigh the loss of profits from an unsound transfer pricing system. For a detailed discussion of negotiated transfer prices see Cook (1975).

Taxation and transfer pricing

The correct transfer price for decision-making

may also conflict with the price which is used to determine profits for taxation assessments. This conflict may arise when the supplying and the receiving divisions are located in different countries with different taxation rates. If the taxation rates in one country are much lower than those in the other country, it would be in the company's interest if most of the profits were allocated to the division which operates in the low taxation country. Taxation legislation restricts the freedom of companies to declare all their profits in the low taxation country (see Income and Corporation Taxes Act 1970, section 485), but, nevertheless, some scope for profit apportionment between divisions clearly exists.

We have established in our discussion so far that it is sometimes appropriate for transfer prices to be based on variable costs. This, however, involves all of the profits being assigned to the receiving division and a loss equal to the fixed costs being allocated to the supplying division. If these divisions are located in different countries, the taxation authorities of the country in which the supplying division is located will find the transfer price to be an unacceptable basis for declaring divisional profits. Also, if the taxation rates for the country in which the supplying division operates are much lower than the taxation rates for the country in which the receiving division operates, it may be in the best interests of the company to alter its transfer pricing system for calculating taxable profits to avoid the majority of profits being assigned to the receiving division. A transfer price based on variable cost will therefore be appropriate for decision-making but unacceptable for calculating tax. For a discussion of the difficulties encountered between subsidiaries in multinational companies in setting transfer prices see Barrett (1977).

Recommended procedure for transfer pricing

When there is a perfect competitive market for the transferred product the transfer price should be based on the market price of the intermediate product. If market imperfections exist, the correct transfer price is where the marginal cost of the supplying division is equal to the sum of the net marginal revenue of the receiving division and the marginal revenue from the sale of the inter-mediate product. If there is *no external market for the intermediate product* Solomons suggests the following alternative transfer pricing procedures.

Transfers of significant amounts occur, but such transfers are not a predominant part of the supplying divisions business

Here the supplying division is not dependent on supplying goods to the receiving division to justify its existence as a profit centre, so converting the supplying division from a profit centre to a cost centre is out of the question. Solomons suggests that the transfer price per unit should be calculated by equating the marginal cost of the producing division with the net marginal revenue of the receiving division. In addition, the receiving division should pay the supplying division an annual lump sum for the franchise to handle the product. This payment should cover the contribution required from the product towards fixed costs and profit. The essential point is that this payment should be fixed by negotiation on the basis of expected transfers so that the receiving division will regard this payment as a fixed cost.

Transfers constitute a predominant part of the supplying division's business, and it can meet all probable requirements

Here Solomons recommends that the supplying division should operate as a cost centre, and transfers to the receiving division should take place at standard variable cost if unit variable cost is constant. If the supplying cost centre's unit variable costs are not independent of the volume of transfers, central headquarters must intervene. Information supplied by the 'cost centre about costs at different levels of output must be collated with information from the receiving division about their requirements at different transfer prices. The transfer price is then determined at that price which will equate demand and supply.

However, if transfers are based on variable cost, the profit performance of the receiving division will be overstated because it will not bear any of the associated fixed costs of the cost centre. Solomons therefore recommends that the cost centre's fixed costs should be charged as a period cost to those divisions which use its products. This charge should be determined in advance based on the proportion of the cost centre's capacity earmarked for each receiving division. This

recommendation will mean that the receiving division will use incremental cost for its output decisions, thus ensuring that sound decisions are made.

The supplying division does not have the capacity necessary to meet all requirements

Here the best allocation of the scarce resources cannot be made by the supplying or the receiving division on its own and it will be necessary for central headquarters to intervene and use linear programming methods to establish the optimum production plan. Once the optimal plan has been established the supplying division must be instructed to supply the specified quantities of the intermediate product to the receiving division. This will mean a change of status for the supplying division to that of a cost centre.

The problem, however, still remains of the transfer price which should be paid by the receiving division for the transfers from the cost centre. Solomons suggests that there is no reason to depart from the methods suggested in the preceding situation where capacity constraints were not operative. Transfer prices should therefore be based on variable cost per unit at the programmed output level, with budgeted fixed costs being allocated as period costs to the divisions which take the transferred products.

Summary

A sound transfer pricing system should accomplish the following objectives:

(1) It should motivate the divisional manager to make sound decisions.
(2) It should enable a report to be made of divisional profits that is a reasonable measure of the management performance of the division.
(3) It should ensure that divisional autonomy is not undermined.

When the market for the intermediate product is perfect, the correct transfer price is the external market price for the product; the supplying and the receiving divisions themselves will determine the optimum output level. Alternatively, the market for the intermediate product might be imperfect or perhaps no market exists. Provided that the supplying division has no capacity constraints, the correct transfer price is the marginal cost of the supplying division for that output at which marginal cost equals the sum of the receiving division's net marginal revenue from converting the intermediate product and the marginal revenue from any sale of the intermediate product on the external market. Where unit variable cost is constant and fixed costs remain unchanged this rule will give a transfer price which is equal to the supplying division's unit variable cost.

Where the unit variable cost of the supplying division is not constant, the marginal cost transfer pricing rule requires that central headquarters set the transfer price by combining the cost and revenue information for the supplying and receiving divisions. This will lead to divisional autonomy being undermined and a performance meausre which does not provide a true reflection of each division's contribution to total company profits. To some extent these conflicts can be reduced if the receiving divisions agree to make a lump sum payment which represents the franchise to the supplying division for meeting the receiving division's requirements. Alternatively, a dual transfer pricing system might be introduced. Full independence can only be achieved by allowing divisions to negotiate their own transfer price, but this may result in non-optimal output decisions being made and this must be balanced against the gains which arise from granting the divisional managers full independence. Where the divisions are located in different countries the relative taxation rates will influence the transfer price that is used to determine profits for taxation purposes.

Finally, you should note that the transfer pricing methods which we have discussed in this chapter are by no means exhaustive. Many writers have suggested more elaborate transfer pricing models which attempt to resolve the decision-making, performance reporting and divisional autonomy conflicts. For a discussion of more elaborate models see Tomkins (1973).

References and further reading

Abdel-Khalif, R. and Lusk, E.J. Transfer pricing — A synthesis. *The Accounting Review* January 1974, 8-23.

Anthony, R.N. and Dearden, J. *Management Control Systems.* R.D. Irwin, 1980, p. 235.

Barrett, M.E. The case of the tangled transfer price. *Harvard Business Review* May/June 1977, 20-6.

Coburn, D.L. *et al.* Dilemmas in multinational transfer prices. *Management Accounting (USA)* November 1981, 53-9.

Cook, P.W. Decentralisation and the transfer price problem. *Journal of Business* April 1975, 87-94.

Emmanual, C. and Gee, K. Transfer pricing: A fair and neutral procedure. *Accounting and Business Research* Autumn 1982, 273-8.

Gould, J.R. Internal pricing on firms when there are costs of using an outside market. *Journal of Business* **37**(1), January 1964, 61-7.

Hirshleifer, J. On the economies of transfer pricing. *Journal of Business* July 1956, 172-84.

Income and Corporation Taxes Act 1970 (Section 485).

Kanodia, C. Risk sharing and transfer price systems under uncertainty. *Journal of Accounting Research* Spring 1979, 74-98.

Lawrence, P.R. and Lorsch, J.W. *Organisation and Environment.* R.D. Irwin, 1967.

Manes, R.P. Birch Paper Company revisited: An exercise in transfer pricing. *The Accounting Review* July 1970, 556-72.

Manes, R. and Verrecchia, R. A new proposal for setting intra company transfer prices. *Accounting and Business Research* Spring 1982, 97-104.

McNally, G.M. Profit centres and transfer prices. *Accounting and Business Research* Winter 1973, 13-23.

Osni, M. A transfer pricing system based on opportunity cost.*The Accounting Review* July 1970, 535-43.

Perrin, J. Transfer pricing. *Accountancy Age* 24 January 1975, 20-22.

Ronen, J. and McKinney, G. Transfer pricing for divisional autonomy. *Journal of Accounting Research* Spring 1970, 99-112.

Rook, A. Transfer pricing, management survey report no. 8. British Institute of Management, 1971.

Schiff, M. Transfer pricing for public reporting: A case study. *Accounting and Business Research* Autumn 1980, 440-43.

Solomons, D. *Divisional Performance: Measurement and Control.* R.D. Irwin, 1968, pp. 187-98.

Stewart, J.C. Multinationals and transfer pricing. *Journal of Business Finance and Accounting* Autumn 1977, 353-72.

Tang, R.Y.W. Environmental variables of multiple transfer pricing: A UK perspective. *Journal of Business Finance and Accounting* Summer 1982, 179-90.

Tomkins, C. *Financial Planning in Divisionalised Companies.* Haymarket Publishing Company, 1973, Chapters 4 and 8.

Watson, D.J.H. and Baumler, J.V. Transfer pricing: A behavioral context. *The Accounting Review* July 1975, 466-74.

Problems

* Indicates that a suggested solution is to be found in the *Students' Manual.*

24.1 B Ltd, producing a range of minerals, is organized into two trading groups: one handles wholesale business and the other sales to retailers.

One of its products is a moulding clay. The wholesale group extracts the clay and sells it to external wholesale customers as well as to the retail group. The production capacity is 2,000 tonnes per month but at present sales are limited to 1,000 tonnes wholesale and 600 tonnes retail.

The transfer price was agreed at £200 per tonne in line with the external wholesale trade price at 1 July which was the beginning of the budget year. As from 1 December, however, competitive pressure has forced the wholesale trade price down to £180 per tonne. The members of the retail group contend that the transfer price to them should be the same as for outside customers. The wholesale group refute the argument on the basis that the original budget established the price for the whole budget year.

The retail group produces 100 bags of refined clay from each tonne of moulding clay which it sells at £4 a bag. It would sell a further 40,000 bags if the retail trade price were reduced to £3.20 a bag.

Other data relevant to the operation are:

	Wholesale group £	Retail group £
Variable cost per tonne	70	60
Fixed cost per month	100,000	40,000

You are required to:

(a) prepare estimated profit statements for the month of December for each group and for B Ltd as a whole based on transfer prices of £200 per tonne and of £180 per tonne when producing at:
 (i) 80% capacity; and
 (ii) 100% capacity utilizing the extra sales to supply the retail trade;

(b) comment on the results achieved under (a) and the effect of the change in the transfer

price; and

(c) propose an alternative transfer price for the retail sales which would provide greater incentive for increasing sales, detailing any problems that might be encountered.

(30 marks)

ICMA P3 Management Accounting November 1980

24.2 An industrial group of companies includes two divisions: A and B. The output of division A is product A, two units of which are used by division B for every one of its product B. Division B has first call on division A's output but there is a separate market outside the group for the balance of division A's output. All the output of division B is sold outside the group.

The maximum capacity of division A is 130,000 units of A and that of division B is 50,000 units of B per annum. Each division maintains a stable level of stocks throughout the year.

The group would like to examine the results of using different bases of transfer pricing under different scenarios (i.e. situaions that could be expected to arise).

The bases of transfer pricing are:

Absorbed standard cost	AS
Market price	MP
Variable cost plus a lump sum of 80% of division A's fixed cost	VC

The scenarios are:

Scenario number	Product A Market price (per unit)	Product A Total demand (thousand units)	Product B Market price (per unit)	Product B Total demand (thousand units)
	£		£	
15	30	100	100	40
23	25	70	90	30
29	35	130	90	30

Costs per unit are:

	Product A	Product B
Variable cost	£20	£12
		(exclusive of 2 units of product A)
Fixed cost	£5	£18
Budgeted volume in units per annum	100,000	40,000

Part 1

You are required to calculate the profits shown by division A and by division B for the following seven situations:

Scenario	Basis of transfer pricing		
15	MP	VC	—
23	—	VC	AS
29	MP	VC	AS

Part 2

Assume that division B receives an overseas order for 20,000 units of B that will in no way influence its other clientele.

(a) As manager of division B state, with supporting calculations, whether you would recommend acceptance of the order in the following two situations:

Scenario	Price per unit (ex factory)	Basis of transfer pricing
(i) 23	£55	AS
(ii) 29	£65	MP

(b) If you were managing director of the whole group state, with very brief reasons, whether you would recommend acceptance of the orders in (a) (i) and (a) (ii) above.

(30 marks)

ICMA P3 Management Accounting May 1982

24.3* White Division is an important supplier to Rose Division in a group in which divisions are operated as autonomous profit centres. The group has established the following rules for calculating transfer prices:

1. If the product is being sold to customers outside the group, the average price for the past six months is to be used as the transfer price.

2. If the product is not sold to outside customers, the transfer price to be used is the standard variable cost plus fixed overhead at minimum budgeted volume plus a 10% profit margin on cost.

The following data are available regarding each division.

White Division

This division produces three products: A, B and C whose variable manufacturing costs per unit and apportioned fixed cost per annum are:

	A	B	C
	£	£	£
Variable manufacturing cost, per unit	6	13	18
Fixed cost, per annum	75,000	105,000	180,000

The direct labour hour content of each of these three products is 3 direct labour hours per unit, but the materials used are different. The production capacity of the factory is 180,000 direct labour hours and it is a requirement that at least 45,000 direct labour hours be used on each product. The remaining capacity can be used for any combination of the three products.

The division has been selling 40% of its output of product A to customers outside the group and the average price over the past 6 months has been £13 per unit. Product A has also been sold to Rose Division as has all White Division's output of products B and C.

Rose Division

This division produces three products: Theta, Sigma and Omega which use products A, B and C from White Division as follows:

Rose Division's product		Number of units of White Division's product used:		
		A	B	C
one unit of Theta	uses	5	5	—
one unit of Sigma	uses	3	5	2
one unit of Omega	uses	2	—	8

The unit selling prices of this division's products, their other unit variable costs (i.e. excluding those from White Division) and apportioned fixed costs per annum are:

	Theta	Sigma	Omega
	£	£	£
Selling price, per unit	280	295	340
Other variable costs, per unit	30	25	45
Fixed costs, per annum	60,000	90,000	120,000

Rose Division has no difficulty in making sales at the above prices and it must sell at least 1,500 per annum of each product. However, because product A is being sold by White Division to customers outside the group, Rose Division has complained that they are operating considerably below capacity.

The group planning executive has therefore intervened and instructed White Division to stop selling outside the group.

A. You are required, on the basis that all White Division's production must be sold exclusively to Rose Division,
 (a) as general manager of White Division, to:
 (i) state what production pattern you would adopt in your sales to Rose Division;
 (ii) calculate what profit per annum would be earned from those sales.
 (b) as general manager of Rose Division, to:
 (i) state what quantities of products A, B and C you would order from White Division;
 (ii) calculate what profit per annum would be earned from your sales.
 (c) as group planning executive, to:
 (i) state what production pattern you would recommend to maximize group profit;
 (ii) calculate what profit per annum would be earned from that pattern.

B. The production engineers of White Division discover a method of increasing the capacity of the factory beyond the present limits of 180,000 direct labour hours, but additional costs would be incurred as follows:

Increase in capacity (in thousands of direct labour hours)	9 : 18 : 27 : 36
Total additional cost, per annum (£000)	15 : 55 : 125 : 210

Increases can only be made in steps of 9,000 direct labour hours to be spread evenly over all three products and the maximum increase is 36,000 direct labour hours.

Assuming that:
 (i) all other data are as given earlier; and
 (ii) the increase must be divided equally among Theta, Sigma and Omega;
you are required, as group planning executive, to calculate what increased production, if any, would optimise group profit.

(25 marks)
ICMA P3 Management Accounting
May 1980

24.4* BUE is a group consisting of four subsidiary operating companies: British Angles, British

Bars, British Circles and British Dies.

British Dies proposes to place a contract for a sub-assembly to be used in one of its new products and, in accordance with BUE policy, has to obtain quotations from any suitable company within the group and at least one outside company.

Within the group, British Angles is approached as the most suitable company and submits a quotation of £2,400 per 1,000 sub-assemblies. In order to do the job, however, British Angles will need to sub-contract some of the work to British Bars and some to British Circles.

The arrangements between the companies for this sub-contract (per batch of completed 1,000 sub-assemblies) are as follows:

British Angles will buy from British Bars special parts at a price of £200.
British Angles will buy from British Circles components at a price of £1,500.
To make up its components, however, British Circles must buy from British Bars standard parts at a price of £380.

From companies outside the group, British Dies obtains the following quotations per batch of 1,000 completed sub-assemblies:

Italmet quotes £1,650 including all carriage and import duties for sub-assemblies manufactured in Italy.
Deutschmet quotes £1,800 for sub-assemblies manufactured in its UK plant, but will buy certain components from British Angles for this job at £550. In order to make these components, British Angles will have to buy parts from British Circles at a price of £350.

The following information is also given:

1. British Cirlces' prices include a 25% profit margin on its total cost (including, where appropriate, any special parts brought in).
2. British Bars' price of £380 is the current market price for these parts. They are in heavy demand by buyers outside the BUE group, and their supply from British Bars is severely limited.
3. The out-of-pocket costs of each group company relating to the work for which it has quoted are:

As a proportion of the total cost of the work it does itself (i.e. excluding parts or components bought from other group companies):

| British Angles | 60% |
| British Circles | 80% |

As a proportion of selling price:

British Bars 75%

4. British Angles' total costs (including purchases from British Bars and British Circles) for the British Dies contract are £2,200, and it assesses that it could make a profit of $33\frac{1}{3}\%$ on the cost of its own work on the Deutschmet contract.

As management accountant of British Dies you are required to:

(a) Recommend whether, from the BUE group point of view, it is more advantageous for the contract to be placed with British Angles, Italmet or Deutschmet.

Show figures to support your recommendations.

(b) List any assumptions you have made in deciding on your recommendations.

(30 marks)

ICMA P3 Management Accounting
November 1977

24.5 Companies RP, RR, RS and RT are members of a group, RP wishes to buy an electronic control system for its factory and, in accordance with group policy, must obtain quotations from companies inside and outside of the group.

From outside of the group the following quotations are received:

Company A quoted £33,200.
Company B quoted £35,000 but would buy a special unit from RS for £13,000. To make this unit, however, RS would need to buy parts from RR at a price of £7,500.

The inside quotation was from RS whose price was £48,000. This would require RS buying parts from RR at a price of £8,000 and units from RT at a price of £30,000. However, RT would need to buy parts from RR at a price of £11,000.

Additional data are as follows:

RR is extremely busy with work outside the group and has quoted current market prices for all its products.
RS costs for the RP contract, including purchases from RR and RT, total £42,000. For the Company B contract it expects a profit of 25% on the cost of its own work.
RT prices provide for a 20% profit margin on total costs.
The variable costs of the group companies in respect of the work under consideration are:
RR: 20% of selling price
RS: 70% of own cost (excluding purchases from other group companies)
RT: 65% of own cost (excluding purchases from other group companies)

You are required, from a group point of view, to:

(a) recommend, with appropriate calculations, whether the contract should be placed with RS or Company A or Company B;

(b) state briefly *two* assumptions you have made in arriving at your recommendations.

(30 marks)
ICMA P3 Management Accounting
November 1983

24.6 AB Ltd which buys and sells machinery has three departments:

New machines (manager, Newman)
Second-hand machines (manager, Handley)
Repair workshops (manager, Walker)

In selling new machines Newman is often asked to accept an old machine in part exchange. In such cases the old machine is disposed of by Handley.

The workshops do work both for outside customers and also for the other two departments. Walker charges his outside customers for materials at cost and for labour time at £8 per hour. This £8 is made up as follows:

Per hour
£

Fixed costs	2.00	(10,000 budgeted
Variable costs	4.50	hours per annum)
Profit	1.50	
	£8.00	

AB Ltd wishes to go over to a profit centre basis of calculations so as to be able to reward its three managers according to their results. It wishes to assess the situation in the context of the following transaction:

Newman sold to PQ Ltd a new machine at list price of £16,000, the cost of which to AB Ltd was £12,000.

To make the sale, however, Newman had to allow PQ Ltd £5,000 for its old machine in part exchange.

PQ Ltd's old machine was in need of repair before it could be re-sold and Newman and Handley were agreed in their estimate of those repairs as £50 in materials and 100 hours of workshops labour time. That estimate was proved to be correct when the workshops undertook the repair.

At the time of taking PQ Ltd's machine in part exchange Handley would have been able to buy a similar machine from other dealers for £3,700 without the need for any repair. When the machine had been repaired he sold it to ST Ltd for £4,200.

You are required to:

(a) show how you would calculate the profit contribution for each of the three departments from the above transaction.

(b) re-calculate the profit contribution for each department if there were the following alternative changes of circumstances:

(i) When the workshops came to repair the old machine they found that they required an extra 50 hours of labour time because of a fault not previously noticed.

(ii) Before deciding on the figure he would allow PQ Ltd for their old machine, Newman asks Walker to estimate the cost of repairs. The estimate is £50 in materials and 100 hours of workshops labour time. When, however, workshops came to repair the old machine, it took them 50% longer than estimated.

(c) recommend briefly how to deal with the following situations in the context of profit centre calculation:

(i) The manufacturer of the new machines allows AB Ltd £200 per machine for which AB Ltd undertakes to do all warranty rerpairs. Over the year the total cost of repairs under warranty exceeds the amount allowed by the supplier.

(ii) Although 4,000 hours of workshop time were budgeted to be reserved for the other two departments, their load increases over the year by 20% (at standard efficiency). The load from outside customers, however, stays as budgeted.

(25 marks)
ICMA P3 Management Accounting
November 1982

24.7* A company has two divisions. South Division manufactures an intermediate product for which there is no intermediate' external market. North Division incorporates this intermediate product into a final product which it sells. One unit of the intermediate product is used in the production of the final product. The expected units of the final product which North Division estimates it can sell at various selling prices are as follows:

Net selling price £	Quantity sold (units)
100	1,000
90	2,000
80	3,000
70	4,000
60	5,000
50	6,000

The costs of each division are as follows:

	South £	North £
Variable cost per unit	11	7
Fixed costs per annum	60,000	90,000

The transfer price is £35 for the intermediate product and is determined on a full cost-plus basis.

You are required to:

(a) Prepare profit statements for each division and the company as a whole for the various selling prices.
(b) State which selling price maximizes the profit of North Division and the company as a whole and comment on why the latter selling price is not selected by North Division.
(c) State which transfer pricing policy will maximize the company's profit under a divisional organization.

24.8 Enormous Engineering (EE) PLC is a large multi-divisional engineering company having interests in a wide variety of product markets. The Industrial Products Division (IPD) sells component parts to consumer appliance manufacturers, both inside and outside the company. One such part, a motor unit, it sells solely to external customers, but buys the motor itself internally from the Electric Motor Division. The Electric Motor Division (EMD) makes the motor to IPD specifications and it does not expect to be able to sell it to any other customers.

In preparing the 1984 budgets IPD estimated the number of motor units it expected to be able to sell at various prices as follows:

Price (ex works)	Quantity sold (units)
£50	1,000
£40	2,000
£35	3,000
£30	4,000
£25	6,000
£20	8,000

It then sought a quotation from EMD, who offered to supply the motors at £16 each based on the following estimate:

	£
Materials and bought-in parts	2
Direct labour costs	4
Factory overhead (150% of direct labour costs)	6
Total factory cost	12
Profit margin (33⅓% on factory cost)	4
Quoted price	£16

Factory overhead costs are fixed. All other costs are variable.

Although it considered the price quoted to be on the high side, IPD nevertheless believed that it could still sell the completed unit at a profit because it incurred costs of only £4 (material £1 and direct labour £3) on each unit made. It therefore placed an order for the coming year.

On revieiwng the budget for 1984 the finance director of EE noted that the projected sales of the motor unit were considerably less than those for the previous year, which was disappointing as both divisions concerned were working well below their capacities. On making enquiries he was told by IPD that the price reduction required to sell more units would reduce rather than increase profit and that the main problem was the high price charged by EMD. EMD stated that they required the high price in order to meet their target profit margin for the year, and that any reduction would erode their pricing policy.

You are required to:

(a) develop tabulations for each division, and for the company as a whole, that indicate the anticipated effect of IPD selling the motor unit at each of the prices listed (10 marks), and
(b) (i) show the selling price which IPD should select in order to maximize its own divisional profit on the motor unit (2 marks),
(ii) show the selling price which would be in the best interest of EE as a whole (2 marks), and
(iii) explain why this latter price is not selected by IPD (1 mark), and
(c) state:
(i) what changes you would advise making to the transfer pricing system so that it will motivate divisional managers to make better decisions in future (5 marks), and
(ii) what transfer price will ensure overall optimality in this situation (5 marks).

(25 marks)

*ICAEW Management Accounting
July 1983*

24.9* (a) Memphis PLC is a multi-division firm operating in a wide range of activities. One of its divisions, Division A, produces a semi-finished product Alpha, which can be sold in an outside market at a price of P_S. It can also be sold to Division B, which can use it in manufacturing its finished product Beta. The outside market in which Alpha is traded is perfect in all respects, except in so far as the buying division would have to incur transportation costs, which are included in the buying price P_B, if it buys Alpha

in the open market. The finished product of Division B, Beta, can be sold only in another perfect external market. Assume also that the marginal cost of each division is a rising linear function of output, and that the goal for Memphis PLC is to maximize its total profits.

You are required to explain how the optimal transfer price for Alpha should be derived in these circumstances, and to outline any rules which should be stipulated by the management of Memphis PLC to ensure attaining its goal of profit maximization (15 marks).

(b) Assume that Divisions A and B operate as above, except (i) that Division A is a monopolist facing a downward sloping demand curve and (ii) that it can sell Alpha externally at a price higher than the price it charges internally to Division B. Relevant information about both divisions is given below.

Output of Alpha (units)	Total cost of Alpha £000	Revenue from outside selling of Alpha £000	Net marginal revenue of Beta £000
60	112	315	47
70	140	350	45
80	170	380	43
90	203	405	40
100	238	425	36
110	275	440	33
120	315	450	30
130	359	455	25

You are required to calculate the optimal transfer price for Alpha and the optimal acitivity level for each division (10 marks).

(25 marks)
ICAEW Management Accounting
July 1982

24.10* The production director of a company is concerned with the problem of measuring the efficiency of process managers. In the production department there are six processes and all products processed pass through a combination of these processes. One specific area of investigation is the measurement of output values which involves the use of transfer prices.

You have been asked by the production director to tabulate the advantages and disadvantages of using each of the following systems of transfer pricing as related to process costing:
(a) absorption cost;
(b) marginal cost;
(c) cost plus profit;
(d) standard cost.

(20 marks)
ICMA P1 Cost Accounting 2
November 1982

24.11* It has been argued that full cost is an inappropriate basis for setting transfer prices. Outline the objections which can be levied at this basis. (9 marks)

ACCA Level 2 Management Accounting
June 1983

24.12* (a) Outline and discuss the main objectives of a transfer pricing system. (5 marks)
(b) Consider the advantages and disadvantages of:
 (i) market price based transfer prices;
 (ii) cost based transfer prices.
Outline the main variants that exist under each heading. (9 marks)
(c) Discuss the relevance of linear programming to the setting of transfer prices. (3 marks)

(17 marks)
ACCA Level 2 Management Accounting
December 1982

24.13* A company operates four factories. Each makes components which are incorporated into the products sold by one or more of the other factories. To encourage a competitive environment the directors have decided that each factory should become a separate profit centre. This will necessitate the use of transfer prices for the inter-factory components.

You are required to:
(a) describe three different methods of establishing the transfer prices;
(b) state which method you would recommend for the company described, giving reasons for your choice; and
(c) prepare for the one method chosen a policy statement outlining how the pricing system would be operated among the different factories.

(20 marks)
ICMA P3 Management Accounting
November 1978

Appendix 24.1: Economic analysis of transfer pricing

It is difficult to discuss the economic analysis of transfer pricing in purely verbal terms without some loss of rigour. To overcome this difficulty a number of theoretical transfer pricing models which are applicable to different situations are presented in diagrammatic form in this appendix.[6] The models are based upon principles which were first suggested by Hirshleifer (1956) and Gould (1964). For simplicity, we will assume that the company consists of only two divisions, a supplying division and a receiving division. The theoretically correct transfer price which will induce divisions to arrive at the optimum output for the company as a whole, when operating in their own best interests, is presented in the foregoing analysis.

Perfect external market for the intermediate product

In our previous discussion in the main body of the chapter we established that, where an external market for an intermediate product exists, the correct transfer price is the intermediate external market price. This situation is presented in Fig. 24A.1.

The external market price for the intermediate product is OP and because the external market for the intermediate product is assumed to be perfect, the marginal revenue for the intermediate product (MR_S) is constant and is represented by the horizontal line PE. The NMR line refers to the net marginal revenue of the receiving division and consists of the marginal revenue of the receiving division (MR_R) less the marginal

conversion cost (MC_R) but excludes the transfer price paid to the supplying division.

The transfer price will be set equal to the market price of the intermediate product on the external perfect market at OP. At this transfer price the receiving division will require quantity OQ_1 (this is where NMR is equal to the transfer price) and will be indifferent as to whether it obtains this supply from the supplying division or the external market. The supplying division will also be indifferent as to whether it sells this quantity to the receiving division or to the external market. However, the supplying division will wish to sell a total quantity of OQ_2 and will sell an additional quantity Q_1Q_2 externally if it supplies OQ_1 internally. (Total quantity OQ_2 is where the marginal cost of the supplying division (MC_S) is equal to its marginal revenue (MR_S).) Note that the NMR schedule for the company as a whole is BCDE and the most profitable output is where it intersects the company's marginal cost schedule ADE at point D. This requires an output of OQ_2 which is identical to the amount produced by the supplying division.

A transfer price of OP, which is equal to the market price of the intermediate product, will mean that the divisions will achieve the total company's optimal output and it will also allow them to deal with each other as they please.

A perfect market for the intermediate product and the presence of selling costs

Gould (1977) considers the situation where a company incurs transportation and selling costs such that there might be a difference between the net price received for the sale of the intermediate product externally and the price at which the product is purchased on the external market. Also, if the intermediate product is transferred internally some selling costs might be avoided. Under these circumstances an optimal production policy may not be achieved if the divisions are allowed to ignore each other's requests for the transfer of intermediate products.

Figure 24A.2 contains identical information to that presented in Fig. 24A.1 with the exception that the market price line is replaced by two lines — a buying price and a selling price. Figure 24A.2 is divided into three sections. The diagram in the first section represents the situation where the NMR and MC_S lines intersect below the net selling price for the intermediate product. From Fig. 24A.2(A) you will see that it is cheaper for the company to manufacture the intermediate product internally as long as the marginal cost of the supplying division (MC_S) is below the buying price of the intermediate product on the external market. Beyond B it is cheaper to purchase the intermediate product on the external market. The company as a whole therefore faces a marginal cost schedule equal to FBC.

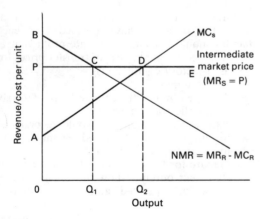

Fig. 24A.1 Perfect external market for the intermediate product

Fig. 24A.2 Perfect market for intermediate product
and the presence of selling costs

As long as the company can obtain a larger marginal revenue by converting the intermediate product into the final product, it should do so. This situation applies so long as the NMR line lies above the net selling price for the intermediate product. This is represented by the segment AD of the NMR line, giving an output of OQ_1 of the *final* product for sale in the external final product market. Additional output of the intermediate product beyond OQ_1 can be sold profitably on the external market, so in this case Q_1Q_2 of the intermdiate product will be sold on the external market at a price of OP_S. The effect of this is that the company as a whole will face an NMR schedule of ADE and as this intersects the intermediate product marginal cost function FBC directly above Q_2 the optimal output for the company as a whole is OQ_2.

At an optimal total output level of OQ_2, OQ_1 will be passed from the supplying division to the receiving division for conversion and sale in the final product market. In addition, Q_1Q_2 of the intermediate product will be sold externally. An internal transfer price of OP_S (where the NMR line ADE intersects the MC line FBC) will induce optimal behaviour by the divisions provided that the supplying division is instructed to provide the receiving division with all the output it requires at the transfer price of OP_S. The reason for this requirement is that the supplying division will correctly determine the optimum output level OQ_2 (where its marginal cost schedule cuts its marginal revenue schedule as represented by the transfer price P_SDE) but will be indifferent between selling to the receiving division or the external market. The receiving division, however, wishes to purchase its total supply OQ_1 from the supplying division. This is in the best interests of the company, and the supplying division's profits will be unaffected if it supplies OQ_1 to the receiving division at a price of OP_S. Because the supplying division will be

indifferent as to who it supplies with the intermediate product a further rule requiring it to meet the receiving division's requirements is necessary to ensure total company optimality.

In Fig. 24A.2(B), the NMR and MC_S lines intersect above the buying price for the intermediate product. The procedure for determining the optimum output level remains unchanged. The NMR schedule for the company as a whole is ACEF and the marginal cost of supplying the product is GBD. These two schedules intersect at point C giving an optimum total company output of OQ_2. The optimal transfer price is given at the point on the vertical axis where these two schedules intersect. The correct transfer price is therefore OP_B. At this price the receiving division will also wish to produce the optimal company output of OQ_2 (this is where its NMR schedule ACE cuts its marginal cost shown by the transfer price line P_BCD) but it will be indifferent as to whether it purchases its requirements from the supplying division or from the external market. The supplying division will want to produce OQ_1 to sell to the receiving division at the transfer price OP_B and this will be in the best interests of the company as the marginal cost of production is lower than the external purchases price. Because the receiving division is indifferent as to whether it purchases the intermediate product from the supplying division or from the external market the receiving division must be instructed to purchase from the supplying division the quantity which it is prepared to supply at the transfer price OP_B. This will be quantity OQ_1 and the receiving division will then obtain its additional supplies, that is Q_1Q_2, on the external market.

In Fig. 24A.2(C) the NMR and MC_S lines intersect between the buying and selling price for the intermediate product. Here the NMR and the marginal cost of supplying intersect at point F giving an optimal

output for the total company of OQ. The transfer price is determined at the point on the vertical axis where these two points intersect. The correct transfer price is therefore OP. At this price there is no need for additional instructions to be given to the supplying or the receiving division about dealing with each other as each division will prefer to deal internally, and no sales or purchases will be made in the external intermediate product market.

No external market for the intermediate product and a perfect market for the final product

This situation is illustrated in Fig. 24A.3. The marginal cost of the supplying and the receiving divisions are represented by MC_S and MC_R. The marginal cost schedule for the company as a whole is represented by $MC_S + MC_R$. The marginal revenue function for the final product is also shown and is represented by MR_R. As it is assumed that the market for the final product is perfect, the marginal revenue line is horizontal and equal to average revenue. The net marginal revenue for the receiving division is represented by NMR and is ascertained by deducting the marginal cost of the receiving division (excluding the cost of purchasing from the supplying division) from the marginal revenue of the receiving division.

The optimum output level for the company as a whole is where the marginal revenue for the company, shown by the horizontal MR_R line, intersects the marginal cost line for the whole company, represented by $MC_S + MC_R$. This indicates an optimum output of OQ and the maximum profit which results is the area ACE. The transfer price at which the supplying division wishes to sell OQ to the receiving division and also the price at which the receiving division wishes to purchase this amount is determined at the point on the vertical

Fig. 24A.4 Imperfect market for intermediate product

axis where the MC_S and the NMR lines intersect. The correct transfer price is therefore OP. The supplying division will view the horizontal transfer price line PD as its marginal revenue schedule and will wish to produce OQ for transfer to the receiving division. The receiving division will want to purchase for conversion to the final product the quantity of output at which the transfer price will be equal to its net marginal revenue. This is also quantity OQ. So both divisions will want quantity OQ to be transferred between them, and the sum of their respective profits will be equal to the total company's maximum profit. The supplying division's profit is represented by area FDP and the receiving division's profit by are BDP, which together equal BDF; area BDF is equal to the area ACE which represents total company profits.

Imperfect market for the intermediate product

In an imperfect market the quantity of the intermediate product which is sold externally will influence the market price, and the marignal revenue for the sale of the intermediate product (MR_S) will decline as output increases (see Fig. 24A.4). The marginal cost and marginal revenue schedules for the company as a whole are represented by the MC_S and $MR_S + NMR$ schedules. The latter schedule represents the marginal revenue of the supplying division plus the net marginal revenue of the receiving division. The optimum output for the company as a whole will therefore occur where the MC_S and $MR_S + NMR$ schedules intersect, that is at level OQ_3.

The optimal transfer price which induces the supplying and the receiving divisions to operate at this output level is shown by the point on the vertical axis where the MC_S and the $MR_S + NMR$ schedules intersect. The correct transfer price is therefore OP_T. At this price the

Fig. 24A.3 No external market for the intermediate product

receiving division will view the horizontal line P_TD as its marginal cost of supply and require output OQ_2 from the supplying division. At this point its NMR schedule intersects the horizontal line PD. The supplying division will face a marginal revenue schedule equal to BED (it will prefer to sell at a transfer price P_T beyond point E as this is in excess of the marginal revenue line below E). This means that the supplying division will prefer to sell OQ_1 of the intermediate product on the external market at a price of OP_E (the selling price at which its marginal revenue line is equal to or above E). In addition, the supplying division will wish to suply Q_1Q_3 at the transfer price OP_T to the receiving division. This will give a total output by the supplying division of OQ_3 (that is, the optimal output for the company as a whole), being the quality of output at which its marginal cost (MC_S) is equal to its marginal revenue BED. This is consistent with the receiving division's demand for OQ_2, because OQ_1 is equal to Q_2Q_3. Therefore OQ_2 equals Q_1Q_3.

Appendices

Present value factors

The table gives the present value of a single payment received n years in the future discounted at x% per year. For example, with a discount rate of 7% a single payment of £1 in six years time has a present value of £0.6663 or 66.63p.

Years	1%	2%	3%	4%	5%	6%	7%	8%	9%	10%
1	.9901	.9804	.9709	.9615	.9524	.9434	.9346	.9259	.9174	.9091
2	.9803	.9612	.9426	.9426	.9070	.8900	.8734	.8573	.8417	.8264
3	.9706	.9423	.9151	.8890	.8638	.8396	.8163	.7938	.7722	.7513
4	.9610	.9238	.8885	.8548	.8227	.7921	.7629	.7350	.7084	.6830
5	.9515	.9057	.8626	.8219	.7835	.7473	.7130	.6806	.6499	.6209
6	.9420	.8880	.8375	.7903	.7462	.7050	.6663	.6302	.5963	.5645
7	.9327	.8706	.8131	.7599	.7107	.6651	.6227	.5835	.5470	.5132
8	.9235	.8535	.7894	.7307	.6768	.6274	.5820	.5403	.5019	.4665
9	.9143	.8368	.7664	.7026	.6446	.5919	.5439	.5002	.4604	.4241
10	.9053	.8203	.7441	.6756	.6139	.5584	.5083	.4632	.4224	.3855
11	.8963	.8043	.7224	.6496	.5847	.5268	.4751	.4289	.3875	.3505
12	.8874	.7885	.7014	.6246	.5568	.4970	.4440	.3971	.3555	.3186
13	.8787	.7730	.6810	.6006	.5303	.4688	.4150	.3677	.3262	.2897
14	.8700	.7579	.6611	.5775	.5051	.4423	.3878	.3405	.2992	.2633
15	.8613	.7430	.6419	.5553	.4810	.4173	.3624	.3152	.2745	.2394
16	.8528	.7284	.6232	.5339	.4581	.3936	.3387	.2919	.2519	.2176
17	.8444	.7142	.6050	.5134	.4363	.3714	.3166	.2703	.2311	.1978
18	.8360	.7002	.5874	.4936	.4155	.3503	.2959	.2502	.2120	.1799
19	.8277	.6864	.5703	.4746	.3957	.3305	.2765	.2317	.1945	.1635
20	.8195	.6730	.5537	.4564	.3769	.3118	.2584	.2145	.1784	.1486
21	.8114	.6598	.5375	.4388	.3589	.2942	.2415	.1987	.1637	.1351
22	.8034	.6468	.5219	.4220	.3418	.2775	.2257	.1839	.1502	.1228
23	.7954	.6342	.5067	.4057	.3256	.2618	.2109	.1703	.1378	.1117
24	.7876	.6217	.4919	.3901	.3101	.2470	.1971	.1577	.1264	.1015
25	.7798	.6095	.4776	.3751	.2953	.2330	.1842	.1460	.1160	.0923
26	.7720	.5976	.4637	.3607	.2812	.2198	.1722	.1352	.1064	.0839
27	.7644	.5859	.4502	.3468	.2678	.2074	.1609	.1252	.0976	.0763
28	.7568	.5744	.4371	.3335	.2551	.1956	.1504	.1159	.0895	.0693
29	.7493	.5631	.4243	.3207	.2429	.1846	.1406	.1073	.0822	.0630
30	.7419	.5521	.4120	.3083	.2314	.1741	.1314	.0994	.0754	.0573
31	.7346	.5412	.4000	.2965	.2204	.1643	.1228	.0920	.0691	.0521
32	.7273	.5306	.3883	.2851	.2099	.1550	.1147	.0852	.0634	.0474
33	.7201	.5202	.3770	.2741	.1999	.1462	.1072	.0789	.0582	.0431
34	.7130	.5100	.3660	.2636	.1904	.1379	.1002	.0730	.0534	.0391
35	.7059	.5000	.3554	.2534	.1813	.1301	.0937	.0676	.0490	.0356
36	.6989	.4902	.3450	.2437	.1727	.1227	.0875	.0626	.0449	.0323
37	.6920	.4806	.3350	.2343	.1644	.1158	.0818	.0580	.0412	.0294
38	.6852	.4712	.3252	.2253	.1566	.1092	.0765	.0537	.0378	.0267
39	.6784	.4619	.3158	.2166	.1491	.1031	.0715	.0497	.0347	.0243
40	.6717	.4529	.3066	.2083	.1420	.0972	.0668	.0460	.0318	.0221
41	.6650	.4440	.2976	.2003	.1353	.0917	.0624	.0426	.0292	.0201
42	.6584	.4353	.2890	.1926	.1288	.0865	.0583	.0395	.0268	.0183
43	.6519	.4268	.2805	.1852	.1227	.0816	.0545	.0365	.0246	.0166
44	.6454	.4184	.2724	.1780	.1169	.0770	.0509	.0338	.0226	.0151
45	.6391	.4102	.2644	.1712	.1113	.0727	.0476	.0313	.0207	.0137
46	.6327	.4022	.2567	.1646	.1060	.0685	.0445	.0290	.0190	.0125
47	.6265	.3943	.2493	.1583	.1009	.0647	.0416	.0269	.0174	.0113
48	.6203	.3865	.2420	.1522	.0961	.0610	.0389	.0249	.0160	.0103
49	.6141	.3790	.2350	.1463	.0916	.0575	.0363	.0230	.0147	.0094
50	.6080	.3715	.2281	.1407	.0872	.0543	.0339	.0213	.0134	.0085

11%	12%	13%	14%	15%	16%	17%	18%	19%	20%	Years
.9009	.8929	.8850	.8772	.8696	.8621	.8547	.8475	.8403	.8333	1
.8116	.7972	.7831	.7695	.7561	.7432	.7305	.7182	.7062	.6944	2
.7312	.7118	.6931	.6750	.6575	.6407	.6244	.6086	.5934	.5787	3
.6587	.6355	.6133	.5921	.5718	.5523	.5337	.5158	.4987	.4823	4
.5935	.5674	.5428	.5194	.4972	.4761	.4561	.4371	.4190	.4019	5
.5346	.5066	.4803	.4556	.4323	.4104	.3898	.3704	.3521	.3349	6
.4817	.4523	.4251	.3996	.3759	.3538	.3332	.3139	.2959	.2791	7
.4339	.4039	.3762	.3506	.3269	.3050	.2848	.2660	.2487	.2326	8
.3909	.3606	.3329	.3075	.2843	.2630	.2434	.2255	.2090	.1938	9
.3522	.3220	.2946	.2697	.2472	.2267	.2080	.1911	.1756	.1615	10
.3173	.2875	.2607	.2366	.2149	.1954	.1778	.1619	.1476	.1346	11
.2858	.2567	.2307	.2076	.1869	.1685	.1520	.1372	.1240	.1122	12
.2575	.2292	.2042	.1821	.1625	.1452	.1299	.1163	.1042	.0935	13
.2320	.2046	.1807	.1597	.1413	.1252	.1110	.0985	.0876	.0779	14
.2090	.1827	.1599	.1401	.1229	.1079	.0949	.0835	.0736	.0649	15
.1883	.1631	.1415	.1229	.1069	.0930	.0811	.0708	.0618	.0541	16
.1696	.1456	.1252	.1078	.0929	.0802	.0693	.0600	.0520	.0451	17
.1528	.1300	.1108	.0946	.0808	.0691	.0592	.0508	.0437	.0376	18
.1377	.1161	.0981	.0829	.0703	.0596	.0506	.0431	.0367	.0313	19
.1240	.1037	.0868	.0728	.0611	.0514	.0433	.0365	.0308	.0261	20
.1117	.0926	.0768	.0638	.0531	.0443	.0370	.0309	.0259	.0217	21
.1007	.0826	.0680	.0560	.0462	.0382	.0316	.0262	.0218	.0181	22
.0907	.0738	.0601	.0491	.0402	.0329	.0270	.0222	.0183	.0151	23
.0817	.0659	.0532	.0431	.0349	.0284	.0231	.0188	.0154	.0126	24
.0736	.0588	.0471	.0378	.0304	.0245	.0197	.0160	.0129	.0105	25
.0663	.0525	.0417	.0331	.0264	.0211	.0169	.0135	.0109	.0087	26
.0597	.0469	.0369	.0291	.0230	.0182	.0144	.0115	.0091	.0073	27
.0538	.0419	.0326	.0255	.0200	.0157	.0123	.0097	.0077	.0061	28
.0485	.0374	.0289	.0224	.0174	.0135	.0105	.0082	.0064	.0051	29
.0437	.0334	.0256	.0196	.0151	.0116	.0090	.0070	.0054	.0042	30
.0394	.0298	.0226	.0172	.0131	.0100	.0077	.0059	.0046	.0035	31
.0355	.0266	.0200	.0151	.0114	.0087	.0066	.0050	.0038	.0029	32
.0319	.0238	.0177	.0132	.0099	.0075	.0056	.0042	.0032	.0024	33
.0288	.0212	.0157	.0116	.0086	.0064	.0048	.0036	.0027	.0020	34
.0259	.0189	.0139	.0102	.0075	.0055	.0041	.0030	.0023	.0017	35
.0234	.0169	.0123	.0089	.0065	.0048	.0035	.0026	.0019	.0014	36
.0210	.0151	.0109	.0078	.0057	.0041	.0030	.0022	.0016	.0012	37
.0190	.0135	.0096	.0069	.0049	.0036	.0026	.0019	.0013	.0010	38
.0171	.0120	.0085	.0060	.0043	.0031	.0022	.0016	.0011	.0008	39
.0154	.0107	.0075	.0053	.0037	.0026	.0019	.0013	.0010	.0007	40
.0139	.0096	.0067	.0046	.0032	.0023	.0016	.0011	.0008	.0006	41
.0125	.0086	.0059	.0041	.0028	.0020	.0014	.0010	.0007	.0005	42
.0112	.0076	.0052	.0036	.0025	.0017	.0012	.0008	.0006	.0004	43
.0101	.0068	.0046	.0031	.0021	.0015	.0010	.0007	.0005	.0003	44
.0091	.0061	.0041	.0027	.0019	.0013	.0009	.0006	.0004	.0003	45
.0082	.0054	.0036	.0024	.0016	.0011	.0007	.0005	.0003	.0002	46
.0074	.0049	.0032	.0021	.0014	.0009	.0006	.0004	.0003	.0002	47
.0067	.0043	.0028	.0019	.0012	.0008	.0005	.0004	.0002	.0002	48
.0060	.0039	.0025	.0016	.0011	.0007	.0005	.0003	.0002	.0001	49
.0054	.0035	.0022	.0014	.0009	.0006	.0004	.0003	.0002	.0001	50

Years	21%	22%	23%	24%	25%	26%	27%	28%	29%	30%
1	.8264	.8197	.8130	.8065	.8000	.7937	.7874	.7813	.7752	.7692
2	.6830	.6719	.6610	.6504	.6400	.6299	.6200	.6104	.6009	.5917
3	.5645	.5507	.5374	.5245	.5120	.4999	.4882	.4768	.4658	.4552
4	.4665	.4514	.4369	.4230	.4096	.3968	.3844	.3725	.3611	.3501
5	.3855	.3700	.3552	.3411	.3277	.3149	.3027	.2910	.2799	.2693
6	.3186	.3033	.2888	.2751	.2621	.2499	.2383	.2274	.2170	.2072
7	.2633	.2486	.2348	.2218	.2097	.1983	.1877	.1776	.1682	.1594
8	.2176	.2038	.1909	.1789	.1678	.1574	.1478	.1388	.1304	.1226
9	.1799	.1670	.1552	.1443	.1342	.1249	.1164	.1084	.1011	.0943
10	.1486	.1369	.1262	.1164	.1074	.0992	.0916	.0847	.0784	.0725
11	.1228	.1122	.1026	.0938	.0859	.0787	.0721	.0662	.0607	.0558
12	.1015	.0920	.0834	.0757	.0687	.0625	.0568	.0517	.0471	.0429
13	.0839	.0754	.0678	.0610	.0550	.0496	.0447	.0404	.0365	.0330
14	.0693	.0618	.0551	.0492	.0440	.0393	.0352	.0316	.0283	.0254
15	.0573	.0507	.0448	.0397	.0352	.0312	.0277	.0247	.0219	.0195
16	.0474	.0415	.0364	.0320	.0281	.0248	.0218	.0193	.0170	.0150
17	.0391	.0340	.0296	.0258	.0225	.0197	.0172	.0150	.0132	.0116
18	.0323	.0279	.0241	.0208	.0180	.0156	.0135	.0118	.0102	.0089
19	.0267	.0229	.0196	.0168	.0144	.0124	.0107	.0092	.0079	.0068
20	.0221	.0187	.0159	.0135	.0115	.0098	.0084	.0072	.0061	.0053
21	.0183	.0154	.0129	.0109	.0092	.0078	.0066	.0056	.0048	.0040
22	.0151	.0126	.0105	.0088	.0074	.0062	.0052	.0044	.0037	.0031
23	.0125	.0103	.0086	.0071	.0059	.0049	.0041	.0034	.0029	.0024
24	.0103	.0085	.0070	.0057	.0047	.0039	.0032	.0027	.0022	.0018
25	.0085	.0069	.0057	.0046	.0038	.0031	.0025	.0021	.0017	.0014
26	.0070	.0057	.0046	.0037	.0030	.0025	.0020	.0016	.0013	.0011
27	.0058	.0047	.0037	.0030	.0024	.0019	.0016	.0013	.0010	.0008
28	.0048	.0038	.0030	.0024	.0019	.0015	.0012	.0010	.0008	.0006
29	.0040	.0031	.0025	.0020	.0015	.0012	.0010	.0008	.0006	.0005
30	.0033	.0026	.0020	.0016	.0012	.0010	.0008	.0006	.0005	.0004
31	.0027	.0021	.0016	.0013	.0010	.0008	.0006	.0005	.0004	.0003
32	.0022	.0017	.0013	.0010	.0008	.0006	.0005	.0004	.0003	.0002
33	.0019	.0014	.0011	.0008	.0006	.0005	.0004	.0003	.0002	.0002
34	.0015	.0012	.0009	.0007	.0005	.0004	.0003	.0002	.0002	.0001
35	.0013	.0009	.0007	.0005	.0004	.0003	.0002	.0002	.0001	.0001
36	.0010	.0008	.0006	.0004	.0003	.0002	.0002	.0001	.0001	.0001
37	.0009	.0006	.0005	.0003	.0003	.0002	.0001	.0001	.0001	.0001
38	.0007	.0005	.0004	.0003	.0002	.0002	.0001	.0001	.0001	
39	.0006	.0004	.0003	.0002	.0002	.0001	.0001	.0001	.0000	
40	.0005	.0004	.0003	.0002	.0001	.0001	.0001	.0001		
41	.0004	.0003	.0002	.0001	.0001	.0001	.0001			
42	.0003	.0002	.0002	.0001	.0001	.0001				
43	.0003	.0002	.0001	.0001	.0001					
44	.0002	.0002	.0001	.0001	.0001					
45	.0002	.0001	.0001	.0001						
46	.0002	.0001	.0001	.0001						
47	.0001	.0001	.0001							
48	.0001	.0001								
49	.0001	.0001								
50	.0001									

31%	32%	33%	34%	35%	36%	37%	38%	39%	40%	Years
.7634	.7576	.7519	.7463	.7407	.7353	.7299	.7246	.7194	.7143	1
.5827	.5739	.5653	.5569	.5487	.5407	.5328	.5251	.5176	.5102	2
.4448	.4348	.4251	.4156	.4064	.3975	.3889	.3805	.3724	.3644	3
.3396	.3294	.3196	.3102	.3011	.2923	.2839	.2757	.2679	.2603	4
.2592	.2495	.2403	.2315	.2230	.2149	.2072	.1998	.1927	.1859	5
.1979	.1890	.1807	.1727	.1652	.1580	.1512	.1448	.1386	.1328	6
.1510	.1432	.1358	.1289	.1224	.1162	.1104	.1049	.0997	.0949	7
.1153	.1085	.1021	.0962	.0906	.0854	.0806	.0760	.0718	.0678	8
.0880	.0822	.0768	.0718	.0671	.0628	.0588	.0551	.0516	.0484	9
.0672	.0623	.0577	.0536	.0497	.0462	.0429	.0399	.0371	.0346	10
.0513	.0472	.0434	.0400	.0368	.0340	.0313	.0289	.0267	.0247	11
.0392	.0357	.0326	.0298	.0273	.0250	.0229	.0210	.0192	.0176	12
.0299	.0271	.0245	.0223	.0202	.0184	.0167	.0152	.0138	.0126	13
.0228	.0205	.0185	.0166	.0150	.0135	.0122	.0110	.0099	.0090	14
.0174	.0155	.0139	.0124	.0111	.0099	.0089	.0080	.0072	.0064	15
.0133	.0118	.0104	.0093	.0082	.0073	.0065	.0058	.0051	.0046	16
.0101	.0089	.0078	.0069	.0061	.0054	.0047	.0042	.0037	.0033	17
.0077	.0068	.0059	.0052	.0045	.0039	.0035	.0030	.0027	.0023	18
.0059	.0051	.0044	.0038	.0033	.0029	.0025	.0022	.0019	.0017	19
.0045	.0039	.0033	.0029	.0025	.0021	.0018	.0016	.0014	.0012	20
.0034	.0029	.0025	.0021	.0018	.0016	.0013	.0012	.0010	.0009	21
.0026	.0022	.0019	.0016	.0014	.0012	.0010	.0008	.0007	.0006	22
.0020	.0017	.0014	.0012	.0010	.0008	.0007	.0006	.0005	.0004	23
.0015	.0013	.0011	.0009	.0007	.0006	.0005	.0004	.0004	.0003	24
.0012	.0010	.0008	.0007	.0006	.0005	.0004	.0003	.0003	.0002	25
.0009	.0007	.0006	.0005	.0004	.0003	.0003	.0002	.0002	.0002	26
.0007	.0006	.0005	.0004	.0003	.0002	.0002	.0002	.0001	.0001	27
.0005	.0004	.0003	.0003	.0002	.0002	.0001	.0001	.0001	.0001	28
.0004	.0003	.0003	.0002	.0002	.0001	.0001	.0001	.0001	.0001	29
.0003	.0002	.0002	.0002	.0001	.0001	.0001	.0001	.0001		30
.0002	.0002	.0001	.0001	.0001	.0001	.0001				
.0002	.0001	.0001	.0001	.0001	.0001					
.0001	.0001	.0001	.0001	.0001						
.0001	.0001	.0001								
.0001	.0001									
.0001										

Cumulative present value factors

The table gives the present value of n annual payments of £1 received for the next n years with a constant discount of x% per year.

For example, with a discount rate of 7% and with 6 annual payments of £1 the present value is £4.767.

Years 0 to:	1%	2%	3%	4%	5%	6%	7%	8%	9%	10%
1	0.990	0.980	0.971	0.962	0.952	0.943	0.935	0.926	0.917	0.909
2	1.970	1.942	1.913	1.886	1.859	1.833	1.808	1.783	1.759	1.736
3	2.941	2.884	2.829	2.775	2.723	2.673	2.624	2.577	2.531	2.487
4	3.902	3.808	3.717	3.630	3.546	3.465	3.387	3.312	3.240	3.170
5	4.853	4.713	4.580	4.452	4.329	4.212	4.100	3.993	3.890	3.791
6	5.795	5.601	5.417	5.242	5.076	4.917	4.767	4.623	4.486	4.355
7	6.728	6.472	6.230	6.002	5.786	5.582	5.389	5.206	5.033	4.868
8	7.652	7.325	7.020	6.733	6.463	6.210	5.971	5.747	5.535	5.335
9	8.566	8.162	7.786	7.435	7.108	6.802	6.515	6.247	5.995	5.759
10	9.471	8.983	8.530	8.111	7.722	7.360	7.024	6,710	6.418	6.145
11	10.368	9.787	9.253	8.760	8.306	7,887	7.499	7.139	6.805	6.495
12	11.255	10.575	9.954	9.385	8.863	8.384	7.943	7.536	7.161	6.814
13	12.134	11.348	10.635	9.986	9.394	8.853	8.358	7.904	7.487	7.103
14	13.004	12.106	11.296	10.563	9.899	9.295	8.745	8.244	7.786	7.367
15	13.865	12.849	11.938	11.118	10.380	9.712	9.108	8.559	8.061	7.606
16	14.718	13.578	12.561	11.652	10.838	10.106	9.447	8.851	8.313	7.824
17	15.562	14.292	13.166	12.166	11.274	10.477	9.763	9.122	8.544	8.022
18	16.398	14.992	13.754	12.659	11.690	10.828	10.059	9.372	8.756	8.201
19	17.226	15.678	14.324	13.134	12.085	11.158	10.336	9.604	8.950	8.365
20	18.046	16.351	14.877	13.590	12.462	11.470	10.594	9.818	9.129	8.514
21	18.857	17.011	15.415	14.029	12.821	11.764	10.836	10.017	9.292	8.649
22	19.660	17.658	15.937	14.451	13.163	12.042	11.061	10.201	9.442	8.772
23	20.456	18.292	16.444	14.857	13.489	12.303	11.272	10.371	9.580	8.883
24	21.243	18.914	16.939	15,247	13.799	12.550	11.469	10.529	9.707	8.985
25	22.023	19.523	17.413	15.622	14.094	12.783	11.654	10.675	9.823	9.077
26	22.795	20.121	17.877	15.983	13.375	13.003	11.826	10.810	9.929	9.161
27	23.560	20.707	18.327	16.330	14.643	13.211	11.987	10.935	10.027	9.237
28	24.316	21.281	18.764	16.663	13.898	13.406	12.137	11.051	10.116	9.307
29	25.066	21.844	19.188	16.984	15.141	13.591	12.278	11.158	10.198	9.370
30	25.808	22.396	19.600	17.292	15.372	13.765	12.409	11.258	10.274	9.427
31	26.542	22.938	20.000	17.588	15.593	13.929	12.532	11.350	10.343	9.479
32	27.270	23.468	20.389	17,874	15.803	13.084	12.647	11.435	10.406	9.526
33	27.990	23.989	20.766	18.148	16.003	14.230	12.754	11.514	10.464	9.569
34	28.703	24.499	21.132	18.411	16.193	14.368	12.854	11.587	10.518	9.609
35	29.409	24.999	21.487	18.665	16.374	14.498	12.948	11.655	10.567	9.644
36	30.108	25.489	21.832	18.908	16.547	14.621	13.035	11.717	10.612	9.677
37	30.800	25.969	22.167	19.143	16.711	14.737	13.117	11.775	10.653	9.706
38	31.485	26.441	22.492	19.368	16.868	14.846	13.193	11.829	10.691	9.733
39	32.163	26.903	22.808	19.584	17.017	14.949	13.265	11.879	10.726	9.757
40	32.835	27.355	23.115	19.793	17.159	15.046	13.332	11.925	10.757	9.779
41	33.500	27.799	23.412	19.993	17.294	15.138	13.394	11.967	10.787	9.799
42	34.158	28.235	23.701	20.186	17.423	15.225	13.452	12.007	10.813	9.817
43	34.810	28.662	23.982	20.371	17.546	15.306	13.507	12.043	10.838	9.834
44	34.455	29.080	24.254	20.549	17.663	15.383	13.558	12.077	10.861	9.849
45	36.095	29.490	24.519	20.720	17.774	15.456	13.606	12.108	10.881	9.863
46	36.727	29.892	24.775	20.885	17.880	15.524	13.650	12.137	10.900	9.875
47	37.354	30.287	25.025	21.043	17.981	15.589	13.692	12.164	10.918	9.887
48	37.974	30.673	25.267	21.195	18.077	15.650	13.730	12.189	10.934	9.897
49	38.588	31.052	25.502	21.341	18.169	15.708	13.767	12.212	10.948	9.906
50	39.196	31.424	25.730	21.482	18.256	15.762	13.801	12.233	10.962	9.915

11%	12%	13%	14%	15%	16%	17%	18%	19%	20%	Years 0 to:
0.901	0.893	0.885	0.877	0.870	0.862	0.855	0.847	0.840	0.833	1
1.713	1.690	1.668	1.647	1.626	1.605	1.585	1.566	1.547	1.528	2
2.444	2.402	2.361	2.322	2.283	2.246	2.210	2.174	2.140	2.106	3
3.102	3.037	2.974	2.914	2.855	2.798	2.743	2.690	2.639	2.589	4
3.696	3.605	3.517	3.433	3.352	3.274	3.199	3.127	3.058	2.991	5
4.231	4.111	3.998	3.889	3.784	3.685	3.589	3.498	3.410	3.326	6
4.712	4.564	4.423	4.288	4.160	4.039	3.922	3.812	3.706	3.605	7
5.146	4.968	4.799	4.639	4.487	4.344	4.207	4.078	3.954	3.837	8
5.537	5.328	5.132	4.946	4.772	4.607	4.451	4.303	4.163	4.031	9
5.889	5.650	5.426	5.216	5.019	4.833	4.659	4.494	4.339	4.192	10
6.207	5.938	5.687	5.453	5.234	5.029	4.836	4.656	4.486	4.327	11
6.492	6.194	5.918	5.660	5.421	5.197	4.988	4.793	4.611	4.439	12
6.750	6.424	6.122	5.842	5.583	5.342	5.118	4.910	4.715	4.533	13
6.982	6.628	6.302	6.002	5.724	5.468	5.229	5.008	4.802	4.611	14
7.191	6.811	6.462	6.142	5.847	5.575	5.324	5.092	4.876	4.675	15
7.379	6.974	6.604	6.265	5.954	5.668	5.405	5.162	4.938	4.730	16
7.549	7.120	6.729	6.373	6.047	5.749	5.475	5.222	4.990	4.775	17
7.702	7.250	6.840	6.467	6.128	5.818	5.534	5.273	5.033	4.812	18
7.839	7.366	6.938	6.550	6.198	5.877	5.584	5.316	5.070	4.843	19
7.963	7.469	7.025	6.623	6.259	5.929	5.628	5.353	5.101	4.870	20
8.075	7.562	7.102	6.687	6.312	5.973	5.665	5.384	5.127	4.891	21
8.176	7.645	7.170	6.743	6.359	6.011	5.696	5.410	5.149	4.909	22
8.266	7.718	7.230	6.792	6.399	6.044	5.723	5.432	5.167	4.925	23
8.348	7.784	7.283	6.835	6.434	6.073	5.746	5.451	5.182	4.937	24
8.422	7.843	7.330	6.873	6.464	6.097	5.766	5.467	5.195	4.948	25
8.488	7.896	7.372	6.906	6.491	6.118	5.783	5.480	5.206	4.956	26
8.548	7.943	7.409	6.935	6.514	6.136	5.798	5.492	5.215	4.964	27
8.602	7.984	7.441	6.961	6.534	6.152	5.810	5.502	5.223	4.970	28
8.650	8.022	7.470	6.983	6.551	6.166	5.820	5.510	5.229	4.975	29
8.694	8.055	7.496	7.003	6.566	6.177	5.829	5.517	5.235	4.979	30
8.733	8.085	7.518	7.020	6.579	6.187	5.837	5.523	5.239	4.982	31
8.769	8.112	7.538	7.035	6.591	6.196	5.844	5.528	5.243	4.985	32
8.801	8.135	7.556	7.048	6.600	6.203	5.849	5.532	5.246	4.988	33
8.829	8.157	7.572	7.060	6.609	6.210	5.854	5.536	5.249	4.990	34
8.855	8.176	7.586	7.070	6.617	6.215	5.858	5.539	5.251	4.992	35
8.879	8.192	7.598	7.079	6.623	6.220	5.862	5.541	5.253	4.993	36
8.900	8.208	7.609	7.087	6.629	6.224	5.865	5.543	5.255	4.994	37
8.919	8.221	7.618	7.094	6.634	6.228	5.867	5.545	5.256	4.995	38
8.936	8.233	7.627	7.100	6.638	6.231	5.869	5.547	5.557	4.996	39
8.951	8.244	7.634	7.105	6.642	6.233	5.871	5.548	5.258	4.997	40
8.965	8.253	7.641	7.110	6.645	6.236	5.873	5.549	5.259	4.997	41
8.977	8.262	7.647	7.114	6.648	6.238	5.874	5.550	5.260	4.998	42
8.989	8.270	7.652	7.117	6.650	6.239	5.875	5.551	5.260	4.998	43
8.999	8.276	7.657	7.120	6.652	6.241	5.876	5.552	5.261	4.998	44
9.008	8.283	7.661	7.123	6.654	6.242	5.877	5.552	5.261	4.999	45
9.016	8.288	7.664	7.126	6.656	6.243	5.878	5.553	5.261	4.999	46
9.024	8.293	7.668	7.128	6.657	6.244	5.879	5.553	5.262	4.999	47
9.030	8.297	7.671	7.130	6.659	6.245	5.879	5.554	5.262	4.999	48
9.036	8.301	7.673	7.131	6.660	6.246	5.880	5.554	5.262	4.999	49
9.042	8.304	7.675	7.133	6.661	6.246	5.880	5.554	5.262	4.999	50

Years 0 to:	21%	22%	23%	24%	25%	26%	27%	28%	29%	30%
1	0.826	0.820	0.813	0.806	0.800	0.794	0.787	0.781	0.775	0.769
2	1.509	1.492	1.474	1.457	1.440	1.424	1.407	1.392	1.376	1.361
3	2.540	2.494	2.448	2.404	2.362	2.320	2.280	2.241	2.203	2.166
4	2.540	2.494	2.448	2.404	2.362	2.320	2.280	2.241	2.203	2.166
5	2.926	2.864	2.803	2.745	2.689	2.635	2.583	2.532	2.483	2.436
6	3.245	3.167	3.092	3.020	2.951	2.885	2.821	2.759	2.700	2.643
7	3.508	3.416	3.327	3.242	3.161	3.083	3.009	2.937	2.868	2.802
8	3.726	3.619	3.518	3.421	3.329	3.241	3.156	3.076	2.999	2.925
9	3.905	3.786	3.673	3.566	3.463	3.366	3.273	3.184	3.100	3.019
10	4.054	3.923	3.799	3.682	3.571	3.465	3.364	3.269	3.178	3.092
11	4.177	4.035	3.902	3.776	3.656	3.543	3.437	3.335	3.239	3.147
12	5.278	4.127	3.985	3.851	3.725	3.606	3.493	3.387	3.286	3.190
13	4.362	4.203	4.053	3.912	3.780	3.656	3.538	3.427	3.322	3.223
14	4.432	4.265	4.108	3.962	3.824	3.695	3.573	3.459	3.351	3.249
15	4.489	4.315	4.153	4.001	3.859	3.726	3.601	3.483	3.373	3.268
16	4.536	4.357	4.189	4.033	3.887	3.751	3.623	3.503	3.390	3.283
17	4.576	4.391	4.219	4.059	3.910	3.771	3.640	3.518	3.403	3.295
18	4.608	4.419	4.243	4.080	3.928	3.786	3.654	3.529	3.413	3.304
19	4.635	4.442	4.263	4.097	2.942	3.799	3.664	3.539	3.421	3.311
20	4.657	4.460	4.279	4.110	3.954	3.808	3.673	3.546	3.427	3.316
21	4.675	4.476	3.292	4.121	3.963	3.816	3.679	3.551	3.432	3.320
22	4.690	4.488	4.302	4.130	3.970	3.822	3.684	3.556	3.436	3.323
23	4.703	4.499	4.311	4.137	3.976	3.827	3.689	3.559	3.438	3.325
24	4.713	4.507	4.318	4.143	3.981	3.831	3.692	3.562	3.441	3.327
25	4.721	4.514	4.323	4.147	3.985	3.834	3.694	3.564	3.442	3.329
26	4.728	4.520	4.328	4.151	3.988	3.837	3.696	3.566	3.444	3.330
27	4.734	4.524	4.332	4.154	3.990	3.839	3.698	3.567	3.445	3.331
28	4.739	4.528	4.335	4.157	3.992	3.840	3.699	3.568	3.446	3.331
29	4.743	4.531	4.337	4.159	3.994	3.841	3.700	3.569	3.446	3.332
30	4.746	4.534	4.339	4.160	3.995	3.842	3.701	3.569	3.447	3.332
31	4.749	4.536	4.341	4.161	3.996	3.843	3.701	3.570	3.447	3.332
32	4.751	4.538	4.342	4.162	3.997	3.844	3.702	3.570	3.447	3.333
33	4.753	4.539	4.343	4.163	3.997	3.844	3.702	3.570	3.448	3.333
34	4.755	4.540	4.344	4.164	3.998	3.845	3.703	3.571	3.448	3.333
35	4.756	4.541	4.345	4.164	3.998	3.845	3.703	3.571	3.448	3.333
36	4.757	4.542	4.345	4.165	3.999	3.845	3.703	3.571	3.448	3.333
37	4.758	4.543	4.346	4.165	3.999	3.845	3.703	3.571	3.448	3.333
38	4.759	4.543	4.346	4.165	3.999	3.846	3.703	3.571	3.448	3.333
39	4.759	4.544	4.346	4.166	3.999	3.836	3.703	3.571	3.448	3.333
40	4.760	4.544	4.347	5.166	3.999	3.846	3.703	3.571	3.448	3.333
41	4.760	4.544	4.347	4.166	4.000	3.846	3.703			
42	4.760	4.544	4.347	4.166	4.000	3.846	3.704			
43	4.761	4.545								
44	4.761									
45	4.761									
46	4.761									
47	4.761									
48	4.761									
49	4.761									
50	4.762	4.545	4.3448	4.167	4.000	3.846	3.704	3.571	3.448	3.333

31%	32%	33%	34%	35%	36%	37%	38%	39%	40%	Years 0 to:
0.763	0.758	0.752	0.746	0.741	0.735	0.730	0.725	0.719	0.714	1
1.346	1.331	1.317	1.303	1.289	1.276	1.263	1.250	1.237	1.224	2
1.791	1.766	1.742	1.719	1.696	1.673	1.652	1.630	1.609	1.589	3
2.130	2.096	2.062	2.029	1.997	1.966	1.935	1.906	1.877	1.849	4
2.390	2.345	2.302	2.260	2.220	2.181	2.143	2.106	2.070	2.035	5
2.588	2.534	2.483	2.433	2.385	2.339	2.294	2.251	2.209	2.168	6
2.739	2.677	2.619	2.562	2.508	2.455	2.404	2.355	2.308	2.263	7
2.854	2.786	2.721	2.658	2.598	2.540	2.485	2.432	2.380	2.331	8
2.942	2.868	2.798	2.730	2.665	2.603	2.544	2.487	2.432	2.379	9
3.009	2.930	2.855	2.784	2.715	2.649	2.587	2.527	2.469	2.414	10
3.060	2.978	2.899	2.824	2.752	2.683	2.618	2.555	2.496	2.438	11
3.100	2.013	2.931	2.853	2.779	2.708	2.641	2.576	2.515	2.456	12
3.129	3.040	2.956	2.876	2.799	2.727	2.658	2.592	2.529	2.469	13
3.152	3.061	2.974	2.982	2.814	2.740	2.670	2.603	2.539	2.478	14
3.170	3.076	2.988	2.905	2.825	2.750	2.679	2.611	2.546	2.484	15
3.183	3.088	2.999	2.914	2.834	2.757	2.685	2.616	2.551	2.489	16
3.193	3.097	3.007	2.921	2.840	2.763	2.690	2.621	2.555	2.492	17
3.201	3.104	3.012	2.926	2.844	2.767	2.693	2.624	2.557	2.494	18
3.207	3.109	3.017	2.930	2.848	2.770	2.696	2.626	2.559	2.496	19
3.211	3.113	3.020	2.933	2.850	2.772	2.698	2.627	2.561	2.497	20
3.215	3.116	3.023	2.935	2.852	2.773	2.699	2.629	2.562	2.498	21
3.217	3.118	3.025	2.936	2.853	2.775	2.700	2.629	2.562	2.498	22
3.219	3.120	3.026	2.938	2.854	2.775	2.701	2.630	2.563	2.499	23
3.221	3.121	3.027	3.939	2.855	2.776	2.701	2.630	2.563	2.499	24
3.222	3.122	3.028	2.939	2.856	2.777	2.702	2.631	2.563	2.499	25
3.223	3.123	3.028	2.940	2.856	2.777	2.702	2.631	2.564	2.500	26
3.224	3.123	3.029	2.940	2.856	2.777	2.702	2.631			27
3.224	3.124	3.029	2.940	2.857	2.777	2.702	2.631			28
3.225	3.124	3.030	2.941	2.857	2.777	2.702	2.631			29
3.225	3.124	3.030	2.941	2.857	2.778	2.702	2.631			30
3.225	3.124	3.030	2.941	2.857	2.778	2.703	2.631			31
3.225	3.125	3.030	2.941	2.857	2.778	2.703	2.631			32
3.225	3.125	3.030	2.941	2.857	2.778	2.703	2.632			33
3.225	3.125									34
3.226	3.125									35
3.226	3.125									36
3.226										37
3.226										38
3.226										39
3.226										40
3.226										41
										42
										43
										44
										45
										46
										47
										48
										49
3.226	3.125	3.030	2.941	2.857	2.778	2.703	2.632	2.564	2.500	50

Appendix III

Areas in tail of the normal distribution

$\frac{(x - \mu)}{\sigma}$.00	.01	.02	.03	.04	.05	.06	.07	.08	.09
0.0	.5000	.4960	.4920	.4880	.4840	.4801	.4761	.4721	.4681	.4641
0.1	.4602	.4562	.4522	.4483	.4443	.4404	.4364	.4325	.4286	.4247
0.2	.4207	.4168	.4129	.4090	.4052	.4103	.3974	.3936	.3897	.3859
0.3	.3821	.3783	.3745	.3707	.3669	.3632	.3594	.3557	.3520	.3483
0.4	.3446	.3409	.3372	.3336	.3300	.3264	.3228	.3192	.3156	.3121
0.5	.3085	.3050	.3015	.2981	.2946	.2912	.2877	.2843	.2810	.2776
0.6	.2743	.2709	.2676	.2643	.2611	.2578	.2546	.2514	.2483	.2451
0.7	.2420	.2389	.2358	.2327	.2296	.2266	.2236	.2206	.2177	.2148
0.8	.2119	.2090	.2061	.2033	.2005	.1977	.1949	.1922	.1894	.1867
0.9	.1841	.1814	.1788	.1762	.1736	.1711	.1685	.1660	.1635	.1611
1.0	.1587	.1562	.1539	.1515	.1492	.1469	.1446	.1423	.1401	.1379
1.1	.1357	.1335	.1314	.1292	.1271	.1251	.1230	.1210	.1190	.1170
1.2	.1151	.1131	.1112	.1093	.1075	.1056	.1038	.1020	.1103	.0985
1.3	.0968	.0951	.0934	.0918	.0901	.0885	.0869	.0853	.0838	.0823
1.4	.0808	.0793	.0778	.0764	.0749	.0735	.0721	.0708	.0694	.0681
1.5	.0668	.0655	.0643	.0630	.0618	.0606	.0594	.0582	.0571	.0559
1.6	.0548	.0537	.0526	.0516	.0505	.0495	.0485	.0475	.0465	.0455
1.7	.0446	.0436	.0427	.0418	.0409	.0401	.0392	.0384	.0375	.0367
1.8	.0359	.0351	.0344	.0336	.0329	.0322	.0314	.0307	.0301	.0294
1.9	.0287	.0281	.0274	.0268	.0262	.0256	.0250	.0244	.0239	.0233
2.0	.02275	.02222	.02169	.02118	.02068	.02018	.01970	.01923	.01876	.01831
2.1	.01786	.01743	.01700	.01659	.01618	.01578	.01539	.01500	.01463	.01426
2.2	.01390	.01355	.01321	.01287	.01255	.01222	.01191	.01160	.01130	.01101
2.3	.01072	.01044	.01017	.00990	.00964	.00939	.00914	.00889	.00866	.00842
2.4	.00820	.00798	.00776	.00755	.00734	.00714	.00695	.00676	.00657	.00639
2.5	.00621	.00604	.00587	.00570	.00554	.00539	.00523	.00508	.00494	.00480
2.6	.00466	.00453	.00440	.00427	.00415	.00402	.00391	.00379	.00368	.00357
2.7	.00347	.00336	.00326	.00317	.00307	.00298	.00289	.00280	.00272	.00264
2.8	.00256	.00248	.00240	.00233	.00226	.00219	.00212	.00205	.00199	.00193
2.9	.00187	.00181	.00175	.00169	.00164	.00159	.00154	.00149	.00144	.00139
3.0	.00135									
3.1	.00097									
3.2	.00069									
3.3	.00048									
3.4	.00034									
3.5	.00023									
3.6	.00016									
3.7	.00011									
3.8	.00007									
3.9	.00005									
4.0	.00003									

Capital recovery factors (Equal annuity rate)

The table gives the equal annual payment to be made for n years in the future to repay loan principal and interest with interest at x% per year.

For example, to repay £1 borrowed now at 7% in six annual payments then the value of an annual payment is £0.2098 or 20.98p.

Years	1%	2%	3%	4%	5%	6%	7%	8%	9%	10%
1	1.0100	1.0200	1.0300	1.0400	1.0500	1.0600	1.0700	1.0800	1.0900	1.1000
2	.5075	.5150	.5226	.5302	.5378	.5454	.5531	.5608	.5685	.5762
3	.3400	.3468	.3535	.3603	.3672	.3741	.3811	.3880	.3951	.4021
4	.2563	.2626	.2690	.2755	.2820	.2886	.2952	.3019	.3087	.3155
5	.2060	.2122	.2184	.2246	.2310	.2374	.2439	.2505	.2571	.2638
6	.1725	.1785	.1846	.1908	.1970	.2034	.2098	.2163	.2229	.2296
7	.1486	.1545	.1605	.1666	.1728	.1791	.1856	.1921	.1987	.2054
8	.1307	.1365	.1425	.1485	.1547	.1610	.1675	.1740	.1807	.1874
9	.1167	.1225	.1284	.1345	.1407	.1470	.1535	.1601	.1668	.1736
10	.1056	.1113	.1172	.1233	.1295	.1359	.1424	.1490	.1558	.1627

Years	11%	12%	13%	14%	15%	16%	17%	18%	19%	20%
1	1.1100	1.1200	1.1300	1.1400	1.1500	1.1600	1.1700	1.1800	1.1900	1.200
2	.5839	.5917	.5995	.6073	.6151	.6230	.6308	.6387	.6466	.6545
3	.4092	.4163	.4235	.4307	.4380	.4453	.4526	.4599	.4673	.4747
4	.3223	.3292	.3362	.3432	.3503	.3574	.3645	.3717	.3790	.3863
5	.2706	.2774	.2843	.2913	.2983	.3054	.3126	.3198	.3271	.3344
6	.2364	.2432	.2502	.2572	.2642	.2714	.2786	.2859	.2933	.3007
7	.2122	.2191	.2261	.2332	.2404	.2476	.2549	.2624	.2699	.2774
8	.1943	.2013	.2084	.2156	.2229	.2302	.2377	.2452	.2529	.2606
9	.1806	.1877	.1949	.2022	.2096	.2171	.2247	.2324	.2402	.2481
10	.1698	.1770	.1843	.1917	.1993	.2069	.2146	.2225	.2305	.2385

Notes

Chapter 1

1 The total profits over the life of a business are identical to total net cash inflows. However, the profits calculated for a particular accounting period will be different from the net cash flows for that period. The difference arises because of the accruals concept in financial accounting. In this book decisions which will lead to changes in profits are also assumed to lead to identical changes in net cash flows.

Chapter 2

1 The statement of standard accounting practice on stocks and work in progress (SSAP 9) requires that all manufacturing costs are regarded as product costs. In Chapter 8 we shall consider a system of variable costing where only variable manufacturing costs are recorded as product costs and fixed manufacturing costs are regarded as period costs.
2 The statement of standard accounting practice (SSAP 9) requires that stocks are valued at the lower of cost or net realizable value. It is assumed that the closing stock which is valued at a *cost* of £400,000 is lower than the net realizable value.
3 It is unlikely that variable cost per *unit* will be constant for all levels of activity. We shall discuss the reasons for using a constant variable cost in Chapter 9.
4 It is assumed that the quantity of direct labour required can be adjusted exactly to meet production requirements.

Chapter 3

1 In certain situations the relevant material cost will be the net realizable value. For a detailed discussion of relevant material costs for decision-making see Chapter 10.

Chapter 4

1 In a non-profit organization the product or service rendered is normally called a program.
2 The Statement of Standard Accounting Practice on Stocks and Work in Progress states that product costs should only include costs associated with manufacturing for stock

valuation. For a discussion of what should be included in stocks for stock valuation see Hendrikson, E.S. *Accounting Theory*. R.D. Irwin, 1982, Chapter 13.
3 This case is published in Anthony, R.N. and Dearden, J. *Management Control Systems*. R.D. Irwin, 1980.

Chapter 6

1 Sometimes scrap is referred to as waste and vice versa. For a discussion of each of these terms please turn to Chapter 7.

Chapter 7

1 Some attempts have been made to establish joint cost allocations which are also acceptable for decision-making. See, for example, Kaplan, R.S. A non-linear programming model for joint cost allocation, pp. 398-409 in *Advanced Management Accounting*, Prentice Hall, 1982.
2 The opening stocks in the next accounting period are £14,550 when net revenue is deducted from costs, and £15,000 when net revenue is regarded as other income. The cost deduction of £450 is therefore reflected in a reduction in the opening stock valuation in the following accounting period, thus giving a lower cost of sales calculation.

Chapter 8

1 Clearly there is a limit to how long managers can continue to increase stocks, and eventually the situation will arise when it is necessary to reduce them, and the deferred fixed overheads will eventually be charged to the periods when the stocks are reduced. Nevertheless, there remains some scope for manipulating profits in the short term.

Chapter 9

1 For an explanation of why total revenue is maximized when

marginal revenue is zero, see Exhibit 11.1 in Chapter 11.
2 Costs can be estimated incorporating other variables besides volume using multiple regression techniques. This topic will be discussed in Chapter 20.

Chapter 10

1 To some extent the reduced output from lower morale and lost sales to customers can be quantified once risk/uncertainty is brought into the analysis. This topic is discussed in Chapter 12.
2 Written down value is the original cost of the asset less cumulative depreciation.
3 You will see in Chapter 14 that the profit or loss on the sale of an asset may affect taxation payments and that this taxation effect should be included in the analysis.

Chapter 11

1 In a monopolistic competitive market there are many sellers of similar but not necessarily identical products with no single seller having a large enough share of the market to permit competitors to identify the effect of other individual sellers' pricing decisions on their sales.
2 It is possible for selling prices to be in excess of *unit* costs but total revenue may still be insufficient to cover total costs. See 'Pricing Floor', p. 234.
3 The relevant cost per unit will be the variable cost if the company is contracted to the hire of the machinery.
4 It is assumed that demand will be in excess of 90,000 units at a selling price of £15 but shortage of production capacity will restrict sales to 90,000 units.

Chapter 12

1 Fixed costs will remain unchanged when activity changes. Consequently the standard deviation calculated is the standard deviation of sales volume multiplied by the unit contribution.
2 You may have noted that project A requires an investment of £40,000 whereas the combination of projects A and B requires an investment of £90,000. Assuming that no other projects are available then the acceptance of project A will enable the company to invest the surplus £50,000 for one year. Given that a one year investment yields a certain return of, say, 10% then £5,000 additional return will be received irrespective of the state of nature if only project A is accepted. Consequently the expected value of A will be increased by £5,000 made up of a £35,000 cash outflow for state of nature 1 (probability 0.5) and a £65,000 cash inflow for state of nature 2 (probability 0.5). Nevertheless a risk averse decision-maker might prefer a certain return of £10,000 from the combination of projects A and B to an uncertain return from investing in project A.

Chapter 13

1 A detailed discussion of this topic was presented in Chapter 1.

2 An investor who requires a return of 10% and invests £110 will require repayment of £133.10 in two years time (that is, (£110 × $(1.10)^2$ = £133.10)).
3 A discussion of the calculation of the cost of capital when projects are financed by a mixture of shareholders' funds and other sources of funds is beyond the scope of this book, but more information on this topic can be found in the business finance literature. Predominant texts include Bromwich (1979), Lumby (1984) and Samuels and Wilkes (1980).
4 All nominal risk free rates are risky in real, purchasing power terms, even though the money rate may be risk free. A discussion on the effect of inflation on capital investment decisions is presented in Chapter 14.
5 The present value is calculated as follows:

$$\text{Year 2: } £120 \times 0.826 \ [£1/(1.10)^2] = £\ 99$$
$$\text{Year 3: } £400 \times 0.751 \ [£1/(1.10^3] = £300$$
$$\underline{\underline{£399}}$$

6 In Chapter 1 it was suggested that objectives were determined by a coalition of various different group — shareholders, employees, customers, suppliers and the local community — each of which must receive payments to get them to participate in the coalition.

Chapter 14

1 See Chapter 1 for a discussion of various different groups — shareholders, employees, customers, suppliers and the local community — each of which must receive minimum payments to get them to participate in the coalition.
2 In 1983 the rate of corporation tax for small companies with profits of less than £100,000 was 38%.
3 From 14 March 1984 until 31 March 1985 an initial first year allowance of 75% can be claimed with the balance being recovered by means of a 25% annual writing down allowance. This initial first year allowance will be reduced to 50% for the year commencing 1 April 1985. From 1 April 1986 the first year allowances will be replaced by annual allowances of 25%.
4 From 1 April 1986 the 100% first year allowance will be replaced by a 25% annual allowance on the written down value of the asset. Capital allowances on this basis would be as follows:

Year 1: £20,000 (25% × £80,000 written down value)
Year 2: £15,000 (25% × £60,000 written down value)
Year 3: £11,250 (25% × £45,000 written down value)

At a taxation rate of 50% the taxation payment will be reduced by 50% of the above figures. Capital allowances from year 4 onwards will be at 25% of the written down value.
5 See Fisher, I. *Appreciation and Interest*. Macmillan, 1896.
6 If the worst possible outcome for each of the three years occurred together then the net present value would be calculated as follows:

$$\frac{10,000}{1.10} + \frac{-5,000}{1.10^2} + \frac{-10.000}{1.10^3} - 20,000 = -22,554$$

7 The calculation of the variance of the cash flows for year 1 is as follows:

Cash flow	Deviation from expected value	Squared deviation	Probability	Weighted amount
10,000	−10,000	100,000,000	0.10	10,000,000
15,000	− 5,000	25,000,000	0.25	6,250,000
20,000	0	0	0.30	0
25,000	5,000	25,000,000	0.25	6,250,000
30,000	10,000	100,000,000	0.10	10,000,000
		Sum of squared deviations (variance)		32,500,000

8 The standard deviation is £49,500 for the combination of project C with the existing projects.

Chapter 16

1 A fixed budget is where the original budget which was drawn up prior to the start of the budget period is compared with the actual results. In other words, a fixed budget is the budget for the planned level of activity and the budgeted costs are not adjusted to the actual level of activity.
2 Actual costs in column (2) are determined by multiplying the actual number of hours by the actual rate.

Chapter 17

1 A normal loss was described in Chapter 6. Examples include liquids which may evaporate in the production process, part of the cloth being lost when cutting it to make a suit, and losses which occur in cutting wood to make furniture.

Chapter 18

1 The quantity variances are regarded as abnormal losses and written off as a period cost following the procedure described for abnormal losses in Chapter 6.
2 The standard quantity of materials for an actual production of 1,800 units is 9,000 kg. The actual usage of materials is 10,000 kg which means an excess usage of 1,000 kg.
3 For an output of 1,800 units 7,200 labour hours should have been used but the actual number of hours used was 7,400. Consequently, 200 excess labour hours were required.
4 The calculation is as follows:

$$\frac{\text{Actual cost (£1,030 or £970)} - \text{Mean cost (£1,000)}}{\text{Standard deviation (£90)}} =$$

$$\pm 0.33 \text{ standard deviation}$$

Chapter 19

1 Scorekeeping information seeks to provide managers with information on how well they are doing in managing their activities whereas attention-directing questions indicate to a manager which areas are not proceeding according to plan.

Chapter 21

1 The steps are:

$$TC = \frac{DO}{Q} + \frac{QH}{2}$$

$$\frac{dTC}{dQ} = \frac{-DO}{Q^2} + \frac{H}{2}$$

$$\text{set } \frac{dTC}{dQ} = 0; \frac{H}{2} - \frac{DO}{Q^2} = 0$$

$$HQ^2 - 2DO = 0$$

$$Q^2 = \frac{2DO}{H}$$

$$\therefore Q = \sqrt{\frac{2DO}{H}}$$

2 This topic was discussed in Chapter 14.

Chapter 22

1 The eight units of materials consist of five units from the 2,000 unused units plus three units released from the reduction in production of product Z by $\frac{3}{4}$ unit.
2 This example was adapted from a problem in Salkin, G. and Kornbluth, J. *Linear Programming in Financial Planning*. Prentice-Hall, 1973, p. 59.

Chapter 23

1 Goal congruence refers to a situation where, if a manager maximizes a performance measure, this will also result in his contribution to the goals of the organization being maximized. Where managers engage in behaviour to improve their performance measures, but such behaviour is not in the best interests of the organization, the performance measures are said to encourage a lack of goal congruence. See Chapter 19 for a more detailed discussion of this topic.
2 A manager can increase profits in the short run by increasing stocks under an absorption costing system, but stocks cannot be continually increased. Ultimately, there will be a decline in stocks and the manager will eventually be charged with the fixed overhead costs which were originally deferred and included in the stock valuation. For a discussion of this see Chapter 8.
3 Adapted from Solomons, D. *Divisional Performance: Measurement and Control*. R.D. Irwin, 1965, p. 82.
4 This exhibit and subsequent comments were adapted from Flower, J.F. Measurement of divisional performance. *Readings in Accounting and Business Research* 1977, 121-30.
5 Assuming that the actual cash flows in Exhibit 24.9 were £15,000 for year 1, instead of £20,000, the capital outstanding will be as follows:

Year	Cash inflow 1	Capital outstanding (WDV) 2	Interest (10%) 3	Depreciation 4 (1−3)	Residual income 5 1−(3+4)
0		£100,000			
1	£15,000	£ 95,000	£10,000	5,000	0

You will see that the capital outstanding is £95,000 compared with £90,000 in Exhibit 24.9. Any difference between this calculation of capital outstanding and Exhibit 24.9 will be due entirely to the actual cash inflow (£15,000) being different from the budgeted cash inflow (£20,000).

6 Amey argues that residual income is an inappropriate measure for profit centres and investment centres whereas for practical reasons Tomkins argues that performance should be measured by a comparison of budgeted and actual cash flows. However, for profit centres where the manager can control the amount invested in working capital Tomkins suggests that residual income is an appropriate measure. For a discussion of each writer's views see Amey (1975), Tomkins (1975b), Emmanuel and Otley (1976).

Chapter 24

1 An explanation of why the marginal revenue curve declines was presented in Chapter 11.

2 Exhibits 24.2 and 24.3 are adapted from illustrations first presented by Solomons (1968).

3 The supplying division will obtain marginal revenue in excess of the transfer price of £27 for the sale of the first five units on the external market and it will not be motivated to follow the optimal company plan for the company as a whole. Similarly, the receiving division will maximize its own profits by accepting all transfers until the net marginal revenue equals the transfer price, and it will therefore wish to sell six units of the final product.

4 The contribution per unit for products F_1 and F_2 are as follows:

	F_1		F_2	
Selling price		£37		48
Receiving division's variable costs:				
Purchases from supplying division				
I_1 4 units at £4.00	16		4 units at £4.00	16
I_2 4 units at £3.75	15		8 units at £3.75	30
Receiving division's variable costs	3	34		2 48
Contribution per unit		3		0

5 On this basis the supplying division's variable cost is £200,000 out of a total of £800,000 variable cost, so 25% of the total contribution of £200,000 is apportioned to the supplying division.

6 The models presented in this appendix are adapted from Tomkins, C. *Financial Planning in Divisionalised Companies*, Chapter 3.

Index